THE PRICE SYSTEM AND RESOURCE ALLOCATION

EIGHTH EDITION

Richard H. Leftwich
Oklahoma State University

Ross D. Eckert
Claremont McKenna College

ⓒ THE DRYDEN PRESS
Chicago   New York   Philadelphia
San Francisco   Montreal   Toronto
London   Sydney   Tokyo   Mexico City
Rio de Janeiro   Madrid

Copyright © 1982 CBS COLLEGE PUBLISHING
All rights reserved

Address orders to:

383 Madison Avenue
New York, New York 10017

Address editorial correspondence to:

One Salt Creek Lane
Hinsdale, Illinois 60521

Library of Congress Catalog Card Number: 81-67238
ISBN: 0-03-059367-0
Printed in the United States of America
2 3 4   144   9 8 7 6 5 4 3 2
CBS COLLEGE PUBLISHING
The Dryden Press
Holt, Rinehart and Winston
Saunders College Publishing

Acquisitions Editor: Glenn Turner
Project Editor: Mary Jarvis
Design Director: Alan Wendt
Managing Editor: Jane Perkins
Text and cover design: Paul Uhl
Copy editing: Bernice Lifton

To Maxine D. Leftwich and Enid F. Eckert

PREFACE

The eighth edition of *The Price System and Resource Allocation* is a joint product of Richard H. Leftwich and Ross D. Eckert. We hope that users will be as well satisfied with the product output as we have been with each other's resource inputs. We will welcome comments and criticisms of both the book's format and its content.

As with previous editions, this one is aimed at second- or third-year undergraduates in intermediate microeconomics courses. It presupposes a principles of economics background. The text itself does not require calculus; however, a complete set of mathematical footnotes is included to speed those trained in calculus along the way toward advanced mathematical treatments of microeconomics. We make liberal use of geometry.

The major change in this edition is the massive infusion of materials applying economic analysis to the everyday life situations that students experience or become acquainted with in many other ways. The applications are placed at chapter ends to avoid breaking the continuity of the theoretical exposition of each chapter and to demonstrate how the analytical tools developed therein are used to understand and evaluate current economic events and problems. They are designed to show students that economics is important and is of direct and continuing use to them.

We are indebted to other economists who contributed to this book in various ways. Professor Shiu-fang Yu of Texas Tech University assumed prime responsibility for the mathematical footnotes.

Important reviews, criticisms and suggestions were given us by Professor Louis De Alessi, University of Miami; Professor George W. Hilton, University of California, Los Angeles; Professor Ronald K. Teeples, Claremont McKenna College; and Professor Richard K. Vedder, Ohio University.

In addition, the following people read the entire manuscript and made valuable comments: Professor Jonathan Cave, University of

Illinois at Urbana; Professor Alvin Cohen, Lehigh University; Professor Donald Holley, Boise State University; Professor Thomas McCullough, University of California, Berkeley; Professor Robert Pennington, George Mason University; and Professor Bruce Seaman, Georgia State University.

For errors and omissions the buck stops with us. Bring them to our attention and we will try to do better next time.

Richard H. Leftwich
Ross D. Eckert

CONTENTS

A Review of
Basic Economic Analysis

The level of economic sophistication that students bring to the intermediate microeconomics course varies greatly from one university to another, and from one student to another within any one university. The first four chapters, which compose Part One, provide a review of the nature and purpose of microeconomic analysis. They also review the fundamentals of demand, supply, and price determination. In some institutions in which students have been uniformly well trained in principles courses, Part One may be omitted at no great cost to the students. But in most universities it will provide and/or reinforce the foundations on which microeconomic analysis is built.

CHAPTER 1

Economic Activity and
Economic Theory

Our economic, political, and social systems are experiencing troubled times. There has been an unparalleled period of prolonged inflation coupled with relatively high rates of unemployment. We have energy problems. Social values and social institutions are being subjected to scrutiny and questioning more intense than any we have seen since the Great Depression. Severe criticism is being leveled at the operation of the capitalist or private enterprise system; some of it pinpoints weaknesses and some of it reveals much ignorance about the nature and performance of such a system.

This book is intended to provide background for the debate. Its purpose is twofold: (1) to spell out the conditions that must be met in *any* economic system if it is to be efficient and (2) to show the operation of the price system, with its strengths and weaknesses, as a means of moving the economy toward those conditions. We should recognize at the outset that there are alternative ways of organizing economic activity; this book, however, is concerned predominantly with the price mechanism.

In this introductory chapter we survey the nature of economic activity, the basic methodology of economics, and the relation of price theory to the general body of economic theory. The next three chapters set the stage for the detailed exposition of price theory that begins in Chapter 5.

Economic Activity

While the boundaries marking off economics from other disciplines or fields of knowledge are hard to draw, general agreement does exist with regard to its main contents. Economics is concerned with humanity's well-being or welfare. It encompasses the social relationships or social organization involved in allocating scarce resources among alternative human wants and in using those resouces toward the end of satisfying wants as fully as possible. The key elements of economic activity are (1) human wants, (2) resources, and (3) techniques of production. Each of these will be discussed in turn.

Human Wants

Economic activity is directed toward the satisfaction of human wants. These provide the driving, motivating force; their fulfillment may be thought of as the end or goal of economic activity. The wants that are important in any economic system may be those of the general public, powerful special interest groups, government leaders, and/or others. Different societies are likely to attach different relative weights to whose wants are the most important.

Wants have two characteristics—they are varied in kind, and in the aggregate over time they are insatiable. Insatiability does not imply that any one individual's desire for a particular commodity is unlimited. The quantity of a good—say, beer—consumed each week that contributes to one's well-being may well be finite. It is commodities in the aggregate for which wants are unlimited, partly because of the great variety of wants that individuals can conjure up.

Origins of Wants The insatiability of wants in the aggregate becomes evident when we consider some of the ways in which wants arise. First, they come into being for the items the human organism must have in order to continue functioning. The need for food is the most obvious case in point. In both extreme and temperate climates two other desires arise from necessity—for shelter and for clothing. One or the other, or both of these, must be fulfilled in some degree if humans are to survive the rigors of low temperatures or the extreme heat of the tropics.

Wants arise, too, from the influence of the culture in which we live, for every society dictates certain requisites for "the good life"—certain standards of housing and food consumption; patronizing of the arts; and possession and consumption of such items as automobiles, charcoal broilers, television sets, and stereo sound systems. The status of individuals in society is thought to depend to a considerable extent upon their levels of consumption. Consequently, many wants are generated in the process of attempting to improve one's status.

The satisfying of our biological and cultural needs requires a wide variety of goods. Individual tastes vary. Some people like roast beef, some prefer ham, and others enjoy mutton. Over time, these same individuals seek to satisfy their hunger with various foods. Tastes in clothing differ, and different social occasions call for different modes of dress. Differences in age, climate, social position, education, and a host of others give rise to variety in the goods desired by society in general.

Finally, wants are generated by the activities engaged in to satisfy other wants, or want-satisfying activity may be said to create new wants. No better illustration can be found than that of a student pursuing higher education. Attending a college or university opens new vistas of potential desires that heretofore the student may not have known existed—intellectual and cultural desires and many others. The generation of new wants in the process of endeavoring to satisfy old ones plays an important role in multiplying human desires.

These sources of wants are not an exhaustive classification. The list, however, illustrates the possibility of the infinite expansion of wants over time and the impossibility of an economy's ever satiating all the wants of all its people.

Want Satisfaction and Levels of Living   The level of want satisfaction achieved in a given economic society is hard to measure. Ordinarily it is expressed as per capita income—sometimes gross and sometimes net, depending on the availability of data. There may be a great dispersion around the average; and the average income figure may be misleading because of distribution problems. Nevertheless, per capita income appears to be one of the best measures available of the performance of an economy from an output point of view.

Sometimes people judge the performance of an economy by whether per capita incomes are at a "satisfactory" level. The implication is that if the level is below "satisfactory," something ought to be done about it—that everyone is entitled to a "satisfactory" level of living. Judgments of this kind are not very valuable from the point of view of economic analysis.

In the first place, the level of living "satisfactory" to a society is entirely relative to the historical time under consideration. A level of living which most people in the United States would have accepted 50 years ago would not be satisfactory today. What is satisfactory today will probably not be satisfactory 50 years from now. As the economy's capacity to produce increases, the concept of what constitutes a "satisfactory" level of living shifts upward. The insatiability of human wants, together with increases over time in productive capacity, leads to an ever-changing concept of what constitutes a "satisfactory" level.

In the second place, the concept of what constitutes a "satisfactory" level varies among different geographic areas. A level of living high enough to make most southeast Asians content for the present will not be high enough for most Europeans or Americans. People become accustomed to certain living levels, and a "satisfactory" one for them becomes one just a little higher than what they currently have.

For most purposes it is not relevant to judge the performance of an economy on the basis of whether it provides a "satisfactory" level of living. Rather, it is more to the point to ask whether it provides the highest level of living that its resources and techniques will permit at a given time, making due allowance for some part of current production to be set aside to augment future productive capacity. One can ask no more of an economy. It should not provide much less. To the extent that some part of current production is used to augment future productive capacity, the level of living that the economy can provide will grow continuously.

Resources

The level of want satisfaction that an economy can achieve is limited partly by the quantities and qualities of its known resources. *Resources* are the means available for producing goods that are used to satisfy wants. Hundreds of different kinds of resources exist in the economy. Among these are labor of all kinds, raw materials of all kinds, land, machinery, buildings, semifinished materials, fuel, power, transportation, and the like.

Classification of Resources Resources can be classified conveniently into two categories: (1) labor, or human, resources and (2) capital, or nonhuman, resources. *Labor resources* consist of labor power or the capacity for human effort, both of mind and of muscle, used in producing goods. The term *capital* can be misleading since it is used in several different ways not only by noneconomists but by economists as well. We use the term to include all nonhuman resources that can contribute toward placing goods in the hands of the ultimate consumer. Specific examples are buildings, machinery, land, available mineral resources, raw materials, semifinished materials, business inventories, and any other nonhuman tangible items used in the productive process.[1] We need particularly to guard against confusing capital and money. Money is not capital as the term is used in this book. Money as such produces nothing. It is a technique[2] facilitating the exchange of goods and services and resources. By and large the use of monetary techniques enables us to obtain higher satisfaction levels than we can reach with barter techniques.

The significance of this classification of resources should not be

---

[1] In a basic sense inventories of goods in the hands of ultimate consumers also constitute capital, since it is the satisfaction yielded by goods rather than the goods themselves that consumers desire. Thus, such goods are still means of satisfying ultimate ends or desires of consumers; that is, they have yet to produce the want satisfaction they are supposed to produce. We shall not cut it this fine in our discussions. Goods in the hands of the ultimate consumer will be called consumer goods rather than capital, and this will avoid some complexities.

[2] See p. 8.

overstated. It is more descriptive than analytical. Within each category there are many different kinds of resources, and the differences between two kinds falling within the same classification may be more significant analytically then the differences between two kinds in separate classifications. Consider, for example, a human ditchdigger and an accountant. Both fall under the descriptive classification of labor. However, from an analytical point of view, the human ditchdigger is more closely related to a mechanical ditchdigger, which comes under the descriptive classification of capital, than to the accountant.

Characteristics of Resources   Resources have three important characteristics: (1) most are limited in quantity; (2) they are versatile; and (3) they can be combined in varying proportions to produce any given commodity. These will be considered in turn.

Most resources are *scarce* in the sense that they are limited in quantity relative to desires for the products that they can produce. These are called *economic resources*. Some resources, such as the air used in internal-combustion engines, are so abundant that they can be had for the taking. These are called *free resources* since they command no price. If all resources were free, there would be no limitation on the extent to which wants could be satisfied and no economic problem would exist. Levels of living could soar to infinite heights. Free resources are of no significance for economic analysis and will be disregarded.

We are interested in economic resources. The scarcity of economic resources makes necessary the picking and choosing of which wants are to be satisfied and to what degree. This is the economic problem in a nutshell.

The population of an economy sets an upper limit on the quantities of labor resources available. Various factors—education, custom, general state of health, age distribution—determine the actual proportion of the population that can be considered as the labor force. Over a short period of time—say, one year—the total labor force cannot expand very much, but over a longer period it may be variable as population has time to change and as changes occur in the factors determining the quantity and the quality of the actual labor force.

Generally, the total capital equipment of the economy is expanding over time, but this expansion occurs slowly. The amount that an economy can add to its total stock of capital equipment in a year, without seriously restricting current consumption, is a fairly small proportion of its existing capital. Therefore, over a short period of time the quantity of capital available to produce goods is limited.

The *versatility* of resources refers to their capacity to be put to different uses. Almost any kind of resource can be used in the production of a wide variety of goods. Common labor can be used in making almost every conceivable good. The more highly skilled or specialized a resource becomes, however, the more limited are its uses. There are fewer alternative jobs for skilled machinists than for common laborers. There are still fewer alternative jobs for the brain surgeon, the ballet dancer, or the professional athlete. Even with a high degree of resource specialization, supplies of one kind of specialized resource can be developed over time at the expense of other kinds. Individuals can be trained as physicians rather than as dentists. More bricklayers can be developed at the expense of the quantity of carpenters. More tractors and fewer combines can be produced. The resources of the economy are quite fluid with respect to the forms that they can take and the kinds of goods that they can produce. The longer the period of time under consideration, the greater their fluidity or versatility.

Possibilities of combining resources in *different proportions* to produce a given good usually exist. Few, if any, goods require rigid proportions of resources. Generally, it is possible to substitute some kinds of labor for capital, or for other kinds of labor, and vice versa. This characteristic of resources is closely related to the characteristic of versatility. Substitution possibilities and versatility generate the potential for the economy to switch productive capacity from one line of production to another; they enable the economy to adjust output to the changing character of human wants. Resources can be transferred into industries producing goods for which wants are expanding and out of those turning out items for which wants are diminishing.

Techniques

Techniques of production and exchange, together with quantities and qualities of resources in existence, set limits on the level of want satisfaction that an economy can achieve. *Techniques* are the know-how and the physical means available for transforming resources into want-satisfying form. The development of techniques for enterprisers is generally considered to lie outside the province of economic theory and in the province of engineering. However, the simultaneous choices of goods to be produced, quantities to be produced, and techniques to be used fall within the scope of economics. Economists usually assume that for the production of any commodity a given range of techniques is available and that for any quantity of the commodity produced the least-cost techniques will be used.

Methodology

To make a useful, systematic study of economic activity, we must learn economic theory and its application. But what is economic theory? Like the theory of any other science, it consists of sets of principles or causal relationships among the important "facts" or variables that surround and permeate economic activity. We shall look first at the construction and functions of sets of economic principles; then we shall turn to the place of price theory within the overall scheme of the discipline.

The Construction of Economic Theory

Any set of principles (a theory) must have a bedrock starting point consisting of propositions or conditions that are taken as given or as being so without further investigation. These we call the *postulates* or the *premises* upon which the theory is erected. In aerodynamics the forces of gravity, the operation of centrifugal force, and air resistance may be among the postulates of a theory involving lift, thrust, and drag. In economics we may build a theory of consumer behavior on the postulate of consumer rationality, defined as the general desire of consumers to secure as much satisfaction as they can in spending their incomes. The first step, then, in the construction of a theory is the specification and definition of its postulates.

The second step is the observation of "facts" concerning the activity about which we want to theorize. For example, if the activity in question is the exchange of groceries between supermarkets and consumers, the activity should be looked into as thoroughly as possible. As facts emerge from continued and repeated observation, it will become apparent that some are irrelevant and can be discarded; others will obviously be significant. In the grocery exchange case, the hair color of consumers is not likely to matter, but the weekly amounts of money that consumers have to spend, the number of supermarkets available to them, and the weekly quantities of groceries available to be purchased will most certainly be important.

The third step—and this one will frequently be taken concurrently with the second—is the application of the rules of logic to the observed facts in an attempt to establish causal relationships among them and to eliminate as many irrelevant and insignificant facts as possible. *Deductive* chains of logic may lead us to believe that certain effects follow certain causes in a regular manner. We may reason that consumers with larger incomes are willing to pay higher prices for specific goods. Therefore, an increase in consumer incomes is likely to lead to higher prices. Or, on the other hand, we may reason *inductively*. Repeated observations may indicate that increases in consumer incomes and increases in prices occur simultaneously. So, putting two and two together, we reach the tentative conclusion that higher incomes cause prices to rise. Such tentative statements of cause-and-effect relationships are called *hypotheses*.

The fourth step in the process of establishing a set of principles is a crucial one. Once hypotheses have been formulated, they must be thoroughly tested to determine the degree to which they are valid, that is, the extent to which they yield good explanations and predictions. The tools of statistics and econometrics are of particular value in this respect. Some hypotheses will not withstand the rigors of repeated testing and, consequently, must be rejected. The testing process may suggest modifications in others; then the modified hypotheses must be tested. Still other hypotheses may be found to hold up most of the time in most of the circumstances to which they are relevant. These we usually refer to as *principles*.

It would be foolish to regard a set of principles as absolute truth. The testing process in economics and in other sciences never ends. At any given point in time we think of principles as the best available statements of causal relations; however, additional data and better testing techniques may enable us to improve on them over time. Economic theory is not a once-and-for-all set of principles. It is viable—evolving and continually growing.

The Functions of Economic Theory

The principal functions of economic theory fall into two categories: (1) to explain the nature of economic activity and (2) to predict what will happen to the economy as facts change. The explanation of the nature of economic activity enables us to understand the economic environment in which we live—how one part relates to others and what causes what. We also want to be able to predict with some degree of accuracy what is likely to happen to the key variables that affect our well-being and to be able to do something about them if we dislike the predicted consequences.

Economists differentiate between *positive economics* and *normative economics* on the basis of whether the users of theory are concerned with causal relations only or whether they intend some kind of intervention in economic activity to alter the course of that activity. Positive economics is supposed to be completely objective, limited to the cause-and-effect relationships of economic activity. It is concerned with the way economic relations *are*. By way of contrast, normative economics is concerned with what *ought* to be. Value judgments must necessarily be made; that is, possible objectives to be achieved must be ranked, and choices must be made among those objectives. Economic policymaking—conscious intervention in economic activity with the intent of altering the course that it will take—is essentially normative in character. But if economic policymaking is to be effective in improving economic well-being, it must obviously be rooted in sound positive economic analysis. Policymakers should be cognizant of the full range of consequences of the policies they recommend.

Price Theory and Economic Theory

Price theory (*microeconomic theory*) and the theory of the economy as a whole (*macroeconomic theory*) constitute the basic analytical tool kit of the discipline of economics. The principles of both are used in special subject areas such as monetary economics, international trade and finance, public finance, manpower economics, agricultural economics, regional economics, and so on. The concentration on microeconomics in this book should in no way be interpreted as minimizing the importance of macroeconomics. Both parts of the kit are essential to a thorough understanding of economic activity.

Microeconomics is concerned with the economic activities of such individual economic units as consumers, resource owners, and business firms. It is concerned with the flow of goods and services from business firms to consumers, the composition of the flow, and the process for establishing the relative prices of the component parts of the flow. It is concerned, too, with the flow of productive resources (or their services) from resource owners to business firms, with their evaluation, and with their allocation among alternative uses.

Macroeconomics treats the economic system as a whole, rather than treating the individual economic units of which it is composed. The particular goods and services making up the flow from business firms to consumers are not integral parts of the analysis, nor are the individual productive resources or services moving from resource owners to business firms. The value of the overall flow of goods (net national product) and the value of the overall flow of resources (national income) receive the focus of attention.

Price index numbers or general price level concepts in macroeconomics replace the relative-price concepts for individual goods used in microeconomics. Macroeconomics concentrates on the causes of change in aggregate money flows, the aggregate movement of goods and services, and the general employment level of resources. Prescription of cures for economic fluctuations and for unemployment of resources follows logically from the determination of their causes. Macroeconomics has much to say about the nature of economic growth and the conditions necessary for the expansion of productive capacity and national income over time.

Price theory is somewhat abstract. We may as well face this point at the outset. Difficulties will be encountered in this respect, but if we recognize the nature of the difficulties, they will be less formidable. Primarily, we shall find that price theory does not give a complete description of the real world. It will not tell us why a price differential of 5 cents per gallon for gasoline exists between Oklahoma City and Cleveland on any given date. However, it should help us understand the real world. It should show us, in general, how the prices of gasoline are established and the role that those prices play in the overall operation of the economy.

Price theory is abstract because it does not and cannot encompass all the economic data of the real world. To take all of the data and factors that influence economic decisions of consumers, resource owners, and business firms into consideration would require minute descriptions and analyses of every economic unit in existence—an impossible task. The function of theory is to single out what appear to be the most relevant data and to build an overall conceptual framework of the price system in operation from these. We concentrate on the data and principles that seem to be most important in motivating most economic units. In eliminating less important data and in building up a logical theoretical structure, we lose some contact with reality. However, we gain in our understanding of the overall operation of the economy because we reduce the factors to be considered to manageable proportions. We may lose sight of some individual trees, but we gain more understanding and a better view of the forest.

The sets of principles comprising price theory should show the directions in which economic units tend to move and should explain the more important reasons why they tend to move in those directions. They should be sets of logically consistent approximations of how the economy operates. The abstraction and precision of theory are essential to clear thinking and to policymaking in the real world, but we should guard against the notion that it provides an unqualified description of the real world. We should make theory our tool—not our master.

Welfare

The central theme of this book is economic *welfare*, defined as the economic well-being of those who live in the society. The welfare, or well-being, of individuals presents no great conceptual difficulties. The simplest case is one in which individuals (or family units) are thought to be the best judges of what does or does not contribute to their own well-being. An individual's welfare is increased or decreased according to the individual's evaluation of the impact of events that affect her or him. As outside observers, we simply ask how events affect individuals and accept their answers at face value.

The welfare of a group is much more difficult to handle. As a starting point we can say that events that increase the well-being of every individual in the group increase that of the group as a whole. But very often an event that increases the well-being of one person decreases that of another. When such is the case, the gain in the welfare of the first must be compared with the loss in the welfare of the second, if any conclusions are to be drawn about the welfare of the group as a whole. Comparisons of this sort raise serious problems. How can changes in the well-being of different persons be compared? In some specific cases we can make rough subjective judgments. Taking a Rembrandt away from a connoisseur of art and giving it to a person who does not understand or value art would surely reduce group welfare. But, in general, we have no objective means of measuring and comparing the gain of one person or group of persons with the loss suffered by another individual or group when an event causes both.

We are left with a group welfare concept known as a *Pareto optimum*.[3] A Pareto optimum is said to exist when no event can increase the well-being of one person without decreasing the well-being of someone else. If we consider the matter another way, a Pareto optimum does not exist if one or more persons can be made better off without making anyone else worse off. If a Pareto optimum does not exist, a movement toward it—making at least one person better off without making anyone else worse off—increases group welfare.

There is no unique Pareto optimal situation in an economy. Suppose that all production and all exchanges that bestow advantage on anyone without disadvantaging anyone else have taken place. If any redistribution of purchasing power now occurs—for example, the imposition of taxes on the rich and the granting of subsidies to the poor—the conditions of the original Pareto optimum are violated. But a new Pareto optimum, given the new distribution of income, is possible. In fact, there will be a different set of Pareto optimal conditions for every different pattern of purchasing power distribution. If the economy moves from one Pareto optimum to another in this fashion, can we say that the welfare of the group has increased or decreased? There are no objective measures that will provide the answer. We can discuss objectively the conditions that lead to Pareto optimality, given the distribution of income, but if we want to dis-

---

[3] Originated by the early twentieth-century Italian economist Vilfredo Pareto.

cuss the impact of income redistribution on welfare, we must fall back on subjective value judgments to support whatever stand we take.

Summary

Economic activity revolves around three key elements: (1) human wants that are varied and insatiable; (2) resources that are limited, versatile, and capable of being combined in varying proportions to produce a given commodity; (3) techniques for utilizing resources to produce goods and services that satisfy wants. The achievement of a level of want satisfaction (level of living) as high as the economy can provide is a primary goal of economic activity in most societies. To approach this end, resources and techniques are not merely used to produce goods and services that satisfy wants; they must also be used to produce the items that contribute most to aggregate want satisfaction. The best possible techniques must be used; resources must be fully employed and properly allocated or distributed among the alternative wants of consumers.

The methodology of economics is like that of other sciences. Sets of principles are developed through the formulation and testing of hypotheses. Theses, in turn, are outgrowths of logic applied to basic premises and observations of facts.

At the outset the relationship of price theory both to the overall discipline of economics and to the real world should be understood. Price theory is an essential part of the economist's tool kit and is used, together with national income theory, in the special subject areas of economics. Rather than explaining in detail the activities of economic units in the real world, it establishes general principles concerning activities on the basis of what appear to be the most important economic data. Activities of economic units in the real world approximate or tend toward those of theory. But this loss in the way of detailed contact with the real world means gain in the understanding of the main forces at work.

This book is concerned with welfare in the Pareto optimum sense; that is, it will have much to say about the conditions of economic efficiency for any given income distribution, but it will not have much to say about whether one income distribution is more efficient than another.

Suggested Readings

Friedman, Milton. "The Methodology of Positive Economics," *Essays in Positive Economics*. Chicago: University of Chicago Press, 1953, pp. 3–43.

Koopmans, Tjalling C. *Three Essays on the State of Economic Science*. New York: McGraw-Hill, 1957, pp. 129–49.

Lange, Oscar. "The Scope and Method of Economics." *Review of Economics Studies* XIII (1945–1946): 19–32.

Marshall, Alfred. *Principles of Economics*. 8th ed. London: Macmillan, 1920, Bk. III, Chap. 2.

Questions and Exercises

1 Make a list of the wants that you have developed as a direct result of attending your college or university. How have these changed since your freshman year?

2 Evaluate the following statement: "The primary cause of poverty in the United States is that people have too little money to spend." Consider in your evaluation the factors limiting the attainable living standard.

3 Explain the effects on the per capita income of an economy of each of the following:
   a a 10 percent increase in the population
   b restrictions on the importation of crude oil
   c development of a substantially improved process for recovery of shale oil deposits
   d large gifts of food to foreign populations experiencing serious nutrition problems

4 Evaluate the following statement: "The most important test of a set of economic principles is whether or not it describes realistically the economic activity to which it is applied."

5 Will income redistribution from the rich toward the poor increase the welfare of a society? Explain why or why not.

6 Distinguish carefully between *positive economics* and *normative economics*. Discuss the interrelationships between these two concepts.

**KEY
CONCEPTS**

Economic system
Private enterprise system
Socialistic system
Public sector
Private sector
Not-for-profit sector
Households
Firms
Economic efficiency

The Organization of an Economic System

Any given society or country develops an institutional framework within which its economic activity is carried on. We call such a framework an *economic system*. Economic systems of the modern world fall somewhere along a continuum between pure private enterprise at the one extreme and pure socialism at the other. The pure private enterprise system is characterized by private ownership of resources as well as goods and services. Private individuals, business enterprises, and associations of various kinds can engage in whatever voluntary production and exchange activities they desire. In the pure socialistic system there is no private property. Resources, goods, and services are owned and/or controlled by the government. Production takes place in government enterprises and the government specifies the conditions under which exchanges can occur. Whereas the private enterprise system is decentralized, the socialistic system is highly centralized.

Present-day economies are a mixture of socialism and private enterprise. Some part of an economy's output will be produced by the *profit-oriented private sector* of the economy. Another part will be produced in a socialistic manner by the *public sector*. In addition, many economies have a *not-for-profit sector*—hospitals, schools, and the like—that is neither fish nor fowl. However, it should be taken into account for any complete analysis of an economic system.

Our primary interest in this book is the operation of a price system in organizing economic activity; that is, in the profit-oriented private sector of a predominantly private enterprise economy. In this chapter we present an overview of such an economy. The overview will enable us to fit details, as we come to them throughout the book, into their proper places and to put them in proper perspective. First, we construct a simple model of a private enterprise system. Next, we discuss the functions of an economic system, with special reference to prices as the mechanism for performing those functions. But much of what we have to say is relevant to socialistic systems, to the not-for-profit sector, and to the public sector of mixed systems. We cannot—and should not—avoid the many points at which the not-for-profit sector and the public sector of an economy affect the profit-oriented private sector. The chapter closes with two brief illustrations of the different role that prices play in the not-for-profit sector.

A Simplified Model

The widely used "circular flow" diagram of Figure 2.1 furnishes a highly simplified model of a private enterprise economic system. Leaving the government aside for the present, economic units are classified into two groups: (1) households and (2) business firms. These interact in two sets of markets: (1) markets for consumer goods and services and (2) resource markets. Households, business firms, consumer goods markets, and resource markets are the component parts of a private enterprise economy, and they form the core around which price theory is built.

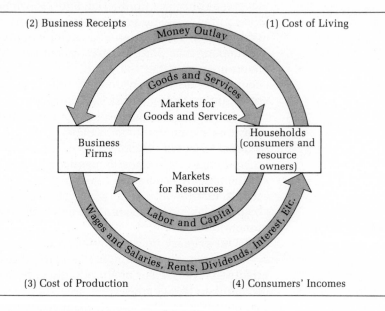

FIGURE 2.1
The circular flow model

(2) Business Receipts (1) Cost of Living

Money Outlay

Goods and Services

Markets for Goods and Services

Business Firms

Households (consumers and resource owners)

Markets for Resources

Labor and Capital

Wages and Salaries, Rents, Dividends, Interest, Etc.

(3) Cost of Production (4) Consumers' Incomes

Households include all individual and family units of the economy. They are the consumers of the economy's output of goods and services. With minor exceptions—for example, the indigent—they also own the economy's resources.

Business firms constitute a more limited group engaged in the buying and hiring of resources and the production and sale of goods and services. They include single proprietorships, partnerships, and corporations at all levels of the production process. In some cases the same economic unit functions both as a firm and as a household, the family farm being a case in point. We shall assume that the unit's activities as a firm can be clearly separated from its activities as a household and that each activity is classified under the appropriate heading.

The upper half of Figure 2.1 represents the markets for consumer goods and services. Households, as consumers, and business firms, as sellers, interact within the markets. Goods and services flow from business firms to consumers; a *reverse* flow of money from consumers to business firms also takes place. Prices of goods and services form the connecting link between the two flows. The value of the flow of goods and services will be equal to the reverse money flow.

The lower half of Figure 2.1 represents the markets for resources. The services of labor and capital in their many forms flow from resource owners (households) to business firms. The reverse flow of money in payment for these resources occurs in such forms as wages, salaries, rents, dividends, interest, and so on, depending on the contractual arrangements under which they are delivered. These are resource prices valuing the services of resources and forming the connecting link between the two flows. In terms of money, the two flows are equal.

Money circulates continuously from households to business firms and back to households again. The sale of goods and services places money at the disposal of business firms for the purchase of resource services to continue production. The sale or hire of the services of resources places money at the disposal of resource owners for the purchase of goods and services.[1] The money flow takes on four familiar aspects as it makes a complete circuit. It is consumers' costs of living at point (1) in Figure 2.1 as it leaves consumers' hands. It is business receipts for business firms at point (2). At point (3) the money flow becomes costs of production; while at point (4) it is consumers' incomes.

If the economy is stationary—neither expanding nor contracting—the flow of money of the upper half of Figure 2.1 will equal the flow of money of the lower half. The aggregate value of goods and services will equal the aggregate value of resource services. Consumers spend all their incomes; no saving occurs. Likewise, business firms pay out all money received to resource owners

---

[1] In some instances the money flow may be circumvented completely by direct exchange of resource services for goods or for "income in kind" to resource owners. To the extent that this type of transaction occurs, the money flows in each half of the diagram will be less than the value of goods and services and the value of resource services. However, since the bulk of exchange in a free enterprise economy will involve money and prices, we shall leave barter exchanges out of consideration.

and there is no business saving.[2] No net investment occurs. In the production of goods and services, capital equipment wears out or depreciates. Some resource services are used to take care of replacement or depreciation, but costs of replacement or depreciation are a part of the cost of producing the goods that caused the depreciation to occur in the first place.

Expanded and more complex circular flow models are frequently used in macroeconomics. Leakages from, and injections into, the income stream help explain contraction or growth of the economy as well as the equilibrium level of economic activity. Leakages include such things as savings, tax collections by the government, and imports of goods from abroad. Injections include investment, government expenditures, and exports.

We are concerned for the most part with the two sets of markets and the interactions that occur within each of them. In product markets the composition of the flow of goods and services, the prices of each, and the outputs of each are of interest to us. Similarly, in resource markets, the prices, the employment levels, and the allocations of resources among different uses are considered.

The Functions of an Economic System

Every economic system, whatever its form, must somehow perform five closely related functions. It must determine (1) what is to be produced, (2) how production is to be organized, (3) how the output is to be distributed, (4) how goods are to be rationed over very short-run periods during which their supplies are fixed, and (5) how the productive capacity of the economy is to be maintained and expanded over time.

Determination of What to Produce

The determination of what is to be produced in an economy is a problem of determining what wants in the aggregate are most important and in what degree they are to be satisfied. Should the amount of steel currently available be used for the production of automobiles or tanks or refrigerators or for the erection of sports arenas? Or should it be used to provide some of each? Since the resources of the economy are scarce, all wants cannot be fully satisfied. The problem is one of picking and choosing from the unlimited scope of wants those that

---

[2] Profits made by business firms flow into the hands of resource owners in the form of higher-than-average dividends to stockholders or higher-than-average prices paid to owners of other resources.

are most important for the society as a whole. The economy must provide some method of placing a set of values on different goods and services that reflects the relative desires of the group for the goods and services it can produce.

The value of an item to society is measured by its price in a private enterprise economy, and the valuation process is accomplished by buyers as they spend their incomes. Consumers, for example, are confronted with a wide range of choices in the goods they can buy. The dollar values they place on each of the various items depend on how urgently they desire each, relative to other goods, their willingness and ability to back up desire with dollars, and the supplies of the things available. The more urgently certain goods are desired, and the more willing consumers are to back up desire with dollars, the higher their prices. The less strong the desire for certain goods, the lower their prices. The greater the available supply of any particular good, the lower its price. Any one unit of the good will be of less importance to the consumer when the supply is great than when the supply is small. The more bread available to eat per week, the smaller the value each loaf will have to consumers. Conversely, the smaller the supply of any particular commodity, the higher consumers will value any one unit of it. Thus, the ways in which consumers spend their incomes establish an array of prices or a price structure in the economy that reflects the comparative values of different goods and services to the consuming public as a whole.

Changes in tastes and preferences modify the patterns of consumer spending. These changes in spending patterns change the structure of prices in turn. The relative prices of goods that consumers now want more urgently go up, while the relative prices of those becoming less desirable decline. The price structure of goods and services changes to reflect shifts in consumers' tastes and preferences.

This analysis is positive in nature, telling us how goods are actually valued by means of a system of prices. It does not tell us how goods *ought* to be valued. The latter problem is an ethical one and lies largely outside the scope of price theory. A consumer with a larger income will exert more influence on the price structure than a consumer with a lower income. Conceivably, biscuits for rich people's dogs may be placed higher in the scale of values than milk for poor people's children, provided there are enough rich people casting their dollar votes in this direction and there are not enough poor people able to spend dollars for milk. The price system, though working perfectly in this case, may lead to social consequences the public considers undesirable and which it may attempt to modify through political processes. Income redistribution, price fixing, and progressive income taxes are examples of such political processes.

Organization of Production

Concurrent with the determination of what is to be produced, an economic system must determine how its resources are to be organized to turn out the desired goods in the proper quantities. The organization of production involves (1) drawing resources from industries producing goods that consumers value less and channeling them into the industries producing goods that consumers value more and (2) efficient use of resources by individual firms. These are considered in turn.

The price system in a private enterprise economy organizes production. Firms producing goods and services that consumers want most urgently receive higher prices relative to costs and will be more profitable than those producing goods and services that consumers want less urgently. The more profitable firms can, and do, offer higher prices for resources in order to expand. Those making less profit or incurring losses are unwilling to pay as much for resources. Resource owners, in the interest of increasing their incomes, want to sell their resources to firms offering the higher prices. Therefore, there is a constant channeling of resources away from firms producing goods and services that consumers want least into the firms producing goods and services that consumers want most. Resources are moving constantly from lower-paying to higher-paying uses, or out of less important into more important uses.

The term *efficiency* in economics differs slightly from the use of the term in physics or mechanics. In both contexts it involves the ratio of an output to an input. With regard to mechanical efficiency, we know that a steam engine is inefficient because it fails to transform a large part of the heat energy of its fuel into power. Mechanically, an internal-combustion engine is more efficient. However, if fuel for steam engines is cheap and fuel for internal-combustion engines is expensive, cheaper power may be obtained from the steam engine.

The concept of *economic efficiency* is also a ratio of output to input. The economic efficiency of a particular production process is the ratio of useful product output to useful resources input. The usefulness of product output, or its value to society, is measured in dollars. Similarly, the usefulness or value of resource input is measured in dollars. Thus, the steam engine, which is less efficient mechanically, will be more efficient economically than an internal-combustion engine if it furnishes *cheaper* power for a particular production process.

The quest for profits provides the incentive for efficient production. The more efficient a firm's operation, given the price of the product, the greater its profits will be. To rephrase the definition of efficiency, it is the value of product output per unit input of resource value. The greater the dollar value of product output per dollar's worth of resource input, the greater economic efficiency is. Likewise, the less the dollar value of resource input needed per dollar's worth of product output, the greater economic efficiency is. Measurement of economic efficiency requires that values be placed on resources of different types and on the same type of resource in different uses. Resources tend to be valued in the market according to their contributions to the production of goods and services.

Economic efficiency within a firm requires that the firm make choices among the different combinations of resources and techniques that can be used in the production process. The choice of techniques to use will depend on relative resource prices and the quantity of product to be produced. The aim of the profit-oriented firm is to produce whatever output it does as cheaply (efficiently) as it can. Thus, if labor is relatively expensive and capital relatively cheap, the firm will want to use techniques making use of much capital and little labor. If capital is relatively expensive and labor relatively cheap, the most efficient techniques are those using little capital and much labor. The techniques to use for most efficient operation will differ at differing levels of output also. Mass production methods and complicated machines cannot be used efficiently for small outputs, but for large outputs they can be very efficient.

Output Distribution

Distribution of output in a private enterprise economy is accomplished by the price system simultaneously with the determination of what is to be produced and the organization of production. Product distribution depends on personal income distribution. Those with larger incomes obtain larger shares of the economy's output than do those with smaller incomes.

The income of an individual depends on two things: (1) the quantities of different resources that he or she can put into the productive process and (2) the prices received for them. If labor power is the only resource owned by the individual, the person's monthly income is determined by the number of hours worked per month multiplied by the hourly wage rate received. If, in addition, the individual owns and rents land to others, the amount of land so rented, multiplied by the monthly rental per acre, will be income from the land. Income from labor added to income from land is total monthly income. The example can be expanded to as many different resources as the individual owns.

Income distribution, thus, depends on the distribution of resource ownership in the economy and whether or not individuals place their resources in employments producing goods that consumers want most—that is, where the highest prices are offered for resources. Low individual incomes result from small quantities of resources owned and/or the placing of resources owned in employments contributing little to consumer satisfaction. High individual incomes result from large quantities of resources owned and/or the placing of resources owned in employments where they contribute much to consumer satisfaction. Thus, income differences result from improper channeling of resources into the production process by individuals and from differences in resource ownership among individuals.

Income differences that arise from improper channeling of certain resources into the production process tend to be self-correcting. Suppose that a number of individuals are capable of doing the same amount of labor per week in a certain skill category, and suppose that two groups are employed in the making of two different products. The value of the product turned out by a worker in the first group is much higher than that of the product turned out by a worker in the second. Since society values the output of any one worker in the first group more highly than it values that of any one worker in the second, the first group of workers will receive greater individual incomes. When workers of the second group perceive the income differential, some move to the higher-paying employment. The increased supply of the first commodity lowers consumers' valuation of it, while the decreased supply of the second commodity has the opposite effect. This, in turn, lowers the incomes of the first (but now larger) group of workers and raises the incomes of the second (but now smaller) group of workers. When the income differential between workers in the two groups disappears, worker movements from the second to the first group cease. The self-correcting mechanism requires time to operate and may, in some cases, be prevented from accomplishing its task by ignorance on the part of the workers of the second group or by institutional barriers that prevent them from moving. In such cases the income differentials tend to become chronic.

A large part of the income differentials arising from differences in resource ownership will not be self-correcting. The major sources of differences in resource ownership are discussed later, in Chapter 18. They can be classified under differences in labor power owned and differences in kinds and quantities of capital owned. Differences in labor power owned by different individuals stem from differences in physical and mental inheritance and in opportunities to acquire specific types of training. Differences in kinds and quantities of capital owned come from many sources. These include initial differences in labor resources owned, differences in material inheritance, for-tuitous circumstances, fraud, and propensities to accumulate.

If society believes that income differences should be smaller, modifications can be imposed on the private enterprise economy without materially affecting the operation of the price system. Society, through the government, may levy income taxes and pay subsidies for redistribution purposes. It may subsidize low-income groups in various ways. Redistribution of income will, however, affect the wants to be satisfied by economic activity by changing the effective pattern of social desires for goods and services. Reduction of high incomes through taxation makes the individuals who are deprived less effective in the marketplace. Augmentation of low incomes with subsidies makes those who are helped more effective in the marketplace. The price system will reorganize production to conform with the new pattern of effective desires for goods and services.

Rationing in the Very Short Run

An economic system must make some provision for rationing commodities over the time period during which the supplies of these cannot be changed. This time period is called the *very short run* by some and the *market period* by others. Suppose that wheat is harvested throughout the country in the same month each year. From one year to the next the supply of wheat available for consumption is fixed, assuming there is no carry-over from one year to the next. The very short run for wheat in such a case is one year. The economy must ration the fixed supply in two ways: (1) it must allocate the fixed supply among the different consumers in the economy; (2) it must stretch the given supply over the time period from one harvest to the next.

In a private enterprise economy, *price* will be the device that allocates the fixed supply among different consumers. Shortages will cause the price to rise, decreasing the amount that each consumer is willing to buy. The price will continue to increase until all consumers together are just willing to take the fixed supply. Surpluses will cause price to fall, raising the amount consumers are willing to buy until they take the entire supply off the market.

Price will also be the device for rationing the good over time. If the entire supply were to be dumped in consumers' hands immediately after harvest, price would be driven low. At the low price consumption would proceed at a rapid pace. As the next harvest approached, the disappearance of most of the commodity in the first part of the period would leave very small supplies for the latter part of the period. Consequently, price would be high in the latter part of the very short-run period.

Speculation plays an important role in smoothing out the consumption of the good over time. Knowing that the price will tend to be low early in the period and high late in the period, speculators will buy up a large part of the supply early in the period, expecting to sell it later at higher prices and thus realize a net gain on their investment in the product. Their purchases will raise the price in the early part of the period above what it would otherwise have been, thus slowing the rate at which the product is consumed at that time. Their sales in the latter period will reduce price below what it would otherwise have been and will provide greater quantities of the product for consumption in the latter part of the period. The actions of speculators modify the price rise that would have taken place over the very short-run period and bring about a more even flow of the product to consumers over time.

Economic Maintenance and Growth

Every economy is expected to maintain and expand its productive capacity. *Maintenance* refers to keeping the productive power of the economic machine intact through provision for depreciation. *Expansion* refers to continuous increase in the kinds and quantities of the economy's resources, together with continuous improvement in techniques of production.

Labor power can be increased through population increases and through the development and improvement of skills by means of training and education. Development and improvement of skills in a private enterprise economy are motivated largely through the price mechanism—the prospects of higher pay for more highly skilled and more-productive work. The extent to which skills can be developed and improved is conditioned by training and educational opportunities, together with physical and mental abilities.

Capital accumulation depends on a variety of complex economic motives, and much debate centers about their relative importances. For capital accumulation to occur, some resources must be diverted from the production of current consumer goods and put to work producing capital goods in excess of the amount needed to offset depreciation.

Improvements in production techniques make possible greater outputs with given quantities of resources. The motives behind the search for and the discovery of inventions and improvements are not always easy to determine. The inventor may invent because that type of activity is interesting. Frequently, improvements in techniques are the by-product of scholarship intended primarily to advance knowledge. However, a large part of the improvements in production techniques is a direct result of the quest for profits, as is well illustrated by the increasing flow of fruitful results coming from the growing research and development departments of large corporations.

The role of the price mechanism and its degree of importance in providing for economic maintenance and growth are not clear. Certainly prices and profit prospects are an important element in determining whether or not maintenance and growth occur. But the area of economic maintenance and growth is virtually an applied subject area in itself. Consequently, we shall be concerned mainly with the first four functions as they are performed by the price system in a private enterprise economy.

The Not-for-Profit Sector

The economic system discussed thus far is composed on the producing side of business firms owned as private property by proprietors or shareholders seeking to earn returns on their investments. These firms create products as diverse as furniture, aspirin, automobiles, plumbing, lettuce, and clothing. But we have conceptualized the economy too narrowly. Many economies contain a large and growing sector of not-for-profit organizations—firms, foundations, government units, and related organizations—that are not "owned" in the conventional private property sense; that is, ownership rights are not in the form of shares that are bought or sold in public securities markets such as the New York Stock Exchange. Private colleges and many hospitals, for example, are owned by their trustees in the technical or legal sense of ownership, but these people cannot sell out their "shares" for gain because such shares, if they exist, are not legally salable. Moreover, many of these organizations have rules against distribution of earnings to such people so that the organizations may maintain a highly valued tax exempt status (sums that they may have "left over" at the end of their fiscal years are rarely called "profits" in their financial statements for this very reason). The same situation exists for governmental units which, although technically owned by all of their citizens, are *effectively* owned by none of them since they have no right to sell their "shares" except by moving to different governmental jurisdictions. It is small wonder then that market criteria—prices, costs, and profits—play a relatively small role in determining resource allocation among and within these organizations.[3]

---

[3] For more reading on this point, see Armen A. Alchian and Reuben A. Kessel, "Competition, Monopoly, and the Pursuit of Pecuniary Gain," in *Aspects of Labor Economics*, A Conference of the Universities-National Bureau Committee for Economic Research, A Report of the National Bureau of Economic Research, New York, Special Conference Series, Volume 14 (Princeton, N.J.: Princeton University Press, 1962), pp. 156–83.

If prices and profits do not guide and direct such organizations, what does? Economists who specialize in the study of these institutions have yet to answer the question fully, but research to date supports two inferences.

First, competition for dollars among these organizations is less important than it is in the for-profit sector. In not-for-profit organizations, resources are less likely to be used in ways that would capture earnings because "owners" cannot take such earnings "home" the way ordinary owners can. For this reason some not-for-profit organizations are less responsive to consumer demands than are ordinary firms that can capture earnings by being responsive. (Have you been as successful with the Postal Service or your county government in persuading them to provide quicker deliveries or better service as you have been with your local department store or filling station?)

Second, the forms of competition that replace "dollar votes" among not-for-profit organizations tend to be unpredictable in the usual economic sense. They cover a wide range of possibilities that depend on the particular institutional situations, and sometimes even the individual personalities, involved. For example, in not-for-profit organizations there is less likelihood that employees will be hired for their productivity (which is very important in a for-profit organization) and a greater chance that they will be hired for their personal characteristics—their "likability," ethnic characteristics, "connections" with existing managers, and so on. We should emphasize that we are not expounding an "all-or-nothing" hypothesis: It is unlikely that all for-profit firms operate strictly by market criteria (prices and profits) or that all not-for-profit organizations operate according to the foregoing standards. Each type of organization will probably display some conduct of each kind. But we would expect relatively more emphasis on the market criteria among for-profit firms than among not-for-profits because the former group of owners can take home the earnings that efficiency brings.

In Hospital Services

The difficulties that a not-for-profit organization may face in rationing a valuable resource by some mechanism other than price is illustrated in the following *Los Angeles Times* summary of a nationwide survey of hospitals providing kidney dialysis in the late 1960s.[4]

> *Many kidney patients selected to go on an artificial kidney machine tend to be better off financially than those who don't get that chance of survival, a UCLA survey shows.*

[4] George Getze, "Factors in Choice of Kidney Machine Patients Surveyed," copyright 10 February 1969, *Los Angeles Times*. Reprinted by permission.

Although the number of available artificial kidney machines is constantly and rapidly increasing, there are not nearly enough of them to go around.

According to A. H. Katz, professor at the UCLA School of Public Health, the lack of machines makes it necessary for doctors to pick and choose among those who need the machines to live. They, in fact, pick and choose those who will survive.

In a nationwide survey of kidney patients and the institutions where they are treated, Katz has found that the criteria most often used in selection of the patients are these:

Absence of disabling disease other than the kidney trouble for which the machine is needed; the age of the patient—that is, young men and women or patients in their primes are preferred to the elderly; the likelihood of vocational rehabilitation—will the patient be able to work with the aid of the machine; social value—that is, is the patient a substantial and contributing member of society, particularly in regard to dependents; intelligence, and financial resources.

Even though financial resources are played down as a criterion, 46 percent of the patients have family incomes above the 1966 national median of $7,800 a year.

Eight percent have family incomes above $15,000 a year, and 5 percent have incomes above $25,000. Both percentages are higher for those incomes than found in the general population.

Conditions definitely excluding a patient from all consideration include a history of joblessness, indigency, a criminal record, mental deficiency, and "poor" family environment, Katz said.

He said some of the judgment is necessarily subjective.

"It is difficult for the treatment centers to apply hard and fast rules governing selection," he said.

The centers or hospitals quite naturally try to minimize the selection aspect.

"Despite the publicity given to selection of patients, and to advisory medical committees, only eight of the 123 treatment centers reported that machinery for selection existed," Katz said.

Eighty of the centers reported they routinely interview the patient's wife or husband, and 53 reported they interview the parents of unmarried patients.

On the subjective side, 18 centers reported that "congeniality" or "likability" is important though they professed it is not consistently considered in all cases. One center said likability is very important.

At the time of the survey there were 805 patients under dialysis in the 123 centers, 30 of which were VA hospitals.

"Since the survey was completed we estimate that another 200 patients have gone on artificial kidneys," Katz said.

"Of the 668 patients who replied to our questionnaires, 499 were males and 165 were females," he said. "Ten percent were *under 19 years old, 22 percent were between 20 and 30, 29 percent were between 30 and 40, 26 percent between 40 and 50."*

Most of the patients live with their wives and children, and 16 percent with their parents or other relatives.

Katz said most of the patients were very sick or near death just before beginning treatment. Despite that, more than 50 percent now are working or being retrained for a new job. Most of the men in physically demanding jobs have had to give them up.

Kidneys provide the crucial function of removing from the blood wastes and unwanted chemicals, which are then secreted in urine. The importance of healthy kidney function is revealed by the fact that Nature gives each of us two. Kidneys are strong organs that can self-correct for a number of malfunctions, but they can be brought down by infections and other diseases that were formerly dreaded as much as cancer is today. By the late 1960s, however, many patients who were otherwise doomed to an early death could be saved by dialysis—circulating their blood through a mechanical filter periodically (commonly three or four eight-hour stints per week)—as a hospital in-patient.

Dialysis machines, highly limited in supply and expensive to use, created in the late 1960s for hospitals and physicians a very short-run rationing problem like that described for other commodities on pages 25–26. But *price* was not allowed to ration access to the scarce kidney machines among competing patients. To permit dying kidney patients to bid against each other for access would have been contrary to the ethics that many of us hold. Moreover, the life-or-death character of such competition would have permitted exorbitantly high prices and earnings to the hospitals providing such services. These would have created an "embarrassment-of-riches" problem for the hospitals, since most of them were not-for-profit organizations. In any case few had incentives to use price as the rationing device since they could not divide the receipts among the hospital owners and/or managers. The rationing of kidney machine time by price, along the lines discussed on pages 25–26, was never a serious possibility.

Instead, hospitals established committees of physicians who effectively decided who would live and who would not by their rationing of the scarce machine-hours. Their judgments were to some extent "subjective," and in some cases depended upon whether the personality of the patient was "congenial" or "likable." (Does the local gas station or furniture store accept your patronage on such criteria?) But a striking feature of most of their rationing criteria was the extent to which they paralleled the outcomes that probably would have resulted under straightforward price competition. The people who received rights to machine time typically were young, had good jobs and incomes, were intelligent, and were diligent workers—economics-oriented criteria that would have been relatively important under an outright ability-to-pay mode of competition. It is also interesting to note that more of the patients were men than women, reflecting the fact that men dominated the labor force during this era, a situation that one would not expect to exist if the test period were in the 1980s instead of the 1960s.

The importance of economic criteria even in institutions that shun profits suggests how powerful those criteria are in our society, although one would hope that the committees assigned weight to noneconomic quality-of-life factors also before rendering their awesome judgments. In any case, within a decade the very short-run rationing problems were alleviated by the marked advances in dialysis technology that emerged largely from the private, profit-oriented sector of the economy. In 1980, for example, portable dialysis units permitting treatment at home could be purchased for $14,500, resulting in treatment costs much less than the former hospital charges and permitting patients much greater mobility and convenience.

In Higher Education

College and university education is another product provided mainly by the nonprofit sector of the economy (both private and public organizations) and rationed by nonmarket criteria. Institutions typically seek students who will lead productive lives rather than students who can pay the most in up-front cash. The available spaces are allocated on the basis of performance in high schools, performance on certain standardized exams (such as the College Boards) and other noneconomic criteria that are believed to be important. In the United States, most of the better colleges reject students who can pay high prices but who have little ability in favor of students who may be less endowed with cash but are long on other abilities. Some students who do not initially meet the admissions criteria of the better schools try to establish a record elsewhere that will justify transfer later on, or are content to graduate from less prestigious institutions. This multitiered layer of higher education—provided through a mix of public and private institutions—appears to be workable.

A different situation exists in Japan, where a college degree from a prestigious institution is the sine qua non of a successful life thereafter. The best Japanese universities admit students strictly on the basis of the competitive examinations described in the following news item.[5]

---

[5] William Chapman, "Scandal Rocks Top Japanese University," copyright 4 April 1980, *Los Angeles Times*. Reprinted by permission. © *The Washington Post*. Reprinted by permission.

When the news broke over Waseda University, one of Japan's most prestigious institutions, the shock to those involved with the school was almost unimaginable.

The president was so choked with emotion he could barely speak at a news conference. A fund-raising drive for Waseda's 100th anniversary was postponed. Public apologies poured out, staff members wept and a dean resigned in the traditional Japanese mode of accepting responsibility for a calamity. Later, an employee committed suicide after leaving a note that ended: "Waseda University—banzai."

The news was this: Entrance examinations for Waseda's School of Commerce had been stolen, copied and peddled, complete with answers, for 10 million yen each (about $40,000) to parents desperate to see their children enrolled.

The scandal evoked a new public debate over the high price of college admissions in Japan, a price usually measured not in money but in emotional strain, family pressures and, often in student despair.

Admission to a top Japanese university is the key to economic success and the "good life," and the pressures to pass entrance exams are intense. Students begin cramming for them in expensive after-hours classes while they are in primary school. Parents go into debt to hire tutors. Suicides and mental breakdowns are common.

The failure rate is high. Of 22,777 who took the Waseda commerce test recently, only 2,130 were accepted.

The pressures of seeking entrance to a top university are accepted because the stakes are so high—perhaps the highest of a lifetime for an ambitious person. Admission is a near-guarantee of lifetime employment at a good salary. Once admitted, students encounter a leisurely academic routine, and few flunk out. Even before graduation they are recruited by the best companies and, barring some calamitous experience on the job, can look forward to regular raises and promotions until retirement.

Social critics who have long deplored the system and advocated reform called the Waseda exam scandal almost inevitable. Kiyoaki Murata, a columnist for the Japan Times, called it the "tip of the iceberg."

"The situation is merely a reflection of the nature of Japanese society, which places inordinate value on a diploma from a name university," he wrote. "As long as there is a market, there will be a supplier, whose monetary incentive can be restrained only by his own ethics."

With the exams having such value, their theft is nothing new. In 1971 someone stole Osaka University entrance exams from a jailhouse printing shop, which was supposed to be the safest place to store them.

There have also been many cases of parents making "backdoor payments" to have their children enrolled in medical and dental *schools. The head of a medical prep school called Tokyo Seminar was accused last year of collecting 2.6 million yen from 110 parents by promising admission into private universities, mostly medical schools.*

But it is rare that a major exam-selling scandal hits one of the major universities such as Waseda, a private college with 40,000 students on three Tokyo campuses.

According to the police version, confirmed by a Waseda official, the latest scandal took form last November when Iichi Watanabe, a Waseda alumnus and warehouse company executive, offered a large sum of money for copies of the School of Commerce exam, scheduled to be given Feb. 24.

He found accomplices in two Waseda clerks, who enlisted a third man, an employee of the university print shop, to smuggle out copies of exams in the areas of mathematics, social studies, English and Japanese. They were quickly copied and returned to the print shop.

Then Watanabe arranged to have model answers prepared by an unknowing group of Waseda students. Authorities believe sets of exams and answers were peddled to at least 10 parents for 10 million yen apiece.

The case took a tragic turn recently when a long-time Waseda employee, Tomokazu Goto, leaped to his death in front of a suburban train, leaving behind a note saying he could not stand the suspicions that he was involved. He had been questioned by the university, but police said he was not a suspect.

Students who fail their examinations are relegated to the career "dustbin," so there is intense pressure on them and their families for a successful exam score. As Mr. Chapman puts it, the "price of college admissions in Japan . . . (is) measured not in money but in emotional strain, family pressures, and often in student despair." Since the pass rate is only about 10 percent, the pressure on families to get their children admitted must be enormous. Not the least of the pressure factors is the fact that a few slots will be filled on the basis of very small and possibly even tiny differences in the exam scores of competing applicants (just as in the United States a few slots are decided on the basis of small differences in grades or other accomplishments).

According to the article, pressures sometimes get out of hand as families attempt to substitute other criteria for the exam scores. Mr. Chapman describes well the tragedies that may arise when the temptations for school officials become great. But his article carries the implication that the Japanese scandal was related to the *existence of markets* in educational admission. This is unfortunate because the bribery scandal resulted from the *interference with markets*. Chapman quotes approvingly the remarks of a Japanese journalist, Mr. Murata, "As long as there is a market, there will be a supplier, whose monetary incentive can be restrained only by his own ethics." On this point Murata, and possibly Chapman, are wrong by 180 degrees. Bribery, an *illegal* payment, is not found where free markets exist but in situations where they are restricted because of either social conventions or laws. Do you have to bribe a furniture store or the plumber? What about your piano teacher or the local Chevrolet dealer? These goods and services are sold in free markets by ordinary firms or proprietorships at roughly market-equilibrium price levels. It is the *absence* of market-clearing prices, owing to price controls or other restrictions, as in the Japanese situation, that creates the potential for bribery.

Although it is risky to draw inferences from a limited sample, it is nonetheless interesting to speculate on why the article about kidney dialysis gave no hint of bribery at the hospitals involved. Was it because Americans are more honest than Japanese? Probably not. Perhaps it was because the scarce resources in the kidney case were allocated by criteria that were a bit closer to those that would have dominated in a market situation than occurred in the case of the Japanese university. This is not an argument for using prices and profits to determine the use of *all* of the economy's resources. It is instead a caveat that corruption tends to be more common in situations where market forces are suppressed.

Summary

The purpose of this chapter has been to obtain a picture of the economic system as a whole and to gain some appreciation of how the price mechanism guides and directs a private enterprise economy. Initially a simple economic model of a private enterprise economy was set up. Economic units were classified into two groups: (1) households and (2) business firms. They interact in the markets for consumer goods and services and in resource markets. Households, as resource owners, sell the services of their resources to business firms. Incomes received are used to buy goods from business firms. Business firms receive income from the sale of goods to consumers. Business incomes, in turn, are used to buy resources from resource owners.

We listed five basic functions of an economic system and discussed the ways in which a private enterprise economy performs those functions. A system of prices is the main organizing force. Prices determine what is to be produced. They organize production and play a major role in the distribution of the product. They serve to ration a particular good over its very short-run period during which the supply of the good is fixed. They are also an element in providing for economic maintenance and growth.

Modern mixed economies have a public sector as well as the private one discussed in the chapter. A not-for-profit sector cutting across the public sector and the profit-oriented private sector can also be identified. Ordinarily, in the not-for-profit sector, prices and profits are not given free reign to guide and direct economic activities. Decision makers usually give other—usually personal—criteria greater weight.

Suggested Readings

Alchian, Armen A., and Kessel, Reuben A. "Competition, Monopoly, and the Pursuit of Pecuniary Gain." In *Aspects of Labor Economics*. A Conference of the Universities-National Bureau Committee for Economic Research, Report of the National Bureau of Economic Research, New York. Special Conference Series, Volume 14. Princeton, N.J.: Princeton University Press, 1962, pp. 156–83.

Clarkson, Kenneth W., and Martin, Donald L., eds. *The Economics of Nonproprietary Organizations*. In Richard O. Zerbe, ed., *Research in Law and Economics: A Research Annual*, Supplement 1, 1980. Greenwich, Conn.: JAI Press, 1980.

Friedman, Milton. *Price Theory*. Chicago: Aldine, 1976, Chap. 1.

Knight, Frank H. "Social Economic Organization." In Harry D. Gideonse and others, eds., *Contemporary Society: Syllabus and Selected Readings*. 4th ed. Chicago: University of Chicago Press, 1935, pp. 125–37.

Stigler, George J. *The Theory of Price*. 3rd ed. New York: Crowell-Collier and Macmillan, 1966, Chap. 2.

Questions and Exercises

1 Use the circular flow model to explain each of the following:
   a inflation
   b unemployment

2 Explain the impact of a set of price controls on
   a the determination of what is to be produced
   b the organization of production
   c the distribution of output

3 Consider one of the world's underdeveloped countries in which the quantities of capital available are small and of unskilled labor, large. What kinds of technology would you expect to find in agriculture and in industry?

4   As minority groups attain improved access to educational opportunities, what will be the effects on their incomes? Why?

5   Why do you suppose it is so difficult for economic growth to be generated in the poor countries of the world?

6   Is profit making an evil or a beneficial kind of behavior in a private enterprise economics system? Explain your answer carefully.

7   How would you have handled the rationing of kidney dialysis machine time in the 1960s?

The Purely Competitive
Market Model

A working knowledge of the operations of the price system as it guides and directs the economic activity of a private enterprise economy rests on the foundations of *demand, supply, markets,* and *competition.* Most people have come in contact with these concepts and, not being sophisticated in economic analysis, toss them around loosely. But these are precise concepts to economists and are the main elements of the market models used so extensively in modern microeconomic theory. We first discuss the concept of competition and then turn to the concepts of demand and supply. The analysis of price determination that emerges when the demand and the supply for a particular item are brought together is the essence of the market model and is considered next. Finally, we examine the concept of price elasticity of demand.

Pure Competition

The term *competition* is used ambiguously not only in ordinary conversation but in economic literature as well. Its common meaning is rivalry, but in economics, when used along with the word *pure,* it carries a different meaning. We shall begin by examining the conditions necessary for the existence of pure competition and then consider its role in economic analysis.

The Necessary Conditions for Pure Competition

There are four conditions that set purely competitive markets apart from other market structures. Perfectly competive markets must meet one additional requirement.

Homogeneity of the Product For competition to exist in a market, all sellers of the product being exchanged sell homogeneous units of the product, or at least the buyers of that product believe that this is so. Buyers think, for example, that the bushels of No. 1 hard winter wheat sold by Farmer Brown are identical to those sold by Farmer Smith. Thus they have no reason for preferring the output of Farmer

Brown to that of Farmer Smith or any other seller of No. 1 hard winter wheat.

Smallness of Each Buyer or Seller Relative to the Market   Each buyer and each seller of the product under consideration is too small in relation to the entire market for the product to influence significantly its price. On the selling side, the individual seller supplies such a small proportion of the total supply that if the vendor drops out of the market altogether total supply will not be decreased enough to cause any rise in price. Or, if the individual marketer sells the maximum amount that it can supply, the total supply will not be increased enough to cause price to fall. The individual sellers of most farm products are in this position. On the buying side, any single buyer takes such a small proportion of the total amount placed on the market that that particular purchaser is unable to influence its price. As consumers, we are in this position with respect to most of the items that we buy. Individually we have no impact on the price of bread, meat, milk, safety pins, and so on. Therefore, the influence in a purely competitive market of any one individual buyer or seller of a product is virtually nonexistent.

Absence of Artificial Restraints   Another condition necessary for the existence of pure competition is that there be no artificial restrictions on the demands for, the supplies of, and the prices of whatever is being exchanged. Prices are free to move wherever they will in response to changing conditions of demand and supply. There is no governmental price fixing nor any institutional setting or administering of price by producers' associations, labor unions, or other private agencies. There is no supply restriction enforced by the government or by organized producer groups. Control of demand through governmental rationing is nonexistent.

Mobility   An additional requirement for pure competition is that there be mobility of goods and services and of resources in the economy. New firms are free to enter any desired industry, and resources are free to move among alternative uses to those where they desire employment. Sellers are able to dispose of their goods and services wherever the price is highest. Resources are able to secure employment in their highest paid uses.

"Pure" and "Perfect" Competition

Economists sometimes distinguish between "pure" and "perfect" competition. The distinction is one of degree. The four conditions just discussed are usually considered necessary for the existence of pure competition, whereas perfect competition requires that one more condition be met—that all economic units possess complete knowledge of the economy.

All discrepancies in prices quoted by sellers will be known immediately, and buyers will buy at the lowest prices. This forces sellers charging higher prices to lower their prices at once. If different purchasers offer different prices for whatever they are buying, sellers will know it immediately and will sell to the highest bidders. The low bidders must, of necessity, raise their price offers. In the market for any particular product or resource, a single price will prevail. Examples of perfect competition are very rare, but stock transactions on the New York Stock Exchange may approximate these conditions. The terms of stock transactions are flashed on the Exchange Board as they are concluded. The information is distributed immediately to interested parties all over the country. Under conditions of perfect competition, adjustments of the economy to disturbances in the conditions of demand and supply will be instantaneous. Under conditions of pure competition, it will take some time for adjustments to occur because of incomplete knowledge on the part of individual economic units.

Pure Competition in Economic Analysis

Competition in economics is impersonal in its nature. There is no reason for enmity to develop between two wheat farmers over the effect that either one has on the market since neither has any effect whatsoever. Each one simply does the best that is possible with what is available. Farmer Brown is not out to get or defeat Farmer Smith. By way of contrast, intense rivalry may exist between two automobile agencies or between two filling stations in the same city. One seller's actions influence the market of the other; consequently, in these cases there is rivalry but not pure competition.

No economist insists that pure competition characterizes any economy, nor does anyone claim that it ever has. The question arises, then, as to why study the principles of pure competition at all. Three important answers may be given. First, the principles of pure competition furnish a simple and logical starting point for economic analysis. Second, a large measure of competition does exist in the United States today, although perhaps not in pure form. Third, the theory of pure competition provides a sort of "norm" against which the actual performance of the economy can be checked or evaluated.

With regard to the first answer, an analogy can be drawn to the study of mechanics. No one questions the procedure of starting a study of mechanics and leaving friction out of consideration. This omission is unrealistic since friction inevitably occurs in the real world, but the temporary postponement of its consideration allows a clear statement of mechanical principles. Friction is later introduced and taken into account. Competitive economic theory principles occupy about the same role in economic analysis as do frictionless principles in the study of mechanics. Once we understand how the frictionless (competitive) economy works, we can observe the effects of friction (imperfect competition and restraints of various sorts) and take them into account. To study the theory of pure competition does not mean that one must believe the real world is one of pure competition, nor does it preclude the very legitimate study of imperfect competition. It brings out fundamental cause-and-effect relationships that are also important in imperfect competition. It is simply the logical place to start if one is to understand the principles of imperfect competition and their applications as well as those of pure competition.

With regard to the second answer, studies indicate that there is substantial competition in the United States economy.[1] Enough competition exists and enough economic units buy or sell under conditions approaching pure competition to give us valid answers to a great many economic problems.

Third, in the theory of a market economy pure competition tends to lead toward the set of conditions defining maximum economic welfare or well-being, given the distribution of income. The actual performance of the economy can then be appraised against its potential "best" performance. Imperfectly competitive or monopolistic forces are important in preventing the attainment of the "best" allocation and use of economic resources. Thus, the purely competitive model frequently is used as the basis for public regulation of imperfectly competitive situations. Presumably it underlies the philosophy and enforcement of the Sherman Antitrust Act of 1890 as amended, government regulation of public utilities, and many other public policy measures.

Demand

Turning now to the development of a market model, we define *demand* for a good as the various quantities of it per unit of time that consumers will take off the market at all possible alternative prices, other things being equal or constant. The quantity that consumers will take will be affected by a number of variables such as (1) the

---

[1] See F. M. Scherer, *Industrial Market Structure and Economic Performance* (Chicago: Rand McNally, 1971), Chap. 3; and G. Warren Nutter and Henry A. Einhorn, *Enterprise Monopoly in the United States, 1899–1958* (New York: Columbia University Press, 1969).

price of the good, (2) consumers' tastes and preferences, (3) the number of consumers under consideration, (4) consumers' income, (5) the prices of related goods, (6) the range or number of goods available to consumers, and (7) consumers' expectations regarding future prices of the product.[2] Additional variables could be listed, but these seem to be the most important ones.

Demand Schedules and Demand Curves

The definition of demand singles out the relationship between possible alternative prices of the good and the quantities of it that consumers will take. Variables (2) through (7) are held constant in defining a given state of demand. Usually we think of quantity taken as varying inversely with price. The higher the price of the good, the less that consumers will take; and the lower the price of the good, the greater the quantity that consumers will take—other things being equal or constant. Some exceptions may occur, in which quantity taken varies directly with price, but these must be few.

Note that the term *demand* is used to refer to an entire demand schedule or demand curve.[3] A demand schedule lists the different quantities of the product that consumers will take opposite its alternative prices. A hypothetical demand schedule is shown in Table 3.1. A demand curve is a demand schedule plotted on an ordinary graph. A demand curve is shown in Figure 3.1. The vertical axis of the graph measures price per unit, and the horizontal axis measures quantity of the good per unit of time. Note that the inverse relationship between the price and the quantity demanded makes the demand curve slope downward to the right.

---

[2] In functional form we can represent the demand relationship as

$$x = f(p_x, T, C, I, p_n, R, E),$$

in which

x is the quantity of good or service X

p_x is the price of X

T represents consumers' tastes and preferences

C is the number of consumers under consideration

I represents total consumers' income and its distribution

p_n represents the prices of related goods

R represents the range of goods and services available to consumers

E represents consumers' expectations.

[3] The equation of the demand curve for X can be written as

$$x = f(p_x),$$

in which the other variables listed in Footnote 2 are parameters. Or, we can reverse the dependency relationship and write

$$p_x = g(x),$$

thus expressing the demand equation in the form in which it is usually shown graphically.

Although the demand equations and curves are represented in this section as being linear, this need not be the case. Linear demand curves are simply easier to draw and explain than are curvilinear ones. The equation for a linear demand curve takes the form

$$p_x = a - bx.$$

TABLE 3.1	Price	Quantity per Unit of Time (hundreds)
Demand schedule for product X	$10.00	0
	9.25	1
	8.50	2
	7.75	3
	7.00	4
	6.25	5
	5.50	6
	4.75	7
	4.00	8
	3.25	9
	2.50	10
	1.75	11
	1.00	12
	0.25	13

FIGURE 3.1
Demand curve for product X

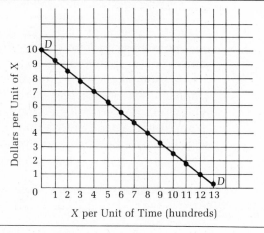

The quantities referred to in Table 3.1 and in Figure 3.1 have no consistent meaning unless they are put in terms of *flows* per time period. They may be stated in terms of a week, month, or year, or whatever time period seems appropriate. It means nothing to say, "At a price of $4 per unit, eight units of product will be taken by consumers." The statement becomes meaningful when we say, "At a price of $4 per unit, eight units of product per week (or month, or whatever the time period happens to be) will be taken by consumers." We are not dealing with quantities as *stocks* but with flows per unit of time. They are rates of purchase, such as 500,000 cars per month or 60 million bushels of wheat per month.

The demand curve separates the purchases that consumers are willing to make from those they are not willing to make. It shows the maximum prices that consumers can be induced to pay for the various quantities indicated on the scale of the horizontal axis, that is, the maximum price at which each of those total quantities can be sold. Or, it can be viewed as showing the maximum quantities that consumers can be induced to take at the price levels indicated on the vertical scale. Any quantity and price shown by a point on, or to the left of and below, the demand curve is a possible or feasible price-quantity combination to consumers. No point to the right of and above the demand curve is a possible or feasible combination.

A Change in Demand versus a Movement
Along a Given Demand Curve

A clear distinction must be drawn between a *movement along* a given demand curve and a *change* in demand. A movement along a given demand curve represents a change in quantity taken resulting from a change in price of the good itself, when all the other circumstances influencing the quantity taken remain unchanged. In Figure 3.2 a decrease in price from p to p_1 increases the quantity taken from X to X_1. This is not called a change in demand since it occurs on a single demand curve, and the term *demand* refers to that entire demand curve. In defining demand we assume that the underlying demand circumstances remain constant while we change the price of the commodity and observe what happens to the quantity demanded.[4]

When any of the circumstances held constant in defining a given state of demand are changed, the demand curve itself will change. Thus, in Figure 3.3 an increase in consumer incomes will shift the demand curve to the right from DD to D_1D_1. With higher incomes, consumers are usually willing to increase their rates of purchase at each alternative price. A shift in consumers' tastes and preferences toward commodity X will have the same results. So, also, will an increase in the number of consumers in the market. An increase in the range of goods available to consumers may cause them to allocate less of their incomes to commodity X, thus shifting the demand curve to the left to position D_2D_2 in Figure 3.3.[5]

---

[4] In the equation

$$p_x = a - bx$$

the coordinates of p_x and x trace out a unique demand curve as long as the parameters a and b remain constant. A change in the value of p_x results in a movement along the curve to the corresponding value of x.

[5] In the equation

$$p_x = a - bx$$

a change in a will shift the price-axis intercept of the curve and a change in b will alter its slope.

FIGURE 3.2
Movement along a
demand curve

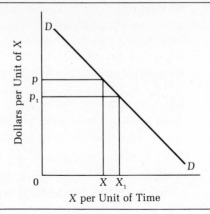

The effects on the demand for X of changes in the prices of goods related to X define the nature of the relationships. A related good is a *competitive* or *substitute* good if an increase in its price causes the demand curve for X to shift to the right. The shift results from consumers turning away from the now relatively higher-priced substitute to X. Suppose, for example, that X is beef and that the price of pork rises. Consumers shift away from pork toward beef, thus increasing the demand for beef.

A related good is a *complementary* good if an increase in its price causes a shift to the left in the demand curve for X. The higher price of the related good induces consumers to take less of it. If in taking less of it they have less desire for X, there is an indication of complementarity. In this case, suppose that X is milk and that the price of cereal rises enough to curtail cereal consumption. The smaller quantity of cereal consumed reduces the desire for milk—the demand curve for milk then shifts to the left.

FIGURE 3.3
Changes in demand

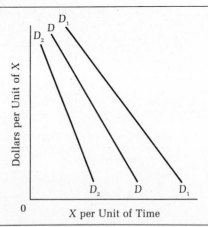

Supply

The supply of a good is defined as the various quantities of it that sellers will place on the market at all possible alternative prices, other things being equal. It is the relationship between prices and quantities per unit of time that sellers are willing to sell. The same distinction is made between a supply schedule and a supply curve that is made between a demand schedule and a demand curve. A supply curve is a supply schedule plotted on a graph. Usually it will be upward sloping to the right, since a higher price will induce sellers to place more of the good on the market and may induce additional sellers to come into the field. A hypothetical supply schedule is listed in Table 3.2 and the corresponding supply curve is shown in Figure 3.4.

TABLE 3.2 Supply schedule for product X	Price	Quantity per Unit of Time (hundreds)
	$4.00	0
	4.25	1
	4.50	2
	4.75	3
	5.00	4
	5.25	5
	5.50	6
	5.75	7
	6.00	8
	6.25	9
	6.50	10
	6.75	11
	7.00	12
	7.25	13

The "other things" that are held constant in defining a given supply curve are basically (1) the set of prices of the resources used to produce the product and (2) the range of production techniques available.[6]

---

[6] The supply function can be written as

$$x = s(p_x, p_r, K),$$

in which

x is the quantity of good or service X
p_x is the price of X
p_r is the set of prices of resources used in producing X
K is the range of production techniques available.

For a short-run supply function we would add M to the list of independent variables, with M representing the number of firms supplying X.

FIGURE 3.4
Supply curve for
product X

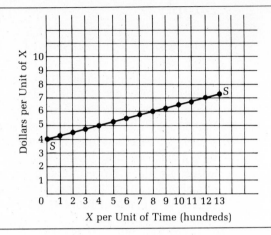

Similarly to the demand curve, the supply curve is a boundary line between what sellers will and will not do. At any given price, sellers would be willing to supply less than the quantity shown by the supply curve at that price, but they cannot be induced to supply more. To be induced to supply any given quantity, sellers must receive at least the price shown by the supply curve at that quantity. They would supply that quantity for a higher price per unit, but they would not supply it for less. Any point on, or above and to the left of, the supply curve represents a possible or feasible quantity supplied at the indicated price. Any point below and to the right of it is not possible or feasible.[7]

For consistency and accuracy in definitions, it is necessary to distinguish between a movement along a given supply curve and a change in supply. In Figure 3.5 a change in the price of X from p_1 to p_2 increases the quantity supplied from X_1 to X_2. This represents a movement along a supply curve—not a change in supply. A change in supply is defined as a shift in the supply curve (for example, from

---

[7] We can express the supply equation as

$$x = h(p_x),$$

or, alternatively, as

$$p_x = s(x),$$

treating the other independent variables of Footnote 6 as parameters. Movements along the supply curve are movements from one set of coordinates to another, with the parameters of the equation remaining constant. A change in supply means a change in the supply equation parameters. Again, when we use linear functions, it is because of their simplicity, not because they are more representative of actual supply conditions. The equation for a linear supply function is

$$p_x = c + dx.$$

FIGURE 3.5
A change in supply
versus a movement
along a supply curve

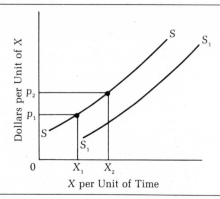

SS to S_1S_1) and results from a change in one of the "other things."[8]

Market Price

Placing the demand curve and the supply curve for any given good or service on a single diagram highlights the forces determining its market price. The demand curve indicates what consumers are willing to do, while the supply curve shows what sellers are willing to do. Consumer demand is assumed to be independent of the activities of sellers. Similarly, the supply curve is assumed to be in no way dependent on consumers' activities. Consumers are assumed to operate independently of one another, and so are sellers.

Market Price Determination

In Figure 3.6 market price determination is illustrated. At price level p_1, consumers are willing to take quantity X_1 per unit of time. However, suppliers will bring quantity X_1' per unit of time to the market; thus, *surpluses* or excess supplies of X_1X_1' per unit of time accumulate. Any seller with a surplus believes that by undercutting other vendors a little, surpluses can be disposed of. Thus, an incentive exists for individual sellers to lower their prices and cut back the

---

[8] In the equation

$$p_x = c + dx$$

the coordinates of p_x and x trace out a unique supply curve as long as the parameters c and d are constant. A change in c shifts the price-axis intercept of the curve, while a change in d alters its slope.

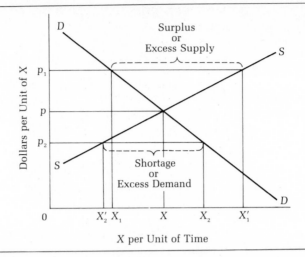

FIGURE 3.6
Equilibrium price
determination

X per Unit of Time

quantity supplied. The price will be driven down by the sellers; quantities supplied will decrease; and quantities demanded will increase. Eventually, when the price has dropped to p, consumers will be willing to take exactly the amount that sellers want to place on the market at that price.

Suppose, alternatively, that sellers initially establish the price at p_2. At this price level consumers want quantity X_2 per unit of time, but sellers will place only X_2' per unit of time on the market. Therefore, *shortages* or excess demand equal to the difference between X_2 and X_2' per time period occur. Faced by the shortages, consumers bid against each other for the available supply, and will continue to do so as long as shortages exist. When the price has been driven up to p by consumers, the shortages will have disappeared and buyers will be taking the quantity that sellers want to sell.

Price p is called the *equilibrium price*. Given the conditions of demand and supply for commodity X, it is the price that, if attained, will be maintained. If the price deviates from p, forces are set in motion to bring it back to that level. A price above the equilibrium price brings about surpluses that induce sellers to undercut each other, driving the price back down to the equilibrium level. A price below the equilibrium level results in shortages that cause consumers to bid the price back up to equilibrium. At a price level of p_1, so much of the good is placed on the market that the value consumers place on any one unit of it is less than the supply price. At price p_2, the quantity placed on the market is so small that the value of a unit of it to consumers is greater than the supply price. At the equilibrium price p, the quantity that suppliers place on the market is such that the supply price and consumers' valuation of a unit of the good are the same.[9]

Changes in Demand and Supply

What happens to the equilibrium price and the quantity exchanged of a good when the demand for it changes? Suppose that DD and SS in Figure 3.7 represent the demand for and supply of apartment units in a given community. Now a private college is established in the

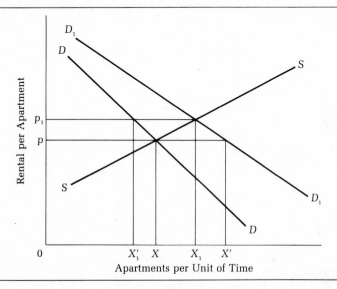

FIGURE 3.7
Effects of a change in demand

community and its enrollment expands rapidly. The influx of apartment consumers brings about an increase in demand to D_1D_1. At the original price or rental rate p, there will be a shortage equal to XX' apartments, and consumers will bid up the price to p_1. The quantity placed on the market and rented out will increase to X_1 as the higher

[9] The equilibrium price and quantity are determined mathematically by solving the demand and supply equations simultaneously. If these are, respectively,

$$p_x = g(x)$$

and

$$p_x = s(x),$$

we have two equations, two unknowns, and a determinate solution.

More specifically, representing demand and supply as lines or curves, let the demand and supply equation be

$$p_x = 10 - \tfrac{3}{4}x \quad \text{(Demand)}$$
$$p_x = \ 4 + \tfrac{1}{4}x \quad \text{(Supply)}.$$

Solving these simultaneously, we find that $x = 6$ and $p_x = 5.50$.

rental rate induces some property owners and builders in the community to construct apartments. After the increase in demand, the new equilibrium price and quantity demanded are thus p_1 and X_1, respectively.

The same diagram can be used to illustrate the effects of a decrease in demand on the price and the quantity exchanged of a product. Let D_1D_1 be the initial demand curve for apartments, while SS is the supply curve. Now suppose that the state university, located in a city 30 miles away, cuts its tuition rates substantially, drawing students away from the private college community. Demand for apartments in the community drops to DD, and at the initial equilibrium price p_1 there is a surplus of $X_1'X_1$. Rental rates will decrease, and fewer apartments will be rented out as property owners find it less worthwhile to make available and maintain some of their apartments. The new equilibrium price and quantity demanded will be p and X, respectively.

Similarly, changes in supply, given the demand curve for a good, will bring about changes in the equilibrium price and quantity exchanged. In Figure 3.8 let DD and SS represent the initial demand curve and initial supply curve for bales of cotton. Suppose that growing conditions become much better than was initially expected, causing supply to increase to S_1S_1. At the initial equilibrium price p, there will be a surplus of XX', causing the price to fall to p_1 and the quantity exchanged to increase to X_1. On the other hand, if S_1S_1 were the initial supply curve and a drought reduced the supply of cotton to SS, a shortage amounting to $X_1'X_1$ bales per unit of time would

FIGURE 3.8
Effects of a change in supply

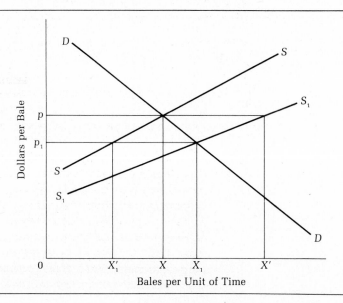

occur at the equilibrium price p_1. The price would rise to p, and the quantity exchanged would fall to X.

Price Elasticity of Demand

The concept of *elasticity* is very useful in economic analysis, as we shall see throughout the rest of this book. Price elasticity of demand measures the responsiveness of the quantity that will be demanded to changes in the price of a good or service, given the demand curve for it. If the quantity taken is highly responsive to a small price change, a price increase will cause the total expenditures on the good to decrease; and a price decrease will cause them to rise. If the quantity demanded is not very responsive to price changes, an increase in the price will increase total expenditures on the good, whereas a price decrease will cause them to fall. These points are of such importance that we develop them at some length below. However, first, we examine the technical aspects of elasticity measurement.

Measurement of Price Elasticity

Intuitively, it appears that the slope of a demand curve is a sufficient measure of the responsiveness of quantity taken to price changes. The slope of a small segment of such a curve can be obtained by observing how much quantity taken changes when the price goes up or down by a certain amount. For example, if a decrease of 10 cents in the price of potatoes causes a 100-bushel increase in quantity taken, the slope of that portion of the curve is $-10/100$ or $-1/10$. However, if we redraw the demand curve, measuring the price in dollars instead of cents, the slope of the same segment of the demand curve becomes $(-1/10)/100$, or $-1/1000$. The shift from cents to dollars in measuring the price causes a drastic decrease in the measurement of the downward slope of the demand curve, even though there has been no real change in the demand curve itself. If we draw the demand curve again, measuring the price in dollars and the quantity taken in pecks, the slope of the same segment of the curve becomes $(-1/10)/400$, or $-1/4000$. Obviously, the slope of the demand curve is a very unreliable indicator of how responsive quantity taken is to changes in price.

  The comparative slopes of demand curves for different goods are also useless as measures of the comparative responsiveness of quantities taken to changes in prices. In comparing the demand curve for wheat with the demand curve for automobiles, suppose that we want to know in which case quantity taken is more responsive to a change in price. The comparative slopes of the two demand curves tell us nothing. A $1 drop in the price of wheat may increase quantity taken by 20 million bushels per month. A $1 decrease in the price of automobiles may increase quantity taken by 5 automobiles per month. This situation, however, does not mean that the quantity taken of wheat is more responsive to changes in its price than is the quantity taken of automobiles to changes in the automobile price. A $1 change in the price of wheat is a very large relative change. A $1 change in the price of automobiles is of little relative consequence. Further, a unit of wheat and a unit of automobile are completely different concepts, and there is no basis for comparing a unit of one with a unit of the other.

The great British economist Alfred Marshall, in response to this difficulty, defined the price elasticity of demand as the percentage change in quantity demanded divided by the percentage change in price, *when the price change is small.*[10] In terms of algebra, the basic definition becomes

$$\epsilon = \frac{\Delta x/x}{\Delta p/p}$$

Consider the movement from A to B in Figure 3.9. The change in quantity from x to x_1 is Δx. The change in price from p to p_1 is Δp. The number or coefficient denoting elasticity is obtained by dividing a percentage by a percentage; it is a pure number independent of

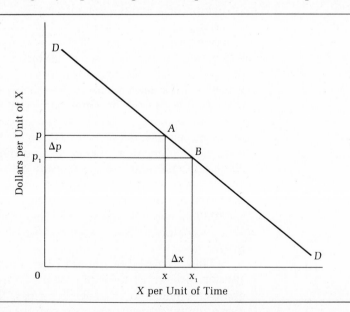

FIGURE 3.9
Measurement of arc elasticity

[10]   Alfred Marshall, *Principles of Economics*, 8th ed. (London: Macmillan, 1920), Bk. III, Chap. IV.

such units of measurement as bushels, pecks, or dollars. Elasticity will be the same between two given points on a demand curve for wheat, regardless of whether the price is measured in dollars or cents and regardless of whether the quantity is measured in bushels or pecks. The elasticity computed between two separate points on the demand curve is called *arc elasticity*. The elasticity computed at a single point on the curve for an infinitesimal change in price is called *point elasticity*. We discuss the two concepts in turn.

Arc Elasticity

Suppose that we want to compute the elasticity of demand between A and B in Figure 3.9, and the coordinates of the two points are as follows:

	p (cents)	x (bushels)
At point A	100	1,000,000
At point B	90	1,200,000

If we move from point A to point B, substituting the appropriate numbers in the elasticity formula, we find that:

$$\epsilon = \frac{\dfrac{200,000}{1,000,000}}{\dfrac{-10}{100}} = \frac{200,000}{1,000,000} \times \frac{100}{-10} = -2. \qquad (3.1)$$

However, if we move in the opposite direction from point B to point A, then

$$\epsilon = \frac{\dfrac{-200,000}{1,200,000}}{\dfrac{10}{90}} = \frac{-200,000}{1,200,000} \times \frac{90}{10} = -1.5. \qquad (3.2)$$

The percentage changes in quantity and price are different, depending on the price and quantity from which we start. The differences in the starting points lead us to different values of the elasticity coefficient.

These computations show that arc elasticity between any two points on a demand curve must be an approximation. The farther apart the points between which arc elasticity is calculated, the greater will be the discrepancy between the two coefficients obtained, and the less reliable either will be. If arc elasticity is to be meaningful, it must be computed between points on the demand curve that are close together.

To avoid these discrepancies, a modification of the basic elasticity formula can be used. With reference to Figure 3.9, suppose that elasticity is calculated as

$$\epsilon = \frac{\Delta x / x}{\Delta p / p_1} \tag{3.3}$$

where p_1 is the lower of the two prices and x is the lower of the two quantities. Using this to compute elasticity between A and B, we find that

$$\epsilon = \frac{200,000}{1,000,000} \div - \frac{10}{90} = \frac{200,000}{1,000,000} \times - \frac{90}{10} = -1.8. \tag{3.4}$$

The modified formula provides a very usable average between the two coefficients obtained with the basic formula.[11]

The demand elasticity coefficient shows the approximate percentage change in quantity demanded for a 1 percent change in price and will be negative in sign since the price and the quantity change in opposite directions. However, when economists speak of the magnitude of elasticity, they mean the absolute value of the coefficient, ignoring the minus sign. Thus, they say that an elasticity of minus one is greater than an elasticity of minus one-half; and an elasticity of minus two is greater than an elasticity of minus one.

Point Elasticity

The point elasticity concept is more precise than that of arc elasticity. If the two points between which arc elasticity is measured are moved closer and closer together, arc elasticity becomes point elasticity as the distance between the points approaches zero.

Elasticity at a point can be measured by a simple geometric method. Figure 3.10 shows a straight line (linear) demand curve. To measure elasticity at point P, we start with the basic formula:

$$\epsilon = \frac{\Delta x / x}{\Delta p / p} = \frac{\Delta x}{x} \times \frac{p}{\Delta p}. \tag{3.5}$$

This can be rearranged to read[12]

$$\epsilon = \frac{\Delta x}{\Delta p} \times \frac{p}{x}. \tag{3.6}$$

---

[11] Another arc elasticity formula frequently used is:

$$\epsilon = \frac{x - x_1}{x + x_1} \div \frac{p - p_1}{p + p_1}.$$

Elasticity computed with this formula between points A and B in Figure 3.9 is -1.7. This formula, too, strikes an average between the coefficients arrived at by means of the basic formula when we work first from A to B and then work in reverse from B to A. See George J. Stigler, *The Theory of Price*, 3rd ed. (New York: Crowell-Collier and Macmillan, 1966), pp. 331–33.

[12] In terms of calculus:

$$\epsilon = \lim_{\Delta p \to o} \frac{\Delta x}{\Delta p} \times \frac{p}{x} = \frac{dx}{dp} \times \frac{p}{x}.$$

FIGURE 3.10
Measurement of point
elasticity

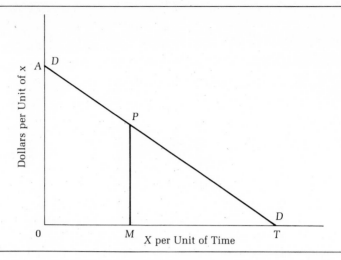

On the demand curve, $\Delta p/\Delta x$ is the algebraic expression of the slope of the curve for small price changes from point P. Geometrically, the slope of the demand curve is MP/MT. Therefore, $\Delta p/\Delta x = MP/MT$, or, inverting both fractions, $\Delta x/\Delta p = MT/MP$. Price at point P is MP and quantity at that point is $0M$. Thus, at point P

$$\epsilon = \frac{MT}{MP} \times \frac{MP}{0M} = \frac{MT}{0M}.$$

Price elasticity coefficients are separated into three absolute value classifications. When they are greater than one, demand is said to be *elastic*. When they equal one, it is said to be of *unitary* elasticity. When they are less than one, demand is said to be *inelastic*. These classifications are illustrated on the linear demand curve of Figure 3.11. Point P is located so that $0M = MT$. Since elasticity of demand at point P equals $MT/0M$, elasticity is unitary at that point. Consider any point farther up the demand curve—point P_1, for example. Since M_1T is greater than $0M_1$, elasticity at point P_1 is greater than one. The farther up the demand curve we move, the greater elasticity becomes, until, as we approach point A, elasticity approaches infinity (∞). Moving down the demand curve to the right from point P, elasticity is less than one and becomes progressively smaller the farther we move. As we approach point T, elasticity approaches zero.[13]

This technique for measuring point elasticity can also be used

[13]   Mathematically, consider that

$$\epsilon = \frac{dx}{dp} \times \frac{p}{x}.$$

For the linear demand curve of Figure 3.11, the dx/dp term of the elasticity coefficient is constant. As $x \to 0$, then the term $p/x \to \infty$ and $\epsilon \to \infty$. As $p \to 0$, then $p/x \to 0$ and $\epsilon \to 0$.

FIGURE 3.11
Elasticity
measurements on a
linear demand curve

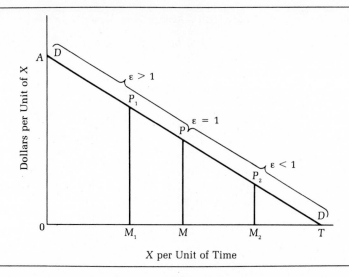

on a nonlinear curve. Suppose that elasticity is to be measured at point P on the demand curve in Figure 3.12. First, draw a tangent to the demand curve at point P and extend it so that it cuts the quantity axis at point T. At point P, the demand curve and the tangent coincide and have the same slopes; therefore, their elasticities must be the same at that point. Measurement of elasticity can proceed as before. Drop a perpendicular from P to $0T$ and call its intersection with the quantity axis point M. Elasticity of demand at point P is equal to $MT/0M$.

FIGURE 3.12
Elasticity
measurement on a
nonlinear demand
curve

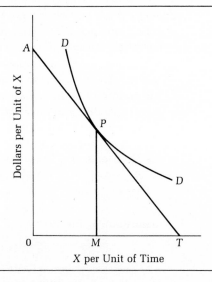

Elasticity and Total Money Outlays

One of the most important aspects of demand elasticity is the relationship that exists among price changes, elasticity, and total amount of money spent for the good. The total amount spent can be viewed either as total buyers' outlay (*TO*) or total sellers' receipts (*TR*) for the item. This amount is found by multiplying the quantity sold by the price per unit at which it is sold.

Suppose that for a certain small price decrease demand is elastic—the percentage increase in quantity sold exceeds the percentage decrease in price. Since the increase in quantity demanded is proportionally greater than the decrease in price, such a price decrease increases sellers' total receipts. Similarly, if demand were inelastic for such a price decrease, the increase in quantity demanded would be proportionally less than the price decrease, and sellers' total receipts would decline. If elasticity were unitary, the proportional increase in quantity sold would equal the proportional decrease in price, and total receipts would remain unchanged. For price increases, the effects on total receipts will be just the opposite.[14]

These results are summarized on the linear demand curve of Figure 3.13(a) and the total receipts curve of Figure 3.13(b). Moving down the demand curve from *A* toward *J*, the elasticity of demand is decreasing but exceeds one; and *TR* will be increasing. For example, at price *B* and quantity *S*, *TR* is equal to the area of rectangle $0BGS$ in Figure 3.13(a), and the vertical distance *SN* in Figure 3.13(b); while at price *C* and quantity *M*, *TR* is the area of rectangle $0CJM$ in the upper diagram and the vertical distance *MQ* in the lower one.

---

[14] The total receipts equation is

$$TR = p \times x.$$

Differentiating with respect to x

$$\frac{dTR}{dx} = p + x\frac{dp}{dx} = p + p\left(\frac{x}{p} \times \frac{dp}{dx}\right) = p + \frac{p}{\dfrac{p}{x} \times \dfrac{dx}{dp}}.$$

Since

$$\epsilon = \frac{p}{x} \times \frac{dx}{dp},$$

then

$$\frac{dTR}{dx} = p + \frac{p}{\epsilon}.$$

The sign of ϵ is negative since dx/dp is negative; however, in terms of the absolute value of ϵ,

$$\frac{dTR}{dx} = p - \frac{p}{|\epsilon|}.$$

Therefore, for any increase in x, if

1. $|\epsilon| > 1$, then $dTR/dx > 0$ and *TR* increases.
2. $|\epsilon| = 1$, then $dTR/dx = 0$ and *TR* is unchanged.
3. $|\epsilon| < 1$, then $dTR/dx < 0$ and *TR* decreases.

FIGURE 3.13
Elasticity, price
changes, and *TR*

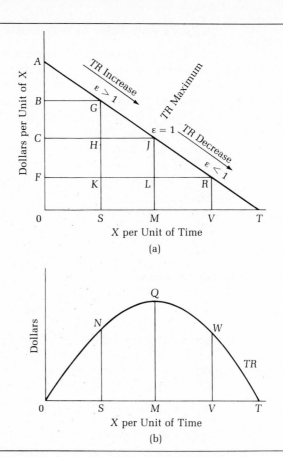

By inspection it is apparent that $0CJM$ is larger in area than $0BGS$. As we move down the demand curve from J toward T, elasticity continues to decrease, is less than one, and TR decreases. At price F and quantity V, TR is the area of rectangle $0FRV$ and the vertical distance VW. It is evident that this area is smaller than that of $0CJM$. It follows that at point J, where elasticity is unitary, TR is maximum.

When a demand curve is a rectangular hyperbola, the elasticity of demand at all points on it is unitary. Such a curve is illustrated in Figure 3.14. Its basic characteristic is that the price multiplied by the quantity demanded yields the same total receipts, regardless of what price is charged. For price increases or for price decreases, total receipts remain unchanged; that is, $x \times p = x_1 \times p_1 = \cdots = x_n \times p_n$.[15]

A seller, contemplating changes in the price of what he sells, needs to know the elasticity of demand for the price change. If de-

---

[15] If the demand curve is a rectangular hyperbola, then

$$x \times p = TR = k,$$

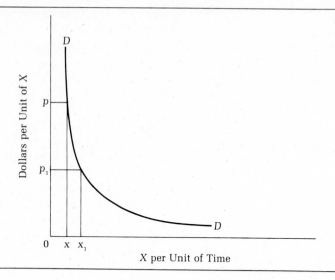

FIGURE 3.14
Unitary elasticity,
price changes, and *TR*

Dollars per Unit of X (vertical axis)

X per Unit of Time (horizontal axis)

mand is inelastic, a price increase is advisable, but a price decrease is not. The former would increase the seller's total receipts, while at the same time it would cut sales. The latter would increase the seller's sales but would cut total receipts.

Factors Influencing Price Elasticity of Demand

The major factors influencing elasticity remain to be considered. These are (1) the availability of good substitutes for the item under consideration, (2) the number of uses to which it can be put, (3) its price relative to buyers' purchasing power, and (4) whether the price established is toward the upper end of the demand curve or the lower end of the curve. These should be thought of as points to look for in trying to determine whether demand will be more or less elastic in the neighborhood of the ruling price.

    The availability of substitutes is the most important of the factors listed. If good substitutes are available, demand for a given

in which k is a constant. Therefore,

$$x = \frac{k}{p}.$$

Differentiating with respect to p,

$$\frac{dx}{dp} = -\frac{k}{p^2}.$$

Thus,

$$\epsilon = -\frac{k}{p^2} \times \frac{p}{x} = -1$$

for all values of x and p.

product or resource will tend to be elastic. If the price of whole wheat bread is decreased while the prices of other kinds remain constant, consumers will shift rapidly from the other kinds to whole wheat bread. Conversely, increases in the price of whole wheat bread while the prices of other kinds remain constant will cause consumers to shift rapidly away from it to the now relatively lower-priced substitutes.

The wider the range of uses for a product or resource, the more elastic demand for it will tend to be. The greater the number of uses, the greater the possibility there is for variation in quantity taken as its price varies. Suppose that aluminum can be used only in the making of airframes for aircraft. Not much possibility exists for variation in quantity taken as its price varies, and demand for it would likely be inelastic. Actually, aluminum can be put to hundreds of uses requiring a lightweight metal. The possible variation in quantity taken is quite large. Increases in its price subtract from, and decreases in its price add to, the list of its economically desirable uses. These possibilities tend to make demand for aluminum more elastic.

Demand for goods that take a large amount of the buyers' budgets is more likely to be elastic than demand for goods that are relatively unimportant in this respect. Goods such as deep freezers, which require large outlays, make consumers price-conscious and substitute-conscious. An increase in the price of deep freezers causes shifts toward the use of commercial lockers. Quantity demanded, therefore, is likely to vary considerably in response to price changes. For goods such as salt or spices, which take a negligible part of consumers' incomes, changes in price are likely to have little effect on the quantity taken. Consumers are likely to be much less substitute-conscious.

If the ruling price is toward the upper end of the demand curve, demand is more likely to be elastic than if it were toward the lower end. This is a mathematical determinant of elasticity, and its validity depends on the shape of the curve. It rests on a different footing from that of the other three determinants. Figure 3.15 shows a linear demand curve.[16] If the original price is p and changes to p_1, and the original quantity demanded is x and changes to x_1, the percentage change in quantity is large because the original quantity is small compared with the quantity change. The percentage change in price is small because the original price is large compared with the change in price. A large percentage change in quantity demanded, divided by a small percentage change in price, means that demand is elastic.

***

[16] The argument of this paragraph does not apply to a demand curve that is a rectangular hyperbola or to one that has greater convexity to the origin than has a rectangular hyperbola. It applies only to those with less convexity.

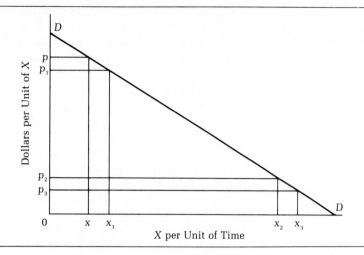

FIGURE 3.15
Dependency of
elasticity on
comparative
percentage changes

If the original price is p_2 and changes to p_3, and the original quantity is x_2 and changes to x_3, the reverse is the case. The percentage change in quantity demanded is small because the original quantity is large. The percentage change in price is large because the original price is small. A small percentage change in quantity demanded, divided by a large percentage change in price, means that demand is inelastic.

With the possible exception of the first point, concerning availability of substitutes, these are not infallible criteria of elasticity of demand; they simply express the nature of the forces affecting it. Additionally, they need not all work in the same direction at the same time. One or more may be working against the others, and the magnitude of elasticity will depend on the relative strengths of the opposing forces.

Cross Elasticity of Demand

Another elasticity concept that is useful in economic analysis is the cross elasticity of demand. It provides a measure of the extent to which commodities are related to each other. If we consider commodities X and Y, the cross elasticity of X with respect to Y is defined as the percentage change in the quantity demanded of X divided by the percentage change in the price of Y. This is expressed mathematically by[17]

$$\Theta_{xy} = \frac{\Delta x/x}{\Delta p_y/p_y}. \tag{3.8}$$

---

[17] Or, in terms of calculus,

$$\Theta_{xy} = \lim_{\Delta p_y \to 0} \frac{\Delta x}{\Delta p_y} \times \frac{p_y}{x} = \frac{\delta x}{\delta p_y} \times \frac{p_y}{x}.$$

Goods and services, or resources for that matter, may be related as substitutes or as complements.

When goods are substitutes for each other, the sign of the cross-elasticity coefficient between them will be positive. Frankfurters and hamburger provide an illustration. An increase in the price of frankfurters will increase hamburger consumption. Changes in the price of frankfurters and in the consumption of hamburger are in the same direction, whether price moves up or down; the cross elasticity is positive.

Goods that are complementary have negative cross-elasticity coefficients. Notebook paper and pencils serve as an illustration. An increase in the price of notebook paper cuts paper consumption and, consequently, the consumption of pencils. A decrease in the price of paper will increase its consumption and, also, the consumption of pencils. The change in the price of notebook paper is accompanied by a change in the consumption of pencils in the opposite direction. Therefore, the cross-elasticity coefficient will be negative.

Cross elasticity of demand is frequently used in attempts to define the boundaries of an industry; however, its use for this purpose has certain complications. High cross elasticities indicate close relationships or goods in the same industry. Low cross elasticities indicate remote relationships or goods in different industries. A commodity whose cross elasticity is low with respect to all other commodities is sometimes considered to be in an industry by itself. A commodity group with high cross elasticities within the group, but with low cross elasticities vis-à-vis other commodities, is often said to constitute an industry. Various kinds of women's shoes will have high cross elasticities among each other but low cross elasticities with regard to other articles of women's clothing. Thus, we have a basis for separating out a women's shoe industry.

One difficulty with cross elasticity as a means of determining industry boundaries is that of establishing how high the coefficients among commodities must be if they are to be considered in the same industry. Cross elasticities among some foods are quite high—those among frozen peas, frozen green beans, frozen asparagus spears, and the like. Others, such as those between frozen vegetables and frozen meat, are likely to be quite low. Is there a frozen food industry? Answers cannot be given unequivocally. Some general economic problems can best be solved by considering all frozen foods in the same industry. Narrower or more specific economic problems will require narrower industry groupings—a frozen-vegetable industry or, perhaps, even a frozen-pea industry. Cross elasticities furnish a guide to, but not a hard and fast determination of, industry boundaries.

Another complication is that of chains of cross relationships. Cross elasticities may be high between passenger cars and station wagons, and between station wagons and pick up trucks. But passenger cars and pick up trucks may have low cross elasticities. Are they in separate industries or in the same industry? Again, the nature of the problem we want to attack must be the guide to the proper definition of industry boundaries.

Applications

In assessing the impact of an economic happening on the price and quantity exchanged of a product, it is useful to single out first its effects on demand and its effects on supply. But, as the following three illustrations indicate, clear analysis requires that the concepts be carefully defined.

Demand versus Quantity Demanded

Failure to make a clear distinction between changes in demand for a product and changes in quantities demanded leads, at worst, to serious errors of economic analysis and, at best, to confusion. The following article from *The Wall Street Journal* demonstrates the point.[18]

> *STRONG PORK DEMAND, DUE TO LOW PRICES, MAY INDICATE PERMANENT SHIFT FROM BEEF*
>
> *Beef remains America's favorite meat, but surprisingly strong demand for pork this fall is intriguing the meat industry.*
>
> *At least some analysts think pork may increase its share of the nation's meat menu. "Beef is still the preferred item, because that's the way we were born and raised," says Chuck Levitt, livestock analyst for Shearson Loeb Rhoades Inc. in Chicago.*
>
> *"But in the long run, you may get a change in consumption habits," he adds. "The new generation is getting a heavy dose of pork."*
>
> *Robin Fuller, livestock analyst for Dean Witter Reynolds Inc. in Chicago, agrees: "The price of pork has become favorable to the price of beef at other times, but never for this prolonged period of time. There may be some permanent switch in consumption patterns after all this is over."*
>
> *Pork's price has been its big lure, of course. The Agriculture Department says the average retail price of pork this year was $1.44 a pound, about the same as last year. But beef's average retail price rose nearly 20%, to $2.26 a pound. Next year, pork is expected to fall to $1.40, while beef climbs to $2.46.*
>
> ***More Than Meets the Pocketbook***
>
> *Apart from the price gap, some officials think there is more to pork's popularity than meets the pocketbook. Millions of hogs*

---

[18] Steve Weiner, "Strong Pork Demand, Due to Low Prices, May Indicate Permanent Shift From Beef," *The Wall Street Journal*, 21 December 1979, p. 24. Reprinted by permission of *The Wall Street Journal*, © Dow Jones & Company, Inc. 1979. All rights reserved.

were slaughtered this fall, they note, and if everything had happened according to plan, the meat market would have been glutted with pork and prices would have plummeted.

Instead, after a modest slump in November, key pork prices are about the same as they were in late September. The brisk demand that caused prices to hold up so well surprised nearly everyone in the industry. Currently, some hog specialists are predicting big things for pork.

Mark W. Thomas, executive secretary of the National Livestock and Meat Board's pork industry group, says it is realistic to think that in five to eight years per-capita pork consumption may reach a steady 100 pounds a year, up from about 65 pounds this year. Beef consumption this year is estimated at 78 pounds a person, measured by retail weight.

Pork Consumption to Grow

Orville Sweet, executive vice president of the National Pork Producers Council, believes pork consumption will grow to over 70 pounds a person next year.

Mr. Sweet says that "whenever we start eating as much as 80 pounds of pork per person or more, we'll have people who have never eaten pork before. I think pork is destined to have a larger share of the red-meat market."

Prices for hogs and pork in the fourth quarter have tended to bolster such producer optimism. As of Sept. 1, the government estimated the number of hogs and pigs in 14 top-producing states at 57 million head, up 16% from last year. And, going into the usual autumn liquidation period, slaughter was correspondingly high, up 15%. The expectation was that hog producers, fearing a price crash caused by 1979's overproduction, would swamp the market by reducing herds—thus reducing prices even further.

Confirming the Theory

The number of animals offered for slaughter semed to be confirming the theory. Daily slaughters early in the year ran from 310,000 to 335,000 head regularly. But in November, daily slaughters began to approach 400,000 head, a high figure even taking into account seasonal factors.

Prices did slip as a consequence, but they didn't collapse, as had been feared. Supermarkets featured pork specials, and booming demand kept retail prices relatively high. With good retail profits to be made, supermarkets sought more pork from packers, who suddenly found profit margins restored as they bought inexpensive animals and sold the meat for good prices.

Prospects are for better prices for producers next year. Greater production also is expected next year. The Agriculture Department says 1980 pork production should reach 16.5 billion pounds, up 9% from this year. Analysts think a quarterly hog and pig report, to be issued today, will show a 10% to 13% higher animal inventory. But they believe it also will show signs that the hog herd's size will level off or be reduced in 1980.

> *The beef industry isn't showing signs of worry about pork's growth, though. The National Cattlemen's Association says it is confident beef will regain its solid following when supplies grow. And Dennis Schmidt, director of meat merchandising for Super Valu Stores Inc., a big wholesaler, says he doubts pork will maintain its gains. "After all, when you want to have a nice dinner, what do you have? Pork chops?" says Mr. Schmidt.*

Can you spot analytical problems in the article? Consider first the title. The first part confuses a *movement along the demand curve for pork* with an *increase in demand.* Either of two editing changes—one in the first clause or one in the second—could make it conform with sound economic analysis. The next part compounds the problem by saying that the movement along the curve *is* an increase in demand attributable to a permanent change in consumer preferences! The article then plays back and forth between these two different demand concepts, using them interchangeably and making it impossible for the reader to come to any sound conclusions.

We can read economic sense into some of the statements made in the article. There is an indication that the quantity demand of pork (even though it is confused with the demand for pork) depends on consumer preferences, the prices of substitutes such as beef, and expectations regarding future pork prices. Some correct statements regarding the effects of changes in supply on prices are made, but these also tend to be confused with movements along supply curves. The critical and most sensible part of the article is the recognition that the *demand* (curve?) for pork depends heavily on the price of *beef*.

The Effects of Expectations on Price

The following article illustrates the importance of *expectations* in the determination of the price of a product.[19]

> *The days of cheap pork will be around a little longer than many analysts had expected, a new Agriculture Department report indicates.*
>
> *The report found a slowdown in the expansion of the nation's herd of hogs and young pigs, but the slowdown wasn't as pronounced as analysts had expected. The result: "Consumers will continue to get a bargain on pork," said Chuck Levitt, a livestock analyst with Shearson Loeb Rhoades Inc.*
>
> *By 1981, though, pork prices should be on the rise, as farmers reduce the size of their herds because current prices for the animals aren't remunerative, most analysts believe. Many of them thought these trends would develop sooner than the report indicates, however.*

[19] "Supply of Cheap Pork May Last Longer Than Analysts Had Thought," *The Wall Street Journal,* 21 March 1980, p. 38. Reprinted by permission of *The Wall Street Journal,* © Dow Jones & Company, Inc. 1980. All rights reserved.

> In its quarterly survey of hog farmers in 14 key states, the Agriculture Department found there were 54.7 million hogs and pigs on farms in those states March 1, up 7% from a year earlier, though analysts had expected them to be only about 3% higher.
>
> Robert Remmele, a department hog specialist, attributed the larger number to mild winter weather that encouraged breeding and to low feed prices. Nevertheless, he expected the number to fall later this year. "Things are leveling off now," he said.
>
> The report also found the number of hogs marketed during the December-through-February quarter totaled 46.6 million, or 9% more than were sold in the year-earlier quarter. Breeding stocks on March 1 totaled 8.1 million head, down 3% from a year earlier, though analysts like Mr. Levitt expected them to be down 6%.
>
> Reported farrowing, or breeding, intentions of the hog farmers tend to confirm expectations of lower hog supplies late this year. The producers, the survey found, intend to have about the same number—3.5 million—of sows breed this spring as last spring, but summer farrowings are expected to decline 3% to 3.1 million.
>
> On the Chicago Mercantile Exchange, hog and cattle futures prices fell after Wednesday's gains that anticipated the government report would show a trend toward reduced pork supplies.

Traders in futures contracts are trying to guess what the price of pork will be at certain dates in the future when they are committed to accepting or making delivery of pork supplies. The price of pork at any given future time depends not only on the position of the demand curve for it but also on the supply curve. As a matter of fact, it is assumed implicitly in the article that demand is given; the article analyzes the impact of expected changes in supply.

Each time the United States Department of Agriculture (U.S.D.A.) gets new information, and it is disseminated through the marketplace, the price of pork for futures contracts adjusts in accordance with the implications that the information carries for the future supply curve of pork. It is clear that the market, on the day of the story, reacted to new information by reducing pork futures prices. This occurred because the U.S.D.A. data indicated that more hogs had been taken to market during the previous three-month period, and breeding stocks of sows were *larger* and, therefore, supplies would be larger than had previously been expected by traders such as Mr. Levitt. The market's reaction after receiving the U.S.D.A. information was in contrast to its behavior on the day before, when traders had bid futures prices up in the expectation that *smaller* supplies would result in higher pork prices.

An Empirical Supply Curve for Blood

College students are often asked for their blood (literally) in either of two ways. First, they are asked to donate freely and altruistically to the American National Red Cross. The blood is used mostly for lifesaving purposes and surgeries. Second, some students at urban universities can sell their blood to commercial blood banks for a price. This blood is used for the production of serums, clotting agents, and other commercial products. The question that arises is whether the tools developed in Chapter 3 can be used to conceptualize the supply of human blood—a "commodity" about which many people have strong altruistic feelings and which is supplied through donations in most countries. Curiously, the Soviet Union, Sweden, and most Eastern European countries have a strong tradition of selling blood for cash rather than donating it. The following excerpt from an article on the supply of blood illustrates one actual attempt by two economists to construct a supply-of-blood curve and the rather interesting twist to the results that their sample of college students revealed.[20]

> *Social institutions can have strange effects on the normal economic forces of supply and demand. A test conducted by one of the authors gives some insight into the way this social attitude to giving and selling blood affects its supply curve. A mass lecture class of principles of economics students, 213 in attendance, were asked to indicate whether or not they would give or sell one pint of blood at various prices. The instructor specified that the question related to giving blood safely, which can be done once each six-week period, and that only one pint could be given or sold at each price by each individual. The results are listed in Table 1.*

TABLE 1 Giving and selling attitudes demonstrated	Dollars/pint	No. of individuals saying they would give one pint
	$0.00	59
	1.00	41
	5.00	65
	10.00	109
	15.00	132
	20.00	145
	25.00	161
	30.00	163
	35.00	163
	40.00	165
	45.00	165
	50.00	170
	55.00	170
	60.00	170

[20] Thomas R. Ireland and James V. Koch, "Blood and American Social Attitudes," in *The Economics of Charity* (London: The Institute of Economic Affairs, 1973), pp. 152–53. © I.E.A., London, England.

There is, of course, an important difference between hypothetical supply curves and individual supply behaviour. (A 'bloodmobile' visited the campus two weeks after the experiment and only seven students, in a check, indicated that they had given blood at a zero price!) What is significant, however, is that 18 individuals listed themselves as willing to give blood at a zero price, but not at a price of $1. Independently from their later action, their responses to the questionnaire indicated an institutional difference between a commercial and a partially philanthropic motivation. Further, some of the students chose to use the questionnaire to air their complaint that the professor's whole discussion of the possibility of buying blood was immoral. Thus, while the actual values might not represent points along the supply curve for the class, the general shape of the supply curve is probably indicative of society as a whole (Figure 1).

The characteristics of this supply curve are that there is a sharp reduction in the quantity supplied when the offer price is raised from zero to the first positive price. From the first positive price through some unspecified range, the response of suppliers is elastic: small increases in price will bring forth fairly large increases in supply. At some point, however, the supply becomes inelastic, after which large increases in the supply price bring forth only small increases in the quantity supplied.

Figure 1

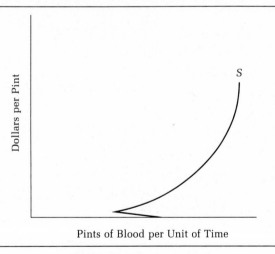

Dollars per Pint

S

Pints of Blood per Unit of Time

Summary

The nature of pure competition and its role in economic analysis should be clearly understood. Pure competition is essentially the ideas of (1) smallness of the individual economic unit in relation to the markets in which it operates, (2) freedom of prices to move in response to changes in demand and supply, and (3) a considerable degree of mobility for both goods and resources in the economy.

The concept of pure competition does not provide an accurate description of the real world, but its usefulness is not negated thereby. It supplies the logical starting point for economic analysis. Enough competition does exist so as to give us valid answers to many economic problems. Additionally, competition provides "norms" for evaluation of the actual performance of the economy.

Demand shows the quantities per unit of time that consumers will take of a commodity at alternative prices, other things being equal. It can be represented as a demand schedule or a demand curve. We must distinguish carefully between changes in demand and movements along a given demand curve. Changes in demand result from changes in one or more of the "other things." Movements along a given demand curve assume that the "other things" do not change.

Supply shows the different quantities per unit of time of a commodity that sellers will place on the market at all possible prices, other things being equal, and, together with demand, determines the equilibrium price of the commodity. The equilibrium price of a commodity is that price which, if attained, will be maintained. Actions of sellers attempting to dispose of surpluses will push a higher-than-equilibrium price toward the equilibrium level. Actions of buyers attempting to buy short supplies will drive a lower-than-equilibrium price toward equilibrium. An increase in demand, given the supply, ordinarily causes an increase in both the price and the quantity exchanged of a good, while a decrease in demand has the opposite effect. An increase in supply, given the demand for a good, ordinarily decreases the price and increases the quantity exchanged. A decrease in supply usually increases the price and decreases the quantity exchanged.

Price elasticity of demand measures the responsiveness of quantity taken of a commodity to changes in its price. Price elasticity of demand is defined as the percentage change in quantity divided by the percentage change in price when the price change is small. Arc elasticity is an approximate measure of elasticity between two separate points. Point elasticity measures elasticity at one single point on the demand curve. Price elasticity of demand is the key element in determining what happens to total business receipts for a commodity when the price of the commodity changes, given demand. When demand is inelastic, increases in price increase total receipts, while decreases in price decrease total receipts. When demand is elastic, the opposite results occur when price is increased or decreased. The degree of demand elasticity for a certain good depends on the availability of substitutes, the number of uses for the good, the importance of the good in consumers' budgets, and the region of the demand curve within which price moves.

The cross elasticity of demand among products is also an important microconcept. High positive cross elasticities indicate a high degree of substitutability between products and are frequently used to mark off the boundaries of particular industries. High negative cross elasticities indicate a high degree of complementarity between products.

Suggested Readings

Baumol, William J. *Economic Theory and Operations Analysis.* 4th ed. Englewood Cliffs, N.J.: Prentice-Hall, 1977, Chap. 9, pp. 179–90.

Knight, Frank H. *Risk, Uncertainty, and Profit.* Boston: Houghton Mifflin, 1921, Chap. 1.

Marshall, Alfred. *Principles of Economics.* 8th ed. London: Macmillan, 1920, Bk. III, Chap. IV; Bk. V, Chaps. I–III.

Questions and Exercises

1 Draw hypothetical demand and supply curves for beef.
   a Show and explain the equilibrium quantity and price. Show and explain the effects of (1) a support price and (2) a price ceiling.
   b What would be the effects on price and quantity exchanged of an epidemic of hoof-and-mouth disease?
   c Show and explain the effects of a beef boycott on the price and quantity exchanged.
   d How would a prohibition of beef imports affect demand, supply, price, and quantity exchanged?

2 Suppose that the carpenters in a large city are unorganized and that there are many employers of carpenters' labor.
   a Under what circumstances would unionization and an increase in wage rates result in an increase in total wages paid to carpenters?
   b Would all carpenters who want to work be able to find employment? Explain.
   c Will a wage-rate increase always raise the total wage bill of the carpenters?

3 In 1973 and 1974 the economy entered a state that Paul Samuelson has dubbed "stagflation," characterized by rising prices and falling outputs (increasing unemployment). With demand and supply curves for a representative product, illustrate and provide a reasonable explanation of this phenomenon.

4 In economic analysis, what does the term *shortage* mean? In the United States, is there a shortage of (a) crude oil, (b) milk, (c) automobiles, (d) sugar, (e) blue jeans? Explain why or why not in each case.

5 Suppose that a ceiling price of $2.00 per thousand cubic feet is placed on natural gas by the government and that the equilibrium price is above that level. Who is helped and who is hurt by the price ceiling? Would you advocate continuing the ceiling over time? Why or why not?

6 In terms of demand and supply, how would you account for the phenomenal increase in the price of gasoline during the decade of the 1970s? Draw a diagram illustrating your answer. List as many forces affecting demand as you can. Do the same for supply.

CHAPTER 4

**CHAPTER
CONTENTS**

**KEY
CONCEPTS**

**Agricultural Price
Supports**

**Oil and Gasoline
Price Ceilings**

Consequences of Price Ceilings

Consequences of Price Decontrol

**Economic Effects of
an Excise Tax**

**Price Controls to
Stop Inflation**

Summary

Suggested Readings

Questions and Exercises

Price floor
Price ceiling
Surplus
Shortage
Excise tax
Tax incidence
Demand elasticity

Policy Applications of the Model

We conclude the Part One review of basic economic concepts and principles with some important current policy applications of those fundamentals. The competitive market model is applicable to a variety of public policies and everyday economic events. Here we focus on (1) agricultural price supports, (2) oil and gasoline price ceilings, (3) the economic effects of an excise tax, and (4) a set of price controls designed to stop inflation. Many such public policies are devised and promulgated with the express aim of correcting inequities in income distribution. However, using the model as an analytical tool, we find that the results of these measures are not always what they are expected to be.

Agricultural Price Supports

The outstanding example of minimum price policies imposed by government is the agricultural price-support program developed by the federal government during and since the Great Depression of the 1930s. Prices of farm products sold were thought by proponents of support programs to be too low relative to the prices of products that farmers buy; that is, they were considered to be inequitable. These relatively low farm prices were deemed an important factor in caus-ing per capita farm income to be lower than the average per capita income in the United States. Consequently, price supports on a wide range of agricultural products have been authorized by Congress to be used as a partial answer to the farm-income problem.

    The essential price theory features of a support program are illustrated in Figure 4.1 with respect to wheat. In an uncontrolled market, with the price free to move, the equilibrium price level is p per bushel and the quantity exchanged is X bushels per year. Sup-pose that price p is thought to be relatively too low, and a support price is set at p_1. The government supports the price by purchasing

FIGURE 4.1
Effects of agricultural
price supports

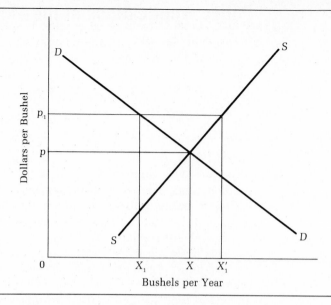

the wheat that farmers cannot sell at price p_1.[1] In Figure 4.1 consumers will buy X_1 bushels per year, leaving a surplus of X_1X_1' for the government to acquire.

A support price will be effective only if it is above the equilibrium level; and if it is effective, surpluses will occur. If it were below p, shortages would induce buyers to bid the price up to the equilibrium level so that the support price would not be effective. Thus, it will be effective only at price levels above p. Yet members of Congress, government officials, farmers, and most of the general public profess amazement that surpluses accumulate from a price-support program and deduce from the existence of surpluses that something about the program is not being handled properly.

What does the government do in the face of the accumulating surplus? We know from the market model that if demand can be increased or supply decreased, there will be smaller surpluses; consequently, we can predict logically that the government would pursue policies to accomplish both. To increase demand, it may stress the virtues of greater wheat consumption. It may try to sell more

[1]   Under the various Agricultural Adjustment Acts, the support price is set by means of a storage-and-loan program. A farmer, instead of selling wheat in the market at price p, can obtain a loan on the wheat from the government at price p_1 per bushel, provided the farmer puts the wheat in storage in government-approved facilities. When the loan is due, the farmer can either sell his wheat and repay it or turn the wheat over to the government as repayment in full. What would be done if the market price of wheat were above p_1 when repayment is due? What would the farmer do if it were below p_1? In effect, the government is guaranteeing that the price will not fall below p_1. Farmers sell what they can in the market at the price, and, in essence, the government buys the surplus.

wheat abroad. To decrease supply, it may place restrictions on the acreage that farmers can plant. It may seek to hold land out of cultivation through a "soil bank." It may establish marketing quotas. It may also seek ways of disposing of the surpluses. Expanding school lunch programs and giving it away via "Food for Peace" foreign aid furnish examples.

The following column from *The Wall Street Journal* describes some aspects of a price support program.[2]

>   *Augustine Marusi, chairman of Borden Inc., aired a gripe when he addressed the company's annual meeting in April.*
>
>   *"On April 1, the (government's) support price for milk went up 87 cents a hundred pounds, to $10.51," he said. "That's almost two cents a quart." But even though the increase raised costs for milk processors such as Borden and thus lifted consumer prices, government inflation-watchers had just fingered the dairy companies for suspicious price increases.*
>
>   *Scoring the "contradiction," Mr. Marusi said, "Higher farm-support prices are politically astute, but they have only helped to put fire on an already-overheating economy."*
>
>   *With Congress and the administration currently considering major farm-price policies, many observers are echoing Mr. Marusi's complaint. They concede that government farm policies aren't the major reason for the steep rises in food prices during the past two years, but they add that those policies are making an already-bad situation worse.*
>
> **Consumers Bear Costs**
>   *"Agricultural policies are undoubtedly adding pressure to rising prices," says Donald Ratajczak, who heads an economic-forecasting project at Georgia State University in Atlanta. Government programs propping up the prices of milk and sugar, he adds, "are the old saw of protecting producers and consumers have to pay for it."*
>
>   *Similarly, a report on price trends prepared by Data Resources Inc., an economic-consulting firm, says, "Food prices have been driven upwards by much of the government's policy making." A prime example, the report says, is the crop "set-aside" program, which gives grain farmers incentives not to plant some of their land. Recently, the Agriculture Department said it would drop the set-aside program for next year because of heavy grain-export demand, but the announcement came only after a sharp run-up in grain prices last spring.*
>
>   *Food prices rose 10% last year, and they soared at an annual rate of 12.5% in the first half of 1979. Most experts expect that rate of increase to slow, but they still see food prices for all 1979*

---

[2]   Paul Ingrassia, "Federal Farm Policies Help Lift Food Prices, Many Observers Gripe," *The Wall Street Journal*, 14 August 1979. Reprinted by permission of *The Wall Street Journal*, © Dow Jones & Company, Inc. 1979. All rights reserved.

averaging 11% above last year. What's more, some are predicting a price rise of nearly that much in 1980.

A basic reason for the price surge is inflation throughout the economy—especially in the costs of fuel, labor and transportation. About 60% of the price of food is added after the food leaves the farm, and as processing and distribution costs rise, so do prices in the supermarkets.

General inflation isn't likely to abate soon, economists say, and neither is the other big spur to higher food bills—too few cows. Beef prices are more than 20% higher than a year ago because of a 16% drop in the number of cattle in the U.S. from the 1975 level. Replacing those animals will take two or three years because cows can produce only one calf a year.

Changes Advocated

Critics of government food policies agree with that assessment—to a point. "We can't get rid of 12% inflation in food prices tomorrow," Georgia State's Prof. Ratajczak says, "but we can start the ball rolling in the right direction by making some policy changes." He estimates that government price-support programs will add 1.5% to 2% to the nation's $290 billion food bill this year. "Obviously, those programs aren't the major reason prices are rising so fast, but they're still important," he adds.

Here are some government programs that experts say are spurring the rise in food prices:

Milk The federal government's price-support program keeps the price of milk rising in step with inflation. The government offers to buy milk products at the support price and thus forces other buyers to meet that price.

By law, the support price is kept at a minimum of 80% of parity, a complex calculation that represents the buying power of farmers in the prosperous years before World War I. As the cost of living rises, so does the support price.

The milk-support price is adjusted twice a year. The next adjustment, due Oct. 1, is expected to raise the price to about $11.50 a hundred pounds from the current $10.51. The market price is likely to start rising before Oct. 1 as buyers anticipate the coming increase.

Until 1977, the government purchased milk products for at least 75% of the parity price, but the Carter administration supported a new law raising the minimum to 80% of parity. That law expires this year, and some observers thought that the administration might seek a return to the 75% minimum level.

Sugar The government uses tariffs and a price-support program to guarantee U.S. sugar growers 15 cents a pound for their product, almost twice the current price of sugar on the world market. Last year, President Carter used administrative authority to raise the support price to 15 cents a pound from 14.7 cents, and now the administration wants legislation that would raise the support price further to 15.8 cents a pound.

Agriculture Secretary Bergland says the administration's deci-sion was "a tough call, but we need a strong domestic sugar indus-try." Economists estimate that the increase would add $220 mil-lion to the nation's food bill through higher prices for such prod-ucts as soft drinks and baked goods as well as for sugar itself.

Higher sugar prices have powerful backers in Congress, includ-ing Russell Long, the Louisiana Democrat who heads the Senate Finance Committee, and Sen. Frank Church of Idaho, chairman of the Foreign Relations Committee. Both men come from major sugar-producing states, and the administration wants their sup-port in Congress on a range of issues.

Consumer groups, however, are lobbying against the higher support price, and they have some secret sympathizers. "For what this program costs consumers, you could buy all the sugar growers out," a high-level Agriculture Department official says.

Grain *Wheat, corn and soybean prices have taken a roller-coaster ride this year, as both the supply and the demand outlooks for the crops have switched back and forth. U.S. farmers took 18 million acres out of wheat and corn production in 1978 in re-sponse to the Agriculture Department's cropland set-aside pro-gram, which encouraged growers of those two crops to leave up to 20% of their land idle. Last March, prices started to move up— exactly as the department had planned.*

Although the Agriculture Department recently announced it wouldn't sponsor a wheat set-aside program to limit production next year (a decision on the corn program will come later), Mr. Bergland also moved to raise the floor under wheat prices. He increased the government's support price for wheat to $2.50 a bushel from $2.35. That's far below the current market price, but the new support level could come into play if wheat prices drop in the future.

Beef *The U.S. limits beef imports, and Agriculture Depart-ment officials say that raising the ceiling on imports won't help consumers much because foreign beef supplies also are tight. "But foreign supplies might be greater if the U.S. didn't have an import ceiling," Georgia State's Prof. Ratajczak says. "Having no ceiling would encourage higher production in other countries, and more beef would be available to import."*

Producers and their representatives in Congress strongly favor such programs because farmers as a group benefit from them. Under most schemes, the government buys up surpluses at the support price. At the same time it attempts to reduce the surpluses through supply reductions. If the latter measures were entirely successful, farmers as a group would benefit only if demands for their products were price inelastic. As the column notes, "set aside" programs in the case of grants may encourage farmers to forgo plantings on as much as 20 percent of their acreage. However, many farmers respond by farming the remaining 80 percent so much more intensively that the government is chronically faced with smaller reductions in agricultural surpluses than it hopes for. In the case of beef, reductions in supply are usually achieved by restricting imports through a quota system, and the same tactic is employed for sugar. Maintaining price-support programs has been one of the chief preoccupations of the members of Congress from states where agriculture is important.

Interesting questions can be raised as to whether or not agricultural price supports actually contribute to greater equity in the economy. Do they reduce income inequalities? Since it is the unit price of the product that is increased, a farmer who raises and sells ten times as much wheat as another will receive ten times the supplemental income that the other receives. The costs of the support program must come from tax revenues. Before the transfer of income from taxpayers to farmers occurs, are the taxpayers richer or poorer than those who are to receive the support payments? What can we say about the overall efficiency of the economy in a situation where farmers are induced either to use resources to produce more than they would have produced at an equilibrium price level or, in the event of supply restrictions, to leave some of the scarce resources of the economy idle?

Oil and Gasoline Price Ceilings

For more than twenty-five years, the United States has followed energy policies that improve temporarily the current position of certain groups in society but seem to have adverse long-run effects for the whole economy. In the late 1950s and 1960s, the dominant policy was an "oil import quota" program, created under pressures from the lobbies of the domestic oil industry. It set quotas, or limits, on the amount of foreign oil that could be imported into the United States each year. This policy raised domestic oil prices somewhat by protecting American producers from foreign competition, although the amounts by which prices were increased must have been relatively small, since gasoline was only about 30 cents per gallon during that period. The irony of the policy, however, was that it tended to induce an over-rapid rate of recovery from domestic reserves and thus contributed to an increased reliance on foreign supplies during the so-called energy crisis of the 1970s. (Would it have made more sense to have imported larger quantities of foreign oil when it was relatively cheaper, leaving larger domestic reserves for the era when foreign oil would become relatively more expensive?)

The import quota policy, which supported oil prices when energy was relatively abundant, was followed by price ceilings when supplies became relatively scarce in the 1970s. Growing affluence (rising incomes) in the United States caused the demand for oil to increase over time. Supply, too, was increasing but not as fast in recent years as demand. Under these circumstances the price per barrel would be expected to rise. Gasoline, the most important petroleum product, was subjected to some degree of price controls from August 1971 through March 1974. During 1973 there were some spot shortages before the fall of the year, but with the Middle East embargo on crude oil shipments to the United States in the fall and winter of 1973–74, shortages of gasoline suddenly became acute. These triggered great public and congressional pressure on the Federal Energy Office (later, the Department of Energy) and the Cost of Living Council to hold the line on the price of gasoline so that the poor as well as the rich could have access to available supplies.

Consequences of Price Ceilings

Actually, effective price ceilings ensure that shortages will persist as long as the controlled price is below the equilibrium market price. In Figure 4.2, DD and SS represent the demand and supply curves for gasoline in July 1971, with p as the equilibrium price. By October 1973, suppose that demand has increased to D_1D_1 and supply has become S_1S_1. If the price is controlled at p cents per gallon, a

FIGURE 4.2
Price controls on gasoline

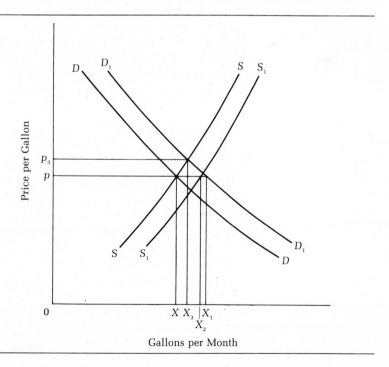

monthly shortage of $X_2 X_1$ gallons occurs. Suppose that an embargo on, or curtailment of, shipments of crude oil to the United States shifts the supply curve of gasoline back to SS. The shortage becomes XX_1 gallons per month.

When the available supplies of a commodity fall short of the quantities that demanders want, a rationing problem emerges. If the price of gasoline had been permitted to rise to p_3, the quantity available per month would have been X_3. At that price consumers would have limited themselves *voluntarily* to that amount, and no rationing problem would have been evident. An equilibrium market price induces consumers to limit themselves to the supplies available. With the price controlled at p, however, the price of gasoline could no longer perform its rationing function.

Having created the shortages with price controls, the federal government was faced with the task of rationing available supplies by nonprice means. A number of devices were employed at different times. One of the first was a ban on Sunday sales of gasoline. Later, retailers were given broad discretionary powers as to which buyers could get gasoline and how much, at the controlled price. This led to much arbitrary conduct—restricted hours of selling that created long and wasteful gas lines at the pump, purchase limits of five gallons that increased wasteful driving to and from filling stations, and preferential treatment to long-standing customers. These practices produced considerable discontent among customers, and in some cases violence became the nonprice method by which scarce supplies were rationed. There were fist fights between anxious buyers, "fender-bender" accidents as drivers vied for better places in the gas queue, and occasional quarrels between customers and station personnel when gas lines were arbitrarily terminated. Some states adopted an "odd-even" method of rationing in which cars with license plates ending in an odd-numbered digit could gas up only on odd-numbered days of the month. But this plan had mixed results. Although intended to shorten gas lines on any given day, it induced motorists to fill up their tanks on every possible day that they could do so. Many more tanks were "topped off" than would have been otherwise, and much gas still was wasted in queuing.

Did the controls help people obtain gasoline at "reasonable" prices? The answer turned upon the costs of queuing that each customer faced and the costs of such inconveniences as extraordinarily early arising to wait for gas before going to work. People accustomed to getting up early may have obtained gasoline at relatively lower costs with price controls than they would have without them, since on the average they lost less valuable time in lines. But others, forced to take time off from work or to adopt other costly behavior to be at the station during its restricted operating hours, could have been net

If a substantial increase in consumers' money incomes now occurs, what happens in the absence of price controls? Demand for X increases to some such level as D_1D_1, and in the absence of price controls consumers bid the price up toward p_1. As this occurs and as it becomes more profitable to produce X, producers seek larger quantities of the resources needed to make the good. The same thing is happening in the production of other goods and services; and as producers bid for resources, resource prices rise. If there were some unemployed resources initially available in the economy, idle units might be drawn into production, permitting expansion of the outputs of some goods and services. But when unemployment has been eliminated, this source of general expansion is no longer possible. Increases in demand when full employment prevails must be reflected in price increases, with no increases on the average in the economy's outputs.

Increases in the prices of resources used in producing any one good or service shift the supply curve for that item to the left. In Figure 4.4 resource price increases move the supply curve of X to S_1S_1. The new equilibrium price is p_2, and the new equilibrium quantity is x_2. Industry X, as we show it, has been able to increase slightly the quantities of the resources it uses and also its product output, but most of the increase in demand is reflected in an increase in the price of the product. The new equilibrium price p_2 induces consumers to ration themselves to the quantity made available at that price.

Effective price controls will change the picture. Consider once more the initial equilibrium situation for X, in which demand and supply are respectively DD and SS. Suppose again that an increase in consumer incomes shifts demand to D_1D_1. This time, however, assume that the price of X is controlled—is not permitted to rise above p_0—and that resource prices, as well, are held down. The immediate impact is a shortage amounting to x_0x_0'. Consumers want more at the controlled price than suppliers will place on the market; they no longer are willing to limit their consumption to the quantity available. Since the price cannot operate to ration the available quantities, how is the rationing to be done? By a first-come first-served policy, with its accompanying queues for the product? By suppliers' whims favoring certain customers? By government-imposed rationing schemes? Or by some other method?

Maximum price policies have an additional impact on the operation of a market system—they make it impossible for relative prices of different products to reflect changes in consumers' relative valuations of different goods and for the price system to reorganize production to accommodate such changes. Figure 4.4 reflects a situation in which an increase in consumers' incomes makes product X

more valuable to consumers relative to all other available goods than it was before. In the absence of controls some additional quantities of resources flow into the production of X, raising the equilibrium quantity produced from x_0 to x_2. With the price of X controlled at p_0, and with resources' prices controlled at whatever their initial levels were, this reallocation will not take place.

As Milton Friedman has aptly put it, placing a set of price controls on a market economy is like locking the rudder on a ship. It does away with the means of steering the economy along the paths desired by consumers.[4] Prices cannot perform their functions of reflecting the relative values of different goods and services and of organizing production according to consumer desires. Some other mechanism—for example, some kind of government rationing program and some kind of arbitrary allocation of resources among producers—must be substituted for it. And, when these are put in place, major distortions and inefficiencies arise and, in fact, did so once the controls began to take hold. Newspaper accounts published almost daily during this period provided a wealth of documentation of the economic wastes that controls cause. The following article is typical.[5]

PRICE CONTROLS: OPPOSITE EFFECT BEGINS TO TELL

Drawn up a Christmas gift list yet? Prepare for a shock. That inexpensive shirt you planned to get for Uncle Harry and some of those other low-cost items you had hoped to get by with may not be too plentiful this year.

Why? Blame it partly on wage and price controls—the program that was supposed to keep prices down.

Kaiser Steel Corp. and other big steel makers have another complaint. To get the zinc needed for galvanized steel used in such things as the common garbage can, they have to shop around in Europe and Australia. That is pretty costly. It also is pretty strange, because producers of zinc in the United States are busy selling much of what they make overseas.

The steel companies, too, can blame the controls program.

What is going on, a rising chorus of troubled business executives and government economists are saying, is that the controls currently are working against themselves. Instead of holding prices down, they are creating a raft of distortions in the American marketplace, most of which mean higher rather than lower prices.

"It's a tough time for price controllers," agreed John R. Brodman, a Cost of Living Council economist. The problem as he and many of those in his profession see it, is trying to hold down prices

---

[4] Milton Friedman, "Why the Freeze Is a Mistake," *Newsweek*, 30 August 1971, p. 23.

[5] John F. Lawrence, "Price Controls: Opposite Effect Begins to Tell," copyright 3 November 1973, *Los Angeles Times*. Reprinted by permission.

at a time when the nation and the world are in a powerful economic boom.

The effects of that combination can be summed up as follows:

Because they cannot raise prices much, companies in many industries are changing the mix of products they make to stress those on which they can make good profits. That is why there will be fewer bottom-of-the-line shirts and other soft goods, for instance.

Producers of raw materials are selling into export markets where prices are much higher and not controlled. This is forcing many manufacturers to chase those same materials across the seas and buy them back.

In industry after industry, even with sales booming, there is a reluctance to build new plants to increase capacity and ease shortages. Shortages, of course, are hardly the thing to encourage lower prices.

When price controls were first instituted in 1971, economists warned that if they lasted long, they would lead to some chaotic distortions in the economy. Now these experts have the evidence to prove it.

Pressure to end the program has been rising for many months, and business leaders now are throwing some tough new arguments at the Nixon Administration.

Henry Ford II told a college audience last month that price controls were a contributor to increased energy consumption just when conservation was needed. His point: by limiting the increase in gasoline prices, the government is encouraging more use than if the prices rose as much as producers and service station operators want them to.

DuPont Co.'s chief economist, Charles B. Reeder, puts it more broadly. "Keep these controls on and they become totally self-defeating," he said. "Demand is higher than it would be because the prices are kept lower and investment in new plants is discouraged because profits are held down."

Already, the Cost of Living Council, charged with administering the controls, is being forced to take steps that are just the opposite of what was intended when the current Phase 4 rules were put into effect last summer.

The idea then was to begin deregulating some industries as soon as it became apparent that price pressures had eased. Instead, the council has faced demands to lift regulations on those industries where the distorting effects of controls have been greatest and the upward price pressures worst of all.

Hence, just last week, the council ended controls on fertilizer. Already there have been price increases of as much as 40% on some kinds. To farmers, however, the alternative was insufficient supply because exports of fertilizer had been running as much as 50% above year-earlier levels. The producers were selling where they could get the higher price.

Now, the council faces intense pressure for deregulation of zinc and aluminum because export prices are so much above domestic ones. And lined up behind those industries are 39 others, from brooms and furniture to baby food and popcorn.

Meantime, the problems are spreading. Faced with shortages of plastic parts and many other items, Ford Motor Co. is building incomplete cars and parking them until the goods arrive.

To some extent, the plastics problem relates to the nation's oil shortage. Raw materials normally used for plastics are being switched to other uses. But price controls are playing a part—"they've screwed up the whole distribution system," said Robert F. Moore, the executive director of Ford's supply staff.

Castings and forgings used in cars also are scarce and Moore attributes that to the effect price controls have had on corporate expansion plans. "If they can't make enough money they are discouraged from expanding."

Textile mills, facing the high cost of wool and cotton, which are not under the control program, have been holding back on producing some items, according to a major clothing retailer.

This retailer is used to getting some sharp bidding among mills for its business. "Now they come in and say, 'Here it is Baby, take it or leave it,'" said an official of the firm.

The paper industry has been complaining loudly in Washington that demand currently is outrunning supply but that it cannot expand at today's prices. The government did permit some price increases recently, but the industry is after more.

"Generally, virtually all expansion plans are being held up at this moment," said a spokesman for International Paper Co., New York.

To stretch supplies, paper producers have sharply reduced the number of grades of paper they are producing—to 75 from 200 in the case of container board used for boxes and other packaging, for instance.

Despite peak demand, the paper industry forecasts annual growth in capacity of only 2.4% over the next three years, well below its average growth rate of recent years.

Actually, throughout the economy, industrial expansion will be only modest next year, according to federal authorities.

Cost of Living Council officials contend that other factors—the unexpectedly sharp rise in demand, the effects of devaluation of the dollar, the need to divert heavy sums from expansion into pollution control and into replacement of old plants closed because of environmental considerations—are major causes of this. But they do concede that the controls are not helping any.

Nevertheless, Administration officials appear likely to keep most of the economy under controls at least into next year. Their hope has been to keep the lid on long enough so that some of the steam goes out of the worldwide inflation, particularly in raw materials prices.

To have that strategy work, the economic boom must subside quickly. Otherwise there will be a bulge in post-controls price increases of awesome proportions, angering labor unions whose wage settlements have been held down by the program.

It is known that the Cost of Living Council is considering ways to end the controls—including the possibility of simply asking each industry to come up with a plan of its own to be submitted for approval. But no early decision is expected.

Meanwhile, some business leaders believe that the distortions the program is causing will persist for a time after it ends. Consumers will find items missing from store shelves and will lose some of the selectivity they have enjoyed.

"You are going to find more of this from next spring to next fall, but you can't tell where," says a spokesman for a big department store chain.

As one would expect, the price and wage controls did not halt inflation. To use another of Milton Friedman's apt metaphors, trying to stop inflation with such techniques is like trying to reduce the size of a balloon by pressing on one of its sides—the pressure of the air simply moves around and exerts force in some other direction. Controls merely cause distortions as economic forces of demand and supply put pressure on other facets of the economy. At the end of the price control experiment in 1974, the rate of inflation was higher than it was at the beginning, in 1971. Moreover, controls had the additional adverse consequence of inducing in governmental circles a false sense of having inflation under control. In 1971, 1972, and 1973 there were large deficits in the federal budget and large increases in the money supply. These caused rapid expansion in demands for goods and services and led to higher inflation rates. The system of price controls failed to accomplish its purpose.

Summary

The competitive market model provides useful insights into the effects of certain economic policymaking by both government and private firms. It shows that effective agricultural price supports of the storage-and-loan type will result in the accumulation of surpluses of the supported products. It also demonstrates that effective price ceilings create shortages that are exasperating to consumers and, in certain cases, politically divisive.

Application of the model to the problem of excise tax incidence shows that there is no difference if the tax is levied on buyers or on sellers, but that the incidence of the tax on each group depends upon the relevant elasticities of supply or demand.

The basic market model can also be applied to the problem of general price controls to stop inflation. It helps explain the inefficiencies and distortions that controls cause. It confirms that price controls attack the symptoms only, and not the causes of inflation.

Suggested Readings

Brozen, Yale. "The Effect of Statutory Minimum Wage Increases on Teenage Unemployment." *Journal of Law and Economics* 12 (April 1969), pp. 109–22.

Knight, Wyllis R. "Agriculture," in Walter Adams, ed., *Structure of American Industry*, 4th ed. New York: Macmillan, 1971.

Miller, James C., III. "Short-run Solutions to Airport Congestions." *Atlanta Economic Review* (October 1969), pp. 28–29.

Radford, R. A. "The Economic Organization of a P.O.W. Camp." *Economica* 12 (November 1945), pp. 189–201.

Questions and Exercises

1 Consider the market for fluid milk. Illustrate with diagrams and explain the effects on price and quantity exchanged of
   a a decline in the birth rate
   b the discovery of a superior breed of milk cow
   c a rise in the price of beef
   d the imposition of substantial taxes on processed milk products.

2 Airline fares are set by the Civil Aeronautics Board. If airlines insist on providing beautiful stewardesses, handsome stewards, gourmet meals, and free movies, what do you know about the level of the fares? What would happen if fares were decontrolled?

3 What has the legalization of abortion done to the demand for, supply, price, quantity, and quality of the service?

4 Many people seem to believe that the enactment and enforcement of minimum housing standards in a given city will be in the best interests of slum dwellers. What effects will the adoption of such standards have on the quality of, quantity of, and price of available housing?

5 Consider the payroll tax levied on both employers and employees to pay Social Security benefits. What would be the effect on a typical employee's take-home pay if the tax were collected entirely from employers? Entirely from employees?

6 In 1978 farmers were quite concerned about their incomes and the prices they received for their products. Through lobbying effforts, public demonstrations, and threats to "strike," they tried to get Congress to increase price supports for farm products. If they were to succeed in getting a support price (say, for wheat) substantially above the equilibrium price, what would be the effects on (1) total farm income, (2) the distribution of income, and (3) shortages or surpluses of wheat? In answering the question, suppose that the support price is enforced through

  a a storage-and-loan type program

  b a subsidy paid to wheat farmers equal to the difference between the equilibrium price of wheat and the support price.

The Underpinnings of Demand

The demand curves for goods and services that were used in Chapters 3 and 4 are rooted in choices made by individuals or households. The more we know about how those choices are made and what affects them the better we can understand the nuances of demands. In Part Two we develop the theory of choice and demand. In Chapters 5, 6, and 7 the analysis is focused on the individual consumer unit, but to complete the demand picture we look at it from the point of view of the individual business concern in Chapter 8.

The modern theory of demand is presented in Chapters 5 and 6. The indifference curve analysis, which forms the core of the modern theory, evolved from the utility approach to demand developed in the latter part of the nineteenth century; however, it is not dependent on the utility approach. Many economists shun the utility approach, or at least relegate it to a secondary position. Because we believe that it contains much of interest and importance we have developed it in Chapter 7. It can, however, be omitted without loss of continuity by those who prefer to do so.

CHAPTER CONTENTS		KEY CONCEPTS
The Consumer's Preferences	**The Consumer's Indifference Map** **Indifference Curve Characteristics** **Complementary and Substitute Relations**	Indifference curve Indifference map Marginal rate of substitution Indifference surface
Constraints on the Consumer	**The Budget Line** **Shifts in the Budget Line**	Substitute goods and services Complementary goods and services Budget line
Maximization of Consumer Satisfaction		Maximization of satisfaction
Applications: Indifference Curve Analysis	**The Hazards of Artificial Sweeteners** The Effects of Information and Warnings The Effects of Prohibitions **The Economics of Fringe Benefits** **Index Numbers** The Laspeyres Price Index The Paasche Price Index	Hazardous products Fringe benefits Laspeyres price index Paasche price index

The Modern Theory of Consumer Choice

The theory of consumer choice provides a logical starting point for the systematic development of microeconomic principles. In this chapter we focus on indifference curve analysis, the general theory of consumer choice. Although indifference curve techniques date from the 1880s, they were not integrated into the main body of economic thought until the 1930s. A British economist, Francis Y. Edgeworth, introduced the concept in 1881.[1] Edgeworth's techniques, with some modification, were adopted by an Italian economist, Vilfredo Pareto, in 1906.[2] It remained for two British economists, John R. Hicks and R. G. D. Allen, to popularize and extend the use of indifference curve analysis in the 1930s,[3] and it has since become the central core of choice and demand theory.

The Consumer's Preferences

We begin the study of an individual consumer's behavior by examining preferences.[4] These are summed up in graphic form as the consumer's *indifference map*. We then examine the main characteristics of the *indifference curves* that make up the indifference map.

The Consumer's Indifference Map

In the modern world, a consumer has available a large number of goods and services among which to express preferences. The number of possible combinations of goods confronting a consumer approaches infinity. What can be said in an analytical way about how the consumer views this wide range of possibilities?

---

[1] Francis Y. Edgeworth, *Mathematical Psychics* (London: C. K. Paul, 1881).

[2] Vilfredo Pareto, *Manuel d'économie politique* (Paris: V. Giard & E. Briere, 1909). The work was first published in Italian in 1906.

[3] John R. Hicks and R. G. D. Allen, "A Reconsideration of the Theory of Value," *Economica*, New Series, No. 1 (February, May 1934), pp. 52–76, 196–219.

[4] The basic consuming unit in an economy is more often a family than a single individual. The term "individual consumer" is used broadly to cover both families and unattached individuals.

To say much of anything, it is necessary to make certain assumptions about the basic nature of the consumer's preferences. We assume *first, that the consumer is able to set up a preference ranking of the combinations available*. The person can determine which combinations are preferable to others and among which combinations he or she is indifferent. *Second,* we assume *that the preferences of the consumer are consistent or transitive*. If combination *A* is preferred to combination *B* and combination *B* is preferred to combination *C*, then combination *A* must be preferred to combination *C*. Again, if combination *D* is equivalent to combination *E* and combination *E* is equivalent to combination *F*, then combination *D* is equivalent to combination *F*. *Third,* we assume *that the consumer prefers more of any good or service to less of it;* that is, the consumer is not satiated with any specific one.[5]

These assumptions enable us to construct an individual consumer's indifference map. To simplify matters, we shall act as though the world contains only two goods—bread (*B*) and wine (*W*). The consumer is asked to rank the many possible available combinations, showing those preferred over others as well as those among which he or she is indifferent.

A set of combinations among which the consumer is indifferent forms an *indifference schedule* or an *indifference curve*. If, for example, the consumer considers all the combinations listed in Table 5.1

TABLE 5.1
An indifference schedule

B (loaves)	W (liters)	Combination
3	7	A
4	4	C
5	2	D
6	1	E
7	½	F

as equivalent to one another, these constitute an indifference schedule. Plotting these combinations (and all those intermediate to the ones in the schedule) in Figure 5.1, we have indifference curve *I*.

Although Figure 5.1 contains only two indifference curves, an infinite number can be drawn. The commodity space enclosed by the

[5] Satiation with any one good is not impossible. We have all seen it occur temporarily with food, liquor, and other items. As we shall see, however, rational economic behavior usually rules out satiation with items that are not abundant enough to be had for the taking.

Also, there are items in the economy, like polluted water and garbage, of which the consumer desires less rather than more. These items are sometimes referred to as "bads" rather than "goods." Controls over them, such as purification and disposal services, become goods and services which we can assume the consumer prefers in greater rather than lesser amounts, up to their saturation levels.

FIGURE 5.1
Indifference curves

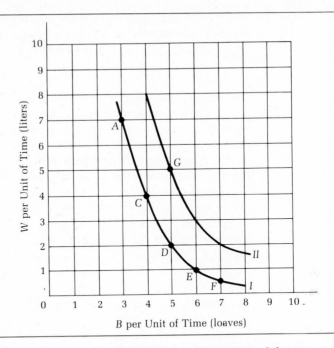

B per Unit of Time (loaves)

B and W axes contains all possible combinations of the two goods. A combination such as G, containing 5 loaves of B and 5 liters of W, will be preferred to combination C, containing 4 loaves of B and 4 liters of W. (Remember the third assumption.) Other combinations equivalent to G can be located, and these trace out indifference curve II. In this manner we can draw as many indifference curves as we wish. All combinations on higher indifference curves—those farther from the origin—are preferable to those lying on lower indifference curves. The whole set of indifference curves constitutes the *indifference map* of the consumer.[6]

Indifference Curve Characteristics

A set of indifference curves exhibits three basic characteristics: (1) *the individual curves slope downward to the right;* (2) *they are*

---

[6] The consumer's preference function or indifference map for two goods, X and Y, can be represented by

$$U = f(x, y),$$

in which U represents levels of preference expressed in ordinal terms only. The equation for one indifference curve is

$$U_1 = f(x, y),$$

in which U_1 is a constant; that is, it represents a given level of preference. Other values assigned to U define other indifference curves, all of these making up the consumer's indifference map. These assigned values show the order of preference magnitudes, not absolute (measurable) magnitudes.

nonintersecting; and (3) *they are convex to the origin of the diagram.* These features will be considered in turn.

Downward slope to the right of indifference curves is assured by the assumption that a consumer prefers more of a good to less of it. If an indifference curve were horizontal, this would mean that the consumer is indifferent between two combinations, both of which contain the same amount of one good, Y, but one of which contains a greater amount of another good, X. A curve could be horizontal only if the consumer were receiving enough X to be saturated with it; that is, additional units of X alone would add nothing to the person's total satisfaction. Similarly, if an indifference curve were vertical, this would mean that the two combinations of X and Y, both with the same amount of X but with one containing more Y than the other, yield equivalent satisfaction to the consumer. Again, this would be the case only if the consumer had reached a saturation point for Y. For the consumer to remain indifferent among combinations after giving up units of one commodity, the loss must be compensated for with additional units of another commodity. The result, shown graphically, is a curve that is downward-sloping to the right.

Indifference curves are nonintersecting if the transitivity assumption holds. In Figure 5.2 we see the logical contradiction of intersecting curves. Combination C is preferred to combination A. Combination A is equivalent to combination B. But combination C is also equivalent to combination B. According to the transitivity assumption, C should be *preferred* to B. Thus, the intersection of indifference curves violates the transitivity assumption. To say that indifference curves are nonintersecting is not to say that they are parallel or that they are equidistant from each other. They may run further apart at some points and closer together at others. The only restriction placed on them here is that they do not intersect.

We cannot prove conclusively at this point that indifference

FIGURE 5.2
Consequences of indifference curve intersection

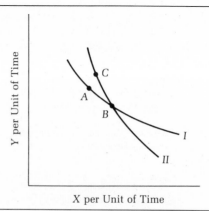

curves are convex to the origin, but we can show that it is likely that they are. To get at the issue, we introduce the *marginal rate of substitution* concept.

The marginal rate of substitution of one product for another, say of X for Y, is abbreviated as MRS_{xy}, and is defined as the maximum amount of Y the consumer is willing to give up to get an additional unit of X—the trade-off between bundles of goods among which he or she is indifferent. In a specific example, say in Figure 5.1, suppose the consumer is taking initially 7 liters of W and 3 loaves of B. To move to a consumption rate of 4 loaves of B, she would be just willing to give up the consumption of 3 liters of W per unit of time. The marginal rate of substitution for this move, or the MRS_{bw}, is 3.

The more of one good and the less of another a consumer has, the more important units of the second become relative to units of the first. For example, at point A in Figure 5.3 the consumer would be willing to give up a relatively large amount of Y to get an additional unit of X. At point B, with much more X and much less Y than at A, a unit of Y would be more important as compared with a unit of X than it was at point A, and the consumer would be willing to give up less Y to get an additional unit of X. The X axis is marked off in equal quantity units between A and B. At point A the indifference curve shows the consumer just willing to give up CD of Y to get an additional unit of X. With more and more X and less and less Y per unit of time, the importance of a unit of Y becomes progressively greater as

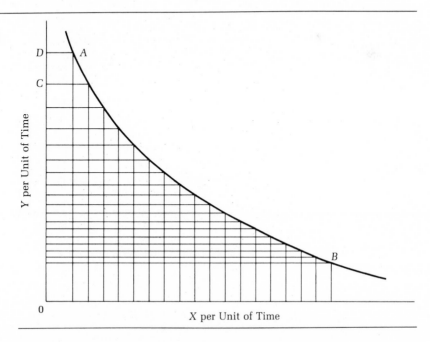

FIGURE 5.3
Diminishing marginal
rate of substitution

compared with that of a unit of X. The amounts of Y the consumer is just willing to give up to get additional units of X become progressively smaller; that is, the marginal rate of substitution of X for Y is decreasing.[7]

If the marginal rate of substitution of X for Y is decreasing, the indifference curve must be convex toward the origin. If it were constant, the amounts of Y the consumer would give up to get additional units of X would be constant instead of decreasing; the indifference curve would be a straight line sloping downward to the right. If the marginal rate of substitution were increasing, the indifference curve would be concave to the origin.[8]

Complementary and Substitute Relations

If a consumer thinks of goods and services as being related to one another, the relationship may be either one of complementarity or one of substitutability. Generally speaking, two goods are comple-

---

[7] It may be helpful to work out the MRS_{bw} arithmetically between different points on indifference curve I of Figure 5.1 before proceeding to the more abstract geometric representation of it in Figure 5.3.

[8] The total differential of the preference function of Footnote 6 is

$$dU = f_x dx + f_y dy.$$

For a given indifference curve, $dU = 0$, so

$$0 = f_x dx + f_y dy$$

and

$$-\frac{dy}{dx} = \frac{f_x}{f_y} = MRS_{xy}.$$

To determine the shape of an indifference curve, we look at the derivative of the MRS_{xy} with respect to x. Since

$$MRS_{xy} = -\frac{dy}{dx},$$

then

$$\frac{d}{dx}(MRS_{xy}) = \frac{d}{dx}\left(-\frac{dy}{dx}\right) = -\frac{d^2y}{dx^2}.$$

If

$$\frac{d^2y}{dx^2} > 0,$$

then

$$-\frac{d^2y}{dx^2} < 0, \quad \text{or} \quad \frac{d}{dx}(MRS_{xy}) < 0,$$

and the indifference curve is convex to the origin. If

$$\frac{d^2y}{dx^2} < 0,$$

then

$$-\frac{d^2y}{dx^2} > 0, \quad \text{or} \quad \frac{d}{dx}(MRS_{xy}) > 0,$$

and the indifference curve is concave to the origin. If

$$\frac{d^2y}{dx^2} = 0,$$

then

$$-\frac{d^2y}{dx^2} = 0, \quad \text{or} \quad \frac{d}{dx}(MRS_{xy}) = 0,$$

and the indifference curve is linear.

ments if an increase (decrease) in the consumption level of one increases (decreases) the relative desirability of the other to the consumer. Goods are substitutes for each other if an increase (decrease) in the consumption level of one decreases (increases) the relative desirability of the other.

These definitions can be made more explicit with the aid of indifference curve concepts. Suppose that the consumer is no longer confined to a two-commodity world but that there are choices among X, Y, and a host of other goods and services. Let the quantities of the other goods and services be measured in money terms, while X and Y are measured in physical terms such as bushels and pints. In Figure 5.4 monetary units M are measured on the vertical axis while the axes of the horizontal plane show units of Y and X. The consumer now has the options of substituting X for M, Y for M, and X for Y. If the

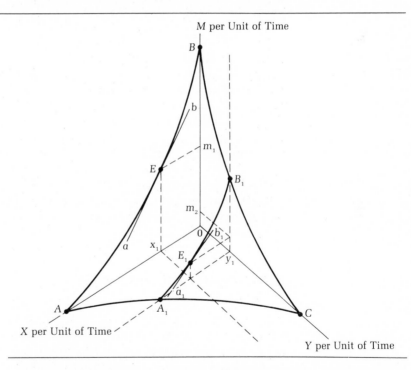

FIGURE 5.4
Substitutes and
complements

consumption level of Y is zero, indifference curve AB represents combinations of M and X that yield the consumer a given level of satisfaction. If the consumption level of X is zero, indifference curve BC shows combinations of M and Y that yield the *same level* of satisfaction as do those of AB. If the consumption level of Y is y_1, indifference curve A_1B_1 shows combinations of M and X that, together with y_1 of Y, yield the *same level* of satisfaction as do those of AB and BC. A family of curves such as A_1B_1, one for each level of consumption of Y, can be drawn tracing out an *indifference surface* bounded by ABC that is convex toward the origin of the diagram.

To determine whether X and Y are complements or substitutes, we hold the consumer's satisfaction level constant; that is, we stay on a given indifference surface. Suppose that initially the consumer is using no Y and has a combination of x_1 units of X and m_1 of M. The MRS_{xm} at point E as measured by the slope of line ab shows the amount of money the consumer is just willing to give up for a unit of X at that point; that is, it shows the *money value* to the consumer of a unit of X. Now, holding the consumption level of X and the consumer's satisfaction level constant, we increase the amount of Y consumed to y_1. To compensate for the increased consumption of Y, the amount of money in the new combination is reduced to m_2. Has the increase in the consumption of Y increased or reduced the money value of a unit of X? The MRS_{xm} at point E_1 as measured by the slope of line a_1b_1 provides the answer. The MRS_{xm} at E_1 is less than the MRS_{xm} at E, meaning that the increase in the consumption of Y, with the consumption level of X and the consumer's satisfaction level held constant, has caused a decrease in the *money value* of a unit of X to the consumer. Therefore, good Y is a *substitute* for good X. If the MRS_{xm} at E_1 had been greater than the MRS_{xm} at E (and this will be the case for many goods), then good Y would be a *complement* to good X.

Examples of complementary and substitute goods abound in the world around us. Tennis rackets and tennis balls, bread and jelly, coffee and doughnuts, automobiles and gasoline are among the many sets of complementary goods. Sets of substitute goods include ham and steak, automobile travel and airplane travel, electric razors and safety razors, and many others.

Constraints on the Consumer

What the consumer is able to do has thus far been left to one side; we have presented a picture of tastes and preferences only. The constraints on the individual's consumption activities are shown by *budget lines*, sometimes called *lines of attainable combinations*.

The Budget Line

The consumer's purchasing power and the prices of what the consumer wants to buy determine his or her budget line. Purchasing power is usually referred to as income. The term is not limited to current earnings but is used broadly to include any supplements to, or deletions from, whatever those earnings may be. We think of the consumer's income, defined in this way, as a weekly, monthly, or yearly average. The prices faced by the consumer are the market prices of the items the individual purchases.

To show how the budget line is established, we again limit the consumer to a two-good world. Suppose that Mary Smith has an income of $100 per week and prices of X and Y are $2 and $1, respectively. If she were to spend her entire income on X, she could consume 50 units per week—she would be at point A in Figure 5.5.

FIGURE 5.5
The budget line

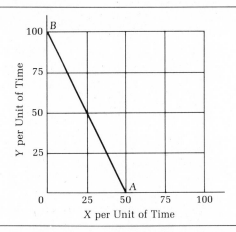

On the other hand, if she were to buy Y and no X, she could consume 100 units of Y and would be at point B. If she is at point B and desires to include X in her consumption pattern, she must decrease her consumption of Y to do so. A decrease of 2 units in her consumption of Y releases $2 that can be used to purchase a unit of X. Every 1-unit increase in the quantity of X consumed requires a 2-unit decrease in her consumption of Y, as long as p_y remains at $1 and p_x is $2. Thus, her budget line is a straight line joining points B and A.

The slope of the budget line is determined by the ratio of p_x to p_y. Suppose that Thomas Green's income is I, the price of X is p_{x1}, and the price of Y is p_{y1}. If he should spend all of his income on Y, then I_1/p_{y1} in Figure 5.6 shows the total number of units of Y that he could purchase. If he were to spend all of his income on X, then I_1/p_{x1} shows the number of units of X that he could purchase. The budget line BA joins the two extreme points.[9]

---

[9]   The budget-line equation for the two-commodity example of the text is

$$xp_x + yp_y = I.$$

Solving for y, we obtain

$$y = \frac{I}{p_y} - \frac{p_x}{p_y} \cdot x,$$

indicating that the Y-axis intercept is I/p_y and that the slope of the line is $-p_x/p_y$.

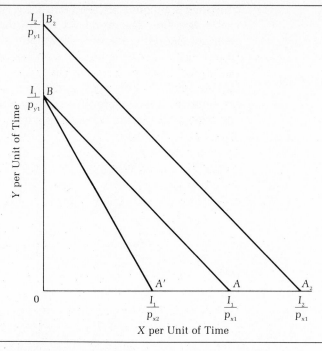

FIGURE 5.6
Changes in the budget line

The slope of the budget line is

$$-\frac{I_1/p_{y1}}{I_1/p_{x1}} = -\frac{I_1}{p_{y1}} \times \frac{p_{x1}}{I_1} = -\frac{p_{x1}}{p_{y1}}$$

or, in more general terms, the slope of any budget line is

$$-\frac{I/p_y}{I/p_x} = -\frac{I}{p_y} \times \frac{p_x}{I} = -\frac{p_x}{p_y}. \qquad (5.1)$$

It measures the amount of Y the consumer would be required to give up in the market to obtain an additional unit of X. Note that the consumer can obtain any combination of goods within or on the boundaries of the triangle $B0A$ in Figures 5.5 or 5.6. All of these constitute his set of *feasible* combinations. The budget line BA separates the feasible combinations—what the consumer is able to purchase—from those combinations beyond his financial reach.

Shifts in the Budget Line

Changes in a consumer's income and changes in the prices of the goods and services available will shift an individual's budget line. Suppose that Thomas Green is again the consumer, that his income is I_1 initially, and that the prices of X and Y are p_{x1} and p_{y1}, respectively. His budget line is BA in Figure 5.6. If the price of X now increases to p_{x2}, while his income and the price of Y remain constant, the budget line becomes BA'. There is no change in the amount of Y that his income will purchase if it is all spent on Y; however, the higher price of X reduces from $0A$ to $0A'$ the amount of X that he could purchase if his money were all spent on X. The new budget line therefore joins B and A'.

From an initial budget line BA, suppose now that Green's income rises from I_1 to I_2 while the prices of X and Y remain constant. The budget line shifts to the right parallel to itself to B_2A_2. The larger income enables him to purchase greater amounts of X, if X alone is purchased, or greater amounts of Y, if Y alone is purchased, so that A_2 lies to the right of A, and B_2 lies above B. Since the prices of X and Y have not changed, both budget lines have a slope of $-p_{x1}/p_{y1}$ and are therefore parallel.[10]

Maximization of Consumer Satisfaction

The theory of consumer behavior is built on the premise that individual consumers, given their budget constraints, seek to maximize their satisfactions. To show the conditions under which a consumer can attain this goal, the consumer's preference factors (the indifference map) and restraining factors (the budget line) are brought together in Figure 5.7. Any combination such as A, B, C, D, or E on the budget line is available. So is any combination, such as G, lying to the left of or below the budget line. Because of the budget constraint, combinations lying to the right of or above the budget line are not available.

The combination chosen must lie on the budget line. A consumer who takes combination G violates the assumption that more of a good is always preferred to less. By moving from G to C, the consumer obtains more X without sacrificing any Y and consequently gets on a higher indifference curve. This sort of move is always possible for a combination below the budget line. Of the combinations on the budget line, the consumer chooses the one that is on the highest indifference curve touched by the budget line. This will be combination C. Combinations A, B, D, and E all lie on lower indifference curves. Combination C is on the highest indifference curve that the consumer can reach and, further, is the only combination available on that indifference curve. Thus, the satisfaction-maximizing combination is always that at which the person's budget line is tan-

---

[10]   Note that in Footnote 9 changes in p_x change the slope of the budget line but not its Y-axis intercept. Changes in I shift the budget line up or down without changing its slope.

FIGURE 5.7
The consumer's
preferred combination

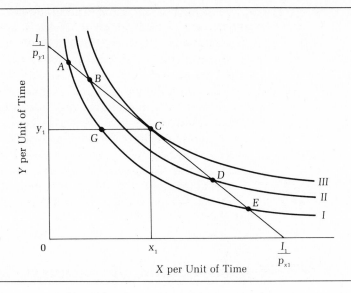

gent to an indifference curve. In Figure 5.7 it contains x_1 of X and y_1 of Y.

Tangency of the budget line to an indifference curve means that the rate at which the consumer is *willing* to give up Y to obtain X is equal to the rate at which he would be *required* by the market to give up Y to obtain X—that is, his $MRS_{xy} = p_x/p_y$.[11] The slope of an indifference curve at any point on it is his MRS_{xy} at that point. The slope of a budget line at any point on it is p_x/p_y. At the point of tangency—that is, at C—the slopes of the two curves are necessarily the same.

Consider point A in Figure 5.7. The slope of indifference curve I is greater than the slope of the line of attainable combinations. In other words, the amount of Y that the consumer *is willing* to give up to get an additional unit of X is greater than the amount of Y that he *would have* to give up to get an additional unit of X (that is, $MRX_{xy} > p_x/p_y$). The consumer would give up units of Y for additional units of X because it is possible to move to a preferred position by doing so. The same would be the case at point B. At point D the slope of indifference curve II is less than the slope of the line of attainable combinations, meaning that the amount of Y that the consumer is willing to give up to get an additional unit of X is less than the amount that would have to be given up (that is, $MRS_{xy} < p_x/p_y$). Therefore, the consumer would not move beyond point C to such a point as D, for such a movement is toward a less-preferred position.

[11] Since the indifference curves and the budget lines both have negative slopes, we shall disregard the minus signs of the slope measurements and consider the absolute values only. This practice is conventional and avoids problems arising from mathematical semantics.

The consumer is maximizing satisfaction at point C, where the marginal rate of substitution of X for Y is equal to the ratio of their respective prices, and he is disposing of his entire income.[12]

Let Y be milk and X be honey in Figure 5.7. Assume that the price of milk p_y is \$1 per pint, while that for honey p_x is \$2 per pound. At point A, $MRS_{xy} > p_x/p_y$; assume that it is 4. Thus, the MRS_{xy} tells us the consumer is just willing to give up 4 pints of milk for an additional pound of honey. The slope of the budget line, p_x/p_y, tells us that if the consumer gives up only 2 pints of milk, the market will let him purchase an additional pound of honey. So the consumer clearly reaches a higher satisfaction level by giving up 2 pints of milk and acquiring one pound of honey in the market. The satisfaction increase is that yielded by the additional 2 pints of milk the consumer would have been willing to sacrifice for the additional pound of honey.

Applications: Indifference Curve Analysis

The theory of consumer choice is not a set of sterile abstract concepts. It can be used in many ways to improve our evaluations of what goes on in the world around us and to enable us to make sound decisions

[12] To solve the consumer's maximization problem mathematically, let his preference function be

$$U = f(x, y). \qquad (1)$$

The budget restraint is

$$xp_x + yp_y = I$$

or

$$xp_x + yp_y - I = 0. \qquad (2)$$

To maximize (1) subject to (2) we use the Lagrange multiplier method, forming a new function in which V is a function of x, y, and λ such that

$$V = g(x, y, \lambda) = f(x, y) - \lambda(xp_x + yp_y - I). \qquad (3)$$

For maximization of V,

$$\frac{\delta V}{\delta x} = f_x - \lambda p_x = 0, \text{ or: } f_x = \lambda p_x \qquad (4)$$

$$\frac{\delta V}{\delta y} = f_y - \lambda p_y = 0, \text{ or: } f_y = \lambda p_y \qquad (5)$$

$$\frac{\delta V}{\delta \lambda} = xp_x + yp_y - I = 0, \text{ or: } xp_x + yp_y = I. \qquad (6)$$

Dividing (4) by (5) and letting (6) stand as it is, the conditions for maximum satisfaction become

$$\frac{f_x}{f_y} = \frac{p_x}{p_y}; \text{ that is } MRS_{xy} = \frac{p_x}{p_y} \qquad (7)$$

with

$$xp_x + yp_y = I. \qquad (8)$$

on economic policy issues of the day. In demonstrating some of its applications, we begin with the recent case of the "hazards" of artificial sweeteners. Next we turn to the economics of fringe benefits and payments in kind—an issue that is of growing importance and that takes a variety of forms. Finally, in an inflation-ridden economy the more we know about price index numbers and the measurement of changes in our living standards, the better off we will be.

The Hazards of Artificial Sweeteners

One of the most fruitful ways of using economic analysis is in perusing the daily newspaper. We use such analysis to seek information on the major issues of the day, about which we will have to make judgments in the course of everyday life. As consumers, we have to decide which goods to buy, whether they be houses, shares of stock, or prescription medicines. As producers, we have to decide what careers to pursue or businesses to establish. As voters, we face at times a bewildering array of candidates, referenda, or initiatives on the ballots. Newspaper reporters are in the business of informing their readers about major events and issues, but the comparative advantage of reporters lies more in description than analysis. This is especially so for economic issues, subjects in which relatively few journalists are trained. The analysis and diagrams presented in this chapter will, when applied to the factual situations that the newspapers recount, enable you to conceptualize better what is *really* going on in your economic world. Economics in many instances can reveal useful angles, nuances, and implications about "the story" that the reporter who wrote it did not fully understand.

Consider, for example, the recent controversy over the use of artificial sweeteners, such as saccharin, in the production of diet soft drinks and other products calling for sugar substitutes. The basic problem is one of trade-offs, so typical of situations that we encounter in daily living. Artificial sweeteners enable diabetics and people who are concerned about their weight to enjoy foods that would otherwise not be suitable for them, but the chemicals used in them may carry other risks, and there has been some evidence to link large doses of these substances to bladder carcinomas. The United States government has wrestled with this problem for about a decade, and the policy it eventually produces (if any) will be of importance not only to consumers of these products but to their manufacturers as well. The following column from *The Wall Street Journal* describes the uncertainties and the bureaucratic wrangling that have surrounded the issue.[13]

---

[13] "Hazards of Artificial Sweeteners Exist, But Not to Extent Suspected, Report Finds," *The Wall Street Journal,* 21 December 1979, p. 10. Reprinted by permission of *The Wall Street Journal,* © Dow Jones & Company, Inc. 1979. All rights reserved.

HAZARDS OF ARTIFICIAL SWEETENERS EXIST, BUT NOT TO EXTENT SUSPECTED, REPORT FINDS

Artificial sweeteners aren't as hazardous as previously suspected but do pose some risks, especially among heavy users and cigaret smokers, according to a federal study.

"There isn't any epidemic going on of saccharin causing bladder cancer in the country," observed Robert Hoover, who directed the $1.5 million study for the National Cancer Institute. Nevertheless, the study concluded, both saccharin and cyclamate, another artificial sweetener, "should be regarded as potential risk factors for human bladder cancer." An earlier Canadian study suggested that men who consume small amounts of saccharin daily have a 60% increased risk of bladder cancer.

The cancer institute also found that individuals who consume 16 ounces or more of dietetic beverages a day as well as six or more servings of a sugar substitute have a 60% greater chance of developing bladder cancer than nonusers. The cancer risk also was higher among heavy smokers, although investigators couldn't determine the specific magnitude of the risk. There also were indications that women who used artificial sweeteners were more prone to developing the disease.

Interviews With 9,000

The investigation involved interviews with 9,000 persons, 3,000 of them bladder-cancer patients. It was conducted in five states and five metropolitan areas.

Congress requested the cancer institute study in 1977, after placing an 18-month moratorium on the Food and Drug Administration's plan to ban the use of saccharin as a food additive. The FDA proposal grew out of findings that the sweetener could cause bladder tumors in laboratory rats.

The moratorium has expired, but the FDA hasn't renewed the proposed ban. The Senate is considering legislation to extend the moratorium through June 1981; the House passed such a bill in July.

Jere Goyan, FDA commissioner, said the agency "will evaluate these new National Cancer Institute data." He reiterated his concern about young people of consuming large amounts of saccharin. "We may have to wait 20 or 30 years to assess the possible effects on our young people on consuming large amounts of a weak carcinogen," or cancer-causing agent, he said.

Calorie Control Council

In Atlanta, Coca-Cola Co. and Royal Crown Cos., manufacturers of diet beverages, referred questions about the companies' views to the Calorie Control Council, an Atlanta-based association of manufacturers and suppliers of dietary foods and beverages.

Robert Gelardi, executive director of the group, expressed surprise at the FDA's interpretation of the report. "They've really tried to pull information out of context" to conclude that saccharin and artificial sweeteners heighten the risk of cancer, he said. "How they can conclude that from the data is very, very surprising."

Several leading producers of cigarets and soft drinks declined immediate comment, saying they needed time to read the study.

The Effects of Information and Warnings   A consumer's choices between diet drinks and sugared drinks is represented by the solid-line indifference map of Figure 5.8. Since these products are ordinarily substitutes for each other, the indifference curves for them exhibit the usual convex-to-the-origin shape, reflecting a diminishing MRS_{sd} at any given level of satisfaction as more diet (D) and fewer sugared (S) drinks are consumed. Given an annual soft drink budget of I dollars, a price per unit of p_s for sugared drinks, and a price per unit of p_d for diet drinks, the soft drink budget line is established. The consumer maximizes satisfaction with combination C, consuming s cans per year of sugared drink and d cans per year of diet drink.

How does the consumer react to the revelation that there may be a link between diet drink consumption and bladder carcinoma? There are at least two significant results.

First, combination C no longer maximizes satisfaction, even though it remains obtainable to the consumer. At that combination—or any other combination for that matter—a can of diet drink now yields less satisfaction to the consumer than it did before, relative to the satisfaction yielded by a can of sugared drink. In

FIGURE 5.8
The effects of information and warnings

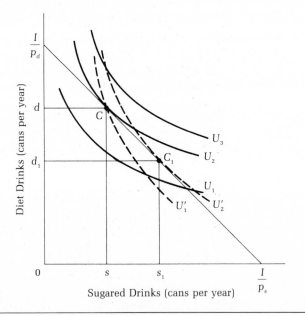

technical terms, the information increases the MRS_{sd} for each and every combination shown on the indifference map. At any combination such as C the consumer is now willing to give up *more* cans of diet drink to obtain an additional can of sugared drink than before. The slope of an indifference curve through point C, or any other point on the map, increases. The indifference map showing the consumer's new preference pattern is the set of dashed curves. To maximize satisfaction the consumer moves down the budget line from combination C to combination C_1, giving up cans of diet drink and purchasing larger quantities of sugared drink.

Second, combination C now represents a lower level of satisfaction than it did before the consumer received the information on the likelihood of cancer. Quantity d of diet drink now yields less satisfaction because of the threat of cancer. Quantity s of sugared drink yields neither more nor less satisfaction than before. Consequently, the total satisfaction level of the consumer at combination C is decreased by the new information. Another way to say this is that the satisfaction level now yielded by indifference curve U_1' is less than that formerly yielded by indifference curve U_2.

At various times the government has considered issuing a permanent, official warning about the possible hazards associated with artificial sweeteners (although this possibility is not mentioned in the foregoing newspaper story). An official warning can be interpreted in the same fashion as for the situation where information is released without the warning. The official warning would tend to occasion an even greater reduction in the rate of diet drink consumption relative to the consumption of sugared drinks. Indeed, this is about what happened following the Surgeon General's admonitions about smoking cigarettes. The official nature of the warning led more smokers to take the dangers of smoking more seriously and, over time, led to reductions in the rate of smoking; although some users of cigarettes merely shifted to increased rates of consumption of other "bad" habits, such as eating more food.

The Effects of Prohibition   The *Wall Street Journal* article also raises the possibility that Congress may permit the FDA to ban artificial sweeteners, enforcing the ban with fines and other penalties on producers or consumers, or both. Two questions arise on which the theory of choice can shed light. First, how large must fines be in order to reduce an individual's consumption level of diet drinks to zero? Second, what are the effects on consumer well-being of prohibiting the product as compared with providing consumers with full information on possible health hazards from ingesting it?

With regard to the first question, it makes sense to suppose that along with making consumption of diet drinks illegal, consumers are given information as to why this is done. A consumer's preferences are altered by the information, as in the previous case. In Figure 5.9, the consumer's indifference map, originally the solid lines, becomes the set of dashed lines. A consumer who purchases illegal diet drinks faces the probability of paying a fine. If we convert the probable fine to a per unit basis so that f is the probable penalty per can, the price of the illegal diet drinks to the consumer becomes $p_d + f$. The higher the fine the closer to the origin the upper left end of the budget line will rest. The size of the fine needed to reduce consumption to zero is that which will just make the budget line tangent to indifference curve U_1' at consumption level S_2 for sugared drinks. Now the consumer would maximize satisfaction with s_2 of sugared drinks and no diet drinks.

What about the satisfaction level of the consumer when the fine is such that the consumption level of the diet drink is zero? As we have previously determined, if the consumer has information on the health hazards of diet drinks and there is no fine, combination C_1 will be purchased. The consumer's satisfaction level index is that of indifference curve U_4'. The imposition of a fine sufficient to cause the consumer to reduce his or her consumption level of diet drinks to zero clearly pulls the consumer down to lower indifference curve U_1'.

FIGURE 5.9
The effects of prohibitions

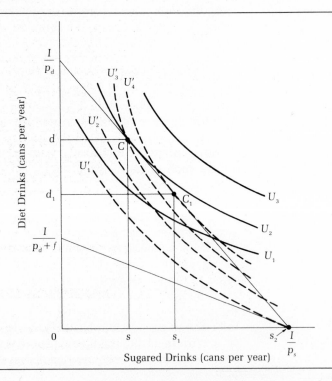

Prohibition of a potentially hazardous product, enforced by means of fines and other penalties, thus means that government functionaries place a higher value than do individual consumers on the risks involved in consuming it—even when all have the same information concerning the risks. Who is the best judge of what you and I should consume?

Using the theory of consumer choice to analyze the diet drink problem reveals, as we earlier suggested that it might, points that would not otherwise have been apparent. The greater the constraints that confront consumers, other things being equal, the lower their satisfaction level will be. In this case, the satisfaction level of a typical consumer is lower when an outright prohibition is imposed than when only an official warning is given. Satisfaction declines when people are prohibited from engaging in some activity altogether, even when the activity carries a certain degree of risk. People tend to prefer (that is, gain more satisfaction by) *reducing* the rate at which they engage in hazardous activities rather than *eliminating* such activities. This is a principle well understood by students and professors of economics, whether or not it is well articulated by newspaper reporters. It is also a principle well understood by politicians, not only those aspiring to office but those attempting to keep the offices they hold. Perhaps this explains the reticence of Congress' part to give the FDA the full authority to institute an outright ban on artificial sweeteners.

The Economics of Fringe Benefits

Fringe benefits—such as guarantees of retirement pay, some free medical services, life insurance, the use of company recreational facilities, and many others—have become commonplace as part of an employee's pay package. These are costs to employers, just as wages and salaries are costs, and the benefits constitute a part of what employees earn. The question that we consider here is whether employees would be better or worse off if employers were to pay them the money value (cost) of the fringe benefits instead of providing the fringe benefits in kind. To keep the choice problem as simple as possible, we assume that there are no tax advantages to employers or employees if some part of wages and salaries are in the form of fringe benefits rather than money.[14]

Suppose initially that an individual's income with no fringe benefits is OI_1 dollars, measured along the vertical axis of Figure

---

[14] The institutional arrangements, such as tax laws, that exist in any society obviously affect the choices that are made. The basic "pure" choice, however, is that between pay in the form of, say, medical services versus pay in the form of money, keeping the choice free of such institutional arrangements. Then one can, if so desired, introduce the appropriate institutional arrangements and examine the impact of these on the choices made.

5.10(a). Units of medical service are measured along the horizontal axis, and the amount that the person's total income will purchase at price p_{m1} per unit is $0D$. With the indifference map shown and budget line I_1D, the individual spends I_1C_1 of income for $0M_1$ units of medical service.

The employer decides to give the individual a pay increase in the form of "free" medical service amounting to $0M_1'$ units per month. The fringe benefit obviously increases the welfare of the individual, but if the pay increase were given in the form of money rather than in the specific form of the good or service, would the individual's welfare be increased by more, or less, or by the same amount?

Figure 5.10(a) illustrates a case in which welfare is increased less by the fringe benefit than it would be by an equivalent amount of money paid to the individual. Free medical services of $0M_1'$, combined with a money income of $0I_1$, shift the budget line to I_1BE. The I_1B segment is determined by the money income $0I_1$—which has not been increased—and the $0M_1'$ (which $= I_1B$) units of medical service that can now be obtained *without using any of the money income available to the individual.*

If, however, more than $0M_1'$ units of medical service per month were consumed, the individual would be required to pay p_{m1} for each

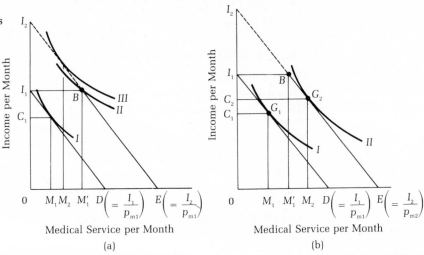

FIGURE 5.10
Fringe benefits versus money income

unit in excess of $0M_1$. These circumstances are shown by the BE segment of the budget line. Note that BE is parallel to I_1D. The slope of both curves is equal to p_{m1}, since the market price of medical services is not changed by the increase in fringe benefits. Note also that $DE = 0M_1'$. The new budget line is "kinked" or has a corner in it at B. Indifference curve II is the highest that the individual can reach so that in this case the entire amount of free medical services is consumed, leaving $0I_1$ dollars to spend on other goods and services.

If the individual receives the pay increase in additional money equal to the value of the fringe-benefit medical services, the budget line becomes I_2E. The increase in money income, I_1I_2, is $0M_1' \times p_{m1}$, that is, what the value of the fringe benefit medical services would be in the market. The BE segment of the budget line is the same as it is in the fringe-benefit case since the individual would, if at point B, be spending I_1I_2 dollars for $0M_1'$ of medical services, leaving $0I_1$ dollars to be spent as desired. The segment of I_2E above point B is the significant one. It represents opportunities open to the consumer that were not available under the fringe-benefit arrangement. The consumption of medical services can be reduced below $0M_1'$ units, and for each unit that it is so reduced the consumer will have p_{m1} more dollars to spend on other things. Given the indifference map of 5.10(a), the individual would indeed reduce consumption of medical services to $0M_2$ per month—where indifference curve III is tangent to the I_2E segment of the budget line. This segment was not available under the fringe-benefit arrangement. In this case the individual's welfare would be greater if the pay increase were in the form of money rather than "free" medical services.

If an individual's preferences are such that after a pay increase more medical services per month are desired than the pay increase would buy or provide, the person's welfare will not be affected by the form of the increase. This situation is illustrated in Figure 5.10(b). Prior to the pay increase the individual has an income of $0I_1$ and maximizes satisfaction at G_1, taking $0M_1$ units of medical services per month. Suppose that a pay increase in the form of medical services amounting to $0M_1'$ is given, changing the employee's budget line to I_1BE. The new satisfaction-maximizing position is G_2, and in addition to the $0M_1'$ of "free" medical services the individual purchases $M_1'M_2$ at the market price of p_{m_1} per unit.

If the pay increase were in the form of money equivalent to the value of the fringe-benefit medical services, the employee's new satisfaction-maximizing position would also be G_2. The budget line becomes I_2E rather than I_1BE, but since the tangency to an indifference curve occurs in the BE segment common to both budget lines, the results are the same either way.

The analytical framework for fringe benefits is applicable to other situations in which grants are made to individuals by governments or by other private parties in kind rather than in money. Examples include food stamps, educational vouchers, and the like. In every such case it can be demonstrated that the welfare of the individual consumer receiving the grant will be at least as high, and may be higher, if it is made in money rather than in kind. Or, to put it the other way around, grants that are made in kind will never make an individual's welfare greater than if they were made in money; however, they may result in lower welfare than if they were made in money.

Index Numbers

The inflation that has been occurring over the last two decades has brought to the foreground two questions on which indifference curve analysis can shed light. First, how is the rate of inflation measured? Second, what impact does inflation have on the welfare of a consumer? The Laspeyres price index and the Paasche price index are commonly used to provide partial answers.

The Laspeyres Price Index In Figure 5.11 the Laspeyres price index is illustrated. The diagram is for one individual and covers a two-year time series composed of year 0 and year 1.

In year 0, suppose that the individual exercises free choice in the spending of income. Let the income level be I_0^L and the prices of X and Y be p_{x0} and p_{y0}, respectively. The most preferred position is combination B_0, containing x_0 of X and y_0 of Y. Total expenditures on this bundle of goods are described by

$$I_0^L = x_0 p_{x0} + y_0 p_{y0}. \qquad (5.3)$$

FIGURE 5.11
The Laspeyres price index

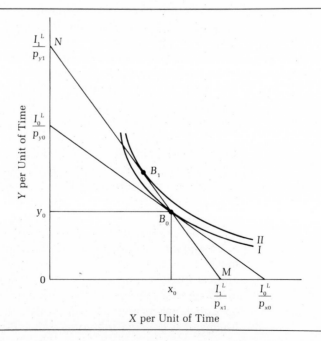

Next consider how much money bundle B_0 would cost in year 1. If the prices of X and Y in that year are p_{x1} and p_{y1}, respectively, and we let I_1^L be the cost of the bundle, then

$$I_1^L = x_0 p_{x1} + y_0 p_{y1}. \tag{5.4}$$

The Laspeyres price index is, in turn,

$$L = \frac{I_1^L}{I_0^L} \times 100 = \frac{x_0 p_{x1} + y_0 p_{y1}}{x_0 p_{x0} + y_0 p_{y0}} \times 100. \tag{5.5}$$

It measures the expenditure that the consumer must make in year 1 as a percentage of the expenditure in year 0, in order to obtain in year 1 the same bundle of goods that maximized satisfaction in year 0.

The Laspeyres index is the *maximum* estimate of the increase in the individual's cost of living, since it erroneously presumes that with expenditure I_1^L the consumer would be at the same level of satisfaction—with bundle B_0 on indifference curve I—in year 1 as in year zero. It is a maximum because in actuality, with an expenditure level of I_1^L in year 1 at prices p_{x1} and p_{y1}, the consumer would not want to stay at bundle B_0. By giving up some of the now relatively higher-priced X for some of the now relatively lower-priced Y, she can move to bundle B_1 and to the higher preference level shown by indifference curve II. Thus, the change in the expenditure level that must occur to enable the consumer to continue to purchase in year 1 the same combination that was purchased in year 0 *overstates the increase* in the cost of maintaining a given level of consumer welfare—unless it should happen that the prices of X and Y increase in the same direction and in the same proportion. In such a case B_1 will coincide with B_0, and the index will measure accurately the change in the cost of living.

What happens to the consumer's welfare from year 0 to year 1? Note that while I_0^L is the actual year-0 expenditure, I_1^L is *not* the actual expenditure in year 1. Rather I_1^L is the *hypothetical* expenditure that would be necessary in that year to purchase the year-0 satisfaction-maximizing bundle of goods. Let the consumer's *actual* expenditure be I_a^L in year 1.

We can be sure that the consumer's welfare is greater in year 1 than in year 0 if

$$\frac{I_a^L}{I_0^L} > \frac{I_1^L}{I_0^L}. \tag{5.6}$$

This means that the percentage increase in the consumer's income exceeds the maximum estimate of the percentage increase in the cost of living. In Figure 5.11 the *actual* budget line for year 1 would lie to the right of NM and would be parallel to it. It would thus be tangent to an indifference curve even higher than *II*. However, if

$$\frac{I_a{}^L}{I_0{}^L} \leq \frac{I_1{}^L}{I_0{}^L},\tag{5.7}$$

we cannot be certain that the consumer's welfare is the same as or less than it was in year 0. It may be greater. The *actual* budget line for year 1 would lie to the left of *NM* and would be parallel to it. If it is tangent to an indifference curve *between I and II*, the consumer is better off in year 1 than in year 0. If it is tangent to indifference curve *I*, there is no change in the consumer's welfare. If it lies far enough to the left of *NM* to be tangent to an indifference curve below *I*, the consumer is worse off in year 0. The fly in the ointment is, of course, the fact that the real increase in the cost of living may be less than

$$\frac{I_1{}^L}{I_0{}^L}.$$

The Paasche Price Index   A different estimate of changes in the cost of living over time is provided by the Paasche price index. Whereas the Laspeyres index shows the relative change in the cost of purchas-

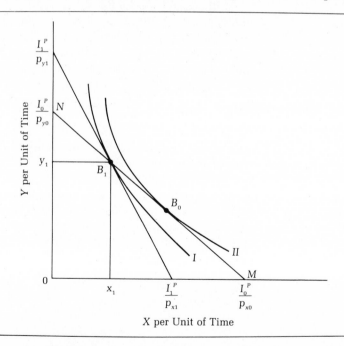

FIGURE 5.12
The Paasche price index

ing a *year-0* bundle of goods between year 0 and year 1, the Paasche index shows the relative change in purchasing a *year-1* bundle of goods between year 0 and year 1.

Suppose the consumer exercises free choice in spending year-1 income. In Figure 5.12, with an income level of $I_1{}^P$ and at prices p_{x1}

and p_{y1} for goods X and Y, combination B_1 is the preferred set of purchases. Combination B_1 contains x_1 of X and y_1 of Y, and the consumer's total expenditures are described by

$$I_1{}^P = x_1 p_{x1} + y_1 p_{y1}. \tag{5.8}$$

The same bundle of goods in year 0 at year-0 prices p_{x0} and p_{y0} would have cost

$$I_0{}^P = x_1 p_{x0} + y_1 p_{y0}. \tag{5.9}$$

The Paasche price index, then, is

$$\frac{I_1{}^P}{I_0{}^P} \times 100 = \frac{x_1 p_{x1} + y_1 p_{y1}}{x_1 p_{x0} + y_1 p_{y0}} \cdot 100. \tag{5.10}$$

The Paasche index represents the *minimum* estimate of the increase in the cost of living from year 0 to year 1. It reflects the increase from $I_0{}^P$ to $I_1{}^P$ in the cost of combination B_1. However, with an expenditure level of $I_0{}^P$ the consumer would have purchased combination B_0 in year 0 and would have been on indifference curve *II* in that year. The expenditure level of $I_1{}^P$ in year 1 yields a lower level of satisfaction than did $I_0{}^P$ in year 0. The actual increase in the cost of living thus exceeds $I_1{}^P - I_0{}^P$ by whatever money value the consumer attaches to the reduction in satisfaction represented by the movement from indifference curve *II* to indifference curve *I*. However, if p_x and p_y change by the same proportional amount and in the same direction between year 0 and year 1, then B_0 and B_1 coincide, and the index correctly measures the change in the cost of living.

Consider again the change in a consumer's welfare between year 0 and year 1. Let the actual income in year 0 be $I_a{}^P$. If

$$\frac{I_1{}^P}{I_{aP}} \le \frac{I_1{}^P}{I_0{}^P}, \tag{5.11}$$

we can be sure that her welfare has decreased between year 0 and year 1, because the increase in actual income is less than the minimum estimate of the increase in the cost of living. In Figure 5.12, the budget line for *actual* income in year 0 would lie on or to the right of NM and would be parallel to it. It would be tangent either to indifference curve *II* at B_0 or to a higher indifference curve. Thus, the welfare loss to the consumer from year 0 to year 1 would be that involved in dropping back from indifference curve *II* or a higher indifference curve to indifference curve *I*. If

$$\frac{I_1{}^P}{I_a{}^P} > \frac{I_1{}^P}{I_0{}^P}, \tag{5.12}$$

we cannot be certain whether or not the consumer's welfare has decreased, increased, or remained constant. The budget line for *actual* income in year 0 will lie to the left of NM and will be parallel to it. If it is tangent to an indifference curve *between* I and II, the consumer's welfare decreases between year 0 and year 1 since the consumer must drop back from that indifference curve to combination B_1 on indifference curve I. If the year-0 actual budget line is tangent to indifference curve I, there is no change in the consumer's welfare between year 0 and year 1, although there would be a change in the combination of goods purchased (a movement up and around indifference curve I). If the actual budget line of year 0 is tangent to an indifference curve lower than I, then the consumer's welfare does indeed increase between year 0 and year 1.

Summary

The indifference curve apparatus provides a useful framework for the theory of consumer choice and exchange. A consumer's tastes and preferences are represented by her or his indifference map. The consumer's opportunity factors—income and the prices of goods purchased—are represented by her or his budget line. The point at which the budget line is tangent to an indifference curve represents the combination of goods that the consumer prefers of those available.

Among the applications of indifference curves is the analysis of information regarding warnings about, and prohibitions of, certain products deemed by the government to be hazardous. Information and warnings tend to change the consumer's preference patterns. Prohibitions tend to lower individual consumers' welfare levels below what they would be in the absence of the prohibitions.

Another application of indifference curve techniques is the analysis of fringe benefits in lieu of money as a part of an employee's total compensation. If an employee voluntarily takes as much or larger quantities of fringe-benefit items than are provided as a part of the employee's compensation, it makes no difference whether that part of the compensation is paid in fringe benefits or in money. Otherwise, the individual is better off if payment is entirely in money.

Still another application is the construction and use of price index numbers. Through the use of indifference curve analysis, it can be shown that a Laspeyres price index provides a maximum estimate of increases in the cost of living over time, while a Paasche price index provides a minimum estimate of such increases.

Suggested Readings

Baumol, William J. *Economic Theory and Operations Analysis*, 4th ed. Englewood Cliffs, N.J.: Prentice-Hall, 1977, pp. 193–213.

Hicks, John R. *Value and Capital,* 2d ed. Oxford, Eng.: The Clarendon Press, 1946, Chaps. 1 and 2.

Henderson, James M. and Quandt, Richard E. *Microeconomic Theory,* 3d ed. New York: McGraw-Hill, 1980, Chap. 2.

Questions and Exercises

1 Draw a consumer's indifference map for pounds of pork and pounds of fish. What can you say about all combinations on a given indifference curve? Select two indifference curves and make whatever inferences of a comparative nature you can about them. Suppose now that a research report, carefully done and widely distributed, clearly demonstrates that pork consumption results in higher cholesterol levels in humans than had previously been thought the case. Show and explain what happens to the consumer's indifference map.

2 A consumer purchases and consumes two goods, food and clothing. Under what circumstances does the consumer maximize satisfaction? Move up the budget line to the left and at some selected point explain the incentives that operate on the consumer.

3 With an indifference curve diagram, show a consumer's equilibrium combination of automobiles and housing. Now suppose the price of automobiles rises rather sharply while that of housing does not. Explain the effects on
   a the consumer's indifference map
   b the consumer's budget line
   c the equilibrium combination.

4 Discuss the likelihood of convexity to the origin of a consumer's indifference curve for two goods, X and Y.

5 Consider an indigent family on relief rolls. Let food and housing be the only items making up the family's budget. Using indifference curve analysis, discuss whether relief payments should be made in (1) kind (that is, a monthly allotment of food and clothing) or (2) money (that is, a monthly welfare check).

CHAPTER CONTENTS		KEY CONCEPTS
Engel Curves	From Indifference Analysis to Engel Curves	Engel curve
	Income Elasticity of Demand	Superior good
		Inferior good
Demand Curves	From Indifference Analysis to Demand Curves	Income elasticity of demand
	Corner Solutions	Demand curve
	Elasticity of Demand and the Price Consumption Curve	Price elasticity of demand
		Substitution effect of a price change
	Income Effects and Substitution Effects	Income effect of a price change
	The Giffen Paradox	Edgeworth box
	Market Demand Curves	Pareto optimum
		Contract curve
Exchange and Welfare		
Applications: Demand Analysis	The Case of Amtrak	
	The Demand for Refuse Collection	
Summary	Suggested Readings	
	Questions and Exercises	

Engel Curves,
Demand Curves,
and Exchange

The indifference curve tools and techniques developed in the preceding chapter underlie Engel curves, demand curves, and exchange. Again we focus on individual consumers. Initially we explain Engel curves. Next we show how demand curves are generated. Finally the incentives for exchange of goods and services among individuals are examined.

Engel Curves

An Engel curve[1] shows the quantities of an item per unit of time that a consumer will take at various levels of income, other things being equal. These curves are of particular importance in an expanding economy and in one in which the inflation rate is greater than consumers think it will be. They help us predict what will happen to the consumption rate of different goods and services as consumers' money incomes rise—for which ones the consumption rate will rise more rapidly and for which ones it may fall. But we will see the significance of Engel curves more clearly if we jump immediately into their construction.

From Indifference Analysis to Engel Curves

Consider the consumer's indifference map depicted in Figure 6.1. Let the vertical axis measure pounds of steak per month and the horizontal axis show units of housing. To keep the analysis manageable, we limit the consumer to a two-commodity world. Assume that the consumer's tastes and preferences, along with the price of steak p_{s1} and the price of housing p_{h1}, are held constant, while income I is allowed to vary.

In Figure 6.1(a) an increase in income from I_1 to I_2 shifts the consumer's budget line to the right, parallel to the original one. The

---

[1] Engel curves are named after Ernst Engel, a German pioneer of the last half of the 1800s in the field of budget studies. See George J. Stigler, "The Early History of Empirical Studies of Consumer Behavior," *The Journal of Political Economy*, 62 (April 1954), pp. 98–100.

FIGURE 6.1
The consumer's Engel
curves for two goods

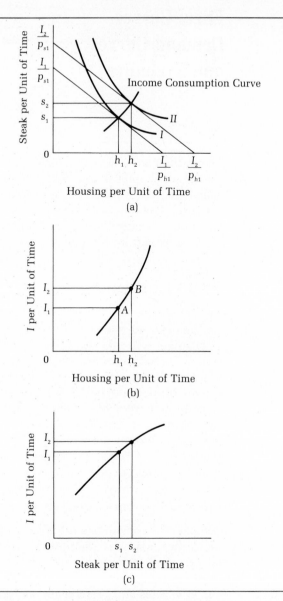

Income Consumption Curve

Housing per Unit of Time

(a)

Housing per Unit of Time

(b)

Steak per Unit of Time

(c)

points of tangency of the budget lines with indifference curves of the consumer show the combination of housing and steak that will be taken at each income level. These combinations, together with the corresponding income levels, provide the data for the construction of the consumer's Engel curves. At an income level of I_1, the consumer will take quantity h_1 of housing. This choice is plotted as point A in Figure 6.1(b). At income level I_2, quantity h_2 will be taken. This choice is plotted as point B. If budget lines corresponding to other levels of income were shown in Figure 6.1(a), corresponding quantities of housing could be determined and plotted against those income levels on Figure 6.1(b).[2]

Goods and services are sometimes classified as *superior* or *inferior*, depending upon how their consumption varies as income changes. A *superior* good is one for which the consumption level increases as consumer income increases. The Engel curves of Figure 6.1(b) and 6.1(c) indicate that housing and steak are superior. The distinguishing characteristic of *inferior* goods is that as the consumer's income increases, the consumption level of them decreases. Hamburger may be a case in point, since at high income levels consumers tend to substitute more expensive meat cuts—prime rib and steak—for it. A graphic picture of the income consumption curve and the Engel curve for such a good is presented in Figure 6.2. At income level I_1, Figure 6.2(a) shows that the consumer takes x_1 pounds of

FIGURE 6.2
Engel curve for an inferior good

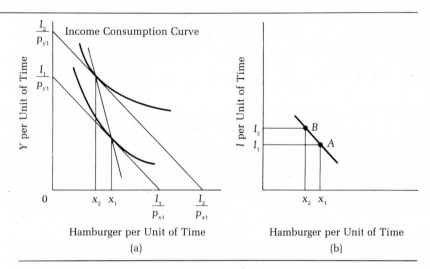

Hamburger per Unit of Time
(a)

Hamburger per Unit of Time
(b)

hamburger in his or her most preferred position. This is plotted as point A in Figure 6.2(b). Similarly, at income level I_2 the consumer takes x_2 pounds, and point B on his Engel curve is located. Note that both the income consumption curve with respect to hamburger and the Engel curve slope upward to the *left*.

---

[2] In footnote 12 of the previous chapter, the solutions of equations (4), (5), and (6) yield values for x, y, and λ in terms of p_x, p_y, and I. Thus, for good X

$$x = x(p_x, p_y, I).$$

If p_x and p_y are held constant, the Engel curve equation for good X becomes

$$x = E(I).$$

The Engel curve for Y is obtained in the same way.

Examples abound of both superior and inferior goods. Among the former are stereo equipment, a college education, housing, the better cuts of meat and, until recently, automobiles. A recent study by the United States Department of Agriculture found that while consumers' aftertax incomes increased by 8 percent, outlays for housing during the period 1960–79 rose by 8.5 percent, health expenditures by 11 percent, and recreation expenditures by 9.5 percent. Food expenditures during the same period fell by an average of 7 percent, suggesting that food as a whole tends to be an inferior good. According to a second USDA study, the income elasticity for food is 0.36, indicating that a 10 percent increase in consumer aftertax income will boost expenditures on food by only 3.6 percent.[3] Within each of these categories there will be exceptions. Although housing as a broad category may be superior, slum housing will be inferior. Recreation as a whole is a superior good but black-and-white television sets are not. Food may be inferior as a category, but liquor and gourmet items are superior goods. Salt, cheap hamburger, cheap wines, and discount airline tickets for "red eye" flights in the wee hours of the morning are all probably inferior. Another clear example of an inferior good is travel between American cities by railroad, which we consider in more detail later in the chapter.

Engel curves provide valuable information regarding consumption patterns for different commodities and for different individuals. For certain basic commodities, such as food, as the consumer's income increases from very low levels, consumption may climb considerably at first; then, as income continues to rise, the increases in consumption may become smaller and smaller relative to those in income. A pattern of this type is illustrated in Figure 6.1(c). One of the Department of Agriculture studies referred to above estimated in 1980 that families in the lowest income group spent 34 percent of their pretax income on food, over three times the 10 percent that families in the highest income group spent. For other items such as housing, as the consumer's income goes up the quantity purchased per unit of time may increase in greater proportion than income does. Figure 6.1(b) reflects a situation of this type. It is also quite possible that an item is a superior good at low income levels and becomes inferior at high income levels.

Income Elasticity of Demand

The responsiveness to the quantity taken of an item to income changes is called the *income elasticity of demand* for that item. The

---

[3] Bill Abrams, "People Spend Less of Their Income on Food Even Though Its Price Keeps Rising Sharply," *The Wall Street Journal*, 16 August 1979. Reprinted by permission of *The Wall Street Journal*, © Dow Jones & Company, Inc. 1979. All rights reserved.

elasticity concept is not a new one at this point, so we need only to spell it out in this particular context. It is defined as

$$\Theta = \frac{\Delta x/x}{\Delta I/I},$$ (5.2)

that is, the percentage change in quantity divided by the percentage change in the level of income, when the change in the level of income is small.[4] For an arc such as EF in Figure 6.3(a), the appropriate

FIGURE 6.3
Income elasticity of demand

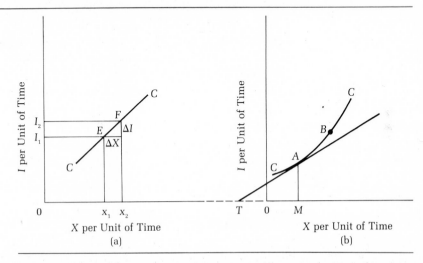

FIGURE 6.3
Income elasticity of demand

data can be fed into the elasticity formula to determine the magnitude of elasticity. In Figure 6.3(b) income elasticity at point A will be $MT/0M$. The derivation of the point income elasticity measurement is exactly the same as it is for a point price elasticity measurement. At point B would the income elasticity of CC be greater than, or less than, one? What would an Engel curve with an income elasticity of one at all points look like?

Demand Curves

An individual consumer demand curve for a good or service shows the quantities that the consumer will take per unit of time at alternative prices, other things being equal. The most important "other things" are (1) the consumer's tastes and preferences, represented by a set of indifference curves; (2) the consumer's income; and (3) the prices of other goods and services. We shall consider in turn the

[4] In terms of calculus it becomes

$$\Theta = \lim_{\Delta I \to 0} \frac{\Delta x/x}{\Delta I/I} = \frac{dx/x}{dI/I} = \frac{dx}{dI} \times \frac{I}{x}.$$

generation of a demand curve, the nature of "corner" solutions, and the elasticity of demand.

From Indifference Analysis to Demand Curves

To obtain a consumer's demand curve for one good, we vary the price of the good and observe the quantity the consumer will take when maximizing satisfaction at each price. In Figure 6.4 measure gallons of gasoline on the horizontal axis. Let Y be all other goods and services measured in terms of identical baskets of them. The consumer's income is I_1; the price of gasoline is p_{g1}; and the price per basket of other goods and services in p_{y1}. The budget line is AB, so we note that at price p_{g1} the consumer takes g_1 gallons per unit of time when maximizing satisfaction.

FIGURE 6.4
The consumer's demand curve for one good

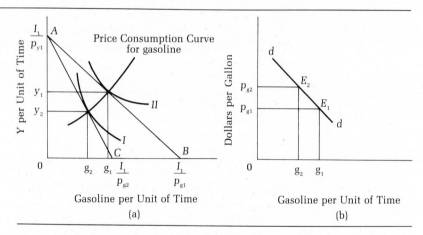

Gasoline per Unit of Time
(a)

Gasoline per Unit of Time
(b)

An increase in the price of gasoline to p_{g2} shifts the budget line from AB to AC. Given the consumer's income of I_1, a higher price per gallon for gasoline means that if the entire income were spent for gasoline, the total amount the consumer could purchase would be smaller. Budget line AC lies below AB and has a steeper slope.[5]

Line AC is necessarily tangent to a lower indifference curve than was line AB, and the new combination of gasoline and other goods and services preferred by the consumer will differ from the original one. Initially, the consumer preferred the combination g_1 of gasoline and y_1 of Y. The new preferred combination will be g_2 of gasoline and y_2 of Y. Different prices of gasoline cause the budget line to assume different positions, with its focal point always remaining at A. Higher prices rotate it clockwise, making it tangent to lower indifference curves. Lower prices rotate it counterclockwise, making it tangent to higher indifference curves.

[5]   The slope of AB is p_{x1}/p_{y1}. The slope of AC is p_{x2}/p_{y1}. Since $p_{x2} > p_{x1}$, then $p_{x2}/p_{y1} > p_{x1}/p_{y1}$.

The line joining satisfaction-maximizing combinations of goods at the various prices of gasoline is called the *price consumption curve* for gasoline and is illustrated in Figure 6.4(a). Note that in reality it shows no prices. It is traced out by preferred combinations of gasoline and Y when the consumer's tastes and preferences, income, and the prices of other goods and services are held constant while the price of gasoline is varied.

The necessary information for establishing the consumer's demand schedule and demand curve for gasoline is obtained from Figure 6.4(a). When the price of gasoline is p_{g1}, the consumer will take quantity g_1 of it. This choice establishes one point on the demand schedule or demand curve. At the higher price p_{g2}, the consumer will take the smaller quantity g_2, establishing a second point on the demand schedule or demand curve for gasoline. These points are plotted as E_1 and E_2 in Figure 6.4(b). Additional price-quantity points can be found in a similar manner and plotted on a conventional demand diagram in the usual way. Most such demand schedules or demand curves show an inverse relationship between price and quantity—the higher the price of a good, the lower the quantity taken, and vice versa.[6]

Corner Solutions

Among the wide array of goods and services from which a consumer can choose, there will be items that the consumer does not buy. The consumer's tastes and preferences my be such that some of these are not desired under any circumstances, even if their prices were zero. As such they simply do not enter into an analysis of that consumer's choices. But other commodities may or may not be purchased, depending upon their prices.

Consider an item such as champagne. In Figure 6.5 quantities per unit of time are measured along the horizontal axis. The vertical axis shows quantities, say identical baskets, of a composite of all other goods and services that enter into the consumer's field of choice. Let the price of each basket of the composite be p_{y1}, and let the consumer's income be I_1. Representative indifference curves are shown by *I, II, III,* and *IV*. Price p_3 for champagne is the price at which the consumer's budget line is just tangent to indifference curve *II* at point *A*. At any champagne price below p_{c3}, champagne enters the consumer's budget. If the price is p_{c2}, the quantity taken is

---

[6] From Footnote 2

$$x = x(p_x, p_y, I).$$

Treating p_y and I as given parameters, the demand equation can be expressed as

$$x = D(p_x).$$

The demand curve for Y can be derived similarly.

FIGURE 6.5
A corner solution

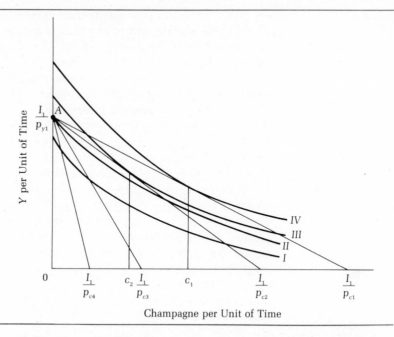

Y per Unit of Time

$\dfrac{I_1}{P_{y1}}$ A

IV

III

II

I

0

$\dfrac{I_1}{P_{c4}}$ c_2 $\dfrac{I_1}{P_{c3}}$ c_1 $\dfrac{I_1}{P_{c2}}$ $\dfrac{I_1}{P_{c1}}$

Champagne per Unit of Time

c_2. If the price is still lower, say p_{c1}, the quantity taken increases to c_1. But if the price is p_{c3} or higher, champagne is ruled out of the consumer's purchases; the quantity taken becomes zero. The consumer will be on the highest possible indifference curve—indifference curve II—with combination A, which contains no champagne. Combination A is called a *corner solution* to the consumer's maximization problem.

A corner solution occurs only if $MRS_{cy} \leq p_c/p_y$ at a point such as A, where the consumer's budget line intersects the Y axis. At such a point, if $MRS_{cy} > p_c/p_y$ the consumer is willing to give up more Y to obtain a unit of champagne than the market requires and will thus maximize satisfaction by moving down the budget line. This would be the case if the price of champagne were p_{c2} or p_{c3}. Translating prices and corresponding quantities of champagne into demand curve form, price p_{c3} is the price at which the consumer's demand curve for champagne intersects the price axis.

Elasticity of Demand and the Price Consumption Curve

If the X axis represents units of any good X and the Y axis represents purchasing power not spent on X,[7] the slope of the price consumption

[7] A given difference curve thus shows combinations of purchasing power and X among which the consumer is indifferent. The budget line is drawn in the usual way. The price of purchasing power, or P_{y1}, in dollars is $1 a unit. Hence, I_1/p_{y1} is the consumer's income. Since the slope of the budget line is p_{x1}/p_{y1} and p_{y1} equals $1, that slope is p_{x1}.

curve indicates whether elasticity of demand for the good is unitary, greater than one, or less than one.

In Figure 6.6(a) the indifference curves are such that the price consumption curve is parallel to the X axis, or has a slope of zero. As the price of X rises from p_{x1} to p_{x2}, the portion of the consumer's income *not* spent on X remains constant at $0y_1$. Thus, the amount spent on X must remain constant also. If a rise in the price of X causes no change in the consumer's spending on X, then the consumer's demand for X must have unitary elasticity for the price increase.

The upward slope of the price consumption curve in Figure 6.6(b) means that demand for X is inelastic. A rise in the price of X from p_{x1} to p_{x2} brings about a decrease in the portion of income not spent on X from $0y_1$ to $0y_2$. In other words, more income is spent on X at the higher price. An increase in expenditures on X, as the price of X rises, can result only when demand for X is inelastic for the price increases.

Figure 6.6(c) shows a downward-sloping price consumption curve, meaning that demand for X is elastic. The rise in the price of X increases the portion of income not spent on X from $0y_1$ to $0y_2$. Therefore, less is spent on X. An increase in the price of X that decreases total expenditure on X results from an elastic demand curve for X between two prices.

Income Effects and Substitution Effects

The inverse relationship that most demand curves show between the price of an item and the quantity of it per unit of time that a consumer will take is the combined result of a *substitution effect* and an *income effect* of a price change. When the price of an item rises and consumers turn away from it toward now relatively lower-priced

FIGURE 6.6
Price consumption
curves and elasticity of
demand

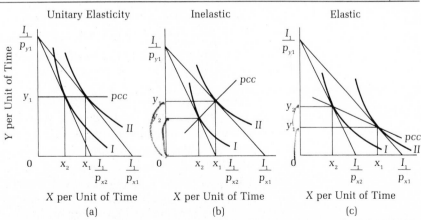

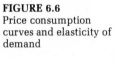

substitutes, a decrease in quantity taken occurs because of the substitution. Additionally, the rise in the price of the item lowers the consumer's real income, or purchasing power, causing the consumer to reduce purchases of all superior goods. To the extent that the reduction in real income affects that individual's consumption of the item under consideration, we have an income effect.

The separation of income and substitution effects is illustrated in Figure 6.7. The consumer's income is I_1 and the prices of X and Y are p_{x1} and p_{y1}, respectively. Combination A, containing x_1 of X and y_1 of Y, is the consumer's preferred combination. Suppose that the price of X now rises to p_{x2}, rotating the budget line clockwise with I_1/p_{y1} as its focal point until it cuts the X axis at I_1/p_{x2}. Note that because of the increase in the price of X, the slope of the new budget

FIGURE 6.7
Income and
substitution effects

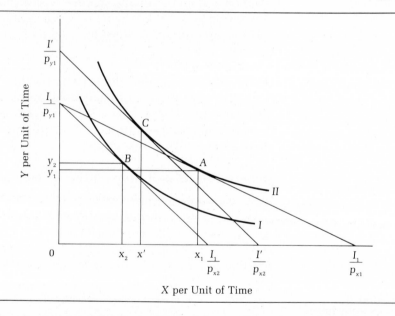

line is greater than that of the old one. The slope of the original budget line is p_{x1}/p_{y1}, while that of the new one is p_{x2}/p_{y1}. Combination B, containing x_2 of X and y_2 of Y is the consumer's preferred combination after the rise in the price of X.

That the consumer's real income has been decreased by the increase in the price of X is illustrated graphically by the fact that combination B lies on a lower indifference curve than combination A does. The movement from combination A to combination B, and the reduction in the quantity of X taken from x_1 to x_2, shows the combined income and substitution effects of the price change.

To isolate the substitution effect and determine its magnitude, we increase the consumer's money income enough to compensate for the loss in purchasing power. The additional purchasing power, or the "compensating increase in income," will move the budget line to the right, parallel to itself; and when just enough has been given the consumer to offset the loss in real income, it will lie tangent to indifference curve II at point C. Combination C is at the same level of preference for the consumer as combination A is; but, because of the now higher price of X, combination A is not available to him. He has been induced to substitute the relatively cheaper Y for the relatively more expensive X in order to avoid a less-preferred position. The income effect of the increase in the price of X has been eliminated by the compensating variation in the consumer's income; hence, the movement from A to C, or the decrease in X taken from x_1 to x', is the pure substitution effect. It results solely from the change in the price of X relative to the price of Y.

The income effect, apart from the substitution effect, can be determined by taking the compensating variation in income away from the consumer. The budget line shifts to the left, and the highest indifference curve to which it is tangent is indifference curve I. Combination B, y_2 of Y and x_2 of X, is the preferred position. The movement from C to B is the income effect and reduces the quantity of X taken from x' to x_2.

The movement of the consumer from combination A to combination B, with the increase of the price of X from p_{x1} to p_{x2} is thus broken down into two steps, one showing the substitution effect and the other showing the income effect. Usually they operate in the same direction. If X is an inferior good, however, the income effect will work in the opposite direction from the substitution effect. In such a case, the increase in the price of X causes a tendency on the part of the consumer to substitute relatively lower-priced goods for X, but at the same time the lower real income of the consumer induces an increase in the consumption of X.[8]

---

[8] To show the separation of substitution effects and income effects for good X mathematically, we return to equations (4), (5), and (6) of Footnote 12 of the preceding chapter. The total differentials of these equations are, respectively:

$$f_{xx}dx + f_{xy}dy - \lambda dp_x - p_x d\lambda = 0 \tag{12}$$
$$f_{yx}dx + f_{yy}dy - \lambda dp_y - p_y d\lambda = 0 \tag{13}$$
$$dI - xdp_x - p_x dx - ydp_y - p_y dy = 0 \tag{14}$$

or

$$f_{xx}dx + f_{xy}dy - p_x d\lambda = \lambda dp_x \tag{12}$$
$$f_{yx}dx + f_{yy}dy - p_y d\lambda = \lambda dp_y \tag{13}$$
$$-p_x dx - p_y dy = -dI + xdp_x + ydp_y. \tag{14}$$

Regarding the right-hand terms as constants, we obtain the determinant

$$D = \begin{vmatrix} f_{xx} & f_{xy} & -p_x \\ f_{yx} & f_{yy} & -p_y \\ -p_x & -p_y & 0 \end{vmatrix}, \tag{15}$$

in which D_{ij} represents the cofactor of the element in the ith row and jth column. Then Cramer's rule is used to solve for dx, dy, and $d\lambda$. With respect to good X:

The substitution effect is usually much stronger than the income effect. A consumer who purchases a great many goods will not ordinarily experience a large drop in real income when the price of one of the goods rises. There may be a large substitution effect, however, when good substitutes are available for the commodity in question.

The Giffen Paradox

Conceivably a price change for an inferior good may generate an income effect that more than counteracts the substitution effect, leading to a demand curve that slopes upward to the right for the price change. This unusual case is called the Giffen Paradox. To the extent that it occurs at all in the real world, it would likely be limited to a small range of prices for the good in question.

The Giffen case is illustrated in Figure 6.8. Let the consumer's income be I_1, and the initial prices of X and Y be p_{x1} and p_{y1}, respectively. In Figure 6.8(a) the consumer maximizes satisfaction with combination A, taking x_1 of X per unit of time at price p_{x1}. Point A' in Figure 6.8(b) is thus determined on the consumer's demand curve for X. Now let the price of X rise to p_{x2}. At the same time suppose we give the consumer a compensating increase in in-

$$dx = \frac{\lambda D_{11}dp_x + \lambda D_{21}dp_y + D_{31}(-dI + xdp_x + ydp_y)}{D}. \tag{16}$$

Now, from equation (16), assuming that p_y and I remain constant and dividing through by dp_x, we obtain the total response in the quantity taken of X to a change in its price:

$$\frac{dx}{dp_x} = \frac{\lambda D_{11}}{D} + x\frac{D_{31}}{D}. \tag{17}$$

If, in equation (16), p_x and p_y are held constant, then

$$\frac{dx}{dI}\bigg|_{dp_x=dp_y=0} = -\frac{D_{31}}{D}. \tag{18}$$

If a change in the price of good X is compensated for by an income change such that the consumer remains on the same indifference curve when the price of X changes—that is, $dU = 0$—then (from Footnote 6) $f_x dx + f_y dy = 0$.
Since, for the consumer to be in equilibrium,

$$\frac{f_x}{f_y} = \frac{p_x}{p_y},$$

then $p_x dx + p_y dy = 0$. This expression is the left-hand side of equation (14); therefore, that equation becomes $0 = -dI + xdp_x + ydp_y$, and from equation (16)

$$\frac{\partial x}{\partial p_x}\bigg|_{dU=0} = \frac{\lambda D_{11}}{D}. \tag{19}$$

Substituting the equalities of equations (18) and (19) in equation (17), we obtain

$$\frac{dx}{dp_x} = \frac{\partial x}{\partial p_x}\bigg|_{dU=0} - x \times \frac{\partial x}{\partial I}\bigg|_{dp_x=dp_y=0,} \tag{20}$$

or

Total effect of a change in p_x	=	substitution effect	−	income. effect

FIGURE 6.8
The Giffen Paradox

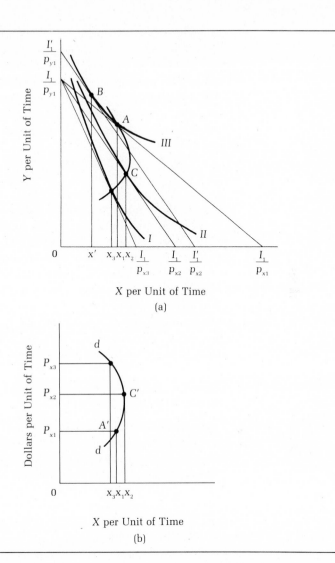

come to offset the loss in real income, that is, sufficient to bring the consumer back to indifference curve III. The consumer would maximize satisfaction at combination B with the substitution effect working in the usual way, reducing consumption of X from x_1 to x'. When we remove the compensating increase in income, combination C maximizes the consumer's satisfaction. Since X is an inferior good, the reduction in the consumer's income from I_1' to I_1 *increases* consumption of X from x' to x_2. A second point, C', on the consumer's demand curve for X is determined. For the price increase from p_{x1} to p_{x2}, we not only show the income effect *working in the opposite direction* from the substitution effect, we also show it *out-*

weighing the substitution effect. When this happens, we have the Giffen Paradox in which an increase (decrease) in the price of a good brings about an increase (decrease) in the quantity per unit of time that will be consumed. Goods for which price changes yield income effects in the opposite direction from and smaller than the substitution effects are inferior goods, but they are not Giffen goods. All Giffen goods are inferior goods, but not all inferior goods are Giffen goods.

The range of prices over which a Giffen effect would operate must be small. In Figure 6.8 we show it occurring for the rise in the price of X from p_{x1} to p_{x2}. For the further price increase from p_{x2} to p_{x3}, we show no Giffen effect—the substitution effect is dominant.

The actual number of Giffen goods in the real world is probably small since they must exhibit relatively large negative income effects on quantities taken. Potatoes in Ireland during the nineteenth century were thought to be a Giffen good. When the price declined, the real income of Irish families increased sufficiently, because so much of it was devoted to this single commodity that the families shifted their consumption away from potatoes to superior forms of food that they could now afford. Not many goods can be found that show strongly inferior characteristics and, at the same time, constitute a large fraction of family budgets.

Market Demand Curves

The market demand curve for a good is built up from the individual consumers' demand curves for it. We defined the demand curve of an individual consumer in much the same way as we defined a market demand curve. It shows the different quantities that the consumer will take at all possible prices, other things being equal. Thus, by summing the quantities that all consumers in the market will take at each possible price, we arrive at the market demand curve.

The process of summing individual consumer demand curves to obtain the market demand curve is illustrated in Figure 6.9. Suppose that there are two consumers only—G and H—who buy commodity X. Their individual demand curves are d_1d_1 and d_2d_2, respectively. At a price of p_1 consumer G will be willing to take x_1 per unit of time while consumer H will be willing to take x_1' per unit of time. Together they will be willing to take quantity $X_1 = (x_1 + x_1')$ at that price, and A is located as a point on the market demand curve. Likewise, at price p_2 consumer G will be willing to take x_2 units per unit of time while consumer H will be willing to take x_2'. Together they will be willing to take $X_2 = (x_2 + x_2')$ at that price, and B is located as a point on the market demand curve. Additional points can be located similarly, and the market demand curve DD is drawn

FIGURE 6.9
Construction of a
market demand curve

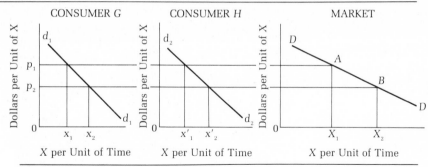

through them. The market demand curve for a commodity, then, is the horizontal summation of the individual consumer demand curves for the commodity.

Exchange and Welfare

The forces giving rise to voluntary exchange of items among individuals and the impact of voluntary exchange on welfare can be readily explained in terms of indifference curve analysis. Suppose that we consider two consumers, A and B, each of whom receives and consumes quantities of two commodities, X and Y, per unit of time.

Individual A's tastes and preferences for X and Y are shown on the conventional part of Figure 6.10. The indifference map of B is rotated 180 degrees and is superimposed on that of A so that the axes of the two diagrams form what is called an *Edgeworth box*. The diagram for B can be placed so that $0M$ represents the entire amount of Y received by the two individuals and $0N$ represents the entire amount of X received. The indifference curves of A are convex to 0, while those of B are convex to $0'$. Any point on or in the rectangle represents a possible distribution of the goods between the two individuals.

The initial distribution of X and Y can be represented by any point, such as F, lying within the rectangle formed by the two sets of axes. Individual A gets $0y_1$ of Y per unit of time, and B gets y_1M. The amount of X received per unit of time by A is $0x_1$ and that by B is x_1N. Individual A is on indifference curve I_1. Individual B is on indifference curve I'. For A the marginal rate of substitution of X for Y at point F is greater than it is for B. Individual A would be willing to give up more Y to get an additional unit of X than B would require to induce him to part with a unit of X. Thus, the stage is set for exchange.

FIGURE 6.10
The basis of exchange

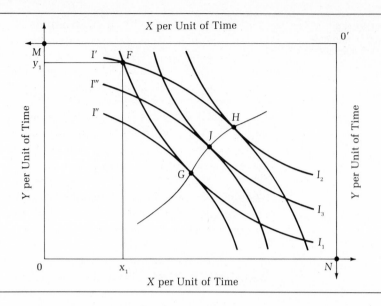

Whenever the initial distribution of the two commodities is such that the MRS_{xy} for one party is not equal to the MRS_{xy} for another party, either or both may gain from exchange. If F is the initial distribution of X and Y, exchanges of Y by individual A to individual B for X could take place in such a way that indifference curve I_1 is followed downward to the right. Individual A would be made no worse off and individual B would be made progressively better off until the distribution of goods between the two is that represented by point G, at which indifference curve I_1 is tangent to indifference curve I''. No further exchange can occur without making one or both parties worse off than they are at G. Similarly, individual A could exchange Y to individual B for X in such a way that indifference curve I' is followed downward to the right. Such exchanges would leave B no worse off than before but would place A on successively higher indifference curves, or in more preferred positions, until the distribution of goods is that represented by point H, at which indifference curve I' is tangent to indifference curve I_2. Any further exchanges will result in a decrease in well-being for one or both parties.

Again, starting at F, both parties could gain from exchanges that follow a path from F to J, falling somewhere within the area bounded by FG and FH. Both parties would reach higher preference levels until some point J, at which an indifference curve of individual A is tangent to an indifference curve of individual B, is reached. Further exchanges would result in one or both parties being made worse off.

Exchanges that alter the distribution of goods from one at which an indifference curve of one consumer intersects an indifference curve of another consumer, toward a distribution within the area bounded by the two indifference curves and within which tangency occurs, lead toward a *Pareto optimum* or an *efficient* distribution of the goods.

In Chapter 1 we defined a Pareto optimum condition as one in which no one can be made better off without making someone else worse off, and it is this condition that occurs at G or J or H or at any other point at which an indifference curve of consumer A is tangent to an indifference curve of consumer B. A line joining all of these tangency points, GJH as extended in Figure 6.10, is called a *contract curve*.

For an efficient distribution of goods between the two parties to exist, or for a Pareto optimum in distribution to exist, the MRS_{xy} for one must be equal to the MRS_{xy} for the other. That is, if the maximum amount of Y that individual A is willing to give up to get an additional unit of X is equal to the minimum amount of Y that B would accept in exchange for a unit of X, then no gain from such an exchange would occur for either party. These conditions are fulfilled at every point along the contract curve. At each such point, an indifference curve of A is tangent to an indifference curve of B; that is, individual A's indifference curve has the same slope as does individual B's, or MRS_{xy} is the same for A as it is for B.

This analysis shows that some redistributions of goods (income) among consumers will increase welfare, but we are left in the dark with respect to other distributions. With the initial distribution F, any point on the contract curve from G to H inclusive is a Pareto optimum, and a movement from F to any such point increases the welfare of the community. However, there are any number of efficient or Pareto optimum distributions of X and Y between consumers A and B; there is one for every point on the contract curve. If a redistribution from J to H is effected, for example, consumer B is made worse off and consumer A is made better off. Who knows whether the increase in A's welfare is just offset, more than offset, or less than offset by the decrease in the welfare of B?

Applications: Demand Analysis

There are many possible examples of demand principles. One of the more interesting is that of the demand for railroad passenger services, an area in which nostalgia often competes with hard economic analysis. So we consider the case of Amtrak in some detail. Next we turn to a piece of recent research, illustrating the law of demand, in the mundane, everyday activity of garbage collection.

The Case of Amtrak[9]

The long-term decline of railroad passenger service in the United States well illustrates the market for an inferior product and its negatively sloped Engel curve. Demand probably peaked in the mid-1890s, when railroads are thought to have provided about 95 percent of intercity trips. More recent data, for 1920 to 1970, are shown in Table 6.1. Electric street railways and interurbans grew rapidly around the turn of the century and, together with cars and trucks after 1910, provided substitutes for passenger trains. Within a decade after World War I, the automobile became dominant for short-haul passenger trips. By 1930 railroads were losing money even on long-haul trains, and by 1940 their passenger level amounted to less than half that of 1920. There was a resurgence of railroad passenger traffic during World War II because of restraints on the use of gasoline and commercial aviation, but the downward trend reappeared soon thereafter. Railroads dieselized their fleets during 1947–52 and made strong attempts to upgrade passenger services, but the growth of airline service accelerated the decline, especially after the introduction in the late 1950s of such commercial jet transports as the Boeing 707.

Most economists of the period explained the decline in terms of the industry's demand conditions. By 1960 the fare differential between Chicago and Los Angeles by air, relative to train, was only about $20, but the time differential was some 40 hours. Most of the people who could afford to spend extra time to save a few dollars were those like the unemployed, the very poor, or the retired elderly—all of whom would place a relatively low value upon the opportunity costs of their time. A few were railroad enthusiasts who rode trains as a form of recreation. Business and vacation travelers who place a relatively high opportunity cost on their time would prefer airplane or auto travel to trains, depending on travel distances, and they have deserted trains in droves. Economists in 1955 estimated that the income elasticity of rail travel was −0.6; that is, for every additional 1 percent increase in income, quantity demanded declined by 0.6 percent, yielding a backward-bending Engel curve like that of Figure 6.2. This elasticity estimate would probably have been even smaller had it been made in the 1960s after the introduction of jet transports. Estimates of the income elasticities for the

---

[9] This discussion is drawn from George W. Hilton, *Amtrak: The National Railroad Passenger Corporation* (Washington, D.C.: American Enterprise Institute for Public Policy Research, 1980). © 1980, American Enterprise Institute for Public Policy Research.

TABLE 6.1 Output and financial performance of American railroad passenger service, 1920–1970	Year	Passengers (millions)	Passenger-Miles (millions)	Net Revenue (thousands of dollars)	Passenger Deficit as Percentage of Freight Net Revenue
	1920	1,270	47,370	N.A.	N.A.
	1925	902	36,167	N.A.	N.A.
	1930	708	26,876	N.A.	N.A.
	1935	448	18,509	N.A.	N.A.
	1940	456	23,816	$−262,058	27.8%
	1945	897	91,826	230,060	18.5
	1950	488	31,790	−508,508	32.9
	1955	433	28,546	−636,693	36.1
	1960	327	21,284	−466,289	32.9
	1965	306	17,162	−398,029	21.6
	1970	289	10,786	−449,579	26.2

N. A. means not available.

Source: George W. Hilton, *Amtrak: The National Railroad Passenger Corporation* (Washington, D.C.: American Enterprise Institute for Public Policy Research, 1980), pp. 3–4. © 1980, American Enterprise Institute for Public Policy Research.

rivals to intercity trains during the 1960s were +1.2 for automobiles and +2.5 for airlines.

During this period an alternative hypothesis for the decline in rail passenger services was put forward. This hypothesis was that railroads were withdrawing the luxury services (such as sleeping and dining cars), which were complements to unadorned passenger travel, as a deliberate discouragement to passenger travel. The view was particularly supported by rail enthusiasts and the affluent elderly, many of whom feared flying, although it was never clear why railroad managements would discourage passengers if the service were profitable. Some of the debate over this issue centered on whether the railroads' losses from passenger services were fact or fiction. These advocates of passenger service formed the National Association of Railroad Passengers to lobby for a nationalized railroad passenger corporation that would give managers explicit incentives to revitalize luxury services. So Congress created the Amtrak system in 1970.

The experience under Amtrak has been more consistent with the demand hypothesis than the discouragement hypothesis. In its early years ridership increased, owing to increases in routes served and substantial subsidies, but by 1975 the pattern of declining demand resumed. Long-haul trains exhibited the greatest decline, as the demand hypothesis would predict.

Amtrak has estimated its own *price elasticity* of demand at about −2.2 for one-way trips, reflecting the abundance of competitive travel modes that it faces as well as the fact that most of its customers travel for recreation or novelty as opposed to more-compelling business reasons. Regionally, Amtrak's lowest estimated price elasticity is -0.67 for the northeast, where business trips are numerous and relatively short and where time lost in riding trains is small. Its estimate of cross elasticity against air travel in the northeast is 0.6 (that is, a 1 percent rise in rail fares will raise air travel by 0.6 percent), but the cross elasticity between rail and bus is 1.29. Thus, Amtrak is much more competitive with bus than with air travel even in the region where business travel by rail is relatively important. Amtrak management appears to take these estimates of elasticity seriously, having held fare increases to two-thirds of the rise in the Consumer Price Index over the period of its operation.

Amtrak has not yet compiled a statistically significant estimate of its *income* elasticity, but for internal working purposes it appears to use a number slightly greater than zero. At first glance this number seems high when compared with the historic decline in rail travel demand, but it is probably a reasonable estimate, given Amtrak's current routes and demand conditions. The population of elderly persons will grow over time, but if more of them work past age 65, they will find rail travel relatively unattractive because of its time-intensiveness. The portion of elderly persons who fear flying is likely to decline absolutely and eventually be replaced by a generation accustomed to air travel throughout their lives. The number of rail enthusiasts is probably static and, in any case, is unlikely to grow enough from its present base (no more than 200,000) to make a dent one way or another in Amtrak's utilization. Moreover, if Amtrak continues to decline, so will the number of train buffs. Thus, Amtrak's demand conditions viewed demographically are not at all favorable.

Working in Amtrak's favor is the rising cost of gasoline, but the net effect of this factor is not clear. Amtrak's patronage increased temporarily during 1973–74 due partly to the surge in world crude oil prices and partly to the shortages of gasoline that price controls created. However, decontrol of petroleum prices and the elimination of shortages will make it easier for motorists to adjust to petroleum supplies in the future, and may thus work to Amtrak's disadvantage. The survival of Amtrak will probably depend less on the net effects of these demand forces and more on congressional largesse. It is unlikely that it can pay its own way.

The Demand for Refuse Collection

Market demand curves are obtained by summing the quantities that individuals in the market want to purchase at alternative prices. The

ing the price of the good while holding constant tastes and preferences, income, and prices of other goods. The resulting points of consumer equilibrium trace out the price consumption curve for the commodity. Information for the demand curve can be taken from the indifference curve diagram.

The slope of the price consumption curve for a commodity indicates the elasticity of demand when the commodity under consideration is measured on the X axis and money is measured on the Y axis. A horizontal price consumption curve means that demand has unitary elasticity. When the price consumption curve slopes upward to the right, demand is inelastic. When it slopes downward to the right, demand is elastic.

The change in quantity taken as a result of a price change, as shown by the demand curve for an item, is the combined result of two forces—an income effect and a substitution effect. For normal goods, these work in the same direction to produce a decrease in quantity for an increase in price, or an increase in quantity for a decrease in price. For inferior goods, the two effects work in opposite directions, but the substitution effect is usually the much stronger of the two.

By means of an Edgeworth box, the conditions for an efficient or Pareto optimum distribution of goods among consumers can be established. These are that the MRS_{xy} of one consumer for any two goods, X and Y, must be the same as the MRS_{xy} of any other consumer for the same two goods. Distributions of goods satisfying these conditions form the contract curve. For any distribution of goods not on the contract curve, a redistribution can occur that moves to the contract curve and increases community welfare. No conclusions regarding community welfare can be drawn from redistributions that occur along the contract curve.

Suggested Readings

Henderson, James M. and Quandt, Richard E. *Microeconomic Theory*, 3rd ed. New York: McGraw-Hill, 1980, Chap. 2.

Hirshleifer, Jack. *Price Theory and Applications*, 2nd ed. Englewood Cliffs, N.J.: Prentice-Hall, 1980, Chaps. 4 and 5.

Questions and Exercises

1 Suppose that Ms. Smythe purchases three goods only: foc clothing (C), and housing (H). At any given level of her i what can you say about the *average* of the income elast the three goods? Explain.

quantity that each individual demands at each alternative price is in turn dependent upon the individual's preference map and budget line. This chain of reasoning and behavior—from preferences to individual demand curves to market demand curves—applies not only to such commodities as eggs, furniture, and automobiles that are produced in the private sector but also to certain goods and services produced in the public sector. However, it is much more difficult for economists (or even political scientists) to assess the demand for governmentally provided goods and services owing to the way in which these preferences are registered. In some elections we vote for candidates more than for particular issues, and in voting for specific candidates we in effect approve the whole bundle of positions the politician takes during the course of the campaign. In other elections there is an all-important issue on which the candidates are divided—for example, certain school board elections—and in such cases electing the person is tantamount to a community decision on the critical issue.

Opinion polls are another commonly used surrogate for detecting trends in electoral opinion, but these devices work imperfectly. Assume that a national polling organization surveys 1,500 persons on whether or not they want more national defense. The answers of respondents to this question usually will not reveal actual demands unless they understand what the implications of their answers might be. Each person is left with his own thoughts about whether his vote for more defense implies cuts in other programs that he might desire more urgently than extra defense spending. Here a more meaningful polling question might be: "Would you prefer that the federal government spend an additional billion dollars in tax revenues on more missiles or on more medical care for poor children?" The typical polling question does not inform the respondent as to what tax price the answer carries. Again, a more meaningful polling question might be: "Would you prefer X additional long-range missiles if it is certain to cost you an additional Y dollars in taxes next year?"

Questions of the last type, while relatively expensive for polling organizations to use for nationwide surveys, are feasible for detecting the demands for certain goods and services provided by local governments. A small college town of 25,000 is renowned in its region for the attention it gives to aesthetic considerations. It is the city's policy for its municipal refuse collectors to pick up garbage, trash, and refuse directly from the backyard of each home rather than from containers that are placed at curbside by each resident. This policy is more convenient for most householders, but primarily it is designed to avoid unsightly rubbish cans and refuse piles along the street on trash day and to prevent the mess that can be caused when animals tip over the cans. However, the policy of backyard pickup is much more expensive than curbside pickup. In addition to the large truck and two or three persons that curbside pickup requires, backyard service requires four or five small gasoline-powered vehicles much like golf carts to carry trash cans from the backyard to the large truck as it moves down the street. Each of the small carts requires its own driver. The cost of the service has become an important consideration in this city since a statewide law in 1978 cut property taxes by one-third, and the property tax is a major source of the city's revenue.

A study was made recently of the demand for backyard versus curbside trash pickups by surveying the residents directly.[10] The survey avoided the relatively meaningless questions described earlier in favor of the *specific price-quantity alternatives* shown in Table 6.2. The demand questions in the survey took the following form: "Would you prefer (1) service X at a price of P_x per month or (2) service Y at a price of P_y per month? The researchers queried a random sample of 500 households throughout the city and obtained 275 usable replies, a large enough number to give their sample statistical meaning.

TABLE 6.2 Relative price combinations for refuse collection from a city survey.	Price Combination	Curbside Service Price	Backyard Service Price	Absolute Price Difference	Percentage Premium for Backyard Service
	1	$5.50	$5.50	$0.00	0
	2	4.50	6.50	2.00	30.8
	3	4.00	7.00	3.00	42.9
	4	4.00	7.50	3.50	46.7
	5	3.50	7.50	4.00	53.3
	6	3.00	7.50	4.50	60.0
	7	3.50	8.50	5.00	58.9

Sources: Ronald K. Teeples, "Preference Intensities for Private and Collective Goods: The Case of Refuse Services," Claremont, Calif.: The Claremont Colleges, Claremont Working Papers in Economics, Business and Public Policy, No. 22, 1980.

The first question was whether or not the resident favored a price-related choice between backyard versus curbside pickups. Almost 73 percent of the sample respondents wanted such a choice, although about 67 percent expressed concern over the aesthetic effects of curbside service. This finding was in sharp contrast to a discussion that had occurred at a city council meeting a year earlier, when the possibility of curbside pickups was first discussed. At that time a few highly vocal residents denounced curbside service, lead-

[10] The following discussion is based on Ronald K. Teeples, "Preference Intensities for Private and Collective Goods: The Case of Refuse Services," Claremont, Calif.: The Claremont Colleges, Claremont Working Papers in Economics, Business and Public Policy, No. 22, 1980.

ing the city council to reject the possibility on the [...]
tion that these views were representative.

The results of the demand survey, listed i[n...]
clearly that the type of service residents prefer is [...]
price differential involved. The survey revealed no [...]
tical difference in the preferences between backyar[d...]
service of households attributable to such nonprice [...]
ing families of different sizes, different ages, differen[t...]
differences in the average number of trash cans that [...]

TABLE 6.3 Preference for refuse collection based on the various price combinations in Table 6.2.	Price Combination	Absolute Price Difference	Percentage Favoring Curbside Service	P[...]
	1	$0.00	9.6%	
	2	2.00	49.5	
	3	3.00	66.2	
	4	3.50	74.4	
	5	4.00	74.5	
	6	4.50	74.4	
	7	5.00	81.8	

Sources: Teeples, "Preference Intensities for Private and Collective Goods," cite[d...]

per week. Table 6.3 thus shows a clear inverse relationsh[ip...]
price and quantity demanded. A price premium of only [...]
for backyard service would cause a majority of the com[...]
prefer the cheaper curbside pickups. The table also reveals [...]
people are highly concerned with aesthetic consideratio[n...]
group is the 18.2 percent of the sample that is willing to p[ay...]
mium of at least 58.9 percent for backyard over curbside s[ervice...]

Summary

The indifference maps of consumers are the foundations on [which...]
various choice and demand patterns of analysis are constr[ucted...]
From them, Engel curves and demand curves can be derived[...]
among other things, such maps can illustrate clearly the benefi[ts to...]
society of voluntary exchange.

Engel curves for commodities are derived by varying the [con-]
sumer's income, and holding tastes and preferences and the pric[es of]
all goods constant. The points of consumer equilibrium form [the]
income consumption curve. The indifference curve diagram [fur-]
nishes the necessary data for setting up Engel curves.

The consumer's demand curve for one good is obtained by va[rying...]

2 Draw and explain a consumer's indifference map for two goods, X and Y, assuming that these are the only goods available. Now draw and explain the consumer's budget line. Explain and illustrate the construction of the consumer's Engel curve for Y. Explain and illustrate the construction of the consumer's demand curve for X.

3 a Consider the following model:
   (i) There are two consumers, Mr. A and Mr. B.
   (ii) They consume two products—gasoline (G) and other (O)—and the total supplies available of these are fixed.
   (iii) Mr. A is much richer than Mr. B.
   (iv) The greater the amount of G consumed by Mr. A, given the amount of O that he consumes, the smaller is his MRS_{go}.
   (v) The greater the amount of G consumed by Mr. B, given the amount of O he consumes, the smaller is his MRS_{go}.

Show with a diagram and explain an equilibrium distribution of the goods between the consumers. Can you say anything about p_g and p_o?

b Suppose that
   (i) The supply of gasoline available to A and B is reduced but that all of the reduction is initially borne by Mr. A—Mr. B's consumption bundle remains fixed.
   (ii) Through price controls both p_g and p_o are prevented from rising. Show diagrammatically and explain the welfare effects of the price controls. Now let the price controls be removed. Show and explain the impact on welfare.

The Utility Approach to
Consumer Choice and Demand—
A Special Case*

The general theory of consumer choice and demand discussed in the last chapter evolved from an older utility approach that has subsequently come to be recognized as a special case of the general theory. The general theory—indifference curve analysis—is self-contained; it does not depend on the utility analysis from which it grew. However, there is much in the utility approach that provides additional insight into consumer behavior. There is also much that is repetitive as one compares this chapter with the preceding one. We try to present the utility approach in a reasonably complete form.

Utility theory, or subjective value theory, came on the scene in the 1870s with the almost simultaneous publication of its basic aspects by three economists working independently—William Stanley Jevons of Great Britain, Karl Menger of Austria, and Léon Walras of France. Present-day utility theory owes much to all three of these economists.

The Utility Concept

The term *utility* means the satisfaction that a consumer receives from whatever goods and services the individual consumes. It is useful analytically to distinguish between total utility concepts and marginal utility concepts under circumstances in which goods are not related to one another and under those where they are related.

Nonrelated Goods and Services

Different kinds of items are unrelated, insofar as their consumption is concerned, if the utility or satisfaction obtained from one is in no way dependent upon the amount that the consumer consumes of the others. It is unlikely, for example, that the utility obtained from consuming nails has any significant bearing on that obtained from the consumption of gasoline.

---

* This chapter may be omitted without loss of continuity.

Total Utility   The *total utility* attained from a commodity refers to the entire amount of satisfaction a consumer receives from consuming it at various rates. The more of an item a consumer consumes per unit of time, the greater will be the total utility or satisfaction received from it, up to a point. At some rate of consumption, total utility will reach a maximum. It yields no greater satisfaction even though more of it is thrust upon the consumer. This state is called the *saturation point* for that commodity.[1]

A hypothetical total utility curve showing these properties is drawn in Figure 7.1(a). In plotting the curve, we assume that utility can be quantified and measured, and that different quantities of utility to the consumer can be added to arrive at a meaningful total; that is, utility is assumed to be *cardinal* in nature.[2] The saturation point is reached at a consumption level of 6 units of X per unit of time. Up to that level, total utility is increasing as consumption increases. Beyond that level, total utility decreases.[3]

Marginal Utility   The change in total utility resulting from a 1-unit change in consumption per unit of time is the *marginal utility* of a good. In Figure 7.1(a), if the consumer were consuming 2 units per unit of time and increased the consumption level to 3, the individual's total utility would increase from 18 to 24 units and the marginal utility would be 6.

The slope of the total utility curve between points A and B shows the increase in utility resulting from the increase in consumption from 2 to 3 units of X and is equal to 6/1 if that segment of the curve is considered to be a straight line. The total utility curve is not necessarily a straight line between A and B, but the error involved in considering it linear is not significant, and becomes progressively less the smaller the distance between points. If the distance on the X axis that measures 1 unit of X is infinitesimal, marginal utility at any given level of consumption is measured by the slope of the total utility curve at that point.[4]

---

[1]   Conceivably, still more units of the good forced upon the consumer can cause total utility to decrease if for no other reason than storage problems. However, the possibility of decreases in total utility beyond the saturation point is of no importance for our purposes.

[2]   Whether utility can be measured cardinally, or whether its measurement has ordinal meaning only, has been an historical source of controversy in the development of economic thought. The theory presented here does not really require measurability but requires that the consumer be able to distinguish between greater and lesser amounts of utility. For expositional purposes we shall treat utility as though it were cardinal.

[3]   In this paragraph, the rate of consumption is increased by discrete units. Total utility is maximum at 5, as well as at 6, units of X per unit of time. However, there are pedagogical advantages to considering the maximum as occurring at 6 units.

[4]   In terms of differential calculus, if the total utility curve were

$$U = f(x) = 12x - x^2,$$

FIGURE 7.1
Total and marginal
utility

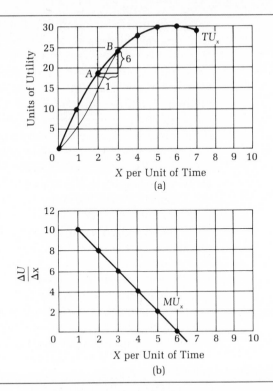

Marginal utility is reflected in the shape of the total utility curve as the rate of consumption is increased or decreased. In Figure 7.1(a) marginal utility decreases as consumption per unit of time increases between 0 and 6. This statement can be rephrased by saying that each additional unit of consumption per unit of time adds less and less to total utility, until finally the sixth unit adds nothing at all. Note also that as consumption per unit of time increases, the average slope of the total utility curve between any two consecutive consumption levels becomes smaller and smaller until, between 5 and 6 units of X, it becomes 0. The concept of diminishing marginal utility and the concavity of the total utility curve, when viewed from below, are the same thing.

Diminishing marginal utility need not be the case for all levels of consumption between 0 and 6 units of X. The lighter curve in Figure 7.1(a) could conceivably be the total utility curve between 0

then

$$MU = \frac{dU}{dx} = f'(x) = 12 - 2x.$$

Marginal utility at 2 units of X is 8 units of utility; at 3 units of X, it is 6 units of utility.

and 3. Suppose, for example, that a single television set in a home with several children causes so much friction over program selection that it adds little to the satisfaction of the family. Two sets—one for the parents and one for the children—may yield more than twice the satisfaction of one. But the successive increases in total utility yielded by three, four, and five sets will surely be successively smaller. Thus, through some range of consumption levels, marginal utility may increase as the consumption increases, and the total utility curve would be convex downward for that range. But if a saturation point for a commodity exists for a given consumer, as the person's consumption level approaches that point, marginal utility must be decreasing even though it may have been increasing at lower levels of consumption.

The marginal utility curve of Figure 7.1(b) is constructed from the total utility curve of Figure 7.1(a). In Figure 7.1(b) the utility axis is stretched so that the vertical distance measuring one unit is greater than it is in Figure 7.1(a). The X axis is the same for the two diagrams. Marginal utility is plotted as a vertical distance above the X axis at each level of consumption. At a consumption level of 6 in Figure 7.1(a), the increase in the total utility curve between 5 and 6 is 0. Hence, marginal utility is 0; in Figure 7.1(b) the marginal utility curve intersects the X axis at that consumption level. In Figure 7.1(b) a line MU_x joining the plotted marginal utilities at each level of consumption is the marginal utility curve for X.

A set of a consumer's marginal utility curves for the different commodities consumed provides a graphic picture of the consumer's tastes and preferences at any given time. For those commodities with which the individual is easily satiated, the marginal utility curves will slope off very rapidly, reaching zero at relatively low levels of consumption. For other products with which the consumer is not easily satiated, the marginal utility curves will slope off gradually and will reach zero at relatively high levels of consumption.[5] Changes in the consumer's tastes and preferences will change the shapes and positions of the marginal utility curves for different goods.

Related Goods and Services

A great many of the goods and services that an individual consumes are related to each other in some way; that is, the quantity that the person takes of one affects the utility that is obtained from others. These may be complementary relationships, or they may be substi-

---

[5] As a practical matter, no consumer will reach the saturation point for any good that commands a price, except by accident. The reason for this statement will become apparent in the next section of the chapter.

tute relationships. In general, goods that are consumed together, such as bread and butter or tennis rackets and tennis balls, are complementary goods, while those that compete with each other in the consumer's scale of preferences, such as beef and pork, are substitute goods.

The nature of relatedness is illustrated in the three-dimensional diagram of Figure 7.2(a). The X and Y axes define a horizontal plane,

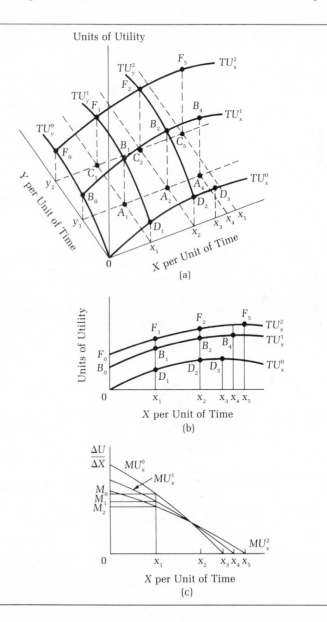

FIGURE 7.2
The utility surface

and total utility is measured as a vertical distance above it. For example, if the individual consumes combination A_1 per week, containing x_1 units of X and y_1 units of Y, the total utility for that consumer from both will be A_1B_1. Points such as B_1, B_2, B_4, F_1, F_2, and F_5—showing total utility for different combinations of X and Y—trace out a *total utility surface* lying above the XY plane.

The utility surface pictured in Figure 7.2(a) shows not only the total utility obtained by the consumer from the consumption of X and Y in various combinations, but also how total utility changes as the rate of consumption of one good is changed, given the rate of consumption of the other.

Consider, for example, variations in the consumption of X at each of three different levels of consumption of Y. If no Y is consumed, the total utility of the consumer, as is shown in Figure 7.2(a), is TU_x^0 for different rates of consumption of X. The same curve is also pictured on the two-dimensional diagram of Figure 7.2(b). If the amount of Y consumed per week is y_1, total utility is y_1B_0 if no X is taken. Changes in quantity of X, with the consumption level of Y held constant at y_1, trace out the total utility curve TU_x^1. We can visualize the consumer as starting from point B_0 on the utility surface and moving up over the surface directly above the dotted line $y_1A_1A_2A_4$. Again the resulting TU_x^1 curve is plotted in two dimensions in Figure 7.2(b). The meaning of the third total utility curve for X, labeled TU_x^2, is now obvious. If no X is consumed, total utility from y_2 of Y alone is y_2F_0. If Y is held constant at y_2, increasing levels of consumption of X will yield the total utility curve TU_x^2 on the utility surface and in the two-dimensional diagram Figure 7.2(b). The curves TU_y^0, TU_y^1, and TU_y^2 are derived in a similar fashion.[6]

Taking the interrelatedness of goods X and Y into account undoubtedly makes utility theory more realistic, but it makes it more complex, too. For one thing, there are innumerable possible total utility curves for each product. There is a different total utility curve for X associated with each different quantity of Y that the individual might consume. Similarly there is a different total utility curve for Y for each different level of consumption of X. There are also innumerable marginal utility curves for each product. Since the total utility curves for X differ at each different level of consumption of Y, so do the corresponding marginal utility curves for X. For example, in Figure 7.2(c) MU_x^0, MU_x^1, and MU_x^2 are derived from TU_x^0, TU_x^1, and TU_x^2, respectively. Here we see that at a consumption level of x_1 of X,

---

[6]   If all goods consumed are related, the consumer's utility function is of the general form

$$U = f(x, y \ . \ . \ . \ n).$$

If all goods consumed are independent of one another, it takes the form

$$U = f(x) + g(y) + \cdots + n(n).$$

the marginal utility of X depends on the amount of Y consumed as well as on the quantity x_1 of X. If no Y is consumed, it is M_0 or the slope of TU_x^0 at point D_1. If y_1 of Y is consumed, it is M_1 or the slope of TU_x^1 at B_1. If y_2 of Y is consumed, it is M_2 or the slope of TU_x^2 at F_1. Similar reasoning applies to Y. If diminishing marginal utility occurs with any increase in the consumption of either X or Y, the utility surface will have the inverted bowl shape exhibited in Figure 7.2(a); that is, any total utility curve drawn for either X or Y will be convex upward.

Indifference Curves

We take a side trip at this point to show how indifference curve analysis evolved from utility theory. However, utility theory itself was a self-contained theory of consumer choice and demand—albeit a special case. In the next section we get back on the main utility theory road, which depends in no way on this section.

In Figure 7.3(a) suppose that a consumer initially consumes good Y only and that she consumes it at a rate of y_1 per unit of time. Her total utility is y_1A_1 or $0U_1$. Is it not possible that by giving up the consumption of a small amount of Y and by increasing the consumption of X in some amount, she can maintain their level of utility constant? Reducing consumption of Y and increasing consumption of X in the manner described, she moves around the indifference surface at a constant distance about the XY plane. Her path traces out the curve A_1B_2. Projected vertically downward on the XY plane, the A_1B_2 curve becomes the dashed line y_1x_2. This curve is redrawn with respect only to the XY plane in Figure 7.3(b).

The curve y_1x_2 shows all combinations of X and Y that yield levels of utility equal to $0U_1$ or y_1A_1. For example, in Figure 7.3(a) at point E the consumer is taking y_0 of Y and x_1 of X; this combination yields a total utility of EF ($= y_1A_1$). Similarly, if she consumes X alone at level x_2, her total utility is x_2B_2 ($= y_1A_1$). Curve y_1x_2 is in every sense an indifference curve like those of the preceding chapter. Since all combinations of X and Y shown by this curve yield the same total utility to the consumer, she is indifferent as to which of them she consumes.

Higher levels of utility are shown by contour lines higher up on the surface, while lower contour lines show lower levels of utility. Projected on the XY plane, the indifference curves corresponding to higher contour lines lie farther from the origin; for example, y_2x_3 as compared with y_1y_2 in Figure 7.3(b). The projections of lower contour lines lie closer to the origin. These observations are based on the assumption that the utility surface tapers toward a summit as we

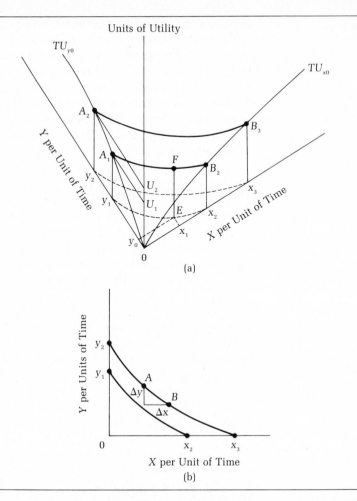

FIGURE 7.3
Indifference curves
from a utility surface

Units of Utility

TU_{y0}

TU_{x0}

A_2

B_3

A_1

F

B_2

y_2

U_2

x_3

y_1

U_1

E

x_2

x_1

y_0

0

(a)

y_2

y_1

A

Δy

B

Δx

x_2

x_3

0

Y per Units of Time

X per Unit of Time

(b)

move up. It is usually thought of as having an inverted bowl shape, although this restrictive shape is not really necessary for the foregoing observations to hold.

The marginal rate of substitution of X for Y is measured by the *ratio* of the marginal utility of X to the marginal utility of Y, or $MRS_{xy} = MU_x/MU_y$. In Figure 7.3(b) suppose that the consumer is originally consuming combination A. If she were to move from combination A to combination B, she would give up Δy of Y and acquire Δx of X with *no change* in her total utility level. The loss in utility from giving up Y is $\Delta y \times MU_y$. The gain from acquiring X is $\Delta x \times MU_x$. Therefore,

$$\Delta y \times MU_y = \Delta x \times MU_x \tag{7.1}$$

$$\frac{\Delta y}{\Delta x} = \frac{MU_x}{MU_y} = MRS_{xy}. \tag{7.2}$$

In this discussion we have continued to assume that utility is measurable. For example, in Figure 7.3(a) the distance $0U_1$ is a definite measurable magnitude, say 8 units of utility, while $0U_2$ is 10 units of utility. Accordingly, in Figure 7.3(b) we would attach the number 8 to the y_1x_2 indifference curve and 10 to the y_2x_3 curve. However, is it essential that we attach absolute utility *magnitudes* to each indifference curve? Would it not be possible, once we have an indifference map, to attach a utility *ranking* to each curve instead?

If we do so, the 8 and the 10 have no significance as absolute measures. They would show only the order of utility magnitudes; that is, 10 is greater than 8. We could accomplish the same thing by attaching the number 1 to y_1x_2 and the number 2 to y_2x_3.[7]

If the order, but not the absolute measure, of utility magnitudes is all that is required, we can forget about how high the utility surface rises above the XY plane. Only its general shape is important. Suppose that we think of it as being collapsible from the top down in such a way that contour lines from bottom to top retain their original shapes. If we do so, we are free of the assumption that utility is measurable. The indifference map is the same in all essential respects as those developed earlier in Chapter 5.

Consumer Choice

Returning now to the main road, the utility concepts provide a basis for determining how a consumer will allocate income among the various goods and services that confront the individual. They are more awkward to use than the more general indifference curve analysis. To keep the discussion as simple as possible, we assume that (1) the goods and services contemplated by the consumer are nonrelated; (2) utility is cardinal; and (3) the marginal utility of each item consumed is diminishing.[8] None of these do any violence to the

---

[7] If the consumer's utility function is represented by

$$U = f(x, y),$$

then the equation for one indifference curve is

$$U_1 = f(x, y),$$

in which U_1 is a constant. Other values assigned to U define other indifference curves, all of these making up the consumer's indifference map. It is necessary only that the assigned values show the order of utility magnitudes; it is not necessary that they show absolute (measurable) utility magnitudes.

[8] Actually, all that we need to assume is that the marginal utility of one good decreases relative to the marginal utilities of other goods as consumption of the one is increased in proportion to the consumption of the others. The marginal utility of X could be increasing. However, if the additional consumption of X raises the marginal utilities of other goods, that of X has decreased *relative* to those of the other goods.

conclusions reached, but they do much to smooth the path toward those conclusions.

Objectives and Constraints

The objective usually postulated for a rational consumer is the maximization of satisfaction or utility. The consumer's preferences are described by utility curves for the various goods and services available. The choice problem is to select from these the kinds and amounts that will yield the greatest total amount of utility.

The consumer is constrained by income (the dollars per unit of time available to spend) and prices of goods and services. Typically, income per unit of time is a more or less fixed amount, as are the prices faced (since the consumer is a pure competitor in the purchase of most things). Subject to these constraints, the consumer chooses the utility-maximizing combination of goods and services.

Maximization of Utility

To avoid unnecessary complexity, we limit the consumer to two goods, X and Y, priced at p_x and p_y, respectively. If p_x and p_y are given and constant, we can measure quantities of the goods in terms of dollars' worths. For example, if a bushel of X costs \$2, we can record that physical quantity as two dollars' worths; a half bushel is equivalent to one dollar's worth. Table 7.1(a) records a consumer's hypothetical marginal utility schedules for X and Y, measuring quantities in dollars' worths and assuming independence between the two goods.[9]

If the consumer has an income of \$12 per unit of time, what is the allocation of it between X and Y that will maximize his utility? Suppose that he spends only \$1 per unit of time. Spent on Y, it will yield only 30 units of satisfaction; whereas if it is spent on X, it will yield 40. Thus, the dollar will be allocated to X. If the consumer increases his expenditure level to \$2, where should the second dollar go? Spent on X, it will increase his total utility by 36 (the marginal utility of a second dollar's worth of X); but spent on Y, it adds only 30 units. The second dollar will be spent on X and so will the third dollar. The situation changes when the total expenditure increases

---

[9] Assuming that the marginal utility schedule of each commodity is independent of the level of consumption of the other commodity, we can go directly and quickly to the conditions necessary for maximization of satisfaction. If X and Y were substitutes, the more of X consumed, the lower the marginal utility of Y would be at various consumption levels of Y. If they were complements, the more of X consumed, the higher the marginal utility of Y would be at various consumption levels of Y. These possibilities do not change the conditions necessary for maximization of satisfaction, but they make numerical exposition of these conditions virtually impossible.

TABLE 7.1
Marginal utility
schedules

(a)

Product X		Product Y	
Quantity (dollars' worth)	MU$_x$ (units of utility)	Quantity (dollars' worth)	MU$_y$ (units of utility)
1	40	1	30
2	36	2	29
3	32	3	28
4	28	4	27
5	24	5	26
6	20	6	25
7	12	7	24
8	4	8	20

(b)

Product X		Product Y	
Quantity (bushels)	MU$_x$ (units of utility)	Quantity (pints)	MU$_y$ (units of utility)
1	50	1	30
2	44	2	28
3	38	3	26
4	32	4	24
5	26	5	22
6	20	6	20
7	12	7	16
8	4	8	10

from $3 to $4. A fourth dollar spent on X will increase the total utility by 28 units; but if the fourth dollar is spent on the first dollar's worth of Y, the increase is 30 units. The fourth dollar will go for Y. As expenditure per unit of time is increased dollar by dollar, the fifth should go for Y; the sixth and seventh, one each on X and Y; the eighth, ninth, and tenth on Y; and the eleventh and twelfth, one each on X and Y. The consumer is now taking five dollars' worths of X and seven dollars' worths of Y. The marginal utility per dollar's worth of X is equal to that of a dollar's worth of Y—both are 24 units of utility.

We know that the consumer's utility for the $12 expenditure is maximum because it was placed dollar by dollar where each dollar made its greatest contribution to total utility.

Generalizing, we can say that a consumer maximizes utility by allocating income among the goods and services (including savings) available in such a way that (1) the marginal utility per dollar's worth of any one is equal to the marginal utility per dollar's worth of any other and (2) all of the income is spent. Savings, which may appear to pose a problem, are simply treated as any other good. A consumer obtains utility from savings. Presumably, the marginal utility of savings, like that of other goods and services, diminishes as their quantity is increased.

Suppose we look at the problem again with data arranged a little differently. Consider another consumer whose marginal utility schedules are based on bushels and pints like those of Table 7.1(b). The price of X is $2 per bushel and that of Y is $1 per pint. This consumer's income is $15 per unit of time. How should it be allocated between X and Y?

Since the marginal utility schedules are in physical measurements of X and Y, rather than in dollars' worths, we need a means of converting the information that they contain into marginal utilities per dollar's worth. To obtain it, consider the fourth bushel of X. If the consumer were taking 4 bushels of X, the fourth bushel has a marginal utility of 32 units. The fourth bushel (like any other bushel) costs $2. At this consumption level the marginal utility per bushel of X divided by the price of X, or MU_x/p_x, is the marginal utility per dollar's worth of X. Thus, the marginal utility per dollar's worth of X is 16 units at this point. Likewise, the marginal utility per pint of Y at any consumption level divided by the price of Y, or MU_y/p_y, can be read as the marginal utility per dollar's worth of Y at that consumption level. The first condition for maximizing satisfaction becomes

$$\frac{MU_x}{p_x} = \frac{MU_y}{p_y} = \frac{MU_z}{p_z} = \cdots \tag{7.3}$$

The requirement that the consumer be spending all of her income—no more and no less—is expressed as

$$x \times p_x + y \times p_y + z \times p_z + \cdots = I. \tag{7.4}$$

The total expenditure on X is the price of X times the amount of X purchased. The same holds for the expenditure on each other good or service, including savings. The total of these must equal the income I.

Since the price of X is $2 per bushel and the price of Y is $1 per pint, we must find some combination of X and Y at which the marginal utility per bushel of X is twice the marginal utility per pint of Y. This combination occurs at 6 bushels of X and 8 pints of Y. However, the total amount spent on X would be $12, and the total amount spent on Y would be $8. The consumer is exceeding her income. Thus, the second condition for maximization of total utility is not met, although the first one is satisfied. Another possible combination is the one containing 4 bushels of X and 7 pints of Y. The first condition is met, since 32/$2 = 16/$1. The second condition is fulfilled also, since 4 bushels × $2 + 7 pints × $1 = $15. Thus, the consumer should take 4 bushels of X and 7 pints of Y to maximize her total utility.

To demonstrate that utility is maximized, transfer a dollar from X to Y. Giving up a dollar's worth of X, or half of the fourth bushel, reduces total utility by 16 units. Spending the dollar for an eighth pint of Y increases total utility by 10. There is a net loss of 6 units. If the dollar were transferred in the opposite direction, there would also be a net loss of utility—3 units in this case.[10]

The data confronting the consumer may not yield the neat solution of this example. Suppose the consumer's income were $14 per unit of time instead of $15. How should it be allocated? She could give up either a half bushel of X or a pint of Y. In either case total utility would be decreased by 16 units. Or if her income were $16, instead of $15, she would take half of the fifth bushel of X. The increase in total utility would be 13 units. If she had taken the eighth pint of Y, her total utility would have increased by 10 units only. Thus, the consumer seeking maximum satisfaction should allocate income among various goods so as to approach as nearly as possible the condition that the marginal utility of a dollar's worth of one good equals the marginal utility of a dollar's worth of any other good purchased.

How would the theory work for a typical family? Suppose that the family budget is composed of the following items: food, clothing, housing, automobile, medical care, recreation, and education. Over a short period of time, expenditures in some of the classifications are more or less fixed in amount. The mortgage payments, for example, are a fixed monthly amount. The grocery bill and medical expenditures are sometimes thought to be dictated by necessity rather than choice. The other categories are likely to be more variable, but habit may be influential in determining them in the short run.

Over a longer period of time, however, expenditures on any or all of the budgeted items are subject to change. The family seeking to get the greatest possible satisfaction from its limited income will reappraise its budget from time to time. The family car begins to rattle more, and at the same time it appears desirable to add a new bedroom to the house for Junior. It is out of the question to purchase both a new car and a new room, and a choice must be made regard-

---

[10] The mathematical problem is that of maximizing the consumer's utility function subject to the budget restraint. Using the symbols of the text, the utility function is

$$U = f(x, y).$$

The budget restraint is

$$xp_x + yp_y = I \quad \text{or} \quad xp_x + yp_y - I = 0.$$

The maximization problem is identical to that shown in Footnote 12, Chapter 5. From that footnote

$$f_x = MU_x = \lambda p_x \quad \text{and} \quad f_y = MU_y = \lambda p_y.$$

Therefore,

$$\frac{MU_x}{MU_y} = \frac{\lambda p_x}{\lambda p_y}, \quad \text{or} \quad \frac{MU_x}{p_x} = \frac{MU_y}{p_y}.$$

ing the direction of expenditure. Further, if either is to be purchased, it may be necessary to cut down on educational expenses for the older daughter, who has been attending a private university. Should she be transferred to the state university where expenses are less? Changes in food and clothing budgeting may also be required to make the new car or the new room possible. Likewise, the family may need to economize on recreation, and even on medical expenses. When Junior has a minor illness, he may have to get over it without a visit to the doctor. A whole chain of decisions will be made on the basis of marginal utility principles if maximum satisfaction for the family is to be attained.

The family subjectively estimates the marginal utilities of dollars spent in each of the various directions. Transfers of expenditures from the items where marginal utility per dollar's worth is less toward items where marginal utility per dollar's worth is greater serve to increase total satisfaction.

Demand Curves

The utility approach to consumer choice can be extended to explain individual consumer demand curves for goods and services. Again, we limit the consumer to a two-commodity world in which X and Y are independent goods. The consumer's utility curves are given and remain constant throughout the analysis. The marginal utility of each good is assumed to be diminishing for increases in the consumption of it.

The Demand Curve for X[11]

To establish the consumer's demand curve for X, suppose that initially the price of X is p_{x1} and the price of Y is p_{y1}. We shall assume that at all times the consumer is operating at the limit of the income

---

[11] The analysis presented here is essentially that of Walras. See Léon Walras, *Abrégé des eléments d'économie politique pure* (Paris: R. Pichon et R. Durand-Auzias, 1938), pp. 131–33. The transition from the theory of consumer behavior to demand curves set out in the text differs from the usual Marshallian treatment, which considers the marginal utility of money constant and simply converts the marginal utility curve for a commodity into the demand curve for it. See Kenneth E. Boulding, *Economic Analysis*, 4th ed., Vol. 1 (New York: Harper & Row, 1966), pp. 520–27.

The Marshallian approach ignores the income effects of price changes. The approach used in the text includes income effects as well as substitution effects. This approach in turn makes the utility analysis of the present chapter more nearly parallel to the indifference curve analysis of the last chapter.

restraint. The consumer will maximize satisfaction or be in equilibrium when taking the quantity of X and that quantity of Y at which

$$\frac{MU_{x1}}{p_{x1}} = \frac{MU_{y1}}{p_{y1}}. \tag{7.5}$$

Thus, at price p_{x1} the consumer is taking a definite quantity of X—that quantity which makes the marginal utility of a dollar's worth of X equal to the marginal utility of a dollar's worth of Y. We shall call this quantity x_1.[12]

The consumer's initial position of equilibrium is shown graphically in Figure 7.4. Assuming that p_{x1} is twice p_{y1}, the consumer takes quantity x_1 of X and y_1 of Y. These quantities are such that MU_{x1} is twice MU_{y1}.[13] One point on the consumer's demand schedule or demand curve for X has now been established. At price p_{x1} the consumer will take quantity x_1.

FIGURE 7.4
Determination of
quantities demanded

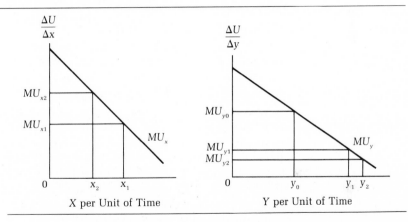

X per Unit of Time   Y per Unit of Time

The problem is to establish the quantities of X that will be taken at other prices of X when the consumer is in equilibrium at each of those prices, with the price of Y remaining constant at p_{y1}, the consumer's marginal utility curves or tastes and preferences remaining constant, and the income also remaining constant.

Suppose that the price of X rises to p_{x2} and that the consumer continues to take the same amount of X as before. The marginal utility per bushel of X will remain unchanged, but the marginal utility per dollar's worth of X, MU_{x1}/p_{x2}, will be less. At the higher price p_{x2} the consumer spends more income on X than before, leav-

[12] The consumer will also be taking some definite quantity y_1 of Y; however, we are primarily concerned with the quantity of X that is taken.

[13] For any given ratio of p_x and p_y, quantities of X and Y taken must be such that

$$p_x/p_y = MU_x/MU_y, \text{ or } MU_x/p_x = MU_y/p_y.$$

ing less to be spent on Y. Since p_{y1} is the given price of Y, the consumer will necessarily cut purchases of Y to some quantity y_0. The decrease in the number of pints of Y consumed raises the marginal utility per pint of Y to MU_{y0} (see Figure 7.4). The marginal utility per dollar's worth of Y is increased to MU_{y0}/p_{y1} and

$$\frac{MU_{x1}}{p_{x2}} < \frac{MU_{y0}}{p_{y1}}; \qquad (7.6)$$

that is, the marginal utility of a dollar's worth of X is now less than the marginal utility of a dollar's worth of Y. The consumer is not maximizing satisfaction.

The consumer clearly will not continue to take quantity x_1 of X after the price has gone up to p_{x2}. Satisfaction can be increased by transferring dollars from X to Y. The loss from taking a dollar away from X is the marginal utility of a dollar's worth of X. The gain from buying an additional dollar's worth of Y is the marginal utility of a dollar's worth of Y. Since $MU_{x1}/p_{x2} < MU_{y0}/p_{y1}$, such a transfer will yield a net gain in total utility.

The transfer of dollars from X to Y will continue as long as the marginal utility of a dollar's worth of X is less than the marginal utility of a dollar's worth of Y. However, as the consumer gives up units of X, the marginal utility per bushel of X increases, causing the marginal utility per dollar's worth of X to increase, since its price remains at p_{x2}. As the consumer buys additional units of Y, the marginal utility per pint of Y declines, as does the marginal utility per dollar's worth of Y. The transfer will stop when the consumer has again equalized the marginal utility per dollar's worth of X with the marginal utility per dollar's worth of Y, and is thus maximizing satisfaction. The quantity of Y taken will have increased from y_0 to some quantity y_2. The quantity of X taken will have decreased from x_1 to x_2. Quantities x_2 and y_2 must be such that

$$\frac{MU_{x2}}{p_{x2}} = \frac{MU_{y2}}{p_{y1}}. \qquad (7.7)$$

The quantities of X and Y that bring MU_x and MU_y into the proper relationship are shown in Figure 7.4 as x_2 and y_2. We now have another point on the consumer's demand curve for X. At price p_{x2} the consumer takes x_2 of X. The analysis has shown that an increase in the price of X causes a decrease in the quantity taken.

Using $MU_{x2}/p_{x2} = MU_{y2}/p_{y1}$ as a new starting point, we can change the price of X again and repeat this process. In the resulting new equilibrium position, the quantity of X taken at the new price is established. Through continued repetition of the process, we can determine a series of price-quantity combinations that represent the demand schedule and that can be plotted as the demand curve. Such a curve is shown in Figure 7.5.

FIGURE 7.5
Individual consumer
demand curve

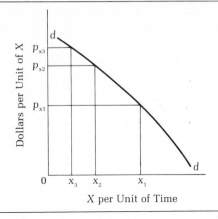

Quantities Taken of Other Goods

As a corollary it may be instructive to take a closer view of what happens to the quantity of Y taken. When the price of X increases to p_{x2}, is the quantity of Y at the new equilibrium position greater than the original quantity? The answer is, "not necessarily," even though we show it to be greater in Figure 7.4. The crucial factor is the elasticity of demand for X. If demand for X is elastic, the increase in the price of X must decrease total spending on X, leaving more of the consumer's income to spend on Y. In this case quantity y_2 would indeed be greater than quantity y_1, as we depict it in Figure 7.4. However, if elasticity of demand for X is unitary, total spending on X and total spending on Y will each remain constant, and there will be no change in the quantity of Y taken. Should demand for X be inelastic, the price increase for X would increase total spending on X and decrease total spending on Y. The new equilibrium quantity of Y taken would be smaller than y_1.

Exchange and Welfare

In any voluntary exchange of goods among individuals, all parties to the exchange expect to increase their satisfaction or welfare. It is this prospect of gain that causes voluntary exchange to occur. The point can be illustrated clearly by means of utility analysis. We limit ourselves to two consumers, A and B, each of whom receives constant quantities per unit of time of two goods, X and Y. Marginal utility schedules for the two goods for each consumer are shown in Table 7.2.

    Comparative marginal utilities of the goods indicate their comparative worths or values to a consumer. Suppose consumer A has 5

TABLE 7.2	Individual A				Individual B			
The basis of exchange	Product X		Product Y		Product X		Product Y	
	Quantity (bushels)	MU$_x$ (units of utility)	Quantity (pints)	MU$_y$ (units of utility)	Quantity (bushels)	MU$_x$ (units of utility)	Quantity (pints)	MU$_x$ (units of utility)
	1	14	1	10	1	20	1	18
	2	13	2	9	2	19	2	17
	3	12	3	8	3	18	3	16
	4	11	4	7	4	17	4	14
	5	10	5	6	5	16	5	12
	6	9	6	5	6	15	6	10
	7	8	7	4	7	14	7	8
	8	7	8	3	8	13	8	6
	9	6	9	2	9	12	9	4
	10	5	10	1	10	10	10	2

bushels of X and 6 pints of Y. A bushel of X at this point contributes 10 units of utility to A's total satisfaction. A pint of Y contributes 5 units of utility. If A were to lose a bushel of X, the loss in satisfaction would be 10 units of utility; or if A were to lose a pint of Y, the loss would be 5 units of utility. Thus, a bushel of X to A is worth 2 pints of Y. Alternatively, we can say that a pint of Y is worth one-half bushel of X.

Suppose that total supplies of goods X and Y are fixed at 12 bushels of X and 12 pints of Y per week and that these are initially distributed between the two consumers so that A has 9 bushels of X and 3 pints of Y, while B has 3 bushels of X and 9 pints of Y. Since for A the marginal utility of a bushel of X is 6 units of utility and a pint of Y is 8 units of utility, a pint of Y is worth 1-$\frac{1}{3}$ bushels of X to A. For B the marginal utility of a bushel of X is 18 units of utility and that of a pint of Y is 4 units of utility. Thus, for consumer B a pint of Y is worth only $\frac{2}{9}$ of a bushel of X.

Under these circumstances both parties will gladly do some exchanging, and exchange will increase community welfare. Individual A will be willing to trade a bushel of X to individual B for a pint of Y, and individual B will be willing to trade a pint of Y for a bushel of X. For individual A the pint of Y gained would be worth 1$\frac{1}{3}$ times the bushel of X given up. For individual B the pint of Y given up would be worth only $\frac{2}{9}$ of the bushel of X gained. To put it another way, in trading a bushel of X for a pint of Y, individual A would give up 6 units of utility in exchange for 7 units, experiencing a net gain of 1 unit of utility. Individual B would give up 4 units of utility in exchange for 17 units, experiencing a net gain of 13 units of utility.[14] The welfare of both is increased by the exchange, and no one's welfare is decreased.

Once this exchange has been consummated, an additional exchange could result in a further gain for both parties. Individual A, with 8 bushels of X and 4 pints of Y, will no longer be willing to exchange on a bushel-for-a-pint basis since the loss from such a transaction would be greater than the gain. However, individual B can still gain from trading pints of Y for bushels of X. Since trade is no longer attractive to A on a bushel-for-a-pint basis, B will alter the terms of the trade. If B, who now has 4 bushels of X and 8 pints of Y, were to give up 2 pints of Y for a bushel of X, then B would give up 14 units of utility, would gain 16 units, and would still experience a 2-unit net gain in utility. Individual A would find this offer attractive, for 11 units of utility would be received in exchange for 7.

Once the second exchange has occurred, no further gains are available from trade between the two parties; a Pareto optimum has been reached and exchange will cease. Individual A has 7 bushels of X and 6 pints of Y with marginal utilities of 8 and 5 units of utility, respectively. Individual B has 5 bushels of X and 6 pints of Y with marginal utilities of 16 and 10 units of utility, respectively. For A the unit of X is worth $1^3/_5$ units of Y. Individual B's relative valuations of X and Y are exactly the same; hence, neither can gain from further exchange.

The general principle underlying the discussion is that for exchange to occur, two or more individuals must place different relative valuations on the goods involved. Relative valuations of goods by a single party depend on relative marginal utilities of the goods. Thus, for all consumers to be in equilibrium—that is, for there to be no incentives to exchange—each individual's holdings of goods must be such that the ratio of the marginal utilities of the goods for him is the same as it is for everyone else. In our simple example, for A and B to be in equilibrium, MU_x/MU_y for A must equal MU_x/MU_y for B. When these conditions do not hold, it becomes worthwhile for the parties to engage in exchange until they do.

Applications: Utility Analysis

Utility analysis has a variety of applications. It can be used in many instances to illustrate points in theory, to distinguish sound from

---

[14] The one-for-one exchange ratio used here is not the only one at which the initial exchange could occur. Both parties can gain from any exchange ratio at which the amount of X that A is willing to give up to get a pint of Y exceeds the amount of X that B would require to give up a pint of Y.

unsound economic policies, and to explain certain behavior patterns of individuals. Examples of such applications follow.

Value in Use and Value in Exchange

The development of a utility theory of choice and exchange enabled economists to explain what the early classical economists of the late eighteenth and early nineteenth centuries called the diamond-water paradox. The paradox was that some goods, like diamonds, have a limited total use value to any one person, yet in markets they have a very high exchange value. Other goods, like water, have a very great total use value to any one person, yet they have a very low exchange value in markets. Early economists were unable to provide a satisfactory explanation of this phenomenon.

The subjective value, or marginal utility, economists of the late nineteenth century used a device like Table 7.3 to provide the answer. Measuring water in 100-gallon units and diamonds in 5-carat units, suppose that when consumer A is maximizing satisfaction, 900 gallons of water and two 5-carat units of diamonds are purchased per year. The total utility of water to A is 196 units of utility. But how does A value any of the 100-unit increments of the total supply? The definition of marginal utility informs us that, at the 900-gallon consumption level, 100 gallons contribute 12 units of utility to A's satisfaction level. Consumer A would be willing to trade 100 gallons of water for units of any other good that provides a marginal utility of 12 or more utility units.

Diamonds, on the other hand, provide a total of 76 units of utility at the 2-unit level of consumption. But the marginal utility of a unit of diamonds is 36 units. Consumer A would not be willing to

TABLE 7.3 The diamond-water paradox	Water			Diamonds		
	Gallons per Year	MU per 100 Gallons	TU	Units per Year	MU per Units	TU
	100	30	30	1	40	40
	200	28	58	2	36	76
	300	26	84	3	24	100
	400	24	108	4	10	110
	500	22	130	5	0	110
	600	20	150			
	700	18	168			
	800	16	184			
	900	12	196			
	1,000	8	204			

trade a unit of diamonds for units of any other good unless the marginal utility of such a good were 36 utility units or more.

The water, which has great use value to A, has a low exchange value because to A its supply is large and its marginal utility is low. The diamonds, which have a much lower use value to A, have a high exchange value because their supply to A is small and their marginal utility is high. Exchange value of a good, then, is really determined by the use value to the consumer of the marginal unit—that is, by the marginal utility of a unit of the good at the current rate of consumption.

Energy Conservation

Since the energy "crisis" of 1973–74, great national concern for energy conservation has been evidenced. To most people conservation means (1) voluntary restraints by individuals on the amounts of gasoline, electricity, and other energy-providing goods that they consume and/or (2) mandatory curbs by the government on the amounts individuals are allowed to consume. Both types of measures imply that prices are fixed below their equilibrium levels. If X represents nonenergy goods and E represents energy goods, at least some persons will be in disequilibrium positions with

$$\frac{MU_x}{p_x} < \frac{MU_e}{p_e}.$$

This means simply that energy goods are undervalued—that consumers want more at current prices than they get.

The disequilibrium positions make the exercise of voluntary restraints on consumption virtually impossible to sustain over time. The temptation is always there to turn the thermostat up to 74 degrees in the winter or down to 76 degrees in the summer. In addition, attempts to secure voluntary restraints promote ill will between those who feel "patriotic" and those who do not. The former will be very upset with the actions of those who do not comply.

Disequilibrium of individuals also creates problems in the enforcement of mandatory curbs on consumption. Users will be divided into a number of special-interest groups. In the case of motor fuel, for example, truckers and farmers represent two such groups. Individuals in each, faced with short supplies, believe that they are victims of discrimination. Group is set against group. And how can those people responsible for allocations determine for whom the fuel is most important?

The obvious way to avoid the problems just posed is to utilize energy prices to do the rationing. We shall assume that the annual (or monthly) supplies to be made available are fixed and that consumers bid for the available supplies. As p_e rises, MU_e/p_e for individuals will fall and so will the amounts of energy that consumers want to consume. *Positive incentives* will exist to turn the thermostat down in the winter and up in the summer. *All* users of motor fuel will have incentives to conserve its use. No one needs to make decisions concerning who gets the available supplies. Energy prices will rise until all consumers together are just willing to take the available supplies. The amount of energy consumed by each consumer will be that at which

$$\frac{MU_x}{p_x} = \frac{MU_e}{p_e}.$$

Charitable Giving

Although most microeconomic theory is oriented toward organized markets like those for gasoline, automobiles, housing, food, and clothing, it can be used advantageously to analyze a much wider range of phenomena. Recently economists have begun to apply it to such utility-enhancing occurrences as friendship, love, marriage, divorce, church attendance, and aesthetics. It is being drawn increasingly into the analysis of crime and punishment—and the study of other aspects of the legal system.

Despite much public opinion to the contrary, economists are human beings too, and generally recognize that people receive satisfaction from nonmarket as well as from market activities. In addition, they understand that most people in making their choices consider in some degree the interests of other members of society. Economic theory does not require that all of us be uniformly selfish. Such a view would contradict much human behavior, like giving aid to others—sometimes even to complete strangers—through blood donations, gifts of food in times of catastrophe, and contributions to health organizations. People sometimes make valiant efforts to save the lives of strangers even at the risk of their own.

Charitable activities constitute a major nonmarket source of satisfaction, or utility, to many people. Charity is the intentional transfer of resources or command over resources at below-market prices, or even zero prices, with the aim of making the recipient better off.[15] Charity may begin at home, but it is regularly extended to those outside the family. In one or another form, it is as old as civilization itself. Organized charities received sizable boosts from such undertakings as the efforts of Florence Nightingale during the Crimean

[15]   This discussion is drawn from Louis De Alessi, "The Utility of Disasters," *Kyklos,* 21 (1968), pp. 525–32; "A Utility Analysis of Post-disaster Cooperation," *Papers in Non-Market Decision Making* 3 (Fall 1967), pp. 85–90.

War of 1854–56, the relief work of American women during the Civil War, and the founding of the International Red Cross by the Swiss banker Jean Henri Dunant in 1858. Much present-day charity is involuntary—carried on by government units and funded by tax receipts. But the following discussion is concerned with private charity.

Charitable activity usually increases after disasters, such as earthquakes, floods, tornadoes, famines, and war, that strike large numbers of people. There is substantial evidence that following such events nonaffected persons tend to provide victims with more shelter, food, medical supplies, and other articles at below-market prices than they were willing to provide before the events occurred. Why does charity increase after such events?

People may obtain additional utility not only when their own income increases but also when the well-being of others is enhanced.[16] For this reason many people give away part of their own incomes. For most of us the marginal utility of charitable giving tends to be diminishing as the giving per unit of time increases. Thus, in Figure 7.6(a), A's total utility curve TU_1^A reflects the utility A obtains from charitable gifts to person B when B's base income is I_1^B. The curve TU_2^A shows A's total utility from giving to B when B's base income is at a higher level I_2^B. Both increase at decreasing rates, reflecting A's diminishing marginal utility from giving. The corresponding marginal utility curves are shown in Figure 7.6(b).

We show TU_1^A peaking at a higher level of giving than does TU_2^A. This pattern says that the worse off B is, the more contributions A would be willing to make before becoming satiated with giving. As such, it seems reasonable and in conformity with everyday observations. Further, if TU_1^A peaks at a higher level of donations than does TU_2^A, as well as lying above TU_2^A, then the increments in TU_1^A per $1 increment must exceed, on the average, the increments in TU_2^A per $1 increment up to the g_1 level of giving. Another way of saying the same thing is that for any level of annual giving below the g_1 level, the marginal utility per dollar given is greater the worse off B is; that is, the MU_1^A curve lies above the MU_2^A curve.

Consider now A's situation when the base income of B is I_2^B. To maximize satisfaction, A allocates income among goods and services, *including charitable giving G,* so that

$$\frac{MU_x}{p_x} = \frac{MU_y}{p_y} = \frac{MU_g}{p_g} = ---- = \frac{MU_n}{p_n},$$

[16] With reference to Footnote 10, the utility function for person A who contemplates giving a portion of his income to person B, thus augmenting B's income I^B, takes the form
$$U^A = f^A(x, y, I^B).$$

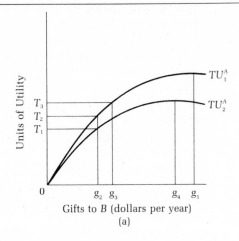

(a)

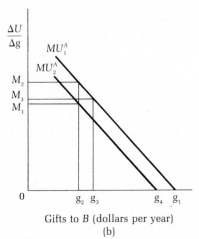

(b)

in which p_g is \$1. Suppose that in Figure 7.6, the satisfaction-maximizing level of giving is g_2, yielding a total utility level from giving of I_1 and a marginal utility of M_1.

Now suppose that a disaster strikes, reducing B's base income to I_1^B—possibly a zero level. At the g_2 level of giving, A's total utility from giving to B increases from I_1 to I_2 and the marginal utility of giving rises from M_1 to M_2. Mr. A now finds that

$$\frac{MU_x}{p_x} = \frac{MU_y}{p_y} < \frac{MU_g}{p_g} > ---- \frac{MU_n}{p_n}.$$

To maximize satisfaction, A will increase the level of giving, transferring dollars from other lines of expenditure. Marginal utilities per dollar's worth of other goods and services increase while the marginal utility per dollar's worth of giving decreases. At some level of giving, g_3, marginal utilities per dollar's worth will again be the same for all goods and services, including giving. The total utility of giving for A will be T_3 and the marginal utility of giving will be M_3.

The foregoing analysis explains why charitable giving tends to increase following some disastrous event. Donors and potential donors perceive the reductions in income of those affected by it. Giving becomes more meaningful to donors because it will provide assistance that is now more "needed." The possibility of its being channeled to worthy recipients is increased. And in widespread catastrophes, there may even be a possibility of friends or relatives of the donor becoming recipients. For all these reasons, the total utility and the marginal utility curves shift upward for any individual donor, thus inducing her or him to engage in a higher level of charitable giving.

Summary

The utility approach to the theory of individual consumer choice and demand is a special case of the indifference curve approach. It can be used to explain, among other things, the consumer's allocation of income among the goods that he or she buys, the consumer's demand curve for any given product, and the exchange of goods among individuals. The conclusions reached depend on the principle of *relatively* diminishing marginal utility of any one good or service as the consumption of it is increased relative to that of other goods and services.

A consumer seeks to maximize the satisfaction derived from the goods and services obtainable with one's given income. Maximization requires that the individual allocate income in such a way that when he or she is spending the entire income, the marginal utility per dollar's worth of one good is equal to the marginal utility per dollar's worth of every other good or service.

To establish the consumer's demand curve for any one commodity, we vary its price, holding constant the prices of other goods, the consumer's income, and tastes and preferences as shown by the individual's utility schedules or curves. At each of the prices the consumer maximizes satisfaction, thus determining the quantity that will be taken at each price. The resulting price-quantity combinations form the consumer's demand schedule and can be plotted as that person's demand curve.

Voluntary exchange of goods among individuals increases the welfare of both parties to the exchange. Incentives for voluntary exchange occur wherever the ratios of the marginal utilities of goods for one consumer differ from the corresponding ratios for another.

The condition for simultaneous equilibrium for all consumers is that the ratios of marginal utilities of all goods be the same for all individuals.

Suggested Readings

Boulding, Kenneth E. *Economic Analysis*, 4th ed., Vol. 1. New York: Harper & Row, 1966, Chap. 24.

Marshall, Alfred. *Principles of Economics*, 8th ed. London: Macmillan, 1920, Bk. 3, Chaps. 5 and 6.

Stigler, George J., "The Development of Utility Theory, I." *The Journal of Political Economy* 58 (August 1950), pp. 307–24.

Questions and Exercises

1 Tom Jones has an income of $50 per day, which he spends on food and clothing. His total utility schedules for each are listed below. The price of food is $2 per pound, and the price of clothing is $4 per yard.

Food		Clothing	
Pounds	TU_f	Yards	TU_c
1	50	1	120
2	95	2	230
3	135	3	330
4	170	4	420
5	200	5	500
6	225	6	570
7	245	7	630
8	260	8	680
9	270	9	720
10	275	10	750

a How much of each should he purchase to maximize satisfaction? Why?

b What will happen to his satisfaction level if he transfers a dollar from food to clothing?

c If a dollar is added to his income, on which item should he spend it? Why?

d If the price of food rises to $3 and his income remains at $50, how should he allocate it between food and clothing?

2 If the marginal utility of a person's income decreases as the person's income increases, would you expect that the individual

would be willing to make a bet in which the chance of winning $100 is exactly the same as the chance of losing $100? Why or why not?

3 Suppose a consumer can allocate income among any number of goods and services. Does it make sense for the consumer to purchase that quantity of any one good that will maximize her total utility for that good?

4 Evaluate this quotation: "The observation that the marginal rate of substitution between any two goods is ordinarily decreasing for a consumer rests on the older observation that the marginal utilities of the goods to the consumer are decreasing."

5 Suppose that two children of primary school age engage in voluntary exchange—one trades a sack of marbles to the other for a pocket knife. Explain the effects of the trade on the welfare of the community.

6 A 1913 Liberty nickel sells for over $50,000, while a nickel of recent mintage is worth only 5 cents. Only five such 1913 nickels were minted. Explain the difference in price. What can you say about the total utility of 1913 nickels as compared with that of nickels currently in circulation? What about the comparative marginal utilities?

Market Classifications and Demand as Viewed by the Seller

Three demand perspectives are important in microeconomics. First, demand can be viewed from the perspective of the individual consumer—the *individual consumer's demand curve* for the product. Second, individual consumer demand curves for a product can be aggregated into the *market demand curve* for it. Third, we must consider how demand looks to the individual seller of a product. It is this *demand curve faced by the firm* that we consider in this chapter. The other two were developed in Chapters 6 and 7.

No special definition of a firm is necessary at this point. It is an individual business concern; it may be a single proprietorship, a partnership, or a corporation. To simplify exposition, we shall assume that it sells one product only.

The demand curve faced by a firm for its product *shows the amounts that it can sell at different possible prices, other things being equal;* thus it could appropriately be called a *sales curve*. Its nature depends on the type of market in which the firm sells. Selling markets are usually classified into four types based on (1) the importance of individual firms in relation to the entire market in which they sell and (2) whether or not the products sold in a particular market are homogeneous. The market types are (1) pure competition, (2) pure monopoly, (3) oligopoly, and (4) monopolistic competition. Markets of the real world do not always fall neatly into one classification or another; they may be a mixture of two or more. However, it is useful in establishing a frame of reference to analyze the demand curve faced by the firm in each of the four theoretical or pure classifications. Detailed analysis of pricing and output under each follows in Chapters 11–14.

Pure Competition

The conditions necessary for pure competition to exist in a market were outlined in Chapter 3. In *pure competition* there are many firms selling the identical product with no one of them large enough relative to the entire market to influence the market price. If one firm drops out of the market, supply is not decreased enough to cause the price to increase perceptibly. Neither is it feasible for one firm to expand output enough to cause any perceptible decrease in market price. No single seller believes that it affects or is affected by other sellers in the market. No rivalries arise. There will be no reactions of other firms to actions taken by any one firm. Relationships among firms are impersonal.

The Demand Curve

In a purely competitive market, the demand curve facing the firm is horizontal at the prevailing market or equilibrium price. At any price above the prevailing market price it can sell nothing. Since all firms in the market sell the identical product, consumers will turn to firms charging the market price if one of them raises its selling price above that level. The proportion of the total market filled by one seller is so small that the firm can dispose of its entire output at the prevailing market price; hence, there is no necessity for lowering the price below that of the other sellers. Any firm attempting to do so will find itself swamped with buyers who promptly bid the price back to the equilibrium level.

A firm selling potatoes faces this sort of demand curve. When it hauls its potatoes to market, it receives the going market price. On the one hand, if it asks for more than the market price and sticks to its request, it will undoubtedly haul the potatoes home again. On the other hand, no amount of potatoes that it alone can bring to market will drive the price down. It can dispose of all it desires to sell at the going market price.

Diagrammatically, the nature of the demand curve faced by the firm is illustrated by dd in the left-hand panel of Figure 8.1. The market demand curve and the market supply curve are DD and SS,

FIGURE 8.1
The demand curve facing the firm—pure competition

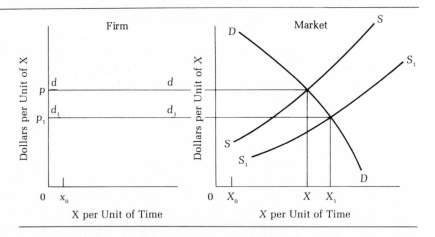

respectively. The market price is p; it determines the horizontal *infinitely elastic* demand curve faced by the firm. The price axes of the two panels are identical; however, quantity measurements of the market panel are compressed considerably as compared with those of the firm panel. For example, if x_0 measures 10 units of X for the firm, let X_0 measure 10,000 units of X for the total market.

In reality the demand curve faced by the firm is an infinitesimal segment of the market demand curve in the neighborhood of quantity X stretched out over the firm diagram. Any one firm can be thought of as supplying the last small portion of quantity X. Stretching this small segment out over the firm diagram makes the demand curve faced by the firm appear to be horizontal.

Influence of the Firm on Demand, Price, and Output

Any forces that change market demand or market supply will change the market price of the product and, consequently, the demand curve faced by the firm. The firm by itself can do nothing about either the demand curve it faces or the market price. It must accept both as given data. If market supply increases to $S_1 S_1$, the market price decreases to p_1; and the demand curve faced by the firm shifts downward to $d_1 d_1$. Any such change is beyond the control of the individual firm. It can adjust its output only, and it will gear its output to the prevailing market price.

Pure Monopoly

A market situation in which a single firm sells a product for which there are no good substitutes is called *pure monopoly*. The firm has the market for the product all to itself. There are no similar products whose price or sales will perceptibly influence the monopolist's price or sales, and vice versa. Cross elasticity of demand between the monopolist's product and other products will either be zero or small enough to be neglected by all firms in the economy. The monopolistic firm does not believe that its actions will evoke retaliation of any kind from firms in other industries. Similarly, the monopolist does not consider actions taken by firms in other industries to be of sufficient importance to warrant taking them into account. The monopolist *is* the industry from the selling point of view. A case in point is the supplier of telephone service to a particular community.

The Demand Curve

The market demand curve for the product is also the demand curve faced by the monopolist. Figure 8.2 shows the market demand curve

FIGURE 8.2
The demand curve
facing the firm—pure
monopoly

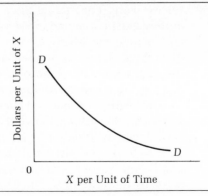

for the product that is produced and sold by a monopolist. It shows the different quantities that buyers will take off the market at all possible prices. Since the monopolist is the only seller of the product, it is possible to sell at different possible prices exactly the amounts that buyers will take at those prices.

Influence of the Firm on Demand, Price, and Output

The monopolist is able to exert some influence on the price, output, and demand for its product. The market demand curve delineates the limits of the monopolist's market. Faced by a given demand curve, the firm can increase sales if it is willing to lower its price, or it can raise its price if it is willing to restrict its sales volume. Additionally, the firm may be able to affect the demand curve itself through sales promotion activities of various kinds. The firm may be able to induce more people to want its product, thus increasing demand; and the firm may be able to make demand less elastic if it can convince enough people that they cannot afford to be without the product. It follows that if the monopolist is able to increase demand, it can increase sales to some extent without lowering the price or, alternatively, it can increase the price to some extent without restricting its sales volume.

Oligopoly

An *oligopolistic* industry is one in which the number of sellers is small enough for the activities of a single seller to affect other firms and for the activities of other firms to affect that firm in turn. Changes in the output and the price charged by one firm will affect the amounts that other sellers can sell and the prices that they can charge. Hence, other firms will react in one way or another to price-output changes on the part of a single firm. Individual sellers are *interdependent*—not independent, as they are under pure competition or pure monopoly.

Oligopolistic industries are frequently classified as (1) *differentiated* or (2) *pure*. A differentiated oligopolistic industry is one in which the firms produce and sell *differentiated products*. The products of all firms in the industry are very good substitutes for each other—they have high cross elasticities of demand—but the product of each firm has its own distinguishing characteristics. The differences may be real or fancied. They may consist of differences in quality and design, as is the case in the automobile industry; or they may consist merely of differences in brand names—for example, aspirin tablets.

A *pure* oligopolistic industry is one in which the firms all make an identical product. Purchasers have no cause for preferring the output of one firm to that of another on any basis except price. Examples of industries approaching the pure oligopoly category are the cement, aluminum, and steel industries.

The Demand Curve

There is no typical demand situation facing an oligopolistic firm. The interdependence of sellers in an oligopolistic market makes the determination of the single seller's demand curve difficult. In some situations the demand curve faced by the firm is indeterminate. In others it can be located with some degree of accuracy.

The oligopolistic seller's demand curve will be indeterminate when the firm cannot predict what the reactions of its rivals will be to price and output changes on its part. The output that the one firm can sell if it changes its price depends on the manner in which other firms react to this price change.

The range of possible reactions is broad. Rivals may: just meet the price change; change price in the same direction but by less than the change of the original seller; exceed the price change; improve the quality of their products; engage in extensive advertising campaigns; or react in other ways. Inability of the individual seller to predict which reactions will occur, and in what degree, amounts to inability to determine the demand curve faced by that seller.

When the single seller knows with some accuracy how its rivals will react to price changes on its part, the demand curve the firm faces becomes correspondingly more certain. If reliable judgments with regard to the probable effect on rivals' reactions to its own sales can be formed, the firm can take these into account. However, each different reaction by each different rival will result in different quantities that the single seller can market. Consequently, ascertaining the

effects of rivals' reactions to the quantities that can be sold at different prices is at best a complex process for the individual firm. A few
examples should improve our grasp of the problems involved.

Suppose that there are two producers in a particular industry
and that price changes by either will be just matched by the other.
Suppose also that the producers are of approximately equal size and
prestige and turn out items virtually identical. The market demand
curve is DD in Figure 8.3. If each firm knows that the other will just
match its price changes, at any given price each will expect to get
approximately half the market. Each will face a fairly determinate
demand curve, dd, for its output, and such a demand curve will lie
about halfway between DD and the price axis.

Next suppose that one producer does not behave in the way just
described. With an initial price of p, suppose that when firm A cuts
the price, firm B cuts the price still further. Firm B will take some of
firm A's customers away. The demand curve faced by firm A will not
then follow dd but will follow some path such as the broken line d'.
Firm A, since its rival reacts by cutting its price still more, loses a
part of its share of the market when it cuts its price. It may undercut
B's price again, and the situation may develop into a price war—an
indeterminate situation.

Suppose that the producers in a given oligopolistic industry
form a cartel. Under the cartel arrangement the firms of the industry
act as a single unit, each having some voice in the setting of price,
output, and other industry policies. When all firms act as a unit, the
amount that one firm can sell at different possible prices becomes
irrelevant. The cartel is concerned with how much the industry as a
whole can sell at different possible prices. Thus, the cartel is in much
the same position as a pure monopolist is, and it is the cartel that
faces the market demand curve. The demand curve faced by a single
firm fails to be a consideration.

FIGURE 8.3
The demand curve
facing the
firm—oligopoly

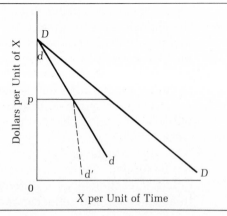

These examples provide a small sample of the possible demand situations faced by an oligopolistic seller. Additional illustrations will be presented in Chapter 13. Our goal at this point is to show that when the demand curve faced by one seller is determinate, the curve's position and its shape will depend on what the reactions of rivals will be to price changes on the part of the single firm.

Influence of the Firm on Demand, Price, and Output

Generally, the oligopolistic firm is able to influence in some degree the demand curve faced by it, its price, and its output. Through sales promotion efforts the firm may be able to shift the demand curve for what it sells to the right—partly by increasing consumer demand for this type of product, but mostly by inducing consumers to desert its rivals and buy its brand. The firm may be able to accomplish this through advertising or through design and quality changes, provided such changes give its brand more customer appeal. Rivals will not be stitting idly by in such cases and may retaliate by vigorous campaigns of their own. The firms with the most effective campaigns will be the ones that succeed in increasing demand for their brands.

Whether the firm does or does not face a determinate demand curve, it knows that in general its demand curve slopes downward to the right. To increase sales, it must usually lower price—unless the sales increase is made possible by a shift to the right of the demand curve. Higher prices can be obtained at the expense of sales, unless they are obtained through or in conjunction with increases in demand. The demand curve faced by an individual oligopolist is likely to be fairly elastic because of the existence of good substitutes produced by other firms in the industry. Elasticity of demand, however, as well as the position of the demand curve, will depend on rivals' reactions to the price and output changes of the single seller.

Monopolistic Competition

Monopolistic competition is a market situation in which there are many sellers of a particular product, but the product of each seller is in some way differentiated, in the minds of consumers, from the product of every other seller. As in pure competition there are enough sellers and each is small enough relative to the entire market so the activities of one have no effect on the others. Relationships among firms are impersonal. Product differentiation may take the form of brand names, trademarks, quality difference, or differences in conveniences or services offered to consumers. The products are good substitutes for each other—their cross elasticities are high. Examples of industries approaching monopolistic competition include the women's hosiery industry, various textile products, and service trades in large cities.

The Demand Curve

The shape of the demand curve faced by the firm under monopolistic competition stems from product differentiation. To see the effects of product differentiation, we first assume its absence. This assumption leaves us with the case of pure competition and a horizontal demand curve such as dd in Figure 8.4. Now we introduce the concept of product differentiation and observe how dd is affected. When products are differentiated, consumers become more or less attached to particular brand names. At any given price for commodity X, some consumers will be on the margin of switching to other brands, while others are attached to X at that price with varying degrees of tightness.

Suppose that for the monopolistic competitor quantity x will be taken at price p. If the firm raises the price, those consumers on the verge of switching to other brands will make the switch, since the other brands are now relatively lower in price. The higher the firm raises its price, the more customers it will lose to relatively lower-priced brands. Since other brands are good substitutes for that of the seller under consideration, the rise in price necessary for it to lose all its customers (pp_1) will not be large. For price increases above p, the demand curve faced by the firm will be the lighter line in the diagram. Similarly, if the firm lowers the price below p, it will pick up marginal customers of other sellers, since its price is now relatively

FIGURE 8.4
The demand curve facing the firm—monopolistic competition

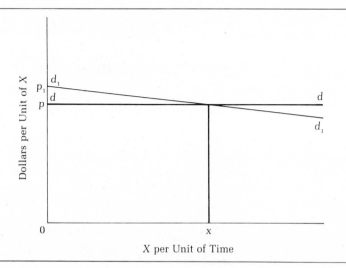

lower as compared with other firms' prices. It will not have to lower price much to pick up all the additional customers it can handle. Thus, for decreases in price below p, the lighter line in the diagram shows the demand curve faced by the one firm. The entire demand curve faced by the monopolistic competitor is one such as d_1d_1.

It may appear that price reductions by one firm that attract customers away from the other firms in the industry would evoke some kind of retaliatory action on the part of the other firms, as it does in oligopoly. Such is not the case, however, because there are many firms in a monopolistically competitive industry. The one that reduces its price will attract so few customers from each of the others that they will not notice or feel the loss. Nevertheless, for the one firm the total increase in customers will be relatively large.

Likewise, it may seem that the price increases by one firm that drive customers away would increase demand for the products of the other firms. The customers shifting to other firms, however, will be widely scattered among those firms. Not enough will go to any other single firm to cause any perceptible increase in demand for its product, even though the loss of customers to the price-raising firm is relatively large.

Influence of the Firm on Demand, Price, and Output

The individual firm in a monopolistically competitive industry may be able to influence demand for its own product to some perceptible degree through advertising. However, the existence of many good substitutes will preclude much success in this direction.

The firm is subjected to highly competitive forces, yet it is to a small extent a sort of monopolist since it has some discretion in setting price and output. But, if the firm raises price very much, it loses all its customers, and it does not have to lower price very far to secure all the customers it can serve. Within that limited price range the firm has price-setting discretion. Outside that price range it is subject to competitive forces. The demand curve faced by a firm under monopolistic competition will be highly elastic throughout its relevant range. The cause is not hard to find. The products of all firms in the industry, even though differentiated, are very good substitutes for each other.

Summary

Analysis of the demand situation facing the individual business firm is organized around four market classifications. The conditions of demand facing the individual firm differ from classification to classification, these differences stemming from two sources: (1) the importance of the individual firm in the market in which it sells and (2) product differentiation or product homogeneity.

Pure competition stands at one extreme of the classification, and pure monopoly at the other. Purely competitive firms sell homogeneous products, and each is so small relative to the entire market that, by itself, it cannot influence market price. Hence, the demand curve faced by the firm is horizontal at the equilibrium market price. A monopolist firm is a single seller of a product not closely related to any other product. It faces the market demand curve for its product.

Oligopoly and monopolistic competition fill the gap between these two extremes. Monopolistic competition differs from pure competition in one respect only—products of different sellers are differentiated. This fact gives the monopolistic competitor a small amount of control over its price; however, each firm is so small relative to the entire market that, by itself, it cannot affect other firms in the industry. It faces a downward-sloping, highly elastic demand curve.

With regard to the number of firms in the industry, oligopoly lies between the extremes of pure competition and monopolistic competition on the one hand, and pure monopoly on the other. Its primary characteristic is that there are few enough firms in the industry for the activities of one to have repercussions on the price and sales of the others. Hence, rivalries develop under oligopoly. The demand curve faced by a single seller depends on what the reactions of rivals will be to market activities on the part of the one firm. If the reactions of rivals cannot be predicted, the demand curve faced by the firm cannot be determined.

Suggested Readings

Fellner, William. *Modern Economic Analysis*. New York: McGraw-Hill, 1960, Chap. 17.

Machlup, Fritz. "Monopoly and Competition: A Classification of Market Positions." *American Economic Review 27* (September 1937), pp. 445–51.

Questions and Exercises

1 Draw and explain the demand curve facing an oligopolistic firm if other firms in the market will match any price decreases but will not follow any price increases by the firm. Is this a plausible situation? Why?

2 Evaluate the following statement: For an industry to be one of monopolistic competition, it is not important that there be *ac-*

tual differences in the items sold by the various sellers; it is only necessary that consumers *think* that differences exist.

3   How would you classify firms that sell aspirin? Haircuts? Wheat? Oil? Automobiles? Steel? Panty hose? In each case, state the reasons for your classification.

4   In which of the four market classifications would you expect firms to advertise their products? Why? Do you think such advertising is in the best interests of consumers? Explain.

5   How would you classify the General Store in Dodge City in 1900?

PART THREE

The firm's output is represented by x, and its inputs are represented by a, b, and c. The equation can be expanded readily to include as many different resources as are used in the production of any given good. It furnishes a convenient way of relating product output to resource inputs.

Firms can usually vary the proportions in which they combine resources in production processes. This flexibility brings about several possible types of relations among inputs, among inputs and outputs, and among outputs. Where inputs can be substituted for one another in the production of a commodity, there will be a number of alternative sets of input quantities that will produce a given level of product output, and the firm must make choices among them. By increasing or decreasing the quantities of all resource inputs used, the firm can increase or decrease its output level. It can also increase or decrease output within limits by increasing or decreasing the quantity used of one or more resource inputs, holding the quantities of other resource inputs constant. And, given the bundle of resources available to it, a firm that produces more than one product can increase its output level of one product by reducing its output level of another, transferring the resources thus released to the production of the first.

The input-input, input-output, and output-output relationships that characterize a firm's production function depend on the techniques of production used. Of the range of techniques available, we assume that the firm will use those that are most efficient—that is, the ones that will provide the greatest value of output for a given value of input. Generally speaking, an improvement in techniques will increase the output possible from given quantities of resources.

The Production Surface

In many ways a firm's production function is analogous to the preference function or the utility function of an individual consumer, although one must be careful not to confuse the two. A firm uses resource inputs to generate product or service outputs. Usually these quantities have cardinal properties—the product output can be measured, added, and, in most cases, seen. An individual consumer purchases and uses products and services to generate a much more nebulous kind of output—satisfaction—that cannot be measured, added, or seen. It has ordinal properties but not cardinal properties.

Suppose, then, that a firm uses two resource inputs, A and B, to obtain outputs of product X. In the three-dimensional diagram of Figure 9.1(a) the coordinates in the horizontal AB plane show input combinations. Product output associated with each input combination is measured vertically above the plane. If no resource A is used,

The Principles of Production

To understand costs and supply, one must first understand the principles of production. The principles of production in microeconomic theory extend beyond costs and supply; they also provide the basis of resource pricing and employment, resource allocation, and product distribution. Production theory, like the theory of consumer behavior, is basically a theory of choice among alternatives. The key economic unit is the individual firm rather than the individual consumer. Whereas the individual consumer attempts to maximize satisfaction by the way in which he or she spends income on consumer goods, the individual firm attempts to maximize the product output it can obtain with any given cost outlay by the way in which it secures and combines resource inputs. A fundamental difference between the two theories is that the purchasing power of the consumer is more or less fixed, while the possible outlays of the firm are variable. This difference will not be of much concern in the present chapter, but it will be important later on.

In this chapter the concept of a firm's production function is first explained, and then the law of diminishing returns is considered. Finally, resource product curves and the comparative efficiencies of different resource combinations are analyzed.

The Production Function

What do we mean by the term "production function"? We look first at the concept and then at the graphic representations of it.

The Concept

The term *production function* refers to the physical relationships between a firm's inputs of resources and its output of good or services per unit of time, leaving prices aside. It can be expressed in general mathematical terms as

$$x = f(a, b, c). \tag{9.1}$$

The Foundations of
Costs and Supply

We do for costs of production in Part Three what we did for demand in Part Two. We examine the individual firm—its production possibilities, its motivations, and its behavior—to see what determines its costs of producing goods and services. These costs in turn form the basis of supply.

The type of selling market in which the firm operates is not important in Part Three. The principles of production and the cost curves of the firm do not depend on the type of market in which it sells its product. However, market structure becomes an important consideration again in Part Four.

FIGURE 9.1
A production surface
and its isoquants

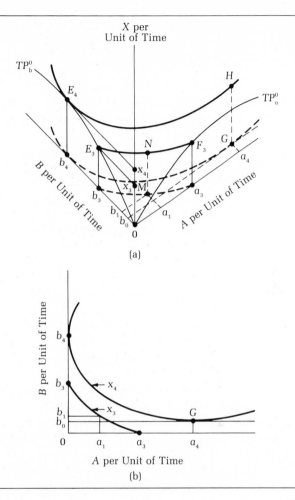

(a)

(b)

total product curve TP_b^0 is generated by varying the quantity of resource B used. An output of $b_3E_3(=0x_3)$ is produced with b_3 of B alone. Similarly, if no resource B is used, TP_a^0 is generated by varying the quantity of resource A used. With a_3 of A, the output level is $a_3F_3(= 0x_3)$. A combination of b_1 of B and a_1 of A yields an output level of $MN = 0x_3$. The whole range of input combinations generates an inverted bowl-shaped production surface, showing the output associated with every possible input combination.

Isoquants Contour lines can be drawn around the production surface of Figure 9.1(a) at each possible level of output. All points on a given contour line are equidistant from the AB plane; that is, any one contour line represents a constant or given level of production. These contour lines can be projected downward onto the AB plane, forming a set of *isoquants*, or product indifference curves. Any one isoquant, say b_3a_3 in Figure 9.1, shows the different combinations of A and B with which the firm can obtain a product output of x_3. If the production surface has an inverted bowl shape, higher contour lines like E_4H, when projected to the AB plane, become isoquants like b_4G, lying farther from the origin of the diagram. A complete set of isoquants for the firm is called its isoquant map.[1]

Isoquant Characteristics   The general characteristics of isoquants are the same as those of indifference curves. First, they slope downward to the right for those combinations of resources that firms will want to use. Second, they do not intersect. Third, they are convex to the origin of the diagram.

Isoquants slope downward to the right for the resources that can be substituted for one another in the production process. For example, usually there are possibilities of substitutions between capital resources and labor resources used. If less of one is used, more of the other must be applied to compensate for the decrease in the first, if the level of output is to remain constant. Exceptions will occur where resources cannot be substituted for one another in production processes.[2] There are no substitutes for raw milk as an input in the production of the pasteurized product. In other cases, in the short run, fixed proportions of resources may be required.

An intersection of isoquants is not logical. An intersection point would mean that a single combination of resources produces two different maximum outputs, thereby implying that an increase in the level of output can be accomplished with no increase in the amount of any resource used. To the right of the intersection point, the implication is that by decreasing the quantities of all resources used product output can be increased. Thus, isoquant intersections are economic nonsense.

Convexity to the origin reflects the fact that different resources are not ordinarily perfect substitutes. Consider labor and capital used in digging a ditch of a certain length, width, and depth. Within limits they can be substituted for each other. But the more labor and

---

[1]   Let the production function be

$$x = f(a, b),$$

in which x is the quantity produced of the good or service and a and b are quantities of resource inputs. An isoquant is the locus of all combinations of resources A and B that yield a given output level; that is,

$$x_3 = f(a, b)$$

defines an isoquant. A family of isoquants, or an isoquant map, is described by treating x as a parameter and assigning different values to it.

[2]   For a discussion of irregularly shaped isoquants, see Sidney Weintraub, *Intermediate Price Theory* (Philadelphia: Chilton, 1964), pp. 34, 40–42.

the less capital used to dig the ditch, the more difficult it becomes to substitute additional labor for capital. Additional units of labor will just compensate for smaller and smaller amounts of capital given up. The same reasoning applies to other resources.

The more of resource A and the less of resource B the firm uses to produce a constant amount of product X, the more difficult it becomes to substitute additional units of A for B; that is, additional units of A will just compensate for smaller and smaller amounts of B given up. This principle is called the principle of *diminishing marginal rate of technical substitution of A for B* ($MRTS_{ab}$). The $MRTS_{ab}$ is measured at any point on an isoquant by the slope of the isoquant at that point. It is defined as the amount of B lost that will be just compensated for by an additional unit of A, with no change in product output occurring.

Product Curves

Product schedules and product curves for either resource A or resource B can be derived from the firm's system of isoquants. With reference to Figure 9.2, suppose that the firm considers the employment of alternative quantities of A per unit of time with a fixed amount b_1 of B. A movement to the right along the line b_1J reflects the use of larger quantities of A. Each isoquant intersected by line b_1J shows the product output obtained with each quantity of A. Thus, when a_4 of A is used with b_1 of B, total product will be x_4. The greater the amount of A used, the greater will be the total product until the firm is using a_6 of the resource. With still greater quantities

FIGURE 9.2
Effects on total product
of quantity changes in
one resource

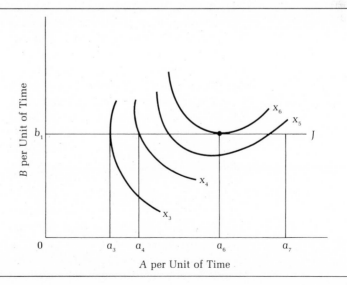

of A, line $b_1 J$ intersects lower and lower isoquants, showing that the total product decreases. Thus, the firm would never use more than a_6 of A with b_1 of B, even if A were free. The total product curve for larger and larger quantities of A used with the fixed amount of B increases, reaches a maximum at a_6 of A, and then decreases. This curve is shown in Figure 9.3.

FIGURE 9.3
Total product curve for one resource

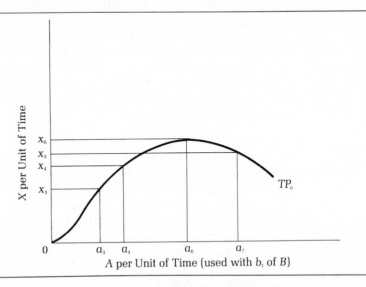

The average product and marginal physical product schedules or curves of a resource are derived from the total product schedule or curve for that resource. Suppose that a firm conducts a series of experiments to determine the total product output it can get from various quantities of labor per unit of time used with a unit of capital. The results are listed in column (3) of Table 9.1 as the *total product* of labor. As the amount of labor is increased up to 7 units, output increases. At 7 and 8 units of labor the maximum total product that a unit of capital will produce is obtained.

The *average product* of labor, computed from columns (2) and (3), is the total product of labor at each level of employment divided by that quantity of labor. Note that in column (4) average product rises as the quantity of labor is increased, reaches a maximum at 3 and 4 units of labor per unit of capital, and then decreases as the employment of labor is increased further.

The change in total product per unit change in the quantity of labor employed, holding the quantity of capital constant, is called the *marginal physical product* of labor. In Table 9.1 an increase in the employment of labor from zero to 1 unit increases total product from zero to 3; thus, the marginal physical product of labor at the 1-unit level of employment is 3 units of product. Two units of labor

TABLE 9.1	(1) Capital	(2) Labor	(3) Total Product (labor)	(4) Average Product (labor)	(5) Marginal Physical Product (labor)	
Product schedules for labor	1	1	3	3	3	
	1	2	7	$3^1/_2$	4	Stage I
	1	3	12	4	5	
	1	4	16	4	4	
	1	5	19	$3^4/_5$	3	Stage II
	1	6	21	$3^1/_2$	2	
	1	7	22	$3^1/_7$	1	
	1	8	22	$2^3/_4$	0	
	1	9	21	$2^1/_3$	−1	Stage III
	1	10	15	$1^1/_2$	−6	

employed, rather than 1 unit, increase total product to 7 units, and the marginal physical product of labor at the 2-unit level of employment is 4 units of product. The rest of column (5) is computed in a similar fashion.

The total, average, and marginal product concepts are shown graphically in Figure 9.4. The vertical axis of Figure 9.4(a) measures product produced per unit of capital (Product/Capital); and the horizontal axis measures labor used per unit of capital (Labor/Capital). The total product curve (TP_l) is in all essential respects like that of Figure 9.3.[3] When l_1 units of labor are used on the unit of capital, total product reaches a maximum. In the illustration additional units of labor per unit of capital cause total product to decrease.

The average product curve for labor (AP_l) of Figure 9.4(b) is derived from the total product (TP_l) of Figure 9.4(a). The vertical axis of Figure 9.4(b) measures product per unit of labor (Product/Labor). The horizontal axis is the same as that of Figure 9.4(a). Since average product is total product divided by the number of units of labor used, average product in Figure 9.4(a) at l' units of labor is $l'A'/0l'$, which measures the slope of the line $0A'$—this ratio is plotted in Figure 9.4(b). As the quantity of labor is increased from zero to l_0, in Figure 9.4(a), the slopes of the corresponding $0A$ lines increase; that is, the average product of labor increases. At l_0 units of

[3]   The total product curve of Figure 9.4 begins at the origin of the diagram, but it is not necessary that it do so. For some resources not absolutely essential in the production of the product, it may begin above the origin—cottonseed meal fed to cows to increase milk production is a case in point. In other cases no product may be obtained until several units of the variable resource are applied to the fixed complex of other resources. For example, one worker in a steel mill will produce nothing. Two workers can do no better. A certain minimum complement of labor is necessary before any production can be obtained. In this case the total product curve of labor begins to the right of the origin.

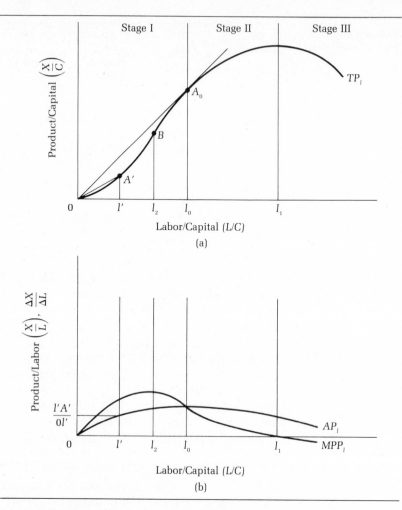

FIGURE 9.4
Product curves for labor

Stage I   Stage II   Stage III

Product/Capital $\left(\dfrac{X}{C}\right)$

A_0

B

A'

TP_l

0   l' l_2 l_0 l_1

Labor/Capital (L/C)

(a)

Product/Labor $\left(\dfrac{X}{L}\right)$, $\dfrac{\Delta X}{\Delta L}$

$\dfrac{l'A'}{0l'}$

0   l' l_2 l_0 l_1

AP_l

MPP_l

Labor/Capital (L/C)

(b)

labor the slope of line $0A_0$ is greater than that of any other $0A$ line drawn from the origin to the total product curve. Thus, the average product of labor is maximum at this point. Beyond l_0 units of labor the average product decreases, but it remains positive as long as total product is positive. The slopes of the $0A$ lines corresponding to the various quantities of labor in Figure 9.4(a) are plotted at the AP_l curve in Figure 9.4(b).

The slope of the total product curve at any given quantity of labor measures the marginal physical product of labor at that point. Both the slope of TP_l and the marginal physical product of labor (MPP_l) are defined as the change in total product per unit change in the quantity of labor used. Marginal physical product reaches a maximum at point B, where the total product curve turns from concave upward to concave downward. At quantity l_1 of labor, the total product is maximum; hence, marginal physical product is zero. Beyond l_1

additional units of labor cause the total product to decrease, meaning that the marginal physical product is negative.[4] The slopes of TP_l at the various quantities of labor in Figure 9.4(a) are plotted as MPP_l in Figure 9.4(b).

An additional guide to the proper location of the marginal physical product curve is its relation to the average product curve. When average product is increasing, marginal physical product is greater than average product. When average product is maximum, marginal physical product equals average product. When average product is decreasing, marginal physical product is less than average product.[5] These relationships are verified by columns (4) and (5) of Table 9.1.

---

[4] Let the production function be

$$x = g(k, l).$$

Total product of labor can be expressed as

$$TP_l = x = g(\bar{k}, l) = f(l),$$

in which $\bar{k}$ represents a fixed amount of capital.

The average product of labor becomes

$$AP_l = \frac{TP_l}{l} = \frac{f(l)}{l},$$

and

$$MPP_l = \frac{dTP_l}{dl} = f'(l).$$

[5] To illustrate these relationships, consider a succession of men entering a room, each taller than the one who preceded him. As each man enters, the average height of the men in the room increases; however, except for the first man, average height will be less than that of the man currently entering. The height of each man as he enters is marginal height and is analogous to marginal physical product. Average height is analogous to average product. Thus, for average product (height) to be increasing, marginal physical product (height) must exceed the average.

Suppose that additional men enter, each successively shorter than the one preceding him and all shorter than the average height before they entered. Average height will decrease but will not be as low as marginal height. When average height is maximum, the height of the last man who entered must have been equal to average height, since he caused neither an increase nor a decrease in average height.

Mathematically, if AP_l is increasing, then

$$\frac{d(AP_l)}{dl} = \frac{d\left(\frac{f(l)}{l}\right)}{dl} > 0,$$

so

$$\frac{l \times f'(l) - f(l)}{l^2} > 0$$

or

$$f'(l) - \frac{f(l)}{l} > 0;$$

therefore,

$$f'(l) > \frac{f(l)}{l};$$

that is, $MPP_l > AP_l$. Similarly, it can be shown that if AP_l is constant or if it is maximum, $MPP_l = AP_l$; and if AP_l is decreasing, $MPP_l < AP_l$.

The Law of Diminishing Returns

The product schedules of Table 9.1 and the product curves of Figure 9.4 illustrate the celebrated *law of diminishing returns*, which describes the direction and the rate of change that the firm's output takes when the input of only one resource is varied. It states that *if the input of one resource is increased by equal increments per unit of time while the inputs of other resources are held constant, total product output will increase; but beyond some point, the resulting output increases will become smaller and smaller.* [6] If the increases in the variable resource are carried far enough, total product will reach a maximum and may then decrease. The law is consistent with observations that there are limits to the output that can be obtained by increasing the quantity of a single resource applied to constant quantities of other resources.

Diminishing returns may or may not occur for the first few one-unit increases in the variable resource used with the fixed quantities of other resources. It is possible for diminishing returns or diminishing increases in total product to occur for all such increments. This is frequently the case with the application of fertilizer to given complexes of seed, land, labor, and machinery.

But a stage of increasing returns may also characterize the initial increases in the variable resource before diminishing returns begin. An example of this situation is the amount of labor used to operate a factory of a given size. Smaller quantities of labor than that for which the factory is designed tend to operate inefficiently because of the multiplicity of jobs to be performed by each individual and because of time lost in changing from one task to another. Equal increments in labor used bring about successively greater increments in total product, up to some point. In Table 9.1, through 3 units of labor, and in Figure 9.4, through l_2 units of labor, we show increasing returns. [7] Beyond these points, increases in the quantity of labor used lead to diminishing returns.

Product Curves and Technical Efficiency

The three product curves defined and described above show the *technical efficiency* of resources for various resource combinations

[6] *The different quantities of the variable resource refer to alternative quantities* used with constant amounts of other resources, not to a chronological application of additional units.

[7] Whether or not we assume that diminishing returns occur at the outset is not important. Usually, for expository purposes we assume first increasing and then decreasing returns as the quantity of the variable resource is increased.

that may be used in making a product. The technical efficiency of any given resource is defined as the ratio of product output to the resource input; that is, it is the average product of the resource. The greater the product output per unit of resource input, the greater the technical efficiency of the resource is said to be.

Suppose that the production function of the firm shows *constant returns to size*. Changes of a given proportion in the quantities of all resources used will change product output in the same proportion. A fifty percent increase in the quantities of all resources used to make the product will result in a fifty percent increase in the output of the firm. Doubling the quantities of all resource inputs will double the product output. Both capital and labor are completely divisible with respect to quantities used; and techniques of production are such that the same techniques will be used for any given ratio of labor to capital, regardless of the absolute amounts of resources used. The same techniques would be used if 2 units of labor work 1 unit of capital as are used if 1 unit of labor works ½ unit of capital, or if 4 units of labor work 2 units of capital. A production function of this type is said to be *linearly homogeneous*.[8]

We are concerned with the *ratio* of the resources as we establish the firm's product curves; we are not really limited to 1 unit of capital or to a fixed amount of capital. We can think of the firm as using any amount of capital it wishes to use; but in establishing the product curves, we convert our observations into terms of product obtainable from 1 unit of the capital resource. For example, if 10 units of labor working 2 units of capital produce 38 units of product per unit of time, for purposes of establishing the product curves we would convert the data to an equivalent of 1 unit of capital—that is, 5 units of labor working 1 unit of capital produce an output of 19 units of product per unit of time.[9] An increase in the quantity of capital used, with the quantity of labor being held constant, is equivalent to a decrease in the quantity of labor, with the quantity of capital being

---

[8] The production function $x = g(k, l)$ is said to be homogeneous of degree n if

$$\lambda^n x = g(\lambda k, \lambda l).$$

It exhibits

1. constant returns to scale, or is linearly homogeneous, when $n = 1$
2. increasing returns to scale when $n > 1$
3. decreasing returns to scale when $n < 1$.

[9] If the production function of Footnote 8 is linearly homogeneous, it takes the form

$$\lambda x = g(\lambda k, \lambda l),$$

which exhibits the following properties:

1. AP_l and AP_k are functions of the *ratio* of capital to labor.
Letting

$$\lambda = \frac{1}{l},$$

held constant, when we think in terms of the ratio used of the two resources.

The Three Stages for Labor

The product schedules of Table 9.1 and the product curves of Figure 9.4 can be divided into three stages. In each of the three, the average product curve and the total product curve of labor provide information on how efficiently the resources are used for various labor-capital ratios. As the ratio of labor to capital is increased—that is, as more and more labor per unit of capital is used—the average product curve yields information regarding the amount of product obtained per unit of labor for the various ratios. The total product curve depicts the amount of product obtained per unit of capital.

Stage I is characterized by increases in the average product of labor as more labor per unit of capital is used. These increases mean that the technical efficiency of labor—the product per worker—rises. The total product obtained per unit of capital, as larger quantities of labor are applied to it, also rises in Stage I. The increases in total product show us that the technical efficiency of capital also increases in Stage I. Thus, increases in the quantity of labor applied to a unit of

then

$$\frac{1}{l} x = g\left(\frac{1}{l} k, \frac{1}{l} l\right) = g\left(\frac{k}{l}, 1\right) = h\left(\frac{k}{l}\right) ;$$

that is,

$$AP_l = h\left(\frac{k}{l}\right) = h(r) \text{ where } r = \frac{k}{l}$$

and

$$AP_k = \frac{x}{k} = \frac{x}{l} \times \frac{l}{k} = AP_l \times \frac{1}{r} = \frac{h(r)}{r}.$$

Thus, both AP_l and AP_k are functions of the capital-labor ratio only. They are constant for all changes in K and L in equal proportions, since such changes do not alter the k/l ratio.

2. The MPP_k and MPP_l are also functions of the k/l ratio, only. Since

$$AP_l = \frac{x}{l} = h(r),$$

then

$$x = l \times h(r).$$

So

$$MPP_l = \frac{\delta x}{\delta l} = h(r) + l \frac{dh(r)}{dr} \times \frac{\delta r}{\delta l} = h(r) + l \times h'(r) \times \frac{-k}{l^2}$$

$$= h(r) - \frac{k}{l} \times h'(r) = h(r) - r \times h'(r).$$

Also,

$$MPP_k = \frac{\delta x}{\delta k} = l \frac{\delta h(r)}{\delta k} = l \frac{dh(r)}{dr} \times \frac{\delta r}{\delta k} = l \times h'(r) \left(\frac{1}{l}\right) = h'(r).$$

capital in Stage I augment the technical efficiency with which *both* labor and capital are utilized.

Stage II is characterized by decreasing average product and shrinking marginal physical product of labor. But the marginal physical product is positive, since total product continues to increase. In Stage II, as larger quantities of labor per unit of capital are used, the technical efficiency of labor—product per worker—decreases. However, the technical efficiency of capital—product per unit of capital—continues to increase.

In Stage III the application of larger quantities of labor to a unit of capital reduces the average product of labor still more. Additionally, the marginal physical product of labor is negative and total product is falling. The efficiency of both labor and capital decrease when the firm pushes into Stage III combinations.

In looking over the three stages, we note two things: (1) the combination of labor and capital that leads to maximum technical efficiency of labor lies at the boundary line between Stages I and II and (2) the combination of labor and capital leading to maximum technical efficiency of capital is the one at the boundary line between Stages II and III.

The Three Stages for Capital

If the production function of the firm is linearly homogeneous, we can rework Table 9.1 and Figure 9.4, determining the product schedules and product curves for alternative quantities of capital applied to one unit of labor. We can show that Stage I for labor is Stage III for capital, that Stage III for labor is Stage I for capital, and that Stage II for labor is also Stage II for capital.

To facilitate comparison of the product curves of labor with those of capital, it will be convenient to set up the product schedules of Table 9.2 and the product curves of Figure 9.5 in an unorthodox way. Table 9.2, showing the effects of increasing the ratio of capital to labor, should be read from bottom to top. Figure 9.5, read in the conventional way from left to right, shows the effects of increasing the ratio of labor to capital, but read from right to left, it shows the impact of increasing the ratio of capital to labor.

The Product Schedules   The results of the reworking of Table 9.1 are shown in Table 9.2. At the bottom of Table 9.1, 10 units of labor are used per unit of capital. In terms of a ratio, this combination means the same thing as using $1/10$ of a unit of capital per unit of labor. These numbers are shown in columns (1) and (2) in the last row of Table 9.2. Similarly, in terms of ratios, 9 units of labor per unit of capital are the same as $1/9$ of a unit of capital per unit of labor; and

TABLE 9.2	(1) Capital	(2) Labor	(3) Total Product (capital)	(4) Marginal Physical Product (capital)	(5) Average Product (capital)	
Product schedules for capital	1	1	3	(−)1	3	Stage III
	1/2	1	3½	(−)3	7	
	1/3	1	4	0	12	
	1/4	1	4	4	16	Stage II
	1/5	1	3⁴/₅	9	19	
	1/6	1	3½	15	21	
	1/7	1	3¹/₇	22	22	
	1/8	1	2³/₄	30	22	Stage I
	1/9	1	2¹/₃	75	21	
	1/10	1	1½	15	15	

so on up through the table until we reach the top, where 1 unit of capital is used with 1 unit of labor. The ratios of capital and labor are the same throughout Tables 9.1 and 9.2.

The total product schedule for various amounts of capital applied to one unit of labor is determined from column (3) of Table 9.1. Ten units of labor applied to 1 unit of capital produce 15 units of product. Obviously, then, $1/10$ of a unit of capital applied to 1 unit of labor should produce a total product of $15/10$ or $1½$ units of product. This result is listed in the last row of column (3) in Table 9.2. Since 9 units of labor applied to 1 unit of capital produce 21 units of product, $1/9$ of a unit of capital applied to 1 unit of labor will produce a total product of $2¹/₃$. Total product of the larger quantities of capital used with 1 unit of labor is computed in a similar way to complete column (3).

The marginal physical product schedule for capital should show the increments in total product per full unit increment in capital at the various ratios of capital to labor used. The first $1/10$ of a unit of capital used increases total product from zero to $1½$ units. Therefore, at this ratio of capital to labor the marginal physical product of a unit of capital is $1½ \div 1/10 = 3/2 \times 10 = 15$ units of product. This quantity is listed in column (4) in the last row of Table 9.2.

An increase in capital from $1/10$ of a unit to $1/9$ of a unit increases total product from $1½$ to $2¹/₃$. The product increment is $7/3 - 3/2 = 14/6 - 9/6 = 5/6$ of a unit of product. The capital increment is $1/9 - 1/10 = 10/90 - 9/90 = 1/90$ of a unit of capital. Marginal physical product of a unit of capital at this point is $5/6 \div 1/90 = 5/6 \times 90 = 75$ units of product. Column (4) is calculated by similar computations on up through columns (1) and (3) of Table 9.2.

Column (5) of Table 9.2, read from bottom to top, presents aver-

FIGURE 9.5
Product curves for
capital

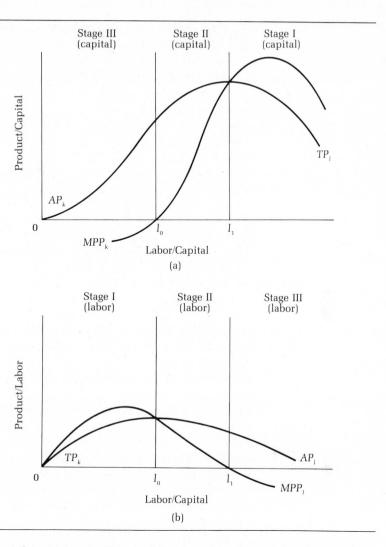

(a)

(b)

age product per unit of capital for the various capital-to-labor ratios. The average product of capital for each ratio is obtained by dividing the total product of capital by the quantity of capital used. Since $1/10$ of a unit of capital produces $1\frac{1}{2}$ units of product, the average product of capital equals $1\frac{1}{2} \div 1/10 = 15$ at this point. Similarly, $2\frac{1}{3}$ units of product divided by $1/9$ of a unit of capital equals an average product of capital at this point of 21 units. The other figures of column (5) are determined by similar computations.

When Table 9.1 is compared with Table 9.2, two columns of Table 9.1 turn out to be identical with two columns in Table 9.2. First, the total product schedule of labor applied to 1 unit of capital [see Table 9.1, column (3)] has become the average product schedule of capital applied to 1 unit of labor [see Table 9.2, column (5)]. Second, the average product schedule of labor applied to 1 unit of capital [see Table 9.1, column (4)] has become the total product schedule of capital applied to 1 unit of labor [see Table 9.2, column (3)]. A little reflection will reveal that these relationships should be expected. The total product of more and more labor applied to 1 unit of capital is the average product of capital (or the product per unit of capital) as the ratio of labor to capital is increased. Likewise, the average product of labor (product per unit of labor) is necessarily the total product of various quantities of capital applied to 1 unit of labor.

A further observation can be made. Stages I, II, and III are marked off approximately for labor in Table 9.1.[10] Stages I, II, and III for capital are marked off approximately in Table 9.2. That which is Stage I for labor in Table 9.1 has become Stage III for capital in Table 9.2. That which is Stage III for labor in Table 9.1 has become Stage I for capital in Table 9.2. Stage II for labor is also Stage II for capital in both tables.

The Product Curves   In Figure 9.5 product curves for capital per unit of labor, as well as those for labor per unit of capital, are shown. The product curves for both labor applied to a unit of capital and capital applied to a unit of labor are drawn in the diagram. Reading the horizontal axes from left to right, the ratio of labor to capital is increasing, giving rise to the three familiar product curves for labor [TP_l in Figure 9.5(a); AP_l and MPP_l in Figure 9.5(b)]. Reading the horizontal axes from right to left, the ratio of capital to labor is increasing; however, equal distances do not measure equal increments. The total product curve of labor when the ratio of labor to capital is increased becomes the average product curve for capital when the ratio of capital to labor is increased. The average product curve for labor when the ratio of labor to capital is increased becomes the total product curve for capital when the ratio of capital to labor is increased. Note that the marginal physical product curve for capital, reading from right to left in Figure 9.5(a), lies above the average product curve for capital when average product is increasing, cuts the average product curve at its maximum point, and lies below the average product curve when that curve is decreasing. Note also that the marginal physical product curve for capital reaches zero at the ratio of capital to labor at which the total product of capital is maximum. The marginal physical product of capital is negative where

---

[10]   The boundary lines between stages must be approximations when product schedules are set up in table form. Only on continuous graphs can the exact boundaries between the stages be established.

increases in the quantity of capital per unit of labor lead to decreases in the total product of capital. The three stages for both capital and labor are shown in Figure 9.5.

Stage II Combinations

Stage II contains all the relevant ratios of labor to capital for the firm. The three stages—their relationships and their characteristics—are summed up in Table 9.3. In Stage I for labor, labor is used too sparsely on the capital, and increases in the ratio of labor to capital will raise its average product. The firm should boost the ratio of labor to capital used, at least to the point at which the average product of labor will no longer rise. Such an increase will place the firm in Stage II.

In Stage III for labor, the marginal physical product of labor is negative, meaning that too much labor is used per unit of capital. The ratio of labor to capital should be decreased at least to the point at which the marginal physical product of labor is no longer negative. Now only Stage II ratios remain with us.

The main points emerging from the foregoing discussion are worth emphasizing. The combination of labor and capital that yields maximum efficiency of labor lies at the boundary between Stage I and Stage II for labor. The one that yields maximum efficiency for capital lies at the boundary between Stage II and Stage III for labor.

The introduction of resource costs into the picture puts the economic issues facing the firm into proper perspective. Suppose that capital is so plentiful that it costs nothing at all, while labor is scarce enough to command some price. Because whatever cost outlay the firm makes will go for labor, the firm will achieve its greatest economic efficiency (lowest cost per unit of product) at the ratio of labor to capital that maximizes product per unit of labor. This ratio occurs at the boundary between Stages I and II for labor. The output per unit expenditure will increase through Stage I and decrease through Stages II and III.

Suppose that labor can be had for the asking and that capital is a scarce resource that commands a price. In this case the entire cost outlay goes for capital, and economic efficiency is greatest when the ratio of labor to capital is such that product per unit of capital is

TABLE 9.3 The three stages for labor and capital	Labor Productivity When the Ratio of Labor to Capital Is Increased		Capital Productivity When the Ratio of Capital to Labor Is Increased	
	Stage I	Increasing AP_l	Negative MPP_k	Stage III
	Stage II	Decreasing AP_l and MPP_l, but MPP_l is positive	Decreasing AP_k and MPP_k, but MPP_k is positive	Stage II
	Stage III	Negative MPP_l	Increasing AP_k	Stage I

maximum. Throughout the first two stages, product per unit of capital (and per unit expenditure) increases as the ratio of labor to capital is increased. At the boundary between Stages II and III for labor, product per unit of capital and product per unit of expenditure are maximum. In Stage III it decreases.

Suppose next that both labor and capital are economic resources; that is, both are scarce enough to command a price. Increases in the ratio of labor to capital in Stage I for labor increase both the product per unit of labor and the product per unit of capital. These increases also raise the product obtained per unit of expenditure on both; hence, the firm will move at least to the boundary between Stages I and II. If the firm moves into Stage II, increasing the ratio of labor to capital, the product per unit expenditure on labor drops while that per unit expenditure on capital increases. Which is more important, the rising efficiency of capital or the dwindling efficiency of labor? We shall return to the question in a moment. If the firm moves into Stage III for labor, the product per unit expenditure on capital and on labor both decrease; hence, when both resources have costs, the firm should not go beyond the boundary line between Stages II and III for labor.

Labor-to-capital ratios of Stage I and Stage III are ruled out of the firm's consideration under all circumstances. The firm will not operate in Stage I for either resource when capital is free and when labor has costs, or when labor is free and capital has costs, or when both resources command prices. The same reasoning applies to Stage III. Stage II is left as the possible range of relevant ratios of labor to capital.

Which of the ratios of labor to capital falling within Stage II will the firm use? The answer depends on the comparative costs or prices per unit of capital and labor. We have already observed that if capital is free and labor must be paid, the firm will use the ratio at which Stage II for labor begins. If capital must be paid and labor is free, the firm will use the ratio at which Stage II for labor ends. From these points we can deduce that the less the price of capital relative to the price of labor, the closer the ratio should be to the beginning of labor's Stage II. The less the price of labor relative to the price of capital, the closer the ratios should be to the end of labor's Stage II. Thus, for any resource that a firm employs we can say that the firm should use some ratio of that resource to other resources that falls within Stage II for it.

A Generalized Stage II

Isoquant diagrams enable us to establish a generalized Stage II—not restricted to a linearly homogeneous production function. Consider the isoquant map in Figure 9.6. From it we can read off the set of

FIGURE 9.6
Stage II on an isoquant
diagram

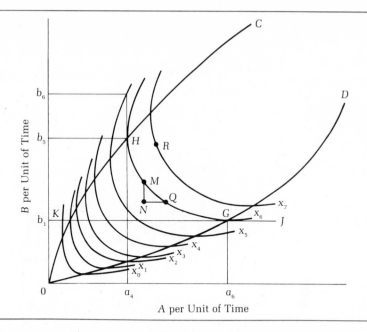

resource combinations that will produce any given level of output. In addition, we can locate the total product curves for resource A—a different one for each different level of resource B with which alternative quantities of A are used. We can also locate the total product curves for resource B—one for each different quantity of A with which alternative quantities of B are used.

On any given isoquant, the marginal rate of technical substitution of A for B is measured by the ratio of the marginal physical product of A to the marginal physical product of B. In Figure 9.6 suppose that combination M of A and B is used to produce x_6 of X. In moving from combination M to combination Q, holding the output level constant at x_6, the firm gives up MN of resource B for NQ of resource A. The reduction in output from giving up MN of B is $MN \times MPP_b$. The increase in output from NQ of A is $NQ \times MPP_a$. Since the reduction in output from giving up B must equal the increase in output from the additional A, then

$$MN \times MPP_b = NQ \times MPP_a,$$

or

$$\frac{MN}{NQ} = \frac{MPP_a}{MPP_b}.$$

Since

$$MRTS_{ab} = \frac{MN}{NQ},$$

then

$$\text{MRTS}_{ab} = \frac{MPP_a}{MPP_b}. \tag{9.2}$$

If the $MRTS_{ab}$ is 2, then MPP_a is twice as large as MPP_b, meaning that an additional unit of A will compensate for the loss of 2 units of B.[11]

The line $0D$ joining the points at which isoquants become horizontal is called a *ridge line*. Consider point G on isoquant x_6. Since the slope of the isoquant, or $MRTS_{ab}$, is zero, it is apparent that MPP_a is also zero at this point. For a movement to the right from point G along line b_1J, the total product of A will decline; and MPP_a is negative for such a movement. This situation means that the firm is moving into Stage III for resource A. The same thing can be said for a movement to the right from every point along $0D$; any combination of A and B to the right of $0D$ is in a generalized Stage III for resource A. The upward slopes of those portions of the isoquants lying to the right of $0D$ reflect the negative MPP_a in Stage III for A.

Line $0C$ joining the points at which isoquants become vertical is also a ridge line. At point H an increase in resource B along line a_4H as extended will decrease the total product of B; that is, MPP_b is negative for the increase. The same thing can be said for any increase in B from a point on $0C$. Consequently, any combination of A and B that lies above $0C$ is in Stage III for resource B.

The combinations comprising this area between ridge lines $0D$ and $0C$ thus constitute a generalized Stage II for both resources. These are the combinations that are relevant for the production decisions of the firm. We need not restrict our thinking to a linearly homogeneous production function or to a production function in which one resource is fixed in quantity. A change in the quantity of

---

[11] The marginal rate of technical substitution of A for B on any given isoquant is found by differentiating the isoquant equation as follows:

$$x_0 = f(a, b)$$

and

$$dx_0 = f_a da + f_b db = 0.$$

Therefore,

$$-\frac{db}{da} = \frac{f_a}{f_b} = \text{MRTS}_{ab}.$$

The partial derivatives f_a and f_b are, respectively, MPP_a and MPP_b. If an isoquant is to be convex to the origin, then

$$\frac{d^2b}{da^2} > 0;$$

that is,

$$-\frac{d^2b}{da^2} = \frac{d}{da}\left(\frac{f_a}{f_b}\right) = \frac{d}{da}(\text{MRTS}_{ab}) < 0,$$

or the $MRTS_{ab}$ is diminishing.

either resource from a combination such as R in the generalized Stage II area will show diminishing returns for that resource.

The Least-cost Combination

Which of the Stage II combinations should a firm use in turning out its product? We assume that the firm's objective is to minimize the cost of producing any given output level; that is, the resource combination should be the one that keeps its cost outlay for that output as low as possible. Another way of stating the objective is to say that whatever cost outlay the firm makes, it should use the resource combination that will produce the greatest amount of product for that outlay.

The problem facing a firm is essentially the same as that facing a consumer. Isoquants show the outputs that the firm gets from "consuming" various combinations of resources. These are analogous to indifference curves, which show the "outputs" of satisfaction a consumer gets from consuming various combinations of goods and services. To complete the analogy we need the firm's counterpart of the consumer's budget line.

This counterpart is called an *isocost*, or "equal cost," curve. Let the firm's total cost outlay on resources A and B be T_1 dollars, while the resource prices are p_a and p_b, respectively. In Figure 9.7 the amount of B that the firm can get if it buys no A is T_1/p_b. The amount of A that the firm can get if it buys no B is T_1/p_a. A line joining these two points shows all combinations of the two that cost outlay T_1 will purchase. This line is the isocost curve.[12] Its slope will have an absolute value of

$$\frac{T_1/p_b}{T_1/p_a} = \frac{T_1}{p_b} \times \frac{p_a}{T_1} = \frac{p_a}{p_b} . \tag{9.3}$$

---

[12] An isocost curve for a firm using two resources, A and B, can be represented by the equation

$$ap_a + bp_b = T_0 \quad \text{or} \quad bp_b = T_0 - ap_a.$$

Dividing through by p_b we obtain

$$b = \frac{T_0}{p_b} - a \frac{p_a}{p_b}$$

in which

$$\frac{T_0}{p_b}$$

is the intercept on the B axis and

$$\frac{p_a}{p_b}$$

is the slope of the curve.

Treating T as a parameter, and assigning different values to it generates a family of parallel isocost curves.

FIGURE 9.7
Cost minimization

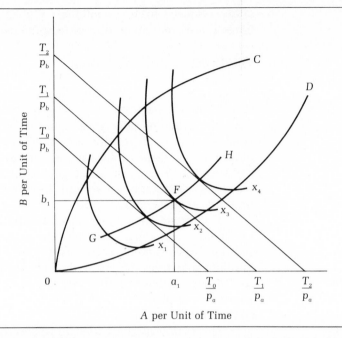

The maximum output obtainable with a given cost outlay is that of the highest isoquant touched by the isocost curve. In Figure 9.7, given the firm's production function, resource prices of p_a and p_b, and a cost outlay of T_1, the maximum amount of X that can be obtained is x_3. This is produced with a_1 of A and b_1 of B. Any other combination that will produce x_3 lies above the isocost curve generated by cost outlay T_1; and as long as p_a and p_b remain constant, other combinations could be obtained only by increasing the cost outlay.

Changes in the firm's cost outlay, given the prices of resources A and B, will shift the isocost curve parallel to itself. If the cost outlay were a smaller amount, T_0, the isocost curve would shift to the left. Thus, in Figure 9.7, T_0 would be the least possible cost of producing output x_2. If the cost outlay were a greater amount, T_2, the isocost curve would shift to the right, and T_2 would be the least possible cost of producing output x_4. The line GH joining all points of equilibrium (least-cost resource combinations) for each possible cost outlay is called the *expansion path* of the firm.

For a firm to minimize the costs of producing a given output level, the marginal rate of technical substitution between any two resources must be equal to the ratio of the prices of those resources. In Figure 9.7 cost outlay T_1 is the minimum cost of producing output level x_3. However, resource combination F, containing a_1 of A and b_1 of B, is the only resource combination that will achieve this result.

What are the conditions that prevail at F? The slope of the isocost curve for outlay T_1 is p_a/p_b throughout its entire length. The slope of isoquant x_3 at point F is measured by MPP_a/MPP_b. Thus, at point F:

$$\frac{p_a}{p_b} = \frac{MPP_a}{MPP_b} = MRTS_{ab}, \tag{9.4}$$

which can be rewritten as

$$\frac{MPP_a}{p_a} = \frac{MPP_b}{p_b}.$$

To secure a given output at the least possible cost, the marginal physical product of a dollar's worth of one resource must be equal to the marginal physical product of a dollar's worth of every other resource used.[13]

Production Possibilities for the Economy

Once we have determined the production functions of individual firms or producing units, we can easily expand the analysis to show what constitutes efficient allocations of resources among producing units. We shall look first at the conditions leading to Pareto optimal-

---

[13] To minimize costs,

$$T = ap_a + bp_b, \tag{1}$$

for a given level of output,

$$x_1 = f(a, b), \tag{2}$$

differentiate (2), obtaining

$$\frac{db}{da} = \frac{f_a}{f_b}. \tag{3}$$

Then take the first partial derivative of T with respect to a, obtaining

$$\frac{\delta T}{\delta a} = p_a + p_b \frac{db}{da}. \tag{4}$$

Substituting (3) in (4) and setting the derivative equal to zero, we have

$$\frac{\delta T}{\delta a} = p_a - p_b \frac{f_a}{f_b} = 0, \tag{5}$$

and the first-order minimum cost condition becomes

$$\frac{p_a}{p_b} = \frac{f_a}{f_b}; \tag{6}$$

that is,

$$MRTS_{ab} = \frac{p_a}{p_b}, \text{ or } \frac{MPP_a}{p_a} = \frac{MPP_b}{p_b}.$$

The second-order condition for minimum cost is that at the point of tangency of the isoquant curve and the isocost line, the isoquant curve be convex to the origin, or

$$\frac{d^2b}{da^2} > 0. \tag{7}$$

ity in the allocation of resources among alternative uses. Then we shall consider the whole range of combinations of goods that an economy may produce efficiently. We shall limit ourselves to a simple economy that produces two goods, X and Y, using two resources, A and B.

Resource Allocation among Products

When two resources, A and B, are used to produce two commodities, X and Y, some distributions of the resources between the two uses will be more efficient than others. An *efficient distribution* is a Pareto optimal distribution—one from which an increase in the output of one good can take place only if the output of the other is decreased. In the discussion that follows, it makes no difference whether the products are produced by the same or by different firms. The isoquant map for product X shows the composite production function for all firms making X. Similarly, the isoquant map for product Y shows the composite production function for that product. We assume that the supplies of resources A and B are fixed amounts per unit of time; that is, the resource supply curves are perfectly inelastic.

The Edgeworth box in Figure 9.8 provides a convenient method of determining which distributions are most efficient. Let the quantity of resource A be $0_x a_5$ or $0_y a'_5$ and the quantity of resource B be $0_x b_5$ or $0_y b'_5$. Isoquants showing production levels of X are convex to the 0_x origin, and those showing production levels of Y are convex to the 0_y origin. Suppose the initial distribution of the two resources is shown at F with $0_x a_1$ of A and $0_x b_1$ of B used in the production of X and with $a_1 a_5$ of A and $b_1 b_5$ of B used in the production of Y.

Are these the most efficient combinations of available resources for the production of X and Y? The output levels are 100 units of

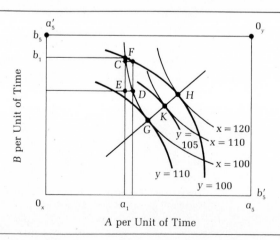

FIGURE 9.8
Efficient resource distributions

each. The slope of the $x = 100$ isoquant at point F, or MPP_a/MPP_b, in the production of X is greater than the slope of the $y = 100$ isoquant, or MPP_a/MPP_b, in the production of Y. This information means that if a unit of A is transferred from the production of Y to the production of X, with the output of X held constant at 100 units, the quantity of B released from the production of X is more than enough to compensate in the production of Y for the release of the unit of A. Suppose, for example, that ED in Figure 9.8 represents the unit of A transferred from the production of Y to the production of X. If the production of X is held at the 100-unit level, EF units of B are released from the production of X. But to hold the output of Y constant at the 100-unit level, only CF units of B are needed to compensate for the unit of A transferred out. Thus, we have a surplus of EC units of B if production of X and Y is held at the original levels.

The released units of B can be used to increase one or both of the product outputs. If the output of X is held at 100 units and the surplus B is turned to the production of Y, this usage constitutes a movement downward to the right around isoquant $x = 100$ and to a Y isoquant above the 100-unit level. Transfers of A from the production of Y to the production of X and of B from the production of X to the production of Y, carried from point F to point G, increase the output of Y to 110 units *without* decreasing the amount of X produced. If the released units of B were used to increase the output of X, holding Y constant at 100 units, a movement from F to H could take place, increasing the production of X to 120 units. The released B can be used to increase the production of both X and Y, moving from point F to some point K between G and H, where an X isoquant is tangent to a Y isoquant. As we have located it, point K represents output levels of 110 units of X and 105 units of Y. Clearly, in all of these cases the efficiency with which resources are used is enhanced.

Any one of the points—G, H, or K—is Pareto optimal. Resource redistributions from F to any one of these points increase the output of at least one of the products without decreasing the output of the other. Once the resource distribution becomes G, H, or K, however, no further transfer of *any kind* can be made without reducing the output of at least one of the goods. A Pareto optimal distribution of resources is said to be an *efficient* distribution.

The condition that must be met for an efficient resource distribution is that $MPP_{ax}/MPP_{bx} = MPP_{ay}/MPP_{by}$; that is, the point locating the efficient distribution in the Edgeworth box must be a point of tangency between an isoquant of one product and an isoquant of the other. In Figure 9.8 the contract curve GKH extended is the locus of all such points. Any point on it, once reached, is Pareto optimal. The analysis tells us nothing about how much X and how much Y the society wants produced. More information is needed to handle this problem. All we have learned is that any distribution of resources, like F, that is not on the contract curve is inefficient. The output of one or both products can be increased by a redistribution of the resources between the two uses to a distribution that lies on a segment of the contract curve like GH—within the arcs of the isoquants that pass through F.

Transformation Curves

The information provided by the contract curve of Figure 9.8 is frequently displayed in the form of a *transformation curve* for the two products, showing the combinations of them that can be produced efficiently, given the resource supplies and techniques of production available for producing them. In Figure 9.8, if all the resources available in the economy are used to produce Y, the total output of the product is shown by the Y isoquant that passes through 0_x. If this amount of Y is y_5, we can plot the combination as point M in Figure 9.9. Product X can be produced only if some of product Y is given up, with resources being transferred from the production of Y to the production of X. In Figure 9.8 the process of giving up successively more Y to produce successively more X is represented by a movement along the contract curve from 0_x toward 0_y. Each pair of tangent isoquants provides the X and Y output combinations that are plotted as the transformation curve in Figure 9.9. The larger the output of X, the smaller the amount of Y that can be produced; thus, the transformation curve must slope downward to the right. If all of the available resources are used to produce X, the total output is x_5 units per unit of time, as is shown by point N in Figure 9.9.

The average slope $\Delta y/\Delta x$ of the transformation curve between two points close together, such as R and S, measures the *marginal rate of transformation* of X for Y, or MRT_{xy}.[14] This is defined as the amount of Y that must be given up to produce an additional unit of X. The MRT_{xy} is shown as increasing in Figure 9.9, meaning that the less Y and the more X the economy chooses to produce, the more Y it must give up to produce an additional unit of X. The primary explanation of this relationship is that some of the economy's resources tend to be more specialized to the production of X, while others are much more useful in producing Y. When all of the economy's resources are used in producing Y, not much Y must be sacrificed to produce a unit of X, since those resources more specialized to the production of X are the ones that are transferred. However, the larger the output of X becomes, and the smaller the output of Y becomes,

---

[14]   In terms of calculus, MRT_{xy} at any given point on the transformation curve is the slope of the curve at that point, that is, dy/dx.

FIGURE 9.9
Transformation curve
for two products

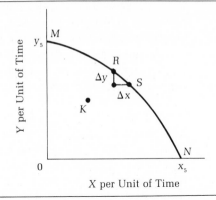

the more necessary it is to transfer those resources more specialized to the production of Y to production of the additional X. Consequently, larger and larger amounts of Y must be given up for one-unit increases in the output of X.

The transformation model provides an excellent summary of the production choices available to a society. If some of its resources are unemployed, the combination of goods will be one such as K lying below the transformation curve. The output of one or both products can be increased without decreasing the output of any other good. An inefficient distribution of resources brings about the same result. The combinations on the curve show the production possibilities or alternatives when resources are fully employed and are distributed or allocated efficiently. They are Pareto optimal production possibilities. We will return to the model in the welfare analysis of Chapter 19.

Applications: Production Principles

Least-cost combinations of resources are basic to efficient production. How they can be used in decision making by production units is illustrated in the following cases.

Natural Gas versus Coal in Power Generation

Many power plants in the late 1970s were ordered by the Department of Energy to shift from the use of natural gas to coal in the generation of electricity. The impact of such an order on an individual firm is to (1) curtail the output attainable with a given cost outlay or (2) increase the total cost of producing a given output. The principles of production illustrate the nature of these options.

Suppose the firm, prior to the order, is spending T_1 dollars on resources in Figure 9.10. Let the horizontal axis measure Btus of energy per day, and let p_{e1} be the price per Btu when the firm uses natural gas. The lower end of the isocost line is determined by T_1/p_{e1}. On the vertical axis we measure total expenditure on other resources. Since the price of a dollar's worth of other resources is \$1, the upper end of the isocost line is $T_1/\$1$ or T_1. The maximum output of the firm for the given cost outlay is x_2 kilowatt hours of electricity. The firm will be purchasing enough natural gas to provide e_1 Btus of energy and will be spending O_1 dollars on other resources.

The order to shift to coal raises the price per Btu to p_{e2}, rotating the isocost clockwise until its lower end becomes T_1/p_{e2}. The expenditure of T_1 dollars will now produce a maximum output of only x_1 kilowatt hours of electricity. Or, if output were to be increased back to the x_2 level, an additional total expenditure on resources amounting to T_1T_2 would be required.

Several interesting points or questions are raised by this case. Since natural gas is more efficient than coal, why should firms be ordered to shift to coal? The usual answer is that supplies of natural gas are running out and remaining reserves need to be conserved. Yet

FIGURE 9.10
Gas versus coal in power generation

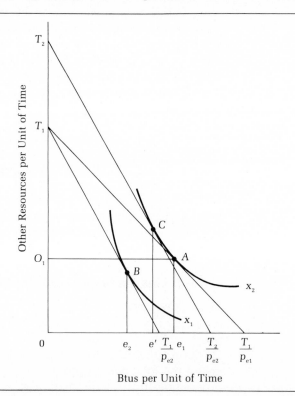

the Federal Energy Regulatory Commission still maintains ceiling prices on natural gas that are below the equilibrium level. Artificially low prices for natural gas encourage greater use of it relative to coal, thus providing incentives contrary to both conservation and the orders to shift to coal. On the other hand, mandatory shifts from gas to coal reduce the demand for gas and make it easier for FERC to hold to its price ceiling for gas. And the price ceiling for gas inhibits the discovery and recovery of additional supplies. Obviously it is much easier to raise questions than it is to answer them.

Road Salt Use in Midwestern Cities

Relatively little salt is manufactured for table consumption. Most of it is sold to cities and counties to be spread on roads for the removal of winter ice, an activity that may strike Californians as odd but is well understood by most midwesterners. A series of strikes and natural disasters during the summer of 1979 caused the manufacture of salt to decline by about 10 percent, as described in the following article.[15]

> To hundreds of highway purchasing agents in the Midwest, lowly salt has suddenly become white gold.
>
> In recent weeks, state and municipal road departments have discovered they'll be paying as much as double last year's prices for de-icing salt, or be forced to go without it altogether. While salt producers say they're sympathetic to the problem, one acknowledges that "as a company, we're delighted with the effect this situation is having on prices."
>
> The situation is this: In 1977, the Department of Energy took over a huge rock-salt mine in Louisiana from Morton-Norwich Products Inc.'s Morton Salt Co. for use as a "strategic" crude-oil storage facility. Then, last June, there was an explosion that halted production at another Louisiana mine owned by Cargill Inc. As a result of the explosion, in which five persons were killed, mining regulations were tightened at other Louisiana salt-mining operations, thus reducing their productivity.
>
> Also this summer, workers at Akzona Inc.'s International Salt Co. operation in Cleveland began a three-month strike. And earlier this month, Hurricane David wiped out a huge crop of salt being extracted from seawater at a solar-salt farm in the Bahamas owned by Diamond Crystal Salt Co.
>
> Thus, the highway salt market will be 10% short on supplies this winter, the Salt Institute, a trade group, estimates.

---

[15] Thomas Petzinger Jr., "Road Departments Find Price for Salt Has as Much as Doubled from Last Year," *The Wall Street Journal*, 28 September 1979. Reprinted by permission of *The Wall Street Journal*, © Dow Jones & Company, Inc. 1979. All rights reserved.

Road Maintenance

Wintertime road maintenance is by far the nation's biggest salt market, accounting for about 11 million tons, or roughly 44% of the industry's annual output of 25 million tons. Table salt and food processing account for less than one million tons a year, and water conditioning and agriculture just two million tons each, so the current shortage isn't expected to have any serious effect on those markets.

The chemical industry consumes about four million tons a year in chlorine and soda ash production and in some quarters is experiencing a supply problem. Pennwalt Corp., for example, was "cut off" by Cargill after the mine explosion and hasn't yet arranged an alternative supply, according to a spokesman.

Among users of de-icing salt, the impact varies widely. The city of Chicago, for example, advertised for bids from salt producers early in the May-to-September bidding season and, as a result, arranged for delivery of the 202,000 tons it will require this winter. However, the city is paying Morton $15.96 a ton, up 27% from last year.

Things are far worse among government units that entered the bidding process later on. Cincinnati, for example, advertised for bids in August, two weeks earlier than in prior years but still late enough that the big suppliers were sold out. The city finally did arrange a winter supply—which it will have to stretch with sand—but only by paying $30 a ton, or double last year's price. And when McKeesport, Pa., opened its bids last week, the low offer was $29.48 a ton, up from $22 a ton paid for each of last year's 1,800 tons.

Stay Out of McKeesport

"Council flatly rejected the bids" as out of line, says Patricia Monoyoudis, McKeesport's Finance Administrator. "We're just going to have to play it by ear day by day until the snow starts flying. My advice to you is: Stay out of McKeesport this winter," she says.

Part of the high cost of salt this year, according to the producers, is a heavy increase in shipping charges, which in many cases account for one-half of the total cost. Most Louisiana salt goes to the Midwest, via barges along the Mississippi and Ohio rivers and then by rail or truck. According to Diamond Crystal, barge rates between Louisiana and southern Ohio have jumped 65% in the last year, partly because of heavy demand by grain shippers.

Some big salt users have been forced to turn overseas for salt, which is high in price to begin with and also must be shipped at an added cost. The Ohio Department of Transportation, for example, recently had to arrange a supply from Chile and Mexico for 22 of the state's 88 counties. The average price was about $37 a ton, compared with an average of about $23 a ton for the domestic variety.

This reduction in supply squeezed many midwestern cities, owing to the higher prices they had to pay for deicing salts for the coming winter. The isoquant/isocost analysis presented in this chapter helps us conceptualize the consequences that the higher salt prices had and sheds light on which of the cities mentioned—Chicago, Cincinnati, and McKeesport, Pa.—have adjusted to the new constraint in the most economical manner.

Municipal governments are generally responsible for maintaining public roads and streets in safe driving conditions. In a sense, cities are in the "business" of "producing," among other things, safe travel for motorists and pedestrians alike. Safety levels—avoiding accidents with their costs in lost property and lives—is the output, and such inputs as labor, machines, bulldozers, ambulances, and road salts are used in its production. This process is conceptualized in Figure 9.11 below, for a single city, let us say, Cincinnati. The two substitute inputs are road salts, measured along the X axis, versus sand (or other resources), measured along the Y axis. The isocost curves show alternative road maintenance budgets that may be spent entirely on salt, entirely on sand, or on some combination of the two inputs. The different levels of road maintenance budgets are indicated by T_0, T_1, and T_2. The initial price of salt is p_{s1} and the price of sand is p_o. The different levels of road safety that can be achieved for

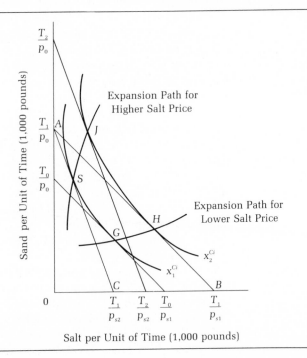

FIGURE 9.11
Salt versus other inputs in Cincinnati

various budget levels are indicated by isoquants such as x_1^{Ci} and X_2^{Ci}. The tangencies between isoquants and total outlay lines show the least-cost combinations for obtaining given levels of safety, or the maximum amounts of road safety that can be obtained for given levels of outlay. If the price of salt before the price increase was p_{s1} and the price of sand was p_{o1}, the relevant expansion path for Cincinnati was GH. If T_1 was the original budget level, the city's optimum combination is H, achieving safety level x_2^{Ci}.

When the price of salt rises from p_{s1} to p_{s2}, the total outlay line shifts from AB to AC. For the same T_1 budget, Cincinnati's optimum combination of salt and sand is S, which contains less salt. Road safety has declined to x_1^{Ci}. By increasing its budget from T_1 to T_2, the city can remain on isoquant level x_2^{Ci} with combination J and is buying less salt than it was originally. Judging from the article, this appears to be what the city fathers decided to do. They bought less salt at the higher price and decided to stretch it by using more sand than previously. They also increased the budget. But they kept road safety at approximately its previous level.

A somewhat different adjustment seems to have occurred in Chicago. The Chicago city fathers appeared determined to purchase the same quantity of salt after the price increase as they did before, and their solution to the higher-salt-price dilemma appears to be economically inefficient. Chicago went straight into the salt market and purchased its full "requirement" of road salts, presumably based on the amount it had needed the previous year, and paid a stiff price for that requirement. Figure 9.12 shows, however, that it would be inefficient for Chicago to use the same quantity of salt after the price increase as it did before *unless* it simultaneously wanted to increase the level of road safety that it produced. Before the price of salt went up from p_{s1} to p_{s2}, Chicago spent T_1 dollars and achieved the x_2^{Ch} level of road safety with combination J of salt and sand. If the city insists on buying the same amount of salt and sand after the price of salt rises, it must increase its budget to T_3 and the total outlay line GH would pass through J. Since it has the same slope as AC, Chicago could achieve the higher level of road safety x_3^{Ch} with an outlay of T_3 and combination M of salt and sand. But if it elects to use combination J after the price increase in salt, it is wasting resources. It would do better with combinations L, using less salt and more sand to produce safety level x_2^{Ch}.

The city of McKeesport entered the road salt market very late in the year, well after Chicago and Cincinnati and after salt prices had climbed substantially. The city found the price to be so high that it decided not to buy road salts at all and simply to "tough it out" and hope for a mild winter. As Figure 9.13 demonstrates, the city necessarily accepts a lower level of road safety because of this decision.

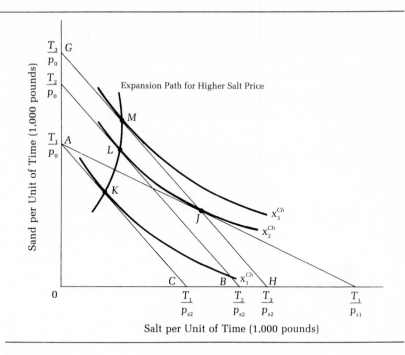

FIGURE 9.12
Salt versus other inputs in Chicago

Sand per Unit of Time (1,000 pounds)

$\dfrac{T_3}{p_0}$ G

$\dfrac{T_2}{p_0}$

Expansion Path for Higher Salt Price

M

$\dfrac{T_1}{p_0}$ A

L

K

J

x_3^{Ch}

x_2^{Ch}

C   B x_1^{Ch} H

0

$\dfrac{T_1}{p_{s2}}$ $\dfrac{T_2}{p_{s2}}$ $\dfrac{T_3}{p_{s2}}$ $\dfrac{T_1}{p_{s1}}$

Salt per Unit of Time (1,000 pounds)

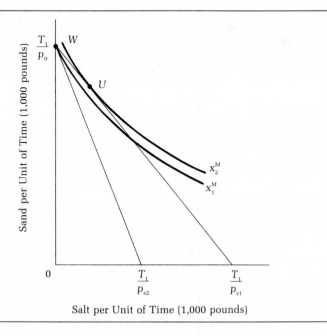

FIGURE 9.13
Salt versus other inputs in McKeesport

Sand per Unit of Time (1,000 pounds)

$\dfrac{T_1}{p_0}$ W

U

x_2^M

x_1^M

0

$\dfrac{T_1}{p_{s2}}$ $\dfrac{T_1}{p_{s1}}$

Salt per Unit of Time (1,000 pounds)

Prior to the increase in the price of salt, the city council would have used combination U of salt and sand, achieving a safety level of x_2^M. If the council correctly understands the city's production function for road safety, then at best its decision to buy no salt at all after the price increase indicates a corner solution at W and acceptance of lower safety level x_1^M. The city's financial expert was wise in advising motorists to stay out of McKeesport during the winter!

Summary

The principles of production lay the foundation for the analyses of costs, supplies, resource pricing and employment, resource allocation, and product distribution. These topics will be considered in later chapters.

The term *production function* is applied to the physical relationship between resource inputs and product output of a firm. Product output is determined partly by the quantities of resource inputs and partly by the techniques of production used by the firm. The production function can be summed up graphically as a production surface and displayed in two dimensions as an isoquant map.

Holding the quantities of all other resources constant, the quantity of any one resource can be varied and the effects on product output can be observed. As the quantity of the variable resource is increased, the law of diminishing returns will become effective. We distinguished among total product, marginal physical product, and average product of the variable resource. The product schedules or product curves of the variable resource were divided into three stages. Stage I is characterized by increasing average product. In Stage II average and marginal physical products of the variable resource are decreasing, but its marginal physical product is still positive. In Stage III the marginal physical product of the variable resource is negative. We deduced that only those ratios of the variable resource to other resources lying within Stage II may be economically efficient for the firm to use.

The precise combination of variable resources that the firm should use depends on the marginal rate of technical substitution among those resources and on their respective prices. To maximize product with a given cost outlay, or to minimize cost for a given amount of product, resources should be combined in ratios such that the $MRTS_{ab} = p_a/p_b$; that is, so that the marginal physical product per dollar's worth of one equals the marginal physical product per dollar's worth of each other resource used.

An Edgeworth box is useful in showing the distributions of resources among products that are efficient in a Pareto optimal sense.

The resulting contract curve provides the necessary information for establishing a transformation curve showing the optimal production possibilities for the economy.

Suggested Readings

Baumol, William J. *Economic Theory and Operations Analysis*, 4th ed. Englewood Cliffs, N.J.: Prentice-Hall, 1977, Chap. 11, pp. 267–89.

Cassels, John M. "On the Law of Variable Proportions," *Explorations in Economics*. New York: McGraw-Hill, 1936, pp. 223–36. Reprinted in *Readings in the Theory of Income Distribution*. Philadelphia: P. Blakiston's Sons, 1946, pp. 103–18.

Heady, Earl O. *Economics of Agricultural Production and Resource Use*. Englewood Cliffs, N. J.: Prentice-Hall, 1952, Chap. 2.

Henderson, James M., and Quandt, Richard E. *Microeconomic Theory*, 3rd ed. New York: McGraw-Hill, 1980, pp. 64–80, 105–33.

Knight, Frank H., *Risk, Uncertainty, and Profit*. Boston: Houghton Mifflin, 1921, pp. 94–104.

Questions and Exercises

1 Draw an isoquant map for a firm that uses two resources, A and B, to manufacture product X. Explain
  a the downward slope of an isoquant
  b nonintersection of any two isoquants
  c convexity to the origin of an isoquant
  d the ridge lines
  e the three stages for each resource
  f output maximization, given the firm's cost outlay and the prices of the resources.

2 If a fixed amount of labor and a fixed amount of capital are available to produce tractors and airplanes, illustrate and explain
  a the conditions for an efficient allocation of the resources between the two products
  b how a transformation curve for the two products is developed
  c the probable slope of the transformation curve.

3 During World War II the United States built a number of airstrips on mainland China utilizing local labor. Both men and women sat around rock piles breaking up rock into gravel with hammers. Concrete was mixed by hand and was carried to the runway forms in baskets on the heads of long lines of workers.

Would it have been more efficient to have brought in rock crushers and concrete mixers to do the job? Explain carefully.

4 The Acme Manufacturing Company has been engaged in the production of metal spools, all of a uniform type, for many years. Production schedules for labor and machinery are independent of each other and of other resources. On a monthly basis they are estimated to be as follows:

Labor Employed	Spools per Month	Machinery (physical units)	Spools per Month
1	200	1	300
2	370	2	430
3	500	3	500
4	600	4	545
5	675	5	570
6	740	6	586
7	800	7	600
8	855	8	612
9	900	9	622
10	940	10	630
11	970	11	635

The company is currently employing 7 workers and 7 units of machinery.

a What is the average product of workers? Of machinery? Explain.

b What is the marginal physical product of workers? Of machinery? Explain.

c If one additional worker were to be employed, how many units of machinery could be given up without loss of production? Explain.

d If a monthly cost outlay of $5,100 is to be made and the respective monthly prices of workers and units of machinery are $600 and $100, what combination of workers and machinery should be used?

e What is the average cost of spools at this point? Explain.

Costs of Production

Costs of production constitute a major determinant of the quantities of a good or service that will be placed on the market. To understand supply and quantities supplied, we must understand costs, which in turn are rooted in the principles of production. We shall consider first the meaning of costs and, second, the short-run and long-run cost curves of the individual firm or production unit.

The Concept of Costs

The concept of costs of production as used in economic analysis differs somewhat from common usage of the term. Common usage ordinarily conveys some idea of the *expenditures* of a firm necessary in turning out a product, but it is not always clear which categories of expenditure are included and which are excluded. The economic concept is more precise and consistent. To build up the concept as it is used in economics, we shall discuss first the alternative cost principle and then the implicit and explicit aspects of costs.

The Alternative Cost Principle

The basic idea of the alternative cost principle is contained in the transformation curve of the last chapter. Under conditions of full employment, and when resources are efficiently allocated among goods and services, an increase in the output of any one product requires the sacrifice of some amounts of alternative products. If a certain kind of labor is used in making both washing machines and refrigerators, an increase in the output of refrigerators entails a reduction in the quantity of washing machines available, since labor must be withdrawn from that use. If steel is used in making automobiles and football stadiums, an increase in football stadiums leaves less steel available for making automobiles, reducing the number of cars that are manufactured. Thus, an increase in the production of any commodity requires the sacrifice of some value of alternative products.

Economists define the costs of production of a particular good as the value of the forgone alternative items that resources used in its production could have turned out. This principle is called the *alternative cost principle*, or the *opportunity cost principle*. The costs of resources to a firm are their values in their best alternative uses. The firm, to secure the services of resources, usually must pay for them amounts equal to what they can earn in those alternative uses. In the earlier example, the cost of the labor in the manufacture of washing machines is the value of refrigerators that the labor could have produced. Unless the manufacturer of washing machines pays approximately that amount for the labor, it will go into or remain in refrigerator production. The steel example is similar. Automobile manufacturers must pay enough for steel to attract or hold the desired amounts away from alternative employments of steel—and its value in the alternative employments is its cost in automobile manufacturing from the economist's point of view.

Explicit and Implicit Costs

The outlays made by a firm (which we usually think of as its expenses) are the *explicit costs of production*. They consist of explicit payments for resources bought outright or hired by the firm. The firm's payroll, payments for raw and semifinished materials, payments of overhead costs of various kinds, and costs charged against sinking funds and depreciation reserves are examples of explicit costs. They are the costs that accountants list as the firm's expenses, and they tend to be determined by the alternative cost principle.

Implicit costs of production are the costs of self-owned, self-employed resources frequently overlooked in computing the expenses of the firm. The costs of a single proprietor who sets aside no salary for himself or herself, but who takes the firm's "profits" as payment for services rendered, is an excellent example. A still more common implicit cost is the return to the owners of a firm on their investment in plant, equipment, and inventories.

The consideration of the firm owner's salary as a cost can be easily explained. In accordance with the alternative cost principle, the cost of the single proprietor's services in putting out the firm's product is the value of the forgone alternative product that would have resulted had the owner worked for someone else in a similar capacity. We consider as a part of the firm's costs, then, a salary for the proprietor equal to the value of the owner's services in his or her best alternative employment. This cost is an implicit cost, which does not take the form of an "expense" outlay.

The consideration of a return on investment as a cost of production is more tricky. Return on investment usually is thought of as coming from the firm's profits rather than as being a cost of production. A simple case is a single proprietor who has invested in (purchased) the land, building, and equipment for the business establishment. A return on the investment equal to what the proprietor could have earned had the same amount been invested elsewhere in the economy is an implicit cost of production. Had the proprietor invested elsewhere, the investment would have been used to purchase resources to produce other goods. What those resources could earn in those alternative uses would determine the return on investment that could have been earned had the proprietor invested there.

The same principle on a larger scale applies to a corporation. Stockholders are the real owners of the corporation's land, plant, equipment, and inventories[1]—they have invested money in resources used by the corporation. Dividends equal to what stockholders could earn had they invested elsewhere in the economy are implicit costs of production from the point of view of the economist. The costs of resources obtained by the firm with stockholders' investments are, according to the alternative cost principle, the value of the alternative products forgone by holding the investment where it is. To hold the investment where it is, the corporation must pay a return to stockholders about equal to what they could earn if they should invest elsewhere in the economy.

Cost, Resource Prices, and Efficiency

Costs of production incurred by the firm consist of both explicit and implicit obligations to resource owners. These obligations are just large enough to obtain and hold resources in the employment of the firm. Usually the firm's "expenses" include the explicit obligations only. Thus, costs of production as viewed by the economist differ somewhat from (and will usually be larger than) the firm's accounting "expenses."

Our discussion of costs is oversimplified to some extent. We shall be concerned with a firm's costs of production at various alternative product outputs. Costs at each output depend on (1) the values of the resources the firm uses—that is, resource prices—and (2) the techniques available for combining resources to produce the output. We shall eliminate the problem of resource pricing by assuming that the firm is a pure competitor in the purchase of resources; that is, the single firm takes such a small proportion of the total amount of any given resource in existence that, by itself, it cannot influence the resource price. The firm can get all it wants of any one resource at a

---

[1] Additionally, the corporation may have borrowed money by selling bonds to increase the amounts of its plant and equipment. Thus, bondholders, too, have invested money in the corporation. Interest payments on the bonds—the return on the bondholders' investments—are explicit payments and are recorded as costs by the corporation, as well as by the economist.

constant price per unit. Thus, differences in costs at different output levels result from differences in the efficiency of the techniques that the firm can use at each of those outputs. The effects on costs of possible changes in resource prices, as a result of output changes on the part of a firm, can be taken into consideration later on, after resource pricing has been discussed.

The Short-run and Long-run Viewpoints

In analyzing a firm's costs of production a distinction is made between the short-run and long-run viewpoints. These are essentially planning rather than calendar time concepts; they refer to the time horizon over which the firm's planning stretches. We shall examine them in turn.

The Short Run

A planning period so short that the firm is unable to consider varying the quantities of some resources used is called the *short run*. It is possible to think of a period so short that no resource can be varied in quantity. Then, as the planning period is lengthened, it becomes possible to adjust the quantity of one. A progressive lengthening of the period permits more and more resources to become variable in quantity until, ultimately, they all fall into the variable category. Any period between that in which the quantity of no resources can be changed and that in which all resources but one are variable can legitimately be called the short run. However, to facilitate exposition we ordinarily use a more restricting definition.

The possibilities of varying the quantities of different resources depend on their nature and the terms of hire or purchase. Some, such as land and buildings, may be leased by the firm for given time periods; or, if they are owned outright, it may take some time to acquire additional amounts or to dispose of a part of the quantities already owned. The number of top management personnel is not ordinarily readily variable. Heavy machinery especially designed for the firm's use cannot be quickly increased or decreased in amount. Typically, the period required for variation in the quantities of such resources as power, labor, transportation, raw materials, and semifinished materials will be shorter than that required for variation in the amounts of land, buildings, heavy machinery, and top management.

The usual interpretation of the short-run concept is a planning period so brief that the firm does not have time to vary the quantities of such resources as land, buildings, heavy machinery, and top management. These are the firm's short-run *fixed resources*. This concept of the short run does allow changes in the quantities of such resources as labor, raw materials, and the like. These are the firm's *variable resources*.[2]

The calendar time length of the short run will vary from one industry to another. For some, the short run may be very short indeed. Such will be the case where the quantities of fixed resources used by a firm in the industry are typically small or can be added to or subtracted from in a short space of time. Various textile and many service industries are cases in point. For others, the short run may be several years. It takes time to add to the productive capacity of an automobile firm or a basic steel firm.

The quantities of fixed resources used determine the size of the firm's plant.[3] The size of plant sets the upper limit to the amount of output per unit of time that the firm is capable of producing. The firm can vary its output up to that limit, however, by increasing or decreasing the quantities of variable resources used in the fixed size of plant.

The fixed resources, or the plant, may be compared with a meat grinder. The variable resource will be analogous to unground meat. In this case the output of ground meat per unit of time can be varied by changing the input of unground meat. There will be some upper limit beyond which the output cannot be increased, regardless of how much unground meat is on hand to push through the grinder.

The capital and labor example of the preceding chapter can also be viewed in a short-run context. We can think of the fixed amount of capital as the fixed size of plant and the variable quantities of labor as the variable resources used with it.

The Long Run

No definitional difficulties are presented by the *long run*. It is a planning period long enough for the firm to be able to vary the quantities per unit of time of all resources used. Thus, all resources are variable. No problem of classifying resources as fixed or variable exists. The firm can vary its size of plant as it desires, from very small to large or vice versa. Infinitesimal variations in size are usually possible.

---

[2] A clear distinction between resources that are fixed and resources that are variable is not always possible. For some firms several of the resources listed here as "variable" may require more time for alterations in quantity taken than some listed as "fixed." For example, contractual arrangements for the purchase of power or labor may be such that quantities of these cannot readily be varied. Yet it may be possible for the firm to lease out, sublease, or sell some part of its "fixed" resources on short notice.

[3] The term *plant* is used here in a broad context to cover the whole scope of the firm's operations. A firm may operate several establishments at different locations; we shall view these all together as the firm's "plant."

Short-run Cost Curves

Classification of resources in the short run as fixed and variable enables us to classify their costs as fixed and variable also. *Fixed costs* are the costs of fixed resources. *Variable costs* are those of variable resources. The distinction between fixed and variable costs is basic to the discussions of total, average, and marginal costs that follow.

Total Cost Curves

In the short run, the total costs of an enterprise depend on the firm's size and on the output level produced. The component parts of total costs are total fixed costs and total variable costs. We shall examine these in turn.

Total Fixed Costs The costs per unit of time of its fixed resources constitute the firm's *total fixed costs.* They include the salaries that must be paid top management to keep it intact over time. They include the costs of holding and maintaining its land—that is, what the land would be worth in alternative uses over time. They include the cost of keeping investment in plant and equipment from shifting away from the firm. Short-run total fixed costs are thus the alternative costs of the fixed resources. They are the obligations that the firm must incur to keep these resources from slipping away in the long run. Note that total fixed costs depend on the size of the firm's operation—its size of plant. They do not depend on the output level at which the plant is operated. So, we can say that a firm's short-run total fixed costs are constant for all possible levels of output.

A hypothetical total fixed cost schedule is presented in Table 10.1; the corresponding total fixed cost curve is plotted in Figure 10.2. Note that the total fixed cost curve is independent of the output level, is parallel to the quantity axis, and lies above it by the amount of the total fixed costs.

Total Variable Costs The alternative costs, or the total obligations that a firm incurs for its variable resources, constitute its *total variable costs.* Unlike its total fixed costs, the firm's total variable costs must vary directly with its output. Larger outputs require greater quantities of variable resources and, hence, larger cost obligations. For example, the larger the output of an oil refinery, the more crude oil input it must use and the larger will be its crude oil costs.

The shape of the total variable cost curve with respect to the firm's output will depend on whether increasing or diminishing returns to variable resources exist as larger and larger quantities of them are used with the firm's given size of plant. Consider the simple case in which a firm uses only one variable resource, resource A. A

Table 10.1 Total cost schedules for a firm	Quantity of X	Total Fixed Cost	Total Variable Cost	Total Cost
	1	$100	$ 40	$140
	2	100	70	170
	3	100	85	185
	4	100	96	196
	5	100	104	204
	6	100	110	210
	7	100	115	215
	8	100	120	220
	9	100	126	226
	10	100	134	234
	11	100	145	245
	12	100	160	260
	13	100	180	280
	14	100	206	306
	15	100	239	339
	16	100	280	380
	17	100	330	430
	18	100	390	490
	19	100	461	561
	20	100	544	644

conventional total product curve for A is drawn on the right-hand side of Figure 10.1, showing increasing returns to A for quantities up to a_3 and diminishing returns for larger quantities. The point of inflection on the TP_a curve is at F.

The TP_a curve is easily converted into the total variable cost curve of the firm once the price of the variable resource A is known. Let the price of A be p_{a1}, so that for any given input of A total variable cost is that quantity of A multiplied by its price. Measure

FIGURE 10.1
Relation between the TVC curve and the total product curve of variable resources

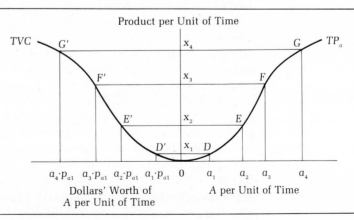

FIGURE 10.2
Total cost curves of a
firm

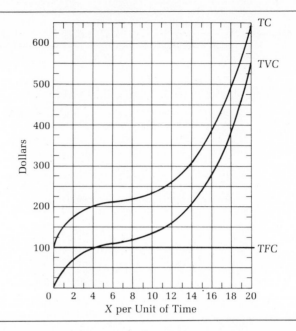

total variable cost (dollars' worth of A) on a horizontal axis stretching to the left of the origin. Total variable cost when a_1 of A is used is
$a_1 \times p_{a1}$, and the corresponding output of product is x_1. On the
left-hand diagram, these coordinates locate point D' on the firm's
total variable cost curve. Points E', F', and G' are located in a similar
manner, and all such points together trace out the firm's total variable cost curve.

The TVC curve in the left-hand panel is a mirror image of the
TP_a curve in the right-hand panel. If, for example, p_{a1} is $1 and we
let the distance on the horizontal axis that measures 1 unit of A to the
right of the origin be equal to the distance that measures $1's worth
of A to the left of the origin, the reflection is exact. The point of
inflection F' on TVC is the precise counterpart of F on TP_a. Both
curves are concave upward from the origin to their respective inflection points and are concave downward beyond the inflection points
because of increasing returns to A for quantities up to a_3 and decreasing returns for still greater quantities. If we rotate the left-hand
side of the diagram 90 degrees clockwise, letting the product axis
become the horizontal axis, the TVC curve is concave downward out
to the inflection point and concave upward beyond that point.

In the usual case, a firm uses several variable resources rather
than only one, but the principles at work are the same as those of the
single resource example. With a given size of plant—a given complex of fixed resources—we can think of increasing the complex of

variable resources used. Since we start from a very small complex, increasing returns to the variable resources may occur—equal increments in outlays on the entire complex may result in larger and larger increments in output—and the *TVC* curve, consequently, will be downward. As larger and larger outlays are made, however, diminishing returns to the complex come into play—equal increments in *TVC* result in smaller and smaller increments in output—and the *TVC* curve becomes concave upward. At some output level the fixed size of plant will have reached its absolute maximum capacity to produce. Now the total variable cost curve turns straight up. Increased obligations incurred for still larger quantities of variable resources will lead to no increases in output at all. The total variable cost schedule of Table 10.1, plotted as the *TVC* curve of Figure 10.2, reflects the results of increasing and diminishing returns to variable resources.

Total Costs   The summation of total fixed costs and total variable costs for various output levels comprise the *total costs* of the firm for those output levels. The total cost column of Table 10.1 is obtained by adding total fixed cost and total variable cost at each level of output. Likewise, the total cost curve of Figure 10.2 is obtained by summing the *TFC* curve and the *TVC* curve vertically. The *TC* curve and the *TVC* curve must necessarily have the same shape, since each increase in output per unit of time raises total costs and total variable costs by the same amount. The output increase does not affect total fixed costs. The *TC* curve lies above the *TVC* curve by an amount equal to *TFC* at all output levels.[4]

Per Unit Cost Curves

In price and output analysis, *per unit cost curves* are used extensively—more so than total cost curves are. Per unit cost curves show the same kind of information as total cost curves, but in a different form. The per unit cost curves are the average fixed cost curve, the average variable cost curve, the average cost curve, and the marginal cost curve.

Average Fixed Costs   The fixed costs per unit of product at various levels of output, or the *average fixed costs*, are obtained by dividing total fixed costs by those outputs. Thus, the average fixed cost col-

---

[4]   The short-run total cost function can be represented mathematically as

$$C = k + f(x),$$

in which

$$TC = C$$
$$TFC = k$$
$$TVC = f(x).$$

umn of Table 10.2 is computed by dividing the total fixed cost column of Table 10.1 by the different quantities of X. The average fixed cost schedule is plotted in Figure 10.3 as the AFC curve.

The greater the output of the firm, the smaller average fixed costs will be. Since total fixed costs remain the same regardless of output, fixed costs are spread over more units of output; and each unit of output bears a smaller share. Therefore, the average fixed cost curve is downward sloping to the right throughout its entire length. As output per unit of time increases, it approaches—but never reaches—the quantity axis. Thus, it becomes apparent that firms with large fixed costs—the railroads, for example, with their tremendous fixed charges on roadbeds and rolling stock—can substantially reduce their fixed costs per unit by producing larger outputs.

Average Variable Costs Variable costs per unit of output are computed in the same way as fixed costs per unit of output. The average variable cost column of Table 10.2 is obtained by dividing total variable costs in Table 10.1 at various outputs by those outputs. Plotted graphically, the average variable cost column of Table 10.2 becomes the AVC curve of Figure 10.3.

The *average variable cost* curve usually will have a U shape.

TABLE 10.2 Per unit cost schedules of a firm	Quantity of X	Average Fixed Cost	Average Variable Cost	Average Cost	Marginal Cost
	1	$100.00	$40.00	$140.00	—
	2	50.00	35.00	85.00	30
	3	33.33	28.33	61.66	15
	4	25.00	24.00	49.00	11
	5	20.00	20.80	40.80	8
	6	16.67	18.33	35.00	6
	7	14.29	16.43	30.72	5
	8	12.50	15.00	27.50	5
	9	11.11	14.00	25.11	6
	10	10.00	13.40	23.40	8
	11	9.09	13.18	22.27	11
	12	8.33	13.33	21.66	15
	13	7.69	13.85	21.54	20
	14	7.14	14.72	21.86	26
	15	6.67	15.93	22.60	33
	16	6.25	17.50	23.75	41
	17	5.88	19.41	25.29	50
	18	5.55	21.67	27.22	60
	19	5.26	24.27	29.53	71
	20	5.00	27.20	32.20	83

FIGURE 10.3
Per unit cost curves of
a firm

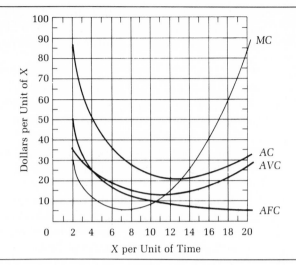

This shape can be explained by the principles of production. Suppose, for example, that a factory is designed to employ approximately 100 workers. The size of plant is fixed, and labor is the only variable resource. The amount of product if only one worker is employed will be extremely small, but if an additional person is hired, the two can divide the jobs to be performed and more than double the single worker's output. In other words, the average product of labor increases with the employment of the additional worker. If a doubling of labor (variable) costs will more than double output, labor costs per unit of output (average variable costs) will decrease. Thus, throughout Stage I for labor the average product per worker increases and the average variable costs decrease. When enough workers are employed to go into Stage II, average product of labor decreases or, what amounts to the same thing, average variable costs increase. The average variable cost curve in this case is a sort of monetized mirror reflection of the average product curve for labor.

The same general principles apply when a complex of several variable resources is used by the firm. At small input levels of the complex, product per unit of cost outlay or "average product" of the complex will be increasing, meaning that average variable costs will be decreasing. As input levels are increased, "average product" reaches a maximum and then decreases. Average variable costs correspondingly reach a minimum and then increase.

When the firm uses a complex of variable resources, combinations of ratios of the variable resources to each other must be considered also. Suppose that the firm for which the cost curves of Figure 10.3 are drawn uses three variable resources—A, B, and C—with its given size of plant. Resource prices are p_a, p_b, and p_c, respectively. If

M dollars. This represents the same number of dollars as does $T_1 - T$ on the total cost diagram.

The marginal cost curve usually is U-shaped, and its shape comes from the TC curve. Up to the x_2 level of output, the TC curve is concave downward; or, what amounts to the same thing, each one-unit increase in output per unit of time up to that point will increase total costs by a smaller amount than did the preceding one. Marginal cost is decreasing as output is increased to that level. Point E on the TC curve is the point of inflection. At output level x_2, at which the point of inflection occurs, marginal cost takes on its minimum value. At outputs greater than x_2, the total cost curve is concave upward, meaning that each one-unit increase in output per unit of time raises total costs by more than the preceding one did. Therefore, marginal cost will be increasing for outputs beyond that level.

Marginal cost at any given output can be thought of, geometrically, as the slope of the total cost curve at that output. The approximate slope of the total cost curve of Figure 10.4(a) between B and D is CD/BC. BC is equal to one unit of output, and CD is equal to $T_1 - T$, or marginal cost of the x_1 unit. The slope of the total cost curve between B and D is thus equal to marginal cost of the x_1 unit. For the typical firm, one unit of output is measured by an infinitesimal distance along the quantity axis. The large size of the unit of output (x to x_1) in Figure 10.4(a) is for purposes of illustration only. If one unit of output is measured by an infinitesimal distance along the quantity axis, marginal cost at any given output is numerically equal to the slope of the total cost curve at that output. The slope of the TC curve of Figure 10.4(a) is decreasing between zero and output x_2 (although TC is rising) and is increasing beyond x_2. Thus, marginal cost first decreases and then increases as output climbs.

Relationship of MC to AC and to AVC

The marginal cost curve bears a unique relationship to the average cost curve derived from the same total cost curve. When AC is decreasing as output increases, MC is less than AC. When AC is increasing as output increases, MC is greater than AC. It follows that at the output at which AC is minimum, MC is equal to AC. These relationships are shown in Figure 10.5.

For example, suppose that the firm's output is x. Its average cost is $0C$. We know that average cost at any output equals the total cost of that output divided by the output; therefore, $0C = TC/x$ at output x. Suppose that the output is increased by one unit to x_1 and that the addition to total costs is $0M_1$, which is the marginal cost of the x_1 unit. Suppose further, as we have shown in Figure 10.5, that marginal cost of the x_1 unit is less than the average cost $0C$ of x units.

FIGURE 10.5
The relationship
between *MC* and *AC*

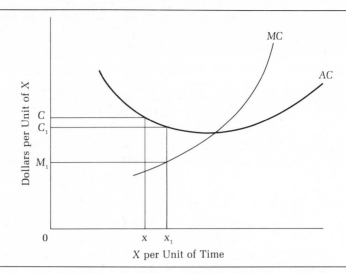

Since the additional unit of output per unit of time adds a lesser amount to total costs than was the average cost of x units, the average cost of x_1 units must be less than the average cost of x units. However, the average cost of x_1 units will not be pulled down as low as the marginal cost of the x_1 unit. Thus, $0C_1 < 0C$, but $0C_1 > 0M_1$; or when average costs are decreasing, marginal cost is necessarily less than average cost. Similarly, when an additional unit of output adds an amount to total costs equal to the old average cost, the new average cost will equal the old and will also be equal to marginal cost of the additional unit of output. Also, when an additional unit of output adds a greater amount to total costs than was the original average cost, the new average cost will be greater than the original but will be less than the marginal cost of the additional unit. These relationships can be verified by reference to Table 10.2 and Figure 10.3.

The relationships between marginal cost and average variable cost will be identical with the relationships between marginal cost and average cost—and for the same reasons. When average variable cost is decreasing, marginal cost will be less than average variable cost. When average variable cost is minimum, marginal cost and average variable cost will be equal. When average variable cost is increasing, marginal cost will be greater than average variable cost. These relationships can also be verified by Table 10.2 and Figure 10.3.

The complete set of short-run per unit cost curves is pictured in Figure 10.3. The marginal cost curve cuts the average variable cost curve and the average cost curve at their respective minimum points. An increase in fixed costs would shift the average cost curve upward and to the right in such a way that the marginal cost curve would still intersect it at its minimum point. No change in the marginal cost curve would be involved, since marginal cost is independent of fixed cost.[6]

As we have presented them, the variations in the component parts of short-run costs, as the firm varies output, do not depend on changes in the price paid per unit for each of the various resources used by the firm. We assumed at the outset that the firm can get all it wants of any resource at a constant price per unit; that is, it buys resources under conditions of pure competition. The shapes of the short-run curves reflect the efficiency with which resources can be used at the alternative output levels obtainable with a given plant size.

In the real world we observe such things as quantity discounts on resources purchased in large amounts by the firm. This represents a departure from pure competition in the buying of resources; it is a departure from the assumptions on which our cost curves are based. Should quantity discounts occur, the total variable cost curve and the total cost curve will increase less as output is increased than they would otherwise. Correspondingly, quantity discounts would cause

---

[6]   Starting from the total cost function

$$C = k + f(x),$$

the marginal cost function becomes

$$MC = \frac{dC}{dx} = f'(x)$$

and is thus seen to depend in no way on k. Further, if average cost is decreasing, then

$$\frac{d\left(\frac{C}{x}\right)}{dx} = \frac{x\,\frac{dC}{dx} - C}{x^2} < 0,$$

or

$$\frac{dC}{dx} - \frac{C}{x} < 0,$$

and

$$\frac{dC}{dx} < \frac{C}{x},$$

which means that $MC < AC$. Similarly, it can be shown that if AC is increasing, then

$$\frac{d\left(\frac{C}{x}\right)}{dx} > 0,$$

or

$$\frac{dC}{dx} > \frac{C}{x};$$

or

$$MC > AC.$$

If AC is constant, then

$$\frac{d\left(\frac{C}{x}\right)}{dx} = 0,$$

or

$$\frac{dC}{dx} = \frac{C}{x},$$

or

$$MC = AC.$$

the average variable cost curve and the average cost curve to show greater decreases, then smaller increases, than they would otherwise show as output is increased. Further modifications of short-run cost analysis will be developed in Chapters 15 and 16.

The Most Efficient Rate of Output

The output at which its short-run average cost is lowest is the output at which any given size of plant is most efficient. Here the value of the inputs of resources per unit output of product is least. As we shall see later, the most efficient rate of output for a given plant size is not necessarily the output at which the firm makes the greatest profits. Profits depend on revenue as well as costs.

Long-run Cost Curves

In the long-run planning period, any size of plant is a possibility for the firm. All resources are variable. The firm can change the quantities used per unit of time, of land, buildings, machinery, management, and all other resources. There will be no fixed costs. We need to concern ourselves with the long-run total cost curve, the long-run marginal cost curve, and the long-run average cost curve.

Long-run Total Costs

We would expect the long-run total cost curve to look like that of Figure 10.6(b), starting at the origin of the diagram and moving upward to the right in much the same fashion as a total variable cost curve. The *LTC* curve, as we have drawn it, reflects first decreasing long-run average costs and then increasing long-run average costs.

The long-run total cost curve of Figure 10.6(b) is based on the isoquant-isocost map of Figure 10.6(a). The production function represented by the isoquant map generates a typical long-run total cost curve. Let numbers on the isoquants indicate the levels of output. The prices of resources A and B are constant at p_{a1} and p_{b1}, respectively, and determine the slope $(-p_{a1}/p_{b1})$ of the family of isocost curves. Alternative possible total cost outlays are shown as the numerators of the various fractions (TCO/p_{b1} and TCO/p_{a1}) along both the B and the A axes. Note that the isocosts showing \$100 increments in total cost outlay are spaced equally from one another.

The spacing of the isoquants reflects, first, economies, and then diseconomies, of size as the firm's plant size is increased. To state it another way, the spacing reflects increasing efficiency and then decreasing efficiency in the use of resources as the plant is expanded. As we move along the expansion path, equal increments in the firm's

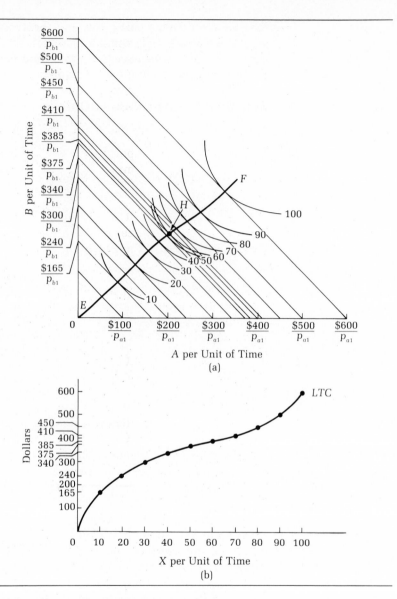

FIGURE 10.6
From isoquants to the LTC curve

output require decreasing increments in total cost outlay until point H is reached. Beyond point H, increasing increments in cost outlay are required to bring about equal increments in output. The resulting total cost curve is that of Figure 10.6(b).

Long-run Average Costs

The long-run average cost curve is derived from the long-run total cost curve in the same way as any average curve is derived from a total curve. At each level of output, we divide *LTC* by output to find *LAC* for that output. The result is the *LAC* curve.

It is instructive, however, to build up the *LAC* curve in an alternative way. Think of the long run as a set of alternative short-run situations into any one of which the firm can move. At any given time we can adopt the short-run viewpoint, considering the alternative output levels that can be produced with the size of plant in existence at that time. Yet, from the point of view of a long-run planning period, the firm has opportunities to change the short-run picture. The long run may be compared with the action sequence of a motion picture. If we stop the film and look at a single picture, we have a short-run concept.

Suppose now that it is technically possible for the firm to build only three alternative sizes of plant. These are represented by SAC_1, SAC_2, and SAC_3 in Figure 10.7. Each *SAC* curve is the short-run average cost curve for a given plant size. In the long run the firm can build any one of these, or it can shift from one to another.

Which one should the firm build? The answer depends on, and will vary with, the long-run output per unit of time to be produced. Whatever the output is to be, the firm will want to produce at an average cost as low as possible for that output.

Suppose the output level is to be x. The firm should construct the plant represented by SAC_1, which will produce output x at a smaller cost per unit (xA) than will either of the other two. Costs would be xB per unit if SAC_2 were used. For output x' the firm would be indifferent between SAC_1 and SAC_2, but for output x_1 it would prefer to use SAC_2. For output x_3 the firm would construct and use the plant represented by SAC_3. We are now in a position to

FIGURE 10.7
The long-run average cost curve, three alternative plant sizes

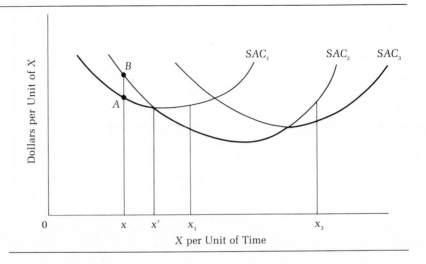

define the *long-run average cost curve*. It shows the least possible cost per unit of producing various outputs when the firm can plan to build any desired size of plant. In Figure 10.7 the heavy portions of the SAC curves form the long-run average cost curve. The light portions of the curves are irrelevant. The firm would never operate in the light portions in the long run because, if it were to do so, it could reduce costs by changing plant size.

The possible plant sizes that a firm can build as a long-run undertaking usually are unlimited in number. For every conceivable size there will be another infinitesimally larger or infinitesimally smaller. Their SAC curves are those of Figure 10.8, and any number of additional SAC curves can be drawn between any two of those in the diagram. The outer portions of the SAC curves form a heavy line, the long-run average cost curve or the LAC curve of Figure 10.8. Since the long-run average cost curve is made up of very small segments of the various SAC curves, it can be considered as a curve just tangent to all possible SAC curves representing the plant sizes that the firm conceivably could build. Mathematically it is an envelope curve to the SAC curves.

Every point on the long-run average cost curve, or the long-run total cost curve for that matter, requires that the firm be using a least-cost combination of resources. For a given output, long-run total cost and long-run average cost are least when *all* resources used are combined in proportions such that the marginal physical product per dollar's worth of one equals the marginal physical product per dollar's worth of every other resource used. This statement means that a dollar spent on management must add the same amount to total product as a dollar spent on raw materials. A dollar spent on labor and a dollar spent on machinery must both yield the same addition to total product, and so on for all resources. Should these conditions not be fulfilled—if a dollar spent on management adds less to total product than a dollar spent on machines—then some

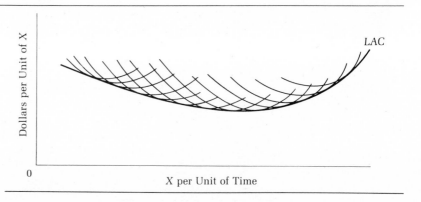

FIGURE 10.8
The long-run average cost curve, infinite alternative plant sizes

Dollars per Unit of X

LAC

0

X per Unit of Time

shifts in expenditures from management to machines will increase total product without increasing total costs; or, if we consider the matter another way, the shifts will provide a decrease in total cost or a decrease in average cost, holding total product constant. Thus, the cost levels shown by the long-run average cost curve for various outputs can be attained by the firm only if the least-cost resource combination is used for each output.

Economies of Size

The long-run average cost curve is usually thought to be a U-shaped curve. Such will be the case if a firm becomes successively more efficient up to some specific size or range of sizes and if it then becomes successively less efficient as the range of plant sizes—from very small to very large—is considered. Increasing efficiency associated with larger and larger plant sizes is reflected by SAC curves lying successively at lower levels and farther to the right. Examples are provided by SAC_1, SAC_2, and SAC_3 in Figure 10.9. Decreasing efficiency, associated with still larger plant sizes, would be shown by SAC curves lying successively at higher levels and farther to the right. The resulting LAC curve would thus have a general U shape.

We call the forces causing the LAC curve to decrease for larger outputs and plant sizes *economies of size*. The discussion of the beer industry at the end of this chapter shows how important economies of size can be in shaping the size and number of firms that an industry contains. These forces are referred to frequently as *economies of scale*, but strictly speaking this latter term is correct only if the production function is homogeneous; that is, if all resources are increased in the same proportion to obtain greater outputs and larger plant sizes. Usually different plant sizes employ different proportions in the resource mix—all resources are *not* increased in the same proportion—for larger plant sizes. Consequently, we use the less re-

FIGURE 10.9
Economies and
diseconomies of size

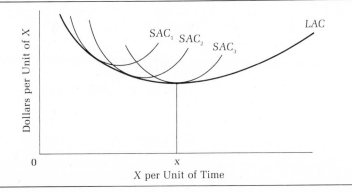

strictive term, economies of size. Two important economies of size are (1) increasing possibilities of division and specialization of labor and (2) increasing possibilities of using advanced technological developments and/or larger machines. The economies will be discussed in turn.

Division and Specialization of Labor   The advantages of division and specialization of labor have long been known to both economists and the general public.[7] A small plant employing few workers cannot specialize the workers on particular operations as readily as can a larger plant employing more people. In the small plant the typical worker performs several different operations in the process of producing the commodity and may not be particularly proficient at some of them. In addition, time may be lost in changing from one set of tools to another in carrying out different operations.

In a larger plant greater specialization may be possible, with the worker concentrating on that process at which he is most adept. Specialization on a particular process eliminates the time lost in changing from one set of tools to another. Also, the worker engaged in a single type of operation develops shortcuts and speed in performing it. The efficiency of the workers is likely to be higher and cost per unit of output correspondingly lower where division and specialization of labor are possible. A word of warning may be necessary, though. In some cases it may be possible to carry specialization to the point at which the monotony of the task begins to counteract increases in the efficiency of the individual's performance.

Technological Factors   The possibility of lowering costs per unit of output by mass-production technology increases as the plant size is increased. In the first place, the cheapest way of producing a small output will usually not be one that employs the most advanced technological methods. Consider, for example, the production of automobile hoods. If the output were to be two or three hoods per week, large automatic presses would not be used. The cheapest way to produce the hoods probably would be to hammer them out by hand. The cost per unit would be comparatively high. There would be no inexpensive way of producing the small output or of operating the small plant for the production of a limited output.

For larger outputs and plant sizes, mass-production technological methods can be used to effect reductions in per unit costs. In this example, if output were to be several thousand units per week, then a larger plant with automatic presses could be installed, and costs per

---

[7]   See Adam Smith, *The Wealth of Nations*, Edwin Cannan, ed. (New York: Modern Library, 1937), Bk. 1, Chaps. 1–3.

unit would be substantially lower than was possible with the small plant.

In the second place, technological considerations are usually such that in order to double the capacity of a machine to produce, a doubling of material, construction, and operating costs of the machine is not necessary. For example, it is cheaper to build and operate a 600-horsepower diesel motor than it is to build and operate two 300-horsepower diesel motors. The 600-horsepower motor has no more working parts than a single 300-horsepower unit. Additionally, the 600-horsepower engine does not require twice the amount of materials used in building a single 300-horsepower motor. The same type of example can be made for almost any machine. Technological possibilities represent a very important explanation of the increasing efficiency of larger and larger plant sizes, up to some limit.

Diseconomies of Size

The question arises as to why, once the plant is large enough to take advantage of all economies of size, still larger sizes are likely to result in less efficiency. It would appear, offhand, that the firm would be able at least to maintain the economies of size. The usual answer to this question is that there are limitations to the efficiency of management in controlling and coordinating a single firm. These limitations are called *diseconomies of size.*

As the size of the plant is increased, management, like the lower echelons of labor, may become more efficient through division of tasks and specialization in particular functions; but the argument commonly made is that beyond some certain size the difficulties of coordinating and controlling the firm multiply rapidly. The contacts of top management with the day-to-day operations of the business become more and more remote, causing operating efficiency in production departments to decrease. Decision-making responsibility must be delegated, and coordination must be established among the decision-making subordinates. The paper work, travel expenses, telephone bills, and additional employees necessary for coordination pile up. Occasionally, plans of separate decision-making subordinates fail to mesh, and costly slowdowns occur. To the extent that greater difficulties of coordination and control reduce the efficiency per dollar outlay on management, as the size of the plant is increased, per unit costs of production will increase.

The discussion so far may be interpreted to mean that as the size of plant expands, economies of size cause the long-run average cost curve to fall, and then, when all economies of size are realized, diseconomies of size begin straightaway. Such is not necessarily the case. Once the plant is large enough to take advantage of all economies of size, there may be a range of larger plant sizes in which diseconomies are not yet evident. As a result the long-run average cost curve will have a horizontal series of minimum points rather than the single minimum point of the conventional long-run average cost curve. When the plant has become sufficiently large for diseconomies of size to occur, the long-run average cost curve turns upward to the right. Another possibility is that some diseconomies begin to occur in a plant too small to realize all economies of size. If the economies of size for larger plants more than offset the diseconomies, the long-run average cost curve slopes downward to the right. Where diseconomies of size more than offset economies of size, the long-run average cost curve slopes upward to the right.

The Most Efficient Size of Plant

The most efficient size of plant is the one generating the short-run average cost curve that forms the minimum point of the long-run average cost curve. It can also be thought of as that size of plant with a short-run average cost curve tangent to the long-run average cost curve at the minimum points of both. The short-run average cost curve of the most efficient size of plant in Figure 10.10 is *SAC*.

Firms will not invariably construct plants of most efficient size and operate them at the most efficient rates of output. As we shall see, they will do so under conditions of pure competition in the long run; however, under pure monopoly, oligopoly, and monopolistic competition, they are not likely, to do so. The size of plant that will operate at the lowest cost per unit for given outputs will vary with the output to be produced. For example, in Figure 10.10, plant *SAC* will produce output x more cheaply than will a plant of any other size, and output x can be produced at a lower cost per unit than can any other output. But for outputs greater or less than x, per unit costs will

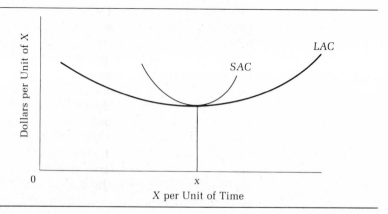

FIGURE 10.10
The most efficient size
of plant

necessarily be higher. Plant sizes other than the most efficient size will produce such outputs at lower costs per unit than will the one of most efficient size.

How can we determine the size of plant to be constructed for a specific output? Consider Figure 10.11. Suppose that the firm is pro-

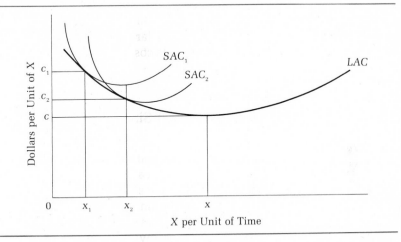

FIGURE 10.11
Appropriate plant size for a given output

ducing output x_1 with plant SAC_1. Plant SAC_1 is being operated at less than its most efficient rate of output. Let the output level be increased to x_2. The increase can be accomplished in either of two ways: (1) by increasing the output rate with plant SAC_1 or (2) by changing to a larger plant size. Either method will allow the firm to reduce costs per unit. Method 1 will cause SAC_1 to be used at its most efficient rate of output. Costs are lower than c_1. However, if the firm should use Method 2, economies of size from the larger plant will allow even greater per unit cost reduction for output x_2 than will Method 1. Costs per unit will be c_2 with plant SAC_2, and this is the lowest cost at which the output can be produced. For outputs between 0 and x, the firm will achieve lowest per unit costs for any given output by using a plant smaller than the most efficient size at less than the most efficient rate of output. Similarly, for any given output greater than x, the lowest cost per unit will be achieved if the firm uses a plant larger than the most efficient size at a greater than most efficient rate of output. The applicable general principle is this: To minimize cost for any given output, the firm should use the plant size for which the short-run average cost curve is tangent to the long-run average cost curve at that output. The importance of this principle can be seen in the discussion of the brewing industry at the end of this chapter.

Long-run Marginal Cost

The *long-run marginal cost curve* shows the change in long-run total cost per unit change in the firm's output when the firm has ample time to accomplish the output change by making the appropriate adjustments in the quantities of all resources used, including those that constitute its plant. Or we can think of the *LMC* curve as measuring the slopes of the *LTC* curve at various output levels.

From the *LTC* curve of Figure 10.12 we can deduce that *LMC* would be less than *LAC* where *LAC* is decreasing—that is, from zero to output x—and would be greater than *LAC* for output levels beyond x where *LAC* is increasing. At output x, *LMC* and *LAC* are equal. These relationships are shown in Figure 10.13 by the *LAC* and *LMC* curves. The *LMC* curve bears the same relationship to its *LAC* curve that any given *SMC* curve bears to its *SAC* curve.

Relationships between *LMC* and *SMC*

When the firm has constructed the proper size of plant for producing a given output, short-run marginal cost will equal long-run marginal cost at that output. Suppose, for example, that the given output is x_2 in Figure 10.13. The firm would use the plant represented by SAC_2, which is tangent to the *LAC* curve at that output. The corresponding total cost curves would be STC_2 and *LTC* in Figure 10.12. We can verify that STC_2 would lie above *LTC* at output levels below x_2 because SAC_2 is greater than *LAC* at those output levels. At output

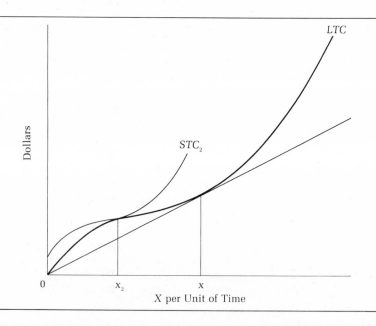

FIGURE 10.12
The relationship between short-run and long-run total costs

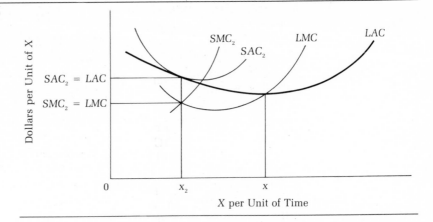

FIGURE 10.13
Relationship between SMC and LMC for a given SAC and LAC

x_2, STC_2 would be equal to LTC because SAC_2 and LAC are equal. At outputs greater than x_2, STC_2 would again exceed LTC because SAC_2 for those outputs again lies above LAC. At output x_2, where SAC_2 is tangent to LAC, curve STC_2 must also be tangent to LTC. At outputs in the neighborhood of, but below x_2, the STC_2 curve must have a smaller slope than the LTC curve. At output levels greater than x_2, the STC_2 curve must have a greater slope than the LTC curve. At x_2, where STC_2 is tangent to LTC, both curves have the same slope.

Because the slope of the STC_2 curve is the short-run marginal cost for the size of plant, and because the slope of LTC is the long-run marginal cost, it follows that $SMC_2 < LMC$ at outputs just smaller than x_2; $SMC_2 > LMC$ at outputs just larger than x_2; and SMC_2 equals LMC at output x_2. These relationships are shown in Figure 10.13.

Applications: Cost Analysis

From the many possible applications of cost analysis, three have been selected for their illustrative content. The first is a common one for all college and university students. The second shows an important economic principle at work. The third is an intriguing case study of an important industry's costs.

Costs of Obtaining a Higher Education

What are the annual costs to a student of attending a college or university? Or, to state the question in a slightly different way, what does it cost a student to invest in human capital to the extent of 30 hours of college or university credit over the course of an academic year? Most students and their parents will underestimate the cost.

The explicit costs to the student are fairly clear. Tuition is a prime consideration. Next in importance (first, at some schools) would be living expenses—room, board, and incidentals. Books and supplies round out the list. Here the family's calculations are likely to stop.

At least two items of an implicit nature are frequently overlooked. The most important one—and the largest cost item in a year of academic training—is the student's forgone earnings. What could the student have earned if she or he had elected to join the labor force in lieu of enrolling in the college or university and investing such a large block of time in studying? Another is the forgone interest on tuition payments. If tuition is paid at the beginning of each semester, the student loses interest on one-half the annual tuition for the academic year, since a semester's tuition could have been kept out on loan at the going interest rate. Similar forgone interest costs may occur if room and board payments are made on a semester-by-semester basis. However, these latter interest costs can be avoided if a student lives off the campus and/or pays room and board on a monthly basis.

Let us summarize and provide perspective. Dollar amounts that may approximate the various cost items for a student at a typical(?) college or university for an academic year (1982) are listed below:

Explicit Costs
Tuition	$4,000
Room and board	3,500
Books and supplies	350
Subtotal	$7,800

Implicit Costs
Forgone earnings	$10,000
Forgone interest	240
($2,000 @ 12%)	
Subtotal	$10,240
Total Costs	$18,090

Cost Minimization by a Multiple-unit Firm

We have derived the cost curves for the overall operation of a firm, aggregating the costs of production of the various production units that the firm may operate if it is indeed a multiple-unit firm. An interesting problem remains, however. How should such a firm allocate its total output level among its production units in order to minimize the cost of producing the output level? Should it always seek to produce in those units that have the lowest average costs?

Suppose that a firm producing crude oil is composed of two units, Unit 1 and Unit 2. The short-run average and marginal cost curves of each unit are illustrated in Figure 10.14. Let the firm's anticipated total output level be X barrels per day.

To minimize its costs, the firm should allocate the X barrels between Unit 1 and Unit 2 in such a way that the *marginal cost* of production in Unit 1 is equal to that of Unit 2; that is, Unit 1 should produce x_1 barrels and Unit 2 should produce x_2 barrels with $x_1 + x_2 = X$. Marginal cost in both Unit 1 and Unit 2 is M, or \$10. Note that the average costs for Unit 1 are higher than the average costs for Unit 2 at these output levels.

Nevertheless, the firm's total costs are minimized. Suppose the output level of Unit 1 is reduced by 1 barrel, while that of Unit 2 is increased by 1 barrel. Since marginal cost at the x_1 output level is \$10, a one-barrel reduction in the output of Unit 1 reduces the firm's total costs by that amount. But a one-barrel increase in the output of Unit 2 pushes marginal cost in Unit 2 above \$10—say, to \$10.25. By the definition of marginal cost, this amounts to a \$10.25 increase in the firm's total costs. The *net* effect of a shift of a barrel of oil per day from Unit 1 to Unit 2 is a 25-cent increase in the firm's total costs. Similarly, from the original output levels, x_1 and x_2, a shift in production from Unit 2 to Unit 1 would increase the firm's total costs. Total costs are thus minimum when production is allocated so that the marginal cost is the same in each production unit.

These conditions for minimizing the firm's total costs are applicable for any total output level. If the firm were to produce X' barrels per day, x_1' should be produced by Unit 1 and x_2' should be produced by Unit 2. If the total output were to be X'', then x_1'' should be produced by Unit 1 and x_2'' should be produced by Unit 2. In each instance the total output is so allocated that marginal costs are the same for the two production units. If UMC_1 and UMC_2 are summed horizontally, we obtain the firm's overall marginal cost curve MC. This curve shows the marginal cost at alternative total output levels when each of those output levels is allocated among production units so as to minimize total costs.

Economies of Size in the Beer Industry[8]

There has long been, as economist Kenneth Elzinga has observed, a special economic relationship between college students and beer. The fortunes of commercial brewers helped to endow Harvard and Vassar, for example, and college students have taken a keen interest in the nature and extent of the industry's output.[9] Watchful consum-

---

[8] Helpful comments on the materials in this section were given by George W. Hilton, editor, *The Breweriana Collector*.

[9] Kenneth Elzinga, "The Beer Industry," in Walter Adams, ed., *The Structure of American Industry*, 4th ed. (New York: Macmillan, 1971). p. 189.

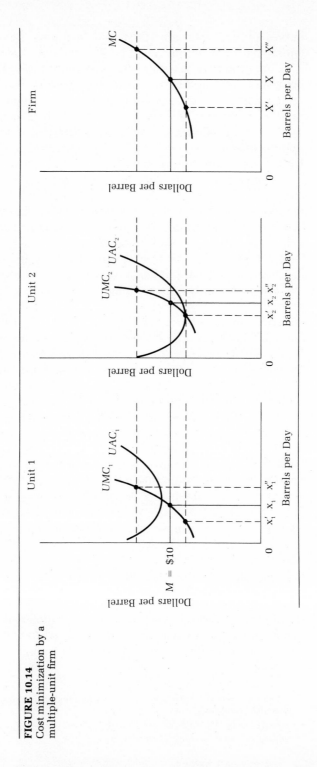

FIGURE 10.14
Cost minimization by a multiple-unit firm

ers of beer may have noticed, however, that the number of brands from which they may choose has been declining. Indeed, the beer industry in the twentieth century, and especially in the period since World War II, has undergone one of the most dramatic shakeouts in American economic history.

The industry reached its peak in this century in 1914, when 1,392 brewery plants were operating. Prohibition reduced it to 331 in 1933, but it rallied temporarily to 756 in 1934 after repeal.[10] Table 10.3 shows the decline since 1946, which has been concentrated among small local or regional breweries. Elzinga found that of the 182 plants eliminated during 1950–61, a total of 119 simply closed their doors, while in another 41 cases the company that bought the brewery continued to operate it from another location. This suggests that 88 percent of the plants that were closed during this period had either an inefficient plant size or insufficient managerial talent at the local brewery.[11] The shakeout was caused by a combination of hostile changes in both demand and supply conditions, although in retrospect the changes in supply conditions appear to have been of paramount importance.

Changes in Demand Conditions One reason why so many firms and breweries closed during the 1940s and 1950s is that demand for beer declined. Per capita consumption peaked in 1908–17 (the decade before Prohibition) at 19.9 gallons per person annually but fell to 15.0 gallons in 1958.[12] Apparently beer was not an inferior good during this era; its income elasticity during 1956–59 was estimated to be 0.4,[13] indicating that the rise in real incomes during the 1940s and 1950s was not the cause of the decline in demand. A better explanation is found in demographic data; persons in the 21–44 age group account for 69 percent of all beer consumption, and this group was roughly of constant size until the 1960s, when the "baby boom" generation born after 1945 came of drinking age.[14]

By 1968, per capita beer consumption had increased to 16.7 gallons per year[15] and was growing at more than twice the rate of growth of population in the 21–44 age cohort. This rise in consumption, which accelerated during the 1970s, was probably caused by a

[10] Ira Horowitz and Ann R. Horowitz, "Firms in a Declining Market: The Brewing Case," *Journal of Industrial Economics,* vol. 13, no. 2 (March 1965), p. 130.

[11] Elzinga, "The Beer Industry," p. 199.

[12] Ibid., p. 192.

[13] Thomas F. Hogarty and Kenneth G. Elzinga, "The Demand for Beer," *The Review of Economics and Statistics,* vol. 59, no. 2 (May 1972), pp. 195–98.

[14] Charles F. Keithahn, *The Brewing Industry* (Washington, D.C.: Staff Report of the Bureau of Economics, U.S. Federal Trade Commission, December 1978), p. 29.

[15] Elzinga, "The Beer Industry," p. 192.

TABLE 10.3	Year	Plants	Firms
Number of breweries and brewery firms in the United States: 1946–1976	1946	471	
	1947	465	404
	1948	466	
	1949	440	
	1950	407	
	1951	386	
	1952	357	
	1953	329	
	1954	310	263
	1955	292	
	1956	281	
	1957	264	
	1958	252	211
	1959	244	
	1960	229	
	1961	229	
	1962	220	
	1963	211	171
	1964	190	
	1965	179	
	1966	170	
	1967	154	125
	1968	149	
	1969	146	
	1970	137	
	1971	134	
	1972	131	108
	1973	114	
	1974 (June)	108	
	1976	94	49

Source: Charles F. Keithahn, *The Brewing Industry*, Staff Report of the Bureau of Economics, U.S. Federal Trade Commission, Washington, D.C.: December 1978, p. 11.

sharp shift in tastes away from distilled liquors to beers and wines and, within each group, toward the beverages that were light in color and dry in taste. Many of the smaller breweries specialized in the stronger-flavored beers.[16]

A second profound change in drinking habits was the rise in home, or off-premises, consumption and the decline in tavern and saloon drinking. Taverns usually were supplied with kegs from local or regional breweries, owing to the high costs of shipping the product

[16] Keithahn, *The Brewing Industry*, pp. 30–31.

relative to its value. Beer is over 90 percent water and is heavy and awkward to transport. Furthermore, keg beer does not require pasteurization to kill the yeast; live yeast in the keg gives the beer a fresher flavor and the action of the yeast keeps up pressure in the keg as the liquid is drawn. By 1979, however, 88.4 percent of beer was sold in cans or bottles for nontavern consumption,[17] and these products had to be pasteurized to kill the yeast and keep the liquid nonexplosive in its container. The per-barrel cost of pasteurization was greater for the smaller brewers due to their lower output.

A third change in demand conditions was the shift in preferences to disposable containers. The shift from kegs to returnable bottles required an investment that caused some local brewers to go out of business. But the advantage for the survivors was limited by the cost of collecting the empties for refilling; this kept down the mileage radius within which brewers could profitably ship their product. Bottles had to be shipped by trucks rather than less expensive railroad boxcars owing to the greater rate of breakage on rails. The surviving smaller breweries lost this advantage, however, with the shift in consumers' preferences to cans, which could be shipped with less breakage by either rail or truck. By 1979, canned beer amounted to more than 60 percent of all the beer produced in the United States.

A fourth change was toward a greater variety of types and sizes of containers. Beer drinkers are fussy. Some prefer only bottles because they are convinced that cans alter the taste. Others prefer cans because they believe that an iced can will chill the liquid faster (a bottle retains heat longer), which improves the flavor. Within each group, customers differ in their favorite sizes—12- or 16-ounce cans plus bottles of various sizes up to a quart. Each different type and size of container requires a separate "closing line"—the complex and highly expensive machinery that fills each container with liquid and then seals it. To maintain between four and six closing lines, and to operate them at optimal speeds, would require an enormous liquid flow-through, and would have imposed on small brewers an additional capital cost in an industry that already was extremely capital intensive.

Sources of plant economies Technological changes in the 1960s and 1970s markedly increased the rate of operation of the closing line. In 1965, the machinery could move about 500 bottles or 900 cans per minute; by 1971, this had increased to either 750 bottles or 1,200 cans;[18] and by the late 1970s the speed of the 12-ounce canning

---

[17] *Brewers Digest*, vol. 40, no. 5 (May 1980), p. 11.

[18] Charles G. Burck, "While the Big Brewers Quaff, the Little Ones Thirst," *Fortune*, November 1972, p. 104. *Fortune*, © 1972 Time Inc. All rights reserved.

line had risen to about 1,500 cans per minute.[19] With these developments, the minimum efficient size of a brewery increased terrifically. Economist Frederick M. Scherer found that a brewery plant, to utilize the modern closing lines at their optimal rates, would have to produce 1.5 million barrels per year to operate the canning line efficiently, between 0.6 and 0.8 million barrels for the bottling line, and 1.0 to 1.2 million barrels for the kegging line. The minimum brewery size for just one size of each type of container was therefore at least 3.3 million barrels, and the minimum size of a brewery designed to produce beer in a variety of container sizes was 4 to 5 million barrels.[20]

Scherer described the options that brewers with small plant capacities faced:

1 operating slower but higher unit cost packaging lines for low-volume products

2 operating additional high-speed lines at rates below their optimal (that is, cost-minimizing) rate

3 operating a limited number of packaging lines and thereby incurring appreciable changeover costs

4 doing without special package sizes and hence suffering loss of sales

5 building a brewery with a capacity of 4 to 5 million barrels so that one can achieve a better balance with respect to utilization of filling equipment.[21]

The comparisons of average cost between the new beer "factories" that have been designed for high annual capacities versus older and smaller plants are startling. In 1972, for example, Schlitz's modern plant at Memphis, with an annual capacity of 4.4 million barrels, employed only 483 production workers. Falstaff had four out-of-date plants, with a combined annual capacity of 4.1 million barrels and about 1,800 production workers. Each Schlitz worker at the Memphis plant produced 9,110 barrels in 1972, whereas each of the Falstaff workers produced only 2,277. The average cost of the Schlitz-Memphis beer was estimated at $1.08 per barrel versus $4.39 for Falstaff.[22] Scherer concluded that the labor crew for a modern brewery with an annual capacity of 4 million barrels could be the

[19] Keithahn, The Brewing Industry, p. 34.

[20] Scherer's unpublished study is described in Keithahn, pp. 34–37.

[21] As cited in ibid., p. 36.

[22] Burck, "While Big Brewers Quaff," pp. 104–106.

same size as the crew for an older plant of 1 million, and that the savings in unit labor costs in moving from the smaller plant to the larger would be 6 cents per barrel.[23] Table 10.4 ranks the various Schlitz breweries by labor costs per barrel in 1973. Generally, the newer and larger the plant capacity, the lower the average labor costs. For the Schlitz firm as a whole, its 1973 average cost per barrel was 2.5 percent *less* than in 1971, in spite of an inflation in labor and materials costs,[24] which shows what a powerful effect on firm costs the larger breweries have had.

TABLE 10.4 Ranking of Schlitz's breweries by labor cost per barrel: 1973	Plant	Year Opened	Labor Cost per Barrel	Total cost per Barrel
	Memphis	1970	$2.17	$20.97
	Winston-Salem	1969	2.19	21.12
	Longview	1966	2.67	21.23
	Tampa	1959	3.50	22.73
	Los Angeles	1954	3.93	21.81
	Kansas City[1]	ACQ	4.42	23.09
	Milwaukee	*	4.80	22.10
	Brooklyn[2]	ACQ*	5.24	17.05
	Honolulu	ACQ	8.27	25.28

ACQ: Acquired.

* Opened prior to World War II.

[1] Closed in 1973; brewery operated for only a portion of the year.

[2] Closed in 1973; brewery operated for only a portion of the year.

Source: Charles F. Keithahn, *The Brewing Industry*, Staff Report of the Bureau of Economics, U.S. Federal Trade Commission, Washington, D.C.: December 1978, p. 47.

Figure 10.15 shows that construction costs for new brewery plants also declined for plants of larger sizes. The data are based on engineering cost estimates given to the U.S. Federal Trade Commission by Schlitz and on three different assumptions about the level of future input prices. The important point here is that construction costs per barrel of capacity decline continuously up to brewery capacities of 5 million barrels per year.[25] Thus, the trend toward lower per-barrel labor costs in breweries of larger capacities has been reinforced by the trend toward lower per-barrel construction costs.

As a final indication of the economies of larger plant sizes in brewing, Table 10.5 shows the new plants or plant expansions that

[23] As cited in Keithahn, *The Brewing Industry*, p. 37.

[24] Ibid., p. 48.

[25] Ibid.

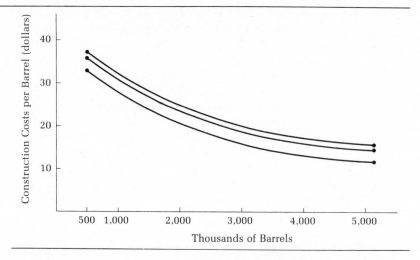

FIGURE 10.15
Estimated costs of construction per barrel for different plant sizes, Schlitz Brewing Company

were underway in 1978 by the major brewers. The minimum addition to capacity is 2.0 million barrels per year, and the average is in excess of 5.2 million barrels. It is also worth noting that all but one of the new breweries or extensions of an existing facility were planned for nonurban areas. This occurred because the location of breweries in older cities was itself a diseconomy owing to higher taxes, higher labor costs, and water that was both more expensive to purchase and more expensive to treat for high levels of chlorine and other urban pollutants. New York City once was the nation's brewery capital, owing to its huge population and the incentives to hold down shipment costs, but production there ceased in the early 1950s.

TABLE 10.5
Plant expansions and new plants

Brewer	Location	Capacity (millions of barrels per year)	Completion Date
A-B	Williamsburg, Va.	Expansion from 2.9 to 7.5	1980
Coors	Golden, Colo.	Expansion from 15 to 25	—
Miller	Albany, Ga.	10	1980
Miller	Fulton, N.Y.	Expansion from 4 to 8	—
Miller	Fort Worth, Tex.	Expansion from 6 to 8	1980
Miller	Eden, N.C.	8.8	1978
Pabst	Pabst, Ga.	Expansion from 4.5 to 8	before 1980
Schlitz	Baldwinsville, N.Y.	Expansion from 2 to 6	by 1980

Source: Charles F. Keithahn, *The Brewing Industry*, Staff Report of the Bureau of Economics, U.S. Federal Trade Commission, Washington, D.C.: December 1978, p. 50.

Sources of Firm Economies   Brewing firms grew in size during the 1946–76 era not only because of increased economies to the operation of a single plant but owing to greater economies in the operation of a multiplant firm. One of the greatest economies of nationwide production and sales came from lower advertising costs per barrel. The shelf life of approximately three months for bottles and cans gave brewers increased incentives to advertise when their inventories grew.

Brewers also are subject to stringent regulation by the federal government and each state authority, and the cost of compliance can be cut on a per-barrel basis by increasing production. The industry is also subject to a federal tax of a flat $9.00 per barrel and various state barrelage taxes that averaged $3.90 in 1970. Taxes represent the single largest cost item in beer—about 35 percent of its price in 1970.[26] From the analysis of tax incidence in Chapter 4, we know that it is unusual for a seller to be able to shift *all* of the burden of taxes onto consumers. The likelihood that taxes pinch smaller brewers inordinately is consistent with a rule that makes smaller brewers eligible for a remission of up to $180,000 per year in federal alcohol taxes.

Scherer estimated that a brewing firm in 1977 needed three to four plants to exhaust all of the available multiplant economies of size and thus to minimize average cost. A firm having four breweries of minimum efficient size (roughly 4.5 million barrels of annual capacity) could produce a total of 18.0 million barrels per year. Such a firm in 1977 would have brewed 11.5 percent of all the beer sold in the United States, and four such firms would have produced 46.0 percent. To wit, four optimally sized firms in 1977 could have supplied about half of the market at minimum long-run average cost.[27]

What is just as surprising as the huge minimum efficient size of the brewery firm in the late 1970s is the extent to which the minimum efficient size has increased. Ira and Ann Horowitz studied the period 1947–62 and estimated that the range of minimum average cost for a firm began at 1.5 million barrels of annual capacity and was exhausted at about 3 million barrels.[28] On the strength of this estimate the Horowitzes predicted in 1965 the coming slaughter of the smaller brewers:

> . . . [T]here are still some 40 out of the 148 companies in the brewing industry with production capacity of less than 100,000 barrels a year, the minimum efficient size of plant, and we can look

[26]   Elzinga, "The Beer Industry," p. 210.

[27]   Keithahn, *The Brewing Industry*, p. 59.

[28]   Horowitz and Horowitz, "Firms in Declining Market," p. 150.

for these firms to leave the industry in the near future. An additional 33 firms have production capacities of less than 200,000 barrels which, while greater than the minimum efficient size of plant, is well below the level necessary to achieve economies of scale. The future for these firms, too, would appear to be none too bright.[29]

Table 10.6 shows how correct the Horowitzes were and how great the slaughter was. Brewing firms with less than 100,000 barrels of annual capacity were half the industry in 1962 but less than 30 percent in 1979. In 1962, there were 27 firms between 100,000 and 200,000 barrels, but in 1979 there were 4.[30]

TABLE 10.6
Changes in annual capacities of brewers; 1962 and 1979

	1962	1979
Total breweries in operation	156	47[a]
Breweries with annual capacity above 100,000 barrels	80	32
Breweries with annual capacity below 100,000 barrels	76	15

a. Of these, 12 firms were still in operation after having been absorbed by another brewing company.

Sources: For 1962: *World Directory of Breweries, 1963–64*, Mount Vernon, N.Y.: American Brewer Publishing Corporation, 1963, pp. 334–35; and *American Brewer*, 1963 and 1964.

For 1979: "Buyers Guide and Brewery Directory for 1980," *Brewers Digest*, vol. 50, no. 1 (Jan. 1980, pt. 2), pp. 10–28.

These dramatic changes can be illustrated in the following pair of cost diagrams. Figure 10.16(a) shows the relevant long-run planning possibilities facing a brewery firm for the period 1947–62, based on the Horowitzes' estimates, before the technological advances permitting a sharp increase in the speeds of the bottle and can-closing lines. Figure 10.16(a) shows cost curve $SAC_{1947-62}$, reflecting the minimum estimated efficient plant size of 0.1 million barrels per year, and the long-run planning curve $LAC_{1947-62}$ shows the exhaustion of economies of firm size at a range of output rates between 1.5 and 3.0 million barrels per year. The position of $SAC_{1947-62}$ clearly shows that a firm having a single plant of minimum efficient size could not compete with the beer sold at lower costs by efficiently sized larger firms during this period. These smaller breweries either were abandoned or were merged into more efficient, larger configurations that allowed their owners to take advantage of economies of advertising, transportation, and use of cans that were available for firms of at least 1.5 million barrels annual capacity.

[29] Ibid., p. 152.

[30] See sources for Table 10.6.

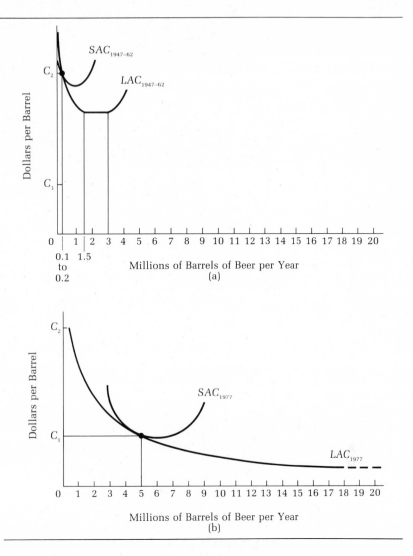

FIGURE 10.16
Minimum plant sizes (SAC) and firm sizes (LAC) for efficient production, 1947–62 and 1977

The technological changes that came about with the development of faster closing lines caused a downward shift in the long-run planning curve to the position shown by LAC_{1977} in Figure 10.16(b). Brewery firms in the 1947–62 era had to plan their output rates within the options shown by $LAC_{1947-62}$. But by 1977 they had to contemplate the most efficient adjustment away from the point on $LAC_{1947-62}$ at which they had been operating to a prospective rate of output selected from the long-run possibilities on the new planning curve LAC_{1977}. The minimum sizes necessary to exhaust available economies in 1977 were estimated by Scherer at about 5.0 million barrels per year for the individual plant, which is illustrated by

SAC_{1977}, and about 18.0 million barrels per year for the firm, which is illustrated by LAC_{1977}. (Scherer's data are not clear about the shape of LAC_{1977} for output rates greater than 18.0 million barrels per year, so we have drawn that segment of the curve as a dashed line to reflect this uncertainty.)

Effects of Size Economies Has the decline in brewing firms produced monopoly or collusive pricing for those that remain? The U.S. Department of Justice's Antitrust Division feared so in the late 1950s and 1960s, when it began a series of legal actions against mergers among brewers, but the government's concerns turned out to be groundless. The net outcome of the changes in demand and supply conditions in brewing has been to increase the price of beer by *less* than the rise in the Consumer Price Index, and even more striking is the fact that the price increases of the larger brewers have been *less* than the industry average. The rise in industry profits that occurred in the 1970s appears to have been the result of making more efficient use of the industry's resources by taking advantage of rising economies of size.[31]

Summary

Costs of production are the obligations incurred by the firm for resources used in making its product. The cost of any given resource is determined by its value in its best alternative use. This principle is called the alternative cost doctrine. Costs of production differ from the usual concept of the firm's "expenses," which usually coincide with explicit resource costs. In determining costs of production, implicit resource costs also must be included. The analysis of costs presented in the chapter assumes that the firm by itself cannot influence the price of any resource that it buys.

In the short run, resources used by the firm are classified as fixed and variable. The obligations incurred for them are fixed costs and variable costs. Total fixed costs and total variable costs for different outputs are the component parts of total costs. From the three total cost curves, we derive the corresponding per unit cost curves—average fixed cost, average variable cost, and average cost. The short-run average cost curve shows the least per unit cost of producing different outputs with a given plant size and is a U-shaped curve. In addition, we derive the marginal cost curve. The output at which

---

[31] Keithahn, *The Brewing Industry*, pp. 89–121.

short-run average cost is least is called the optimum rate of output for a given size of plant.

All resources can be varied in quantity by the firm in the long run; consequently, all costs are variable. The long-run average cost curve shows the least per unit cost of producing various outputs when the firm is free to change its plant to any desired size. It is the envelope curve to the short-run average cost curves of all possible sizes of plant, and it is usually U-shaped. The factors causing its U shape are called economies of size and diseconomies of size. The long-run marginal cost curve shows the change in total costs resulting from a one-unit change in output when the firm is free to vary the quantities used of all resources.

For whatever output the firm produces in the long run, if the least per unit cost is to be obtained for that output, the plant size must be such that its short-run average cost curve is tangent to the long-run average cost curve at that output. For such a plant size, short-run marginal cost will equal long-run marginal cost at the output of tangency.

Suggested Readings

Stigler, George J. *The Theory of Price*. 3rd ed. New York: Crowell-Collier and Macmillan, 1966, Chaps. 6, 9.

Viner, Jacob. "Cost Curves and Supply Curves." *Zeitschrift für Nationalökonomie*, 3 (1931), pp. 23–46. Reprinted in American Economic Association, *Readings in Price Theory*, George J. Stigler and Kenneth E. Boulding, eds. Homewood, Ill.: Richard D. Irwin, 1952, pp. 198–232.

Questions and Exercises

1 A steel mill uses labor and capital to produce tons of steel. The prices of labor and capital are p_{l1} and p_{k1}, respectively. With an isoquant-isocost diagram show how
   a its short-run total cost curve is generated and explain the shape of the curve
   b its long-run total cost curve is generated and explain the shape of the curve.

2 It is often argued that the reason for being of state universities is that they provide higher education at a lower cost than do private universities. Assuming that the quality of output is the same for each type of university, discuss this issue in terms of the annual costs
   a to a student and his or her family
   b to the society as a whole.

3 For automobiles of comparable size, it would appear that General Motors produces at a lower cost per unit than does American Motors. If such is the case, what are some of the possible explanations for the cost differential?

4 The long-run average cost curve of a firm is given. Locate an output level to the left of its minimum point. What scale of plant should the firm use to produce that output? Show these points diagrammatically and draw in the long-run marginal cost and the short-run marginal cost curves. Explain your answers.

Appendix to Chapter 10
The Geometry of Short-run per Unit Cost Curves

The relationships between total cost curves and per unit cost curves can be shown geometrically. Using the three total cost curves as starting points, we shall derive from them the corresponding per unit cost curves. Then we shall show geometrically the relationship between the average cost curve and the marginal cost curve.

The Average Fixed Cost Curve

In Figure 10.17(b) the average fixed cost curve is derived from the total fixed cost curve of Figure 10.17(a). The quantity scales of the two diagrams are the same. The vertical axis of Figure 10.17(a) measures total fixed costs, whereas that of Figure 10.17(b) measures fixed cost per unit.

Consider output x in Figure 10.17(a). At that output total fixed cost is measured by xA. Now consider the straight line $0A$. The slope of $0A$ is $xA/0x$, which is numerically equal to average fixed

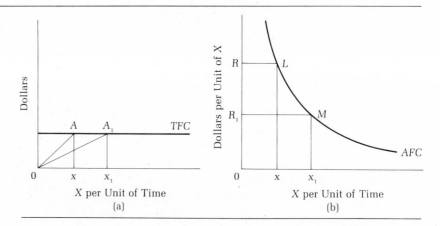

FIGURE 10.17
The geometry of *TFC* and *AFC*

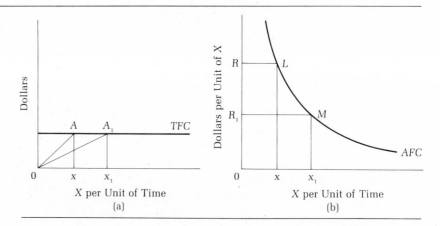

cost $0R$ in Figure 10.17(b). Likewise, at output x_1 average fixed cost $0R_1$ in Figure 10.17(b) equals the slope of $0A_1$ or $x_1A_1/0x_1$.

At successively larger outputs, the slopes of the corresponding $0A$ lines become smaller and smaller, showing that average fixed cost decreases as output increases; however, it can never reach zero. The numerical slopes of the $0A$ lines plotted against the respective outputs for which they are drawn comprise the average fixed cost curve of Figure 10.17(b).

Geometrically, the AFC curve is a rectangular hyperbola. It approaches, but never reaches, both the dollar axis and the quantity axis. It is convex to the origin of the diagram. The distinguishing feature of a rectangular hyperbola is that at any point on the curve, such as L, the values represented on each axis, when multiplied together, produce the same mathematical product as the multiplication of the corresponding values at any other point on the curve, such as M. In other words, $0x \times 0R = 0x_1 \times 0R_1$. Such must necessarily be the case for the average fixed cost curve. Because total fixed costs are constant and because average fixed cost at any output multiplied by that output equals total fixed cost, the mathematical product of any output times its corresponding average fixed cost must equal the mathematical product of any other output times its corresponding average fixed cost.

The Average Variable Cost Curve

In Figure 10.18(b) the average variable cost curve is derived from the total variable cost curve in Figure 10.18(a). The process of derivation is similar to that used in obtaining the AFC curve. At output x, TVC equals xB; hence, AVC at output x equals $xB/0x$, equals the slope of

FIGURE 10.18
The geometry of TVC and AVC

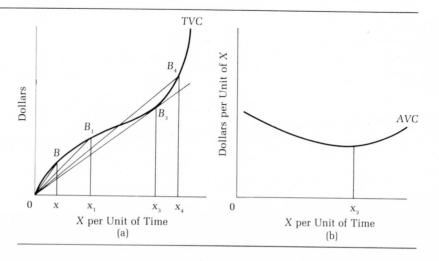

line $0B$. At x_1, AVC equals $x_1B_1/0x_1$, equals the slope of $0B_1$. At x_3, AVC equals $x_3B_3/0x_3$, equals the slope of $0B_3$. At x_4, AVC equals $x_4B_4/0x_4$, equals the slope of $0B_4$. The numerical slopes of the $0B$ lines plotted against their respective outputs trace out the AVC curve of Figure 10.18(b).

The geometric derivation of the AVC curve makes it clear that the curve takes its shape from the TVC curve. Between 0 output and output x_3, the $0B$ line for each successively larger output must have a smaller slope than the one for the preceding output. Hence, between 0 and x_3 the AVC curve must be decreasing. At output x_3, line $0B_3$ is just tangent to the TVC curve and, thus, has a smaller slope than any other $0B$ line can possibly have. At x_3, AVC is as low as it can get. At outputs greater than x_3, the $0B$ lines will increase in slope, meaning that AVC is increasing. The AVC curve must have a U shape if we have correctly established the shape of the TVC curve.

The Average Cost Curve

In Figure 10.19(b) the average cost is derived from the total cost curve in the same way that the AVC curve is derived from the TVC curve. At output x, TC equals xC, so AC equals $xC/0x$, equals the slope of line $0C$. At output x_1, AC equals $x_1C_1/0x_1$, equals the slope of $0C_1$. At output x_4, AC equals $x_4C_4/0x_4$, equals the slope of $0C_4$. At output x_5, AC equals $x_5C_5/0x_5$, equals the slope of $0C_5$. The slopes of the $0C$ lines plotted against the corresponding outputs locate the AC curve in Figure 10.19(b).

If the shape of the TC curve is correct, the AC curve must be a U-shaped curve. The $0C$ lines decrease in slope as output increases

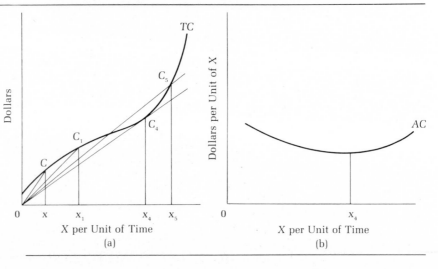

FIGURE 10.19
The geometry of TC and AC

up to output x_4. At output x_4, $0C_4$ is tangent to the TC curve and, consequently, is the one of least slope. Here AC is minimum. At greater outputs, the slopes of the $0C$ lines are increasing; that is, AC is increasing.

The Relationship of AC and MC

The relationship between AC and MC can be shown geometrically with the aid of the TC curve of Figure 10.20. Consider output x_1.

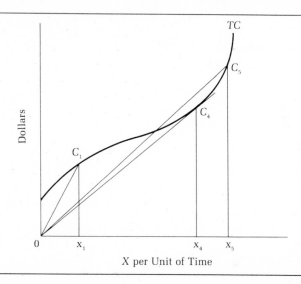

FIGURE 10.20
The geometry of AC and MC

Average cost at x_1 is equal to the slope of line $0C_1$. Marginal cost at output x_1 is equal to the slope of the TC curve at that output. The line $0C_1$ has a greater slope than does the TC curve at output x_1; hence, average cost at x_1 is greater than marginal cost at the same output. This will be the case for any output up to x_4. At output x_4 the slope of the line $0C_4$ is equal to the slope of the total cost curve at that output, meaning that average cost and marginal cost are equal at that output. As we have seen already, average cost is minimum at output x_4. At output x_5 the slope of line $0C_5$ is less than the slope of the TC curve, meaning that marginal cost is greater than average cost at that output. This relationship will hold at any output above x_4—that is, at outputs for which average cost is increasing. Thus, when average cost is decreasing, marginal cost is less than average cost. When average cost is increasing, marginal cost is greater than average cost.

Prices and Output Levels of Goods and Services

We bring demand and costs together in Part Four. Building on the foundations laid in Parts Two and Three, we develop models of the market mechanism to show how prices and output levels of goods and services are determined under each of the four basic selling market structures that were introduced in Chapter 8.

Pricing and Output
under Pure Competition

The purely competitive model of prices and outputs is constructed in this chapter. It explains how production is organized by prices and profits in a purely competitive, or frictionless, private enterprise economy. Ways in which monopoly elements modify the operation and the results of the system are taken into account in the following three chapters.

Pure competition was defined in Chapter 3. Its prime characteristics are (1) product homogeneity among the sellers of an industry; (2) many buyers and sellers of the product—that is, enough of each so that no one is large enough relative to the entire market to influence product price; (3) an absence of artificial restraints on demand, supply, and product price; and (4) mobility of goods and resources.

The Very Short Run

The *very-short-run*, or *market*, period, refers to situations in which supplies of products are already in existence. For example, demand for a product may be seasonal, with production scheduled ahead of the months in which the item is to be sold. The clothing industries are cases in point. Spring, summer, fall, and winter production are based on estimated seasonal demands and occur well in advance of the season of sales. Other examples are retail markets for fresh fruit and vegetables. Retailers purchase stocks of perishable goods. Once the stocks are on hand, they must be disposed of before they spoil. Still another example is that of a product produced seasonally for a demand that continues the year around. Production of wheat and other farm crops typifies this situation. Two basic problems must be solved by the economy in the very short run: (1) how are existing supplies of goods to be allocated or rationed among the many consumers who want them, and (2) how are given supplies to be rationed over their entire very short-run periods?

Rationing among Consumers

Price is the mechanism for rationing or allocating a fixed supply among the consumers who want it. Suppose that the period during which the supply is fixed is one day and that the demand curve of Figure 11.1 shows the different quantities per day that consumers will take from the market at different possible prices. The supply curve is vertical since the supply for the day is fixed. Price p will clear the market. Everyone who wants the commodity at that price will receive it in the desired amounts. At a price below p a shortage will develop, and consumers will drive the price up. At a price above p surpluses will exist, and individual sellers will lower their prices to get them off their hands. At price p consumers voluntarily ration themselves to the fixed supply.

Rationing over Time

Prices also serve to ration a fixed supply over time, but the process is more complex. Suppose that the market period is one year. Suppose, however, that the demand curve of Figure 11.2 is based on a four-month period only. To simplify matters, imagine further that the demand curves for each of the three four-month periods of the year are alike. Assume that sellers more or less correctly anticipate the market for each four-month period and sell or hold their supplies accordingly.

Since the diagram applies to a four-month period only, the supply curve for the first period will not be vertical. Sellers have the option of selling during any of the three four-month periods. The higher the price offered during the first period, the greater the quantity of the good they would be expected to place on the market during that time span. Thus, the supply curve for the first four-month

FIGURE 11.1
Very-short-run rationing among consumers

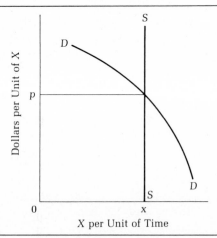

FIGURE 11.2
Very-short-run
rationing over time

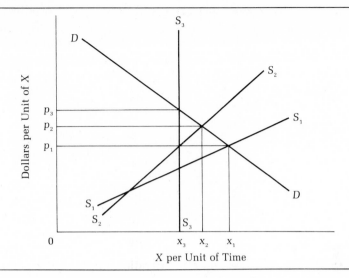

period will be upward-sloping to the right as is S_1S_1. The market price will be p_1, and the quantity sold will be x_1.

The supply curve for the second four-month period would be expected to lie above S_1S_1, except at low prices, and to be less elastic. It would lie above S_1S_1 because sellers, to be induced to hold quantities over, would require sufficiently higher prices for different quantities to cover storage costs and a normal rate of return on investment in the goods carried over. At relatively low prices, however, the quantities supplied for the second four-month period may lie to the right of S_1S_1. The possibility of low prices in the second period is more serious to sellers than is a similar possibility in the first period because the opportunities for disposing of supplies held over have been reduced. Consequently, sellers may be induced to place more on the market than they would have been willing to at those same prices in the first period. The smaller elasticity at various prices is also a result of the narrowing of opportunities for disposing of the supplies held over. The periods during which supply can be disposed of now have been reduced to two. The supply curve for the second period would look something like S_2S_2. The price would be p_2, and the quantity sold would be x_2.

The third four-month period will be identical with the case shown in Figure 11.1. The remaining supply must be disposed of in the third period; consequently, the supply curve will be S_3S_3 in Figure 11.2. Note that S_3S_3 lies above S_2S_2 except at low prices and that it is less elastic than S_2S_2. In fact, S_3S_3 is completely inelastic. The price will be p_3, and the quantity sold will be x_3.

The successively higher prices for the four-month periods will occur as shown only if sellers correctly anticipate demand and the amounts that should be held over. If sellers misjudge the future market and hold large quantities over to the second and third periods, the prices during those periods may fall below that of the first period. If sellers' anticipations are correct, the price for each successive period should be sufficiently higher than that of preceding periods to pay storage costs, a normal rate of return on investment in held-over supplies, and compensation for the risks in holding supplies over to succeeding periods.

Thus, price is the rationer of fixed supplies over time. Sellers or speculators, as the case may be, in holding supplies off the market during the early part of the overall very-short-run period cause the price to be higher during that time than it would otherwise have been. By their speculative activity they smooth out both the prices and quantities sold over the entire period. In the absence of any speculative activity, relatively large quantities would be placed on the market early in the period, holding the price down. Relatively small quantities available in the latter part of the period would cause the price to be high. The speculative activity described, while not eliminating the upward price trend over time, does much to narrow the differential between the early and late parts of the period. Activity of this type occurs regularly in the markets for those storable farm products lying outside the price-support program.

A Corollary

A corollary to this discussion is that once a good is on the market in fixed quantity, costs of production play no part in the determination of its price. The price will be determined solely by the fixed supply, together with demand for the product.[1] It is futile for holders of such a product to try to recoup production costs. A purely competitive seller, who cannot alone consume the product, will prefer to dispose of the holdings at any price above zero rather than keep it indefinitely. Old bread and overripe bananas are cases in point. Costs of production enter the picture only when there is some possibility of varying the supply produced over the time period under consideration. Such a possibility exists in both the short and the long run, which we have yet to consider.

The Short Run

A time period in which a firm can vary its output but does not have time to change its size of plant is the *short run*. The number of firms

---

[1] Note that in the example of Figure 11.2 market supply is fixed at an absolute quantity for the third period only.

in an industry is fixed because new firms do not have time to enter and existing firms do not have time to leave. Any changes in industry output must come from the fixed plant capacity of existing firms. Since each firm is too small, relative to the market in which it sells, to be able to affect the market price of the product, the problem facing the firm is that of determining what output to produce and sell. For the market as a whole, the market price and market output must be determined.

The Firm

As a starting point, we use the premise that a firm's objective is to maximize its profits or minimize its losses if it cannot make profits. This premise can be modified to include such objectives as sales maximization with a minimum profit constraint, concern for the environment, enhancement of community cultural activities, and the like. But usually we expect a firm to make those choices that will enable it to make more profits rather than less, and such choices lead toward profit maximization.

Profits   Since the concept of profit is ambiguous enough to require explicit definition, a note on profits is in order before proceeding further. *Economic profits* are a pure surplus or an excess of total receipts over *all* costs of production incurred by the firm. Included as costs are obligations incurred for all resources used equal to what those resources could earn employed in their next best alternative uses, that is, the opportunity or alternative costs of all resources used. These costs include returns to the owners of capital used, equivalent to what they could get had they invested in capital elsewhere in the economy. They include implicit returns to labor owned by the operator of the business. Thus, profits are so much "gravy" for the firm.

  The contrast between the concept of economic profits, as defined, and the accountant's concept of a corporation's net income or "profits" should help make this definition clear. Corporation income taxes will be ignored. A corporation's "profits" are determined by the accountant as follows:

Gross income
− Expenses (including interest payments on bonds,
  amortization expenses, depreciation expenses, and so on)
───
= Net income or "profits"

However, from the point of view of economics, certain costs have been left out of consideration. Obligations incurred to the owners of the corporation's capital (its stockholders) are as much costs of production as are those incurred for labor or for raw materials. The corporation is usually thought to make payments to capital owners in the form of dividends from the corporation's "profits," but from the point of view of economic theory this is incorrect. To arrive at economic profits, dividend payments equal to what investors could earn had they invested elsewhere in the economy should be subtracted from the corporation's net income as follows:

$$\frac{\begin{array}{l} \text{Net income or ``profits''} \\ -\ \text{Average dividends} \end{array}}{=\ \text{Economic profits}}$$

What happens to profits made by an individual firm? They accrue primarily to the owners of the firm in the form of (1) higher returns to investors in the business or (2) increases in the value of the owners' holdings. The former means higher-than-average dividends to stockholders in the case of the corporation or, in the case of a single proprietor or partner, a higher income than could have been earned had that individual invested and/or worked elsewhere. The latter means that some of the economic profits are plowed back into the firm to expand or improve it. This action increases the value of the owners' holdings. Profits may be used sometimes to pay other resource owners' returns that are more than the opportunity costs of their resources.

Profit Maximization: Total Curves Profit maximization requires a comparison of total costs with total receipts at various possible output levels and choice of the output at which total receipts exceed total costs by the greatest amount. Total receipts, or total revenue at different outputs, are plotted against short-run total costs at various levels of output in Figure 11.3. The total cost curve is the short-run total cost curve of the preceding chapter. The total receipts curve needs further elaboration.

Since the purely competitive firm can sell either large or small outputs at the same price per unit, its total receipts curve will be a linear upward-sloping curve starting at zero. If sales of the firm are zero, so are total receipts. If sales are one unit of output per unit of time, the firm's total receipts are equal to the price of the product. At two units of output and sales, total receipts will be twice the price of the product. Each one-unit addition to the firm's sales per unit of time will increase total receipts by a constant amount—the price per unit of product—hence, the total receipts curve is upward-sloping and linear.[2]

---

[2]   The total receipts curve can be written as

$$R = f(x) = xp.$$

FIGURE 11.3
Short-run profit
maximization: total
curves

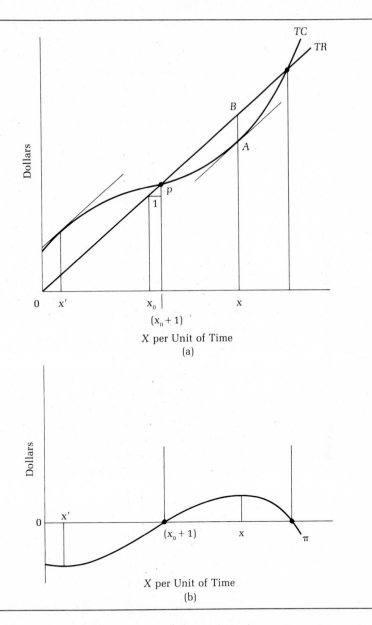

X per Unit of Time
(a)

X per Unit of Time
(b)

Profits of the firm are maximum at output x, where the vertical distance of TR above TC is greatest. The amount is measured by AB. At output x the slopes of the two curves are equal. At outputs just smaller than x, the slope of TR exceeds that of TC; hence, the two curves spread farther and farther apart as output increases. At outputs just greater than x, the slope of TC exceeds that of TR; hence, the two curves come closer and closer together as output rises.

The amount by which the firm's total receipts change when its sales are changed by one unit is called *marginal revenue*. Under conditions of pure competition, since the product price is fixed in the firm's view, the change in total receipts brought about by a one-unit change in sales is necessarily equal to the product price. Marginal revenue and the product price for the purely competitive seller are the same thing. In Figure 11.3(a) an increase in sales from x_0 to $(x_0 + 1)$ increases TR by an amount equal to p. Thus, both marginal revenue and product price are equal to the slope of the TR curve.[3]

The necessary conditions for profit maximization can be restated in terms of marginal revenue and marginal cost. Since marginal cost is equal to the slope of the TC curve and marginal revenue is equal to the slope of the TR curve, profits are maximized at the output at which marginal cost equals marginal revenue.[4] At outputs between x' and x, we can see that marginal revenue is greater than marginal cost. Therefore, larger outputs in this range up to x will add more to the firm's total receipts than to the firm's total costs and, consequently, will make net additions to profits or net deductions from losses. Beyond output x marginal cost is greater than marginal revenue. Larger outputs beyond x add more to total costs than to total receipts and cause profits to fall.[5]

Profit Maximization: Per Unit Curves Analysis of the firm's profit-maximizing output is usually put in terms of per unit cost and revenue curves. The basic analysis is the same as above, but the diagrammatic treatment is in a different form. The firm's short-run average cost curve and short-run marginal cost curve are shown in Figure 11.4, as is the demand curve faced by the firm. Since marginal

---

[3] The relationship between marginal revenue and total revenue is the same as that between marginal utility and total utility, between marginal physical product and total product of a resource, and between marginal cost and total cost. Since

$$R = f(x) = xp,$$

in which p is a constant, then

$$MR = \frac{dR}{dx} = f'(x) = p.$$

[4] This statement must be used with caution. Consider output x' in Figure 11.3. At output x' losses are maximized rather than profits, although marginal cost equals marginal revenue. The relationship between the TR curve and the TC curve at the output of equality between MR and MC must be considered carefully.

[5] Denoting profits by π and letting the total cost function be $C = g(x)$, then

$$\pi = R - C = f(x) - g(x).$$

The first-order conditions for profit maximization are

$$\frac{d\pi}{dx} = f'(x) - g'(x) = 0,$$

or

$$f'(x) = g'(x);$$

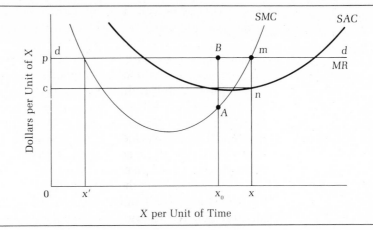

FIGURE 11.4
Short-run profit maximization: per unit curves

revenue is equal to the price per unit, the marginal revenue curve coincides with the demand curve faced by the firm. Both are horizontal at the level of the market price of the product.

Profits are maximum at the output level at which marginal cost equals marginal revenue, that is, at x, where SMC equals MR.[6] At any output less than x, say x_0, marginal revenue x_0B exceeds marginal cost x_0A. Larger outputs up to x will increase total receipts more than they do total costs; hence, profits will rise up to that point. Beyond output x, SMC is greater than MR, and movement to those larger outputs will increase total costs more than they do total receipts, causing profits to decrease. Therefore, x is the output of maximum profits. Total profits of the firm appear in Figure 11.4 as the area of the rectangle $cpmn$. Profit per unit is the price p minus average cost c at output x. Total profit is equal to profit per unit multiplied by sales; that is, total profit equals $cp \times x$. Note that at output x profit per unit is not maximized, nor is there any reason

that is,

$$MR = MC.$$

If the second-order conditions show

$$\frac{d^2\pi}{dx^2} < 0,$$

the output is one of maximum profit—like x in Figure 11.3(b). If the second-order conditions show

$$\frac{d^2\pi}{dx^2} > 0,$$

losses are maximized. This is the case at x' in Figure 11.3(b).

[6] Note that MC equals MR at output x', but this is an output of maximum loss. For profit maximization MC must equal MR and, *additionally*, the MC curve must intersect the MR curve from below.

why it should be. The concern of the firm is with total profits, not with profit per unit.

Loss Minimization   If it should happen that the market price of the product is less than short-run average costs at all possible output levels, the firm will incur losses instead of making profits. Since the short run is defined as a time period so short that the firm cannot change its size of plant, liquidation of the plant in the short run is not possible. The choices open to the firm are whether to (1) produce at a loss or (2) discontinue production. Fixed costs will be incurred even if the second alternative is chosen.

The firm's decision rests on whether or not the price of the product covers average variable costs (or whether total receipts cover total variable costs). Suppose the market price of the product is p_0 in Figure 11.5. If the firm produces x_0, at which SMC equals MR_0, total receipts equal $p_0 \times x_0$. Total variable costs also equal $p_0 \times x_0$; hence, total receipts just cover total variable costs. Total costs are equal to total variable costs plus total fixed costs; therefore, if variable costs are just covered, the firm's loss will be equal to total fixed costs. It makes no difference whether the firm produces or not. In either case, losses equal total fixed costs.

If the market price is less than minimum average variable costs, the firm will minimize losses by discontinuing production. The loss will equal total fixed costs when the firm produces nothing. If the firm should produce at a price less than p_0, average variable costs would be greater than price and total variable costs would be greater than total receipts. Losses would equal total fixed costs plus that part of total variable costs not covered by total receipts. Price p_0 is called the *shutdown price*.

FIGURE 11.5
Short-run loss
minimization

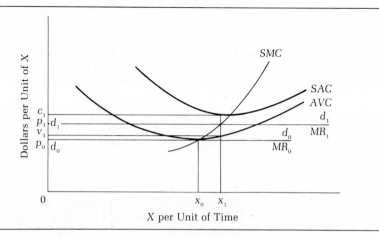

At a price greater than minimum average variable costs, but less than minimum SAC, it pays the firm to produce. At a price such as p_1, an output of x_1 results in losses that are less in amount than total fixed costs. Total receipts are $p_1 \times x_1$. Total variable costs are $v_1 \times x_1$. Total receipts exceed total variable costs by an amount equal to $v_1 p_1 \times x_1$. The excess of total receipts over total variable costs can be applied against total fixed costs, thus reducing losses to an amount less than total fixed costs. Loss in this case equals $p_1 c_1 \times x_1$.

Suppose, for example, that the producer under consideration is a wheat farmer who owns his farm and his machinery. The farm is mortgaged and the machinery not yet paid for. Mortgage and machinery payments constitute fixed costs and must be met whether or not the farmer produces wheat. Outlays for seed, gasoline, fertilizer, and his own labor represent variable costs. If the farmer produces nothing, there are no outlays on variable resources.

Under what circumstances should the farmer produce nothing at all and hire his labor out to someone else? If expected receipts from the wheat crop are not sufficient to cover the costs of seed, gasoline, fertilizer, and his own labor, he should not produce. If he produces under these circumstances, his losses will equal mortgage and machinery payments plus that part of his variable costs not covered by his receipts. If he does not produce, his losses will equal mortgage and machinery payments only. Thus, he should not produce.

Under what circumstances will it be to his advantage to produce even though incurring losses? If expected receipts will more than cover the variable costs, the excess can be applied to the mortgage and machinery payments, and production should be undertaken. Under these circumstances, a decision not to produce means that the loss will be the full amount of the fixed costs. If the farmer produces, the loss will be less than the total fixed costs.

At output level x_1, when the market price is p_1, equality between SMC and MR shows that losses are minimum. At a lower output MR is greater than SMC, and increases in output will add more to total receipts than to total costs, thus reducing losses. Beyond x_1, SMC is greater than MR, meaning that increases in output add more to total costs than to total receipts. The increases in output will increase the losses. Hence, losses are minimum at the output where SMC equals MR.

To summarize, the firm maximizes profits or minimizes losses by producing the output at which SMC equals MR, or the price. There is one exception. If the market price is less than the firm's average variable costs, losses will be minimized by stopping production altogether, leaving losses equal to total fixed costs.

Short-run Supply Curve of the Firm   That part of the firm's *SMC* curve that lies above the *AVC* curve is the firm's *short-run supply curve* for the product. The *SMC* curve shows the different quantities that the firm will place on the market at different possible prices. At each possible price, the firm will produce the amount at which *SMC* equals p (and *MR*) to maximize profits or minimize losses. Supply drops to zero at any price below *AVC*.

The Market

The market price has been taken as given thus far, but we now have the tools necessary to see how it is determined. Market price emerges from interactions between demanders of a good, on the one hand, and its suppliers, on the other. We discussed the forces underlying a market demand curve in previous chapters, but we have yet to establish the market supply curve. The short-run market supply curve for a commodity is a short step beyond the individual firm supply curve. After we establish it, we shall consider short-run equilibrium for an entire market.

Short-run Market Supply Curve   As a first approximation, we can think of the *short-run market supply curve* as the horizontal summation of the short-run supply curves of all firms in the market. This supply curve shows the quantities of the commodity that all firms together will place on the market at various possible prices. Such a short-run market supply curve is valid if resource supplies to the group of firms in the market are perfectly elastic, that is, if changes in resource inputs and product output by all firms simultaneously have no effect on resource prices. We shall return to this point shortly.

Short-run Equilibrium   Diagrammatically, Figure 11.6 shows the determination of market price, market output, and the output of one representative firm of the industry. The output axis of the market diagram is considerably compressed as compared with that of the firm diagram. The price axes of the two diagrams are identical. The market demand curve for the product is shown as *DD* in the market diagram. The *SAC* and *SMC* curves of the representative firm are drawn in the firm diagram. The horizontal summation of all individual firm supply curves establishes the short-run market supply curve *SS*. The short-run equilibrium market price is p. The demand curve and the marginal revenue curve faced by the firm are horizontal at that level. To maximize profits, the representative firm, and each firm in the market, produces the output at which $SMC = MR = p$. The firm output is x. The combined outputs of all firms are the market output X. The market as a whole and each individual firm in it are in short-run equilibrium.

FIGURE 11.6
Short-run equilibrium:
firm and industry

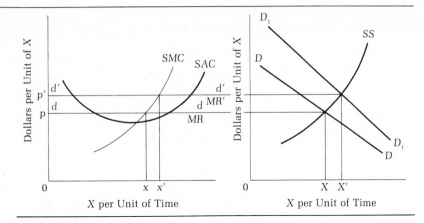

An increase in market demand for the product to D_1D_1 will increase the short-run equilibrium price and output. The increase in demand will cause a shortage of the good at the old price p, which will be driven up by consumers to p'. The demand curve and marginal revenue curve faced by the firm shift up to the level of the new market price. To maximize profits, each firm will expand its output up to the level at which its SMC equals its new marginal revenue and the new market price. The new output level for the representative firm will be x', and the new market output will be X'.

Supply Curve Modifications   When an expansion or contraction of resource inputs by all firms acting simultaneously causes resource prices to change, the short-run market supply curve is no longer the horizontal summation of individual firm supply curves. Even though one firm cannot affect resource prices through expansion or contraction of the quantities it buys, all firms acting at the same time may be able to do so. If the expansion of the market output and resource inputs raises resource prices, individual firm cost curves will shift upward. If expansion reduces resource prices, firm cost curves will shift downward. The possibility exists, too, that some resource prices will rise and some will fall. The effect may be to change the shape of the cost curves slightly and cause some shift up or down, depending on whether resource price increases or decreases are predominant.

The net effect of resource price increases, when expansion occurs, will be to make the short-run market supply curve less elastic than it would otherwise be. In Figure 11.6 the rise in demand increases price and marginal revenue, inducing firms to expand output. But suppose the output expansion pushes resource prices up, shifting SAC and SMC upward. The upward shift in SMC is also a shift to the left, meaning that the new SMC curve will equal marginal revenue or price at a smaller output than would be the case had the

SMC curve not shifted. Similarly, resource price decreases resulting from expansion of the market output will cause the market supply curve to be more elastic than the one shown in Figure 11.6. The short-run market supply curve in this case is obtained by summing individual firm profit-maximizing outputs at each possible level of the market price.

The Long Run

The possibilities of output variation in a purely competitive industry are much greater in the long run than in the short run. In the *long run*, output can be varied through increases or decreases in the utilization of existing plant capacity—as is the case in the short run. More important, however, in the long run firms have time to alter their plant sizes and there is ample time and opportunity for new firms to enter, or for existing ones to leave the industry. The two latter possibilities greatly increase the elasticity of the long-run market supply curve as compared with that of the short-run. Long-run adjustments in the size of plant by individual firms will occur simultaneously with the entrance or exit of firms to and from the industry, but they can be more easily understood if they are considered first by themselves.

The Firm: Size of Plant Adjustments

The firm's determination of the size of plant to use can be put into proper focus by assuming that entry into the industry is blocked in some way. Suppose that the firm is faced with a certain market price, say p, in Figure 11.7. Its long-run average cost curve and long-run marginal cost curve are *LAC* and *LMC*, respectively. To maximize

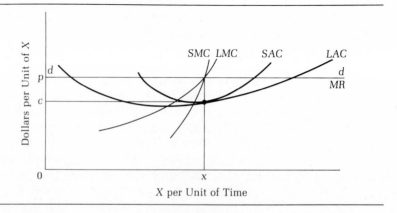

FIGURE 11.7
Plant size adjustment in the long run

long-run profits, the firm should produce output x, at which long-run marginal cost equals marginal revenue. The plant size that enables the firm to produce output x at the least possible cost per unit is SAC and for that size of plant, short-run marginal cost also is equal to marginal revenue. Profits of the firm are $cp \times x$.

The Firm and the Market

For the market as a whole, long-run adjustments to a disturbance depend on whether the industry is one of increasing costs, constant costs, or decreasing costs.

Long-run Equilibrium For a firm, *long-run equilibrium* means that it has either no incentive or no opportunity to change what it is doing. If profit maximization is its objective, the firm of Figure 11.7 is in long-run equilibrium. Its $LMC = MR = p$, so there is no incentive to change the size of its plant. Its $SMC = MR = p$, so there is no incentive to move from an output level of x per unit of time.

Long-run equilibrium for the industry implies more than that the firms in the industry are in that state. In addition, there must be no incentive for new firms to enter the industry or for existing firms to leave. In other words, there must be no lure of economic profits to induce the entry of new firms, nor can there be the pain of losses to prompt present firms to leave.

If entry into the industry is open—and in pure competition it is not blocked—profits like those made by the firm of Figure 11.7 will attract new firms. The industry promises a rate of return to investors greater than that they can earn on the average elsewhere in the economy. The entry of new firms increases the supply of product X and causes the price to move downward from its original level p. Each individual firm in the industry, faced with downward-shifting demand and marginal revenue curves, will cut its output level below x and will reduce its size of plant below SAC. In the interest of maximizing profits, outputs will be cut to levels at which the long-run marginal cost curve cuts the successively lower marginal revenue curves.

Economic profits can be made by firms in the industry until enough producers have entered to drive the price down to p_1, as is seen in Figure 11.8. At that point individual firms will have cut their plants back to the most efficient sizes, as is shown by SAC_1, and they will operate at the most efficient rate of output. Economic profits have been eliminated by the entry of new firms, and there is no inducement for more firms to enter. No losses are being incurred, and, thus, there is no incentive for firms to leave the industry. The firms in the industry are doing satisfactorily; they are earning returns

FIGURE 11.8
Long-run equilibrium

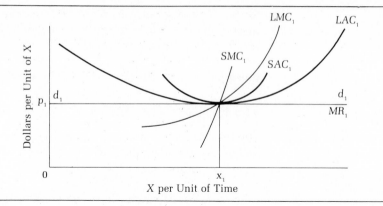

for all resources equal to what those resources could earn in alternative employments.[7]

The industry is in long-run equilibrium when all its firms are in the position shown in Figure 11.8. In general terms, for every firm $LAC = SAC = p$ at the output being produced, and at no other output can lower average costs be obtained. Also, for each firm there is no incentive to increase or decrease the size of plant or output since $LMC = SMC = MR$.

For long-run industry equilibrium to exist, individual firms must also be in long-run equilibrium. The converse of this assertion will not hold. An individual firm could be in long-run equilibrium while making profits—as in Figure 11.7, for example. But in this case,

---

[7] In the discussion of the long run we shall assume that for all firms, both already in the industry and potentially in it, the minimum points of the *LAC* curves lie at the same level. This condition is a necessary one for defining the long-run equilibrium position of an industry.

In reality long-run equilibrium is never likely to be achieved in any industry. It is a will-o'-the-wisp that industries forever chase but never catch. Before an industry can reach equilibrium, conditions defining the equilibrium position change. Demand for the product changes, or costs of production change as a result of resource price changes, or techniques of production alter. Thus, the chase goes on toward a new equilibrium position. The long-run (and other) equilibrium concepts are important, however, because they show us the motivation for, and direction of, the chase. Additionally, they show us how the chase works toward (in most cases) solution of the economic problem.

The argument usually made regarding equality of minimum long-run average costs of firms in the industry rests on the alternative cost doctrine. Initial inequalities in such costs may result from superior management of particular firms, from favorable locations of certain firms with respect to power, markets, and sources of raw and semifinished materials, or from other similar causes. According to the alternative cost doctrine, these differentials will not persist. The superior manager who can make profits for the firm could do the same for other firms in the industry and, perhaps, in others outside the industry. The manager's prospective value to other firms becomes his or her cost to the firm in which the manager works; thus, the cost of the manager's services to the one firm increases to the point at which the manager can make pure profits for none. The same argument applies to a favorable location. The cost of the favorable location becomes its value to other firms that could use it to advantage. Its value to other firms is the capitalized value of the returns it could earn for them. Hence, the profits it can earn for any one firm disappear as its cost is correctly determined.

the industry would not be in equilibrium. The existence of long-run industry equilibrium requires long-run individual firm equilibrium at a no-profit, no-loss level of operation.

Similarly, long-run equilibrium for an industry and an individual firm requires that short-run equilibrium exist at the same time. Short-run equilibrium for an individual firm and an industry can exist even though there is long-run disequilibrium for the individual firm and/or industry. Long-run equilibrium of an industry is a more general concept than is either long-run equilibrium for a firm or short-run equilibrium for both a firm and an industry.

Although this analysis serves to introduce the concept of long-run equilibrium in a purely competitive industry, it is by no means a complete analysis of the long-run adjustments that occur within the industry as a result of some disturbing force. Usually changes in cost as well as price will take place as new firms, attracted by profits, enter the industry. The nature of the cost adjustments, if any, will depend on whether the industry is one of increasing costs, constant costs, or decreasing costs. Each of these will be analyzed in turn below.

Increasing Costs   Consider first an industry of *increasing costs*. The nature of increasing costs will become evident as we move through the analysis. Suppose that the industry is initially in long-run equilibrium. Then suppose that the disturbing force is an increase in demand for product X. We shall trace through the short-run and long-run effects of the increase in demand. Then the long-run market supply curve for the product will be established.

Long-run equilibrium diagrams for the industry and for a representative firm of the industry are shown in Figure 11.9. The market demand curve is DD, and the short-run market supply curve is SS. The firms' long-run average cost curve and short-run average cost curve are LAC and SAC, respectively. The firm's short-run marginal cost curve for size of plant SAC is SMC. The long-run marginal cost curve is omitted. It is not essential for the analysis and unduly complicates the diagram.

Since the industry and the firm are in long-run equilibrium, they are necessarily in short-run equilibrium, too. Therefore, we can think of the market demand curve and the short-run market supply curve as establishing the industry price p. The demand curve and the marginal revenue curve faced by the firm are horizontal and are equal to price p at all levels of output for the firm. The firm produces the output at which SMC (and LMC) equals marginal revenue or price. Individual firm output is x. Industry output X is the summation of individual firm outputs at price p. There are just enough firms in the industry to make the price equal to minimum short-run and

FIGURE 11.9
Effects of changes in demand: increasing costs

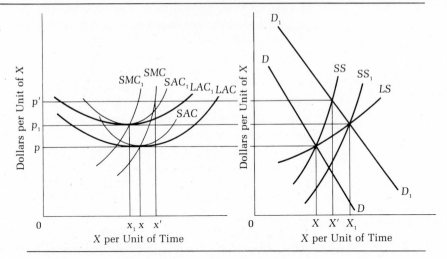

long-run average costs for the firm at output x. The firm is using the most efficient size of plant at the most efficient rate of output. There are no economic profits or losses being incurred.

What will be the short-run effects of an increase in demand to D_1D_1? The market price will rise to p'. To maximize profits, the firm will increase output to x', the output at which SMC equals the new marginal revenue. Industry output will increase to X'. The firm will be making profits equal to output x', multiplied by the difference between price p' and short-run average costs at output x'. The short-run effects of the increase in demand are (1) an increase in price and (2) some increase in output as existing plant capacity is worked with greater intensity.

Consider now the long-run effects. The existence of profits will bring new firms into the industry. As new firms enter, increasing the industry's productive capacity, the short-run market supply curve will shift to the right. The more firms that enter, the farther to the right the curve will move. The increases in supply will cause price to move downward from the short-run high of p'. As the price falls, individual firms will reduce output from the short-run high of x'.

In an increasing cost industry the entry of new firms causes the whole set of cost curves for existing firms to shift upward. Such a shift will occur in an industry that uses significant proportions of the total supplies available of the resources necessary for making its product. Suppose, for example, that one such resource is a special steel alloy. The entry of new firms in the industry increases the demand for such resources, thus raising their prices. As resource prices rise, the set of cost curves shifts upward accordingly.

Any given set of cost curves presupposes that the firm can get all it wants of any one resource at a constant price per unit. No single firm causes the prices of resources to change, since it does not take a large enough amount of any resource to be able to affect its price. It is the greater demand for resources brought about by the entry of new firms into the industry and, perhaps, by the simultaneous expansion of output by existing firms that causes resource prices to rise. The forces causing resource prices to rise lie completely outside the control of the individual firm and are said to be *external* to the firm. The increases in resource prices and the consequent upward shifts of the cost curves are thus the result of *external diseconomies* of increasing production in the industry.

A two-way squeeze is put on profits by the entry of new firms as the price falls and costs rise. New firms enter until the price decreases enough and costs rise enough for the price to be equal again to minimum long-run average costs for individual firms. All profit is squeezed out. In Figure 11.9 the new price is p_1, and the new cost curves are LAC_1, SAC_1, and SMC_1. The entry of new firms stops, and the industry is once more in long-run equilibrium. The new long-run market price of p_1 lies between the original long-run price of p and the short-run high of p'. The new firm output is x_1, at which SMC_1 is equal to the new long-run marginal revenue and price. Industry output will have increased to X_1, since the increased capacity of the industry has moved the short-run supply curve to SS_1.[8]

Will the new long-run output of the firm be equal to, greater than, or less than the old long-run output x? The answer depends on the way in which the cost curves shift upward. Whether these curves shift straight up, a little to the left, or a little to the right depends on the comparative price increases of different classes of resources. If all resource prices increase proportionally, the same combinations of resources will be the least-cost combinations. The cost curves will shift straight up, and the new long-run firm output will be equal to the old. Suppose, however, that short-run fixed resources go up relatively more in price than do those that are considered variable in the short run. The firm will want to economize on the now relatively more expensive fixed resources. The proportions of these resources to the relatively cheaper variable ones will be decreased to secure

---

[8]   To keep an already complex exposition as simple as possible, a long-run development of a transitory nature has been ignored in the argument of the text. The short-run high price, resulting from the increase in demand for the product, not only attracts profit-seeking new firms into the industry but also creates an incentive for existing firms to increase their plant sizes beyond the most efficient size. This situation will be the case, since for the individual firm maximum long-run profits are obtained at the output at which long-run marginal cost equals marginal revenue and price (see Figure 11.7). Then, as the entrance of new firms lowers price, the output at which long-run marginal cost equals price becomes smaller. The firm is induced to reduce its plant size. When enough firms have entered to eliminate profits, the firm once more will be building the most efficient size of plant.

enter, causes the cost curves to shift downward. Both the price of X and costs of production are decreasing. Eventually, the declining product price overtakes the declining cost curves, and profit is squeezed out. The new long-run equilibrium price is p_1 and is less than the original price of p. Individual firm output is x_1, at which both short-run and long-run marginal costs equal marginal revenue or price. The new industry output is X_1. The long-run supply curve LS will be downward-sloping to the right.

What are the circumstances that could conceivably give rise to decreasing costs? Suppose the industry in question is a young one growing up in a new territory.[9] Transportation facilities and the organization of markets, both for resources and the final product, may not be well developed. An increase in the number of firms in the industry and, consequently, in the size of the industry may make feasible the development of improved transportation and marketing facilities that will substantially reduce the costs of individual firms. For example, industrial growth of an area may stimulate development and improvement of railway, highway, and air transportation service into and out of the area. However, good explanations of decreasing costs are rather hard to find; whatever the explanations given for particular cases, they usually stem basically from improvements in the quality of resources furnished or from greater efficiencies developed in the resource-furnishing industries.

Decreasing costs, or *external economies* of increasing production, as discussed above, should not be confused with the *internal economies* of size possible for a single firm with a size of plant smaller than the most efficient one. The individual firm has no influence over external economies. These result solely from expansion of the industry or from forces outside the control of the firm. Internal econmies of size are under the control of the firm. The firm can secure them by enlarging its plant.

Probably, increasing-cost industries are the most prevalent of the three cases analyzed. Decreasing costs are most unlikely to occur. Industries of constant cost and of decreasing cost are likely to become industries of increasing cost as they become older and more well established. If it is possible to have decreasing costs, once the decreasing costs or external economies of increasing production have been taken advantage of, the industry must surely become one of constant or increasing costs.

The disturbing force triggering these chains of adjustments was assumed to be an increase in demand for the product. It could just as well have been a decrease in demand, in which case there would be losses for individual firms, and exit from the industry would have

---

[9] In this case the chances of its being one of pure competition are small.

occurred until long-run equilibrium was again established. Or, in lieu of changes in demand, we could have assumed that major technological developments caused disequilibrium, and these would induce new firms to enter the industry until long-run equilibrium was reestablished.

The Welfare Effects of Pure Competition

In a private enterprise economic system, what effects on welfare would be expected if the market structure in which producers and sellers operate were purely competitive? A complete assessment of the expected effects must wait until we have examined resource pricing and employment in detail; however, some tentative statements can be made at this point.

The welfare effects of purely competitive forces can be brought out by summarizing how the purely competitive mechanism operates. Suppose that initially disequilibrium exists; there is a random array of prices, outputs, and distribution of productive capacity (resources). There are two "givens" throughout the discussion: (1) pure competition exists in all markets, and (2) the distribution of purchasing power does not change. We shall focus attention on two goods, food (F) and clothing (C).

The Very Short Run

In the very short run, consumers—confronted with the initial prices of goods and services—attempt to allocate their incomes so as to maximize satisfaction. Since supplies are initially fixed, prices move to the levels that will just clear the markets and create no surpluses. All exchanges that are mutually beneficial occur as prices move toward their equilibrium levels. Since such exchanges benefit the exchanging parties without decreasing the welfare of anyone external to the exchanges, community welfare increases. Community welfare with fixed supplies is maximum when, for each consumer,

$$MRS_{fc} = \frac{p_f}{p_c};$$

or, in marginal utility terms,

$$\frac{MU_f}{MU_c} = \frac{p_f}{p_c}$$

or

$$\frac{MU_f}{p_f} = \frac{MU_c}{p_c}$$

All consumers are on their contract curves, and the distribution of goods is complete.

The Short Run

If the plant capacity in food and clothing production is fixed, and outputs of both commodities are not at short-run profit-maximizing levels, will the consequent adjustments increase welfare? Suppose that firms producing food are operating at outputs such that $SMC_f < p_f$, and that clothing firms are producing outputs at which $SMC_c > p_c$. The production of clothing will be reduced, and the production of food will be increased. Community welfare will be increased in the process. Consumers value variable resources used in producing F more than they value them used in making other goods. This differential valuation is the meaning of $SMC_f < p_f$. The price p_f is the value that consumers place on any one unit of F at the current supply level. At current production levels of F, the short-run marginal cost of F is the value of the products that the resources used in producing the last one-unit increment in F can turn out in their best alternative uses. Consequently, consumer welfare can be increased by transfers of resources from those other uses into the production of F—that is, from uses in which those resources produce a smaller value of product into the use where their output is of greater value. Similarly, $SMC_c > p_c$ means that consumers value resources used in producing C less than they value them used in producing other goods. Consumer welfare can be increased by resource transfers from C into the production of other goods.

The purely competitive market mechanism induces producers to accomplish the output changes that consumers desire. To maximize profits or to minimize losses in the short run, producers of F want to increase their outputs to levels at which $SMC_f = p_f$. Producers of C desire to contract their outputs to levels at which $SMC_c = p_c$. Producers in industry F offer slightly higher prices for the necessary variable resources. In industry C output contraction decreases demand for variable resources used in that industry, which, in turn, depresses the prices offered for those variable resources. To the extent that F and C use the same kinds of variable resources, voluntary reallocation by resource owners, from the lower-paying to the higher-paying uses sufficient to equalize their remuneration in the two uses, will occur. If the two industries use different kinds of variable resources, a general reallocation of variable resources may take place throughout the economy. Reallocation may occur, from industry C to other industries, that can use the kinds of variable resources needed in producing C. In turn, reallocation of the kinds of resources used in industry F, from other industries to industry F, may happen. The overall short-run resource reallocation that occurs will be limited, however, by the existing plant capacity in the two industries. Short-run equilibrium exists in the two industries when $SMC_f = p_f$ and $SMC_c = p_c$.

The Long Run

Although the short-run reorganization of production increases the welfare of consumers, it stops short of maximizing it because of fixed plant capacity in each industry. In the long run there is ample time for productive capacity to move, that is, for firms to enter and to exit whenever incentives to do so occur.

Suppose that short-run equilibrium exists and that firms in industry F show profits, while those in C incur losses. The profits in F and the losses in C mean that consumers value investment in plant and equipment more in industry F and less in industry C than they value it in other uses; their welfare will be increased by transfers of investment out of C, where they value it less, and into F, where they value it more. The incentives motivating producers bring about this result.

The short-run losses in C bring about rates of return on investment in that industry below what investment elsewhere in the economy will earn. Consequently, disinvestment in C will occur—through failure to take care of depreciation on plant and equipment and through the eventual liquidation of some existing firms. As firms leave industry C, the supply of C decreases, causing its price to rise. The decreased demands for resources in industry C lower their prices, decreasing costs of production for individual firms. The exit of firms will cease when the decreasing supply has raised the price and lowered costs enough so that losses are no longer being incurred. A smaller number of firms in C will be producing with plants of most efficient size and most efficient rates of output, but in total they will produce a smaller combined output at a higher price than in the short run.

At the same time, short-run profits in industry F will be attracting resources (productive capacity) into that industry. The profits indicate a higher return on investment than investors can earn elsewhere in the economy. This is a lucrative field in which to invest. New firms are established in the industry. Increasing demands for resources raise their prices and the cost curves of both entering firms and firms already in the industry. The entry of new firms increases industry supply, driving the price down. New firms enter until the increasing supply reduces the price of F to the level of the higher average costs. Entry stops when profits no longer appear to be obtainable to entering firms. Firms are forced to use most efficient plant sizes and operate them at most efficient rates of output to avoid losses. More firms are in the industry; their combined outputs are greater; and the product price is lower than it was in the short run.

The reallocation of resources may be direct or indirect. If the plant capacity of firms in industry C can be easily converted to the production of product F, firms in industry C may simply switch over to producing the more profitable F. Or, if the production processes of the two industries are unrelated, reallocations will be of the indirect nature described above, with firms folding in industry C and new firms emerging in industry F. In either case, profits and losses, and differential prices for resources in the two industries, bring about the desirable reallocation of resources or productive capacity.

With the establishment of long-run equilibrium, the economy is operating at maximum economic efficiency. Individual firms in each industry operate most efficient plant sizes at most efficient rates of output. Consumers receive units of each product at prices equal to the minimum obtainable average cost per unit. Each consumer is induced to consume those quantities of goods at which the marginal rate of substitution between any two is equal to the price ratio of the two. Thus, the marginal rate of substitution between any two goods is the same for all consumers. Producers are induced to produce quantities of each good at which long-run marginal costs are equal to their respective prices. Marginal rates of transformation between any two goods are thus equal to their price ratios and, in turn, are equal to consumer marginal rates of substitution between the goods.

The achievement of long-run equilibrium conditions in purely competitive markets appears to lead to maximum consumer welfare. As we examine the other market structures, we shall find that they fall short of reaching the summit; one of our tasks is to assess the extent to which they fall short. The purely competitive model provides an excellent bench mark for this purpose, and several conditions resulting from long-run purely competitive equilibrium that have welfare implications are worth noting.

First, pure competition leads to that organization of productive capacity at which *prices of products are equal to their per unit costs—marginal and average.* There are no profits or losses. Productive capacity (resources) is so allocated that it is valued equally by consumers in all its alternative uses, and no reallocation can increase welfare.

Second, *each firm operates at peak efficiency,* producing its output at the least possible cost per unit. In long-run equilibrium the firm is induced to operate a most efficient plant size at the most efficient rate of output in order to avoid losses. It takes advantage of all possible economies of size, as well as using the most efficient resource combination for the output level it produces.

Third, *resources are not diverted into sales promotion efforts.* No necessity exists for individual firms to engage in aggressive activities to promote sales when they sell in purely competitive markets. One firm alone cannot influence product price, and the products of all firms in the industry are homogeneous. Since the individual firm can sell all it wishes to at the going market price, sales promotion to increase its volume is unnecessary. The homogeneity of the product put out by all sellers largely precludes sales promotional activities on the part of one to raise his price. Buyers have so many alternative sources of supply that price increases on the part of one seller reduce his sales to zero.

Applications: Competitive Markets versus Monopolizing Incentives

Competitive industries are not always left free to remain competitive over time. First, in an industry of many firms, smaller single firms may be unable to protect themselves from efforts of larger firms to eliminate them from the industry through political means. Second, firms in a competitive industry may be able to reduce competition among themselves—that is, to become an effective cartel—through legislative or government regulatory activities. Each of these possibilities is illustrated in the competitive markets for personal transportation by car: the jitneys of the World War I era, and taxis in the Great Depression of the 1930s.

Jitneys[10]

Jitneys were unlike any present-day form of transportation. In the form of the Ford Model T, the first "family car" that was the rage of its day, they combined the features of buses, taxis, and delivery vehicles. Jitneys could hold about five seated passengers plus a few more standing on the running boards. Typically, the owner of a car would pick up fares who were heading in the same direction as he was during the morning and evening home-to-work commute at 5 cents each. In this sense jitneys were the first car pools. However, some owners drove jitneys on a full-time basis. A few would follow well-known routes and schedules, but most would select their "routes" according to the destination of the first passenger(s) to board (indicating the destination by posting a sign on the windshield much like

---

[10] This discussion is drawn from Ross D. Eckert and George W. Hilton, "The Jitneys," *The Journal of Law and Economics*, 15 (October 1972), pp. 293–325.

modern buses do) and then solicit other passengers who were headed in that general direction.

Jitneys were highly competitive among themselves, but most of their patrons came from the street railway lines. The trolleys dominated American urban transportation during this period, but they operated with fixed schedules and, of course, their routes were absolutely inflexible. An automobile trip often was more direct, quicker, and, like present-day taxi services, permitted lateral mobility away from main thoroughfares into residential areas. Moreover, the jitneys were aided by the trolleys' pricing scheme—5 cents per passenger regardless of distance. Although this was a bargain for a ten-mile trip, it was a relatively high price for a short jaunt of two to three miles. It was for trips of the latter type that jitneys were in greatest demand. Jitneys regularly worked the trolley lines, too, and often drove just ahead of the streetcar soliciting passengers at rail stops. Beginning in Los Angeles, in July 1914, the use of jitneys spread quickly until a nationwide peak of 62,000 units were in service a year later. The financial losses to the trolleys were huge, running at a rate of about $2.5 million annually in California alone in 1916.

The trolley companies initially viewed the jitneys as a "fad" that would quickly pass when the vehicle owners began making economically rational calculations of their operating and ownership costs. The street railways estimated these costs in a businesslike manner, including the expenses of depreciating cars and the implicit wages that jitney drivers could earn elsewhere. They concluded that most drivers were operating their vehicles at a "loss." But this was a serious miscalculation for two reasons.

First, the implicit wage that jitney drivers assigned themselves as a part of the costs of their enterprises was nonexistent or low, since most of them were either fully or partially unemployed. Unemployed jitney owners would put their vehicles into service if revenues were sufficient to pay them implicit wages equal to or above the money value they would place on their "leisure" time. Those to whom part-time employment was available would require implicit wages from jitney operations equal to or above what they could earn in the alternative employments. Consequently, during periods of recession more jitneys would be available than during periods of higher employment and better alternative earning opportunities. Trolley companies overestimated the implicit wages that would be required to induce persons to operate in the jitney trade—especially during the 1914–15 recession.

The trolley companies' second miscalculation was to assume that the family car, when used as a jitney, would be depreciated as an investment expense just as if it had been purchased for strictly jitney-driving purposes. The usual accounting calculation of profit-

or-loss, the so-called bottom line, would produce an erroneous economic result if it failed to take into account that the family car had been purchased and would continue to be used for nonjitney purposes whether or not the head of the household also drove the car as a public conveyance. The trolley companies failed to recognize that the costs most jitney drivers had to cover to remain "in business" were relatively low, and that the potential supply of jitneys was almost as great as the supply of family cars for part-time driving.

By the spring of 1915, the trolleys had switched from a policy of benign neglect to one of active hostility, and their trade press referred to jitneys as "a malignant growth" and "this Frankenstein of transportation." Most cities had only one trolley firm and few had more than two or three. Typically, trolleys received monopoly franchises from the city in exchange for tax payments of 1 or 2 percent of gross receipts. Thus, the city fathers and the trolleys had a mutual interest in annihilating the jitney, and they formed alliances for this purpose. The jitneys were numerous, but they were transient and wholly lacking in political clout.

Instead of prohibiting jitneys outright, the cities and trolley companies pushed through ordinances restricting jitney operations, thereby taking away the advantages that made them popular. Basically they raised the typical jitney's average costs to a point at which it became unprofitable to operate. Some of these ordinances were diabolically clever. Requiring that jitneys take out official licenses and pay annual fees (and in some cases take out franchises and pay direct taxes as a percentage of gross receipts) sharply raised jitney operating costs. Compelling them to operate full eight-hour days eliminated most of the part-timers. Establishing fixed routes for the small vehicles reduced their attractiveness to many passengers, and in many cities these routes were not permitted to parallel those of trolleys. Requiring that jitneys follow long routes all the way to suburban areas unprofitable for jitneys and trolleys alike eliminated even more. Many cities prohibited jitneys from soliciting passengers at rail stops and some even forbade them from entering downtown business areas. In some cities jitneys reacted by forming "car clubs" that did not charge fees for travel but did accept "donations" from their "members." But the courts held that this was an attempt to evade the law. By the end of 1915, the jitney fleet had been cut in half, and by the early 1920s, it was gone.

Taxicabs

The jitneys' survivors were called taxicabs. They provided personalized door-to-door services for fewer people at higher fares and did not threaten the trolley systems. Taxicab markets in most major cities were relatively unregulated before 1929. In that year major fleet owners established a nationwide trade association to lobby for ordinances to restrict additional entry to "their" markets.[11] With the Depression of the early 1930s, more and more unemployed people were flooding taxi markets just as they had the jitney markets two decades earlier. Entry costs were low and the competition was keen, and this time the "injured" parties were the established taxi firms rather than the transit companies. These firms lobbied their local city councils for ordinances to limit the number of licenses that could be issued, give preferential rights for new licenses to *existing* firms rather than new entrants, and set minimum fare levels to diminish price competition.[12]

In New York City, for example, a 1937 ordinance limited the number of taxi licenses to 13,566—the total of cabs then on the streets—as compared with about 11,900 in operation since 1961. The license, called a "medallion" because it consists of a steel plate bolted to the vehicle's front hood, may legally be sold. Through the years the demand for taxi service and the fares that cabs may charge have increased, but the supply of cabs has declined, largely because of restrictions on the use of automobiles and tires during World War II, which caused some licensees to abandon their medallions. The exchange value of the medallion reached $68,000 in 1980, although the annual license fee that the city charges is only $150; and banks, expecting that the city will not reissue dormant medallions or create new ones, have been willing to finance more than half the purchase price.[13] A similar licensing system exists in Chicago, where the number of cabs has been limited since the 1930s. In 1970, a maximum of 4,600 licenses was allowed; a license exchanged in the market then for about $25,000.[14] In Los Angeles a different system of regulation evolved. Licenses were limited in the late 1920s. In the early 1930s, there was a series of bankruptcies and mergers among taxi firms. In 1934, the city created five territories and gave each of five remaining firms a franchise to operate exclusively in one of the territories. That system of territorial monopolies endured for nearly fifty years.

The taxicab market in Washington, D.C., is a prominent exception to the producer pattern that we have seen. It is a competitive market organized to benefit customers. Washington taxi firms faced the same problems during 1930–33 as those in other cities. The

[11]   Edmund W. Kitch, Mark Isaacson, and Daniel Kasper, "The Regulation of Taxicabs in Chicago," *The Journal of Law and Economics*, 14 (October 1971), p. 317.

[12]   Ross D. Eckert, "On the Incentives of Regulators: The Case of Taxicabs," *Public Choice*, 14 (Spring 1973), pp. 83–99.

[13]   Joe Mysak, "Trafficking in Taxis: The Market for Medallions Is a Two-Way Street," *Barron's*, 23 February 1981, pp. 15–18.

[14]   Ibid.

number of operators swelled owing to unemployment, and the preexisting firms urged the local government to protect them from the influx of competitors. But Washington is a federal city, governed chiefly by members of Congress who are elected in the states and who are not beholden to local businesses for political support or other favors. Congresspersons keep the taxi market competitive by refusing to restrict entry; so supply is high and the fares (which Congress also determines) are low. This suits the self-interests of members of Congress since they use cabs intensively for business trips around town. Congress forbade taxi operators to install taxi meters, out of a concern that this would raise the cost of trips, and has instead maintained a system of "zone" fares which, as one might expect, has the lowest per mile prices on the trips that congresspersons take most often—generally the run between Capitol Hill and the federal offices downtown. Not surprisingly, a political system in which the interests of producers are relatively strong will yield outcomes in favor of those producers, just as a political system in which consumers hold the trump cards will tend to accommodate consumer self-interests quite nicely.

Summary

This chapter draws together the analyses of demand and of costs to show how the price system organizes production under the special conditions of pure competition. Pricing and output are discussed from the time viewpoints of the very short run, the short run, and the long run.

Supplies of goods are fixed in amount in the very short run. Price serves to ration existing supplies among consumers. Additionally, price rations the fixed supply over the duration of the period of the very short run.

Individual firm outputs can be varied within the limits of their fixed sizes of plant in the short run. To maximize profits, individual firms produce the outputs at which their short-run marginal costs equal marginal revenue or product price. Industry price of a product is determined by the interactions of all consumers and all producers of the good. Individual firms may make profits or incur losses in the short run.

In the long run, additional firms will enter industries that make profits, and some existing firms will leave industries in which losses occur. Thus, productive capacity expands in the former industries and contracts in the latter. Expansion of productive capacity lowers market price of the product and decreases individual firm profits. Contraction of productive capacity increases market price and reduces losses. Long-run equilibrium exists in each industry when the number of firms in the industry is just sufficient for profits not to be made nor losses incurred. When an industry is in long-run equilibrium, product price equals average cost of production. Each firm must be operating a most efficient size of plant at the most efficient rate of output if losses are to be avoided.

An industry may be characterized as one of increasing cost, constant cost, or decreasing cost. Increasing costs occur when the entrance of new firms into an industry raises the price of resources used to produce the product. The resulting higher costs are called external diseconomies. In constant cost industries, the entrance of new firms does not increase demand for resources enough to raise their prices. Consequently, no changes in the costs of existing firms occur. Decreasing costs, which must be rare in the real world, occur when the entrance of new firms causes resource prices and costs of production to fall. These are termed external economies.

Pure competition has certain welfare effects or implications that are important. First, consumers get products at prices equal to their per unit costs of production. Second, pure competition, where pure competition can exist, results in the greatest economic efficiency. Third, there is little motivation for sales promotion efforts on the part of individual firms.

Suggested Readings

Friedman, Milton. *Price Theory*. Chicago: Aldine 1976, Chap. 5.

Marshall, Alfred. *Principles of Economics*. 8th ed. London: Macmillan, 1920, Bk. 5, Chaps. 4 and 5.

Viner, Jacob. "Cost Curves and Supply Curves." *Zeitschrift für Nationalökonomie*, 3 (1931), pp. 23–46.

Questions and Exercises

1 A corporation's managers, contemplating a substantial increase in the company's plant and equipment, are puzzling over means of financing the new investment. The problem is whether they should float a bond issue to raise the money or sell additional shares of common stock. How will the corporation income tax affect the decision that they make on this issue?

2 To maximize profits, the firm produces an output level at which total revenue exceeds total costs by the greatest possible amount. At the same time profits are maximized at the output level at which marginal cost equals marginal revenue. Can you reconcile these two statements?

3 The Flight School at State University has asked to lease an individually owned Cessna 150 on a part-time basis for flight instruction purposes. The individual is free to use the airplane whenever she so desires. The Flight School proposes to pay a rate of $15 per hour for the use of the plane, plus the gasoline and oil that it uses. The costs to the individual of owning and operating the airplane are as follows:

Depreciation:	$1,000 per year
Insurance:	$600 per year if she leases to the Flight School
	$350 per year if she does not lease to the Flight School
Tiedown:	$150 per year
Annual inspection:	$250 per year
Maintenance and repair:	$5 per flight hour
Gasoline and oil:	$8.50 per flight hour

a If the owner does not lease the airplane to the Flight School and flies the airplane 100 hours per year, what is her hourly cost?

b Should she lease it to the Flight School at the proposed rate
  (i) If she flies the airplane 100 hours per year and the Flight School flies it 100 hours per year? Explain.
  (ii) If she flies it 100 hours per year and the Flight School flies it 50 hours per year? Explain.
  (iii) If she flies it 100 hours per year and the Flight School flies it 25 hours per year? Explain.

4 Explain why the long-run supply curve of a purely competitive industry is more elastic at each price level than the short-run supply curve.

Pricing and Output under
Pure Monopoly

The nature of pure monopoly was explained in Chapter 8; but we shall review briefly its essential characteristics before examining pricing and output in a pure monopoly situation. Pure monopoly is a market situation where there is a single seller of a product for which there are no good substitutes. The product sold by the monopolist is clearly different from other products sold in the economy. Changes in the prices and outputs of other goods leave the monopolist unaffected. Conversely, changes in the monopolist's price and output leave the other producers in the economy unaffected.

Pure monopoly in the real world is rare. Local public utility industries approximate it. Other industries that approach this type of market structure include the manufacturing of locomotives, telephone equipment, and shoe machinery, as well as the production of magnesium and nickel.[1] But monopoly is not pure unless substitutes are nonexistent. Even in the public utility field, gas and electricity are to some extent mutual substitutes. Aluminum also has substitutes, as do the metal alloys produced with the aid of molybdenum and magnesium.

Nevertheless, the pure monopoly model provides tools of analysis that are indispensable for the study of prices, outputs, resource allocation, and economic welfare. We shall discuss in turn basic monopoly concepts, short-run and long-run pricing and output, price discrimination, effects of monopoly on welfare, and the control of monopoly pricing.

Costs and Revenues under Monopoly

How, if at all, do monopolists' costs and revenues differ from those of pure competitors?

---

[1]   F. M. Scherer, *Industrial Market Structure and Economic Performance* (Chicago: Rand McNally, 1970), p. 59.

Costs of Production

The cost concepts that we developed in Chapter 10 are as applicable to pure monopoly as they are to pure competition. The difference between pure monopoly and pure competition lies in the conditions under which goods and services are *sold*, not in the conditions under which resources are purchased. In this chapter we assume that the monopolistic seller of a product is a purely competitive buyer of resources and has no effect on resource prices.[2] The monopolistic firm can get as much of any resource as it desires without affecting its price per unit.

Revenues

What is the difference between the purely competitive firm and the monopolistic firm on the selling side? A purely competitive firm faces a horizontal demand curve and a marginal revenue curve that coincides with it since the firm can sell any desired amount at the market price. However, the monopolist faces the market demand curve. With that demand curve, the price must be decreased to increase sales. The downward slope of the demand curve facing the firm has important implications for the monopolist's marginal revenue in relation to the price.

Marginal revenue at different levels of sales per unit of time for the monopolist will be less than the price per unit at those sales levels. Consider Table 12.1. A typical demand schedule faced by a monopolist is shown by columns (1) and (2). Total revenue at differ-

	(1) Price	(2) Quantity per Unit Time	(3) Total Revenue	(4) Marginal Revenue
TABLE 12.1 Demand, total revenue, and marginal revenue schedules	$10	1	$10	$10
	9	2	18	8
	8	3	24	6
	7	4	28	4
	6	5	30	2
	5	6	30	0
	4	7	28	(−)2
	3	8	24	(−)4
	2	9	18	(−)6
	1	10	10	(−)8

[2] Modifications of cost curves to take account of a single firm's influence on resource prices are deferred to Chapter 16. If used here, the modifications would make no essential difference in the development of the chapter.

ent levels of sales is listed in column (3), and at any given level of sales equals the price multiplied by the quantity sold. The marginal revenue column shows the changes in total receipts resulting from one-unit changes in the sales level. With the exception of the first unit, marginal revenue is less than the price at each level of sales. Suppose that the firm's current level of sales is 3 units of X. Price per unit is $8 and total receipts are $24. If the firm desires to increase sales per unit of time to 4 units of X, it must reduce the price per unit to $7 in order to expand sales. The fourth unit sells for $7. However, the firm takes a $1 loss per unit on its previous sales volume of 3 units. The total loss of $3 must be deducted from the selling price of the fourth unit in order to compute the net increase in total receipts resulting from the 1-unit increase in sales. Thus, marginal revenue at a sales volume of 4 units is $7 − $3 = $4 (the difference between $28 and $24).[3]

When the demand schedule and marginal revenue schedule of Table 12.1 are plotted on the same diagram, the marginal revenue curve lies below the demand curve. In fact, the marginal revenue curve bears the same relationship to the demand curve as does any marginal curve to its corresponding average curve. The demand curve is the firm's average revenue curve. When any average curve—average product, average cost, or average revenue—decreases as the firm's output increases, the corresponding marginal curve lies below it.

The relationship of a firm's marginal revenue and price is stated in a convenient form by

$$MR = p - \frac{p}{\epsilon};$$

that is, marginal revenue is equal to price minus the ratio of price to the elasticity of demand at any given level of sales.[4] Consider the

---

[3] Let the demand curve be

$$p = f(x).$$

Then

$$TR = xp = xf(x)$$

and

$$MR = \frac{d(TR)}{dx} = p + x\frac{dp}{dx} = f(x) + xf'(x).$$

A geometric method of finding the marginal revenue curve for a given demand curve is developed in Appendix I of this chapter.

[4] From Footnote 3

$$MR = \frac{d(TR)}{dx} = p + x\frac{dp}{dx} = p + \frac{p}{\frac{dx}{dp} \times \frac{p}{x}} = p - \frac{p}{\epsilon}$$

demand curve faced by a purely competitive firm, as is shown in Figure 12.1(a). Elasticity of demand at all outputs approaches infinity (∞). Because $MR = p - p/\epsilon$ and because $\epsilon \to \infty$, p/ϵ approaches zero and MR approaches p; that is, for all practical purposes $MR = p$ at all outputs. Now consider a monopolist faced by the straight-line demand curve of Figure 12.1(b). At output M, halfway between zero and T, $\epsilon = 1$. At smaller outputs $\epsilon > 1$ and at larger outputs $\epsilon < 1$.[5]

FIGURE 12.1
Implications of demand elasticity for marginal revenue

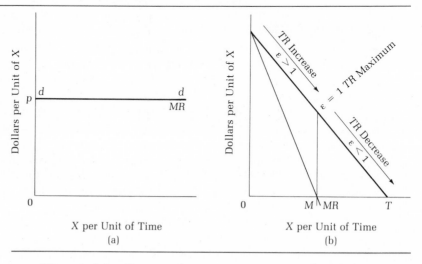

We noted in Chapter that an increase in sales, when $\epsilon > 1$, causes TR to increase. This means that when $\epsilon > 1$, MR must be positive. The equation $MR = p - p/\epsilon$ states the same thing. If $\epsilon > 1$, then p/ϵ must be less than p and MR must be positive. The greater ϵ is, the smaller p/ϵ will be, and the smaller will be the difference between p and MR. At the output where $\epsilon = 1$, TR is maximum and MR should be zero. The formula supports this point. If $MR = p - p/\epsilon$ and $\epsilon = 1$, then $MR = p - p = 0$.

In Chapter 3 we also learned that increases in sales, when $\epsilon < 1$, cause TR to decrease. MR must be negative in this case. If $MR = p - p/\epsilon$ and $\epsilon < 1$, then $p/\epsilon > p$ and MR is negative. The formula is consistent with our earlier observations regarding the relationships between elasticity and total revenue when sales are increased.

since

$$\epsilon = -\frac{dx}{dp} \times \frac{p}{x} \, .$$

This proposition is proved geometrically in Appendix II of this chapter.

[5] See pp. 57–58.

The Short Run

What are the effects of the different set of demand and revenue curves on a monopolist's output level and price?

Profit Maximization: Total Curves

The rules for profit maximization are the same for a pure monopolist as they are for a pure competitor. When plotted, the total receipts schedule of Table 12.1 becomes a total receipts curve like that of Figure 12.2. Note the difference between the monopolist's TR curve and that of a purely competitive firm. The difference results from the fact that to sell greater outputs the monopolist must charge lower prices. Therefore, total receipts increase at a decreasing rate and at some output level, such as x_1, they reach a maximum. Still larger sales cause total receipts to fall rather than rise. The monopolist maximizes profits at output x, where the difference between TR and TC is greatest. The output at which the difference between the TR and TC curves is greatest is that at which their slopes are equal (tangents to the curves at this output are parallel). Since the slope of the TC curve is marginal cost and the slope of the TR curve is marginal revenue, profits are maximum at the output at which marginal revenue equals marginal cost.[6]

FIGURE 12.2
Short-run profit maximization: total curves

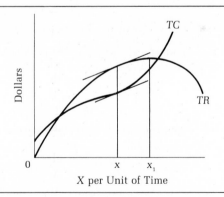

Profit Maximization: Per Unit Curves

Diagrammatic representation of short-run profit maximization by a monopolist in terms of per unit costs and receipts is presented in Figure 12.3. Profits are maximum at output x, at which SMC equals MR. The price per unit that the monopolist can get for that output is

---

[6]   The mathematics of profit maximization for a monopolist are the same as for a purely competitive firm (see pp. 288–89).

FIGURE 12.3
Short-run profit
maximization: per unit
curves

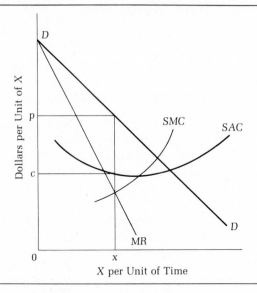

p. Average cost is c, and profits are equal to cp multiplied by x. At smaller outputs MR is greater than SMC; thus, larger outputs up to x add more to total receipts than to total costs and increase profits. At larger outputs MR is less than SMC; hence, increases beyond x add more to total costs than to total receipts and cause profits to shrink.[7]

Two Common Misconceptions

There is a common misconception that a monopolist always makes profits. Whether or not this is so always depends on the relationship between the market demand curve faced by the monopolist and the conditions of cost. The monopolist may incur losses in the short run and, like the purely competitive firm, continue to produce if the price more than covers average variable costs. In Figure 12.4 the monopolist's costs are so high and the market so small that at no output will the price cover average costs. Losses are minimum, provided the price is greater than the average variable costs, at output x, at which SMC equals MR. Losses are equal to $pc \times x$.

Another common misconception is that the demand curve faced by a monopolist is inelastic. Most demand curves, with the exception of those faced by firms under conditions of pure competition, range from highly elastic toward their upper ends to highly inelastic to-

---

[7] The intersection of MR and SMC tells us nothing other than that profits are maximum or losses are minimum at that output. The price is shown by the demand curve at that output and not by the MR curve. Profits are determined by the price and *average cost*, not by the price and *marginal cost*.

FIGURE 12.4
Short-run loss
minimization: per unit
curves

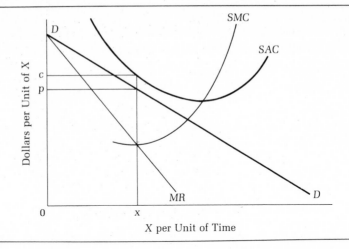

ward their lower ends,[8] and cannot be said to be either elastic or inelastic. They are usually both, depending on the sector of the demand curve under consideration. The output that maximizes a monopolist's profits will always be within the elastic sector of the demand curve if there are any costs of production. Marginal cost is always positive; therefore, at the output at which marginal cost equals marginal revenue, marginal revenue must also be positive. If marginal revenue is positive, then the elasticity of demand must be greater than one.

Short-run Supply

A monopolistic firm has no short-run supply curve. That part of the SMC curve lying above the average variable cost curve does *not* show the quantities that the monopolist would place on the market at the various alternative prices above minimum AVC. Instead, it shows the quantities that would be placed on the market at alternative levels of *marginal revenue* for the monopolist. Any given level of marginal revenue at the profit-maximizing output level is consistent with several alternative demand and price possibilities.

By way of illustration, suppose that a monopolist faces demand curve D_1D_1 in Figure 12.5. Profits are maximum at output x; product price is p_1; and the level of marginal revenue at that output level is r. Now suppose that the demand curve is D_2D_2, such that the marginal revenue curve MR_2 for the new demand curve also is equal to SMC at output level x and marginal revenue level r. The price at which

---

[8]   The situation could conceivably be reversed, but such an occurrence would be unusual. A demand curve that is inelastic toward the upper end and elastic toward the lower end would necessarily be one with a greater degree of curvature than that of a rectangular hyperbola.

FIGURE 12.5
Absence of the supply
curve in monopoly

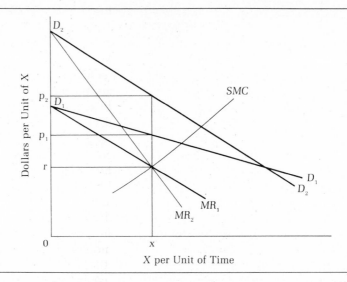

output x will be sold is now p_2 instead of p_1. Thus, the monopolist's output is not determined by marginal cost and price. Instead, it is determined by marginal cost and marginal revenue. For purposes of comparison, consider again the discussion of a purely competitive firm's short-run supply on page 292.

The Long Run

Long-run adjustments of monopolists, when profits are made in their respective industries, differ from those of competitive firms because of different entry conditions into their industries as well as because of differences in demand and revenue curves faced by the firms.

Entry into the Industry

Whereas the entry of new firms into an industry of pure competition is easy in the long run, entry into a monopolistic industry is blocked. The monopolist must be able to forestall the entry of new firms when profits are being made or the firm does not remain a monopoly. Entry into the industry will change the market situation in which the firm operates.

    The monopolist may block entry in several ways. It may be possible to control the sources of raw materials necessary for the production of the commodity. The Aluminum Company of America, for example, prior to World War II was reputed to own or control over

90 percent of the available supplies of bauxite, the basic raw material used in the making of aluminum.[9] Or patents held by the monopolist prevent other firms from duplicating the product. In the manufacture of shoe machinery, a single company once held patents simultaneously on virtually all equipment used in the manufacture of shoes. Instead of selling machinery outright to shoe manufacturers, the company leased it to them and collected royalties. The shoe manufacturer who obtained any equipment from another source then found it impossible to obtain key equipment from the company.[10] The market of a monopolist may be so limited relative to its most efficient size of plant that even though one firm makes profits, the entry of another would drive prices so low that both would incur losses. Thus, entry is blocked. Still other methods of blocking entry are possible. In the public utility field, exclusive franchises granted by the governmental unit concerned will do the job. These are some of the more important monopolizing devices.[11]

The requirement that entry be completely blocked, if pure monopoly is to remain just that, helps explain why it is rare. Except in cases where the government blocks entry, it is extremely difficult for a monopolist to suppress the rise of substitutes when profits can be made in the field. Patents similar to those of the monopolist can be secured, although putting them to use in making substitute products may be difficult in some cases. Some patents may become obsolete as new ideas and processes supersede those of the past. Where sole ownership of raw materials is the monopolizing device used, substitute raw materials frequently can be developed to make a product that is a reasonably good substitute for the original.

Size of Plant Adjustments

Since entry into the industry is blocked, the monopolist adjusts long-run output by means of size of plant adjustments. Three possibilities exist. First, the relationship between the monopolist's market and long-run average costs may be such that a plant smaller than the most efficient size will be built. Second, the relationship may be such that a most efficient size of plant will be appropriate. Third, the monopolist may, under certain circumstances, be induced to build a plant larger than the most efficient size.

---

[9]   Clair Wilcox, *Competition and Monopoly in American Industry*, Temporary National Economic Committee Monograph No. 21 (Washington, D.C.: Government Printing Office, 1940), pp. 69–72.

[10]   *Ibid.*, pp. 72–73.

[11]   A more complete list of devices for restricting entry into particular industries is discussed on pp. 373–75.

Less than Most Efficient Size of Plant Suppose the monopolist's market is so limited that the marginal revenue curve cuts the long-run average cost curve to the left of its minimum point. Figure 12.6 illustrates this situation. Long-run profits are maximum at the output at which LMC equals MR. The output is x and the price is p. The monopolist should build the size of plant that will produce output x at the least possible average cost for that output; that is, its short-run average cost curve SAC should be tangent to the LAC at output x. If SAC is tangent to LAC at output x, SMC is necessarily equal to LMC at that output.[12] Also, because output x is the output at which LMC equals MR, curve SMC is equal to MR at the same output. Thus, a monopolistic firm in long-run equilibrium is necessarily in short-run equilibrium, too. Profits are equal to cp × x. Any change in the size of plant or in the rate of output of SAC will decrease profits.

FIGURE 12.6
Long-run profit maximization: less than most efficient plant size

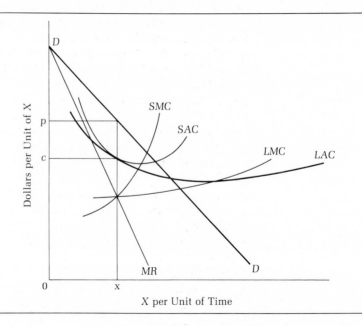

In this case the monopolist will build a less than most efficient size of plant and operate it at a less than most efficient rate of output. The market is not large enough to expand the plant sufficiently to take advantage of all economies of size. The size of plant used will have some excess capacity. If it were made smaller than SAC, so that no excess capacity occurs, there would be a loss of some of the economies of size that SAC offers. The loss would more than offset any "gains" from fuller utilization of a smaller plant size.

---

[12] See Chapter 10, pp. 258–59.

Local power companies in small- and medium-sized towns often operate plants smaller than the most efficient size at less than the most efficient rates of output. The relatively small local market for electricity limits the generating plant to a size too small to use the most efficient generating equipment and techniques. Yet the well-planned plant will have some excess capacity—both to take advantage of economies of size and to meet peak output requirements.

Most Efficient Size of Plant   Suppose that the monopolist's market and cost curves are such that the marginal revenue curve hits the minimum point of the *LAC* curve as in Figure 12.7. The long-run profit-maximizing output is x, at which *LMC* = *MR*; this will necessarily be the output at which *LAC* is minimum. The monopolist, to produce x at the least possible cost per unit for that output, should build plant *SAC*, the most efficient size of plant. In this case *SMC* = *LMC* = *MR* = *SAC* = *LAC* at output x. The firm is in both short-run and long-run equilibrium. The price is p; the average cost is c; and profits are equal to cp × x. Under the assumed conditions, the firm operates a most efficient size of plant at the most efficient rate of output.

Greater than Most Efficient Size of Plant   Suppose that the monopolist's market is large enough for the marginal revenue curve to cut the *LAC* curve to the right of its minimum point. This situation is diagrammed in Figure 12.8. The long-run profit-maximizing output is x. The proper plant to build is *SAC*, which is tangent to *LAC* at

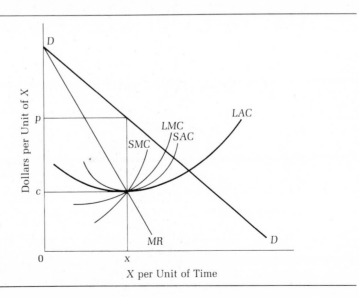

FIGURE 12.7
Long-run profit maximization: most efficient size of plant

FIGURE 12.8
Long-run profit
maximization: greater
than most efficient
plant size

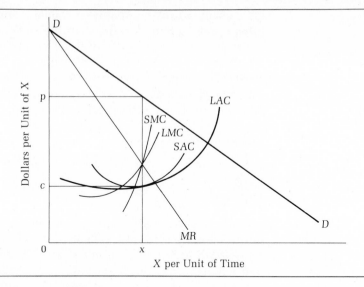

output x. At output x, $LMC = SMC = MR$; hence, the monopolist is in short-run as well as long-run equilibrium.

Under the assumed conditions, the monopolist builds a plant larger than the most efficient size and operates it at more than the most efficient rate of output if profits are maximized. The plant is so large that diseconomies of size occur. It pays to use a plant a little smaller than the one that would produce output x at its most efficient rate of output. By operating SAC at more than its most efficient rate of output, a lower per unit cost can be attained than would be possible with a larger plant. The diseconomies of size of a still larger plant are of a greater cost magnitude than is the operation of SAC beyond its most efficient rate of output.

Price Discrimination

In some cases a monopolist may find it possible and profitable to separate and keep separate two or more markets for its product and to charge a different price for the product in each of the markets. Two conditions are necessary for such *price discrimination* to occur. First, the monopolist must be able to keep the markets apart. Otherwise, the product will be purchased in the market with the lower price and resold in the one with the higher price, thus ironing out the price differential that the monopolist attempts to establish. Second, as we shall soon discuss, for price discrimination to be profitable the elasticities of demand at each price level must differ among the markets.

Distribution of Sales

Consider first the way in which a discriminating monopolist would distribute sales between two (or more) markets. Up to any given volume of sales (we shall ignore costs for the moment), it pays always to sell in the market in which an additional unit of sales per unit of time adds most to total receipts. This amounts to saying that sales should be distributed among the markets in such a way that marginal revenue in each market is equal to marginal revenue in the other market(s). This distribution yields the greatest total receipts from a given volume of sales.

Diagrammatically, suppose that the monopolist can sell in the two separate markets of Figure 12.9. The demand curves are D_1D_1 and D_2D_2, respectively. For convenience, the quantity axis of Market II is reversed, with units of X measured from right to left instead of from the usual left to right. If the volume of sales is less than x_0, the entire amount should be sold in Market I, since the additions to total receipts from sales in that market will exceed any addition to total receipts made from selling in Market II. If the total volume of sales equals x_1 plus x_2, the monopolist should sell x_1 in Market I and x_2 in Market II so that marginal revenue in Market I equals marginal revenue in Market II. The level of marginal revenue will be r in each market. To show that this distribution brings in the greatest possible total receipts, suppose that the sales volume in one market is cut by one unit and that in the other it is increased by one unit. Cutting sales by one unit in either market reduces total receipts from that market by an amount equal to r. Increasing sales by one unit in the other market will add less to total receipts than r, since marginal revenue from an additional unit of sales per unit of time in that market will be

FIGURE 12.9
Distribution of sales among markets: price discrimination

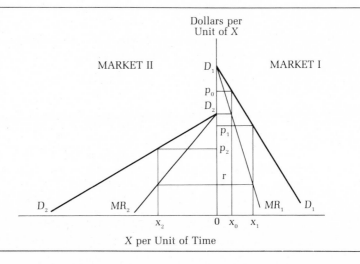

less than r. With the proper distribution of sales, the price in Market I will be p_1 and the price in Market II will be p_2.

The reasons why elasticity of demand at each possible price must differ between the two markets now become clear. Since $MR = p - p/\epsilon$, if elasticities were the same in the two markets at equal prices, the corresponding marginal revenues would also be the same. The distribution of sales that makes marginal revenue in Market I equal to marginal revenue in Market II would make the price in Market I equal to the price in Market II. If such were the case, there would be neither point nor profit in separating the markets.

Profit Maximization

The monopolist's cost curves, together with the marginal revenue curve for the total sales volume, are needed to solve the profit-maximizing problem. Let the average cost curve and the marginal cost curve be those of Figure 12.10. They depend in no way on how the monopolist's output is distributed among markets. The marginal revenue curve for the monopolist's total sales volumes, when sales are properly distributed among markets, is ΣMR in Figure 12.10. The demand curve and the marginal revenue curve for Market II have been drawn in the usual way. Then MR_1 and MR_2 are summed horizontally to obtain ΣMR.

The profit-maximizing problem is now reduced to a simple monopoly problem. The total output of the monopolist should be x,

FIGURE 12.10
Profit maximization: price discrimination

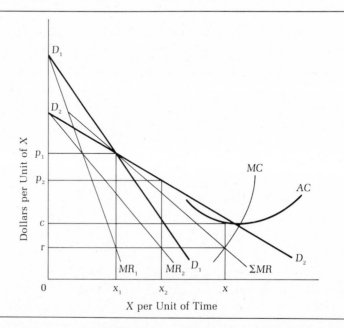

at which $MC = \Sigma MR$. The distribution of sales and the prices charged should be x_1, sold at price p_1 in Market I, and x_2, sold at price p_2 in Market II. Marginal revenue in Market I equals marginal revenue in Market II equals r with this distribution of sales. If total output and sales were less than x, marginal revenue in one market or the other (or both) would be greater than r, and marginal cost would be less than r. Increases in production up to x would, therefore, add more to total receipts than to total costs and would increase profits. If total output and sales were expanded beyond x, marginal cost would exceed r and marginal revenue in one market or the other (or both) would be less than r. Such increases in production would add more to total costs than to total receipts and would reduce profits. With output x properly distributed between the two markets, profits in Market I will equal $cp_1 \times x_1$ and profits in Market II will equal $cp_2 \times x_2$. Total profits will be $cp_1 \times x_1$ plus $cp_2 \times x_2$.[13]

Examples of Price Discrimination

Price discrimination is frequently encountered in public utility industries. Electric power companies usually separate commercial from domestic users of electricity. Having a separate meter for each customer enables the company to keep the markets apart. Elasticity of commercial users' demand for electricity is higher than that of domestic users; consequently, a lower rate is charged commercial

---

[13] Let the monopolist's total receipts for both markets be

$$R = R_I + R_{II},$$

in which

$$R_I = R_I(x_I)$$

and

$$R_{II} = R_{II}(x_{II}).$$

Let the total cost equation be

$$C = C(x),$$

in which

$$x = x_I + x_{II}.$$

The profit equation is

$$\pi = R - C = R_I(x_I) + R_{II}(x_{II}) - C(x_I + x_{II}).$$

To maximize profits

$$\frac{\delta \pi}{\delta x_I} = R_I{}'(x_I) - C'(x) = 0$$

$$\frac{\delta \pi}{\delta x_{II}} = R_{II}{}'(x_{II}) - C'(x) = 0,$$

or

$$R_I{}'(x_I) = R_{II}{}'(x_{II}) = C'(x),$$

which means that marginal revenue in Market I equals marginal revenue in Market II equals marginal cost for the monopolist's entire output.

users. This discrimination stems from the greater possibilities of commercial users adopting substitutes for the power company's product. Large commercial users may find it possible not only to find substitute sources of power but to generate their own electric power. Although domestic users may, and sometimes do, generate their own electric power, generating plants for their power needs are so small that costs per unit tend to be prohibitive.

Another example of price discrimination occurs in the field of foreign trade in the classic case of "dumping." Goods are sold abroad for a lower price than the domestic or home price. The markets are separated by transportation costs and tariff barriers. Elasticity of the demand curve facing the seller in the foreign market is usually higher than that in the domestic market. Although the seller may be a monopolist in the domestic market, he may find himself confronted abroad with competitors from other countries. Substitutes for his product on the world market increase the elasticity of the foreign demand curve he faces.

The Welfare Effects of Pure Monopoly

What impact would the introduction of pure monopoly into the purely competitive world discussed in the last chapter have on consumer welfare? The effects appear most striking when we assume that some markets are characterized by pure competition, and others by pure monopoly. As in the purely competitive case, a complete statement of the welfare effects of pure monopoly must wait until resource pricing and employment have been discussed.

Short-run Output Restriction

If all industries were initially purely competitive and were in long-run equilibrium, monopolization of one or more of them would reduce consumer welfare. Suppose, for example, that X in Figure 12.11 represents one industry in a purely competitive economy. The market demand curve is DD and the market short-run supply curve (the sum of the individual firm marginal cost curves) is SS. The market price is p, and the industry output level is X. Although the average cost curves are not drawn, suppose that the industry is in long-run equilibrium and that Pareto optimality exists throughout the economy.

What would be the short-run impact of monopolization of industry X? If the productive capacity of the industry were brought under the control of a single firm, demand would look different to the

FIGURE 12.11
Monopolistic output
restriction

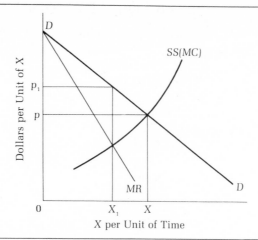

monopolist than it did to the individual firms making up the industry when it was purely competitive. The purely competitive firms each saw a horizontal demand curve at the market price p. Each firm saw a marginal revenue curve that coincided with that demand curve and produced an output level at which short-run marginal cost was equal to marginal revenue or price p. The monopolist sees the market demand curve sloping downward to the right and a marginal revenue curve that lies below the demand curve like MR in Figure 12.11. When we assume that the monopolist takes over intact the physical facilities of the industry and that no diseconomies of size are thereby engendered, SS (the industry supply curve or marginal cost curve under pure competition) is also the marginal cost curve of the monopolist. To maximize profits, the monopolist would reduce the industry's output level to X_1 and raise the price to p_1. The reduction in the output of X would release some of the resources used in the industry, and these would be used to increase the outputs of other goods, reducing their prices in the process.

As resources are transferred out of X into other uses, welfare is reduced. The marginal cost of X at any output level is the value in other uses that consumers attach to the resources used to produce a unit of X. The price of X at that output level is the value they attach to the same resource bundle used to produce X. We note, in Figure 12.11, that as the output level of X is reduced from X toward X_1 the marginal cost of X falls below its price, indicating that resources are being transferred from uses where their values to consumers are greater to uses where their values to consumers are less. This change must necessarily reduce the level of well-being of at least some members of the society.

Long-run Output Restriction

Welfare will also be held below its optimum level in the long run by blocked entry into an industry in which profits are being made. Where long-run profits occur, the product price exceeds average costs, indicating that productive capacity in the industry is too small relative to productive capacity elsewhere in the economy. Consumers value those resources making up plant capacity more when they are used in the profit-making industry than when they are used elsewhere—therefore, welfare is less than it could be.

A major problem posed by monopoly in a private enterprise economy, then, is that it prevents the price mechanism from organizing production in a Pareto optimal way. The monopolized industries are induced to maintain output levels that are too small—marginal costs are less than the respective product prices—and the monopolies prevent productive capacity itself from expanding where consumers desire expansion, that is, where profits are made. The use of insufficient resources in the monopolized industries necessarily means the use of too much in competitive industries if full employment of resources exists.

Inefficiency of the Firm

In addition to the welfare impact of output restriction, the monopolistic firm ordinarily will not use resources at their peak potential efficiency. The purely competitive firm in long-run equilibrium uses the most efficient size of plant at the most efficient rate of output. The size of plant and the output that maximize the monopolist's long-run profits are not necessarily the most efficient ones.[14] However, if monopoly is to be compared with pure competition on this point, the comparison is legitimate only for industries in which pure competition can exist. In an industry with a limited market relative to the most efficient rate of output of the most efficient size of plant, monopoly may result in lower costs or greater efficiency than would occur if there were many firms, each with a considerably less than most efficient size of plant. In such a case, even though monopoly may result in greater efficiency than any other type of market organization, resources still are not used at peak potential efficiency.

Sales Promotion Activities

It may be to the advantage of the monopolist to engage in some sales promotion activities, whereas under pure competition there is little

[14] See pp. 323–26.

point to activities of this kind. The monopolistic firm may use sales promotion to enlarge its market, that is, to shift its demand curve to the right. Also, if the firm can convince the public that consumption of its product is highly desirable or even indispensable, elasticity of demand at various prices may be decreased. Aditionally, such activities may be used to shield it from potential competition and to protect its monopoly position. Its objective in this case will be to get its name so closely tied to its product that potential competitors will find it futile to attempt to enter the market. At this point it is difficult to assess the impact of sales promotion activities on welfare. We shall be in a better position to analyze these effects when we have completed the chapter on oligopoly.

Regulation of Monopoly

The tools of monopoly analysis so far discussed provide some indications of how monopoly might be regulated to offset, at least in part, its adverse effects on welfare. Two possible governmental regulatory devices are (1) direct regulation of monopoly price and (2) regulation through taxation.

Price Regulation

Authority is frequently vested in state regulatory commissions to govern the rates or prices charged by public utilities, such as gas and electric power companies. The economic problem involved is determination of the rate that will induce the monopolist to furnish the greatest amount of product consistent with its costs and with consumer demand.[15]

The profit-maximizing output of a monopolist in the absence of price regulation is shown in Figure 12.12.[16] The monopolist maximizes profits at output level x, where marginal cost equals marginal revenue. The price will be p, and profits are $cp \times x$. Since entry into the industry is blocked, the profits may persist over time.

By establishing a maximum price below p but greater than r, the regulatory commission can induce the monopolist to increase output. Suppose a maximum price of p_1 is established—at the level at which the marginal cost curve cuts the demand curve. The demand curve faced by the monopolist becomes p_1AD. Between output

---

[15] Economic aspects of the problem frequently are subordinated to political aspects, but we shall omit the latter.

[16] The analysis can be presented in either long-run or short-run terms. A short-run explanation has the virtue of being less complex.

FIGURE 12.12
Regulation of
monopoly by price
control

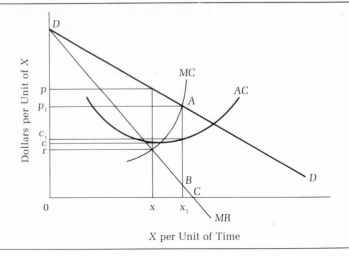

levels of zero and x_1, sales will be made at p_1 per unit. The monopolist cannot charge more, but the public will take its entire output at that price. For output levels greater than x_1, the monopolist must lower the price below p_1 to clear the market; hence, the market demand curve is relevant.

The change in the demand curve faced by the firm alters the marginal revenue curve as well. From 0 to x_1, the new demand curve is infinitely elastic—it is the same as the demand curve faced by a firm under pure competition—and marginal revenue equals p_1. Beyond output x_1, the market demand curve and the original marginal revenue curve are relevant. After the maximum price is established, the marginal revenue curve of the monopolist is p_1ABC.

The monopolist's profit-maximizing position must be reexamined in view of the altered demand and marginal revenue situation. With the establishment of the maximum price, x is no longer the profit-maximizing output. Profits will be maximized at the level of output at which the marginal cost curve cuts the new marginal revenue curve. At x, marginal revenue exceeds marginal cost; consequently, increases in output up to x_1 increase profits. At outputs beyond x_1, marginal cost would exceed marginal revenue—which drops off sharply, or is said to be "discontinuous" at x_1—causing profits to decrease. The new profit-maximizing output is x_1, a larger output than before. Even though profits $c_1p_1 \times x_1$ occur, welfare has been increased.

Taxation

Taxes levied on monopolists are often thought to be appropriate regulatory devices to prevent them from reaping the full benefits of their monopolistic positions. We shall consider two types: (1) a specific tax or a fixed tax per unit on the monopolist's output[17] and (2) a lump-sum tax levied without regard to output.[18]

A Specific Tax Suppose that a specific tax is levied on the monopolist firm of Figure 12.13. Its original average cost and marginal cost curves are AC and MC, respectively. The original price and output are p and x. The tax is a variable cost and shifts the average and marginal costs upward by the amount of the tax. Faced with the new cost curves, AC_1 and MC_1, the monopolist cuts output to x_1 and raises price to p_1 in order to maximize profits.

FIGURE 12.13
Regulation of monopoly by a specific tax

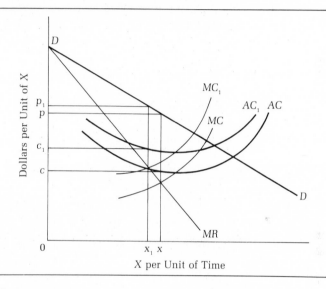

The monopolist is able to pass a part of the specific tax to the consumer through a higher price and a smaller output. At the same time the monopolist's profits will be smaller after the tax than before. Pretax profits were $cp \times x$. Aftertax profits are $c_1p_1 \times x_1$. To make certain that aftertax profits are smaller than pretax profits, think for a moment of the firm's total revenue and total cost curves. Total receipts of the monopolist at various outputs are unchanged by the tax, but total costs at all outputs will be greater. Profits at all possible outputs will be smaller than before, and maximum profits after the tax necessarily will be smaller than they were before. If all the monopolist's profits were taxed away through specific taxes, prices

[17] The general effects would be the same if an *ad valorem* tax, a fixed percentage of the product price, were levied.

[18] The general effects would be the same if the tax were a fixed percentage of the monopolist's profits.

still higher and outputs still smaller than those shown in Figure 12.13 would result. It appears that a specific tax on the monopolist's product would reduce welfare rather than increase it.[19]

A Lump-Sum Tax   Suppose that a lump-sum tax is imposed on the monopolist of Figure 12.14—for example, a license fee imposed by a city on its only public swimming pool. The original average and marginal cost curves are AC and MC. The original price and output are p and x. Since the lump-sum tax is independent of output, it is a fixed cost to the monopolist. It shifts the average cost curve to AC_1, but it has no effect on the marginal cost curve. Consequently, the profit-maximizing price and output remain at p and x, but profits fall from $cp \times x$ to $c_1 p \times x$.

FIGURE 12.14
Regulation of monopoly by a lump-sum tax

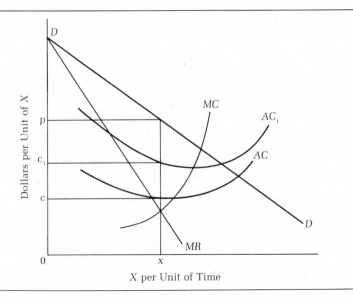

The lump-sum tax must be borne by the monopolist alone. It is not possible to pass any part of it on to the consumer through higher prices and smaller outputs. Attempts to do so will decrease profits even more. All of the monopolist's profits may be taxed away in this manner, with no effect whatsoever on output and price. The lump-sum tax by itself has no impact on welfare.

[19]   Consider, however, the possible effects of specific taxes levied on the outputs of pure competitors in the economy, which would induce them to reduce their output levels, releasing resources to the monopolized industries and inducing the latter to expand their outputs. Or consider the impact of per unit subsidies paid to monopolists.

Application:
Finding the Right Monopoly Price

It is easy for other firms to look upon a monopolist's situation with envy. After all, the absence of competitors and product substitutes permits higher than competitive profits from higher prices and lower quantities. The exact price and quantity to maximize profits looks easy enough from Figure 12.3. But the detailed information a monopolist must have to maximize profits is almost never instantly available and often can be obtained only at a sizable dollar cost.

How many times have we heard in casual conversation, or read in newspapers, that a monopolist "always will charge the highest price that the market will bear"? But the *right* price to maximize profits is not provided by the market automatically. The monopolist can "set" the market price because of control over quantity supplied. But which market price should be chosen?

A monopolist usually has more accurate information about the nature of costs than about demand. Is the demand curve straight or curved? Where does it lie? What are the elasticities at each price? In practice, most monopolists attempt to answer these questions by shrewd guesses and estimates, trial-and-error changes in price as new conditions develop, and sometimes by sophisticated market research to delineate specific arcs of the demand schedule. But these are costly processes requiring time and resources. Sometimes expert consultants and brokers who specialize in acquiring this information about demand and in making better-than-average predictions about particular price elasticities are hired. Since such data are valuable to sellers, those managers, executives, or brokers who have successful records in choosing profit-increasing prices and quantities often command high fees.

The following excerpts from an article in *Fortune* by Stephen Solomon show in a microcosm the basic problem that all monopolies face in attempting to find the price that maximizes profits.[20]

*　　*　　*

> *Nearly all speakers hire agents who take a cut, usually one-third, of the lecture fee. The agent who first recognized and exploited the incipient demand for the new kind of speaker was Harry Walker, president of Harry Walker, Inc., of Manhattan, now probably the largest "lecture bureau" in the country. Walker claims he booked 2,000 dates this past year for a lineup of speak-*

[20]　Stephen Solomon, "Speech Is Golden on the Lecture Circuit," *Fortune*, 31 December 1979, pp. 40–43. *Fortune*, © 1979 Time Inc. All rights reserved.

ers that almost amounted to a shadow government: [Alexander] Haig, [Michael] Blumenthal, [Henry] Kissinger, Joseph Califano, James Schlesinger, William Simon, and Gerald Ford, to name a few. He also represents leading economists (e.g., Milton Friedman, Walter Heller) and prominent newsmen (e.g., Mike Wallace, Marvin Kalb, George Will).

Fees for such performers have practically kept pace with the price of OPEC oil. In 1970, the high was about $2,500; today it is around $15,000, and Kissinger once got $20,000. This tremendous increase, combined with the sharp growth in Walker's bookings—up more than 40 percent in 1979 alone—has enabled his family-owned company to triple its revenues and profits in the past five years. Walker won't disclose the figures, but Fortune estimates that his total billings this year will come to around $9 million. Of this, his own cut would be $3 million and his pretax profit just under $1 million. Not bad for a man who employs sixteen people and operates out of a jumble of unkempt cubbies on the thirty-sixth floor of the Empire State Building.

Walker, who is sixty-three, is more entertaining than many of his products. Short and thickset, with an enormous store of energy, he is not given to underselling himself. He obviously relishes his access to those who count. ("Every day," he says, "I have conversations with thirty to thirty-five of the most powerful people in the world.") He is prone to skewer the English language—"I was chewing more than I could bite off," he said recently, describing a business mistake.

Walker represents speakers from both political parties and holds them in equally high regard; above their heads he sees price tags that gradually melt into halos. He is a shrewd judge of talent. "Milton Friedman," he says, comparing two economists, "is worth two Joe Pechmans."

"Genius" is a word Walker uses frequently in describing how he built the business. He would have you believe he has no serious competition—"Kissinger asked me why he shouldn't sign up with one of my competitors instead of with me. I said, 'I don't have any competitors.'" The man who had handled Brezhnev and Chou En-lai signed on—but not before he had talked Walker into cutting his agent's commission well below the standard 33 1/3 percent.

In truth, the notion that there is no serious competition in this business is nothing more than a facade. When he envisions reality, Walker sees himself as a Spanish galleon surrounded by pirates who are about to climb on board and carry away his treasure. There are ten or so major lecture bureaus around the U.S. and scores of one-person, one-room, one-telephone operations. "It's a cutthroat business," Walker will admit. "They try to contact my speakers and tell them they will take a lower commission."

The predominant contractual arrangement in the business is called a "listing," in which speakers allow more than one agency to advertise their availability and then choose among the offers.

Walker handles financial commentator Louis Rukeyser and columnist Jack Anderson on this basis. But, wherever possible, he presses for exclusive management rights. His agreement with Kissinger and Ford stipulates that he is their only agent, though they may accept speaking engagements on their own without paying him a commission. Blumenthal and Haig have agreed to make all their bookings through Walker and give him his cut.

In return, Walker and his staff aggressively "package" his clients, bombarding trade associations and Fortune 500 companies ("I worship that list," he says) with brochures, biographical sketches, letters from satisfied listeners, and tapes of prior speeches. A new speaker will be trotted out to show his stuff at the annual convention of the American Society of Association Executives, which draws the presidents of nearly all the major trade associations. The exposure is as valuable to newcomers on the lecture circuit as an appearance on the Tonight Show is to budding show-business talent. Walker has three video recorders in his Long Island home to catch all the news programs, lest he miss something that might make one of his clients a particularly timely attraction. He handles itineraries and travel plans—all of his speakers fly first class, stay at the best hotels, and ride in limousines (at the sponsoring group's expense).

With few exceptions, Walker refuses to represent a lecturer who cannot command at least $3,500 a speech. He turns down obscure Congressmen and refused to handle the man who "invented" Pet Rocks. It's not surprising that 90 percent of his bookings come from trade associations and corporations. They stand alone in their ability to pay fees that one of Harry's speakers, futurist Leo Cherne, admits are "quite frankly outlandish."

The Economics of Talk

Why are the fees so high? One reason is that heavy demand is outstripping the supply of speakers. For trade-association conventions, a big-time attraction is worth his fee if he builds attendance that helps off-set the costs of rental space and food. Even at the prices they charge, top dogs on the circuit get many more offers than they have the time to fulfill. "I can't believe it," says Walker of clients who blithely turn down $10,000 fees. "I actually have to convince people to take the money." Potentially hot speakers who neither hire agents nor hit the lecture circuit strike him as a shamefully wasted resource. Paul Samuelson, the Nobel economist, says he is "not interested in the commercial aspect." He speaks only when he thinks it important to do so, charges small colleges nothing, and donates to charity the fees he collects from those that can afford to pay.

The agents themselves tend to drive up prices. Speakers are reluctant to get involved in the gaucheries of haggling over fees, and might feel compelled to lower their price if they came under pressure from friends or acquaintances. The agent provides a convenient shield from such demands. The speaker need only say he is under contract, and much as he would like to talk cheap, there is nothing he can do about it.

"There's very little bargaining," says Ken Gerbino, part owner of Corporate Seminars, Inc., a Beverly Hills company that puts on seminars for business. "Walker knows what the speakers' time and effort are worth—and that's what we pay." If a charity or nonprofit group pleads lack of funds, Walker is not about to cave in. He might suggest that money be raised through corporate grants or gifts from individuals. Perhaps someone in the community has recently lost a loved one and would like to establish a lecture fund as a memorial.

Walker has quasi-cartelized a major segment of the industry. As is the case in any other business, not all products are interchangeable in the lecture industry—warlocks don't compete with diplomats, for example. But lots of business groups might consider some former Cabinet officers fairly substitutable—say, Blumenthal and Simon. To the extent that Walker can sign interchangeable speakers to exclusive contracts, he can control their output and exercise a degree of monopoly power over prices. It's as if there were only one Mercedes dealer in the country, and he gained exclusive rights to sell Cadillacs and Lincolns as well.

While some speakers seem embarrassed by the fees they get, a lot of them argue that they earn the money. Although they seldom find themselves in hardship posts—like migratory birds, they tend to fly south in the winter—they complain that the traveling takes them away from work and family. And they point to the years they have spent developing expertise. If a twenty-one-year-old kid with a mediocre college education can pull down a million dollars playing professional basketball, who's to quibble over paying a $10,000 fee for a trenchant analysis of monetary policy?

*　　*　　*

The famous persons listed in the lecture bureau of Harry Walker, Inc. all knew from the start they could get big fees by giving talks to meetings of corporate executives, labor union conventions, college commencements, and the like. But which groups should they talk to and what prices should they charge? Mr. Walker, judging by the nature and number of his clients, knows demand elasticities about as well as anyone in the business. All of his clients save Henry Kissinger, whose bargaining power seems to have been stronger, pay Walker one-third of their earnings to choose suitable engagements, set their prices, and bargain with buyers in their behalf. Note that this lessens the temptation to give price breaks to friends and former associates. The article in *Fortune* lists the fees that Walker obtains for some of his clients but does not mention the number of speeches that each client gives at his or her fee level. For example, among economists, Nobel laureate Milton Friedman is said to command twice the fee of Joseph Pechman, but it is possible that Pechman gives more speeches than Friedman and is thus at a point on the demand curve for his services representing a higher quantity but a lower price.

It is clear in the next-to-last paragraph of Mr. Solomon's article that Mr. Walker is keenly aware that the demand curves for his clients' services are downward sloping and that each captures some amount of monopoly gain. The article does not mention price discrimination, but the nonresalable character of each speech raises the possibility that Mr. Walker can obtain different fees for his clients, depending upon the particular audience or event. Walker's own fees are constrained by competition from other lecture bureaus that have their own prestigious clients and may attempt to lure away some of Walker's.

Finally, did you locate a technical error in Mr. Solomon's piece where he refers to "demand outstripping supply"? What does he mean by this remark? Would not higher lecture fees induce speakers to offer higher *quantities supplied*? How would you rephrase the author's point in precise economic terms?

Summary

Pure monopoly is rare in the real world; however, the theory of pure monopoly is applicable to those industries in which it is approximated and to firms that act as though they were monopolists. Additionally, the theory furnishes necessary tools of analysis for the study of oligopoly and monopolistic competition.

The differences between the theory of pure monopoly and the theory of pure competition rest on the demand and revenue situations faced by the firm and on the conditions of entry into industries in which profits are made. Marginal revenue is less than price for the monopolist. The firm's marginal revenue curve lies below the demand curve that it faces. Entry into monopolistic industries is blocked.

The monopolist maximizes short-run profits or minimizes short-run losses by producing the output and charging the price at which marginal revenue equals short-run marginal cost. A monopolist may incur losses and, if so, continue to produce if price exceeds average variable cost. The monopolist operates within the elastic sector of its demand curve.

In the long run the monopolist maximizes profits at the output at which long-run marginal cost equals marginal revenue. The size of plant to be used will be the one with its short-run average cost curve tangent to the long-run average cost curve at the profit-maximizing output. Short-run marginal cost will equal long-run marginal cost and marginal revenue at that output.

A monopolistic firm finds it profitable to practice price discrimination when the firm can keep markets for its product separate and when elasticity of demand for each market is different at each possible price. The price-discriminating monopolist produces an output and distributes it among markets in such a way that marginal revenue in each market equals that prevailing in every other market and is also equal to marginal cost.

Monopoly has important implications for welfare in a private enterprise economy. Where it exists along with competitive industries, it leads to output restriction and prices that are higher than marginal costs. The possibility of long-run profits under monopoly exists because of blocked entry into monopolized industries. Where profits occur, consumers are willing to pay more for a product than is necessary to hold the resources making that product in the industry concerned. Blocked entry limits transfer of resources into and expansion of output of a monopolized profit-making industry, and thus reduces welfare. A monopolistic firm is not likely to operate most efficient sized plants at most efficient rates of output. Some sales promotion efforts may be made to enlarge the market, to decrease elasticity of demand for the monopolist's product, and to discourage potential competition.

The theory of monopoly sheds some light on effective means of monopoly regulation. A maximum price set below the monopoly price will benefit consumers through both the lower price and an increased product output. A specific tax levied on the monopolist's product will be shifted partly to consumers through output restriction and higher prices. A lump-sum tax must be borne entirely out of the monopolist's profits.

Suggested Readings

Dewey, Donald. *Monopoly in Economics and Law*. Chicago: Rand McNally, 1959.

Harrod, R. F. "Doctrines of Imperfect Competition." *Quarterly Journal of Economics*, 48 (May 1934), pp. 442–70.

Irwin, Manley R. "The Telephone Industry." In Walter Adams, ed., *The Structure of American Industry*, 5th ed. New York: Macmillan, 1977, pp. 312–33.

Marshall, Alfred. *Principles of Economics*. 8th ed. London: Macmillan, 1920, Bk. 5, Chap. 14.

Robinson, Joan. *The Economics of Imperfect Competition*. London: Macmillan, 1933, Chaps. 2–3, 15–16.

Questions and Exercises

1 Suppose that there is a single supplier of natural gas in a community and that a regulatory commission is contemplating a ceiling price for the product. The commission decides to use "average cost pricing" methods, that is, to set the ceiling at the level at which the firm's average cost curve intersects the demand curve. If there is more than one such intersection, the one occurring at the largest output level will be used. What can you say about (1) the regulated price and output versus the unregulated price and output and (2) the shortages or surpluses resulting from the price regulation under each of the following circumstances?
   a The average cost curve is falling at its point of intersection with the demand curve.
   b The average cost curve is rising at its point of intersection with the demand curve.
   c The average cost curve is minimum at its point of intersection with the demand curve.

2 Consider the transformation curve for a two-product world in which product *X* is manufactured and sold by a monopolist while product *Y* is manufactured and sold by pure competitors. If firms in each industry maximize profits, what, if anything, can we say about the output mix in the economic system?

3 In Hometown, U.S.A., the motion picture theater charges higher prices for the movie in the evening than in the afternoon. Explain why the management would want to do so and the circumstances that make such pricing practices possible. Illustrate your discussion diagrammatically.

4 Are there any circumstances under which a single firm in an industry would be expected to sell at a lower price than would be possible if there were many smaller firms, each of the same size, in the industry? If so, give examples and explain the circumstances fully.

5 Would you expect a monopolist firm to engage in extensive advertising of its product? Why or why not? What would determine the size of the monopolist's advertising budget?

6 What effect do you think monopoly has on the distribution of income? Explain.

Appendix I to Chapter 12
Derivation of the Marginal Revenue Curve

The marginal revenue curve can be derived geometrically from a given demand curve. A straight-line demand curve will be used to develop the method that will then be modified to cover the case of a nonlinear demand curve.

Straight-line Curves

Consider first what a marginal revenue curve is. In Figure 12.15 the quantity units are purposely large. Suppose a single unit of sales adds an amount $0K$ to the firm's total receipts. Both total receipts and marginal revenue are equal to area I, or $0K \times 1$. When sales are increased to 2 units of X per unit of time, suppose total receipts increase by an amount $0L$. Marginal revenue of a unit now equals area II, or $0L \times 1$. Area II does not overlap area I but lies entirely to the right of it. The dotted line from the top of area II to point L is a reference line only, to assist in reading marginal revenue from the dollar axis. Total revenue from the 2 units equals marginal revenue when sales are 1 unit, plus marginal revenue when sales are increased to 2 units; in other words, total revenue equals area I plus area II. Marginal revenue, when sales are increased to 3 units per unit of time, equals $0M$, or, what amounts to the same thing, equals area III. Total revenue is now equal to area I plus area II plus area III. The stair-step curve from K to N is the marginal revenue curve for the firm through 3 units of sales.

For a typical firm, a single unit of output is measured by an

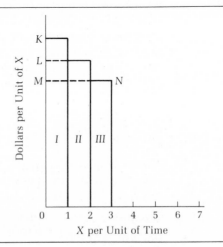

FIGURE 12.15
Marginal and total revenue

infinitesimal distance along the X axis. If the distance measuring a single unit of output is infinitesimal, the marginal revenue curve no longer looks like the discontinuous or stairstep curve of Figure 12.15 but looks as smooth as the MR curve in Figure 12.16. The point to be made from Figure 12.15 is that at any given level of sales total receipts are equal to the area under the marginal revenue curve up to that quantity. In Figure 12.15 total receipts from 3 units of sales equal the sum of areas I, II, and III, as we have said. The same is true in Figure 12.16, where total receipts when sales are $0M$ are equal to area $0ASM$.

Assume that the demand curve faced by a monopolist is the straight line DD of Figure 12.16, and that we want to determine marginal revenue at sales level $0M$. Ignore the MR curve of the diagram temporarily. Price at quantity $0M$ will be MP or $0N$. Suppose now that MR is drawn in Figure 12.16 as a tentative marginal revenue curve. It should start from the vertical axis at a common point with the demand curve.[21] Reference to Table 12.1 shows that the marginal revenue curve for a straight-line demand curve also will be a straight line spreading away from the demand curve as the sales level increases.

FIGURE 12.16
Derivation of the marginal revenue curve from the demand curve

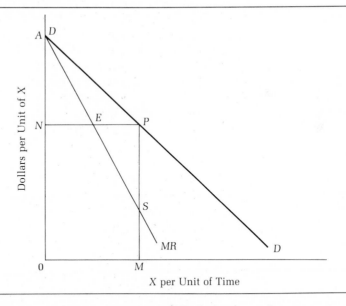

What conditions must be fulfilled if marginal revenue is to be correctly measured at sales level $0M$? If MR were the marginal reve-

<hr/>

[21]   Actually, it coincides with the demand curve at a sales level of one unit. However, if the distance measuring a unit of sales on the quantity axis is infinitesimal, we can assume that both curves start from a common point on the vertical axis.

nue curve, area $0ASM$ would equal total receipts. Also, area $0NPM$ (that is, price times quantity) equals total receipts. Hence, area $0NPM$ must equal area $0ASM$. Area $0NESM$ is common to both the larger areas, and if subtracted from each, the area of triangle ANE must be equal to the area of triangle EPS. Angle NEA equals angle SEP because the opposite angles formed by two intersecting straight lines are equal. Since triangles ANE and EPS are right triangles, with an additional angle of one equal to the corresponding angle of the other, they are also similar triangles. If MR is correctly drawn, triangles ANE and EPS are equal in area as well as similar and thus will be congruent. If they are congruent, SP must equal NA since the corresponding sides of congruent triangles are equal. Therefore, to locate correctly marginal revenue at sales level $0M$, we must measure the distance NA and set point S below point P so that SP equals NA. Marginal revenue at $0M$ will be MS.

Use of the geometric method for deriving marginal revenue from a given demand curve is simpler than the proof. Suppose that we locate the marginal revenue curve for demand curve DD in Figure 12.17. Select several points such as P, P_1, and P_2 at random on the demand curve. The corresponding levels of sales are $0M$, $0M_1$, and $0M_2$. Corresponding prices will be $0N$, $0N_1$, and $0N_2$. Now drop below P by an amount equal to NA and call the newly located point S. Marginal revenue at sales level $0M$ is MS. Drop below P_1 by an amount equal to N_1A. Call this point S_1. Marginal revenue at $0M_1$ equals M_1S_1. Repeat the process at P_2 so that S_2P_2 equals N_2A. A line joining the S points is the marginal revenue curve.[22]

Nonlinear Curves

The procedure with a slight modification can be used to locate the marginal revenue curve for a nonlinear demand curve. Suppose that the demand curve is DD in Figure 12.18. The demand curve and the marginal revenue curve start from a common point on the vertical axis, and we should locate marginal revenue at several different sales

---

[22] Mathematical determination of the marginal revenue function, from a linear demand function, is a simple calculus exercise. Let the demand equation be

$$p = a - bx.$$

Then

$$TR = xp = ax - bx^2$$

and

$$MR = \frac{dTR}{dx} = a - 2bx.$$

Thus, for a linear demand function the marginal revenue function is also linear, has the same intercept a on the price axis, and has twice the slope b of the demand function.

FIGURE 12.17
Location of the MR
curve for a linear
demand curve

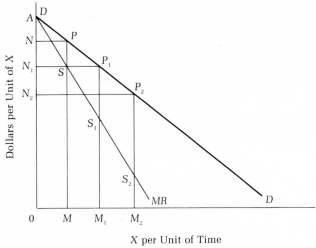

quantities, say $0M$, $0M_1$, and $0M_2$. The corresponding points on the
demand curve are P, P_1, and P_2. The corresponding prices are $0N$,
$0N_1$, and $0N_2$. Draw a tangent to the demand curve at point P so that
the tangent cuts the vertical axis. Call this point A. If the tangent
were the demand curve, we could easily find marginal revenue for it
at sales level $0M$. We would drop below P by an amount equal to NA
and set point S so that SP equals NA. Actually the tangent and
demand curve DD are the same curve and have the same slope at the

FIGURE 12.18
Location of the MR
curve for a nonlinear
demand curve

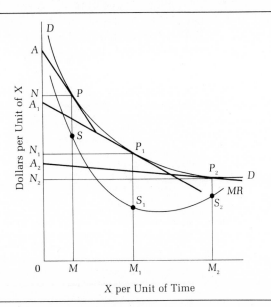

point of tangency. Therefore, MS will be marginal revenue for DD at sales level $0M$, as well as being marginal revenue for the tangent when the tangent is thought of as being the demand curve. Marginal revenue at sales $0M_1$ can be found by drawing at tangent to DD at P_1. The tangent intersects the vertical axis at A_1. Drop below P_1 by an amount equal to N_1A_1 and marginal revenue at $0M_1$ is M_1S_1. Repeat the procedure at P_2, so that S_2P_2 equals N_2A_2. Marginal revenue at $0M_2$ is M_2S_2. A line joining the S points is the marginal revenue curve for DD. Note that when the demand curve is not a straight line, the A points on the vertical axis shift as different levels of sales are considered.[23]

Appendix II to Chapter 12
Price, Marginal Revenue, and Elasticity of Demand

The proposition that marginal revenue equals price minus the ratio of price to elasticity of demand at that price is proved geometrically with the aid of Figure 12.19. Suppose that the sales level is $0M$. The demand curve is either DD or D_1D_1—which are tangent at that level of sales. At sales level $0M$, the elasticity of both curves is the same, and the corresponding marginal revenues will also be the same. For convenience, draw the marginal revenue curve corresponding to D_1D_1. Elasticity of demand at $0M$ equals $MT/0M$. However, $MT/0M$ is equal to PT/AP, since a line (PM) parallel to one side of a triangle $(A0)$ cuts the other two sides into proportional segments. Likewise, $PT/AP = 0N/NA$. Because $0N = MP$ and $NA = SP$, $0N/NA = MP/SP$.

[23] A common mistake in locating the marginal revenue curve for a given demand curve is that of merely drawing the marginal revenue curve so that it bisects the distance between the demand curve and the vertical axis. This procedure will locate the marginal revenue curve accurately for a linear demand curve only. If the demand curve has any curvature to it—that is, if it is convex or concave when viewed from below—such a procedure is not valid. If the demand curve is convex from below, the marginal revenue curve will lie to the left of a line bisecting the distance between the vertical axis and the demand curve. If the demand curve is concave from below, the marginal revenue curve will lie to the right of such a line.

Even in the case of a linear demand curve the procedure described here is correct in a mathematical sense only. It is not sound logically from the point of view of economics. For example, in Figure 12.16 point E lies on the marginal revenue curve for demand curve DD. Sales level $0M$ (or NP) and price $0N$ (or MP) are used in locating point E. However, there is no economic reason why sales level $0M$ or price $0N$ (or MP) should have any connection at all with marginal revenue at one-half of sales level $0M$. The connection is purely a mathematical one stemming from the fact that DD is a straight line. With regard to sales level $0M$ and price $0N$, the only marginal revenue value that could be derived from them logically is marginal revenue at that sales level and that price.

FIGURE 12.19
Price, elasticity of
demand, and marginal
revenue

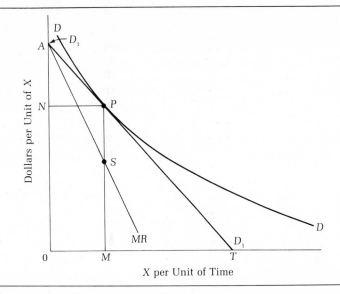

Elasticity of demand at $0M$ is equal to $MT/0M = PT/AP = 0N/NA = MP/SP$, or $\epsilon = MP/SP$. Dividing through by ϵ and multiplying through by SP, $SP = MP/\epsilon$. From the diagram it can be seen that $MS = MP - SP$. Because $SP = MP/\epsilon$, then $MS = MP - MP/\epsilon$, or:

marginal revenue = price − price/elasticity.

<table>
<tr><td>

**CHAPTER
CONTENTS**

</td><td></td><td>

**KEY
CONCEPTS**

</td></tr>
</table>

Costs and Demand	**Cost of Production**	Pure oligopoly
	Demand	Differentiated oligopoly
		Centralized cartel
Pure & Differentiated Oligopoly		Market-sharing cartel
		Price leadership
		Price wars
Collusion versus Independent Action	**Perfect Collusion**	"Kinked" demand curve
	Imperfect Collusion	Nonprice competition
	Independent Action	
	Classification Limitations	
The Short Run	**Perfect Collusion**	
	Imperfect Collusion	
	Independent Action	
The Long Run	**Size of Plant Adjustments**	
	Entry into the Industry	
Nonprice Competition	**Advertising**	
	Differences in Quality and Design	
The Welfare Effects of Oligopoly	**Output Restriction**	
	Efficiency of the Firm	
	Cartelization Wastes	
	Sales Promotion Wastes	
	Range of Products	
Applications	**Interdependence in the Brewing Industry**	
	OPEC: A Cartel?	
Summary	**Suggested Readings** **Questions and Exercises**	

Pricing and Output
under Oligopoly

Market situations in which there are few enough sellers of a particular product for the activities of one to be of importance to the others are called *oligopoly* situations. A single seller occupies a position of sufficient importance in the product market for changes in the firm's market activities to have repercussions on the others in that market. Other sellers react to the market activities of the one, and their reactions in turn have repercussions on it. The individual seller is aware of this interdependence and, when changing price, output, sales promotional activity, or quality of product, must take into account the reactions of others.

The analysis of pricing and output under oligopoly lacks the neatness and precision of the theories of pure competition and of monopoly. The imprecision is partly because of oligopolistic uncertainty—in many cases an oligopolistic firm cannot be sure what rivals' reactions will be to various kinds of activities on its part—and partly because oligopoly covers a wide range of cases, each with its own unique characteristics. There is not now, nor is there likely to be in the foreseeable future, a general theory of oligopoly. Consequently, in this chapter we try to develop a sense of the problems and principles involved in analysis of oligopolistic industries. Several selected models are examined with this objective in mind.

First we shall briefly discuss costs and demand as they are to be used in the analysis. Next we shall consider collusion versus independent action by oligopolists. Then we shall examine short-run pricing and output, long-run pricing and output, and nonprice competition. Finally we shall consider the effects of oligopolistic market structures on the operation of the economy.

Costs and Demand

In what important respects do oligopolistic market structures differ from competitive and monopolistic market structures?

Costs of Production

We continue to assume in this chapter that the oligopolistic firm buys its resources competitively. Its cost curves are like those of the purely competitive firm and the pure monopolist.

Demand

Differences in the conditions of demand as seen by the individual firm constitute the main feature setting oligopoly apart from the other types of market structure. Since what one firm is able to do in the market is conditioned by the ways in which its rivals react to the market activities of the one, the extent of this oligopolistic uncertainty is highly variable from case to case. In some situations the firm is quite knowledgeable as to the reactions it can expect from other firms, and so it can determine the demand curve it faces with some confidence. In other situations the firm does not possess this knowledge, and the position and shape of the demand curve it faces are highly conjectural. Interdependence of demand among the firms of an industry and oligopolistic uncertainty give rise to a whole host of problems and strategies for firms that we do not find in the other market classifications.

Pure and Differentiated Oligopoly

The distinction between differentiated oligopoly and pure oligopoly will not play a prominent role in our analysis. As a practical matter, sellers in most oligopolistic industries sell differentiated products.[1] Nevertheless, some of the fundamental principles of differentiated oligopoly, as well as of pure oligopoly, are seen most clearly when we assume that pure oligopoly exists. For example, instead of a single market price for a good produced under differentiated oligopoly, a cluster of prices may occur. Automatic toasters may range in price from $29.95 to $34.95. The various price levels reflect consumers' views regarding the respective qualities of the different sellers' wares and the availabilities of different makes. Analysis may be simplified and basic pricing principles not distorted seriously if we assume that pure oligopoly exists, thus reducing the cluster of

---

[1] Industries approaching pure oligopoly include cement, basic steel, and most of the other basic metal-producing industries. Even here, there are elements of differentiation among the products sold in a particular industry. Locational factors, service, and personal friendships may differentiate the products of the various sellers in an industry.

prices to a single market price for the product.[2] Wherever necessary, we shall specify whether conditions of differentiated or pure oligopoly are assumed.

Collusion versus Independent Action

An oligopolistic market structure in an industry invites collusion among the industry's firms, but collusive arrangements are seldom perfect and are usually difficult to maintain over time. There are at least three major incentives leading oligopolistic firms toward collusion. (1) They can increase their profits if they can decrease the amount of competition among themselves and act monopolistically. (2) Collusion can decrease oligopolistic uncertainty. If the firms act in concert, they reduce the likelihood of any one firm's taking actions detrimental to the interests of the others. (3) Collusion among the firms already in an industry will facilitate blocking newcomers from that industry. However, once a collusive arrangement is in existence, any single firm has a profit incentive to break away from the group and act independently, thus destroying the collusive arrangement. We shall distinguish among cases of perfect collusion, imperfect collusion, and situations characterized by independent action on the part of individual firms.[3]

Perfect Collusion

Cartel arrangements may approach perfect collusion among the sellers in an industry. A *cartel* is a formal organization of the producers within a given industry. Its purpose is to transfer certain management decisions and functions of individual firms to a central association in order to improve the profit positions of the firms. Overt formal cartel organizations are generally illegal in the United States, but they have existed extensively in countries outside the United States and on an international basis. In the United States, covert collusion may result in cartellike arrangements. The electrical equipment case of the 1960s provides an example.[4] In addition, the aid of

[2] One such distortion is that product differentiation may affect the individual seller's control over price. Attachment of consumers to the products of single sellers will reduce the changes in quantities sold for price adjustments upward or downward within a certain price range; that is, it will make the demand curve faced by the individual seller less elastic within that price range.

[3] See Fritz Machlup, *The Economics of Sellers' Competition* (Baltimore: The Johns Hopkins Press, 1952), pp. 363–65.

[4] See F. M. Scherer, *Industrial Market Structure and Economic Performance* (Chicago: Rand, McNally, 1970), pp. 158–61.

the government itself may be enlisted to support what are essentially cartel arrangements. Oil prorationing by state commissions in the major petroleum-producing states has served this purpose.[5]

The extent of the functions transferred to the central association varies in different cartel situations. We shall consider two representative cartel types. The first, selected to illustrate almost complete cartel control over member firms, will be called *the centralized cartel*. The second illustrates cases in which fewer functions are transferred to the central association. It will be designated as *the market-sharing cartel*.

In the centralized cartel, the decision making with regard to pricing, output, sales, and distribution of profits is accomplished by the central association, which markets the product, determines prices, specifies the amount that each firm is to produce, and divides profits among member firms. Member firms are represented in the central association, the cartel policies presumably result from exchanges of ideas, negotiation, and compromise. However, a firm's power to influence cartel policies is not necessarily proportional to its representation in the central association. Its economic power in the industry may significantly influence cartel policies.

The market-sharing cartel is a somewhat looser form of organization. The firms forming the cartel agree on market shares with or without an understanding regarding prices. Member firms do their own marketing but observe the cartel agreement.

Imperfect Collusion

Imperfectly collusive cases are made up mostly of tacit informal arrangements under which the firms of an industry seek to establish prices and outputs and yet escape prosecution under the United States antitrust laws. The price leadership arrangements that have existed in a number of industries—steel, tobacco, oil, and others—are typical of this class. However, tacit unorganized collusion can occur in many other ways. Gentlemen's agreements of various sorts with regard to pricing, output, market sharing, and other activities of the firms within the industry can be worked out on the golf course and on "social" occasions of different kinds.

Independent Action

Cases of independent action are just what the name implies. The individual firms of an industry each go it alone. In some industries independent action often touches off price wars when the reactions of

---

[5] Walter S. Measday, "The Petroleum Industry," in Walter Adams, ed. *The Structure of American Industry*, 5th ed. (New York: Macmillan, 1977), pp. 144–45.

rivals to the economic activities of one firm are retaliatory in nature. In other industries independent action may be consistent with industry stability over time. Firms may have learned by experience what the reactions of rivals will be to moves on their part and may voluntarily avoid any activity that will rock the boat. Or it may be that the management of each firm is reasonably well satisfied with present prices, outputs, and profits, and is content to let things continue as they are rather than chance the start of a chain reaction.

Classification Limitations

Collusion is a matter of degree, with cases of perfect collusion and cases of independent action at the polar limits. We cannot with certainty say that all price leadership cases or all gentlemen's agreements fall under the heading of imperfect collusion. Ordinarily we would expect that to be the case, but in some instances the terms of agreement and adherence to those terms may be strict enough to present a case of perfect collusion. Similarly, cartel arrangements may not always be enforced strictly enough to warrant calling them perfect collusion, but rather they may fall in the category of imperfect collusion.

Reference to the number of firms in an industry is conspicuously absent from the classification that we have made. Yet the degree of collusion achieved is not entirely divorced from the number of firms involved. The greater the number of firms in a given industry, the harder it will be ordinarily to achieve a high degree of collusion. The smaller the number of firms involved, the easier it is for the activities of individual firms to come under the scrutiny of the others. Small numbers are more easily policed by the group as a whole; hence, collusive arrangements are less likely to be violated by individual firms.

The Short Run

We turn now to outputs and pricing in specific oligopoly cases in the short run. Typical examples under each of the three classifications of the preceding section will be examined so that a general grasp of the fundamental problems and principles involved in oligopolistic situations can be obtained. In the short-run analysis of the present section, we should keep in mind that individual firms do not have time to change their plant sizes, nor is it possible for new firms to enter the industry. The number of firms in the industry under consideration is fixed.

Perfect Collusion

There are two major types of perfect collusion cases in oligopolistic markets. These are: (1) the centralized cartel and (2) the market-sharing cartel.

The Centralized Cartel Collusion in its most complete form is exemplified by the centralized cartel. Its purpose is the joint or monopolistic maximization of industry profits by the several firms of the industry. "Ideal" or complete monopolistic price and output determination by a cartel will rarely be achieved in the real world—although it may be approached in some instances.

Suppose that the firms of an industry have surrendered the power to make price and output decisions to a central association. Quotas to be produced are determined by the association, as is the distribution of industry profits. Policies adopted are to be those that will contribute most to total industry profits. To simplify the analysis, we shall assume that the firms of the industry produce a homogeneous product.

Maximization of the cartel's profits is essentially a monopoly problem, since a single agency is making decisions for the industry as a whole. Profits are maximum where the industry output and price are such that industry marginal revenue equals industry marginal cost. These two concepts need explanation.

The association is faced with the industry demand curve for the product; the industry marginal revenue curve is derived from it in the usual manner. The industry marginal revenue curve shows how much each one-unit increase in the volume of sales per unit of time will increase industry total receipts. The industry demand curve and the industry marginal revenue curve are shown by DD and MR, respectively, in Figure 13.1.

FIGURE 13.1
The centralized cartel

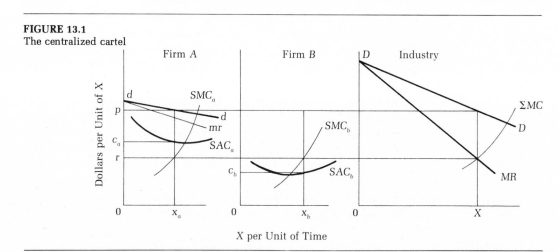

X per Unit of Time

The industry marginal cost curve is constructed from the short-run marginal cost curves of individual firms in the industry. The two-firm case in Figure 13.1 shows how this construction is done. For any given output level the central agency should minimize industry costs. This goal can be accomplished by allocating quotas to the member firms in such a way that the marginal cost of each firm, when producing its quota, is equal to the marginal cost of every other firm when each is producing its respective quota. If quotas are allocated to individual firms in any other way, industry costs for the given output will not be minimized. Suppose, for example, that the quota of firm A with respect to that of firm B is such that A's marginal cost is greater than that of B. Industry costs could be decreased by reducing A's quota and by increasing B's. Reducing A's production rate by one unit will reduce industry total cost by an amount equal to A's (higher) marginal cost. Increasing the production rate of B by one unit will increase industry total cost by an amount equal to B's (lower) marginal cost. Thus, the reduction of firm A's quota will decrease total cost by more than the increase in firm B's quota will raise it. When quotas are correctly allocated for each possible industry output, the industry marginal cost curve will be the horizontal summation of the individual firm's short-run marginal cost curves. The industry marginal cost curve is ΣMC in Figure 13.1.[6]

The profit-maximizing price for the cartel will be p, and the industry output will be X. Each individual firm should produce the quota at which its short-run marginal cost is equal to industry marginal revenue r. The quota of firm A will be x_a and that of firm B will be x_b. Ignore dd and mr in the firm A diagram for the present. If industry output exceeds X, marginal costs of one or more firms will be greater than r and industry marginal revenue will be smaller. More will be added to industry total costs by these outputs than to industry total receipts; hence, profits will decrease. If industry output is less than X, some or all firms' short-run marginal costs will be less than r, while industry marginal revenue will exceed r. Larger outputs up to X will add more to industry total receipts than to industry total costs, and profits will increase.[7]

[6]   Cf. the multiple-plant case discussed on pp. 260–261.

[7]   Let π = profits:

$$R = f(x_a + x_b) = \text{total revenue of the cartel}$$
$$C_a = g(x_a) = \text{total cost for firm } A$$
$$C_b = h(x_b) = \text{total cost for firm } B.$$

Then,

$$\pi = R - (C_a + C_b) = f(x_a + x_b) - g(x_a) - h(x_b).$$

To maximize profits

$$\frac{\delta\pi}{\delta x_a} = f'(x_a + x_b) - g'(x_a) = 0,$$

Profits can be computed on a firm-by-firm basis and totaled for the industry. Profit per unit of output for a single firm will equal the industry price minus the firm's average cost at the output that the firm produces. Profit per unit multiplied by the firm's output equals the profit that the firm contributes to total industry profits. Profit of firm A is $c_a p \times x_a$, while that of firm B is $c_b p \times x_b$. Total industry profits are the sum of the profits contributed by all individual firms. Industry profits may be distributed among firms on an "as earned" basis or according to any other scheme deemed appropriate.

The "ideal" monopolistic determination of industry output and price just described is seldom achieved in practice. Decisions made by an association result from negotiation, give-and-take, and compromise among the points of view and interests of cartel members. Therefore, the association would probably not be able to act precisely as would a monopolist. Profits, for example, may be distributed according to production quotas assigned to individual firms. Some firms, able to exert great pressure on the central association, may receive quotas that run their marginal costs above those of other firms, thus raising industry costs and lowering industry profits. In addition, pressure on the central association to increase the quotas of some firms may result in decisions to expand industry output beyond the profit-maximizing level. Prices and profits below the full monopolistic level would result. Inefficient high-cost firms may be assigned quotas that run their marginal costs above industry marginal revenue, even though principles of economy may indicate that such firms should be shut down completely. These possibilities by no means exhaust the field, but they do serve to illustrate the point that political decisions on the part of the association, made to placate certain member firms, may sometimes take precedence over economic considerations.[8] These possibilities also give a glimpse of just how difficult it will be for even the most efficient central association to pursue a profit-maximization strategy successfully.

In a cartel composed of several firms, there exists an incentive for individual firms to leave the cartel and operate independently. With the larger part of the industry adhering to the cartel price, an individual firm operating independently would be faced with a de-

$$\frac{\delta \pi}{\delta x_b} = f'(x_a + x_b) - h'(x_b) = 0,$$

and

$$f'(x_a + x_b) = g'(x_a) = h'(x_b),$$

or MR from cartel sales must equal the marginal cost of firm A's output and the marginal cost of firm B's output.

[8] See Machlup, *Sellers' Competition*, pp. 476–80.

mand curve for its output that is much more elastic than the industry demand curve in price ranges around the cartel price.

Consider firm A in Figure 13.1, for example. If firm A could break away from the cartel, it would be faced with a demand curve such as dd, provided other firms in the cartel adhere to price p. The demand curve facing any one individual firm under these circumstances would be much more elastic than the industry demand curve at the cartel price, since a cut in price by the individual firm would attract buyers away from the rest of the cartel. Consequently, marginal revenue for firm A, operating independently at output level x_a, would be higher than marginal revenue for the cartel at output level X. Firm A's marginal revenue would exceed its marginal costs at output x_a, and the firm could increase its own profits by expanding its output beyond x_a.

The incentives for price cutting for any one firm of a cartel are illustrated in Figure 13.2. The demand curve facing the firm for

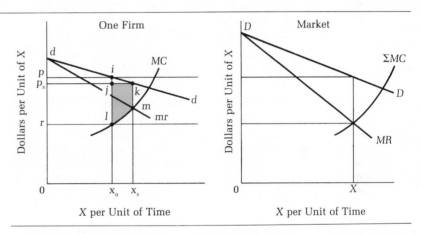

FIGURE 13.2
The rewards for secret price-cutting in a cartel

clandestine price cutting or price increasing is dd, generated on either side of point i, which is the quota and price assigned the firm by the cartel central association. Operating in the cartel, the firm's total revenue is $0pix_a$. With a secret price cut to p_s, the firm's total revenue is increased by area $x_a jkx_s$ − area $p_s pij$. Its total costs are increased by the additional area under the marginal cost curve; that is, by $x_a lmx_s$. So the firm's profits would be raised through secret price cutting by $(x_a jkx_s - p_s pij) - x_a lmx_s$.

If the firm can practice price discrimination, separating the old from the new customers, it can obtain even larger gains. Suppose it can sell quota $0x_a$ at the cartel price, and can then secretly cut price and sell an *additional* $x_a x_s$ units. Now area $ljkm$, the shaded area, represents the additional revenues minus the additional costs. It is not necessary for the firm to relinquish the revenues represented by the rectangle $p_s pij$. This price discrimination tactic can benefit the firm in two ways: (1) it results in greater profits than price cutting without discrimination; and (2) it reduces the risk that the cartel central association will detect the price cutting, since the price break is given on fewer units of sales, $x_a x_s$ instead of $0 x_s$. The less sold outside the cartel the smaller will be the reduction in the total sales of the association and thus the lower the probability that other firms will realize what is happening. Smaller sellers in a cartel are more likely to avoid detection in secret price cutting than are large sellers. They tend to have disproportionate leverage in obtaining cartel quotas and use their strategic position within the cartel to grow at the group's expense.[9]

The price-cutting incentives for one firm apply to each member of the group. Each firm is likely to recognize that its competitors have similar incentives to deal secretly; so, for self-protection, some may try to cut price by some amount first. These cuts increase industry output, lower industry price, and weaken the power of central association. The gains from collusion tend to be destroyed. Cartels are apt to hold together best when there are few sellers and few buyers, thus reducing the costs of monitoring the participating firms.

The Market-sharing Cartel Market-sharing arrangements are more common then centralized cartels. The difficulties that a central association encounters in selecting a price that all members can agree upon, dividing quotas equitably, and preventing secret dealing often make market-sharing arrangements emerge by default. Under certain circumstances, market-sharing can result in an "ideal" monopoly price and output for the industry; that is, the industry profit-maximizing level of price and output. In practice, it is likely to deviate from the monopoly position.

Suppose that the firms of the industry produce a homogeneous product and agree on the share of the market that each is to receive at each possible price. Homogeneity of the product will establish the rule of a single price in the product market. To simplify the analysis, assume further that there are only two firms in the industry. The two have equal costs and agree to share the market half and half.

Under the assumed conditions, the two firms will have identical views regarding the price to charge and the output to produce. The industry demand curve for the product is DD in Figure 13.3. Each firm faces demand curve dd for its own output. Each has a short-run average cost curve and a short-run marginal cost curve of SAC and SMC, respectively. The marginal revenue curve faced by each is mr.

[9] George J. Stigler, "A Theory of Oligopoly," *The Journal of Political Economy*, 72 (February 1964), pp. 44–61.

FIGURE 13.3
The market-sharing
cartel

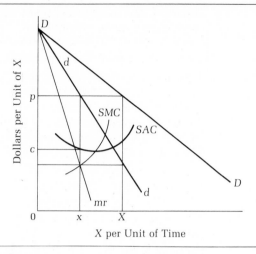

The profit-maximizing output for each firm will be x, at which SMC is equal to mr. Each will want to charge price p. Profits for each will equal $cp \times x$. Together the firms will produce an industry output of X that will fill the market at price p. Such will be the case since dd lies halfway between the market demand curve and the price axis.

Under the assumed conditions the market-sharing cartel, like the centralized cartel, will determine price and output at the levels that a monopolist would set if the monopolist were in complete control of the producing facilities of the industry. Such a monopolist's marginal cost curve would be the horizontal summation of the two SMC curves of the two plants—it would lie twice as far to the right at each price level as the SMC curve of Figure 13.3 does. The monopolist would face the industry demand curve DD, and at output X, industry marginal revenue would be at level r—the same level as individual firm marginal revenue at output x. Such would be the case because DD has the same elasticity at price p as does dd.[10]

At output X, industry marginal cost would be at level r. Output X would be the profit-maximizing output for the monopolist, since industry marginal revenue and industry marginal cost are equal at that output. The monopolist would sell output X at price p per unit.

Several factors, however, may stand in the way of the achievement of an "ideal" monopolistic price and output. Costs of production for the individual firms are likely to differ rather than being

---

[10] Two demand curves with equal elasticities at each of various price levels are said to be isoelastic. Demand curves are isoelastic when the quantities taken at each of various prices form a constant ratio to each other. [See Joan Robinson, *The Economics of Imperfect Competition* (London: Macmillan, 1933), p. 61.] Because dd lies halfway between DD and the price axis at different prices, the quantities taken as shown by dd are in constant ratio to the quantities taken as shown by DD. The ratio is one-half.

identical, as we assumed that they were. Market sharing largely precludes the transferring of output quotas from firms with higher marginal costs to those with lower marginal costs at the outputs produced by each. Differing points of view and differing interests of the firms comprising the cartel may result in compromises that prevent maximization of industry profits. Individual firms, assigned market shares and given a product price, may deliberately or in good faith overestimate the quantities of product that constitute their respective proportions of the total market, and thus they may encroach on the markets of others.[11] Additionally, the degree of independent action left to individual firms may whet their desires to break away from the cartel and may increase the possibilities of their doing so.

Under a market-sharing cartel arrangement markets need not be shared equally. High-capacity firms may receive larger market shares than those of low capacity. Market sharing may be accomplished on a regional basis, with each firm allocated a particular geographic area instead of sharing a common market. A whole host of difficulties may arise as a result of different demand elasticities at particular prices: different costs, inferior territories, encroachment upon each other's territories, and so on—all of which make pricing and output problems much more uncertain than they appear to be in the model. The range and magnitude of the uncertainties imply that the number of collusive arrangements attempted generally will exceed the number that are successful.

Imperfect Collusion

Price-leadership arrangements are predominant where collusion is imperfect. Two illustrative cases follow.

Price Leadership by a Low-cost Firm   In the absence of formal cartel arrangements, price leadership by one firm in the industry frequently provides the means of colluding. Suppose that there are two firms in the industry, that a tacit market-sharing arrangement has been established with each firm assigned half the market, that the product is undifferentiated, and that one firm has lower costs than the other.

A conflict of interest will occur with regard to the price to charge. The market demand curve is DD in Figure 13.4. Each firm faces demand curve dd. The cost curves of the high-cost firm are SAC_1 and SMC_1. Those of the low-cost firm are SAC_2 and SMC_2. The marginal revenue curve of each is mr. The high-cost firm will want to

<hr />

[11]   To minimize sales in excess of market shares or quotas, most cartels exact penalties from the member that exceeds its quota.

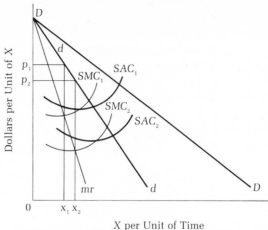

FIGURE 13.4
Price leadership by a low-cost firm

produce an output of x_1 and charge a price of p_1, whereas the low-cost one will want to produce an output of x_2 and charge a price of p_2.

Since the low-cost firm can afford to sell at a lower price than the high-cost firm can, the latter will have no recourse other than to sell at the price set by the low-cost firm. Thus, the low-cost firm becomes the price leader. This type of situation has several ramifications, depending on the comparative costs of the firms, the number of them in the industry, the shape and position of the market demand curve, and the share of the market that each firm is to receive.[12]

Price Leadership by a Dominant Firm   Many oligopolistic industries are made up of one or more large firms, together with a number of small ones. To avoid large-scale price cutting, tacit collusion may occur in the form of price leadership by one or more of the large firms.[13] To simplify the analysis, assume that there is a single large dominant firm in the industry and a number of small firms. Suppose that the dominant firm sets the price for the industry and allows the small ones to sell all that they desire at that price. The dominant firm then fills out the market.

Each small firm tends to behave as though it were in a competitive atmosphere. It can sell all that it wants to sell at the price set by the dominant firm; it faces a perfectly elastic demand curve at the level of the established price. The marginal revenue curve of the small firm coincides with the demand curve faced by it; hence, to

[12]   See Kenneth E. Boulding, *Economic Analysis*, Vol. I, *Microeconomics*, 4th ed. (New York: Harper & Row, 1966), pp. 475–82.

[13]   Price leadership has been common in the fabrication of nonferrous alloys, steel, agricultural implements, newsprint, and other industries. *See* Scherer, pp. 164–73.

maximize profits, the small firm should produce the output at which its marginal cost equals marginal revenue and the price set by the dominant firm.

A supply curve for all small firms combined is obtained by summing the marginal cost curves of all the small firms horizontally. It shows how much all small firms together will place on the market at each possible price. This curve is labeled ΣMC in Figure 13.5.

FIGURE 13.5
Price leadership by a dominant firm

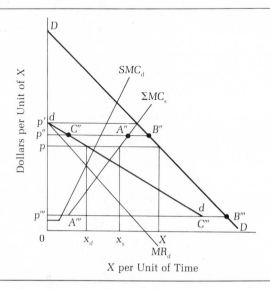

The demand curve faced by the dominant firm can be derived from this information. The market demand curve DD shows how much of the product consumers will take off the market at each possible price, whereas the ΣMC curve indicates how much the small firms combined will sell at each possible price. The horizontal differences between the two curves at all possible prices reveal how much the dominant firm can sell at those prices. The demand curve faced by the latter is dd and is obtained by subtracting the ΣMC curve from the DD curve horizontally. To show in detail how dd is obtained, suppose that the dominant firm sets the price at p'. At this or any higher price, the small firms would fill the market, leaving no sales for the dominant firm. At a price of p'', the small firms would sell quantity $p''A''$, leaving $A''B''$ for the dominant firm to sell. In order to place the demand curve for the dominant firm's product in proper relationship to the quantity and dollar axes of the diagram, we can set point C'' so that $p''C''$ equals $A''B''$. This process can be repeated at various assumed prices. A line joining all points thus established will be dd, the demand curve faced by the dominant firm. At any price below their respective average variable costs, the smaller firms will drop out of the market, leaving the entire market to the dominant firm.

The profit-maximizing price and outputs are determined in the usual way. The marginal revenue curve of the dominant firm is MR_d, and its marginal cost curve is SMC_d. Profits are maximum for this firm at an output level of x_d, at which SMC_d equals MR_d. The price it charges is p. Each small firm maximizes profits by producing the output at which its marginal cost is equal to its marginal revenue, and marginal revenue for each small firm is equal to price p. Total output for the small firms combined is x_s, the output at which ΣMC equals p. Total industry output is x_d plus x_s and equals X. Profit for the dominant firm is x_d times the difference between price p and its average cost at output x_d. Profit for each small firm is equal to its output times the difference between price p and its average cost at that output. Average cost curves are omitted from Figure 13.5 to avoid cluttering the diagram.

Many variations of the dominant-firm model are possible. For example, if there are two or more large firms surrounded by a cluster of small ones, the small firms may look to one or to a group of the large firms for price leadership. The large firms collectively may estimate the amounts that the small firms will sell at various prices and proceed to share or divide the remaining market in any one of various possible ways. The present analysis assumes no product differentiation. But product differentiation may occur in similar price leadership cases, causing price differentials for the products of the various firms. The gasoline industry furnishes a case in point. Retail prices of the major companies—one or more of which often serves as the price leader—will be very close together in a given locality, while those of small independents will tend to be a few cents per gallon below that of the majors.

Independent Action

It would be a mistake to characterize all oligopolistic industries as collusive. In many such industries, collusion has never existed. In others, collusive arrangements, when effected, have broken down. It appears, too, that the antitrust laws may have deterred concerns in some industries from engaging in collusion and may have forced firms in other industries to cease doing so. Empirical data on the extent to which collusion occurs in oligopolistic industries are not available, for this is the kind of information that colluding firms want to suppress rather than publicize. In any case, a very substantial segment of oligopolistic market structures is likely to contain firms that act independently of others.

Price Wars and Price Rigidity Price wars present a persistent danger in oligopolistic industries characterized by independent action on the part of individual firms. Little of a precise analytical nature can be said about these. One seller may lower the price to increase sales. But this move takes customers away from rivals, and the rivals may retaliate with a vengeance. The price war may spread throughout the industry, with each firm trying to undercut others. The end result may well be disastrous for some individual firms.

The specific causes of price wars are varied, but they originate from the interdependence of sellers. A new filling station opening up in a given locality, or an existing one attempting to revive lagging sales, may be the initiating factor. Surplus stocks at existing prices and limited storage facilities have touched off price wars in the sale of crude oil in the petroleum industry. In a young industry, sellers may not have learned what to expect of rivals, or they may be scrambling to secure an established place in the industry and may inadvertently start a price war.

Maturity on the part of an industry may substantially lessen the likelihood of price wars. Individual firms may have learned what not to do and may carefully avoid activities that could touch off hostilities. They may have established a price or a cluster of prices that is tolerable to all from the point of view of profits. Such prices are believed by many to be rather rigid over time, although there is no clear-cut evidence that this is the case. Individual firms are thought to engage in nonprice competition rather than in price rivalry in order to increase their respective shares of the market and profits. Soft drinks and cigarettes are often cited as examples of mature rigid-price industries.

The "Kinked" Demand Curve An analytical device frequently used to explain oligopolistic price rigidity is the "kinked" demand curve. This case is thought to occur when certain assumptions concerning the industry and the firms in the industry are fulfilled. First, the industry is a mature one, either with or without product differentiation. A price or a cluster of prices fairly satisfactory to all has been established. Second, if one firm lowers its price, other firms will follow or undercut it in order to retain their shares of the market. For price decreases, the individual firm cannot hope to do more than hold its former share of the market—and it may not succeed in doing that much. Third, if one firm increases its price, others will not follow the price increase. The customers of the price-raising firm will shift to the other, now relatively lower-priced firms, and the price-raising concern will lose a part of its share of the market.

The demand curve faced by a single firm in such a situation is pictured diagrammatically in Figure 13.6 as *FDE*. The firm is selling

FIGURE 13.6
The kinked demand
curve: cost changes

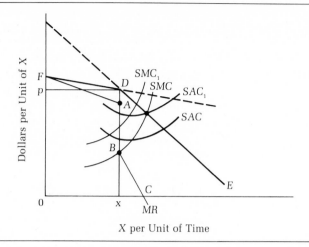

quantity x at price p. If it decreases the price below p, other firms
follow, and it retains only its share of the market. For price decreases,
then, the demand curve faced by the firm is DE, and it will have
about the same elasticity at different prices as the market demand
curve. Should the firm increase the price above p, others will not
follow, and it loses a part or all of its share of the market to the other
firms. The demand curve faced by the firm for price increases is FD,
and at each possible price it will have a considerably greater elasticity than the market demand curve. The demand curve FDE is not a
smooth one; it has a "kink" in it at the established price p.

The kinked demand curve has important implications for the
marginal revenue curve of the firm. The marginal revenue curve is
discontinuous at output x; that is, it has a gap in it at that point. This
gap can be visualized by imagining, first, that only the FD portion of
the demand curve exists and by drawing the appropriate marginal
revenue curve for it. Second, imagine that the DE portion of the
demand curve extends smoothly on up to the price axis, and draw
the appropriate marginal revenue curve for it. Since the imagined
part of the DE curve does not exist, no marginal revenue curve exists
for it at outputs less than x. Since the FD part of the demand curve
does not go beyond x, neither does its marginal revenue curve. The
two nonvertical sections of the marginal revenue curve can be
thought of as the appropriate marginal revenue curves for two distinct continuous demand curves, and there would be no reason to
expect them to be equal to each other at output x.

The discontinuous marginal revenue curve can be thought of
also in terms of elasticity of demand. If the demand curve were
continuous, its elasticity would be changing continuously as we
move from higher to lower prices. Since $MR = p - p/\epsilon$, the marginal

revenue curve would also be continuous as we move down the demand curve. However, the demand curve breaks at D. Elasticity at an output infinitesimally below x is substantially greater than elasticity at an output infinitesimally above x. Thus, marginal revenue must drop sharply at output x.

Cost curves SAC and SMC show a situation such that at price p some profit can be made. The marginal cost curve cuts the marginal revenue curve within its discontinuous part. Output x and price p are, in fact, the firm's profit-maximizing output and price. If the output level were less than x, marginal revenues would exceed marginal cost, and the firm's profits would be increased by expanding output to x. For output increases above x, marginal cost exceeds marginal revenue, and profits will decrease.

Discontinuous marginal revenue curves may result in rigid pricing policies on the part of individual firms in the industry. Suppose that one firm's costs rise because of increases in the prices it must pay for resources. The cost curves will shift upward to positions such as SAC_1 and SMC_1. As long as the marginal cost curve continues to cut the discontinuous part of the marginal revenue curve, there is no incentive for the oligopolist to change either price or output. The reverse situation also holds. Resource price decreases will shift the cost curves downward, but as long as the marginal cost curve cuts the marginal revenue curve in its discontinuous part, no price-output changes will occur. If costs should go up enough for the marginal cost curve to cut the FA segment of the marginal revenue curve, the oligopolist will restrict output to the point at which marginal cost equals marginal revenue and will raise the price. Likewise, if costs decrease enough for the marginal cost curve to cut the BC segment of the marginal revenue curve, the oligopolist will lower the price and increase output up to the level at which marginal cost equals marginal revenue. Thus, there is room for the cost curves to shift up or down without changing the oligopolist's profit-maximizing price and output. Such will be the case as long as the marginal cost curve cuts the marginal revenue curve in its discontinuous part.

Price rigidity may also persist when demand changes. The initial position of the oligopolistic firm is pictured by Figure 13.7(a). Assume its costs do not change and market demand for the product increases. The demand curve faced by the oligopolist shifts to the right to $F_1 D_1 E_1$, as is shown in Figure 13.7(b), but it remains kinked at price p. The marginal revenue curve moves to the right also, with its discontinuous segment always occurring at the output at which the demand curve is kinked. If the increase in demand is limited enough so that the marginal cost curve still cuts the marginal revenue curve in the discontinuous segment $B_1 A_1$, the firm will continue

FIGURE 13.7
The kinked demand
curve: changes in
demand

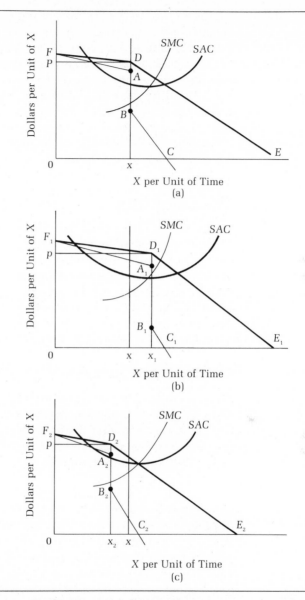

to maximize profits at price p but at a larger output x_1. If the increase in market demand should shift the firm's demand curve farther to the right than $F_1 D_1 E_1$, the marginal cost curve would cut the marginal revenue curve's $F_1 A_1$ segment; and to maximize profits the firm should increase the price as well as the output. A decrease in market demand shifts the firm's demand curve to the left to $F_2 D_2 E_2$, as is shown in Figure 13.7(c). Here there is no incentive to change the price, although output decreases, until the demand curve shifts far

369   CHAPTER 13   Pricing and Output under Oligopoly

enough to the left for the marginal cost curve to intersect the $B_2 C_2$ segment of the marginal revenue curve. This amount of shift would induce the firm to lower the price along with output.

The case of the kinked demand curve is only one of many possible oligopolistic situations, and it rests on a special set of assumptions regarding the behavior of rivals when confronted with certain actions on the part of the firm under analysis. Often students (and some professors) become intrigued with the case and tend to think of it and the term "oligopoly" as being synonymous. We should avoid this inaccuracy in our thinking.

The Long Run

Two types of adjustment are possible in oligopolistic industries in the long run. Individual firms are free to build any desired size of plant; thus, the relevant cost curves for the firm are the long-run average cost curve and the long-run marginal cost curve. Second, some industry adjustments may be possible in the form of entry of new firms into the industry or exit of old ones. These types of adjustment will be considered in turn.

Size-of-plant Adjustments

The size of plant that the individual firm should build depends on its expected rate of output. For any given rate of output we can say, as a first approximation, that the firm attempts to produce that output at the least possible average cost; that is, it builds the plant size that makes its short-run average cost curve tangent to the long-run average cost curve at that output.

Under perfect collusion, and often under imperfect collusion, quotas, market shares, and outputs of individual firms may be predictable with some degree of accuracy. In such cases the firm would be expected to adjust its size of plant accordingly. Not much can be said with regard to whether the size of plant would be of most efficient size, less than most efficient size, or greater than most efficient size. It may be any one of the three, depending on the nature of the oligopolistic situation involved. Certainly, there is no reason to expect that the firm would tend to construct a most efficient size of plant.

For a firm in an industry characterized by independent action, there will be no more certainty regarding the size of plant to build than there is regarding the output to produce and the price to charge. Growth possibilities of the industry may influence the decisions of the firm to a large extent. The existence of a large growth potential would make the individual firm optimistic with respect to anticipated sales and would result in plant enlargements. "Live-and-let-live" policies or fear of "rocking the boat" on the part of individual firms may lead to fairly determinate outputs and, consequently, to some degree of certainty as to the sizes of plant to build. Again, there is no reason for believing that most efficient sizes would be built.

Entry into the Industry

When individual firms in an industry make profits or when they incur losses, incentives exist for new firms to enter the industry or for old ones to leave. Exit from an oligopolistic industry will usually be much easier than entry and need not detain us. Ease or difficulties of entry are much more important. The very existence of oligopolistic markets depends to some extent on whether or not entry into the industry can be partially or completely blocked. In addition, the degree of collusion that can be attained or maintained within the industry tends to be an inverse function of the ease of entry.

Entry and the Existence of Oligopoly   If entry into an oligopolistic industry is comparatively easy, it may not remain oligopolistic in the long run. Whether it does or not will depend on the extent of the market for the product, as compared with the most efficient size of plant for an individual firm. Profits will attract new firms, lowering the market price or the cluster of prices as industry output increases. When the price no longer exceeds long-run average costs for individual firms, entry will cease. If the market is limited, the number of firms may still be small enough to make it necessary for each firm to take account of the actions of the others. If so, the market situation remains one of oligopoly. If the market is extensive enough so that the number of firms can increase to the point at which each of them no longer considers that its activities affect the others, or that the activities of other firms affect it, the market situation will have become one of either pure or monopolistic competition.

Entry and Collusion   Easy entry tends to break down collusive arrangements. We have seen already that in a collusive arrangement a strong incentive exists for any one individual firm to break away from the group. The same sort of incentive operates to attract new firms into a cartelized industry and to induce those entering firms to remain outside the cartel. The entering firm, if it remains outside the group, will face a demand curve more elastic at various price levels than that of the group and, consequently, will be confronted with higher marginal revenue possibilities. At prices slightly below the cartel price, it can pick up many of the cartel's customers. At prices slightly above the cartel price, it can sell little or nothing. Entering firms that remain outside the collusive group will encroach more and more on the profits of that group or will cause the group to incur losses and force its eventual dissolution.

Even when the entering firms are taken into the cartel, a strong presumption exists that dissolution of the cartel will follow eventually. Refer to Figure 13.8. Suppose the ΣMC is the horizontal summa-

FIGURE 13.8
Long-run cartel equilibrium and the effects of entry

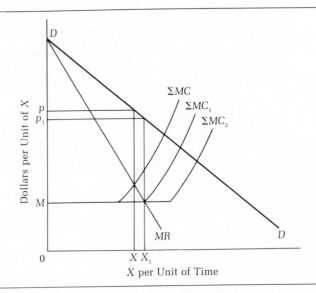

tion of individual firm short-run marginal cost curves. The price will be p, and industry output will be X. The entry of new firms will move the ΣMC curve to the right,[14] increasing the industry profit-maximizing output and lowering the profit-maximizing price. When enough firms have entered to shift the industry marginal cost curve to ΣMC_1, forcing the price down to p_1 and increasing the level of output to X_1, profits for the industry may still exist. More firms will enter, shifting the industry marginal cost curve to some position ΣMC_2; however, industry profits will decrease if output is expanded beyond X_1. Industry marginal revenue for the additional output will be less than the industry's marginal cost. The more profitable course of action for the cartel is to keep the additional firms idle and simply cut them in on the industry's profits. Plant costs of additional firms augment industry total costs, and, eventually, enough firms will have entered the industry to cause all profit to be eliminated. A strong incentive now exists for individual firms to break away from the cartel. Any single firm, if it markets its own output, faces a more

[14] Assume that M is the minimum price at which any firm will enter the industry.

elastic demand curve in the neighborhood of the cartel price than does the cartel. Marginal revenue for the firm exceeds marginal revenue for the cartel. Also, average cost for the firm is lower than average cost for the cartel.[15] The firm that can break away can make profits, provided others remain in the cartel and the cartel price is maintained. The temptations facing each individual firm are likely to result in a breakup of the cartel.[16]

Barriers to Entry   Since ease of entry into an industry tends to be the nemesis of collusive oligopoly, collusion usually can be maintained only when entry is restricted; collusion has as one of its purposes the erection of barriers to potential entrants. Barriers to the entry of new firms may be inherent in the nature of the industry, or they may be established by its existing firms. These will be called "natural" barriers and "artificial" barriers, respectively. Natural barriers to entry may be inevitable in particular industries. Artificial barriers conceivably can be removed.

Probably the most important natural barrier to entry is the smallness of the product market in relation to the most efficient size of plant for a firm in the industry. Suppose, for example, that there are two firms in the industry, and each is operating with a plant size somewhere near the most efficient size. Price exceeds average costs for each, and some profit exists. Heretofore we have considered the existence of profit as the signal for the entrance of new firms. Prospective entrants eye the profit and consider the possibility of entering. They discover that if a new firm enters with a less than most efficient plant size, average costs of the entrant will be so high that no profit could be made. Further, if a new concern enters with a most efficient size of plant, industry output will be increased to the extent that price will be below average costs both for existing firms in the industry and for the entrant. Therefore, no new firms will enter.

Another natural barrier to entry consists of the difficulty of putting together a large and complex plant and of obtaining funds to build it. The automobile industry is a case in point. The initial investment outlay for a potential entrant is extremely high. Large amounts of space, several buildings, and specialized heavy equipment must be obtained. Highly skilled and well-paid personnel are necessary. A nationwide organization of dealership, maintenance, and repair facilities must be established. The difficulties of entry have been so great that only a few firms had the financial backing to try it from World War II to the mid 1970s, despite record profits in the

[15]   The individual firm's cost is lower since the cartel is holding the plant capacity of a number of firms idle, thus adding to cartel average costs.

[16]   See Don Patinkin, "Multiple-Plant Firms, Cartels, and Imperfect Competition," *Quarterly Journal of Economics*, 41 (February 1947), pp. 173–205.

industry during that period. This barrier to entry is not the only one for the automobile industry, but it has been major.

Among the artificial barriers to entry, those enforced or supported by the state loom large. Patent rights to key machines or technological processes may be obtained by certain firms of an industry. Those firms may then maintain control of the machines or processes by leasing them to a limited number of other firms.[17] Or the firms of an industry, through cross-licensing arrangements, may give each other access to the patents of each but refuse to allow any new firms to use them.[18]

Government-supported barriers to entry exist extensively in the field of transportation. On a local basis, taxicab and bus companies operate under franchises guaranteeing limited "competition" in the industry. Entry into the interstate public transportation field, with the exception of air carriers, is regulated by the Interstate Commerce Commission. The Civil Aeronautics Board regulates entry into the air transportation field.

Local governments regulate entry into a host of local oligopolistic industries. Building codes in many cities prevent the entrance of firms producing prefabricated houses or parts of houses. Local licensing laws are frequently used to limit the number of barbers, taverns, plumbers, morticians, and others in service trades. Entry-restricting devices are usually rationalized as maintaining standards of competency, keeping undesirables out of the trades, and protecting the public in other ways.

A second artificial barrier to prospective entrants is the control by the firms already in the field of strategic sources of raw materials necessary for making the product. This barrier will be of greatest importance where raw material sources are highly concentrated geographically, or, at least, where the better sources are so clustered. Concentration of raw material sources facilitates concentration of ownership. Magnesium, nickel, molybdenum, and aluminum provide examples.

Third, so-called limit pricing policies of established firms in an industry may be used to bar the door. Established firms may deliberately produce outputs greater than those that maximize profits, lowering price sufficiently so that it is not profitable for a potential newcomer to enter.[19] Or, similar tactics may be used by large, financially powerful firms to drive smaller rivals out of an industry. The classic

---

17   Entry into the glass-container industry has been controlled in this manner. *See* Wilcox, pp. 73–78.

18   *See* Joe S. Bain, *Industrial Organization*, 2d ed. (New York: John Wiley & Sons, 1968), pp. 335–37.

19   *See* Donald Dewey, *Microeconomics* (New York: Oxford University Press, 1975), pp. 114–19, 141–51.

example is the Standard Oil case of the late 1800s. Additionally, recurrent price wars may create such an atmosphere of uncertainty about the profit possibilities of an industry that new firms will steer clear of it.

Fourth, product differentiation may form an artificial barrier to entry. The industry's product may have become so closely identified with particular sellers' names that consumers will refuse to buy "off brands." Even though standard brands are differentiated from each other, the standard brands are well known to almost all consumers. What consumers fear and refuse to consume are the new, unknown, and, consequently, "inferior" brands. This reluctance is an important barrier to entry into the automobile industry.

Restricted entry into an oligopolistic industry makes it possible for profits to exist in the long run for the firms in the industry. This is not to say that pure profits will always exist in oligopolistic industries. Losses can and do occur. Or, the firms of an industry may be just covering average costs, showing neither profit nor loss. When no profits are being made, entry will not be desired regardless of whether it is restricted or open. The possibility of profits provides the motivation for entry, and when entry is restricted, profits may persist over time. Restricted entry prevents profits from playing their essential role in the organization of productive capacity in a private enterprise economy.

Nonprice Competition

Although oligopolists may be reluctant to encroach upon each other's market shares by lowering the product price, they appear to have little hesitancy in using other means to accomplish the same results. While open undercutting of the price(s) of rivals raises the specter of price wars that may be disastrous to some firms, product differentiation offers a more subtle and a much safer way of accomplishing approximately the same results. Product differentiation occurs in two major forms: (1) advertising and (2) variation in design and quality of product. Both forms may, and do, occur simultaneously, but for purposes of analysis we shall treat them separately.

Advertising

The primary purpose of advertising is to shift the demand curve faced by the single seller to the right and to make it less elastic. Thus, the seller can sell a larger volume at the same or a higher price without the danger of touching off a price war. Each seller tries to encroach on the markets of others through advertising. When one firm launches an ingenious and successful advertising program, ordinarily there will be a time lag before rivals can embark on similar programs, and profits can result during the time-lag interval.

Frequently the products of sellers in an industry can be differentiated effectively by advertising alone. Each seller attempts to attract customers to its particular brand name, although basically the product of each seller may be the same as that of other sellers in the industry. The success of sellers in this respect is especially evident in the aspirin industry. All 5-grain aspirin tablets conform to certain United States pharmacopoeia specifications, and one is as effective for the patient as another; nevertheless, some nationally known sellers are able to attract and hold customers at prices far greater than those of other sellers in the same industry.

In some instances, rival advertising campaigns succeed only in increasing the costs of individual sellers. Attempts on the part of a single seller to encroach on the markets of others may be anticipated by the other sellers. They launch counteradvertising campaigns of their own, and all sellers succeed only in holding their original places in the market. The overall market for the product may not be expanded at all by advertising activity—the present-day cigarette industry is a case in point. Once rival advertising is started, however, no single seller can withdraw without losing its place in the market. The advertising outlays become "built in" to the cost structures of individual firms and lead to higher product prices than would otherwise prevail.

How far should nonprice competition through advertising be carried by the individual seller seeking to maximize profits? The same principles that have guided us thus far in profit maximization apply in this case. Advertising outlays are expected to add to the seller's total receipts, but successively larger outlays per unit of time beyond some point will add successively less to total revenues. That is, marginal revenue from advertising will decrease as outlays increase. Similarly, larger advertising outlays add to the seller's total costs; that is, marginal costs of advertising are positive. The profit-maximizing outlay on advertising will be that outlay at which the marginal cost of advertising is equal to the marginal revenue received from it.[20]

Differences in Quality and Design

Variations in quality and design of particular products are usually used, along with advertising, to differentiate the product of one seller

[20] In practice, probably less is known about the effects of advertising outlays than about the effects of any other cost outlays made by the firm. Nevertheless, any intelligent approach by management to the "correct" magnitude of the advertising budget must be made on the basis of estimated marginal revenue and estimated marginal cost resulting from its contraction or expansion.

from another. The objective of variations on the part of one seller is that of causing consumers to prefer its product over those of others—that is, to shift its demand curve to the right (or to enlarge its share of the total market) and to make its demand curve less elastic. Additionally, quality variation may be used to extend the market vertically—different qualities to appeal to different classes or groups of buyers.

When quality and design variations are used to increase an individual firms's market shares, rival firms are not expected to sit by idly while their markets shrink. Retaliation by rivals will occur. Successful innovations will be imitated and improved on. Individual firms may succeed in increasing their market shares temporarily, but if a permanent increase is to be obtained, such firms must be able to keep ahead of their rivals.

The automobile industry furnishes an excellent example of product variation to increase market shares of particular firms. One producer initiates power steering. Consumers take to the innovation, and other producers follow to regain their market positions. Another mounts the motor on rubber, and the process is repeated. Low-pressure tires, automatic transmissions, high horsepower, and many other improvements, both real and fancied, are introduced initially to enlarge the market share of one producer, and are in turn copied by others to regain or hold their shares of the market.

When quality differences are introduced to extend the market vertically for a product, we may find the same firm producing a range of product qualities to sell to different groups of buyers at various prices, or we may find different firms specializing in particular qualities of the product. Initially a product, say deluxe garbage disposals, may be produced for middle-income group markets. Sellers find that by producing "super deluxe" models the market can be expanded into upper-income levels. Likewise, by stripping the deluxe model of fancy gadgets, a standard model can be sold to lower-income groups at a lower price. When different firms specialize in a particular quality of the product, quality differences may become the basis for market sharing.

Product variation often operates in the best interests of consumers. When it passes along the fruits of industrial research in the form of an improved product to the consuming public, consumer desires may be more adequately met than before. The electric mixer in lieu of the old hand-driven egg beater, the more portable and more versatile tank type of vacuum cleaner in lieu of the upright model, the no-frost refrigerator, the high-fidelity stereo sound system, the self-starter on the automobile, and many other variations in product probably represent improved fulfillment of consumer wants.

Some product variation falls in the same class as retaliatory advertising. It increases costs but adds little to the fulfillment of consumer desires. Design changes adding nothing to the quality of the product may occur. The purpose of the design change may simply be to differentiate last year's from this year's model. Each seller believes that other sellers will make some changes and decides it should do the same to hold its share of the market.

The principles of profit maximization with respect to design and quality changes are the familiar ones. Any changes that will add more to total receipts than to total costs will increase profits (or reduce losses), or any changes that will reduce total costs more than total receipts will increase profits (or reduce losses). To maximize profits with respect to changes in the product, the firm should carry out changes to the point at which the marginal revenue from the changes is equal to the marginal cost of making them.

The Welfare Effects of Oligopoly

Oligopolistic market structures, as compared with purely competitive market structures, would be expected to have adverse effects on consumers welfare. The problems are essentially the same as those brought about by pure monopoly. There is output restriction, internal inefficiency of the firm, and resource waste in sales promotion activities. There may, however, be some welfare gains from product differentiation.

Output Restriction

An oligopolistic firm ordinarily faces a demand curve for its output that is downward sloping to the right, or that is less than perfectly elastic. As a consequence, marginal revenue at each level of sales is less than the price; and since the profit-maximizing firm produces the output level at which marginal revenue equals marginal cost, marginal cost will be less than the product price. The important point is that resources going into this product are more valuable to consumers in this use than in alternative uses. Welfare would be increased by transfers of resources into the product and expansion of its output to the point at which marginal cost is equal to the product price.

In addition, an oligopolistic firm may make profits in the long run because entry into the industry is restricted. The price of the product exceeds the average costs of production, indicating that an expansion of the productive capacity of the industry would increase welfare. However, restricted entry keeps this desirable reallocation of resources from taking place.

Efficiency of the Firm

The maximum potential economic efficiency for individual firms in the production of particular commodities is realized when those firms are induced to build most efficient sizes of plant and operate them at most efficient rates of output. As we have observed, there is no automatic tendency for this state of affairs to occur in the long run under oligopoly. The firm's output depends upon its quota, its market share, or its anticipations with regard to its marginal revenue and its long-run marginal costs. Once a long-run output is decided on, the firm will want to produce that output as cheaply as possible; that is, it will build the size of plant whose short-run average cost curve is tangent to the long-run average cost curve at that output. Coincidence of the desired output with the output of a most efficient size of plant, operated at the most efficient rate of output, would be sheer accident.

It should be emphasized that firms in an oligopolistic type of market, even though they do not use most efficient plant sizes, operated at most efficient rates of output, may provide more efficiency in producing a certain product than would firms of any other type of market organization. The most efficient size of plant may be so large in comparison with the market for the product that not enough firms can exist to make the market one of pure competition. If the firms of the industry were broken up or atomized so that no one firm could appreciably influence market price, each might have a plant of much smaller than most efficient size. Consequently, costs and price(s) of the product might be higher, and output levels smaller, with such an arrangement than they would be with the oligopolistic market structure.

Cartelization Wastes

One of the implications of our analysis of cartels is that they will almost always misallocate resources by generating idleness.[21] The group of firms attempts to achieve the monopoly price and output but without the coordination and control that a single firm can provide. In the short run, the higher prices require that each member reduce output. Even so, some firms may expand the number and size of their plants just to obtain leverage for a larger quota from the association in the case of a centralized cartel or from the informal meetings of the group in the case of a market-sharing cartel. These moves increase the idleness of resources even more. In the long run, cartel profits attract new entrants, which reduces the sales of existing

---

[21] W. H. Hutt, *The Theory of Idle Resources: a Study in Definition*, 2d ed. (Indianapolis, Ind.: Liberty Press, 1977), pp. 145–54.

firms (assuming no reduction in price) and thus raises excess capacity even more. The cartel may in the end achieve the monopoly level of equilibrium price and output, but if this occurs it typically carries with it a total industry plant that vastly exceeds the resources that a monopoly would have employed. In other words, the cartel may finally reach the monopoly price and output, but it does so with less efficiency. These extra resource misallocations justify a harsher public policy against cartels relative to monopolies, and it is probably for this reason that the United States antitrust statutes (primarily the Sherman Act) provide far stiffer penalties against cartels and collusions.

Sales Promotion Wastes

Firms in oligopolistic markets engage in extensive sales promotion activities designed to extend their own markets at the expense of the markets of rivals. As we have seen, the major forms of such activities are advertising and changes in product quality and design. To the extent that they add nothing to consumer satisfaction, resources used in these activities are obviously wasted. Often, however, they yield certain satisfactions to consumers in the forms of entertainment and improved product quality. In these instances the important question with regard to economic efficiency and welfare is whether or not the values of the additional satisfactions obtained from resources used in sales promotion activities are equal to their marginal costs, that is, equal to the satisfactions that the resources could have produced in alternative employments. A strong case can be made that since decisions regarding entertainment and product quality variations are made by business firms rather than by consumers in the market places of the economy, expenditures on resources so used will be too large and will be misdirected. The value of the additional consumer satisfaction obtained will consequently be less than the marginal costs of providing it. To the extent that this phenomenon occurs, economic waste will be the result—welfare will be less than optimum.

Range of Products

Differentiated oligopoly provides each consumer with a broader range of products among which to choose than does either pure competition or pure monopoly. Rather than being limited to a single kind and quality of automobile, each consumer can choose the kind and quality that best suits individual needs and income. The same observations apply to television receivers, washing machines, refrigerators, or even entertainment. Gradations in product qualities, with each lower quality selling at a correspondingly lower price, increase the divisibility of the consumer's purchases of particular items. Consequently, the opportunities for allocating income among different products may be so enhanced that the consumer can achieve a higher level of want satisfaction than would otherwise be possible. Additionally, product differentiation enables a consumer to give vent to individual tastes and preferences with regard to alternative designs for a particular product. The range of products available under differentiated oligopoly appears to work in the consumer's favor or to increase individual welfare over what it would otherwise be.

Applications

Since oligopolistic market structures are so varied in their characteristics, a wealth of applications are available. Among the more interesting ones are the brewing industry and the OPEC crude oil cartel.

Interdependence in the Brewing Industry

Uncertainty is the curse borne by oligopolists. The terrific interdependency among four of the largest and one of the smallest United States brewers in 1980 is seen in the following article from the *Los Angeles Times*.[22]

> The nation's largest beer producers appear to be brewing a price war that experts fear may cause industry stocks to lose their gusto.
>
> Lower beer prices would mean thinner profit margins, which industry analysts say could cause investors to lose their enthusiasm for buying stock in the brewing companies.
>
> Price competition also would reverse a trend begun when New York-based Philip Morris Inc. acquired Miller Brewing in 1969. Philip Morris brought to the beer industry its own style of marketing—one that emphasized flashy advertising rather than the traditional method of competing by lowering prices.
>
> **Industry Growth Slowing**
> "Miller came in and showed them how to do it," explained Donald W. Rice, a beverage industry analyst with the Milwaukee brokerage [firm] of Blunt Ellis & Loewi.
>
> As a result, Miller, which had only 4% market share when it was acquired 10 years ago, grew in 1979 to the nation's second largest brewer, holding 16% of the market.

[22] Kaven Tumulty, "Investors May Find Beer Stock Flat as Industry Price War Heats Up," copyright 25 August 1980, *Los Angeles Times*. Reprinted by permission.

But with industry growth slowing to a projected 2% this year from an average of 4.4% annually over the last three years, even Miller has gone back to price discounting.

"It could be very painful if it gets extensive," Rice said, "particularly for Anheuser (-Busch of St. Louis) and Miller, because they've locked themselves into these horrendous advertising budgets."

Fewer Price Increases

Analyst Lawrence Adelman of Dean Witter Reynolds agreed. "I'm pessimistic," he said. "I think there will be fewer price increases announced than has been the case in the last several years," when brewers raised their prices about 5% every six months.

But George Thompson of E.F. Hutton dismissed the price war threat. "I think there is a lot more being made out of that than is actually (warranted by) reality," he said.

Thompson is particularly optimistic about the prospects for Anheuser-Busch, which is the nation's largest brewer, producing beers such as Budweiser, Michelob and Busch. Its steady growth during the past few years has been eclipsed by that of Miller, while the two companies engaged in an advertising slugfest. Miller's dollar sales increased 44% in 1979, nearly double Anheuser-Busch's 23% growth.

Industry observers disagree about the prospects for the Adolph Coors Co. of Golden, Colo., which has geared up its advertising and has launched a light beer to compete with similar brews from Miller and Anheuser-Busch.

"The jury is still out," Thompson said. "The Coors Light brand has done very, very well. Coors has to continue spending a lot of money on marketing."

Similar uncertainty exists over the fate of Milwaukee's Joseph Schlitz Brewing Co., which reigned during the 1950s as the nation's premier brewer, but has slipped far behind Anheuser-Busch and Miller since. Schlitz's dollar sales were down 1.8% in 1979 from the 1978 level.

"The basic problem is the Schlitz brand itself," Thompson said, explaining that the company lost many customers during the mid-1970s when it shortened its brewing cycle, and caused a "real taste erosion."

Since then, it has corrected that, "so now what they have is a beer that tastes like other beers," Thompson said.

But the consumer's negative impression of the beer has not changed he said, adding, "I think what we have here is a tremendous brand disloyalty. It's something that I can't recall happening before. People are really unwilling to try the product, and that really is a problem to overcome."

He predicted the company's stock will regain its strength, but said the upturn probably would occur no earlier than the second quarter of next year.

> Getting good marks from all the analysts interviewed was G. Heileman Brewing Co. of La Crosse, Wis. Heileman increased its sales 32% during the first quarter of the year, excluding the contributions of Carling National Breweries, which it acquired in March, 1979.
>
> Rice described the firm's executives as "street fighters," and said their concept of brewing is "not that it's a business, it's a war."
>
> Heileman produces about 30 brands, the largest of which is Old Style, described by Rice as "probably the fastest growing major brand in America." Other brands include Tuborg Gold and Blatz.
>
> Rice said Heileman would be fairly immune to price competition, because it has so many brands.

The article is all about uncertainty, even though it mentions the word only once. The firms are taking into account interdependencies as each anticipates a decline in the rate of growth in sales (demand). The experts in the industry and the major brokerage firms, however, have conflicting opinions as to what the equilibrium prices and market shares will be. Will each firm attempt to maintain its former rate of sales by changes in price, advertising, the number of its brands, the tastes of its brands, or some combination of these strategies? How will rivals react to each of these new moves? Will these repercussions in turn cause the initial strategies to change and thus cause the reactions to change again? This problem, which is typical of oligopolies where firms act independently, is so recursive and has so many possible outcomes that it is essentially impossible to model satisfactorily. This is why so many studies of oligopoly economics end up as descriptions or a range of theories, rather than contributions to a central theory of oligopoly.

OPEC: A Cartel?

The uncertainties facing the thirteen members of the Organization of Petroleum Exporting Countries (OPEC) are significant, but they are very different from those facing the United States brewers. Each industry is clearly oligopolistic because most of the members in each occupy positions of sufficient importance in the product market for their actions to have repercussions on the others. The difference is that the brewers act independently, whereas OPEC members meet several times a year for the express purpose of setting a joint price. To some extent this removes the uncertainty of what the various OPEC members will charge for their oil—an uncertainty that the unorganized brewers are unlikely to eradicate. But OPEC has been unable to solve the problems of (1) agreeing to a joint pricing strategy and charging a single, *unified* price across the group as a whole for each grade of oil; (2) determining the particular *quantities* that each member will sell at the prices charged; and (3) preventing secret price dealing within the group. Although OPEC's success has been great by historical standards, it remains an imperfect collusive arrangement that has not achieved *the* monopoly price and output.

OPEC's Precursor "Cartel" Cartels, as we have emphasized throughout the chapter, fail more often than they succeed. OPEC grew out of failure, during the 1950s, by the major international oil companies to make their attempted cartel effective.[23]

The problem that these companies faced in the late 1950s, a problem common to most attempts at cartelization, was excess productive capacity. Between 1948 and 1958, the production of oil from the Middle East grew at a rate almost double that of the rest of the world. The area was attractive not only because of the vastness of its resources and their extremely low marginal extraction costs but because of the lower transport costs of shipping oil to Europe and the United States. The drilling and selling of oil usually was performed by the major international oil firms through contracts that they made with each of the area's "host" governments. The hosts usually took their share of the gains from extraction in the form of a 50 percent royalty on total revenues: the number of barrels multiplied by half of the market price.

The system worked well in generating higher-than-competitive oil prices since the number of participating oil companies was relatively small, reducing both collusion costs and the gains from secret dealing. Given the low short-run elasticity of demand, higher-than-competitive revenues were obtained for both the oil firms and the host governments from the control of supply.

But the major oil companies were unsuccessful in setting prices through control of quantity sold, and the "cartel" became unstable for all of the typical reasons we have described earlier in this chapter. A primary source of instability was the behavior of the individual host governments. Each had an incentive to grant additional oil concessions beyond those held by the major companies. Additional oil output would yield the host even more royalty revenue as long as market price did not decline. The *whole group* of hosts had incentives to avoid increases in output since this would inevitably cause market price to fall. With inelastic oil demand schedules, lower prices would reduce total receipts of all companies combined and thus reduce the revenues captured by the hosts. But it was in the

---

[23] This summary is drawn from the materials contained in William G. Dauster, *The Origins of OPEC: An Economic History* (Los Angeles: University of Southern California, Department of Economics, M.A. thesis, draft mimeo, 1981), Chapters 2 and 3.

interests of *any single* host government to cheat on the group by making additional oil concessions in the same way that any single firm in a collusive arrangement has an incentive to cut price secretly. Lured by the profits that the major oil firms had been making, many smaller "independent" oil companies began to offer host governments new exploration contracts on more favorable terms than the majors had offered. Since host governments did not coordinate policies among themselves at the time, there were no restraints on their incentives to accept such deals. Moreover, some hosts probably dealt with the independents on a defensive basis in the expectation that it would be only a matter of time before their rivals did.

The response of the major oil companies was to try to preempt the independents through new production of their own in the Middle East, the Sahara, and South America. But this increased total productive capacity, and thus total oil supplies, even more. To sell their oil, the independents cut prices. There were now so many sellers in the "cartel" that the costs of restructuring it were not worth incurring.

Policies in still other countries compounded the supply problem. In the late 1950s, the Soviet Union began to export oil. In the United States in 1958–59, the domestic oil import restrictions that we described in Chapter 4 were tightened, causing oil exports from the Middle East that might have gone to the United States to go instead to other countries, raising supplies and lowering prices in those countries. United States antitrust agencies also were concerned over the possible participation of American oil firms in international price-fixing arrangements, so American companies increased both domestic and foreign production to avoid legal tangles at home. By late 1959, the "cartel" was a shambles.

The major oil companies still produced the lion's share of Middle East output; but to sell it in competition with the independents, they had to meet the independents' price cuts. Given the inelasticity of demand, this reduced their total receipts and the royalties of the host governments as well, angering the hosts and leading to acrimony over division of the spoils. Continuing price cuts by the majors led five of the hosts, Saudi Arabia, Iran, Iraq, Venezuela, and Kuwait, to organize a series of meetings in 1959–60 for the purpose of "stabilization of prices and regulation of production." It was out of these meetings that OPEC was formed. OPEC's more drastic moves to raise prices did not begin until 1970–71, when the United States and other consuming countries were soft-pedaling their opposition to price hikes.[24] Then came a series of nationalizations of oil company

---

[24] M. A. Adelman, "Politics, Economics, and World Oil," *American Economic Review, Papers and Proceedings*, vol. 64, no. 2 (May 1974), pp. 58–67.

property, the 1973 Arab–Israeli war and Middle East embargo, and the Iranian supply disruption of 1979. Each of these events indicated to the OPEC countries how expensive it would be for consumers to shift from petroleum to substitutes, and thus how very inelastic the *short-run* demand schedule for crude oil is.

Which Oligopoly Model Fits OPEC?   Just as OPEC is not a group of independent and uncoordinated firms, neither is it a centralized cartel. It has no central association, no mechanism for assigning quotas of sales, no rules to keep a member from adding new productive capacity, and few means other than diplomatic or military action for enforcing sanctions against secret price dealing or even overt price cutting. OPEC is a very loose association of governments—six in the Middle East, two in Northern Africa, two in Southwestern Africa, two in South America, and one in Southeast Asia—and there are real limits to the extent of member-nation cooperation, aside from the limits imposed by geography.

At first glance it seems as though the dominant-firm price-leader model would be appropriate.[25] OPEC sells about half the world's petroleum and is clearly the dominant organization in this market. The kingdom of Saudi Arabia sells about one-third of OPEC's share and thus appears to be the dominant country within the dominant organization. Moreover, Saudi Arabia, as we will observe later, usually presses OPEC for lower prices, so the demand curve for its oil must be more elastic than that for the rest of OPEC collectively—an observation that also fits the dominant firm model. But closer scrutiny reveals inconsistencies. The Saudis often behave in a way that is contrary to the notion of a residual supplier implied by the model. They have frequently increased substantially the quantity they supply in order to hold world oil prices *down* from the levels that other OPEC nations would impose. This strategy has often worked.

OPEC is more than a dominant firm model but weaker than a market-sharing cartel model, too. The countries meet regularly to establish prices, but they often cannot agree in total. When they do concur on price levels, they rarely can agree on sales quotas, as the public quarrels over these matters attest. There is private and public discounting of prices, failure to transfer quotas from high- to low-cost sellers, and different pricing policies pursued by different sellers or groups of sellers. If OPEC is a cartel, it is a highly imperfect cartel. Relative to standard oligopoly models, it is a hodgepodge.

[25] For a perceptive comparison of these models, *see* Thomas D. Willett, "Conflict and Cooperation in OPEC: Some Additional Economic Considerations," *International Organization*, vol. 33, no. 4 (Autumn 1979), pp. 581–87; and "Structure of OPEC and the Outlook for International Oil Prices," *The World Economy*, January 1979, pp. 51–64.

How Effective Is OPEC? The two strongest forces for stability within OPEC are its homogeneous products (which is almost a sine qua non of successful collusion) and the low elasticity of demand for crude oil *in the short run*. The cost of altering machinery to reduce energy uses, the cost of designing and constructing plants to produce synthetic fuels, the slow rate at which new competing oil fields are developed, and the concerns in some Western countries over the use of nuclear fuels all have helped OPEC raise the price of oil by 500 percent in real terms between 1973 and 1980.

But OPEC also contains destabilizing forces. First, thirteen member countries is a large number for an effective cartel. Second, the economic interests of these countries diverge sharply. There are two key divisions within OPEC.[26] The first is a group of short-run profit maximizers who generally have smaller oil reserves, larger populations, and greater demand for cash for economic development purposes than the others. The second group consists of long-term maximizers who generally have greater oil reserves, smaller populations, and less demand for cash to finance development. The group of *short-run maximizers* includes Algeria, Indonesia, Iran, Iraq, Nigeria, and Venezuela. They tend to focus on the very high short-run inelasticity of demand in consuming countries and argue that OPEC should raise prices to the limit right away since they have little to lose if substitutes for oil become common in a decade or two. The *long-run maximizers* include, Kuwait, Libya, Saudi Arabia, and the United Arab Emirates. This group focuses mainly on the *relatively* greater long-run elasticity of demand and argues that OPEC generally should keep prices at levels that do not encourage the creation of substitutes in the near future. It is very difficult within the loose structure of OPEC—the group relies on the rule of unanimity rather than majority—for these viewpoints to be reconciled; and for the most part, the two camps have agreed to disagree.

Third, OPEC occasionally achieves a unified structure of prices, but it is rarely able to agree on quantities. No country wants to be the only, the first, or the most generous member in cutting back on quantities produced. The higher prices are raised, the greater the cutbacks needed, however; and some structure of quotas is called for unless the self-restraint of individual countries is very strong. It is here that the *sovereignty* of member countries interfaces with economic self-interest *of the group*, because few of them are willing to surrender their national power over production to something like a central cartel association. Saudi Arabia is particularly opposed to greater centralization, for fear that great political pressure from the group

---

[26] Robert S. Pindyck, "OPEC's Threat to the West," *Foreign Policy*, 30 (Spring 1978), pp. 36–52.

will be brought against the kingdom to bear the largest fraction of the needed reduction in sales.[27]

Fourth, OPEC's "weapon" against secret price cutting is public criticism of the offender. The higher group prices are raised and the less the group's total production becomes, the more elastic market demand grows and the more elastic the demand curve faced by any single seller willing to cut price secretly. As OPEC prices go higher, some countries are likely to "chisel" defensively. These incentives are particularly troublesome in OPEC, owing to the large discrepancy between the market price and hence the marginal revenue, for a single price cutter, and the marginal cost of extracting oil. For Saudi Arabia, for example, the mid-1980 price of $28 per barrel was about 140 times their marginal extraction cost of perhaps 20 cents per barrel. Outbursts of price cutting, sometimes in the form of discounts on credit terms or the shaving of premiums or taxes, occasionally get reported in the newspapers. In 1975, evidently Ecuador and Libya were making deals,[28] and in 1976, the Saudis accused Iraq of increasing its sales by 30 percent at the same time as the Saudis had cut their production by nearly 3 million barrels per day. As Sheik Ahmed Zaki Yamani, the Saudi oil minister, said in 1976, "This means they lowered prices. Others did, too."[29] Such statements represent additional bits of evidence to suggest that OPEC has yet to achieve the monopoly combination of price and quantity sold that would maximize the wealth of the group as a whole.

The Special Position of Saudi Arabia   Saudi Arabia has about one fourth of the world's proven oil and gas reserves—that is, the hydrocarbons that are "inventories," already located and drilled and waiting to be pumped from the ground. This is enough oil to last past the end of this century at present pumping rates. Thus, when the Saudis think of the price elasticity of the demand for petroleum, it is the very long-run elasticity that they keep uppermost in mind. In 1974, for example, some economists in the United States Treasury calculated that the wealth-maximizing price of oil for Saudi Arabia was between $5 to $10 *less* per barrel than for the typical short-run maximizing member of OPEC.[30]

The Saudis clearly understand that a monopoly price is a relatively high price but not necessarily a relatively rising price. The conversion of an industry from competitive to cartelized conditions should cause a one-shot increase in price as quantity is reduced to

[27]   Willett, "Conflict and Cooperation," p. 585.

[28]   Robert A. Rosenblatt, "OPEC Defies Law of Supply and Demand," *Los Angeles Times*, 21 September 1975.

[29]   Joe Alex Morris, Jr., "Oil Price Rise Will Hold at 5%, Saudi Official Says," *Los Angeles Times*, 18 December 1976.

[30]   Willett, "Conflict and Cooperation," p. 586.

the desired level. Beyond this, price should not increase further unless either inflation occurs or demand or supply conditions change. In particular, rapid increases in relative prices of oil tend to be undesirable because they lead the consuming countries to accelerate their conversion to low-fuel forms of machinery or synthetic fuels, and they increase the likelihood of economic recessions in countries in the West in which Saudi Arabia and other long-run maximizing countries within OPEC have invested enormous wealth. Instead, Saudi Arabia seems to want petroleum prices to increase slowly to reflect the gradual reduction of inventories in the ground up to the limit of the per-barrel cost of substitute fuels, adjusted of course for inflation of the currencies of importing countries. A more moderate rise in the price of oil also places fewer strains in the form of reduced sales, internecine quarrels over cutbacks, and, possibly, defensive chiseling on the collusive arrangement.

Thus far there have been two sharp splits within OPEC over pricing. In 1977, Saudi Arabia and the United Arab Emirates raised prices by only 5 percent while the remainder of OPEC increased prices by 10 percent.[31] At the time, Saudi Arabia also raised its production "target" beyond the rate of 8.5 million barrels per day by as much as 1.5 million in order to pressure the rest of the group to reduce their prices. It is thought the kingdom could have expanded supply to about 11 million barrels per day in 1977 but elected not to. To give some idea of the magnitudes involved, 8.5 million barrels per day exceeds the *entire* United States oil output in 1980, and 1.5 million surpasses the 1980 level of production from Alaska. The extra production was not enough to cause other countries to lower prices, but it did prevent them from rising by very much. Between 1973 and 1978, the *real,* or inflation-adjusted, price of oil declined by 25 percent in terms of the United States dollar.

The next crucial event in oil pricing occurred when Iran ceased production during its 1979 revolution. The short-run maximizing oil exporters viewed this as an opportunity to double the level of world oil prices through a series of "leapfrogging" adjustments by individual OPEC members. This produced a situation that the oil minister of one exporting country likened to having "13 different OPECs," a paradox described in the following column from *The Wall Street Journal.*[32]

---

[31]   Morris.
For an excellent summary of the recent history of pricing by the Persian Gulf producers, *see* Richard D. Erb, "The Gulf Oil Producers: Overview and Oil Policy Implications," *AEI Foreign Policy and Defense Review,* vol. 2, nos. 3 and 4 (1980), pp. 5–8.

[32]   James Tanner and Ray Vickers, "OPEC Talks Next Week Will Try to Start Bringing Order to Oil Markets and Prices," *The Wall Street Journal,* 12 December, 1979. Reprinted by permission of *The Wall Street Journal,* © Dow Jones & Company, Inc. 1979. All rights reserved.

It may come as a surprise to Americans who have seen gasoline and heating-oil prices rise in a seemingly endless spiral, but the oil-producing nations aren't especially happy with their situation.

As the Organization of Petroleum Exporting Countries prepares for its semiannual meeting, beginning in Caracas, Venezuela, on Monday, most of the oil ministers of the 13 member nations indicate in interviews that a major goal is to start on a course toward stabilizing world oil markets.

The meeting no doubt will result in another rise in the official price for OPEC's oil (which currently is well below prices in the spot market) and plenty of rhetoric in support of the increase. But most representatives of the seven Arab and six non-Arab OPEC nations are clearly concerned and somewhat confused about the swift pace of events that has resulted in runaway petroleum prices this year.

A First Step

For one thing, says Sheik Ahmed Zaki Yamani, Saudi Arabia's oil minister, "we have lost control over petroleum prices." Trying to restore some order to short-term pricing therefore will be the first order of business in Caracas. But the ministers view that as only a first step in attempting to chart OPEC's course in longer-range oil markets as well as its roles in world political and economic affairs.

So the ministers at Caracas will begin efforts toward:

—Developing a program to "fine-tune" OPEC's total output to avoid the wide swings in production that have taken world oil supplies from surplus to shortage to surplus.

—Instituting an automatic pricing mechanism that would adjust petroleum prices over the long term, quarterly if necessary, to avoid sudden jumps in prices. The system would aim to keep the producers in pace with inflation and eventually put oil quotes in line with costs of alternative energy sources (currently estimated at the equivalent of $30 a barrel, against OPEC's average official price of $22 a barrel).

—Improving the relations that have deteriorated with both the industrial and developing nations as a result of this year's soaring of petroleum prices.

Report on 18-Month Study

Some of these concepts are included in a little-noticed study that OPEC's so-called Long-Range Strategy Committee is completing after 18 months. The committee's findings will probably get more attention from the oil ministers at Caracas than their pricing announcements might suggest.

Although the final draft of the report isn't completed, Sheik Yamani, chairman of the committee, says he hopes it will be ready for presentation to the ministers at this session.

Venezuela and Saudi Arabia are the main sponsors of the 44-

page working paper, which has been reviewed by the ministers of Algeria, Iraq, Iran and Kuwait, also members of the strategy committee. The oil ministers from the remaining OPEC nations (Ecuador, Gabon, Indonesia, Libya, Nigeria, Qatar, and the United Arab Emirates) may review the study at next week's session. If not, they will probably take it up at a special session in the spring. Final action then would probably come at an OPEC summit meeting scheduled for later this year to mark OPEC's 20th anniversary.

Basis for a Dialogue

The study hasn't been made public, but Petroleum Intelligence Weekly, a trade publication, says that it sets the basis for a broad dialogue with industrial countries, aimed in part at stabilizing oil supplies. The report also covers oil and energy perspectives for the next 10 years, relations with developing and industrial nations, and consideration of a longer-term "rational" oil-producing system.

Whether OPEC is likely to adopt unified long-range plans is debatable, of course. The OPEC nations have diverse goals and interests, and the Iranian crisis has injected new dissensions. Iran and Libya, at least, appear content with the threat of oil scarcity driving petroleum prices even beyond their targets. But many others in OPEC fear they may be approaching the point of diminishing returns. They expect at least a temporary oil surplus to surface next year, and prices may be forced lower again.

In the past, OPEC was able to maintain a floor under prices even during times of surplus. But its official pricing actions this year have been mainly a rubber stamping of what its members had already chosen to charge individually. Consequently, says one oil minister, "there are now 13 different OPECs," with each producer setting its own prices without much regard for the cartel's benchmark quote.

Fears of a Glut

With oil supplies tight, individual pricing measures haven't been much of a problem for the group. But if an oil glut develops, price-cutting by members could follow as they try to keep their market shares. Many in OPEC fear that this could bring on severe strains, perhaps endangering the cartel.

Renewed oil shortages could also bring real problems for OPEC. The oil ministers cite recurring talk in some industrial nations, particularly the U.S., about possible military actions in the oil fields if supplies are disrupted. Some ministers also worry about the effects on the economic health of the Western nations from ever-rising prices and possible supply shortages. That isn't necessarily altruistic. Many of the producers have much of their wealth invested in Western countries.

As all of this suggests, the oil ministers are indeed concerned about supply and price stability. "Oil demand will fall sharply in the year ahead," one minister says. "Supplies will be abundant, *and this may cause some people to think that the oil crisis is over. Actually, the world will only be sitting in the eye of the hurricane, and we will be heading toward catastrophic shortages of oil if consumers don't cut back consumption.''*

Sheik Yamani echoes this view and sees gasoline prices in the U.S. possibly reaching $10 a gallon if the 1980s do bring major oil shortages. The grim prospect of a future disastrous shortage, in fact, dominates the long-range planning as the OPEC nations reap the riches from this year's 70% increase in oil prices.

Consumer Awareness

Sheik Ali Khalifah Al-Sabah, Kuwait's oil minister, suggests that the surge in spot oil prices (which are beyond OPEC's control) to as much as $45 a barrel has helped consumers understand that there really is an oil problem. As a result, he says, "consumers are certainly going to curtail their oil consumption." He sees demand for OPEC oil dropping as much as 15% to 20% in 1980.

That is one reason why several in OPEC want to coordinate production rates with lower demand to avoid a glut. They also seem willing to let output rise, within reason, to match a rebound in demand.

The OPEC planners want oil consumers, including the developing nations, to get together with oil producers to prepare ways to deal with such possible market disruptions. The producers suggest automatic price-increase procedures with gradual rises that consumers would know were coming.

OPEC tried such an approach for this year, when prices were scheduled to rise quarterly, for a cumulative 14.5% increase for the year. But the effort fell apart after the Iranian oil stoppage as frantic buyers scrambled for oil at any price.

Demand was high during this period because the consuming countries were replenishing inventories that had been run down during the Iranian cutback and were increasing their stockpiles as a hedge against future reductions. Demand increased so much that the "spot" price for oil in the market for inventories and resales surged to $45, nearly double the average of official OPEC prices in the market for contract oil. (In reading this article notice the confusions by the authors and several of the officials whom they quote between demand versus quantity demanded.)

Saudi Arabia viewed the late-1979 turn of events with alarm. Sheik Yamani was quoted in the preceding article as having claimed, "We have lost control over petroleum prices." A fortnight later The Sheik was quoted as stating "There will be a glut. And there will be a definite drop in spot-market prices. I can see this very clearly, and it will happen probably at the end of the first quarter (of 1980). . . . Inventories have reached the highest level ever."[33] Sheik Yamani's predictions are not to be taken lightly for he is in a position to make

[33] Ibid.

them come true—at least in part. This was done when the kingdom increased its daily production from 8.5 million to 9.5 million barrels, similar to its action in 1977. By the spring of 1980, the "glut" that the oil minister predicted, and that the kingdom's production policy was designed to create, had arrived; and by July 1980, spot prices were falling. Consuming countries had adopted many conservation measures in response to the higher prices that, in terms of economic analysis, amounted to moving up the existing long-run demand curve; but the demand curve for oil also shifted leftward, owing partly to the economic recession that reduced the rate of growth in industrial production, generally, thus also depressing the rate of growth in the demand for petroleum.

The long-run maximizers within OPEC, led by Saudi Arabia, sought to end the price leapfrogging and to restore an OPEC pricing policy that was more congenial to their economic interests. This involved establishing the long-term pricing arrangements that the preceding article describes. Price increases would be tied to formulas that both exporters and importers could count on, and the "fine-tuning" would attempt to end the disruptions that wide price swings caused. This issue is so important within OPEC that the group has devoted an entire three-day meeting to the reports of the Long-Range Strategy Committee. However, agreement on the formulas and rules that the kingdom, the emirates, and certain other long-run maximizers desire is often frustrated by bickering within the organization over the "base price" from which all price changes will be figured. The short-run maximizers want the base price to be relatively high. Saudi Arabia and its allies want a lower price, and their bargaining position for it is very strong, owing to their supply capabilities. The kingdom did not increase production by enough to choke off all of the increase in prices that followed the Iranian disruption,[34] perhaps because of opposition from Iran and other short-run maximizers to such a policy. The rivalries in OPEC are illustrated in the following article from *The Wall Street Journal*. It provides quotations and background information that illustrate very nicely the internal acrimony that is typical of attempts to cartelize.[35]

> —*Opening their special meeting here, oil producers made little progress toward resolving differences on either long-term or current oil-pricing policies.*
>
> *But the 13 members of the Organization of Petroleum Exporting Countries did seem to be moving toward a goal of possibly matching oil production to demand to cope with current and possible future oil surpluses.*

[34] Erb, "The Gulf Oil Producers," p. 7.

[35] James Tanner, "OPEC Seems to Be Moving Toward Goal of Matching Its Oil Output to Demand," *The Wall Street Journal*, 16 September 1980. Reprinted by permission of *The Wall Street Journal*, © Dow Jones & Company, Inc. 1980. All rights reserved.

"There is a strong trend to cut production, at least two million barrels a day," asserted Mana Said Otaiba, oil minister for the United Arab Emirates. He had said over the weekend that cutbacks by any producers shouldn't be considered until it's determined how much demand there will be for OPEC oil when winter arrives.

Saudi Arabia remains the key, of course, to pricing and production policies by OPEC in the long and short term. Saudi officials didn't completely clarify the kingdom's positions in these matters, but Sheik Ahmed Zaki Yamani, Saudi oil minister, continued to maintain that the kingdom wouldn't raise its relatively low oil prices until price unity is restored in OPEC. He also reiterated that Saudi Arabia won't reduce its relatively high rate of oil production until agreement has been reached on OPEC's long-term strategy.

Prices in Disarray

Sheik Yamani, the architect of the long-term strategic plan being considered here, continued to maintain that he is "hopeful" the producers will be able to achieve a unified pricing structure. OPEC prices have been in disarray since the Iranian revolution triggered tight oil supplies last year, sparking price leapfrogging among oil producers.

Although Saudi Arabia is OPEC's biggest producer, its pricing has been far more moderate than that of most other producers. Its key grade of oil, the OPEC benchmark crude, currently is at $28 a barrel, compared with the $32-a-barrel base used by most other OPEC members. Additionally, producers of top-quality crudes, such as Algeria, Nigeria and Libya, added up to $5 a barrel as a "differential" or premium for their better-grade crudes.

The Saudi oil minister told reporters that the kingdom won't raise its prices despite pressure from some in OPEC, particularly Iran, unless prices of the highest-priced oils are reduced. "Definitely the $5 differential is far from reality," he said. He added, however: "We are fairly hopeful that a compromise could be achieved on this matter."

Whether such a "compromise" would involve a possible increase of $2 or $4 a barrel in Saudi oil prices, as has been widely speculated, probably won't be known at the earliest until tomorrow, when the oil ministers are scheduled to hold a "consultative meeting" on current pricing and production.

Saudi Arabia's current rate of oil production, 9.5 million barrels a day, compared with the usual 8.5 million barrels a day, also will be a major topic at the oil ministers' consultative session because of the current world oil glut.

The meeting that opened yesterday is a joint session of the oil ministers with the foreign and finance ministers of the 13 producing nations. Neither Saudi Arabia's current oil prices nor its high rate of production was to be part of the discussions of this meeting, *which was to take up only long-term pricing and production policies.*

Tirade by Iranian Aide

Nonetheless, Saudi production and prices were hot topics during the day yesterday, mainly because of Iran. At one point yesterday afternoon, Ali Akbar Moinfar, Iran's chief delegate, mounted an hour-long tirade against Saudi Arabia. "As a matter of fact," he said, "Saudi Arabia is enjoying tremendous profit because of the Iranian revolution. Saudi Arabia is exploiting the market 'shortage' by overproduction and underselling. Roughly, I calculate Saudi Arabia is making a profit of $100 million a day."

Sheik Yamani answered: "I think we all understand English in this room. When the OPEC Algiers meeting (in June) said the ceiling is $32 that means it is a ceiling and doesn't forbid OPEC members from selling under that. But Iran does sell above the ceiling and that's where the problem starts."

Earlier, Mr. Moinfar had told reporters that Iran might consider reducing its oil price, currently $35 a barrel, if Saudi Arabia would reduce its production two million barrels a day.

Iranian and Iraqi officials also tangled, right at the start of yesterday's conference. Because Sheik Yamani has devoted such an effort to the long-term-strategy plan, he had wanted the Iraqi oil minister to be chairman of this joint conference. That is because an OPEC summit meeting is to be held in Baghdad in November, where members are to endorse the long-term-strategy plan and observe OPEC's twentieth anniversary.

But Mr. Moinfar, angered by the Iranian-Iraqi border conflict, already has objected to the holding of the summit in Iraq. And yesterday he strongly objected to the appointment of an Iraqi as chairman of this meeting. A Venezuelan suggestion that Algeria's foreign minister head this conference was accepted and settled the dispute.

The joint meeting, which may end today, even though its work may have to be completed by another triministerial meeting before the Baghdad summit, was intended to lay the groundwork for the Baghdad summit, as well as polish the long-term-strategy plan.

Key Parts of Plan Cited

Key parts of the plan under review and possible revision here are increased OPEC aid to developing countries and an automatic pricing system that would raise prices quarterly, based on Western economic growth, inflation rates, and currency fluctuations. Both have sparked controversies of another sort.

At yesterday's session, which went into the night, the conference agreed to appoint two separate committees to meet this morning in an attempt to resolve differences and then report to the conference.

The Iran-Iraq border war of 1980 presented OPEC with problems and Saudi Arabia with opportunities that were almost a replay of those accompanying the Iranian revolution in 1979. To prevent another round of disruptive price hikes, the Saudis increased their production, again, to in excess of 10 million barrels per day.[36] As the war continued into November 1980, oil buyers prepared for smaller future exports and protected their inventories from a sudden possibility of a wider war by stepping up their rate of purchases in the spot market, which again drove the spot price above OPEC's contract prices.[37] The prospect of rising prices and leapfrogging strengthened the hand of the short-run maximizers and led OPEC to delay the implementation of Sheik Yamani's long-term pricing strategy.[38] The Sheik, knowing that higher prices and more leapfrogging would damage his own country's interest in lower prices, began to warn his colleagues that another oil "glut" would occur by 1981 or 1982.[39] Apparently the Saudis also decided to help the glut along by maintaining their production at a rate of about 10.3 million barrels per day, even though production by Iran and Iraq had increased to roughly half of its prewar level by March 1981.[40]

By April 1981, as this book went to press, the shiek's predictions of another oil glut were coming true more rapidly than perhaps even he had anticipated. Oil inventories within the United States were rising, world spot prices (and some contract prices) were declining, and wholesale and retail gasoline prices within the United States were beginning to fall for the first time in six months.[41] Higher prices had led consumers to cut back on purchases and had stimulated non-OPEC countries to raise output: Mexico by 32 percent;

---

[36] "Daily Saudi Oil Boost Expected to Hit 1.5 Million Barrels to Ease Shortfalls," *Los Angeles Times*, 7 October 1980.

[37] Karen Elliott House, "Saudi Oil Official Warns of Price Boosts If Firms Don't Start Tapping Inventories," *The Wall Street Journal*, 11 November 1980.

[38] James Tanner, "Plan of OPEC for More Orderly Pricing Is Seen Likely Casualty of Iran-Iraq War," *The Wall Street Journal*, 9 October 1980.

[39] James Tanner, "OPEC's Worries About a Possible Oil Glut May Moderate Members' Price Increases," *The Wall Street Journal*, 22 December 1980.

[40] *The Wall Street Journal*: Youssef M. Ibrahim, "Oil Exports from Iraq, Iran Are Rising Amid News Peace Talks Are Being Held," 6 March 1981; "Saudis Warn West About Stockpiling Crude-Oil Supplies," 6 January 1981. Initially the two belligerents bombed each other's oil fields, but then each realized the long-run costs of this strategy and shifted tactics to bombing each other's oil refineries, the loss of which would limit abilities to wage war. Iraq's exports held up during the war better than Iran's, owing to Iraq's pipelines to the Mediterranean via Turkey and Syria, although these were intermittently subjected to sabotage.

[41] *The Wall Street Journal*: Bill Paul, "Oil Production May Be Trimmed by Saudis, Others," 20 February 1981; Bill Paul, "Ecuador, Mexico Cut Oil Prices Due to Glut," 9 April 1981; "Oil Firms Cut Prices, Offer Rebates to Lift Gasoline Demand," 10 April 1981; Bill Paul, "Retail Gasoline Prices Begin to Decline for First Time in Six Months, Analyst Says," 17 April 1981.

Norway, 30 percent; Britain, 12 percent, and Argentina, 4 percent.[42] Sheik Yamani, using this opportunity to press for his country's interest in lower long-run prices, declared his intention not to cut back Saudi production until OPEC took favorable action on his long-run pricing strategy proposals.[43] To avoid even the possibility of confusion on this score, he announced on an American television interview program: "We engineered the glut, and we want to see it stabilize the price of oil"; and he predicted that prices would fall for some time until a general pricing agreement is reached.[44]

External Destabilizing Forces on OPEC The strains on OPEC arise not only from its internal weaknesses but from external forces as well. Increased petroleum production by the United Kingdom, Norway, and Mexico—not one of which is a member of OPEC—could, to some extent, reduce the cartel's share of world sales. Additional conservation measures and deregulation of crude oil prices in the United States are likely to reduce this country's imports below their 1980 levels. Anything that reduces OPEC's share of world sales will put increasing strains on its internal decision-making arrangements and enhance its instability.

Although the preceding discussion has focused on the strategy of sellers in the international market for oil, buyers have cards of their own that they may play. On the whole, the oil-importing nations have acted passively: they have avoided steps that could be interpreted by OPEC as hostile and have often beseeched certain of its members, particularly Saudi Arabia, to increase production. A different strategy would be for large buyers, such as the United States or the European Economic Community, to try to play particular members of OPEC off against the rest of the group. This could be done by making long-term contracts at very favorable prices with certain relatively "hungry" members of the cartel that have demands for current income, for example, Venezuela or Nigeria. Such negotiations, if successful, could weaken the rest of OPEC by inducing the remaining members to meet the prices or restrain production even more.[45] But the strategy is full of risks. First, it would place all the United States' "eggs" in the "basket" of the single country with which the deal was made, and a political upheaval in that country could have disastrous consequences for U.S. buyers. Second, it

---

[42] G. Kent Sorey, "Three Forces Work to Stall New OPEC Price Shock," *Los Angeles Times,* 7 April 1981.

[43] "Saudi Arabian Oil Output to Stay at Higher Level," *The Wall Street Journal,* 31 March 1981.

[44] Robert A. Rosenblatt, "OPEC Prices to Drop, Saudi Official Says," *Los Angeles Times,* 20 April 1981.

[45] Adelman, "Politics, Economics, and World Oil."

would require a complete reorientation of the pro-Saudi Arabia policy that the United States government has pursued on a bipartisan basis since the Eisenhower administration. This policy has included not only oil sales but weapons contracts and, at times, certain political assurances that come close to outright guarantees of Saudi security. The present United States policy would be very difficult to change. Perhaps it is better than the alternative, in spite of what a cynical economist might view as a naive and timid pursuit of the nation's economic self-interest.

Summary

In oligopolistic market structures, there are few enough firms in the industry for the activities of one to influence and evoke reactions from others. The demand curve faced by a single firm will be determinate when the firm can predict with accuracy what the reactions of rivals will be to market activities on its part. Otherwise it will be indeterminate.

We classified oligopolistic industries according to the degree of collusion that exists among firms in each of the industries. Under perfect collusion we included groups of firms such as cartels. Under imperfect collusion we included situations typified by price leadership and gentlemen's agreements. Under independent action we included noncollusive cases.

In the short run, perfectly collusive oligopolistic cases approximate the establishment of monopoly price and monopoly output for the industry as a whole. The less the degree of collusion, usually, the lower the price and the greater the output. In industries characterized by independent action on the part of individual firms, price wars are likely to be common occurrences. As the industry matures, the situation may become collusive, or it may develop into a "live-and-let-live" attitude on the part of the firms in the industry. In the latter case, price rigidity may occur. Firms may be afraid to change price for fear of touching off a price war.

In the long run, the firm can adjust its plant size as desired and new concerns can enter the industry, unless entry is blocked. The size of plant chosen by the firm will be the one that will produce its anticipated output at the least possible average cost for that output. Easy entry into the industry is largely incompatible with a high degree of collusion. Collusion exists partly to block entry. Barriers to entry may be classified as "natural" and "artificial." Restricted entry may enable firms in the industry to make long-run pure profits.

The firms of particular oligopolistic industries frequently engage in nonprice competition through product differentiation, to avoid touching off price wars. Nonprice competition takes two major forms: advertising and variation in quality and design. To the extent that firms using them succeed only in holding their respective market shares, costs of production and product prices will tend to be higher than they would otherwise be. The firm desiring to maximize profits will use each to the point at which the marginal revenue from it equals the marginal cost of extending its use.

Some of the welfare effects of oligopolistic markets on the economy are these:

1   Outputs are restricted below, and prices are increased above, the levels that will yield Pareto optimality, since product price tends to be higher than marginal cost. With entry partially or completely blocked, pure profits and additional output restrictions occur.

2   Individual firms are not induced to produce at their maximum efficiency plant sizes, although in many cases they produce more efficiently than they would if the industry were atomized.

3   Imperfect collusive arrangements and cartels may generate underutilized, or even unused, plant capacity.

4   Some sales promotion wastes occur.

5   The range of products available to consumers is broader under differentiated oligopoly than it would be under pure competition or pure monopoly.

Suggested Readings

Bain, Joe S. *Industrial Organization,* 2d ed. New York: John Wiley & Sons, 1968.

Machlup, Fritz. *The Economics of Sellers' Competition.* Baltimore: The Johns Hopkins Press, 1952, Chaps. 4, 11–16.

Scherer, F. M. *Industrial Market Structure and Economic Performance.* Chicago: Rand, McNally, 1970.

White, Lawrence J. "The Automobile Industry," in Walter Adams, ed., *The Structure of American Industry,* 5th ed. New York: Macmillan, 1977, Chap. 5.

Wilcox, Clair. *Competition and Monopoly in American Industry.* Temporary National Economic Committee Monograph No. 21. Washington, D.C.: U.S. Government Printing Office, 1940.

Questions and Exercises

1   Suppose that the auto repair shops in Universityville form an association. They agree to, and post, a schedule of minimum hourly labor charges for shop work.

    a How, if at all, could this action be advantageous to them as a group?

    b If it is advantageous to them as a group, why may it be necessary for them to police the arrangement; that is, why may some shops want to "chisel"?

2   In many states barber shops must be licensed by the state to "protect the public from incompetent barbers." In some states county organizations of barbers determine the minimum prices to be charged for various barbering services. These minimum prices then have the force of law—it is illegal to charge less. The rationale of these laws is that minimum prices must be set at a level that will enable individual shops to be kept clean and sanitary.

    a Do you believe that licensing is necessary to protect the public? Why or why not? Can you think of any other reason why licensing laws might be affected?

    b Would you expect minimum prices to be set with the stated rationale in mind? Why or why not? Can you think of alternative ways of insuring sanitation that may lead toward higher consumer welfare?

3   From World War II to the mid-1970s, no new automobile-manufacturing firms have been able to enter the industry and survive. What possible explanations can be offered in view of the fact that established firms in the industry, except for Chrysler and American Motors in some years, were generally profitable during that period?

4   Would you favor breaking General Motors into several companies, each producing a specific line of automobile—for example, Chevrolets? Why or why not?

5   Outline in some detail the set of policies that you think the government should pursue with respect to oligopolistic market structures. State and explain what you would expect each policy to accomplish.

CHAPTER CONTENTS		KEY CONCEPTS
Some Special Characteristics		Monopolistic competition Short run Long run Welfare Most efficient size of plant Most efficient rate of output
The Short Run		
The Long Run	Adjustments with Entry Blocked	
	Adjustments with Entry Open	
Welfare Effects of Monopolistic Competition	Output Restriction	
	Efficiency of Individual Firms	
	Sales Promotion Wastes and Benefits	
	Range of Products Available	
Application: Restraints on Advertising in the Health Service Professions		
Summary	Suggested Readings	
	Questions and Exercises	

Pricing and Output under
Monopolistic Competition

There are many sellers of the product in an industry characterized by monopolistic competition, and the product of each one is in some way differentiated from the product of every other seller. Several questions arise. What does "many sellers" mean? How can we distinguish between differentiated oligopoly and monopolistic competition? How many sellers must there be in an industry to warrant calling the case one of monopolistic competition? These questions cannot be answered objectively by numbers alone. When the number of sellers is large enough so that the actions of any one have no perceptible effect upon other sellers, and their actions have no perceptible effect upon the one, the industry becomes one of monopolistic competition.

The theory of monopolistic competition provides few new analytical tools; it is very similar to that of pure competition. It furnishes a better description of those competitive industries in which product differentiation occurs—food processing, men's clothing, cotton textiles, and the service trades and health professions in large cities, for instance—in that it recognizes small monopoly elements and the consequent different prices charged by different sellers of a particular type of product.

Some Special Characteristics

The conditions of demand faced by the firm set monopolistic competition apart from the three market situations discussed previously. Product differentiation leads some consumers to prefer the products of one seller in an industry over those of others. Consequently, the demand curve faced by an individual seller has some downward slope to it and enables it to exercise a small degree of control over its product price. Ordinarily the demand curve faced by the firm will be very elastic within its relevant range of prices because of the numerous good substitutes available for the product.

Product differentiation by the sellers in an industry increases the complexity of presenting the analysis in graphic terms. For ex-

does, occur. Where it occurs, it is usually the result of legislative activity of one kind or another. Owners or operators of the firms in a particular industry may belong to a trade association that has some political influence on a local, statewide, or perhaps even a nation-wide basis. The industry may be fairly profitable, and the trade association may foresee the possibility of wholesale entry into the industry. Therefore, it may use its influence to secure the enactment of legislation that is rationalized as insuring an adequate supply of the commodity at prices allowing those in the trade to make fair and reasonable profits. In the service trades in a particular city or state, one can easily find laws that tend to block entry.[1]

In such situations individual firms seek to adjust their respective plant sizes to those required for long-run profit maximization. The long-run average cost curve and the long-run marginal cost curve are the relevant ones for the firm. These are shown as LAC and LMC in Figure 14.2. The demand curve faced by the firm is dd, and

FIGURE 14.2
Long-run profit maximization: entry blocked

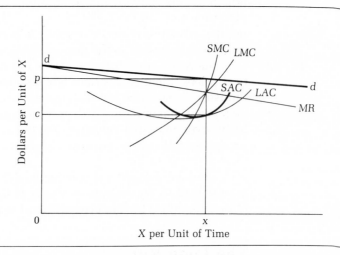

the marginal revenue curve is MR. Profits will be maximum at output x, at which long-run marginal cost equals marginal revenue. Output x can be sold for price p per unit. To produce output x at the least possible cost per unit, the firm should build the plant size that has its short-run average cost curve tangent to the long-run average cost curve at that output. Since SAC is tangent to LAC at output x, short-run marginal cost is equal to long-run marginal cost and to marginal revenue at that output. Profits are equal to $cp \times x$.

If the firm should deviate from output x by increasing or de-

---

[1]   See Milton Friedman, *Capitalism and Freedom* (Chicago: University of Chicago Press, 1962), Chap. 9.

creasing its rate of output with the given size of plant, SMC would be greater than or less than MR, and profits would decline. If it should raise or lower its rate of output by changing the size of plant, LMC would be greater than or less than MR, and profits would decline. Long-run equilibrium for the firm, when entry into the industry is blocked, means that the firm produces the output at which SMC equals LMC equals MR, and at which SAC equals LAC.

Adjustments with Entry Open

Ordinarily we would expect entry into, or exit from, a monopolistically competitive industry to be easy. Existing firms without the benefit of a trade association are likely to feel unconcerned about a few firms more or less in the industry; or, in the event they are concerned about the entry of new firms, they feel powerless to do anything about it. The mere fact that a large number of firms exists in the industry suggests that the size of each is something less than gigantic and that effective collusion without government support would be extremely difficult. Thus, most of the bars to entry that exist in oligopolistic markets are not effective in markets of monopolistic competition.

When pure profits exist for firms in the industry and potential entrants believe that they, too, can make pure profits, entry will be attempted. As new firms enter, they encroach on the markets of existing firms, causing the demand curve and the marginal revenue curve faced by each to shift downward. The downward shift of each firm's demand curve results from the increase in industry supply of the product as new firms enter. The increase in supply (and in the number of suppliers) pushes the whole cluster of price ranges for individual firms downward.[2]

The entry of new firms into the industry will affect costs of production for existing firms. As in pure competition (and in oligopoly to the extent that entry is possible), an industry classification of increasing cost, constant cost, and decreasing cost can be used. If the industry were one of increasing costs, the entry of new firms would cause resource prices to rise, which would shift the cost curves of existing firms upward and would raise the level of costs of entering firms. Under constant costs the entry of new firms would have no effects on resource prices or on the cost curves of individual firms. In the unlikely case of decreasing costs, the entry of new firms would cause resource prices to decrease and the cost curves to shift downward. We shall examine only the case of increasing costs.

---

[2] This analysis parallels that of pure competition. Larger market supply under pure competition shifts demand curves faced by the individual firms downward.

The entry of new firms will shift the demand curves faced by individual firms downward and their cost curves upward. These shifts will cause profits to decrease, but new firms will continue to enter as long as profit possibilities remain. Eventually, enough firms will have entered to squeeze out pure profits.

This situation for the individual firm is pictured graphically in Figure 14.3. Compared with Figure 14.2, the demand curve faced by the firm has shifted downward as new firms enter, from dd in Figure 14.2 to d_1d_1 in Figure 14.3. The long-run cost curves have shifted

FIGURE 14.3
Long-run profit maximization: entry open

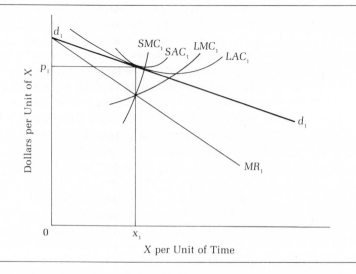

upward to LAC_1 and LMC_1. The short-run cost curves have also shifted upward, and adjustments in the size of plant have occurred. When enough firms have entered to cause the demand curve faced by each firm to be just tangent to its long-run average cost curve, firms of the industry will no longer be making profits, and entry will stop.

Long-run equilibrium will be achieved by individual firms and by the industry as a whole when each firm in the industry is in the position shown in Figure 14.3. For each individual firm long-run marginal cost and short-run marginal cost equal marginal revenue at some output such as x_1. Any deviation from that output with size of plant SAC_1 will cause losses. Any change in the size of plant will also cause losses. Short-run average cost equals long-run average cost at that output, and both are equal to the price per unit received by the firm for its product. The industry as a whole will be in equilibrium since no profits or losses occur to provide the incentive for entry into or exit from the industry.

Welfare Effects of Monopolistic Competition

Monopolistic competition does not differ greatly from pure competition with respect to its welfare effects. It does, however, have some slightly restrictive impacts.

Output Restriction

If one of the industries of a purely competitive economy in long-run equilibrium were to become monopolistically competitive, welfare would tend to be reduced by a slight restriction of output and a slight increase in the prices charged for the product. The demand curve faced by the monopolistic competitor, though very elastic, is less than perfectly elastic. Marginal revenue for the individual firm is less than price, and the rate of output is stopped short of that at which marginal cost equals the product price. The more elastic the demand curve faced by the firm, the less will be the deviation from purely competitive price and output.

In the long run the price will equal the average costs of production unless entry into the industry is blocked. When entry is free and easy—as appears to be the usual case—new firms enter the profit-making industries and reduce profits to zero. Consumers pay just enough to enable firms to hold the desired quantities of resources in the production of the good. Organization of the economy's productive capacity can follow consumers' tastes and preferences with a high degree of accuracy.

When entry into profit-making industries is blocked, the consequences with respect to prices and average costs are much the same as they are under pure monopoly and oligopoly. Productive capacity of the economy cannot be organized to conform accurately to consumers' tastes and preferences. Additional quantities of resources are prohibited from moving into the profit-making industries where they would be more productive than they are in alternative employments.

Efficiency of Individual Firms

There will be some inefficiency of individual firms in the long run when entry into the industry is easy; that is, the firm will not be induced to build the most efficient size of plant nor to operate the one it does build at the most efficient rate of output. This point can be seen best by reference to Figure 14.3. A most efficient size of plant would generate losses for the firm since average cost at such an output would be greater than price. If the long-run average cost curve lies below the demand curve for any range of outputs, pure profits can be made by any firm that builds the correct size of plant for any one of those outputs. New firms will enter until profits are eliminated. Profit possibilities are eliminated when long-run average cost curves for individual firms are tangent to the demand curves they faced. Losses are incurred when the long-run average cost curve lies above the demand curve for all outputs. Exit of firms from the industry will continue until the long-run average cost curve for each firm is again tangent to the demand curve it faces.

In long-run equilibrium the output at which losses are avoided by the firm ($SMC = LMC = MR$) is the output at which the average cost curves are tangent to the demand curve. Since the demand curve faced by the firm is downward sloping, the average cost curves must be downward sloping, also, at their point of tangency with the demand curve. Thus, with easy entry into the industry, individual firms will build a less than most efficient size of plant, such as SAC_1 in Figure 14.3, and they will operate at less than the most efficient rate of output.

Some overcrowding with regard to the number of firms in the industry, and some excess plant capacity, may occur when entry is easy. Since each firm builds a less than most efficient size of plant, there is room for more firms to exist than there would be if all were building plants of most efficient size. Also, since each firm tends to operate the plant that it does build at less than the most efficient rate of output, it follows that excess plant capacity may exist. Empirical examples of both situations are not hard to find. The various textile industries illustrate both an excess of firms in an industry and excess capacity for individual firms.

The inefficiencies of the firm pointed out above should not be overemphasized, nor is the foregoing paragraph an argument for restriction of entry into monopolistically competitive industries. The demand curve faced by the firm is highly elastic; and the more elastic it is, the nearer the firm will come to building an optimum size of plant to operate near the optimum rate of output. Free entry into the industry will cause the total industry output to be greater than it would be if entry were restricted, and it will cause prices to be correspondingly lower.

When entry is restricted, the firm will build the appropriate size of plant to produce the output at which long-run marginal cost equals marginal revenue. There is no inducement for the firm to build an optimum size of plant. The plant built will be optimum only in the event that its marginal revenue curve passes through the minimum point on its long-run average cost curve. Such an occurrence would be purely accidental.

Sales Promotion Wastes and Benefits

Some waste advertising or design changes may occur under monopolistic competition. Efforts on the part of individual firms to expand their markets in this way may be counteracted by similar efforts on the part of the others, and the resources so used merely add to costs of production. Any such waste of resources will be much smaller under monopolistic competition than under oligopoly, where efforts on the part of one firm to expand its share of the market induces others to put forth similar efforts to prevent such expansion. Such rivalries do not exist under monopolistic competition. Advertising done by one firm induces no retaliatory action by others. When the advertising of one is counteracted by that of others, this is simply the result of all firms trying to do the same thing—expand their own markets. None are reacting to encroachments of other firms on their particular markets.

But advertising may also have certain beneficial consequences for consumers. It may lower the costs of acquiring knowledge about prices and other characteristics of the differentiated products the market makes available. The application in the following section shows that restraints on advertising in certain health service trades can prevent the price competition that would occur even with blocked entry. What little evidence we have about the impact of advertising in the real world suggests that the benefits it provides to consumers in the form of better and cheaper price information outweighs its costs. Thus, advertising on net may in some cases improve buyer welfare.

Range of Products Available

Consumers will have a broad range of types, styles, and brands of particular products from which to choose in market situations of monopolistic competition. The consumer can choose the type, style, or color of package that most nearly suits his or her fancy and pocketbook.

The different kinds of a specific product may be so numerous that they prove confusing to the consumer, and problems of choice may become very complicated. Ignorance with regard to actual differences of quality results in a willingness by the consumer to pay higher prices for particular brands, which in reality are not superior to lower-priced brands of the same product. What shopper can possibly be familiar with the comparative qualities of all the many different brands of soaps and detergents, floor waxes, electric irons, and so on, to say nothing of the differences in skills and locations of dentists and physicians?

Application: Restraints on Advertising in the Health Service Professions

Economists have long debated the question of whether consumers on net gain or lose welfare as a result of advertising. Clearly advertising cuts two ways. First, it is a selling expense to a firm and requires the use of resources; consequently, the higher costs may cause prices to be higher than without advertising. Second, advertising may benefit consumers by saving them search costs. The better informed consumers are about prices, the smaller price differences among sellers should be. Searching for better prices is expensive in the time, trouble, and transportation required for visiting or communicating with sellers. Consumers who do enough searching often can find a seller who will quote a lower price, but the costs of the extra search may not be worth the money savings.[3] Advertising, by increasing the amount of information that consumers have at hand, lowers search costs and should, to some extent, reduce price differences. Whether or not the extra value of these benefits to consumers exceeds the extra costs of resources that firms devote to advertising budgets is a matter that cannot be settled a priori. Economic theory alone cannot predict whether the net of these two conflicting forces caused by advertising will be to raise prices or to lower them, and the debate among economists cannot be settled without some hard evidence.

Professor Lee Benham attacked this problem by comparing the prices found in markets in which advertising is allowed versus those found in markets for similar products in which it is prohibited.[4] Restraints on advertising are common in most of the health service professions. Advertising increases knowledge and competition. The trade associations of physicians, nurses, and pharmacists (with regard to prescription drugs) have convinced most state legislatures to prohibit advertising and enforce it by the threat of withdrawing or suspending licenses to practice. The professions typically have too many members to be able to establish and enforce their own restraints on advertising without governmental assistance. But restraints on advertising by optometrists and opticians vary considerably among states, so Benham used the prices of eyeglasses in markets of each type to determine whether advertising on net would cause prices to be higher or lower.

Benham's study is important for expanding our understanding

---

[3] George J. Stigler, "The Economics of Information," *The Journal of Political Economy*, 69 (June 1961), pp. 213–25.

[4] Lee Benham, "The Effect of Advertising on the Price of Eyeglasses," *The Journal of Law and Economics*, 15 (October 1972), pp. 337–52.

of monopolistic competition as well as of advertising. The market for eyeglasses in most large cities fits the monopolistically competitive market structure rather well. There are a number of sellers, but each may have a sufficiently differentiated product to make its demand curve less than perfectly elastic. Small monopoly elements could be caused by differences in office location (especially in prime shopping centers), variations in the brands of lenses and frames that are stocked, and even differences in optical skills. These distinctions may be important to some buyers in spite of the fact that the number of substitutes available is very large. Without advertising, the cost to consumers of acquiring information about these differences is relatively high.

Benham's data base was a sample of eyeglass prices collected from a survey of the uses of, and expenditures on, health services in 1963. In that year, three-fourths of the states had regulations of some type against eyeglass advertising; some restraints applied only to price advertising, while others prohibited advertising of any kind. Two jurisdictions, Texas and the District of Columbia, had no restraints whatsoever. In general, Benham found that eyeglass prices were between 25 percent and 100 percent higher in states where advertising was completely forbidden than in states having no restrictions. The wide range is caused by the fact that some states impose restrictions other than advertising that sharply increase eyeglass prices, whereas other states have adopted a policy of almost complete laissez-faire in eyeglass markets. The nature of Benham's results did not change when the cost of an eye examination was included in the price of eyeglasses. But he did discover disparities in eyeglass prices between states that permitted nonprice advertising as opposed to those that prohibited advertising of all kinds. The resulting price differentials were still in favor of the states with the fewer restraints on advertising, although the differentials were much smaller than those reported above.

Benham concluded that his results were ". . . consistent with the hypothesis that, in the market examined, advertising improves consumers' knowledge and that the benefits derived from this knowledge outweigh the price-increasing effects of advertising."[5] This result came as a surprise to his university colleagues. A poll he had taken before the study showed that 40 percent of the economists polled and 100 percent of the professors of marketing polled expected prices to be the same or lower where advertising was prohibited!

Benham's study was important, but it would be risky to generalize from its results either too widely or too quickly. After all, he

[5] Ibid., p. 349.

focused only on one market in one year. Even so, his results were so striking that the United States Federal Trade Commission is moving against restraints on advertising in other health professions, as the following article from *The Wall Street Journal* shows.[6]

—*The Federal Trade Commission ruled that the American Medical Association's restrictions on doctors' advertising violate federal antitrust law and ordered the AMA to end the restrictions.*

The commission generally upheld a decision made last year by Ernest Barnes, an FTC administrative law judge, who found that the AMA's rules restrained competition among doctors. The rules restrict most forms of advertising and ban price advertising and the solicitation of patients. In contrast to Mr. Barnes' decision, however, the commission said it would allow the association to move immediately to adopt "reasonable ethical guidelines" for advertising. Mr. Barnes had recommended that the AMA be barred for two years from issuing such guidelines.

The FTC's order, which may be appealed to the federal courts, also requires the 200,000-member association to expel any local medical association that violates the order. As a result, the commission decided it wasn't necessary to issue an order against the Connecticut State Medical Association and the New Haven County (Conn.) Medical Association, which were named in the FTC's complaint when it was filed in 1975.

The commission's order also bars the AMA from taking disciplinary action against a doctor for participating in a health-maintenance organization, which is a group of doctors who work together on salary instead of getting paid for services performed. Patients pay a set annual fee to the organizations for all covered medical services. FTC officials see such organizations as a way to hold down medical costs, which have soared in the past several years.

The commission had charged in its complaint that the advertising restrictions, which have been eased since then by changes in the AMA's ethical canons, illegally fixed fees for doctors' services. The rules also stifled competition among doctors and deprived patients "of information pertinent to the selection of a physician and the benefits of competition," the agency charged.

In its opinion, by Commissioner David Clanton, the agency upheld the charges. "Ethical principles of the medical profession had prevented doctors and medical organizations from disseminating information on the prices and services they offer, severely inhibiting competition among health-care providers," according to the opinion.

In Chicago, the AMA said it would appeal the FTC's ruling. "There isn't one bit of evidence to support" the agency's conclu-

---

[6] "FTC Tells American Medical Association to End its Curbs on Doctors' Advertising," *The Wall Street Journal*, 25 October 1979. Reprinted by permission of *The Wall Street Journal*, © Dow Jones & Company, Inc. 1979. All rights reserved.

sion that the AMA has restricted competition, said Newton Minow, a lawyer representing the AMA.

He took issue with the FTC's contention that the AMA has prevented physicians from disseminating information on prices and services. He said he didn't know "where or when" the AMA would appeal the FTC's decision.

The case is an example of increasing interest shown by federal antitrust officials in recent years in what they view as antitrust abuses by professionals. The Justice Department had sued the American Bar Association over its advertising ban, but the case was dropped after the Supreme Court decided in another case that the ban violated free speech rights of lawyers. In addition, the FTC has issued a trade rule that overturns bans on eyeglass advertising, but that rule has been challenged in court. The commission also is considering whether it should propose a rule that would sever the medical profession's control over Blue Shield programs, which critics of the profession charge keeps medical costs artificially high.

The article shows that the FTC was aware of Benham's study before it decided to move against the American Medical Association, and it is clear that the AMA will not relinquish its rules against physician advertising without a legal battle.

Summary

In a market situation of monopolistic competition, there are enough sellers of differentiated products so that the activities of each have no effect on others and their activities in turn have no effect on one. The demand curve faced by a firm in the market has some downward slope because of product differentiation and the attachment of consumers to particular brand names. However, it is highly elastic within the relevant price-output range.

Short-run profit maximization by the firms in the industry will occur at the prices and outputs at which each is equating its marginal cost to its marginal revenue. There is no single industry price. There will be a cluster of market prices reflecting consumer opinions of comparative qualities of the product.

In the long run the nature of the adjustment of firms and the industry to a position of equilibrium will depend on whether entry into the industry is blocked or easy. With entry blocked, individual firms will produce the output and sell at the price at which long-run marginal cost equals marginal revenue. The firm will build the appropriate size of plant for that output, and, with the appropriate size of plant, short-run marginal cost will also equal marginal revenue.

With entry easy, the existence of profits will induce new firms to enter, decreasing the demand curve faced by the firm and shifting the cost curves upward, if the industry is one of increasing costs. Entry will continue until profits are squeezed out. The long-run and the short-run average cost curves for each firm will be tangent to the demand curve faced by it at the appropriate output. Long-run and short-run marginal costs will equal marginal revenue.

Monopolistic competition, existing along with pure competition tends to reduce welfare through (1) output restriction and price increases, (2) inefficient plant size, and (3) some advertising wastes. There will also be a broader range of products among which consumers may choose than will occur in the other three market situations, a condition that may or may not affect welfare.

Suggested Readings

Benham, Lee. "The Effect of Advertising on the Price of Eyeglasses." *The Journal of Law and Economics*, (October 1972), pp. 337–52.

Chamberlin, Edward H. *The Theory of Monopolistic Competition*, 8th ed. Cambridge, Mass.: Harvard University Press, 1962, Chaps. 4–5.

Machlup, Fritz. *The Economics of Sellers' Competition*. Baltimore: The Johns Hopkins Press, 1952, Chaps. 5–7, 10.

Stigler, George J. "Monopolistic Competition in Retrospect." *Five Lectures on Economic Problems*. New York: Macmillan, 1947, pp. 12–24. Reprinted in George J. Stigler, *The Organization of Industry*. Homewood, Ill.: Richard D. Irwin, 1968.

Questions and Exercises

1 University City boasts 35 barber shops. In each shop there are three barbers of equal ability, and the barbers in any one shop are as technically competent as those in any other. Would you expect the demand curve for the services of each barber to be horizontal, or would you expect it to slope downward to the right? Catalog completely the reasons for your answer.

2 Check the licensing laws of your state, and compile a list of all the occupations, trades, and businesses for which licenses are required. What reasons are cited in the statutes for requiring licenses? Do you agree that these are the actual reasons for licensing? Why or why not?

3 Casual observations in most cities and towns often show new automobile service stations being built. At such occurrences we hear people say time and again, "We don't really need all those

stations." In terms of the theory of monopolistic competition, can you put analytical content into observations and comments of this type?

4 Assume that firms of industry X sell under conditions of monopolistic competition and that the industry is in long-run equilibrium. Assume that firms in industry Y sell under conditions of pure competition and that the industry is also in long-run equilibrium. Each is an industry of increasing costs. An increase in demand now occurs in each. Using diagrams, compare and contrast between the two industries

  a the short-run effects on prices and outputs of the demand increases

  b the long-run effects on prices and outputs of the demand increases.

The Determination of and the Functions of Resource Prices

For the analysis of the markets for goods and services, we assumed that resource prices were given without much concern for how those prices were determined or for the functions they perform in a market economy. The purpose of Part Five is to fill the void by examining resource markets in detail. It may be useful to review Chapter 8, "The Principles of Production," since Part Five builds on the foundation established in that chapter.

Resource prices play a key role in guiding and directing a private enterprise economy. They are an essential element in determining the levels of employment of different kinds of labor and capital. They serve to allocate resources among different uses. They provide the inducements or incentives for individual firms to use efficient resource combinations. And, as the farmers' demonstrations of 1978 and the coal miners' strike of the winter of 1977–1978 illustrate, they are important to us personally. Since all of us are resource owners, the prices we get for the resources that we own affect our income and how we share in the economy's output.

CHAPTER 15

Pricing and
Employment of Resources:
Pure Competition

How are resource prices and employment levels determined when pure competition in both product and resource markets prevails?[1] Pure competition in resource markets implies several things. No one firm takes enough of any given resource to be able to influence its price. No one resource supplier can place enough of a given resource on the market to be able to influence its price. Variable resources are mobile among different employments, and their market prices are flexible. On the basis of these conditions we shall analyze the simultaneous employment of several variable resources by the firm; next, we shall consider the pricing and employment of any given variable resource.

Simultaneous Employment of
Several Variable Resources

Up to this point, profit maximization by the firm has been considered in terms of product outputs and sales, with little specific attention given to resource inputs. In this section, profit maximization will be viewed in terms of resource inputs and least-cost resource combinations.

Profit Maximization and Least-cost Combinations

The least-cost combination of variable resources for a given output was discussed in Chapter 9.[2] Resources must be so combined that the marginal physical product per dollar's worth of one is equal to the marginal physical product per dollar's worth of each of the other resources used if such a combination is to be achieved. The given output is not necessarily the profit-maximizing output of the firm. Suppose, in Figure 15.1, that the firm produces an output of x_0 and

---

[1] A simple definition of the market for a resource will suffice for most purposes. The market for a resource is the area within which the resource is free to move (or is mobile) among alternative employments. The extent of the market for a given resource will vary, depending on the time span under consideration. The longer the period of time, the broader the market will be.

[2] See pp. 215–17.

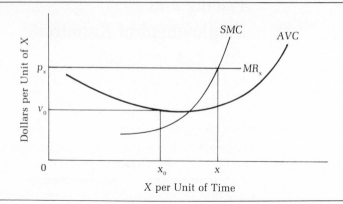

FIGURE 15.1
Least-cost combinations and profit maximization

uses two variable resources, A and B. To produce output x_0, resources A and B must be combined so that MPP_a/p_a equals MPP_b/p_b, if average variable costs are to be kept down to v_0. If the product price is p_x, the firm's output is too small for profit maximization. Although A and B are used in proper proportions, not enough of either is being used.

To maximize profits, the firm's output must be increased to x. Additional output can be obtained by using more of both resource A and resource B. To keep average variable costs as low as possible while output is expanded, increases in the quantities of resources A and B must be in proportions such that the marginal physical product per dollar's worth of A continues to equal the marginal physical product per dollar's worth of B. When output x is reached, the firm will be using the resources not only in the least-cost combination but also in correct absolute quantities.

Marginal Physical Products and Marginal Cost

The least-cost combination conditions for resources A and B—MPP_a/p_a equals MPP_b/p_b—are the reciprocal of the marginal cost of product X. Consider resource A first. Any one unit of resource A contributes an amount to the firm's total cost equal to p_a. It adds an amount to the firm's total product equal to MPP_a. Thus, the fraction p_a/MPP_a should be read as "the change in the firm's total costs per unit change in the product." This is the same thing as the marginal cost of product X; hence, we can state that MC_x equals p_a/MPP_a. Likewise, MC_x equals p_b/MPP_b. Since MPP_a/p_a equals MPP_b/p_b, when the firm is using a least-cost combination of A and B, we can state that

$$\frac{MPP_a}{p_a} = \frac{MPP_b}{p_b} = \frac{1}{MC_x}. \tag{15.1}$$

Or we can consider the reciprocals of the foregoing terms and state that

$$\frac{p_a}{MPP_a} = \frac{p_b}{MPP_b} = MC_x. \quad (15.2)$$

The last statement means that at whatever output the firm is producing, if it uses the least-cost combination of resources, the amount of A or the amount of B or the combined amounts of both necessary to add a single unit to the firm's output brings about the same addition to the firm's total costs. Suppose that the product is men's suits and the variable resources used are labor, machines, and materials. The last one-unit increment in quantity produced per unit of time should increase total costs of the firm by the same amount, regardless of whether the increment in product is obtained by increasing the ratio of labor to materials and machines, materials to labor and machines, or machines to labor and materials. Total costs should be raised by the same amount if the increment in product is obtained by simultaneous increases in the quantities of all three resources. When resources are used in the correct combination, they are equally efficient at the margin. The last dollar outlay on one resource adds the same amount to total product as the last dollar outlay on any other resource. The increment in cost necessary to bring about the last unit increase in product output per unit of time is the marginal cost of the product.

Suppose that we again consider profit maximization by the firm in terms of the quantities of resources that should be used. With reference to Figure 15.1 at output x_0, MC_x is less than MR_x or

$$\frac{MPP_a}{p_a} = \frac{MPP_b}{p_b} = \frac{1}{MC_x} > \frac{1}{MR_x} = \frac{1}{p_x}. \quad (15.3)$$

The firm is using the resources in correct proportions to produce output x_0; however, output x_0 is too small for profit maximization since MC_x is less than MR_x. In the pursuit of maximum profits, the firm will add to its output by increasing the inputs of A and B. Additional quantities of A and B used with the constant quantities of fixed resources cause the marginal physical product of each to fall. The prices of A and B remain constant since the firm purchases them under conditions of pure competition; consequently, MPP_a/p_a and MPP_b/p_b decrease, as does $1/MC_x$.

Decreases in $1/MC_x$ mean increases in MC_x. Thus, decreases in the marginal physical products of A and B are the same as increases in the marginal cost of product X. Larger quantities of A and B will be employed to expand the firm's output up to the point at which

$$\frac{MPP_a}{p_a} = \frac{MPP_b}{p_b} = \frac{1}{MC_x} = \frac{1}{MR_x} = \frac{1}{p_x}, \quad (15.4)$$

or up to the point at which the firm's marginal cost equals its marginal revenue or product price. At the profit-maximizing output the firm will be using its variable resources both in the correct combination and in the correct absolute amounts.

Pricing and Employment of a Given Variable Resource

Demand and supply analysis is used to show how the market price and employment level of a given resource are determined. First, the individual firm demand curve, the market demand curve, and the market supply curve for the resource must be constructed. Once we have accomplished these objectives, we can then determine the market price, the firm's employment level, and the market level of employment of the resource.

The Demand Curve of the Firm: One Resource Variable

The demand curve of a firm for a given variable resource should show the different quantities of it that the firm will take at various possible prices. But the factors influencing the quantities that a firm will take when confronted by various alternative prices of the resource differ when the given resource is the only variable resource used by the firm from the factors that prevail when the given resource is one of several variable resources used by the firm. Assume for the present that the given resource is the only variable one used; that is, the quantities of all other resources employed remain constant.[3] Assume also that the firm's objective is to maximize its profits.

The firm considers different quantities of the resource—for example, resource A—with regard to their effects on its total receipts and total costs. If larger quantities of A per unit of time will add more to the firm's total receipts than to its total costs, those quantities will increase profits (or decrease losses). On the other hand, if larger quantities of A will add more to the firm's total costs than to its total receipts, they will cause profits to fall (or losses to increase). The firm should employ that quantity of the resource at which a one-unit increase in its employment level increases both total receipts and total costs by the same amount.

Marginal Revenue Product The change in a firm's total receipts, when it changes the employment level of some resource A by one

---

[3] The assumption is the same as that made in defining the law of diminishing returns.

unit, is called the *marginal revenue product* of the resource to the firm, or MRP_a. To compute it, note first that the change in the output of the firm caused by a one-unit change in the employment level of A is the marginal physical product of resource A, or MPP_a. This change in output alters the firm's total receipts by an amount per unit equal to the marginal revenue the firm receives from its sale. Thus, a one-unit change in the employment level of A changes the firm's total receipts by the marginal physical product of A multiplied by the marginal revenue received from the sale of the product. If X is the product and A is the resource under consideration, then

$$MRP_a = MPP_a \times MR_x.$$

Value of Marginal Product   When the employment level of some resource A is changed by a firm producing some product X, it is often important to consider the *market's* valuation of the change as well as the impact of the change on the firm's total receipts. Again, a one-unit change in the employment level of A changes the output level of X by MPP_a. The change in the output of X is valued by the market, or by buyers of the product, at p_x per unit. The market's valuation of the employment level change, or the *value of the marginal product of A*, is the marginal physical product of A multiplied by the product price. Symbolically,

$$VMP_a = MPP_a \times p_x.$$

For the purely competitive seller of product X, the marginal revenue product of a resource is equal to its value of marginal product. Such must be the case since $MR_x = p_x$. Consequently, VMP_a and MRP_a can be used interchangeably for the purely competitive seller; however, we shall note in the next chapter that the distinction between the two concepts becomes very important in analyzing resource pricing and employment by monopolistic sellers of product X.

In Table 15.1, which represents Stage II for resource A, column (2) lists the marginal physical product of A when various quantities of it are used with constant quantities of other resources. The price per unit and the marginal revenue of the final product of the firm are shown in column (3). The marginal revenue product and the value of marginal product of resource A are shown in column (4).

In Stage II for resource A, the marginal revenue product falls as larger amounts of A per unit of time are employed. The fall is caused by the operation of the law of diminishing returns—in Stage II for resource A, the marginal physical product of A declines as larger quantities of it are employed. Thus, A's marginal revenue product drops even though the price at which the final product is sold, and its marginal revenue, remain constant.

TABLE 15.1	(1) Quantity of A	(2) Marginal Physical Product (MPP_a)	(3) Product Price and Marginal Revenue ($p_x = MR_x$)	(4) Marginal Revenue Product and Value of Marginal Product ($VMP_a = MRP_a$)	(5) Resource Price (p_a)
Value of marginal product, resource price, and profit maximization	4	7	$2	$14	$4
	5	6	2	12	4
	6	5	2	10	4
	7	4	2	8	4
	8	3	2	6	4
	9	2	2	4	4
	10	0	2	0	4

Level of Employment A one-unit increase in the employment level of a resource adds to the firm's total costs an amount equal to its price when resources are purchased under conditions of pure competition. One firm takes such a small proportion of the total supply of the resource that, by itself, it cannot affect the resource price. If the price of the resource is $4 per unit, each one-unit increase in the amount of A employed adds $4 to the firm's total cost. These amounts are shown in column (5) of Table 15.1.

The profit-maximizing level of employment of A by the firm is that level at which the marginal revenue product of the resource is equal to its price per unit. Refer to Table 15.1. A fourth unit of A per unit of time adds $14 to the firm's total receipts but only $4 to its total costs; therefore, it adds $10 to the firm's profits. A fifth, sixth, seventh, and eighth unit of A each adds more to total receipts than to total costs and, consequently, makes a net addition to profits. A ninth unit of A adds the same amount to both total receipts and total costs. A tenth unit, if employed, will decrease profits by $4. Hence, when p_a is $4, profits are maximized with respect to resource A at an employment level of 9 units. We can write the profit-maximizing condition in either of the following forms:

$$MRP_a = p_a$$

or

$$MPP_a \times MR_x = p_a. \tag{15.5}$$

The second form is simply an elaboration of the first.

The Demand Curve The marginal revenue product schedule for resource A, as listed in columns (1) and (4) of Table 15.1, is the firm's demand schedule for A if A is the only variable resource employed.

It shows the different quantities that the firm will take at different possible prices. If p_a were \$10 per unit, 6 units would be employed. If p_a were \$14 per unit, the employment level would be 4 units.

The demand curve of the firm for the resource is the marginal revenue product schedule plotted. Figure 15.2 shows such a curve.

FIGURE 15.2
Marginal revenue
product curve

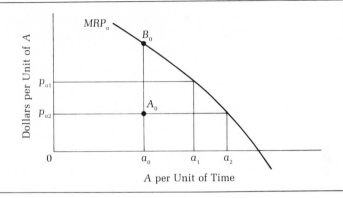

With reference to the quantity axis, it occupies Stage II for resource A. With reference to the dollars-per-unit axis, the marginal revenue product at each quantity of A is found by multiplying the marginal physical product at that level of employment by the marginal revenue at the corresponding level of product sales.

It may be instructive to consider profit maximization by the firm with respect to resource A again—this time in terms of the demand curve or the marginal revenue product curve. If the price of A in Figure 15.2 were p_{a2}, the firm would maximize profits by using quantity a_2. If the firm were to use quantity a_0, the a_0 unit would add a_0A_0 to the firm's total costs but would add a_0B_0 to the firm's total receipts. It would add A_0B_0 to the firm's profits. Increasing the employment level of A up to a_2 adds more to total receipts than to total costs, and, therefore, increases profits. Beyond a_2, larger quantities add more to the firm's total costs than to its total receipts and cause profits to decline. If the price of A were p_{a1}, the firm would maximize profits by using that quantity at which the marginal revenue product of A equals its price per unit.

The Demand Curve of the Firm: Several Resources Variable

When a firm uses several variable resources, its demand curve for any one of them is no longer the marginal revenue product curve of the resource. In such a case, a change in the price of one, assuming the prices of the others remain constant, will bring about changes in the quantities used of the other resources; these changes will, in turn, affect the utilization of the one as the firm attempts to maximize profits and to reestablish a least-cost combination of resources. Suppose we call such changes the *firm* or *internal effects* of a change in the price of a resource.

To illustrate the internal effects, suppose that we want to derive the firm's demand curve for resource A, which is one of several variable resources. Suppose that initially the firm is producing the profit-maximizing output of product X and is using the appropriate least-cost combination of variable resources. As shown in Figure 15.3, the price of A is p_{a1} and the quantity employed is a_1. The

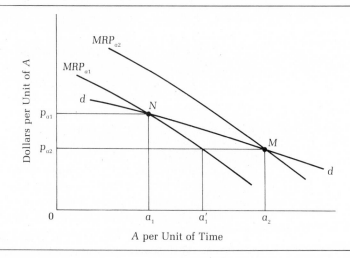

FIGURE 15.3
The firm's demand curve for one of several variable resources

MRP_{a1} curve shows the marginal revenue product of A when the quantity of A only is varied.

Suppose that for some reason the price of A falls to p_{a2}. Since $MRP_a > p_a$, the firm will tend to expand employment of A toward a_1'. This greater utilization of A will shift the marginal physical product, and the marginal revenue product curves of variable resources complementary to A, to the right. The corresponding curves of substitute resources will be shifted to the left. Since the prices of other resources remain constant, the utilization of complementary resources will increase, while that of substitute resources will decrease. Such changes in the utilization of other resources will shift the marginal physical product and the marginal revenue product curves of A to the right. Each different level of utilization of each other variable resource will result in a different marginal physical product curve and marginal revenue product curve for A.

When these and higher-order complementary and substitute effects have worked themselves out, the firm will be on some such marginal revenue product curve as MRP_{a2} and will be employing that quantity of A at which its marginal revenue product equals its price—that is, quantity a_2.[4] The employment levels of other variable resources will also be such that, for each one, its value of marginal product equals its price when the firm is again maximizing profits and using the appropriate least-cost combination.

Points N and M are on the firm's demand curve for resource A. They show the quantities of A that the firm would take at alternative prices of A when the prices of other resources are held constant and the quantities of all other resources are adjusted appropriately for each price of A. Other points on the firm's demand curve for A can be established in a similar fashion, and would trace out a curve such as dd. Ordinarily the firm's demand curve for a resource will be more elastic than will any single marginal revenue product curve of the resource. The better the substitutes available for a resource, the more elastic its demand curve will be.

The Market Demand Curve

A first approximation to the market demand curve for a resource is the horizontal summation of individual firm demand curves for it. However, a straightforward horizontal summation leaves out what we shall call the *market* or *external effects* of changes in the price of a resource.

In a purely competitive world, an individual firm is small enough, relative to the markets in which it operates, to anticipate that its actions will have no effect on the price of anything it buys or sells. Consequently the firm's demand curve for a resource should show the different quantities that it would take at various alternative resource prices when it anticipates that its actions will have no effect on the price of whatever product it sells. The firm considers only the firm or internal effects of resource price changes.

The market or external effects come about as a result of simultaneous expansion or contraction of industry outputs of products by all firms using a given resource as the price of the resource changes. If industry X is one of those using resource A, a decrease in the price of resource A will cause all firms using A to increase their employment of it. Although no one firm's increase in output is sufficient to cause a reduction in the price of X, the simultaneous increases in output of all firms may cause such a price decrease to come about. Each such fall in the price of X and the marginal revenue from X will cause shifts to the left or decreases in the whole family of individual

---

[4]   The increasing ratios of resource A to fixed resources of the firm will insure that the marginal physical product and the marginal revenue product of A decline, even though the changing utilization of other variable resources tends to shift the curves for A to the right.

firm marginal revenue product curves, and consequent shifts to the left or decreases in individual firm demand curves for resource A.

The external effects of changes in the price of a resource and the construction of the market demand curve for the resource are illustrated in Figure 15.4. Suppose that the firm of the diagram, and every

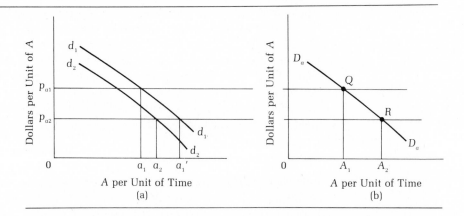

FIGURE 15.4
The market demand curve for a resource

other firm that uses resource A, is in equilibrium and that the price of A is p_{a1}. The firm's demand curve for A is $d_1 d_1$; the firm is employing a_1 of A. By summing the amounts that all firms employ at price p_{a1}, we determine the total amount taken off the market at that price, A_1. Thus, Q is a point on the market demand curve for A.

Suppose next that the price of A falls to p_{a2}. Each firm will expand its employment of A; but as the firms in each industry that uses A expand employment of it and, consequently, the industry outputs of product, market prices of products decrease. Individual firm demand curves for resource A shift to the left toward positions such as $d_2 d_2$. Thus, the individual firm employment levels of A will increase toward such quantities as a_2 rather than toward a_1'.

Restricted expansion in the employment of A results from the market or external effect of the decrease in the resource price. When each individual firm has made the necessary adjustments to achieve a least-cost combination of resources and a profit-maximizing product output, and when each firm's level of employment is some such level as a_2, the amounts that all employ together at price p_{a2} can be totaled to obtain quantity A_2. Then R is a second point on the market demand curve for A. Other points on the market demand curve can be found in a similar way; they trace out the market demand curve $D_a D_a$.

The Supply Curves

The market supply curve for resource A, or for any other resource, shows the different quantities per unit of time that its owners will place on the market at different possible prices. Generally it will be upward sloping to the right, indicating that at higher prices more of it will be placed on the market than at lower prices. Nonhuman resources used in any one industry are in general the outputs of other industries. Their supply curves, then, will be the appropriate industry or market supply curves. Except in cases of constant cost and decreasing cost, they will slope upward to the right. In the petroleum industry, for example, increases in crude oil prices lead to a more rapid rate of recovery and vice versa. The precise shapes of resource supply curves are not of paramount importance for our purposes, although for certain types of economic problems they will be. They may be upward sloping to the right; they may be absolutely vertical; or, in unusual circumstances, they may bend back on themselves at high prices. The basic analysis will be the same in each case.

The labor supply curve of an individual is an interesting analytical case—people do not always offer to work more hours when wage rates rise. This is because of possible trade-offs between work and leisure. Any one hour of the day can be devoted to either leisure activities or work; the alternative or opportunity cost of an hour of leisure time is the additional income that could have been earned from using it for work, and the opportunity cost of an hour of work is the value of the satisfaction that could have been obtained from devoting it to leisure. Thus, both income and leisure are items that people would usually prefer more of rather than less. An increased wage rate permits a person either to obtain more income by working the same number of hours or to obtain the same income by working fewer hours. Thus, the effect of the increase on the quantity of labor supplied depends upon the individual's preferences.

The indifference curve techniques of Chapters 5 and 6 lend themselves well to the analysis of choices between income and leisure time. Suppose, for example, that the indifference map in Figure 15.5(a) shows a person's preference structure for combinations of daily income and leisure. Income is measured on the vertical axis, and leisure on the horizontal axis. Any one indifference curve shows combinations of income and leisure that are equivalent to the individual. Higher indifference curves show preferred sets of income-leisure combinations.

A budget line, or income line, shows the income level that can be obtained by working (giving up leisure) different numbers of hours at a given wage rate. The distance $0H$ represents the maximum number of hours of leisure per day that it would be possible for the individual to trade for work. Some minimum number of hours is required for eating and sleeping. If this number were 10 hours per day, then $0H$ would be 14 hours. At a wage rate of w_1, the individual can earn an income of I_1 $(= 0H \times w_1)$ by working $0H$ hours per day,

FIGURE 15.5
Work, leisure, and
labor supply

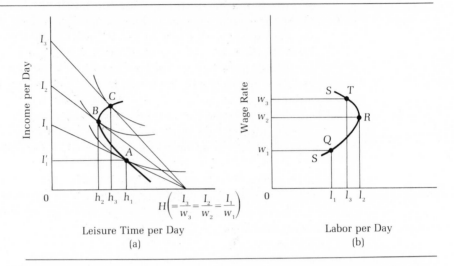

Leisure Time per Day
(a)

Labor per Day
(b)

keeping his or her tradable leisure at zero. If h_1H hours per day are worked, income earned is I_1' $(= h_1H \times w_1)$ and the tradable leisure time is $0h_1$ hours. Note that the slope of the income line is the wage rate w_1.

The individual would be expected to seek out the most preferred combination of income and leisure from all of the combinations that the income line will permit. Given the wage rate w_1, combination A is preferred over all of the others available; this is the highest indifference curve that can be reached. The person will work h_1H hours earning an income of I_1' dollars per day. At this point the marginal rate of substitution of leisure for income is equal to the wage rate—the amount of income that the individual would be willing to sacrifice to obtain an additional hour of leisure is the amount that he or she would be required to sacrifice in the labor market.

By considering the income lines generated for different wage rates, points on the individual's labor supply curve can be determined. At wage rate w_1, the amount of labor supply will be h_1H $(= 0l_1)$ per day, and this point is plotted as point Q in Figure 15.5(b). A higher wage rate, w_2, will shift the income line clockwise to I_2H, increasing the amount of labor supplied to h_2H $(= 0l_2)$. In Figure 15.5(b), this is plotted as point R. A still higher wage rate, w_3, generates income line I_3H and induces the individual to supply h_3H

$(= 0l_3)$ hours of labor per day, giving rise to point T. These and other points located in a similar fashion trace out the labor supply curve SS.

The total impact of a wage rate change on the amount of labor supplied (or leisure demanded) is the combined result of an income effect and a substitution effect. A higher wage rate increases the income that an hour of work provides and thus makes an hour of leisure more expensive. The individual has an incentive to work more hours and indulge in less leisure time–the substitution effect. But the higher wage rate also generates an income effect. It enables the person to obtain the same income with less work than before, providing an incentive to reduce the number of hours of work. In the theory of consumer behavior, the substitution and income effects of a price change operate in the *same* direction for goods that are not inferior. In the case of income-leisure choices, however, the income and substitution effects of a wage-rate change operate in *opposite* directions.

The substitution and income effects of a wage change are illustrated in Figure 15.6, which is essentially the same diagram as Figure

FIGURE 15.6
Substitution and income effects of a wage-rate change

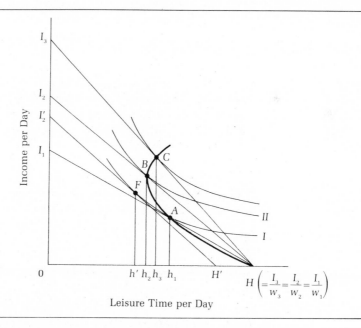

15.5(a). As before, the time available for work each day is $0H$, and the indifference curves show the individual's preference structure between income and leisure. At wage rate w_1, the individual selects the combination of work hours and leisure hours indicated by point A on indifference curve I. At a higher wage, w_2, the person selects the combination B on indifference curve II. To decompose the movement from combination A to combination B into the substitution effect and the income effect, we first eliminate the income effect. To accomplish this, we take away the real income increase generated by the wage-rate increase, leaving only the substitution effect. The appropriate compensating decrease in income is $I_2'I_2$, which shifts the income line from I_2H parallel to itself to $I_2'H'$ and makes it tangent to indifference curve I at some point F. The pure substitution effect of the wage-rate increase is thus an increase in the hours of work the individual would offer, amounting to h_1h'. The income effect is now obtained by returning the withdrawn income to the individual, moving the income line from $I_2'H'$ back to I_2H. The pure income effect of the wage-rate increase is a decrease in work effort amounting to $h'h_2$ hours. In Figure 15.6 we show the substitution effect outweighing the income effect for the wage-rate increase from w_1 to w_2, so that the net impact of the raise is an increase of h_1h_2 in the hours of labor offered.

In some cases the income effect of a wage change may outweigh the substitution effect so that a wage-rate increase results in a *decrease* in the amount of labor offered. We show this in Figures 15.5 and 15.6, for an increase in the wage rate from w_2 to w_3. To avoid clutter in the diagram, the income effects of the wage-rate increase have not been separated from the substitution effects; however, the decomposition can be easily accomplished. The increase in the wage rate from w_2 to w_3 brings about a *net reduction* in hours of labor offered of h_2h_3. Since the substitution effect of an increase in wage rates is *always* toward more hours of work offered, this result can be obtained only if the income effect, working in the opposite direction, is greater. As we show in Figure 15.5(a) between points B and C, where the income effect of wage changes outweighs the substitution effects, the corresponding labor supply curve of Figure 15.5(b) bends backward, or upward to the left, for wage-rate increases.

The importance of backward-bending individual labor supply curves should not be exaggerated. Within relevant wage-rate ranges, they may not be backward bending for many persons. Further, even if individual labor supply curves do bend back above some wage-rate level, there is no assurance that the market supply curve will show the same characteristic. Increases in wage rates that may cause some individuals to place fewer hours of labor on the market will also induce new individuals to enter the labor market. The entrance of new workers into the market at higher wage-rate levels may very well affect tendencies of workers to reduce their individual offerings. Nevertheless, empirical investigations show that (1) historically as wage rates have risen and affluence has increased, average working hours per week have declined for individuals, and (2) workers earning relatively high wage rates tend to work fewer hours per week than those earning relatively low rates.

Resource Pricing and the Level of Employment

The conditions of market demand and market supply, as summed up in the market demand curve and the market supply curve, determine the market price of the resource. Its equilibrium price will be that at which resource buyers are willing to take the same quantity per unit of time that sellers want to sell.

In Figure 15.7(b) the market demand curve and the market supply curve are D_aD_a and S_aS_a, respectively. Resource A will be priced at p_a. At a higher price, sellers will want to sell more than buyers will want to take at that price. Some unemployment will occur, and the owners of idle units will undercut each other to secure full employment of their particular supplies. Thus, the price will be driven down to the equilibrium level of p_a. At prices lower than p_a there will be a shortage of the resource. Resource buyers will bid against each other for the available supply, driving the price up to the equilibrium level.

An individual firm, purchasing resource A competitively, can get as much as it wants at a price of p_a per unit. A single construction firm in Chicago will not be able to influence the market price of steel. The supply curve of the resource from a single firm's point of view is shown in Figure 15.7(a) as a horizontal line at the equilibrium market price. The dollars-per-unit axes on the firm and market diagrams are identical. The scale of the quantity axis of the market diagram is greatly compressed, as compared with that of the single firm. The level of employment of the resource by the single firm is quantity a, assuming that dd is the demand curve of the firm associated with

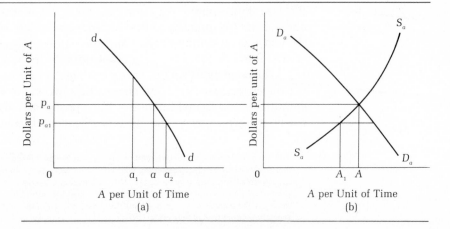

FIGURE 15.7
Determination of market price, market level of employment, and firm level of employment of a resource

price p_a; and at that quantity, marginal revenue product is equal to its price per unit. The market level of employment of the resource is the summation of the quantities employed by the individual firms and is shown as quantity A in the market diagram.

The belief that resources are often paid lower than equilibrium prices is widespread enough to warrant its consideration in some detail. Suppose, in Figure 15.7, that resource A is priced at p_{a1}. At that price individual firms want quantities, such as a_2, in order to maximize their profits with respect to the resource. All firms cannot get as much as they desire since the entire quantity placed on the market at that price is only A_1. Some firms will necessarily get quantities even less than a, say a_1. For such firms the marginal revenue product of A is greater than the resource price. If these firms expand their employments of the resource, they will increase their profits. Each firm believes that by offering a price slightly higher than p_{a1} it will be able to get as much of the resource as it desires. In the absence of collusion among the firms employing the resource—and in pure competition there is no collusion—each attempts the same strategy. No firm succeeds in getting as much as it wants until the price has been driven up to p_a. Under pure competition in resource buying, independent action on the part of each firm, together with the incentive to maximize profits, precludes the permanent location of a resource price below its equilibrium level.

It is worth noting that under pure competition, a particular resource receives a price per unit equal to both its marginal revenue product and its value of marginal product. Thus, a unit of resource A is paid just what it contributes to the value of the economy's product. The market demand curve for A shows the value of marginal product for A in all its uses combined. The market demand curve and the market supply curve determine the price; hence, the resource price is equal to its value of marginal product in any one, or in all, of the firms that use the resource. Any one firm takes the market price as given and adjusts the quantity of the resource employed in such a way that the marginal revenue product and the value of its marginal product in that firm are equal to the market price of the resource.[5]

The conditions set out in the first part of the chapter for employing the correct amounts and correct proportions of several resources simultaneously to maximize the firm's profits can also be established considering resources one by one. Suppose the firm uses two re-

---

[5] This point is frequently misconstrued. A firm is said to pay a resource a price equal to its marginal revenue product—implying that the firm determines the marginal revenue product of the resource, then pays it accordingly. This implication misrepresents the nature of marginal productivity theory under pure competition. The firm has nothing to say about the price. It must pay the market price, but it adjusts the quantity taken to the point at which the marginal revenue product equals that price.

sources, A and B. To maximize profits with respect to A, it should employ A up to the point at which

$$MPP_a \times MR_x = p_b, \text{ or } \frac{MPP_a}{p_a} = \frac{1}{MR_x} = \frac{1}{p_x}. \qquad (15.6)$$

Likewise, B should be employed up to the point at which

$$MPP_b \times MR_x = p_b, \text{ or } \frac{MPP_b}{p_b} = \frac{1}{MR_x} = \frac{1}{p_x}. \qquad (15.7)$$

Equations (15.6) and (15.7) can then be combined as follows:

$$\frac{MPP_a}{p_a} = \frac{MPP_b}{p_b} = \frac{1}{MR_x} = \frac{1}{p_x}. \qquad (15.8)$$

Since MPP_a/p_a and MPP_b/p_b are the same as $1/MC_x$, then

$$\frac{MPP_a}{p_a} = \frac{MPP_b}{p_b} = \frac{1}{MC_x} = \frac{1}{MR_x} = \frac{1}{p_x}. \qquad (15.9)$$

When the firm employs each of its variable resources in the correct absolute amount for profit maximization, it necessarily will be using them in the correct combination.

Alternative Costs Reconsidered

The alternative cost doctrine, which we discussed in Chapter 10, can be stated in terms of the value of marginal product of any given resource. Under pure competition, each firm using a given resource employs that quantity of it at which its marginal revenue product and its value of marginal product equals its price. Any discrepancy in resource prices offered by different firms induces units of the resource to move from the lower-paying to the higher-paying uses until a single price prevails throughout the market. The resource price, or its cost to any firm, will be equal to the value of its marginal product in its alternative employments.

Economic Rent

Perfect mobility of all resources does not occur in the short run even under conditions of pure competition. Those resources constituting the firm's size of plant are not mobile—they are fixed in quantity for particular uses or users. The longer the time period under consideration, the fewer will be the fixed resources.

The returns received by fixed resources are not determined according to the principles set out above. Since those resources are not free to move into alternative employments, their short-run remuneration will be whatever is left over after the mobile resources have been paid whatever it takes to hold them to the particular firm. The mobile resources must be paid amounts equal to what they can earn in alternative employments—that is, amounts equal to the values of their marginal product in alternative employments. The residual left for the fixed resources is called *economic rent.*[6]

A short-run cost-price diagram for an individual firm should help make clear the concept of economic rent. The short-run average cost curve, average variable cost curve, and marginal cost curve are drawn in Figure 15.8. Suppose that the market price of the product is

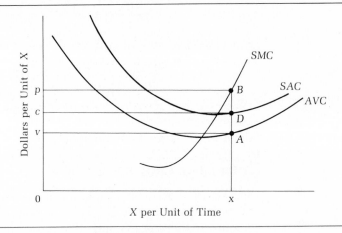

p. The firm's output will be x. Total cost of the variable (mobile) resources is 0vAx. This is the outlay necessary if the firm is to hold its variable resources.

Should the firm attempt to reduce the payments made to variable resources, some or all of them would move into alternative uses where their marginal revenue products and remunerations are greater. Thus, the average variable cost curve shows the necessary outlays per unit of product output that the firm must make for variable resources. The fixed resources get whatever is left from the firm's total receipts; that is, they receive economic rent. Total rent for the fixed resources is vpBA. The lower the market price of the product, the less the rent will be. The higher the market price of the product, the higher the economic rent will be.

A problem now arises with regard to the nature of the SAC curve. What does it show? To get at the problem, suppose that we consider the firm's investment in the fixed resources. The rent repre-

---

[6] These returns are sometimes called *quasi rents.* This term, introduced by Alfred Marshall, is used so ambiguously in economic literature that we shall avoid it altogether.

sents the return on investment in the firm's fixed resources. Only that part of the rent, which represents a return on investment equal to what that amount of investment could earn elsewhere in the economy, or in alternative uses, constitutes fixed costs for the firm. Thus, letting the part of rent represented by $vcDA$ be the fixed costs for the firm, the rest of the rent is what we have defined previously as pure profits. Average cost at any output is equal to average fixed cost plus average variable cost at that output.

Economic rent may be equal to, greater than, or less than enough to cover the firm's fixed costs. When investment in the firm yields a higher rate of return than investment on the average elsewhere in the economy, rents are greater than total fixed costs; we then say that the firm is making pure profits. The firm's profits are zero when rents equal total fixed cost; that is, when investment in the firm yields the same rate of return as investment elsewhere. When product price is not sufficient for rents to equal total fixed costs or when investment elsewhere in the economy yields a higher rate of return than it does with the firm, we say that the firm is incurring losses.

Applications

Straits, the Suez Canal, and Economic Rent from Ocean Shipping[7]

The age-old doctrine of "freedom of the seas," a principle of international law first set down in the time of Elizabeth Tudor, has been transformed during the past forty years. Coastal nations, through the first half of this century, generally asserted control over foreign shipping and fishing out to the three-mile limit only. By the late 1970s, however, all but a handful of coastal states asserted control out to twelve nautical miles. At present there are 121 straits that are international waterways under a three-mile limit but which would be overlapped by a twelve-mile limit and thus be under the exclusive control of the adjacent coastal nations. Such control could be used either to collect tolls or to exact political concessions from maritime and oil-importing countries.

The gains that states can capture from the straits they control are in the form of economic rent. The available data suggest that such gains are not especially large. The maximum amount that any one state can extract from a shipowner is the difference between the costs of taking the next best, but more circuitous, route and the costs of

---

[7] This material is based on Ross D. Eckert, *The Enclosure of Ocean Resources: Economics and the Law of the Sea* (Stanford, Calif.: Hoover Press, 1979), Chapter 3.

traveling the direct route through the strait. Economists at the United States Treasury in 1974–75 attempted to estimate some of these available rents. Closing off the English Channel, through which between 22 and 27 percent of United States imports pass, would have cost the United States only $35 million to $45 million per year extra in shipping costs. This is the maximum rent that the controlling country or countries could extract from the United States. Closing off all four of the straits that link the Pacific and Indian oceans without circumnavigating Australia would have increased the cost of United States oil imports to the West Coast by about 35 cents per barrel, or about 30 percent of the cost of the shorter trip. This would have amounted to an extra $137 million per year in 1975 for the United States. Again the $137 million figure is the maximum rent that could have been extracted from this country. The figure pertaining to Japan would have been larger since almost all of its oil imports come through these straits from the Persian Gulf. These data are not conclusive, but they suggest that the economic power of straits states, if they were to exercise it fully, is far from overwhelming.

The inherent limits on the rents that stem from such a geographical monopoly are clear from the experience of Egypt with the Suez Canal. The canal was closed when ships were sunk in it during the 1973 Six Day War, but the Egyptians cleared and reopened it in 1975 with the intention of profiting from its operation. The director of the Egyptian canal authority declared his policy on tolls in 1974: "We expect to be able to set dues that will make it in the interest of a ship to use the canal if it physically can,"[8] a policy that is about as oriented toward profit maximization as one could imagine. The actual tolls in 1976 were about $200,000 for the passage of a tanker of 249,000 deadweight tons, or something close to $1.00 per ton. But revenues collected at these prices were far short of the $400 million annually that the canal authority anticipated, and ship traffic was only about one-third of the prewar levels. What explains the director's miscalculation in setting tolls?

The key error was his failure to estimate correctly the extra cost of the detour—circumnavigating Africa via the Cape of Good Hope. The cost of circumnavigation declined after 1974 owing to a reduction in oil shipments out of the Persian Gulf. As oil-consuming nations cut their imports, the demand for tankers declined and the cost of tanker charters dropped markedly. Lower daily costs of hiring tankers reduced the opportunity costs of the longer trip, causing more shipowners to choose the lower-cost alternative. Using the canal cuts about twelve days off the length of a trip between the Persian Gulf and Rotterdam; and, at the time, the daily operating costs

[8] Ibid., p. 77.

of a large tanker were about $7,000. The canal toll of about $1.00 per ton meant that tankers of more than 100,000 deadweight tons could usually save by taking the longer trip. The experience evidently weighed heavily in the decision of the Egyptians in 1976 to deepen the canal in order to accommodate larger tankers and at the same time, to adjust downward the schedule of tolls. As the director of the canal authority put it, "After the improvement [canal deepening] program we have to reexamine the toll structure because perhaps it may be a bit high."[9]

Labor Supply among the Rats

Experiments are now something of a vogue among economists. Increasingly, economists too are getting back to the basics by testing in real situations some of the most elementary and essential propositions on which the structure of economic theory rests. Experimental economists have studied, for example, the direction and speed of price adjustments away from market-disequilibrium situations, the stability properties of collusive managements having different numbers of participants, and the efficiency properties of auctions. To approximate real-world conditions, the experimenters often give participants, usually students, actual cash grants with which to play the game at hand, and permit shrewd transactors to take home their winnings.

Some of these experiments have been unusual, to say the least, involving patients in mental hospitals and even laboratory rats who are given "incentives" along the lines of the behavior-modification theories of psychologist B. F. Skinner. They are described in the following excerpts from an article by Tom Alexander, "Economics According to the Rats," which appeared in *Fortune*. We leave it to you to draw any inferences you may wish about the behavior of "normal" persons from the relatively exotic experiments summarized in the article.[10]

> *Two centuries after the founding of their discipline, half a century after being installed as court wizards in the palaces of policy, a great many members of the economics profession are beginning to wonder what, if anything, they really know. Their inability to comprehend or deal with problems like stagflation has sent them off on a new search for understanding. Like astronomy or meteorology, economics has always been a "field" science, gathering its data from the bewildering real world rather than from the laboratory. But unlike astronomers and meteorologists,*

[9] Ibid., p. 78.

[10] Excerpts from Tom Alexander, "Economics According to the Rats," *Fortune*, December 1, 1980, pp. 127–32. Tom Alexander, *Fortune*, © 1980 Time Inc. All rights reserved.

who can interpret observations in light of laboratory-tested laws of physics, economists have few proven principles to go by.

Lately there's been an explosion of interest in the subdiscipline of experimental economics. While laboratory studies in economics have been carried out from time to time for decades, now a growing number of researchers at some prestigious universities are devoting their careers to experimental investigation of everything from market behavior to the decision-making of rats and pigeons. "This work didn't get much attention until the early Seventies, but now we're swamped with requests to do projects," says Charles Plott, a pioneering experimental economist at Caltech. "What happened was that the academic theorists began to look at some of the results and say, 'God almighty, we've got all these big general theories and we can't even explain that!'"

Experimental economists have found that they are usually better at predicting how markets will behave than at forecasting the behavior of individuals. So a number of experimenters have turned their attention to the question of what motivates people. For example, two Texas A&M economists, Ray Battalio and John Kagel, investigated a token economy in a female mental ward at Central Islip State Hospital on Long Island. There, inmates earn token money for performing chores—say, one token for making their own beds, or seven tokens for working an hour in the laundry. They are free to earn as much or as little as they like and can spend their tokens on candy, cigarettes, or even private dormitory rooms.

Among Battalio and Kagel's fascinating discoveries is that the pattern of earnings in the institution closely mirrors income distribution in the U.S. as a whole. For instance, the highest fifth of the Islip State earners got 41.2% of all earnings, compared with 41.5% for the highest fifth in the U.S. as a whole. The lowest fifth in the institution got 7.4%, compared with 5.2% in the real economy.

Kagel and Battalio have also investigated token economies with both male and female workers and found that the earnings differences between males and females were similar to those in the larger society. The median token income of the women was 69.5% that of the men, compared with about 59% for the U.S. as a whole. Write Battalio and Kagel: "Many explanations might account for the observed difference—differences between the sexes in physical stamina or desire for leisure—but . . . it cannot be accounted for by sex bias or segregation of the sexes into different jobs."

Battalio and Kagel have concluded that leisure is both a biological and an economic good, like food, that human beings consume in amounts depending upon price and need. When Kagel gave a talk sounding this theme at the State University of New York at Stony Brook, one interested listener was an experimental psychologist at SUNY named Howard Rachlin. Rachlin believed that he could duplicate many of the token-economy results with laboratory animals. So Rachlin, Battalio, and Kagel, together with one of Rachlin's former psychology students, Leonard Green of Washington University, have joined forces to investigate some long-standing economic controversies using rats and pigeons.

One such controversy concerns the effect of rising wages: Will they encourage workers to work harder, or will they diminish the relative value of money vs. leisure? To look into that question, the economist-psychologist team is using techniques developed by Harvard psychologist B. F. Skinner, who trained animals to push at levers or peck at buttons to earn rewards of food or drink in devices now called Skinner boxes.

The experiments with rats and pigeons seem to have proved both sides right in the leisure-income controversy. As the wage rate goes up—that is, as the experimenters reduce the number of pecks required to obtain a pellet of pigeon food or the number of pushes to get a serving of rat food—hungry pigeons and rats will push and peck faster and more diligently, but only up to a point. When that point is reached—and it tends to be different for each individual but still well short of satiation—the animals invariably slow down and substitute increasing amounts of leisure for all that hard work. The result resembles the "backward-bending labor-supply curve" some theoretical economists predict will befall increasingly prosperous societies. The researchers concluded that "non-human workers are willing to trade more income for leisure if the price is right."

The team has also used Skinner boxes to investigate the effects of a negative income tax on work output, a topic of intense interest among policymakers contemplating the overhaul of present welfare programs. The researchers programmed the Skinner boxes to supply varying amounts of "free" food at intermittent intervals while the animals were working. Even though hungry and underweight, rats and pigeons reduced their work output more or less in proportion to the amount of free food received.

Work for work's sake

Significantly, this work-reduction effect is greater among low-wage rats, that is, rats that have to work a lot for a little food. Rats getting lots of food, it appears, retain a certain love of work for work's sake. The free income also has a puzzlingly disproportionate effect upon total consumption: even when the free food is included in their earnings, the total amount is less than what rats earn when they receive no free food at all.

Summary

This chapter applies the principles of production to the pricing and employment of resources under conditions of pure competition both in product selling and resource buying. First, the principles fundamental to the employment of several variable resources by a firm were established. Second, the principles underlying pricing and employment of any given variable resource were determined.

When a firm uses several variable resources, it solves two problems simultaneously in the process of maximizing its profits. It must use resources in the correct (least-cost) combination; and it must use the absolute amounts necessary to produce the quantity of the product that maximizes profits. Use of resources in the correct absolute amounts means that they are used in the correct combination also. The firm should employ those amounts of resources and produce that amount of product at which

$$\frac{MPP_a}{p_a} = \frac{MPP_b}{p_b} = \cdots = \frac{MPP_n}{p_n} = \frac{1}{MC_x} = \frac{1}{MR_x} = \frac{1}{p_x}.$$

The individual firm demand curve, the market demand curve, and the market supply curve for a resource are necessary for determining the market price, the individual firm level of employment, and the market level of employment of the resource. When the firm employs one variable resource only, the marginal revenue product curve for the resource is the firm's demand curve for it. If the firm employs several variable resources, the firm's demand curve for a given resource shows the different quantities that the firm would take at various alternative prices when prices of other resources are held constant. At each price of the given resource, the firm makes all the adjustment necessary in the quantities of all resources used in order to maximize its profits. The market demand curve is obtained by summing the quantities that all firms in all industries using the resource will take at each possible resource price. The market supply curve shows the quantities of the resource that its owners will place on the market at various possible prices. Once the market price is established, the firm will employ a quantity of the resource at which its marginal revenue product is equal to its market price. The market level of employment is the summation of individual firm levels of employment.

Suggested Readings

Hicks, John R. *Value and Capital*, 2d ed. Oxford, Eng.: The Clarendon Press, 1946, Chaps. 6, 7.

Scitovsky, Tibor. *Welfare and Competition*, rev. ed. Homewood, Ill.: Richard D. Irwin, 1971, Chap. 7.

Stigler, George J. *The Theory of Price*, 3d ed. New York: Crowell-Collier and Macmillan, 1966, Chap. 14, pp. 239–44.

Questions and Exercises

1 "Rising marginal costs result from the operation of the law of diminishing returns." Analyze this statement in detail.

2 Suppose that bricklayers' labor is purchased competitively and that the bricklayers' union is able to push wage rates above the equilibrium level. Show and explain the effects on
  a the market level of employment
  b the individual firm's level of employment
  c the total wage bill for bricklayers
  d the cost of housing.

3 The relationship between a commercially mixed feed for dairy cows and the quantity of milk produced per day by a cow, holding all other inputs constant, is as follows:

Feed	Milk
2	1.0
4	2.0
6	2.8
8	3.5
10	4.0
12	3.9

The price of milk is $1 per gallon. The price of the feed is 35 cents per pound. Determine the most profitable quantity of feed to use. Explain your reasoning.

4 A purely competitive manufacturer of product X uses two variable resources, A and B, to turn out its product. State and explain the complete set of conditions, both with respect to the level of product output and the levels of resource inputs, that must be met if profits are to be maximized.

5 Would you expect that price ceilings placed on crude oil would help solve the energy problem? Explain your answer in detail.

CHAPTER CONTENTS		KEY CONCEPTS

Monopoly
Least-cost combination of resources
Marginal revenue product
Demand curve for a resource
Exploitation
Monopsony
Supply curve of a resource
Marginal resource costs
Mobility

Pricing and
Employment of Resources:
Monopoly and Monopsony

For markets other than pure competition, some additions to and modifications of the principles of resource pricing and employment are in order. We shall examine how they work (1) when firms sell products as monopolists while buying resources under conditions of pure competition and (2) when firms buy resources as monoposonists while selling products either as pure competitors or as monopolists. For product monopoly the relationship between the value of marginal product and the marginal revenue product of a resource must be examined further. To take monopsony into account, a modified view of the resource supply curve facing the firm is necessary. Monopoly and monopsony will be considered in turn.

Monopoly in the Selling of Products

Individual firm demand for a resource, when monopoly occurs in the sale of products, is almost the same as when pure competition prevails. The most significant difference between the two selling market structures is evidenced in the market demand curves for the resource.

Simultaneous Employment of Several Variable Resources

A monopolist firm that uses several variable resources must determine the combinations of resources necessary to produce alternative outputs at the least possible costs. If it purchases resources under purely competitive conditions, its least-cost conditions are the same as those faced by a pure competitor. The least-cost combination for a given output is that at which the marginal physical product per dollar's worth of one variable resource is equal to the marginal physical product per dollar's worth of every other variable resource used. If A and B are two such resources, they should be combined so that

$$\frac{MPP_a}{p_a} = \frac{MPP_b}{p_b}. \tag{16.1}$$

To maximize profits, however, the monopolist must do more than determine least-cost combinations of variable resources. It must use enough of each to produce the product output at which marginal revenue from its sales and marginal cost of its output are equal. With reference to Figure 16.1, suppose that the firm uses the least-cost combination for the production of x_0 units of product. The marginal cost of the product, $0c$, is less than the marginal revenue, $0r$, from it. The output level of X and the quantities used of resources A and B are all too small. These conditions can be summarized as follows:

$$\frac{MPP_a}{p_a} = \frac{MPP_b}{p_b} = \frac{1}{MC_x} > \frac{1}{MR_x}. \qquad (16.2)$$

The monopolist can expand output by increasing the quantities of A and B used in combination with its fixed resources. The marginal physical product of both A and B will diminish, causing the marginal cost of the product to rise. The larger output and sales of the monopolist cause marginal revenue from the product to fall. The quantities of A and B, together with the firm's output, will be increased until the marginal cost and the marginal revenue are equal. At output x and price p, profits will be maximized. Variable resources will be used in the least-cost combination, as well as in the correct absolute quantities. The profit-maximizing conditions, with respect to resource purchases, resource combinations, and product output, can be summarized as follows:

$$\frac{MPP_a}{p_a} = \frac{MPP_b}{p_b} = \frac{1}{MC_x} = \frac{1}{MR_x}. \qquad (16.3)$$

These principles of profit maximization apply to all types of sellers' markets—pure competition, pure monopoly, oligopoly, and

FIGURE 16.1
Least-cost combinations and profit maximization

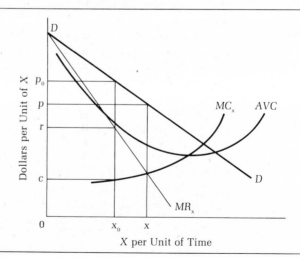

448   PART FIVE   Determination of and Functions of Resource Prices

monopolistic competition—as long as pure competition prevails in the buying of resources.

Pricing and Employment of a Given Variable Resource

The price and employment level of a given variable resource are determined in much the same way when resource purchasers are monopolistic sellers of product as when they are purely competitive product sellers. The monopolist's demand curve for a resource, while defined in the same way as that of the pure competitor, is slightly more difficult to compute. As in the purely competitive market, we differentiate between the case in which the given resource is the only variable one employed by the firm and the case in which it is one of several variable resources employed.

The Demand Curve of the Firm: One Resource Variable   To maximize profits with respect to a single variable resource, the monopolist must employ that quantity at which a one-unit change in the quantity employed per unit of time changes total revenue and total cost in the same direction by the same amount. The effects on total receipts and on total costs of one-unit changes in the quantities employed are determined in the same way as they were for the pure competitor.

Changes in the firm's total receipts and the causes of those changes are shown in Table 16.1. Columns (1) and (2) show a portion of the marginal physical product schedule for resource A, lying in Stage II for that resource. Resource A is the only variable resource used by the firm; the quantities of all other resources are fixed. Columns (3) and (4) show the portion of the product demand schedule of the monopolist corresponding to the quantities of A shown in column (1).

Column (6) is the important one for the present. It shows the additions to the firm's total receipts made by one-unit increments in the quantity of A employed per unit of time, that is, the *marginal*

TABLE 16.1 The computation of the marginal revenue product of a resource	(1) Quantity of A	(2) Marginal Physical Product (MPP_a)	(3) Total Product	(4) Product Price (p_x)	(5) Total Revenue	(6) Marginal Revenue Product (MRP_a)
	4	8	28	$10.00	$280.00	—
	5	7	35	9.80	343.00	$63.00
	6	6	41	9.60	393.60	50.60
	7	5	46	9.50	437.00	43.40
	8	4	50	9.40	470.00	33.00

revenue product of resource A. The marginal revenue product of a given quantity of A can be computed directly from column (5), but in a fundamental sense it is the marginal physical product of A at that quantity multiplied by the marginal revenue from the final product obtained from sale. Marginal revenue product of A or MRP_a when, say, 5 units are employed, equals marginal physical product of A at that point multiplied by the marginal revenue from each of the additional units of sales.[1]

Increases in the level of employment of A by the monopolist cause the marginal revenue product of A to decrease for two reasons. First, they cause the marginal physical product of A to decline because of the operation of the law of diminishing returns. Second, marginal revenue for the monopolistic firm ordinarily will fall as it markets larger quantities of product.

The marginal revenue product curve is the monopolistic firm's demand curve for A when it buys the resource competitively and when resource A is the only variable one used by the firm. The monopolist will buy that quantity of A at which the addition made to total receipts by a one-unit increment is equal to the addition made to total cost by the increment. Since the resource is purchased competitively, the addition to total cost made by each additional unit of A purchased per unit of time is the same as the price per unit of A. Thus, in Figure 16.2 if MRP_a is the monopolist's marginal revenue product curve for A and p_a is the price per unit of A, the monopolist will use quantity a. The profit-maximizing conditions can be written as

$$MRP_a = p_a$$

or

$$MPP_a \times MR_x = p_a \qquad (16.4)$$

---

[1] A fifth unit of A per unit of time increases output and sales of X from 28 units to 35 units, and total receipts of the firm from \$280 to \$343. The increment in revenue per unit increment in sales, or MR_x, equals \$63 ÷ 7 or \$9 per unit for each of the 7 units. Marginal revenue product of A, then, when 5 units are employed, must equal $MPP_a \times MR_x$; that is, $7 \times \$9 = \$63$.

In terms of calculus,

$$x = f(a) = \text{the firm's production function}$$

and

$$p_x = h(x) = \text{the demand curve facing the firm.}$$

Thus,

$$R = x \times p_x = x \times h(x) = \text{the firm's total revenue}$$

and

$$\frac{dR}{dx} = p_x + x \times h'(x) = \text{marginal revenue.}$$

Therefore,

$$MRP_a = \left(\frac{dR}{dx}\right)\left(\frac{dx}{da}\right) = [p_x + x \times h'(x)]f'(a).$$

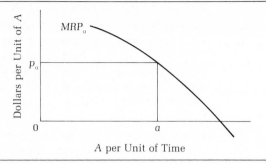

FIGURE 16.2
The marginal revenue product curve for a resource

At different possible prices of A, the marginal revenue product curve shows the different quantities that the monopolist will purchase per unit of time.

The Demand Curve of the Firm: Several Resources Variable   The procedure for establishing the monopolist's demand curve for a given resource when several variable resources are employed is the same as that used in the purely competitive case. Assuming that the prices of all other resources remain constant, changes in the price of the given resource will give rise to the same sort of firm or internal effects.

These effects are shown in Figure 16.3, in which A is the given variable resource. Suppose that the initial price of A is p_{a1}; the firm is using a least-cost combination of variable resources and is producing the profit-maximizing quantity of product X. The quantity of A employed is a_1. The curve MRP_{a1} is valid for changes in the quantity of A only.

A reduction in the price of A to p_{a2} will provide an incentive for the monopolist to increase employment of the resource toward $a_1{}'$.

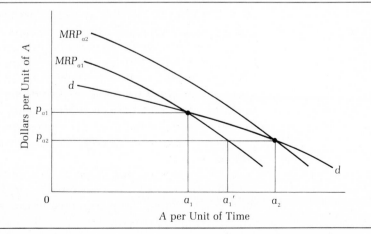

FIGURE 16.3
The firm's demand curve for a resource

But, as the employment of A is expanded, the marginal physical product curves and marginal revenue product curves of complementary resources will be shifted to the right, causing larger quantities of these to be used at their given prices. The corresponding curves of substitute resources will be shifted to the left by the greater utilization of A, and smaller quantities of substitute resources will be employed at their given prices by the monopolist. Both effects will shift the marginal physical product curve and the marginal revenue product curve of resource A to the right. When the monopolist has again established a least-cost profit-maximizing combination of variable resources, the marginal revenue product curve for A will be in some position such as MRP_{a2}, and the quantity of A employed will be a_2. Thus, the firm's demand curve for resource A will consist of points tracing out a curve such as dd.

The Market Demand Curve and Resource Pricing If all purchasers of resource A were purely monopolistic sellers of product, the market demand curve for A would be the horizontal summation of all individual firm demand curves for it. There would be no external or industry effects resulting from a decrease in the price of A, for each monopolist is the sole supplier of product for his industry. The effect of a decrease in the price of A on the quantity of product turned out by any given industry and, consequently, on the price of the commodity has already been taken into account in the marginal revenue product curves and in that monopolist's demand curve for the resource.

If the purchasers of resource A are oligopolists or monopolistic competitors, the market demand curve for the resource is no longer the horizontal summation of individual firm demand curves for it. A change in the resource price changes not only the output that any single firm in a given industry will produce but the outputs of all other firms in the industry as well. These adjustments will occur in every such industry that uses the resource. As in the purely competitive case of Chapter 15, changes in product outputs of other firms in the industry will shift the product demand curve facing any given firm and, consequently, the firm's demand curve for resource A. Thus, at any given price the quantities employed by all firms in all industries using A, when each firm is maximizing its profits, must be totaled to locate a point on the market demand curve for A. Other points on the market demand curve can be obtained in the same fashion.

The procedure just outlined is applicable for establishing the market demand curve for a resource regardless of the type of product market in which the firms using the resource sell. The usual case will be that some of the firms using resource A will sell in one type of product market and some will sell in other types. The only market structure requirement to be met is that all firms purchase the resource competitively.

With regard to market supply, resource pricing, and resource employment, monopoly in the product market adds nothing new to the analysis presented in the preceding chapter. The market supply curve for resource A again shows the different quantities of it that its owners will place on the market at various alternative prices. The market price of the resource moves toward the level at which firms are willing to employ the quantity per unit of time that its owners are willing to place on the market.

The market price of A determines its level of employment. The monopolist, like a firm selling under conditions of pure competition, is faced with a horizontal supply curve for resource A at a level equal to its market price. The monopolistic firm will employ the resource up to the point at which it is maximizing profits with respect to it. At this point the marginal revenue product of the resource is equal to its price. The market level of employment of the resource is the summation of all individual firm employment levels, whether those firms be monopolists, pure competitors, oligopolists, or monopolistic competitors.

When the monopolist is maximizing profits with respect to each variable resource used, those resources will necessarily be used in a least-cost combination. Suppose that A and B are the only two variable resources used by a monopolist producing product X. When profits are maximized with respect to A, then

$$MPP_a \times MR_x = p_a. \tag{16.5}$$

Similarly, maximization of profits with respect to B means that

$$MPP_b \times MR_x = p_b. \tag{16.6}$$

Consequently,

$$\frac{MPP_a}{p_a} = \frac{MPP_b}{p_b} = \frac{1}{MC_x} = \frac{1}{MR_x} . \tag{16.7}$$

Monopolistic Exploitation of a Resource

Monopoly in a product market is said to result in exploitation of resources used by the monopolist. In this respect *exploitation* means that units of a resource are paid less than the value of the product that any one of them adds to the economy's output. A monopolist employs that quantity of a resource at which its price equals its marginal revenue product—marginal physical product multiplied by marginal revenue from the sale of the product. But the value of product added to the economy's output by a unit of the resource is its value of marginal product—marginal physical product multiplied by price per unit at which the product is sold. The marginal revenue product of the resource to a particular firm facing a downward-sloping product demand curve is less than the value of marginal product of the resource, since marginal revenue is less than product price in such cases. Hence, the prices paid resources used by monopolistic firms are less than the values of the products that they add to the economy's output.

Nevertheless, the price paid a resource must be equal to what it can earn in its alternative employments. Exploitation does not mean that the monopolist pays units of the resource less than do competitive firms hiring units of the same resource. Exploitation under monopoly occurs because the monopolist, faced by the market price of the resource, stops short of the employment level at which the value of marginal product of the resource equals the resource price. Units of the resource contribute more to the value of the economy's output when employed by the monopolist than they do when employed by the purely competitive firm, but they are paid the same price in each market situation. Thus, market forces will not induce resources to move into their more valuable uses.

Monopsony in the Buying of Resources

A resource market situation in which there is a single buyer of a particular resource is called one of *monopsony*.[2] A monopsonistic situation is the opposite extreme to pure competition among resource buyers—the situation that we have heretofore assumed exists. Two additional resource market situations can be distinguished. The first is oligopsony, in which there are a few buyers of a particular resource that may or may not be differentiated. One buyer takes a large enough proportion of the total supply of the resource to influence the market price of the item. The other situation is one of monopsonistic competition. Here there are many buyers of a particular kind of resource, but there is differentiation within the resource category that causes specific buyers to prefer the resource of one seller to that of another. Our analysis will center around monopsony—one buyer of the resource—but it may also be applied to oligopsony and monopsonistic competition.

---

[2] The term *monopsony* is applied also to cases in which there is a single buyer of a particular product; however, our discussion will be confined to monopsony in resource markets.

Resource Supply Curves and Marginal Resource Costs

As the only buyer of a resource, the monopsonist faces the market supply curve for it. Ordinarily that supply curve is upward sloping to the right. A producer who furnishes virtually the entire source of employment in an isolated area would be in this position, in the short run at least. Contrast the supply curve faced by a monopsonist with that faced by the firm that buys a resource under conditions of pure competition. Under pure competition the firm can get as many units of the resource per unit of time as it desires at the going market price; hence, it is faced with a horizontal or perfectly elastic resource supply curve even though the market supply curve may be upward sloping to the right or less than perfectly elastic.

The upward slope of the resource supply curve faced by the monopsonist gives monopsony the characteristics that distinguish it from pure competition. To obtain larger quantities of the resource per unit of time, the monopsonist must pay higher prices. Columns (1) and (2) of Table 16.2 present a portion of a typical resource supply schedule illustrating this situation. Column (3) shows the total cost of resource A to the firm for different quantities purchased. Column (4) shows marginal resource cost of A to the firm.

Marginal resource cost is defined as the change in the firm's total costs resulting from a one-unit change in the purchase of the resource per unit of time. When the resource supply curve faced by the firm is upward sloping to the right, marginal resource cost will be greater than the resource price for any quantity purchased by the firm. This relationship can be explained with reference to Table 16.2.

Suppose that the firm increases the quantity of A that it purchases from 10 units to 11 units. The eleventh unit costs the firm $0.65. However, to obtain 11 units per unit of time, the firm must pay $0.65 per unit for *all 11 units*. Therefore, the cost of obtaining the other 10 units has increased from $0.60 to $0.65 per unit. An additional cost of $0.50 is incurred on the 10. Add this to the $0.65 that the eleventh unit costs, and the increase in the firm's total cost is

TABLE 16.2	(1) Quantity of A	(2) Resource Price (p_a)	(3) Total Resource Cost (TC_a)	(4) Marginal Resource Cost (MRC_a)
The computation of marginal resource cost	10	$0.60	$6.00	—
	11	0.65	7.15	$1.15
	12	0.70	8.40	1.25
	13	0.75	9.75	1.35

$1.15. The marginal resource cost of the twelfth and thirteenth units can be computed in a similar way.[3]

A graphic illustration of the resource supply curve and the marginal resource cost curve faced by a monopsonist is shown in Figure 16.4. The market supply curve for resource A is $S_a S_a$. The marginal resource cost curve is MRC_a and lies above the supply curve. The marginal resource cost curve bears the same relationship

FIGURE 16.4
Marginal revenue product, marginal resource cost, and profit maximization for a monopsonist

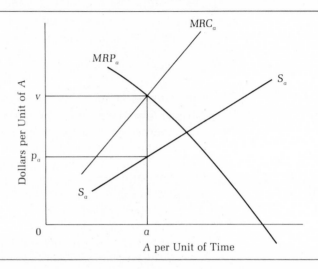

to the supply curve that a marginal cost curve bears to an average cost curve. In fact, the market supply curve of resource A is the average cost curve of resource A alone; and the marginal resource cost curve is the marginal cost curve of resource A alone. Obviously then, if the supply (average cost) curve of A is increasing, the marginal resource cost (marginal cost) curve must lie above it.[4]

[3] Let the supply curve for resource A be

$$p_a = \phi(a).$$

Then

$$TC_a = a \times \phi(a)$$

and

$$MRC_a = \frac{dTC_a}{da} = \phi(a) + a \times \phi(a) = p_a + a \times \phi'(a);$$

that is, marginal resource cost of A at the a level of employment is equal to the price of A at that level of employment plus the incremental cost of A for the entire a units of the resource.

If the firm buys resource A under conditions of pure competition, the supply curve of A to the firm is horizontal,

$$\phi'(a) = 0,$$

and

$$MRC_a = p_a.$$

[4] See pp. 246–249.

Pricing and Employment of a Single Resource

Profit maximization with respect to resource A is governed by the same general principles for the monopsonist as for firms buying resources competitively. Larger quantities of A per unit of time will be purchased if they add more to the firm's total receipts than to its total costs. Additions to the monopsonist's total receipts as more A is employed are shown by the curve MRP_a in Figure 16.4. Additions to total costs are shown by the marginal resource cost curve. Profits are maximized when quantity a of the resource is employed. Larger quantities would add more to total costs than to total receipts and would cause profits to decline. We can state the profit-maximizing conditions in equation form. When the monopsonist's profits are maximized, that quantity of A is employed at which

$$MRP_a = MRC_a$$

or

$$MPP_a \times MR_x = MRC_a. \tag{16.8}$$

The monopsonist differs from the competitive buyer of resources with respect to the price paid for the resource at the profit-maximizing level of employment. For quantity a of the resource, it is necessary for the monopsonist to pay a price of only p_a, although the marginal revenue product of the resource at that level of employment is v. Should the monopsonist employ that quantity of A at which its marginal revenue product is equal to its price—as does the competitive resource buyer—less profit would be made. To maximize profits, the quantity of the resource used is restricted, and it is paid a price per unit that is less than its marginal revenue product. The important consideration for profit maximization is the employment of that quantity at which the marginal resource cost equals the marginal revenue product—and for the monopsonist, the resource price is less than the marginal resource cost. Monopsony profits, resulting from the excess of the marginal revenue product of the resource over its price per unit, are equal to $p_a v \times a$.

Simultaneous Employment of Several Variable Resources

The conditions that must be met by the monopsonist, if he is to employ least-cost combinations of variable resources for given outputs, differ slightly from those that apply to purely competitive resource buyers. As before, the least-cost combination for the monopsonist is that combination at which the marginal physical product per dollar's worth of one resource is equal to the marginal physical product per dollar's worth of every other resource. The difference between the monopsonistic and the competitive buyer rests on what constitutes the marginal physical product per dollar's worth of a resource.

An illustration will help make this difference clear. Suppose that a coal-mining firm buys miners' labor monopsonistically. At the current level of employment a single miner's labor adds a ton of coal per day to the firm's output. This is the marginal physical product of the miner's labor. It adds \$20 to the firm's total costs. This is the marginal resource cost of the miner's labor, and it exceeds the daily wage rate. The addition made to the firm's total production per additional dollar's expenditure on labor is $1/20$ of a ton of coal, or is equal to MPP_l/MRC_l. The same calculation applies to any other resource purchased monopsonistically. The marginal physical product per dollar's worth of any resource is found by dividing its marginal physical product by its marginal resource cost.

If a firm purchases variable resources A and B monopsonistically, to achieve the least-cost combination for a given output it must use them in such proportions that

$$\frac{MPP_a}{MRC_a} = \frac{MPP_b}{MRC_b}. \tag{16.9}$$

The reciprocal of either or both of the fractions in the equation represents the marginal cost of the product at whatever output the firm is producing. A unit of A used adds an amount MRC_a to total costs and an amount MPP_a to total product. Therefore, the addition to total costs per unit increase in output is MRC_a/MPP_a. Similarly, the marginal cost of the product in terms of resource B is MRC_b/MPP_b.

Suppose that initially the monopsonistic firm is using too little of A and B for profit maximization, but it is using the least-cost combination for the product output it is producing. Marginal cost of the product is less than marginal revenue from its sale. These conditions can be summed up as follows:

$$\frac{MPP_a}{MRC_a} = \frac{MPP_b}{MRC_b} = \frac{1}{MC_x} > \frac{1}{MR_x}. \tag{16.10}$$

Profit maximization requires the employment of greater quantities of the variable resources per unit of time. The additional resource units will increase the output and decrease the marginal revenue received from the product. Additional quantities of A and B cause the marginal physical products of both resources to decline. At the same time the marginal resource costs of A and B increase. Thus, the marginal cost of the product to the firm rises as a result of two forces working simultaneously—declining marginal physical products and rising marginal resource costs. Additional quantities of A and B will be employed per unit of time until the marginal cost equals the marginal revenue. At this point the resources are used in the correct absolute quantities, as well as in the least-cost proportions. The conditions necessary for profit maximization can be stated as follows:

$$\frac{MPP_a}{MRC_a} = \frac{MPP_b}{MRC_b} = \frac{1}{MC_x} = \frac{1}{MR_x}. \qquad (16.11)$$

The conditions necessary for profit maximization by the monopsonist also can be established by considering resources A and B one at a time. Resource A should be used up to the point at which

$$MPP_a \times MR_x = MRC_a \qquad \text{or} \qquad \frac{MPP_a}{MRC_a} = \frac{1}{MR_x}. \qquad (16.12)$$

Likewise, resource B should be used up to the point at which

$$MPP_b \times MR_x = MRC_b \qquad \text{or} \qquad \frac{MPP_b}{MRC_b} = \frac{1}{MR_x}. \qquad (16.13)$$

From (16.12) and (16.13) we arrive again at the conditions expressed in (16.11).

The profit-maximizing conditions set forth above for the monopsonist are general enough to apply to all classifications of both product sellers' markets and resource buyers' markets. Under conditions of pure competition in resource buying, MRC_a and MRC_b become p_a and p_b, respectively. Under conditions of pure competition in product selling, MR_x becomes p_x.[5]

---

[5]   In terms of calculus, the general solution to the problem of profit maximization by a firm with respect to several variable resources is as follows:

$$x = f(a, b) = \text{the firm's production function}$$
$$p_x = h(x) = \text{the product demand curve facing the firm}$$
$$p_a = \phi(a) = \text{the supply curve facing the firm for resource } A$$
$$p_b = \psi(b) = \text{the supply curve facing the firm for resource } B.$$

On the revenue side,

$$R = x \times p_x = \text{total revenue of the firm}$$

$$\frac{dR}{dx} = p_x - x \times h'(x) = \text{marginal revenue of the firm}$$

and

$$\frac{\delta R}{\delta a} = \left(\frac{dR}{dx}\right)\left(\frac{\delta x}{\delta a}\right) = [p_x - x \times h'(x)]\frac{\delta x}{\delta a}$$

$$= \text{marginal revenue product of } A \text{ to the firm.}$$

Similarly,

$$\frac{\delta R}{\delta b} = \left(\frac{dR}{dx}\right)\left(\frac{\delta x}{\delta b}\right) = [p_x - x \times h'(x)]\frac{\delta x}{\delta b}$$

$$= \text{marginal revenue product of } B \text{ to the firm.}$$

On the cost side,

$$C = k + a \times p_a + b \times p_b = \text{total costs of the firm}$$

$$\frac{\delta C}{\delta a} = p_a + a \times \phi'(a) = \text{marginal resource cost of } A$$

$$\frac{\delta C}{\delta b} = p_b + b \times \psi'(b) = \text{marginal resource cost of } B.$$

To maximize profits,

$$\pi = R - C = x \times p_x - (k + a \times p_a + b \times p_b)$$

$$\frac{\delta \pi}{\delta a} = [p_x - x \times h'(x)]\frac{\delta x}{\delta a} - [p_a + a \times \phi'(a)] = 0,$$

Conditions Giving Rise to Monopsony

Monopsony results from either or both of two basic conditions. First, monopsonistic purchases of a resource may occur when units of the resource are specialized to a particular user. This statement means that the marginal revenue product of the resource in the specialized use is enough higher than it is in any alternative employments in which it conceivably can be used to eliminate the alternative employments from the consideration of resource suppliers. Thus, the resource supply curve facing the monopsonist will be the market supply curve of the resource and usually will be upward sloping to the right. The more the user is willing to pay for the resource, the greater will be the quantity placed on the market.

A situation of the kind described may occur when a special type of skilled labor is developed to meet certain needs of a specific firm. The higher the wage rate offered for the special category of labor, the more individuals there will be who are willing to undergo the necessary training to develop the skill. No other firm utilizes labor with this or similar skills; consequently, once trained, the workers' only options are to work for this firm or to work elsewhere at jobs where their marginal revenue products and their wage rates are significantly lower.

Specialization of resources to a particular user is not confined to the labor field. A large aircraft or automobile manufacturer may depend on a number of suppliers to furnish certain parts used by no other manufacturer. In the tightest possible case, such suppliers sell their entire outputs to the manufacturer, and complete monopsony by the manufacturer exists. Given time, the suppliers may be able to convert production facilities to supply other types of parts to other

$$\frac{\delta \pi}{\delta b} = [p_x - x \times h'(x)] \frac{\delta x}{\delta b} - [p_b + b \times \psi'(b)] = 0$$

$$[p_x - xh'(x)] \frac{\delta x}{\delta a} = p_a + a\phi'(a)$$

$$[p_x - xh'(x)] \frac{\delta x}{\delta b} = p_b + b\psi'(b)$$

$$MRP_a = MRC_a \quad \text{and} \quad MRP_b = MRC_b.$$

If the firm is a purely competitive seller of product, then

$$P_x = h(x) = k \quad \text{and} \quad h'(x) = 0.$$

If it is a purely competitive purchaser of A, the supply curves of A and B are horizontal; so

$$\phi'(a) = 0 \quad \text{and} \quad \psi'(b) = 0.$$

Thus, the profit-maximizing conditions can be stated as

$$p_x \times \frac{\delta x}{\delta a} = p_a \quad \text{and} \quad p_x \times \frac{\delta x}{\delta b} = p_b$$

or

$$VMP_a = p_a \quad \text{and} \quad VMP_b = p_b.$$

manufacturers, and the degree of monopsony enjoyed by the one may be decreased correspondingly.

The second condition from which monopsony may stem is the immobility of certain resources. It is not necessary that resources in general be immobile. It is only necessary that mobility out of certain areas or away from certain firms be lacking, thus creating unique monopsonistic situations. Various forces may hold workers in a given community or to a given firm. Among these are emotional ties to the community together with a fear of the unknown. Ignorance regarding alternative employment opportunities may exist. Funds may not be sufficient to permit job seeking in, and movement to, alternative job areas. Seniority and pension rights accumulated with a firm may make workers reluctant to leave. Specific cases of immmobility among firms within a given geographic area may result from agreements among employers not to "pirate" each other's work forces. For many years the most famous of all "no-pirating" pacts between employers occurred in organized professional baseball. Formal collusion among the clubs, sanctioned by an antitrust immunity from Congress, reduced substantially wage competition for players and resulted in a sizable redistribution of income from players to clubs. This case will be examined later in the chapter.

Monopsonistic Exploitation of a Resource

Monopsony in the purchase of a resource also is said to result in exploitation of that resource. Monopsonistic exploitation can be understood best by comparing monopsony with pure competition in resource buying. In a purely competitive situation each firm will add to its profits by taking larger quantities of the resource up to the point at which the marginal revenue product of the resource is equal to the resource price. The resource receives a price per unit equal to what any one unit of it contributes to the firm's total receipts.[6]

In contrast, the monopsonist maximizes profits by stopping short of the resource employment level at which marginal revenue product of the resource is equal to its price per unit. This situation is shown in Figure 16.4. The profit-maximizing level of employment is that at which the marginal revenue product equals the marginal resource cost. Since the marginal resource cost exceeds the resource price, the marginal revenue product of the resource does also. Hence, units of the resource are paid less than what any one of them contributes to the total receipts of the firm. This situation is called monopsonistic exploitation of the resource. The monopsonist restricts the quantity of the resource used and holds down its price.

[6] Monopolistic exploitation will occur if the resource-buying firms face downward-sloping product demand curves, but there is no monopsonistic exploitation.

Measures to Counteract Monopsony

What can be done to counteract monopsonistic exploitation of resources? Two alternatives will be considered. First, administered or fixed minimum resource prices can be used. Second, measures successful in increasing resource mobility will reduce the monopsonistic power of particular resource users.

Minimum Resource Prices Minimum resource prices can be established by the government or by organized groups of resource suppliers. The typical monopsonistic situation is pictured in Figure 16.5. The level of employment of resource A is quantity a. Its price per unit is p_a; however, marginal revenue product is v, and the resource is being exploited. Suppose that a minimum price is set at p_{a1} and that the firm must pay a price of at least p_{a1} per unit for all units purchased. Should the firm want more than a_1 units, it faces the mn sector of the resource supply curve. The entire supply curve now faced by the firm will be $p_{a1}mn$.

The alteration in the resource supply curve facing the firm also alters the marginal resource cost curve. For quantities between zero and a_1, each additional unit of A employed per unit of time adds an amount equal to p_{a1} to the firm's total costs. The new marginal resource cost curve coincides with $p_{a1}m$, the new supply curve, out to quantity a_1. For quantities greater than a_1, the regular supply curve mn is the relevant one, and the corresponding sector of the marginal resource cost curve becomes lk. The altered marginal resource cost curve is $p_{a1}mlk$. At quantity a_1, it is discontinuous between m and l.

The quantity of A that the firm should now employ to maximize profits will differ from the quantity used before the minimum price

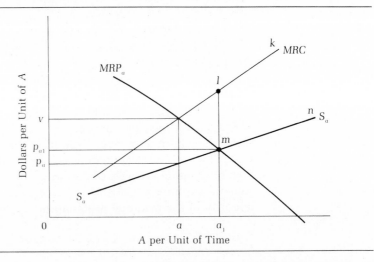

FIGURE 16.5
Control of monopsony by minimum resource prices

was set. The firm should use quantity a_1, at which the new marginal resource cost is equal to the marginal revenue product of A. The minimum price not only eliminates monopsonistic exploitation of the resource, but it also increases the level of employment in the process.

This analysis assumes that the minimum price of resource A is set at just the correct level to counteract monopsony completely. Such precision may or may not be achieved in fact. However, any minimum price between p_a and p_{a1} will counteract monopsony to some extent. The nearer to p_{a1} the price is set, the more nearly will exploitation be eliminated. Prices set between p_{a1} and v will counteract exploitation also, but at the expense of employment. Unemployment will occur, since at any price level above p_{a1} resource sellers will want to put more on the market than buyers are willing to buy.

Countering of monopsony by price regulation is at best a difficult job. The precise price level at which monopsony is offset completely is hard to determine. In the labor field—where monopsony is most publicized—minimum wage laws may be the counteracting device used. However, different degrees of monopsony for different kinds of labor and for different situations make blanket price fixing of this type impractical as an overall monopsonistic offset. Collective bargaining on a firm-by-firm basis could more nearly meet and offset individual monopsonistic cases. But even here the problem of determining—leaving aside the difficulty of obtaining—the "correct" minimum price for the resource remains.

Measures to Increase Mobility   Measures to increase resource mobility among alternative employments get directly at the causes of monopsony. Immobility of resources is thought by many economists to be most serious in labor markets; hence, our discussion will be centered on the labor resource. We shall present a few general lines of approach rather than specific and detailed programs. With regard to the labor resource, mobility among geographic areas and firms, horizontal mobility among occupations at the same skill level, and vertical occupational mobility to higher skill classifications will be of value in counteracting monopsony.

An efficient system of federal employment exchanges should provide one avenue of attack on labor immobility. An important function of such a system is the collection and dissemination of information regarding alternative employment opportunities. It should make data available to the entire labor force—including those in now isolated communities—with regard to high-wage, scarce-labor-supply areas, and give descriptions of the requisite skills for obtaining employment in such areas. In addition, the system should perform the more common function of bringing together job opportunities and workers seeking alternative jobs.

The educational system offers a second avenue of attack. It can increase both the vertical and horizontal mobility of labor resources. With regard to vertical mobility, the availability and use of educational opportunities can channel larger numbers of the younger generation toward higher-paying, higher-level occupations. By means of vocational and trade schools the educational system can provide older workers with training for upward movement through skill classifications. To increase horizontal mobility, vocational guidance can assist in steering the potential labor force away from lower-paying occupations toward those providing higher remuneration at approximately the same skill level. Additionally, adult education programs can furnish the retraining necessary to escape from particularly low-paying occupations that are no longer in demand.

Still a third line of attack is that of a limited amount of subsidization of worker migration out of areas characterized by monopsony, since one of the causes of immobility is lack of funds needed by workers to move into alternative employment areas. Subsidization of migration may occur in the form of government loans or outright grants of funds to assist in worker relocation.

The Concept of Mobility

A few observations regarding the meaning of mobility are in order so that no wrong impression be given. To some people a mobile labor force may imply a drifting one with a high job turnover rate—an undesirable social situation. Mobility, as the term is used in economics, does not mean a complete lack of ties to particular communities and social institutions; nor does it mean that all workers must be ready to pack up and move at the slightest provocation. The amount of actual movement necessary to prevent monopsony usually will be quite small. The possibility or likelihood of migration is the important factor. Also, there is at all times considerable change and turnover of the labor force—workers changing jobs, new workers entering the labor force, and old workers retiring. This constant change constitutes mobility. The primary problem is that of directing the mobility that already exists into economically desirable channels.

Applications

The empirical evidence of the following two cases demonstrate well the usefulness of the theory of resource pricing and employment.

The Minimum Wage in Practice[7]

The legal minimum wage rate, first introduced in 1938 as an integral part of the New Deal, is among the most pervasive of American social programs. With reference to Tables 16.3 and 16.4, we divide time into two eras. In the first, 1938 to 1960, the minimum wage rate increased from $0.25 to $1.00 per hour, but the number of workers in firms covered by the law expanded from only 43.4 percent of the nonagricultural work force to 53.1 percent. Industries in certain product categories were deliberately excluded from coverage, and within covered industries certain small firms were exempt unless their sales reached a given threshold. In the second era, 1961 to 1981, the minimum wage rate was increased from $1.00 to $3.35 per hour and, more important, coverage was expanded to almost 84 percent of the nonagricultural work force.

The 1938–60 Era   The likely consequences of a legal minimum wage rate have never been a mystery to economists. Owing to the law of demand, a wage floor that is imposed above the free-market rate and enforced by legislation should, if other conditions do not change simultaneously, cause a reduction in employment in the firms that are subject to coverage. Moreover, the reduction in employment in the covered sector will be larger the greater the elasticity of labor demand. The effect of the legislation in the first era can be illustrated with the diagrams of Figure 16.6. Although the wage floor is applied

FIGURE 16.6
Effects of a legally enforced minimum wage on covered and uncovered industries

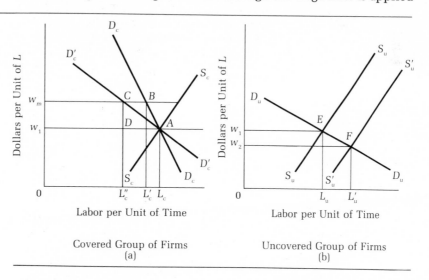

Covered Group of Firms
(a)

Uncovered Group of Firms
(b)

[7] This section is based on the excellent summary of the research on the effects of minimum wages by Finis Welch, *Minimum Wages: Issues and Evidence* (Washington, D.C.: American Enterprise Institute for Public Policy Research, 1978).

TABLE 16.3 The basic minimum wage and aggregate coverage, 1938–1981	Month/Year of Change in Minimum	Basic Minimum Changed to	Basic Minimum as a Percentage of Average (straight-time) Manufacturing Wage	Percentage of All Nonsupervisory Employees in Private, Nonagricultural Work Covered
	10/38	$0.25	41.7	43.4
	10/39	0.30	49.5	47.1
	10/45	0.40	42.1	55.4
	1/50	0.75	54.0	53.4
	3/56	1.00	52.9	53.1
	9/61	1.15	51.2	62.1
	9/63	1.25	52.7	62.1
	2/67	1.40	51.5	75.3
	2/68	1.60	55.6	72.6
	5/74	2.00	47.2	83.7
	1/75	2.10	45.1	83.3
	1/76	2.30	46.0	83.0
	1/78	2.65	48.4[a]	83.8[b]
	1/79	2.90	49.7[a]	83.8[b]
	1/80	3.10	49.9[a]	83.8[b]
	1/81	3.35	51.9[a]	83.8[b]

[a] Manufacturing wages are extrapolated, based on log-linear trend, 1965–1976. During this period wages grew 6.3 percent a year (R^2 for the trend line is 0.989).

[b] Coverage rate under 1977 amendment estimated by Employment Standards Administration. The 1977 amendment did not significantly alter the definition of covered jobs, although provisions for reductions in minimum size for necessary coverage will inflate these levels.

Source: Finis Welch, *Minimum Wages: Issues and Evidence,* Washington, D.C.: American Enterprise Institute for Public Policy Research, 1978, p. 3. © 1978, American Enterprise Institute for Public Policy Research.

TABLE 16.4 Estimated percentages of nonsupervisory workers covered by minimum wage laws by major industry: selected years, 1947–1976	Industry	1947–1960	1961–1966	1967–1968	1976
	Mining	99%	99%	99%	99%
	Contract construction	44	80	98	99
	Manufacturing	95	96	97	97
	Transportation and public utilities	88	95	97	98
	Wholesale trade	69	69	72	80
	Retail trade	3	33	49	72
	Finance, insurance, and real estate	74	74	74	76
	Services (excluding domestic)	19	22	63	72

Source: Finis Welch, *Minimum Wages: Issues and Evidence,* Washington, D.C.: American Enterprise Institute for Public Policy Research, 1978, p. 4. © 1978, American Enterprise Institute for Public Policy Research.

to the covered sector of Figure 16.6(a), the effects spill over to the uncovered sector of Figure 16.6(b).

Figure 16.6(a) shows a relatively low-wage group of firms that are initially in equilibrium at the free-market rate w_1 with the associated quantity of labor L_c. For simplicity we assume that all labor in the market is of equal quality so that it can be represented by a single demand schedule, either D_cD_c or $D'_cD'_c$. Now assume that a legal minimum rate is established at w_m. The law guarantees the minimum to all who can get jobs at that rate, but it does not guarantee jobs. The wage rate w_m brings about a reduction in the quantity of labor hired. The economic question of importance is the extent to which employment in the covered industries falls, and this depends upon the elasticity of demand for labor. We draw two possible demand curves in which $D'_cD'_c$ is more elastic than D_cD_c for each possible wage rate. The reduction in employment is $L_cL'_c$ if D_cD_c is the appropriate curve; but the reduction is the larger quantity $L_cL''_c$ if $D'_cD'_c$ is the demand curve.

Is demand likely to be relatively elastic for workers affected by the minimum wage? The elasticity of demand for labor generally has three major determinants. First, the elasticity tends to be larger the better the substitutes available for labor. Second, it tends to be larger the greater the elasticity of demand for the products for which the labor is employed. Third, it tends to be larger the greater the percentage of total costs that are accounted for by wages. All three of these suggest that labor demand curves are relatively elastic in the neighborhood of the minimum wage rate.

To test this hypothesis economists have investigated before-and-after employment in low-wage firms, industries, and regions each time the legal minimum wage has been increased, and found predictable results. For example, a study of employment in sawmills and clothing plants that made men's garments and seamless hosiery in the 1950s showed that all suffered reductions in employment after a hike in the minimum wage, and the low-wage plants had the largest reductions.[8] In a county-by-county study in Florida, the minimum wage increases of the 1950s caused twice the reduction in employment in the low-wage counties as in the relatively high-wage ones. Further, the larger the difference between the legal minimum wage and the previously prevailing market wage, the greater the drop in employment.[9] Also the low-wage firms having the largest difference between the new minimum wage and the previous free-

[8] J. M. Peterson, "Employment Effects of Minimum Wages, 1938–50," *Journal of Political Economy,* 65 (Oct. 1957), pp. 412–30.

[9] Marshall R. Colberg, "Minimum Wage Effects on Florida's Economic Development," *The Journal of Law and Economics,* 3 (Oct. 1960), pp. 106–17.

market wage effected the more extensive substitution of capital for labor resources each time the minimum wage increased.[10]

Rise in Minimum Wage Spurs Some Firms to Cut Work Hours and Hiring of Youths[11]

LOMBARD, Ill.—Last summer Janet Straka started work at the Steak n Shake restaurant here in this Chicago suburb at 9 a.m. to get ready for the 10 o'clock opening.

But in January the federal minimum wage rose to $2.65 an hour from $2.30. Steak n Shake, seeking to blunt the impact, decided to open an hour later, since there were few early customers anyway. Steak n Shake also cut the opening waitress's preparation time to 30 minutes. So Miss Straka, a school-teacher who works summers part-time at the hamburger chain, now starts work at 10:30 a.m., and her weekly earnings are down to about $36 from $40 last summer.

Her shortened workday shows one way in which the higher minimum wage is affecting employment in the U.S. There haven't been wholesale layoffs of low-wage workers, but some workers are putting in fewer hours on the job.

Another effect is that teen-agers, especially blacks, are having more trouble finding work as companies like Steak n Shake look for older, more-qualified workers likely to stay at a job longer. Hiring this type of worker is becoming easier because the combination of higher wages and more inflation is drawing more housewives and people like Miss Straka to work. The consumer also is affected; since last year, Steak n Shake's prices have risen 7%, partly because of higher costs of food, especially beef.

Hot Debate

Whether the minimum wage fuels unemployment and inflation has been hotly debated for years because its effects are so hard to isolate from other factors affecting the economy. Now the debate is heating up again. Federal Reserve Board Chairman G. William Miller and Treasury Secretary W. Michael Blumenthal both recently suggested that the next scheduled increase in the minimum wage, to $2.90 an hour in January, be postponed. Both cited the inflationary stimulus.

Their suggestion has drawn sharp retorts from both the AFL-CIO and Labor Secretary Ray Marshall. "No one cries inflation when interest rates on a car or house go up by half a point, but listen to them when the minimum wage is raised to the princely sum of $2.65 an hour," Mr. Marshall said recently. He also noted Labor Department figures showing that the economy added some

---

[10] David E. Kuan, "Minimum Wages, Factor Substitution, and the Marginal Producer," *Quarterly Journal of Economics*, 79 (Aug. 1965), pp. 478–86.

[11] Paul Ingrassia, "Rise in Minimum Wage Spurs Some Firms to Cut Work Hours and Hiring of Youths," *The Wall Street Journal*, 15 August 1978. Reprinted by permission of *The Wall Street Journal*, © Dow Jones & Company, Inc. 1978. All rights reserved.

1.6 million jobs since December (including 150,000 jobs for teen-agers). "These new jobs are a telling answer to those who claim that the minimum-wage laws put people on the unemployment lines," Mr. Marshall concluded.

Most economists, though, do contend that higher wages lead to higher prices, unless workers' productivity rises proportionately. And they feel sure that minimum-wage increases add to unemployment. "The question is how much they add," says Walter E. Williams, a Temple University economist who has studied the minimum wage for Congress's Joint Economic Committee. He says the increase in employment since December—and the drop in the nation's unemployment rate to the current 6.2% from 6.4%—would have been larger if the minimum wage hadn't risen. "The economy always adds some jobs during a period of growth," Mr. Williams observes.

Big Numbers Involved

The debate is more than academic. An estimated 4.6 million U.S. workers, more than 5% of the nation's work force, got a pay raise when the minimum wage was increased last January. In all, those workers are pocketing an extra $2 billion this year, and the Labor Department says 5.2 million workers will get another $2 billion next year when the $2.90 minimum takes effect. Beyond that, under a law passed last year, the hourly minimum is to rise to $3.10 in 1980 and to $3.35 in 1981. The increases also tend to raise wages of workers paid only slightly above the minimum and of low-wage workers not covered by the law (such as some farm workers and some household help).

The $79-billion-a-year fast-food and restaurant industry has plenty of minimum-wage workers, and it's clear that as the minimum increases, so do companies' efforts to cut the number of workers at a restaurant. Employes aren't flying out of restaurants like hamburgers off a grill, but productivity efforts are beginning to show results.

At the Lombard Steak n Shake, for instance, total employe hours worked each week actually trail a year ago, even though business is up. The amount of the decline varies from week to week, but total hours are generally down 10%. As well as opening an hour later, the restaurant is closing an hour earlier—at 11 p.m. during the week and at midnight on Fridays and Saturdays.

Some Shortcuts

To reduce work hours further, the restaurant has taken some shortcuts. The waitresses used to mix powdered coffee creamer with water for cream pots on each table. Now the pots have been replaced by individual packets of liquid coffee creamer, which don't require preparation. Likewise, sugar pourers on the tables are being replaced by paper packets. The chain still hand-slices pickles lengthwise, but now it uses fewer pickles for garnish to reduce slicing time.

All these maneuvers have helped the Steak n Shake at Lombard. In the 24 weeks ended last week, the restaurant's labor costs rose only 5% from a year earlier, against an increase of more than 15% in the minimum wage.

Steak n Shake also is trying to hire older workers; because they generally are more productive and tend to stay on the job longer, they reduce hiring and training costs. The Lombard store's 37 employes now average 21 years of age; a year ago there were 39 employes, and the average age was 18. The Indianapolis-based company as a whole employs about one-third fewer teenagers than a year ago, Thomas R. Delph, vice president, says.

The higher minimum wage is helping Steak n Shake attract older workers. Ironically, so is the higher inflation rate, itself partly a product of minimum-wage increases. Housewife Jane Andrews, for example, hadn't worked for 10 years until she started as a Steak n Shake waitress last year. "You always say you're going back to work to get out of the house, but that extra money really helps," Mrs. Andrews says. "I know other women who are going back to work to help keep up with inflation."

Young Workers Hurt

As a result, job opportunities are reduced for teen-agers, who usually are less qualified than adults, and especially for black youths, who tend to be the least qualified. The unemployment rate in the 16-to-19 age bracket now stands at 16.3%, and for blacks of that age it is 37%. The minimum-wage law, Prof. Williams says, makes companies "less willing to hire and train the least-productive employee, which includes teen-agers and particularly black teen-agers."

That's exactly what's happening in five Dairy Queen stores in Decatur, Ill. The owner, Stacy Smith, believes that students with higher grades tend to be better workers; so when the minimum wage went up, he raised his hiring requirements. He now looks for at least a "B" grade average. As a result, Mr. Smith says, fewer blacks qualify. This year only six of his 75 student workers are black, down from 10 of 75 a year ago.

Mr. Smith also has begun using another cost-cutting tool. By law, employers can get Labor Department permission to hire students to work up to 20 hours a week (more in the summer) at 85% of the minimum wage, provided that their work hours don't exceed 10% of a company's total. "I didn't see the need to take advantage of this before the minimum wage went up," Mr. Smith says.

Red Lobster's Changes

Like Steak n Shake, General Mills Inc. has cut morning preparation time at its Red Lobster Inns. The restaurants still open at 11 a.m., but preparation now begins at 9 a.m. instead of 8 a.m. Red Lobster also cut restaurant crew meetings to twice a month from once a week; waitresses and waiters are paid to attend the meetings, where they can air gripes, learn new procedures and the like. In addition, Red Lobster thinned its supervisory staff to one supervisor for every four restaurants; each supervisor used to oversee only three inns.

Another company, International Multifoods Corp., has pared the work force 7% in its nine restaurants by combining jobs. Regular full-time employes now do some work, such as preparing salads, that used to be handled by part-timers. So even though the minimum wage has risen—as have sales at the company's Boston Sea Party and T. Butcherblock resaurants—the restaurants' payroll costs are "about even" with last year, Multifoods says.

Some fast-food and restaurant companies are trying to change their hiring patterns. McDonald's Corp. is seeking to attract older workers to reduce crew turnover, but "it's too early for us to see any trends," a spokesman says. A similar move by Pillsbury Co.'s Burger King also hasn't been going on long enough to pass judgment.

Self-Service Trend

A trend to self-service restaurants is clear, however. Eliminating waiters and waitresses is especially important to employers because restaurants are faced with stiffer "tip-credit" requirements as well as the minimum-wage increase. Currently, restaurants must pay table help only half the minimum wage, and tips are credited with providing the other half. But next year, employers must pay table help 55% of the minimum wage, and in 1980 the requirement will rise to 60%.

General Mills says it is accelerating new openings of its self-service York Steak House restaurants and slowing down Red Lobster openings (the company won't provide figures). Also, General Mills is testing a new beef and seafood restaurant called Hanahan's and designed around the self-service concept.

"Self-service is part of our strategic planning," says Eugene E. Woolley, executive vice president for restaurants. "It's a long-term effect of these minimum-wage increases."

The above article from *The Wall Street Journal* gives an almost textbooklike description of the effects that the $2.65 minimum wage had on employment in the fast-food industry in 1978. Owners of these restaurants shifted their help from teenagers to older employees who were less mobile, reduced the number of hours worked by many employees, tended to change from fast-food to self-service type restaurants that had relatively lower labor costs, and cut back on foods and services that were relatively labor intensive—for example, they served fewer sliced pickles on hamburgers. Each observation is consistent with the adjustments that one would expect from effective minimum wage rate changes in low-wage, competitive firms.

We return to Figure 16.6 to consider what happens to people who must work fewer hours or take other jobs as a result of the higher minimum wage. In Figure 16.6(a) the persons in group $0L_c''$ who continue to hold jobs in the covered sector after the minimum wage has been raised will gain the amount w_mCDw_1 over and above their former wage payments, but the position of the people in group $L_c''L_c$ is more difficult to determine. Basically they have three options.[12]

First, they could continue to seek employment in the covered sector in a lotterylike, queuing process for the reduced number of jobs that are now available there. Searching for these jobs entails costs, and each person will have to make calculations a priori weighing the expected search costs versus the probabilistic gains from obtaining one of the higher-paying jobs.

Second, after a period of unemployment while searching for jobs in the covered sector, they could cease their search for work and withdraw from the labor force. Persons making this decision are no longer "unemployed," as that term is defined by the U.S. Department of Labor, and are therefore not counted in the ranks of the unemployed. Consequently, we cannot equate the reduction in employment $L_c''L_c$ with a rise in unemployment as reflected in official statistics reported by the U.S. Department of Labor. For this reason, the official statistics understate the real extent of unemployment that higher minimum wages cause.[13] We can measure with confidence only the reduction in employment.

The third alternative for people who end up in the group $L_c''L_c$ is to leave the covered sector for jobs in the uncovered sector. This is shown in Figure 16.6(b). The supply of labor in the uncovered sector increases from S_uS_u to $S_u'S_u'$ and the wage rate declines from w_1 to w_2. The lower wage rate gives firms an incentive to hire more labor until the marginal revenue product of labor once again is equal to the market wage rate. The new equilibrium quantity of labor is L_u'. The rise in employment in the uncovered sector, in the amount L_uL_u', will be equal to the reduction in employment in the covered sector, in the amount $L_c''L_c$ only if no one chooses to become unemployed or to leave the labor force.

The economic inefficiency caused by minimum wage rates is now apparent. The marginal revenue product of labor in the covered sector, w_m, is greater than the marginal revenue product of labor in the uncovered sector at w_2. There is a strong presumption that the same relationship exists between values of marginal product. Inequality among values of marginal product means that society has

---

[12] Jacob Mincer, "Unemployment Effects of Minimum Wages," *Journal of Political Economy*, vol. 84, no. 4, part 2 (Aug. 1976), pp. S87–S104.

[13] The official statistics will overstate the rise in unemployment if people who formerly were not looking for work decide to reenter the labor force and search for jobs because they know that any job they find will pay a higher wage than previously, owing to the hike in the legal minimum. In any case, the official United States statistics are unreliable as a gauge to the effects of the minimum wage. Ibid.

suffered a reduction in real net national product. A higher value of marginal product in the covered sector has been given up in exchange for a lower value of marginal product in the uncovered sector. Society cannot achieve maximum welfare since the allocation of labor resources in the economy is inefficient. Inefficiency will be least serious if the $L_c''L_c$ units of labor losing jobs in the covered sector move to the uncovered sector. The inefficiency will be larger if some drop out of the labor force instead of taking jobs in the sector that is exempt. The waste is larger in the latter case because a dropout from the labor force yields society a negative value of marginal product.

Figure 16.6 is broadly consistent with what economists learned about the employment consequences of the minimum wage during the 1938–60 era when the coverage was relatively narrow. As economist Finis Welch put it, there was an enormous "run from cover."[14] This movement is apparent from Table 16.5. Teenagers, who are usually less skilled and lower paid, gradually shifted out of the covered manufacturing sector each time the legal minimum wage was increased, and moved into such uncovered industries as services and the wholesale and retail trades. This movement would tend to reduce

TABLE 16.5
Percentage of employed teenagers working in manufacturing, wholesale and retail trade, and services: 1930, 1940, and 1955.

Industry	1930	1940	1955
Teenagers 14–17 years old			
Manufacturing	42%	26%	17%
Wholesale and retail trade	21	28	45
Services	22	36	33
Teenagers 18–19 years old			
Manufacturing	39	30	28
Wholesale and retail trade	18	26	31
Services	22	28	22

Source: Finis Welch, "Minimum Wage Legislation in the United States," Economic Inquiry, vol. 12, no. 3 (Sept. 1974), p. 298.

wage rates in the uncovered sector and produce the less efficient resource allocation described earlier. The minimum wage has also increased the vulnerability of teenagers to recessions. From 1954–68 teenagers were about four times more likely than adults to lose their jobs during an economic downturn. Marvin Kosters and Finis Welch concluded in 1972 that "minimum wage legislation has undoubtedly resulted in higher wages for some of the relatively low productivity workers who were able to obtain employment than these workers would have received in its absence. The cost in terms of lost em-

[14] Welch, Minimum Wages, p. 29.

ployment opportunities and cyclical vulnerability of jobs, however, has apparently been borne most heavily by teenagers."[15]

A similar conclusion was drawn by Yale Brozen after studying the employment of household workers.[16] Employment in this industry usually displays a countercyclical pattern. When the economy is strong, people tend to avoid household jobs in favor of better-paying work elsewhere; but the reverse applies when the economy is in recession. This inverse correlation between economic fluctuations and employment in domestic work is broken, however, each time the legal minimum wage is raised. This is because household work has always been an uncovered activity. Domestic wage rates also tend to decline each time the legal minimum wage goes up.

The 1961–81 Era   The second era in minimum wage legislation, during which the legal minimum rate was increased and its coverage expanded sharply, can also be analyzed with the help of Figure 16.6(a). The more firms and industries covered by the legislation, the fewer "safety valves" there are available to accommodate the reduction in employment that minimum wage rate increases cause in the covered sector. For example, Finis Welch found that between 1961 and 1967 teenage employment in retail trade declined when coverage in this sector was increased from 30 percent to 58 percent.[17] But the precise extent of the fall in teenage employment, owing to post-1960 increases in the legal minimum wage rate and the expansion in its coverage, is difficult to measure. In excess of a half-dozen studies have been done on the post-1960 era, but they have produced diverse results as authors used different data bases and slightly different techniques. Still, several generalizations are possible.

One of the most important findings is that teenagers are not the only group adversely affected by the minimum wage.[18] Teenagers held only about one third of the low-wage jobs in 1973. The remaining two thirds were held by people of all ages, with those over 65 being an important group. Increases in the minimum wage rate seem to cause reduction in employment for males between the ages of 20 and 24, males over 65, and females over 20. Moreover, higher minimum wage rates also cause people who cannot find work to withdraw from the labor force rather than continuing to search for the fewer jobs available in the covered sector. A reduction in full-time work tends to occur with only a partly offsetting rise in part-time work. For the economy, working hours decline relatively just as with

[15]   Marvin Kosters and Finis Welch, "The Effects of Minimum Wages on the Distribution of Changes in Aggregate Employment," *American Economic Review*, 62 (June 1972), p. 330.

[16]   Yale Brozen, "Minimum Wage Rates and Household Workers," *The Journal of Law and Economics*, 5 (Oct. 1962), pp. 103–109.

[17]   Welch, *Minimum Wages*, p. 32.

[18]   Ibid., pp. 34–38.

the fast-food firms of *The Wall Street Journal* article. Altogether it is likely that some 10 to 15 percent of the labor force is affected by the minimum wage law, and most of those involved are low-wage labor. The minimum wage makes some persons better off, but at the same time it makes others worse off. Thus, Finis Welch claims that "the minimum wage serves only as a tax from the poor to the poor."[19]

Monopsony in Professional Baseball[20]

Professional baseball players officially were "liberated" in 1975— liberated from a monopsonistic restriction in their contracts that indentured them to the employers holding their contracts for the duration of their athletic careers. The restriction, dating back to 1879, survived for seventy-six years and might have endured indefinitely had it not been for a strategic miscalculation by the club owners. This era in the baseball players' labor market has been carefully studied by several economists and represents a "textbook case" of monopsony.

The Reserve Clause   The incentives of baseball clubs to collude on wages were enormous owing to the players' large *economic rents*— the difference between the values of their skills in baseball as compared with their next best employments. Players like Ruth, Feller, Spahn, Koufax, and Mays had superb skills which made them worth a great deal in baseball, but the next best alternative for most of them would have been a relatively low-wage job. Thus the clubs, by suppressing wage competition, could capture for themselves some of the economic rents that would otherwise have gone to the players.

The baseball players' labor market actually consisted of three separate markets, depending upon each individual player's contractual status. Players who had never signed a contract with any team in organized baseball, usually youngsters out of high school, were called *free agents*. They were free to sell their services to whichever club bid highest, and the clubs competed in this market by offering *bonuses* to those signing up. Bonuses were usually modest and represented the portion of the player's economic rent that he retained.[21]

Once a player signed a contract his market options changed drastically. All players were required to sign a *uniform contract* that was drawn up by organized baseball and used by all clubs. The

---

[19]   Ibid., p. 25.

[20]   These materials are based on Simon Rottenberg, "The Baseball Players' Labor Market," *Journal of Political Economy*, vol. 64, no. 3 (June 1956), pp. 242–58; David S. Davenport, "Collusive Competition in Major League Baseball—Its Theory and Institutional Development," *The American Economist*, vol. 14, no. 2 (Fall 1969), pp. 6–30; and Gerald W. Scully, "Pay and Performance in Major League Baseball," *American Economic Review*, vol. 64, no. 6 (December 1974), pp. 915–30.

[21]   Rottenberg, "Baseball Labor Market," p. 244, notes that bonuses during the 1940s and 1950s of as much as $100,000 were not unknown, but usually were much smaller.

contract had a one-year duration, and it could be terminated unilaterally by the club. But its key feature was a clause that *reserved* the latter's unilateral right to renew the contract for another year at a wage established by the club, subject to the condition that next year's salary could not be less than 75 percent of the current year's figure. In addition, there was and still is an absolute minimum annual salary. This arrangement tied each player's baseball services to the club with which he initially signed, and it gave the club an exclusive right to deal with the player. Some athletes occasionally bargained with their club by threatening to quit baseball altogether unless they were paid higher wages. Such "holdouts" gained attention on the sports pages, but the club's "final" offer would signal that the player either could accept it or withdraw from baseball to his next best employment. In fact, very few athletes withdrew.

The third labor market consisted of *player contracts*. The uniform contract gave the club the unilateral right to transfer the player to one of its own minor league teams, sell his contract to another team, or trade it for the contract of another player(s). Players whose contract was sold or traded were required by the uniform contract rules to report for work to the acquiring club within seventy-two hours. By acquiring the player's contract, the new club also gained the reserved right to renew the contract every year at a noncompetitive wage. Clubs seeking to purchase or trade for a player's contract could deal only with the club that owned the contract. *Tampering*, or negotiating directly with players, was prohibited by general agreement among clubs, and the Commissioner of Baseball would levy a substantial fine on an offender. Club owners took tampering so seriously that some were, and still are, unwilling to discuss even with sportswriters their plans to deal for player contracts without first opening formal negotiations with the cognizant club.

As Gerald W. Scully put it, "The (reserve clause) restriction grants some monopsony power to the owner and the exercise of that power results in a divergence between *MRP* and salary. The marginal revenue product continues to be an essential factor in player salary determination, but under the reserve clause, players and owners share the player's *MRP*."[22] This portion of the monopsony gain equals the economic rent that is lost by the players, which could be capitalized into the prices that clubs could obtain by trading or selling contracts to other teams. The bonus, as we noted earlier, is the portion of the player's economic rent that he retains.

The Extent of Exploitation Ideally, each baseball club would use its monopsony power in the labor market to engage in salary discrimination in the same manner that other firms use their monopoly power in

[22] Scully, "Pay and Performance," p. 916.

the product market to engage in price discrimination. Each player logically should be presented a take-it-or-leave-it offer reflecting his next best alternative, his outside income from product endorsements and other pecuniary activities, and changes in his marginal revenue product to the team. However, it is difficult for many monopsonists to arrive at this lowest possible salary offer. Moreover, to reduce salaries to such a level could destroy team morale, result in a poorer season win-loss record, and hence reduce gate receipts. Thus, we should expect that the salaries of players would exceed somewhat their next best earning possibilities. This expectation is clearly supported by data from a variety of sources.

The reserve clause was first introduced in the National League in late 1879 after a season of intense wage competition among teams.[23] David S. Davenport reports that about 68 percent of one of the team's total expenses in 1878 went for team salaries, but that it had declined to 54 percent in 1880. From 1883 to 1950 the gross receipts of baseball clubs rose by eighty times the initial level, but player salaries increased only seven times. Increases in baseball salaries also have lagged behind the trend increases in salaries in motion pictures and other recreation industries.[24] The following excerpt from Davenport's article[25] offers a back-of-the-envelope calculation of the MRP versus the wage paid to Sandy Koufax, the ace pitcher of the Los Angeles Dodgers during the 1960s. He estimates that the Dodgers obtained about $500,000 of the annual economic rent that would have accrued to Koufax under a regime of competitive wages—an amount about four times his highest salary.

> It is difficult to determine if a player is economically exploited. I made an attempt with one particular player—Sandy Koufax. I chose Koufax because as a starting pitcher, he only plays in one quarter or fifth of all games, providing an opportunity to assess individual drawing power and to try to determine whether he was "exploited." . . . I made a "guesstimate" of the value of Koufax's MRP by comparing the attendance at Dodger games when he pitched with that at games when he did not. I also made a rough estimate of his indirect contribution by comparing the attendances and overall playing records in two consecutive years—one in which he played and the next in which he was retired. The results . . . are dramatic, although admittedly inexact. Koufax in 1966 drew an average of 6,000 more customers per game in nineteen games at home and 7,000 more in nineteen road games. Tak-

[23] Rottenberg, "Baseball Labor Market," p. 247.

[24] Davenport, "Collusive Competition in Baseball," p. 17.

[25] Reprinted from David S. Davenport, "Collusive Competition in Major League Baseball—Its Theory and Institutional Development," The American Economist, vol. 14, no. 2 (Fall 1969), pp. 17–18.

ing $2.00 as the average ticket price and figuring the Dodgers' percentage of receipts to be 80% at home and 20% on the road, the additional revenue from games which Koufax started is $236,178. Since his salary was reported to be $120,000, later said to be $130,000, it appears that Koufax's wage was far below the value of his MP. But this $236,000 is in no rational sense the extent of the Dodgers' marginal revenue from Koufax. In 1966, he won 27 and lost 9, leading the Dodgers to the pennant with a 95-67 record for a winning percentage of .586. Koufax retired. The following season, the Dodgers finished in eighth place with a record of 73-89 and a .451 percentage. For 36 games, the number pitched by Koufax in 1966, the average Dodger pitcher (a .451 winner) would have won 16 and lost 20.

The difference between this record and that of Koufax in '66 is eleven victories and losses, or half the difference between the club's season records in 1966 and 1967. The difference in Dodger home attendance alone was 953,430. One might argue that with Koufax pitching, the improved playing record would recover half the attendance difference. I think this is a high estimate, as I suspect club attendance increases at an accelerated rate as the club gets closer to first place. And there is probably some duplication from the direct analysis above. But if we only credit his pitching with recovering, say, a fourth of the attendance difference, he would increase Dodger home attendance by 238,360 and revenues (attendance times $1.60, the Dodger share of the $2.00 average ticket) $381,376. His total marginal revenue, then, could be guesstimated at $617,554.

Compared with Koufax's salary of $130,000, the Dodgers received almost $500,000 of his marginal revenue. And Koufax did not get his $130,000 through his own bargaining power alone. . . . Koufax got his $130,000 only through a bargaining coalition with fellow star pitcher, Don Drysdale. The importance of their combined talent to Dodger playing fortunes was so high that the Dodgers were forced to increase their offer, especially since Koufax and Drysdale were not in the position of having nowhere else to go but had already signed movie contracts. Even with the help of this added bargaining strength, Koufax was exploited for an estimated $500,000. It is reasonable to argue that this was not all exploitation. . . . Other portions could be assigned to interest on the original investment in the franchise, rent from the use of the club's own stadium, return on the club's favorable franchise location, and part of the salaries for other players who through cooperation contributed to [his] value. But it remains most doubtful that Sandy Koufax came anywhere close to realizing the value of his marginal product.

Gerald W. Scully's research shows how sophisticated statistical techniques, when cleverly applied to basic economic concepts, can yield a striking estimate of the monopsony gain in baseball.[26] To do this Scully had to compare salaries with *MRPs* for players of different qualities. Organized baseball keeps extensive historical data on player productivities (for example, batting averages or strikeouts), and salaries are announced publicly, although there is no assurance that they are accurate. Scully estimated the productivities of players based on the productivities of entire teams. This required a comparison between each team's revenues from attendance and broadcasting on the one hand and the team's win-loss percentage in that season on the other. Using data for 1968–69, Scully estimated that a one-point rise in the team's win-loss percentage would increase revenues by $10,330.

Table 16.6 shows Scully's estimates of the strength of the wage collusion. The difference between his estimates of gross versus net marginal revenue product reflect his attempt to remove the costs of training, operating farm clubs, and search activities that clubs engage in as they develop players. Thus his comparisons between net *MRP* and salary yield his estimate of the gain to clubs from wage collusion only. The gains are large and are probably understated because Scully was generous in his estimate of the training and search costs—the difference between gross *MRP* and net *MRP*. Based on different assumptions about career lengths and productivities not shown in Table 16.6, Scully concluded that "average players receive salaries equal to about 11 percent of their gross and about 20 percent of their net marginal revenue products. Star players receive about 15 percent of their net marginal revenue products. . . . On the whole, therefore, it seems that the economic loss to professional ballplayers under the reserve clause is of a considerable magnitude."[27] Interestingly enough, Scully's estimate of the portion of Sandy Koufax's economic rent that the Dodgers obtained, based on these complex statistical techniques, was only about $125,000 (or 25 percent) more than the estimate given by David Davenport using a simple arithmetic procedure.[28]

Baseball's Defense of the Reserve Clause   The baseball club owners long had argued that the reserve clause was necessary to equalize the distribution of player talent within the league and to prevent a single team from dominating league play. Without the clause, the club owners claimed, the financially strongest teams—usually those in the largest metropolitan areas—could buy up all the best players, win

[26]   Scully, "Pay and Performance," pp. 920–21.

[27]   Ibid., p. 929.

[28]   Ibid., p. 922.

TABLE 16.6 Scully	Performance[a] SA or SW	Gross Marginal Revenue Product[b]	Net Marginal Revenue Product	Salary
	Hitters			
	270	$213,800	$85,500	$31,700
	290	230,000	101,700	34,200
	310	245,200	116,900	36,800
	330	261,400	133,100	39,300
	350	277,500	149,200	41,900
	370	292,700	164,400	44,400
	390	308,900	180,600	47,000
	410	325,000	196,700	49,600
	430	340,200	211,900	52,200
	450	356,400	228,100	54,800
	470	372,600	244,300	57,400
	490	387,800	259,500	60,000
	510	403,900	275,600	62,700
	530	420,100	291,800	65,300
	550	435,300	307,000	67,900
	570	451,400	323,100	70,600
	Pitchers			
	1.60	$185,900	$57,600	$31,100
	1.80	209,200	80,900	34,200
	2.00	232,400	104,100	37,200
	2.20	255,700	127,400	40,200
	2.40	278,900	150,600	43,100
	2.60	302,200	173,900	46,000
	2.80	325,400	197,100	48,800
	3.00	348,600	220,300	51,600
	3.20	371,900	243,600	54,400
	3.40	395,100	266,800	57,100
	3.60	418,400	290,100	59,800

[a] SA is the lifetime slugging average of hitters, and differs from the "batting" averages that are usually calculated in that the slugging average takes into account the number of bases advanced on each hit rather than simply the number of hits. SW is the lifetime strikeout-to-walk ratio of pitchers, the clearest measure of the productivity of pitchers in isolation from the rest of the team. The average life of hitters is assumed by Scully to be 8 years and of pitchers 6 years.

[b] The estimated average cost of player development and training is $128,300 per year. This is the difference between the column of gross marginal revenue products and the column of net marginal revenue products.

Source: Gerald W. Scully, "Pay and Performance in Major League Baseball," *The American Economic Review*, vol. 64, no. 6 (Dec. 1974), p. 923.

pennants perpetually, and wreck the value of franchises in other cities.

The fallacy of this argument was exposed in 1956 in a classic article on baseball economies by Simon Rottenberg, from which an excerpt is reprinted here.[29]

> Is it clear that the reserve rule is necessary to achieve more or less equal quality of play among teams? Assume that teams are distributed among locations, as they are in fact, so that the revenues of some are very much larger than those of others. Assume a free players' labor market, in which players may accept the offer of the highest bidder and teams may make offers without restraint.
>
> At first sight, it may appear that the high-revenue teams will contract all the stars, leaving the others only the dregs of the supply; that the distribution of players among teams will become very unequal; that contests will become less uncertain; and that consumer interest will flag and attendance fall off. On closer examination, however, it can be seen that this process will be checked by the law of diminishing returns, operating concurrently with each team's strategic avoidance of diseconomies of scale.
>
> Professional team competitions are different from other kinds of business ventures. If a seller of shoes is able to capture the market and to cause other sellers of shoes to suffer losses and withdraw, the surviving competitor is a clear gainer. But in baseball no team can be successful unless its competitors also survive and prosper sufficiently so that the differences in the quality of play among teams are not "too great."
>
> If the size of a baseball team is thought of as the number of players under contract to it, each player being weighted by some index of his quality, then diseconomies of scale set in at some point when a team too far outstrips its competitors, and they become larger in proportion to the size of the differences.
>
> Two teams opposed to each other in play are like two firms producing a single product. The product is the game, weighted by the revenues derived from its play. With game admission prices given, the product is the game, weighted by the number of paying customers who attend. When 30,000 attend, the output is twice as large as when 15,000 attend. In one sense, the teams compete; in another, they combine in a single firm in which the success of each branch requires that it be not "too much" more efficient than the other. If it is, output falls.
>
> A baseball team, like any other firm, produces its product by combining factors of production. Consider the two teams engaged in a contest to be collapsed into a single firm, producing as output games, weighted by the revenue derived from admission fees. Let the players of one team be one factor and all others (management,

[29] Reprinted from Simon Rottenberg, "The Baseball Players' Labor Market," *Journal of Political Economy*, vol. 64, no. 3 (June 1956), pp. 254–55, by permission of The University of Chicago Press. © 1956 by The University of Chicago.

transportation, ball parks, and the players of the other team), another. *The quantity of the factor—players—is measured by making the appropriate adjustment for differential qualities among players, so that a man who hits safely in 35 per cent of his times at bat counts as more than one who hits safely only 20 per cent of the time. Given the quantity of the other factors, the total product curve of the factor—players of one team—will have the conventional shape; it will slope upward as the "quantity" of this factor is increased, reach a peak, and then fall. It will not pay to increase this factor without limit. Beyond some point—say, when a team already has three .350 hitters—it will not pay to employ another .350 hitter. If a team goes on increasing the quantity of the factor, players, by hiring additional stars, it will find that the total output—that is, admission receipts—of the combined firms (and, therefore, of its own) will rise at a less rapid rate and finally will fall absolutely. At some point, therefore, a first star player is worth more to poor Team B than, say, a third star to rich Team A. At this point, B is in a position to bid players away from A in the market. A's behavior is not a function of its bank balance. It does what it calculates it is worthwhile to do; and the time comes when, in pursuing the strategy of its own gains, it is worthwhile, whatever the size of its cash balance, to forego the services of an expert player and see him employed by another team.*

The wealthy teams will usually prefer winning to losing. If they do, they will prefer winning by close margins to winning by wide ones. If their market behavior is consistent with this objective—that is, if they behave like rational maximizers—playing talent will be more or less equally distributed among teams.

It does not require collusion to bring about this result. It is not senseless to expect it to be produced by a free labor market in which each team is separately engaged in gainful behavior. The position of organized baseball that a free market, given the unequal distribution of revenue, will result in the engrossment of the most competent players by the wealthy teams is open to some question. It seems, indeed, to be true that a market in which freedom is limited by a reserve rule such as that which now governs the baseball labor market distributes players among teams about as a free market would.

Rottenberg argues that teams have an incentive to be balanced relatively evenly because attendance receipts are maximized by barely winning a pennant, not by mopping up the league. He uses the concept of diminishing returns to make his point. Rottenberg demonstrates in the excerpt that the distribution of playing talent around the league will be the same with the reserve clause as without it, although the incomes of the clubs relative to those of the players will be larger with the clause. David S. Davenport has shown that the effects of the reserve clause have been just the opposite from the clubs' stated intention:

> In practice, the reserve clause has made possible what it was theoretically designed to prevent—it has allowed dominant clubs to control player talent and competition through such practices as the farm system and the buying of player contracts, while the control and lowering of cost curves for labor have allowed weaker clubs to survive. An empirical look at the competition supposedly promoted is indicative of the failure of a policy that does not attack the problem source. Between 1920 and 1968, the rich market area Yankees have won 29 American League flags in 48 seasons. In the National League, three teams—St. Louis, . . . and the rich market area New York-San Francisco Giants and Brooklyn-Los Angeles Dodgers—have won 33 of 48 pennants.[30]

Rottenberg's analysis is consistent with the evidence that Davenport gathered.

Competition Replaces Monopsony Baseball, for one reason or another, has always enjoyed an antitrust immunity. Initially that immunity was established by a 1922 case in which the Supreme Court employed an archaic definition of interstate commerce that removed baseball "games" from the ambit of the Sherman Act. Although the Court's definition of interstate commerce was broadened over time, Congress never intervened to remove the original immunity granted baseball clubs. In Curt Flood's challenge of the reserve clause, the Supreme Court in 1972 refused to overturn it on grounds that although Congress realized the inconsistency between baseball's immunity and the general antitrust policy, the legislature deliberately chose to maintain the inconsistency.

The Baseball Players Association never attacked the reserve clause through a strike. They obtained increases in the minimum salary paid to players from the $7,500 level that prevailed in the early 1950s to $30,000 in the early 1970s. The Association also strove for better pensions and grievance procedures that would benefit all players.

In 1973 the clubs acceded to a request of the players to allow outside arbitration of a broad range of contractual disputes. This was a major blunder. Within two years Andy Messersmith mounted a challenge of the reserve clause on the ground that it ought to apply *for only one renewal year* rather than in perpetuity at the discretion of the club. Defending the reserve clause with the same "equal distribution" arguments that Simon Rottenberg's article debunked, the

---

[30] Davenport, "Collusive Competition in Baseball," p. 9.

clubs adamantly refused to negotiate with the players over this issue and demanded that the arbitrator give an immediate all-or-nothing answer. On December 23, 1975, impartial arbitrator Peter Seitz ruled that the reserve clause was indeed a fit subject for negotiation between the clubs and the players, an outcome that was upheld on each of two occasions in which the clubs appealed the ruling to federal courts. Organized baseball had lost the reserve clause even though its antitrust exemption was still intact! Mr. Seitz, for his part, was fired by the clubs.[31]

Within a year the clubs and the players had reached the type of agreement that Seitz's ruling required. Briefly, the players could become free agents after six years of play, and players after five years could demand to be traded. They could veto any six clubs they did not want to be traded to. Any player taking either step would have to wait an additional five years before asking to be traded again. This was a collective bargaining compromise in which the players got less than complete freedom of contract on an annual basis and the owners gave up on the reserve clause for fear the players would strike.[32]

The effects of the Seitz ruling were dramatic. Bidding for the initial group of twenty-four free agents occurred in a New York hotel in November 1976. The owners spent a total of $23 million. Reggie Jackson won the sweepstakes with $3 million for his new contract. Gene Autry, owner of the California Angels, put down $5.2 million for three players. Charlie Finley, owner of the Oakland "A's" and whose controversial contracts with several of "his" players—mainly Catfish Hunter—may have led to the challenge of the reserve clause,[33] apparently emerged from the bidding room in a state of gloom. He said, "This is the worst thing that's ever happened to baseball. It was like a den of thieves in there . . . everyone trying to cut one another's throats (sic). It's like having someone come in your house and snap up all your children. I feel I was contributing to the demise of baseball. I don't have the money to get into the bidding but then I don't have an alternative either."[34] Bowie Kuhn, Commissioner of Baseball, observed: "That the weaker clubs are trying to improve through this system is gratifying. And it may be that we are going to see the beginning of a process where the stronger clubs will be outbid by the weaker clubs. The important concept of preserving some sort of balance will be benefited by the process. . . ."[35] This observa-

[31] Jerome Holtzman, "Summation of Year's Activities," *Official Baseball Guide—1976* (St. Louis: The Sporting News, 1976), pp. 283–92.

[32] Ron Rapoport, "Baseball's Free Agent Jitters,'" *Los Angeles Times*, 23 November 1976.

[33] Ross Newhan, "Baseball's Golden Era," *Los Angeles Times*, 6 December 1976.

[34] Ross Newhan, "Baseball's Free Agent Scramble Is On," *Los Angeles Times*, 5 November 1976.

[35] Newhan, "Baseball's Golden Era."

tion was, of course, 180 degrees away from the old "equal distribution" argument that the clubs had used to defend the reserve clause.

By 1980 the results of the new competition were plain. At the
end of 1979 more than 100 players had changed club uniforms since
1975,[36] and the average player's salary had increased from $51,000 in
1976 to between $130,000 and $150,000 in 1980.[37] Salaries also had
risen for players who had not yet become free agents. In November
1980, Dodger left-fielder Dusty Baker signed a five-year contract with
the Dodgers for $4 million after eight months of negotiations and just
a few minutes before the moment that he was scheduled to become a
free agent.[38] Baseball's antitrust immunity was still intact, but it was
not worth much anymore.

Summary

The principles of resource pricing and employment in situations
other than pure competition are a modification of the principles established in the preceding chapter. Monopoly in product markets
alters the nature of individual firm demand curves for resources.
Monopsony in the purchase of resources alters the nature of the resource supply curve faced by the firm.

The monopolistic firm employing several variable resources
must determine the least-cost resource combinations for various possible outputs and also the profit-maximizing quantities of variable
resources to use. The least-cost combination for a given product output is the one at which the marginal physical product per dollar's
worth of one resource is equal to the marginal physical product per
dollar's worth of every other resource used. To maximize profits, the
firm must use both a least-cost combination and the correct absolute
amounts of each resource. Resources must be used so that

$$\frac{MPP_a}{p_a} = \frac{MPP_b}{p_b} = \cdots = \frac{MPP_n}{p_n} = \frac{1}{MC_x} = \frac{1}{MR_x}.$$

Monopoly in product markets is said to result in monopolistic
exploitation of resources, since the resource price equals its marginal
revenue product for the firm and is less than the value of its marginal product for the economy as a whole.

The market price and the employment level of a resource are
determined simultaneously. Where monopoly occurs in product

[36] Frederick C. Klein, "Baseball Is Prospering Despite Shifts Caused by New 'Free Agents'," *The
Wall Street Journal*, 4 April, 1979.

[37] Mike Littwin, "The Free-Agent Draft: Baseball's No-Star Wars V," *Los Angeles Times*, 13
November 1980.

[38] Mike Littwin, "Baker Signs 5-Year Dodger Contract," *Los Angeles Times*, 11 November 1980.

markets, marginal revenue product of each variable resource used must be equal to its price if profits are to be maximized. If the monopolist uses only one variable resource, the marginal revenue product curve of the resource is the firm's demand curve for it. If several variable resources are used, internal or firm effects of price changes in any given resource must be taken into account in determining the firm's demand curve for it.

The market demand curve for a resource is obtained by summing the quantities of it that all firms will employ at each possible price, whether those firms operate as monopolists or as pure competitors in selling products. Resource price is determined by the conditions of market demand and market supply. As the market price is established, the firm adjusts its employment of the resource to the level at which the marginal revenue product equals the resource price. The market employment level is the summation of individual firm employment levels.

Monopsony means a single buyer of a particular resource; hence, the monopsonistic firm faces a resource supply curve that slopes upward to the right. It also faces a marginal resource cost curve that lies above the supply curve. The firm maximizes profits by employing the quantity of the resource that equates its marginal revenue product to its marginal resource cost. The marginal resource cost and the marginal revenue product of the resource exceed the resource price at the profit-maximizing level of employment, thus resulting in monopsonistic exploitation of the resource.

Suggested Readings

Cartter, A. M., and Marshall, F. R. *Labor Economics*. Homewood, Ill.: Richard D. Irwin, 1967, Chap. 10.

Fellner, William. *Modern Economic Analysis*. New York: McGraw-Hill, 1960, Chap. 19.

Rees, Albert. *The Economics of Work and Pay*. New York: Harper & Row, 1973, Pt. 2.

Robinson, Joan. *The Economics of Imperfect Competition*. London: Macmillan, 1933, Chaps. 25–26.

Welch, Finis. *Minimum Wages: Issues and Evidence*. Washington, D.C.: American Enterprise Institute for Public Policy Research, 1978.

Questions and Exercises

1 Would you expect a monopolist to use
    a an efficient mix of variable resources? Why or why not?
    b Pareto optimal quantities of resources? Why or why not?

2 Commutative justice is said to be attained when units of a resource are paid what they are worth to the society. Consider two of many purchasers of common labor. One sells the product as a monopolist. The other sells the product as a pure competitor. Explain the wage rate that each would pay, the level of employment in each firm, and whether or not commutative justice is attained. Illustrate your answer with a diagram.

3 **a** Explain and illustrate with a diagram the following concepts:
   (i) monopolistic exploitation of a resource
   (ii) monopsonistic exploitation of a resource.
b Explain and illustrate how price fixing may be used in each case to counteract exploitation. Would you expect such price fixing to be feasible? Why or why not?

4 Would you expect that there is much monopsony in the purchase of common (unskilled) labor in the United States? Why or why not?

5 What kinds of government policies other than price fixing might be used to counteract monopsonistic exploitation of resources?

CHAPTER CONTENTS		KEY CONCEPTS

Value of marginal product
Pure competition
Monopoly
Monopsony
Marginal revenue product
Marginal resource cost
Pareto optimality

Resource Allocation

One of the most important functions performed by resource prices in a private enterprise economy is that of allocating resources among different uses and different geographic areas. If a high level of efficiency is to be attained in the economy, constant reallocation of resources must be in process in response to changes in human wants, the kinds and quantities of resources available, and the available techniques of production. In developing the principles of resource allocation, we shall first discuss the conditions of "correct" resource allocation; then consider the concept of resource markets and the allocation of resources among them, leading to maximum efficiency in resource use; and, finally, examine certain circumstances that prevent resources from being correctly allocated.

The Conditions of Maximum Welfare

What are the allocation conditions that must be met if units of any given resource are to make their maximum contributions to welfare? In general terms, the requirement is that the value of marginal product of the resource in any one of its uses must be the same as its value of marginal product in all of its other uses. Suppose that some other allocation prevails—for example, that a tractor used on a farm contributes at the margin $2,000 worth of farm products annually to the economy's output, and that an identical tractor used in construction can contribute a yearly $3,000 worth of products to the economy's output. If a tractor were switched from farming to construction, there would be a net gain to consumers of $1,000 worth of product. Obviously, some consumers can be made better off without making anyone worse off. Transfers of resources from lower value of marginal product uses to higher value of marginal product uses always yield a welfare increase; and maximum welfare results when these transfers have been carried to the point that for each resource its value of marginal product is the same in all its alternative uses.

Resource Markets

When the price system is used to allocate resources, the concept of a resource market becomes important. The extent of a resource market depends on the nature of the resource under consideration and on the time span relevant to the problem at hand. Within a given time span some resources are more mobile than others, and, consequently, their markets tend to be larger. Mobility depends on a number of things— shipping costs, perishability, social forces, and the like—and resources differ with respect to these characteristics.

Ordinarily, the mobility of any given resource varies with the time span for which its owners are making decisions. Over a short period of time its mobility is more limited than over a longer period. Consider labor of a certain kind, say, machinists. Over a short time period of a few months, or perhaps a year, machinists in the United States will not move readily from one geographic area to another, although they may be fairly free to move from one employer to another within a single locality. The longer the period of time under consideration, the larger the geographic area within which they are free to move. Over a period of twenty-five years they will be fairly mobile throughout the entire economy.[1]

Over short periods of time all the machinists, or all the units of any other resource in the economy, do not necessarily operate in the same market. The economy can be divided into a number of submarkets, each being the area within which units of a resource are mobile in the given time span. The longer the time span considered, the greater the interconnections among the submarkets. Over a sufficiently long period the submarkets tend to fuse into a single market.

The submarkets for a resource tend to be conceptual rather than real in the sense that boundaries between them are blurred. Each submarket overlaps others. However, if we think of them as being separate and apart from each other, we can make better progress with the analysis of resource allocation. Also, in place of the whole continuum of time periods, only two need be considered: (1) a short period during which the submarkets for a given resource are separate and (2) the long period in which resources have sufficient time to move freely among the submarkets and create a fusion of these into a single market.

---

[1] Mobility does not require the physical transference of a machinist from one area to another or even from one employer to another. As old machinists retire from the work force and new ones enter, mobility can exist; for in certain areas the retiring machinists may not be replaced, while in others the number of entries into the trade may exceed retirements.

Resource Allocation under Pure Competition

Will the price system allocate resources among their various uses so that optimal welfare tends to be approached? If pure competition exists in both product markets and resource markets, and if there are no externalities in consumption and production, such an allocation will tend to occur; therefore, the competitive model with no externalities provides a convenient starting point. We shall begin with the short-period allocation of a resource within a given submarket. Then the analysis will be extended to include long-period allocation among submarkets or over the entire economy.

Allocation within a Given Submarket

When units of a resource are so allocated that the value of marginal product in one use is greater than it is in other uses, the allocation is incorrect from the point of view of economic efficiency and welfare. The resource units would be worth more to the society in the higher value of marginal product use; and if they were transferred from the lower to the higher value of marginal product uses, the total value of the economy's output would be increased.

Resource prices furnish the mechanism for reallocation when resources are incorrectly allocated under a purely competitive system. Suppose that units of a given resource are allocated between two industries in such quantities that the value of marginal product of the resource is higher in one than in the other. Given this allocation, firms in the industry in which the value of marginal product is higher will also be willing to pay more per unit for the resource because in each industry the resource will be paid an amount equal to its value of marginal product. Consequently, resource owners, seeking maximum income, transfer resource units from the lower-paying to the higher-paying uses.[2] As units of the resource are transferred, its value of marginal product decreases in the employments to which it is moved and increases in the employments from which it is taken. The transfer continues until the resource's value of marginal product is equalized in all its uses, and all firms in the submarket are paying a price per unit equal to that value of marginal product. At this point the resource is correctly allocated and, within the submarket, is making its maximum contribution to net national product.

---

[2] New resource units just entering the market, say, college graduates, may be attracted to the jobs offering higher pay. This attraction, together with the failure to replace resource units retired from the market in lower-paying employments, provides an important method of transfer.

To illustrate the technical economics of the allocation process, suppose that the firms in two different industries, X and Y, operate in the same submarket for resource A. Suppose also that, initially, units of A are correctly allocated among the firms of the two industries. The VMP_{ax}, or value of marginal product of A in firms of the industry producing X, is equal to VMP_{ay}, or the value of marginal product of A in firms of the industry producing Y. Suppose further that there is neither a surplus nor a shortage of A on the market, so that

$$VMP_{ax} = VMP_{ay} = p_a$$

or

$$MPP_{ax} \times p_x = MPP_{ay} \times p_y = p_a,$$

where p_a is the price per unit of resource A, and p_x and p_y are the respective prices of product X and product Y.

Suppose that an increase occurs in the market demand for commodity X, while demand for commodity Y remains unchanged. The level of aggregate demand remains constant, and the increase in demand for X is offset by decreases in demand for commodities other than X and Y. The price of X rises, thereby increasing VMP_{ax}. Resource A has become more valuable to society in the production of X than it is in the production of Y. The original allocation of A no longer maximizes welfare; that is, this allocation is no longer the correct one. At price p_a for the resource, employers in the industry producing X find that a shortage of A exists. Consequently, they will bid up the price of A enough to cause owners of A to transfer units of it from the industry producing Y to the industry producing X. As the quantity of A employed by firms in the industry producing X increases relative to the quantities of other resources used, MPP_{ax} declines. As the output of X increases, p_x declines. Thus, VMP_{ax} declines.

Changes within the industry producing Y will accompany changes in the industry producing X. As units of A are transferred from the production of Y to X, the proportions of A to other resources used by firms in the industry producing Y fall, and MPP_{ay} increases. Smaller amounts of Y are produced and sold; consequently, p_y rises. Increases in MPP_{ay} and p_y mean higher VMP_{ay}.

Reallocation of A from the production of Y to X continues until units of the resource are again correctly distributed between the two industries. Units of A move from the industry producing Y to the industry producing X until the VMP_{ax} has gone down enough and the VMP_{ay} has gone up enough for the two to be equal. The new price per unit of A will be somewhat higher than the old one, for its value of marginal product is now higher in both industries than it was previously. In bidding against each other for the available supply of A, firms in both industries have raised the price of A to the level of its value of marginal product in both uses.

Resource A will again be making its maximum contribution to net national product. When VMP_{ax} was greater than VMP_{ay}, every movement of a unit of A from the industry producing Y to the industry producing X increased A's contribution to net national product. Withdrawal of a unit of A from the industry producing Y decreased A's contribution to net national product by an amount equal to VMP_{ay}. Putting the unit of A to work in the industry producing X increased A's contribution to net national product by VMP_{ax}. Hence, a net gain in A's contribution to net national product resulted from such transfers until A's value of marginal product was once more equalized among firms in the two industries.

Allocation among Submarkets

We extend the analysis by increasing the time span under consideration, joining short-period with long-period analysis. Consider two resources: (1) a certain kind of labor and (2) capital. All units of labor are homogeneous. Capital is fixed in specific forms and is immobile for the short period; but over the long period it is mobile, can change its form, and can be reallocated from one use to others.[3]

Allocation of Labor   Suppose that Area I and Area II initially constitute separate but identical short-period submarkets. The goods produced in the two submarkets are the same, as are capital facilities; and their labor demand curves, D_1D_1 and D_2D_2, as in Figure 17.1, are also the same. However, labor supplies for the two areas differ. Area I has a larger labor supply than Area II; thus, the labor supply curve S_1S_1 of Area I lies farther to the right than S_2S_2 of Area II.

Labor is poorly allocated, and its maldistribution causes its value of marginal product and its price to differ between the two areas. The price of labor, or the wage rate, in Area I will be w_1, and in Area II it will be w_2. The level of employment in Area II is L_2, while

---

[3]   Capital is usually considered in two contexts: (1) as concrete agents of production and (2) as a fluid stock of productive capacity. The first context is a short-run concept, with capital taking such specific forms as buildings, machinery, wheatland, and so on. The second is a long-run concept. Concrete pieces of equipment have time to wear out and be replaced. But replacement of the same kind and in the same place does not necessarily occur. Replacement can be in the form of new and different kinds of concrete agents. In agriculture, horse-drawn machinery was allowed to depreciate as the use of tractors became widespread and special machinery adapted to the tractor gradually came into use. Or capital may flow from one industry to another and from one location to another through depreciation in the one and the building of new equipment in the other. Thus, while capital may be almost completely immobile in the short run, in the long run it becomes quite mobile. *See* Frank H. Knight, *On the History and Method of Economics* (Chicago: University of Chicago Press, 1956), pp. 56–57.

FIGURE 17.1
Allocation of labor
between submarkets

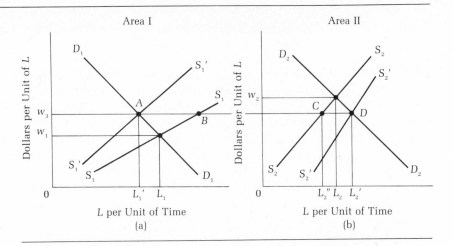

that in Area I is higher at L_1. The higher ratio of labor to capital in Area I causes the marginal physical product and value of marginal product of labor to be lower in that area. The reverse holds in Area II. The ratio of labor to capital is smaller; consequently, the marginal physical product and value of marginal product of labor are higher.

The disparate submarket prices for labor furnish the incentive for long-period movement or reallocation of labor from Area I to Area II; and reallocation tends to eliminate the wage differential. As workers leave Area I, the short-period supply curve for that submarket shifts to the left. As they enter Area II, its short-period supply curve shifts to the right. As the ratio of labor to capital declines in Area I, labor's value of marginal product and the wage rate increase. In Area II the increasing ratio of labor to capital decreases labor's value of marginal product and the wage rate. Reallocation continues until wage rates of the two submarkets are equal at w_3. The labor supply curve of Area I is now $S_1'S_1'$, and that of Area II is $S_2'S_2'$.

The reallocation of labor between Areas I and II increases real net national product and welfare. Before the movement began, the value of marginal product of labor in Area I was w_1. In Area II it was substantially higher at w_2. The movement of a unit of labor from Area I to Area II causes a loss of w_1 dollars' worth of product in Area I and a gain of almost w_2 dollars' worth of product in Area II. This gain more than offsets the loss in Area I and creates a net increase in total value of product produced in the economy. Each transfer of a unit of labor from Area I to II brings about such a net increase until the values of marginal product and the wage rates of labor are the same in the two submarkets. Labor is then correctly allocated between the two areas—it is making its maximum contribution to welfare. No further transfer of labor in either direction can increase net national product, but will decrease it instead. Also, equalization of the wage rates will have removed the incentive for labor migration to occur.

Allocation of Capital   The entire burden of adjustment will not be thrown on labor in the long period as the foregoing analysis suggests; it will be partly absorbed by reallocation of capital. The high ratio of labor to capital in Area I amounts to the same thing as a low ratio of capital to labor. Likewise, the low ratio of labor to capital in Area II means a high ratio of capital to labor. Therefore, we would expect the value of marginal product of capital in Area I to exceed that in Area II. Differing productivities of capital and returns on investment between the two areas furnish the incentive for capital to migrate from Area II to I.

Long-period capital migration affects the short-period labor demand curves and the wage rates of the two areas. As units of capital leave Area II, the demand curve (value of marginal product curve) for labor in that area shifts to the left, augmenting the decline in wage rates caused by the increasing labor supply. As units of capital enter Area I, the demand curve for labor in Area I increases. The increases in demand join the decreases in supply in raising the wage rates of Area I.

When the reverse migrations of labor and capital have been sufficient to equalize wage rates and the returns on investment between the two areas, both labor and capital will be correctly allocated. Further transfers of either resource in either direction will reduce the real net national product yielded by the two submarkets combined.

Conditions Preventing Correct Allocation

A number of forces in the real world prevent the price system from allocating resources correctly. Even with the price system free to operate and with resource prices free to guide resource allocation, three important causes of incorrect allocation can be cited: (1) monopoly in product markets, (2) monopsony in resource markets, and (3) certain nonprice impediments to resource movements. Additionally, direct interference with the price mechanism by the government or by private groups of resource owners and resource purchasers constitutes a cause of incorrect allocation. We shall consider these causes in turn.

The term *monopoly* is used in a broad context to include pure monopoly, oligopoly, and monopolistic competition—all cases in which individual firms face downward-sloping product demand curves. Similarly, the term *monopsony* is used broadly. Complete monopsony in resource purchases precludes any reallocation whatsoever. With less than complete monopsony, units of a given resource may be free to move along a limited number of buyers, any one of which can influence market price of the resource.

Monopoly

Monopoly in product markets may not affect resource movements directly. Resources may be free to move among alternative employers even though the firms employing them enjoy a degree of product monopoly. Steel, common labor, certain raw materials, and other resources are employed by many firms and may flow readily from one to another without regard to the types of product market in which individual firms sell. Where price discrepancies for any such resource exist within or among submarkets, long-period reallocation of the resource tends to occur to whatever extent necessary to eliminate the discrepancies. Every firm in every submarket has an incentive to employ that quantity of the resource at which its marginal revenue product equals its marginal resource cost. Reallocation tends to occur until the price of the resource is the same in all its alternative employments.

When some degree of product monopoly exists, real net national product and welfare would not be maximized even if all resources were so allocated that the marginal revenue product of each is the same in all its alternative employments. Individual firms face downward-sloping product demand curves. For each firm marginal revenue is less than product price. Thus, for any given resource, value of marginal product in each of its uses would exceed marginal revenue product. But discrepancies would occur among the values of marginal products of the resource in its various uses even though its marginal revenue product were the same in all of them. This will be the case because of the differing demand elasticities of the various products that the resource aids in making. Differing demand elasticities mean that product prices and corresponding marginal revenues are not proportional to each other among the different products. Hence, values of marginal products of the resource in its various uses are not proportional to its marginal revenue products. When the latter are equal, the former will be unequal. Inequalities among values of marginal product of a resource in its various uses show that net national product could be increased by transferring units of the resource from lower value of marginal product uses to higher value of marginal product uses.

It is *value of marginal product* of a resource that measures the contribution of a unit of it to the value of the economy's output—its marginal physical product multiplied by the price of the final product. *Marginal revenue product* shows the contribution that a unit of the resource makes to the total receipts of a single firm; but where monopoly exists, this is less than the value of the product added to the economy's output by the resource unit. Thus, when a resource is so allocated that its price is equalized in all alternative uses, the price system has done its job. Even though further reallocation from lower value of marginal product uses to higher value of marginal product uses will increase net national product, there is no automatic motivation to make it occur.

Suppose that machinists in Detroit work both for firms selling as oligopolists and those selling as pure competitors. An automobile manufacturer furnishes an example of the former type of firm, whereas any one of many small independent machine shops is an example of the latter. Suppose that an equilibrium allocation of machinists exists—they are paid $8 per hour in all alternative employments. The small machine shop hires that quantity at which the value of marginal product of machinists is $16 per hour. The automobile manufacturer hires that quantity at which marginal revenue product equals $16 per hour. Since the automobile manufacturer faces a downward-sloping product demand curve, value of marginal product of machinists employed by the firm exceeds their marginal revenue product. Value of marginal product may thus be $20 per hour. Society would gain in terms of net national product if some machinists would transfer from the small independent machine shops to automobile manufacturers. However, since both pay $16 per hour, the price system will not motivate the transfers.

In addition, partially or completely blocked entry into monopolistic industries may prevent other resources from being so allocated that their respective marginal revenue products and prices are equalized within and among submarkets. We can think of such resources as being inseparable from the existence of individual firms—they are short-run "fixed" resources. They can enter industries only in the form of plant for new firms. The existence of long-run profits for the firms in an industry indicates that the marginal revenue products of such resources are greater in that industry than they are elsewhere in the economy.

Monopsony

The existence of monopsony in resource purchases may also prevent the price system from allocating resources correctly. Where some degree of monopsony is present, an individual firm purchases that quantity of a resource at which its marginal revenue product equals its marginal resource cost. When the resource supply curve to the firm slopes upward to the right, marginal resource cost exceeds the price that the firm pays the resource. When equilibrium in the purchase of the resource is reached on the part of any single firm, the price paid the resource is below its marginal revenue product.

Differential prices of the resource guide its allocation among the few firms using it, just as they did in the previous analysis. Voluntary reallocation of the resource will cease when its price is the same in its alternative uses. Resource owners will have no incentive to transfer units of it from one employment to another, and an equilibrium allocation will have been achieved.

Even though an equilibrium allocation may be achieved and all firms may be paying the same price for the resource, it will not be making its maximum contribution to net national product. To the extent that the supply curves of the resource facing different firms have differing elasticities, marginal resource costs and marginal revenue products of the resource among different firms will not be equal. Some degree of monopoly in product markets will create further distortions in the pattern of values of marginal products. Hence, there is no reason for believing that the values of marginal products of the resource will be the same among its alternative employments even though it is everywhere paid the same price. About the most that we can say on this point is that resource transfers from lower value of marginal product uses to higher value of marginal product uses would increase real net national product. However, since the resource price is the same in its alternative employments, resource owners will not make such transfers voluntarily.

Nonprice Impediments

Resources may be incorrectly allocated for reasons other than discrepancies among prices, marginal resource costs, marginal revenue products, and values of marginal product. Some of the important "nonprice" factors follow.

Ignorance Lack of knowledge on the part of resource owners may prevent resources from moving from lower-paying to higher-paying uses. In the most obvious case resource owners may lack information concerning the price patterns of the resources over the economy as a whole. Bricklayers may not be aware of the areas and firms paying the highest wages for bricklayers. Farmers may sell products in some areas at unnecessarily low prices when they are not aware of the higher prices that can be obtained elsewhere. Investors make mistakes when they are ignorant of alternative investment opportunities throughout the economy.[4]

---

[4] The classic examples here are the many single proprietorships that fail in such fields as neighborhood grocery stores, eating and drinking establishments, and filling stations.

Lack of knowledge may also prevent potential resources from being channeled into the resource supply categories in which they will contribute most to net national product. Various kinds of labor resources illustrate the point. For what trade or profession should potential entrants to the labor force be trained? Do those responsible for influencing or selecting the vocation possess full knowledge of the future returns to be derived from alternative vocations? Usually they do not. Children may follow parents as sharecroppers or machine operators, when alternative occupations would be more lucrative. Or, where children do not follow parents' occupations, the information on which decisions are made is often sketchy. Frequently the potential entrant and his or her advisers do not discover until the training program is well advanced or completed that the choice of occupation has been an unfortunate one economically—and at this point it may be too late to change.

Sociological and Psychological Impediments Sociological and psychological factors may throw blocks in the way of the allocation of resources that will maximize net national product.[5] They include those ties to particular communities, to friends, and to the family that restrict mobility regardless of the monetary incentives to move. Or, the virtues of a particular occupation, community, or way of living may be so extolled by various social groups that mobility is restricted. Glorification of the family farm, or of southern California, or of the teaching profession may be cases in point.

Institutional Factors Various institutional barriers to reallocation of resources are evident in the economy. In the industrial world, workers accumulate certain rights with particular firms. These include pension and seniority rights. In some cases labor unions may restrict entry directly into particular occupations. Patent rights held by one firm or a group of firms in an industry may block the entry of new firms into the industry and thus condemn quantities of certain resources to other occupations in which their values of marginal products and rates of pay are lower. The list can be extended considerably, but these cases illustrate the point.

Price Fixing

Sometimes the price mechanism is not allowed to perform its function of signaling the spots where quantities of certain resources should be transferred in or out. Some resource prices are fixed or

---

[5] We are not saying that such blocks constitute mistakes on the part of society. The "good life" is not necessarily achieved through maximization of net national product. It may be desirable to sacrifice some product, if necessary, for the achievement of other objectives or values.

controlled by the government. Control may be exercised through such devices as minimum wage legislation, agricultural price supports, or the general price and wage controls that many advocate during inflation. Some resource prices may be partially or completely controlled by organized private groups of resource owners and resource purchasers. A number of labor unions fall within this category, as do certain farm-marketing cooperatives and some employer associations. Three hypothetical examples will illustrate some of the effects of controlled resource prices on the equilibrium allocation of resources and on net national product. We shall assume that, in the absence of control, pure competition would exist; however, even if some degree of monopoly in product markets were to be found, the results would be approximately the same.

Two submarkets for a given resource are shown in Figure 17.2. As a matter of convenience we shall call the resource labor. The two

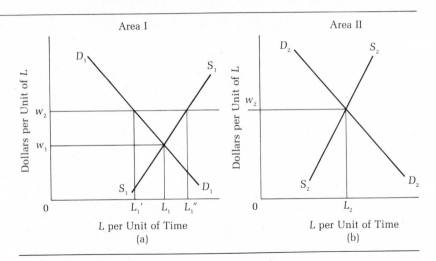

FIGURE 17.2
The impact of minimum resource prices on labor allocation

submarkets are alike except for the initial distribution of labor. They produce the same products and have identical supplies of capital. The demand curves for labor are the same for each submarket. Since Area I has a greater labor supply than Area II, the short-period price of labor will be lower in Area I and the employment level will be higher. We shall consider three possible cases.

Case I Assume that the workers of Area II are organized and that those of Area I are not. The initial labor demand and labor supply situations are shown in Figure 17.2. The equilibrium wage rate and employment level in Area I are w_1 and L_1, respectively. In Area II they are w_2 and L_2, respectively. Assume further that organized workers, through collective bargaining, succeed in placing a floor of rate w_2 under Area II wage rates. The immediate or short-period effects of the minimum wage rate of w_2 in Area II will be nil. Since w_2 is initially the equilibrium wage rate in Area II, the union should have little difficulty in obtaining it. At that rate of pay, employers of Area II are willing to employ as much labor as is willing to go to work. The wage differential between the two areas continues to reflect the existence of the initial maldistribution of labor.

The effects of the minimum wage rate set in Area II are felt in the long period. The wage differential creates an incentive for workers to migrate from Area I to Area II. However, if additional workers were hired in Area II, the ratio of labor to capital would increase, the marginal physical product of labor would decrease, and the value of marginal product of labor would decrease. Since the wage rate of such additional workers would be w_2 and since this rate would exceed their values of marginal product, they would not be hired. Any workers migrating from Area I to Area II would find themselves unemployed, and this prospect would keep migration from occurring. Employment in Area I at the lower wage rate of w_1 would be preferable to no employment at all in Area II, regardless of how high wage rates are. Labor would remain poorly allocated between the two areas, and welfare would be permanently below its optimum level.

This situation sets the stage for interesting repercussions with regard to capital. An incentive for capital to migrate in the long period will be present in this case, also. In fact, capital migration is the only adjustment in resource allocation that can occur. As capital migrates from Area II to Area I, demand for labor will shrink in Area II and grow in Area I. This demand change will increase wage rates and employment in Area I. However, unemployment will develop among the organized workers of Area II, and welfare will still be below its maximum potential level.[6]

Case II Assume that the organized workers of Area II succeed in extending their union to Area I. Once Area I is organized, assume that workers in both places can bring wage rates in Area I up to w_2 (Figure 17.2). Immediate short-period effects occur. There will be no initial impact on the employment level in Area II. In Area I unemployment amounting to $L_1'L_1''$ will occur. In Area I at the old wage level of w_1, employment level L_1 equates value of marginal product of labor to the wage rate. The minimum wage rate of w_2 makes the wage rate greater than the value of marginal product of labor at the

---

[6] The women's full-fashioned hosiery industry furnishes an excellent example of the migration of capital from high-cost union areas to low-cost nonunion areas. *See* Sumner H. Slichter, *Union Policies and Industrial Management* (Washington, D.C.: The Brookings Institution, 1941). pp. 353–60.

old employment level of L_1. Employers find that a reduction in employment will decrease their total receipts by less than it reduces their total costs; hence, workers are laid off. The decreasing ratio of labor to capital increases the value of marginal product of labor until, when only L_1' workers are employed, their value of marginal product is again equal to the wage rate. Here the layoffs will stop.

The long-period effects of the minimum wage rate of w_2 will be approximately the same as the immediate effects. Since the wage differential is eliminated, there is no incentive for employed workers of Area I to migrate to Area II. Employers of Area II will not find it profitable to hire more workers than L_2 at a wage rate of w_2; hence, unemployed workers of Area I will not find migration to Area II of any benefit.

With regard to capital, the minimum wage rate of w_2 in Area I and the reduced ratio of labor to capital (increased ratio of capital to labor) eliminate the incentive for capital to migrate to Area I in the long period. The ratio of capital to labor in Area I is increased sufficiently by the worker layoffs to make the value of marginal product of capital in Area I equal to that in Area II.[7] Thus, the minimum wage rate of w_2 extended to both areas prevents the effects of the initial misallocation of resources from being alleviated by either labor or capital migration; and, in addition, it creates unemployment.

Case III A third possibility, in which controlled resource prices may not affect resource allocation adversely, deserves some consideration. Assume that both areas are organized or, alternatively, that the government sets a minimum wage rate applicable to both. The wage rate is set through collective bargaining or by the government at level w_3, as is shown in Figure 17.3—that is, at precisely the level that would prevail in free markets in the long period after workers had had sufficient time to migrate. The initial demand and supply relationships are D_1D_1 and S_1S_1, respectively, in Area I. In Area II they are D_2D_2 and S_2S_2, respectively. In Area I the minimum wage rate of w_3 will cause unemployment equal to AB. In Area II a labor shortage equal to CD will occur at wage rate w_3, and the wage rate in that submarket will rise to w_2.

Unemployment will assist the price system in reallocating labor from Area I to Area II in the long period. The unemployed and the lower-paid workers of Area I will seek the higher-paying jobs of Area II. The supply curve for labor in Area I will shift leftward to $S_1'S_1'$

---

[7] Since the initial capital facilities and products produced in the two areas were assumed to be the same, the labor demand curves are also the same. At wage rate w_2 each market employs the same quantity of labor; that is, L_1' units of labor equals L_2 units of labor in Figure 17.2. Consequently, ratios of labor to capital in the two areas, when the wage rate for both is w_2, will be the same; and the value of marginal product of capital will also be the same.

FIGURE 17.3
Job opportunities as incentives for labor migration

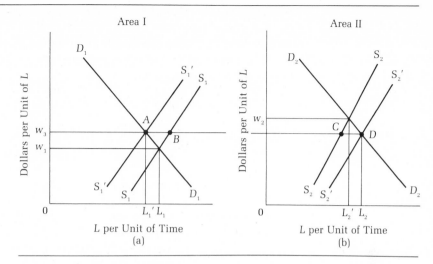

and that of Area II will shift rightward to $S_2'S_2'$. Labor will be reallocated so that its value of marginal product is equalized between the two submarkets, allowing labor to make its maximum contribution to net national product.

Again, some migration of capital from Area II to Area I may occur in the long period. At wage rate w_3 the initial employment level is L_1' in Area I and is greater than the initial employment level of L_2 in Area II. Therefore, the ratio of capital to labor is smaller, and the marginal revenue product of capital is greater in Area I than in Area II. Capital migration will reduce the demand for labor in Area II and will increase it in Area I, thus reducing the amount of labor migration necessary to secure full employment and maximum net national product.

Summary

Any given resource is "correctly" allocated—makes its maximum contribution to economic welfare—when its value of marginal product is the same in all of its alternative uses. In a private enterprise economic system resource prices serve the function of directing the allocation of resources.

Only under pure competition in product markets and resource markets will resources automatically be allocated so that maximum real net national product or welfare will tend to be realized. Under pure competition a misallocation of any given resource causes its values of marginal products in different employments to differ from each other. Consequently, employers for whom its value of marginal product is higher bid resources away from those for whom its value of marginal product is lower. Transfers of resource units from lower to higher value of marginal product uses increase the contributions of the resource to welfare. Its maximum contribution occurs when value of marginal product of the resource is the same in all its possible uses. Price of the resource will also be the same in all its alternative uses; therefore, no incentive will exist for further transfers to be made.

With some degree of monopoly in product markets, a resource will be reallocated among its alternative uses until its price is the same in all of them. However, where employers are monopolists in some degree, they employ those quantities of the resource at which its marginal revenue product equals its price. Marginal revenue products of the resource will be the same in alternative employments. Differing product demand elasticities cause values of marginal products of the resource to differ in alternative employments. Thus, the resource does not make its maximum contribution to net national product.

Where employers have some degree of monopsony, but there is no resource differentiation, a resource will again be reallocated until its price is the same in alternative employments. But a monopsonist employs the resource up to the point at which marginal revenue product equals marginal resource cost. Different monopsonists may face resource supply curves of differing elasticities; and, if so, marginal resource cost will be different for each, even though all pay the same price per unit for the resource. With equilibrium allocation of the resource achieved, marginal revenue products differ. The usual case will be that differences in values of marginal product also occur, and the resource will not be making its maximum contribution to net national product.

Nonprice impediments to correct allocation of resources include ignorance, sociological and psychological factors, and institutional restrictions. In some instances the achievement of noneconomic values may be of more importance to society than correct resource allocation.

Direct interferences with the price mechanism by the government and by private groups may prevent resources from being correctly allocated in some cases. In other cases such interference may not lead to adverse effects.

Suggested Readings

Clark, John Bates. *The Distribution of Wealth*. New York: Macmillan, 1923, Chap. 19.

Pigou, A. C. *The Economics of Welfare,* 4th ed. London: Macmillan, 1932, Pt. 3, Chap. 9.

Rees, Albert. *The Economics of Work and Pay.* New York: Harper & Row, 1973, Pt. 3.

Questions and Exercises

1   Suppose that coal miners in Kentucky are initially unorganized and that an equilibrium wage rate w_1 prevails. Then suppose that a union is formed and succeeds in organizing approximately one-half of the miners. The rest are unorganized. The union succeeds in raising wage rates in unionized mines to w_2. Explain the effects on
    a   resource allocation
    b   national income.

2   Much of the nation's crude oil is produced in Louisiana, Texas, and Oklahoma. In an uncontrolled market, the price per barrel of crude oil to buyers in New York is typically greater than it is in one of the producing states—for example, Oklahoma.
    a   What explanation can you offer for the difference?
    b   Does the price difference (to users) mean that crude oil is misallocated? Why or why not?
    c   What would be the effect on the allocation of crude oil if a ceiling price equal to the initial Oklahoma market price is placed on the resource?

3   One of the traditional objectives of labor unions is to obtain "equal pay for equal work" for their members. Suppose that all carpenters belong to the Carpenters' Union and that, to begin, this objective has been attained. Assume that initially, at the union wage scale, equilibrium exists in the market for carpenters in both Oldtown and Newcity. Over time Newcity grows and expands, while Oldtown deteriorates. What mechanism exists for reallocating carpenters
    a   if the union wage scale is strictly maintained?
    b   if the union loses members and the wage scale is no longer enforced?

CHAPTER CONTENTS		KEY CONCEPTS
Individual Income Determination		Marginal productivity theory
		Marginal revenue product
Personal Distribution of Income	**Distribution among Spending Units**	Value of marginal product
		Marginal resource cost
	Income Equality and Income Differences	Personal distribution of income
Causes of Income Differences	**Differences in Labor Resources Owned**	Lorenz curve
	Horizontal Differences in Labor Resources	Functional distribution of income
	Vertical Differences in Labor Resources	
	Differences in Capital Resources Owned	Horizontal differences in labor resources
	Material Inheritance	Vertical differences in labor resources
	Fortuitous Circumstances	
	Propensities to Accumulate	Administered prices
	Price Manipulations	Negative income tax
	Administered Prices: Pure Competition	
	Supply Restrictions: Pure Competition	
	Administered Prices: Monopoly	
	Administered Prices: Monopsony	
	Price Increases Accompanying Demand Increases	
Movements toward Less Inequality	**Resource Redistribution**	
	Labor Resources	
	Capital Resources	
	Administered Prices	
	The Negative Income Tax	
	Income Redistribution and the Price System	
Application	**The New Jersey-Pennsylvania Experiment**	
Summary	**Suggested Readings**	
	Questions and Exercises	

Distribution of Income and Product

Of the four functions of an economic system with which we are concerned, we have yet to consider the distribution of the economy's product or income. Income distribution among the families and individuals of economic systems has been an age-old source of unrest and concern. A promise always extended by socialist economic systems is that they will improve the distribution of income. In recent years the governments of most private enterprise countries have been promising the same thing. In this chapter we examine the way in which a private enterprise system distributes income, the possibilities of redistribution, and the welfare implications of both.

Individual Income Determination

The principles of individual income determination and of income distribution in a private enterprise economic system are called *the marginal productivity theory.* These principles were set out in previous chapters; in this one we shall draw them together and summarize them.

The principles of income determination where pure competition prevails, both in product markets and resource markets, were developed in Chapter 15. The owner of a given resource is paid a price per unit for the units employed equal to the marginal revenue product and the value of marginal product of the resource. The price of the resource is not determined by any single employer or by any single resource owner. It is determined by the interactions of all buyers and all sellers in the market for the resource.

If for some reason the price of a resource should be less than its marginal revenue product, a shortage will occur. Employers want more of it at that price than resource owners are willing to place on the market. Employers, bidding against each other for the available supply, will drive the price up until the shortage disappears and each is hiring (or buying) that quantity of the resource at which its marginal revenue product equals its price.

A price high enough to create a surplus of the resource will set forces in motion to eliminate the surplus. Employers take only those quantities sufficient to equate its marginal revenue product to its price. Resource owners undercut each other's prices to secure employment for their idle units. As price drops, employment expands. The undercutting continues until employers are willing to take the quantities that resource owners want to place on the market.

Where some degree of monopoly[1] exists in product markets, the determination of the equilibrium price of the resource occurs in the same way. Like the purely competitive firm, the monopolistic firm employs those quantities of the resource at which its marginal revenue product is equal to its price. However, the price per unit received by owners of the resource is less than its value of marginal product, and the resource is exploited monopolistically.

Some degree of monopsony in the purchase of a given resource will cause it to be paid still less than its marginal revenue product. The monopsonist, faced with a resource supply curve sloping upward to the right, employs that quantity of the resource at which its marginal revenue product is equal to its marginal resource cost. Marginal resource cost is greater than the price paid for the resource. Monopsonistic exploitation of the resource occurs to the extent that its marginal revenue product exceeds its price. If the resource purchaser is also a monopolist, marginal revenue product of the resource will in turn be less than its value of marginal product, and the resource will be exploited monopolistically as well as monopsonistically.

As we noted in Chapter 2, an individual's income per unit of time is the sum of the amounts earned per unit of time from the employment of the various resources which the person owns. If a single kind of resource is owned, the income will be equal to the number of units placed in employment multiplied by the price per unit which the individual receives. If the individual owns several kinds of resources, the income from each one can be computed in the same manner, and then all can be totaled to determine that person's entire income.

Personal Distribution of Income

The personal distribution of income refers to income distribution among spending units of the economy. We shall survey the distribu-

---

[1] Again, we use the term to refer to all cases in which the firm faces a downward-sloping product demand curve. They include cases of pure monopoly, oligopoly, and monopolistic competition.

tion of income by size and then point up certain problems involved in discussing income differences and equality.

Distribution among Spending Units

Some idea of the distribution of income in the United States is provided by Table 18.1. It is worth noting that 76 percent of the families had incomes of $10,000 or more per year in 1978. Note also that 8.2 percent of families fell below the $5,000 per year level. Among unre-

TABLE 18.1
Distribution of total money income in the United States before taxes: 1978

Total Money Income	Families		Unrelated Individuals	
	Number (thousands)	Percent	Number (thousands)	Percent
Under $5,000	4,718	8.2%	9,489	38.6%
$ 5,000 to $ 9,999	9,154	15.8	6,929	29.2
$10,000 to $14,999	9,656	16.6	4,086	16.6
$15,000 to $19,999	9,769	16.9	2,211	9.1
$20,000 to $24,999	8,392	14.5	936	3.8
$25,000 to $49,999	14,033	24.3	787	3.2
$50,000 and over	2,082	3.6	148	0.6
Total	57,804	100.0	24,585	100.0
Median Income	$17,640		$ 6,705	

Source: U.S. Department of Commerce, Bureau of the Census, *Consumer Income*, Series P–60, No. 123 (June 1980), p. 3,

lated individuals—persons 14 years of age or over who are not living with any relatives—over one-third had incomes under $5,000 per year. Using the poverty thresholds defined by the federal government for 1978—$6,662 for an urban family of four, with appropriate adjustments for other sizes of households—some 24.5 million persons lived in poverty in 1978. These constitute about 11.4 percent of the total population of the United States. Median family income was $17,640. The median income for unattached individuals was $6,705.

Income Equality and Income Differences

Inequality in the distribution of income among households is of great concern to many people. The device usually used to indicate the extent of inequality is the Lorenz curve of Figure 18.1, in which we measure the percentage of the total number of families and unattached individuals on the horizontal axis and the percentage of total family and unattached individuals' income on the vertical axis. If income were equally distributed among families, the relation between the percentage of families and the percentage of income would form the straight diagonal line 0A —20 percent of the families would

FIGURE 18.1
Inequality in the
before-tax distribution
of income, 1978

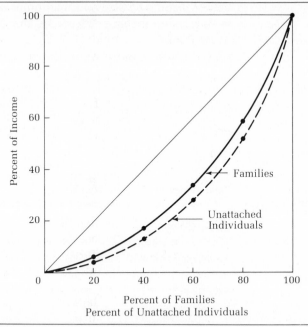

Source: U.S. Department of Commerce, Bureau of the Census, *Consumer Income,* Series P-60, No. 123 (June 1980), pp. 63, 65

have 20 percent of the income; 50 percent of the families would have 50 percent of the income, and so on. But the actual distribution of income is not an equal apportionment. The actual distribution of family income is shown by the solid curved line. Note that the lower 20 percent of families received only 5.4 percent of total income and that the lower 60 percent of families received only 34.8 percent of total income. The extent to which the actual income distribution deviates from a perfectly equal one is reflected by the curvature of the Lorenz curve. The dotted line shows the distribution of the total income of unattached individuals among that group. Note that income of unattached persons was even more unequally distributed than was family income.

Even if the Lorenz curves show perfect equality in the distribution of income, there is no assurance that all spending units are treated equally by the economic system. Unattached individuals vary in many ways. There are differences in ages, regional locations, cultural tastes, and the like. Therefore, equality of money income among them may lead to very different levels of fulfillment or of economic well-being. When we consider family spending units, the differences in family sizes and age distributions further compound the problem of lack of homogeneity among spending units.

The difficulties encountered in trying to define and measure income equality or income differences will not be of major importance for our purposes. We are interested in the causes of differences rather than in their ethical implications. We shall have occasion to refer to "movements toward greater equality," but this phrase should be accepted for what it is—a loose statement meaning some mitigation of income differences among heterogeneous spending units. It means some lopping off of incomes at the top and some augmenting of incomes at the bottom. It does not mean that we can state with any precision the point at which income distribution is "equalized."

Causes of Income Differences

With reference to the determinants of individual[2] incomes, it becomes clear that differences in incomes arise from two basic sources: (1) differences in the kinds and quantities of resources owned by different individuals and (2) differences in prices paid in different employments for units of any given resource. The former are the more fundamental; the latter arise from various types of interference with the price system in the performance of its functions and from any resource immobility that may occur.

It will be convenient to discuss labor and capital resources separately. To enable us to see the importance of each in perspective, it is worthwhile to note the *functional distribution* of income in the United States, that is, distribution according to the resource classes into which resources are divided. In Table 18.2 compensation of employees represents income received by the owners of labor resources for the listed years, while corporate profits, interest, and rental income represent income received by capital owners. All are understated substantially because proprietors' income includes income both from labor and from capital. Since accounting records for such enterprises often do not differentiate between returns to labor and returns to capital, we cannot split this item into categories labeled capital and labor. We can guess roughly that labor resources account for 80 percent of national income and that capital resources account for some 20 percent.

In this section we shall first consider differences in the kinds and quantities of labor resources owned by different individuals. Next, differences in capital resources owned will be discussed. Finally, we shall examine the effects on income distribution of certain manipulations of the price mechanism.

---

[2]   The term *individual* will be used throughout the rest of the chapter to refer to a spending unit, regardless of its size or composition.

TABLE 18.2
National income by type
of income: 1939–1979

Type of Income	1939 Income (billions)	1939 Percent of Income	1949 Income (billions)	1949 Percent of Income	1959 Income (billions)	1959 Percent of Income	1969 Income (billions)	1969 Percent of Income	1979 Income (billions)	1979 Percent of Income
Compensation of employees	$48.1	66.3%	$140.8	64.7%	$278.5	69.6%	$565.5	72.8%	$1,459.2	75.8%
Business and professional proprietors' income	7.3	10.0	22.7	10.4	35.1	8.8	50.3	6.5	98.0	5.1
Farm proprietors' income	4.3	5.9	12.9	5.9	11.4	2.8	16.8	2.0	32.8	1.7
Rental income	2.7	3.7	8.3	3.8	11.9	3.0	22.6	2.9	26.9	1.3
Net interest	4.6	6.3	4.8	2.2	16.4	4.1	29.9	3.8	129.7	6.7
Corporate profits	5.7	7.9	28.2	13.0	47.2	11.8	78.6	12.0	178.2	9.3
Total[a]	$72.8	100.0	$217.7	100.0	$400.5	100.0	$763.7	100.0	1,924.8	100.0

[a] Columns may not total due to rounding.

Sources: Economic Report of the President (Washington, D.C.: Government Printing Office, 1965), p. 203; U.S. Department of Commerce, *Survey of Current Business* (May 1975), p. S–2, and (July 1980), p. 14.

Differences in Labor Resources Owned

The labor classification of resources is composed of many different kinds and qualities of labor. These have one common characteristic—they are human. Any single kind of labor is a combination or complex of both inherited and acquired characteristics. The acquired part of a worker's labor power is generally referred to as human capital. We shall make no attempt to separate inherited from acquired characteristics.

Labor can be subclassified horizontally and vertically into many, largely separate, resource groups. Vertical subclassification involves grading workers according to skill levels from the lowest kind of undifferentiated manual labor to the highest professional levels. Horizontal subclassification divides workers of a certain skill level into the various occupations requiring that particular degree of skill. An example would be the division of skilled construction workers into groups—carpenters, bricklayers, plumbers, and the like. Vertical mobility of labor refers to the possibility of moving upward through vertical skill levels. Horizontal mobility means the ability to move sideways among groups at a particular skill level.

Horizontal Differences in Labor Resources   At any specific horizontal level, individuals may receive different incomes because of differences in the demand and supply conditions for the kinds of labor that they own. A large demand for a certain kind of labor relative to the supply of it available will make its marginal revenue product, and its price, high. On the same skill level, a small demand for another kind of labor relative to the supply available will make its marginal revenue product and its price low. The differences in prices tend to cause differences in income for owners of the kinds of labor concerned.

Suppose, for example, that bricklayers and carpenters initially earn approximately equal incomes. A shift in consumers' tastes occurs from wood to brick construction in residential units. The incomes of bricklayers will rise, while those of carpenters will fall because of the altered conditions of demand. Over a long period of time, horizontal mobility between the two groups tend to decrease the income differences thus arising, and welfare will be increased in the process.

Quantitative differences in the amount of work performed by individuals owning the same kind of labor resource may lead to income differences. Some occupations afford considerable leeway for individual choice of the number of hours to be worked per week or month. Examples include independent professionals, such as physicians, lawyers, and certified public accountants, along with independent proprietors, such as farmers, plumbing contractors, and garage owners. In other occupations, hours of work are beyond the control of the individual. Yet in different employments of the same resource, variations in age, physical endurance, institutional restrictions, customs, and so on can lead to differences in hours worked and to income differences among owners of the resource.

Within a particular labor resource group, qualitative differences or differences in the abilities of the owners of the resource often create income differences. Wide variations occur in the public's evaluation of individual dentists or physicians or lawyers or automobile mechanics. Consequently, within any one group, variations in prices paid for services and in the quantities of services sold to the public will lead to income differences. Usually a correlation exists between the ages of the members of a resource group and their incomes. Quality tends to improve with accumulated experience up to a point. Data reported by Milton Friedman and Simon Kuznets suggest, for example, that the incomes of physicians tend to be highest between the tenth and twenty-fifth years of practice and that those of lawyers tend to be highest between the twentieth and thirty-fifth years of practice.[3]

Vertical Differences in Labor Resources   The different vertical strata themselves represent differences in labor resources owned and give rise to major labor income differences. Entry into high-level occupations, such as the professions or the ranks of business executives, is much more difficult than is entry into manual occupations. The relative scarcity of labor at top levels results from two basic factors: (1) individuals with the physical and mental characteristics necessary for the performance of high-level work are limited in number; (2) given the necessary physical and mental characteristics, many lack either the opportunities for training or the necessary social and cultural environment for movement into high-level positions. Thus, impediments to vertical mobility keep resource supplies low, relative to demands for them at the top levels; and they keep resource supplies abundant, relative to demands for them at the low levels.

Differences in labor resources owned because of disparities in innate physical and mental characteristics of individuals are accidents of birth. The individual has nothing to do with choosing them. Nevertheless, they account partly for restricted vertical mobility and for income differences. The opportunities for moving toward top positions and relatively large incomes are considerably enhanced by the inheritance of a strong physical constitution and a superior intel-

---

[3]   Milton Friedman and Simon Kuznets, *Income from Independent Professional Practice* (New York: National Bureau of Economic Resarch, 1945), pp. 237–60.

lect; however, these by no means insure that individuals so endowed will make the most of their opportunities.

Opportunities for training are more widely available to individuals born into wealthy families than to those born to parents in lower-income groups. Some of the higher-paying professions require long and expensive university training programs that are often beyond the reach of the latter groups. The medical profession is a case in point. However, we often see individuals who have had the initial ability, drive, and determination necessary to overcome economic obstacles thrown in the way of vertical mobility.

Differences in social inheritance constitute another cause of differences in labor resources owned. These are closely correlated with differences in material inheritance. Frequently, individuals born "on the wrong side of the tracks" face family and community attitudes that sharply curtail their opportunities and their desires for vertical mobility. Others, more fortunately situated, acquire the training necessary to be highly productive and to obtain large incomes because it is expected of them by the social group in which they move. The social position alone, apart from the training induced by it, may be quite effective in facilitating vertical mobility.

When vertical mobility would otherwise occur but is blocked, income differences persist and welfare is below its potential maximum. If those who are denied access to jobs and occupations with higher value of marginal products were able to attain these, the result would be higher real net national product as well as greater equality in income distribution.

Differences in Capital Resources Owned

In addition to inequalities in labor incomes, large differences occur in individual incomes from disparities in capital ownership. Different individuals own varying quantities of capital, such as corporation or other business assets, farmland, oil wells, or other property. We shall examine the fundamental causes of inequalities in capital holdings.

Material Inheritance   Differences in the amounts of capital inherited or received as gifts by individuals create disparities in incomes. The institution of private property on which private enterprise rests usually is coupled with inheritance laws allowing holdings of accumulated property rights to be passed from generation to generation. The individual fortunate enough to have a wealthy parent inherits large capital holdings; that person's resources contribute much to the productive process; and the individual is rewarded accordingly. The child of a southern sharecropper—who may be of equal innate intelligence with the child of a wealthy parent but inherits no capital—contributes less to the productive process and receives a correspondingly lower income.

Fortuitous Circumstances Chance, luck, or other fortuitous circumstances beyond the control of individuals constitute a further cause of differences in capital holdings. The discovery of oil, uranium, or gold on an otherwise undistinguished piece of land brings about a large appreciation in its value or its ability to yield income to its owner. Unforeseen shifts in consumer demand increase the values of certain capital holdings while decreasing the values of others. National emergencies, such as war, lead to changes in valuations of particular kinds of property and, hence, to differential incomes from capital. Fortuitous circumstances can work in reverse also, but, even so, their effects operate to create differences in the ownership of capital.

Propensities to Accumulate Differing psychological propensities to accumulate, and differing abilities to do so, lead to differences in capital ownership among individuals. On the psychological side a number of factors influence the will to accumulate. Stories circulate of individuals determined to make a fortune before they reach middle age. Accumulation sometimes occurs for purposes of security and luxury in later life. It sometimes stems from the desire to make one's children secure. The power and the prestige accompanying wealth provide the motivating force in some cases. To others, amassing and manipulation of capital holdings is a gigantic game—the activity involved fascinates them. Whatever the motives, some individuals have such propensities and others do not. In some instances the will to accumulate may be negative, and the opposite of accumulation occurs.

The ability of an individual to accumulate depends largely on the person's original holdings of both labor and capital resources. The higher the original income, the easier saving and accumulation tend to be. The individual possessing much in the way of labor resources initially is likely to accumulate capital with his or her income from labor; investments are made in stocks and bonds, real estate, a cattle ranch, or other property. Or the individual possessing substantial quantities of capital initially—and the ability to manage it—receives an income sufficient to allow saving and investment in additional capital. In the process of accumulation, labor and capital resources of an individual augment each other in providing the income from which further accumulation can be accomplished.

Price Manipulations

Various groups of resource owners throughout the economy, dissatisfied with their current shares of national income, seek to modify income distribution through manipulation or fixing of the prices of resources that they own or the prices of products that they produce and sell. Groups of farmers—wheat, cotton, dairy, and others—have been able to obtain government-enforced minimum prices for the products that they sell. Groups of retailers have been able to secure state laws forbidding product-selling prices below a fixed percentage of markup over cost. Labor organizations seek to increase, or in some cases to maintain, their shares of national income by fixing wages through the collective bargaining process. People throughout the economy, concerned with the small distributive shares of low-paid workers, support minimum wage legislation. We shall examine typical cases of administered prices[4] in an attempt to assess their effects on income distribution.

Administered Prices: Pure Competition   Suppose that owners of a given resource, dissatisfied with their shares of national income, seek and obtain an administered price above the equilibrium level for their resource. Will the incomes of the resource owners involved increase relative to the incomes of the owners of other resources? In other words, will the owners of the given resource receive a larger share of the economy's product? Equally important, what will happen to the share of total earnings of the resource received by each of its owners? What will be the effects on the efficiency of the economy's operation or on welfare?

If demand for the given resource remains constant,[5] the effect of the administered price on total income earned by the resource will depend on the elasticity of demand. If elasticity is less than one, total income will rise and owners of the resource as a group will have increased their distributive share. If elasticity equals one, no change in total income will occur. If elasticity is greater than one, total

---

[4] *Administered prices* are prices fixed by law, by groups of sellers, by groups of buyers, or by collective action of buyers and sellers. They are the antithesis of free-market prices established by free interactions of buyers and sellers in the marketplaces.

[5] There seems to be no valid reason for assuming that a change in the price of the resource will change the demand for it, especially if the resource concerned constitutes a small proportion of the economy's total supplies of resources—and such is usually the case for any given resource. Even if the administered price raises the total income of the resource owners involved, it seems unlikely that demand for the products that the resource assists in producing will be increased to any significant degree. In a stationary economy, particularly, it seems logical to assume independence between resource price changes and consequent changes in demand for the resource.

income and the distributive share of owners of the resource as a group will decline.

Reference to Figure 18.2 will help to answer the second problem—the effects of the administered price on the distribution among the owners of the resource of the total income earned by it. The demand curve and supply curve in the figure for resource A are DD and SS, respectively. The equilibrium price is p_a, and the level of employment is quantity A.

FIGURE 18.2
Effects of administered prices on income distribution

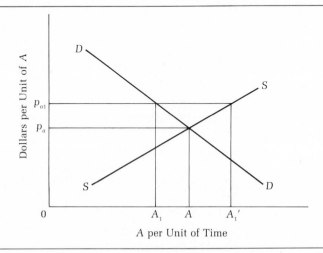

Suppose that an administered price of p_{a1} is set for the resource—none can be sold for less. Whether the administered price is set by the government, through bargaining between organized groups of buyers and sellers, or through unilateral action on the part of either resource buyers or resource sellers is of no consequence. The effects will be the same. Confronted by the higher price, each firm using resource A finds that if it employs the same quantity as before, marginal revenue product for the resource will be less than its price. Consequently, each firm finds that reductions in the quantity of the resource used will lower total receipts less than they decrease total costs and will increase the firm's profits. When all firms have reduced employment sufficiently for the marginal revenue product of the resource in each to equal p_{a1}, they will again be maximizing profits. The market level of employment will have dropped to A_1.

The administered price p_{a1} will create unemployment, thus causing income differences between those whose resources are employed and those whose resources are not.[6] At price p_{a1} employers will take quantity A_1, but quantity A_1' of the resource seeks em-

---

[6] Unless the unemployment is shared equally by all owners of the resource.

ployment. Unemployment amounts to A_1A_1'. Those whose units of the resource remain employed gain greater distributive shares of the economy's product; however, those owning idle units now receive nothing for them. Units of the resource still are paid according to their marginal contributions to the total receipts of the firm. For the employed units, marginal revenue product is greater than formerly because of the reduction in the ratio of resource A to the other resources used by individual firms. The marginal revenue product of the unemployed units is zero.

The unemployed units of resource A may seek to be used in another resource classification. Suppose, for example, that units of resource A are carpenters. Carpenters denied employment in that skill category, at a wage rate of p_{a1}, may seek work as common laborers rather than remain as jobless carpenters. Their marginal revenue product and their wage rate will be less in the lower skill classification. The administered wage rate increases income differences in two ways: (1) employed carpenters receive higher wage rates and incomes than they would otherwise receive; and (2) the wage rates and incomes of common labor are lower than they would otherwise be, as unemployed carpenters join their ranks and increase the supply of common labor.

The effects of the administered price on welfare are clear. The unemployed units of A contribute nothing to the value of the economy's output, or, to the extent that they shift into lower productivity classifications, they contribute less than they would otherwise have done. If the resource price were allowed to drop to its equilibrium level, greater employment in the uses with higher value of marginal product would raise the real value of the economy's output—and at the same time would contribute toward greater income equality among owners of the resource.

Supply Restrictions: Pure Competition   Resource prices in given employments may be increased indirectly through restriction of the resource supplies that can be used in those employments. Examples are furnished by governmental acreage restrictions placed on cotton and wheat farmers. Or the same result may be obtained by labor union activity. The milk-truck drivers' union in a large city may succeed in making union membership a condition of employment, while at the same time it restricts entry into the union. The effects on income distribution and total output of the economy are about the same as those resulting from directly administered prices. The employment level of the resource in its restricted use is decreased, leaving some of the resource units either unemployed or seeking employment in alternative uses. Land excluded from cotton and wheat farming may be switched to the production of other products. Light-truck drivers excluded from driving milk trucks may secure such alternative employments as delivery-truck or taxi driving. Value of marginal product and price of resource units in the restricted use increase,[7] while value of marginal product and price of those placed in other employments decrease. These changes lead to differential prices for the resource and to greater income differences. At the same time they lead to net national product smaller than the economy is capable of producing.

Administered Prices: Monopoly Do administered resource prices set above the equilibrium level offset the restrictive effects of monopoly when resource buyers sell a product as monopolists? The argument is frequently made that they do and that the advance in resource prices comes from the monopolists' profits. Suppose that initially the equilibrium price for a given resource prevails. Firms with some degree of monopoly in product markets are among those who buy the resource, and the resource is so allocated that its price is the same in its alternative uses. The resource price equals its marginal revenue product in its various employments, and those units of the resource employed by monopolistic sellers are exploited monopolistically—they receive less than they contribute to the value of the economy's output.

Will an administered resource price above the equilibrium price regain what is lost by resource owners from monopolistic exploitation? Suppose such an administered price is obtained. Marginal revenue product of the resource for individual firms will be less than the administered price if firms continue hiring the same quantities as before. Consequently, each firm reduces its employment of the resource to the level at which its marginal revenue product equals the administered price. But note that it is still marginal revenue product and not value of marginal product of the resource that is equal to its price. Despite the administered price, monopolistic exploitation of the resource continues to occur.[8]

---

[7] In the case of wheat land or cotton land, the ratio of land to other resources is decreased both through decreased acreage allowances and through more intensive application of labor and fertilizer. Greater marginal physical product of the land and possibly higher prices for smaller crops increase the value of marginal product of land.

About the same thing happens with regard to milk-truck drivers. Firms faced with restricted supplies attempt to make each driver as productive as possible. Slightly larger trucks may be used to minimize the number of trips back to the plant for reloading. Trucks may be made more convenient to get into, to get out of, and to operate. Idle truck time is avoided through better maintenance and repair facilities for trucks. Such measures increase the marginal physical product of the drivers. Additionally, the employment of fewer drivers may lead to smaller milk sales and higher milk prices. Thus, the value of marginal product of milk-truck drivers will be higher than before.

[8] Thus, measures to offset monopolistic exploitation of resources must attack the monopolistic

In addition, the level of employment of the resource by monopolistic firms, already too low for maximum welfare, is reduced still further. At the higher price the firms employ fewer units of the resource. More units seek employment. Unemployment and even greater differences in income among owners of the resource occur. If the unemployed units then find employment in resource classifications or uses with lower marginal revenue product, income differences are mitigated to some extent; but they still occur.

Administered Prices: Monopsony   In monopsonistic cases administered resource prices can offset monopsonistic exploitation of a resource. The employment level of the resource can be increased at the same time that its price is raised above the market level. The income and the distributive shares of the owners of the resource are increased relative to those of other resource owners in the economy. At the same time the level of real net national product and welfare will be increased.

The detailed explanation of how an administered resource price offsets monopsonistic exploitation was presented in Chapter 16. To recapitulate the analysis, an administered price set above the market price makes the resource supply curve faced by the firm horizontal at that price. For prices higher than the administered price, the original supply curve is the relevant one. For the horizontal section of the resource supply curve, marginal resource cost and resource price will be equal. By judicious setting of the administered price, the firm can be induced to employ that quantity of the resource at which marginal revenue product equals resource price. Without the administered price the firm restricts employment and pays units of the resource less than their marginal revenue product.

Price Increases Accompanying Demand Increases   The effects of administered resource price increases, when demand for the resource remains constant, are often confused with the effects of resource price increases that accompany increases in demand for the resource. Suppose that demand for a given resource is rising while, simultaneously, resource owners organized as a group succeed in *bargaining out* a series of price increases with the buyers of the resource. Suppose further that the contract prices at no time exceed the rising equilibrium price. No adverse distributive effects for the owners of the resource arise. Their positions are continuously improving as individual resource owners and as a group. However, it is erroneous to conclude from situations of this kind that administered resource

product demand situation. They must eliminate the difference between marginal revenue and price for the monopolist and, hence, between marginal revenue product and value of marginal product of resources.

price increases will, in general, have no adverse effects on total income of the owners of the resource in question or on the distribution of income within the group. We must distinguish carefully between those administered price increases that are accompanied by increases in demand for the resource and those that are not. Although the former may have no adverse effects on total income of the owners of the resource or on the distribution of income among such owners, adverse effects—except in the case of monopsony—are likely to arise from the latter.

Movements toward Less Inequality

In most societies that rely heavily on the market mechanism to organize economic activity, there is a general belief that some reduction of income differences is desirable. The result is a spate of antipoverty and income-redistribution measures. What do we learn from microeconomics that will help us evaluate the effectiveness of alternative income-redistribution policies?

Resource Redistribution

Since the market mechanism tends to reward households in proportion to their contributions to production processes, a major part of any redistribution program must consist of measures to improve the distribution of resource ownership. Some 80 percent of income is earned by labor resources, so it becomes apparent that differences in labor resources owned constitute the most important source of income differences. Differences in capital resources owned are also of some significance. How can these differences be reduced? In turn, we shall look at: (1) redistribution of labor resources and (2) redistribution of capital resources.

Labor Resources   The ownership of labor resources can be redistributed through measures that enhance vertical mobility. Greater vertical mobility will increase labor supplies at higher skill levels and decrease them at lower levels. Greater supplies at the higher levels will reduce values of marginal product or marginal revenue products, thereby lowering the top incomes. Smaller supplies at the lower levels will increase values of marginal product or marginal revenue products, thereby increasing incomes at the lower skill levels. The transfers from lower to higher skills will mitigate income differences and will add to net national product in the process.

At least two methods of increasing vertical mobility can be suggested. First, greater equality in educational and training opportunities for the poor and the rich can be provided. Second, measures may be taken to reduce the barriers to entry established by groups and associations of resource owners in many skilled and semiskilled occupations.[9]

Measures to enhance horizontal mobility also can serve to lessen income differences. These include the operation of employment exchanges, perhaps some government subsidization of movement, vocational guidance, adult education and retraining programs, and other measures of a similar nature. The argument is really for a better allocation of labor resources, both among alternative jobs within a given labor resource category and among the labor resource categories themselves. Greater horizontal mobility, as well as greater vertical mobility, will increase net national product at the same time that it decreases income differences.

Capital Resources   Policy measures to redistribute capital resources meet considerable opposition in a private enterprise economy. Many advocates of greater income equality will protest measures designed to redistribute capital ownership—and these measures are the ones that will contribute most toward such an objective. The opposition centers around the rights of private property ownership and stems from a strong belief that the right to own property includes the right to accumulate it and to pass it on to one's heirs.

Nevertheless, if income differences are to be reduced, some means of providing greater equality in capital holdings among individuals must be employed. The economy's system of taxation may move in this direction. In the United States, for example, the personal income tax, the capital gains tax, and estate and gift taxes, both federal and state, are intended to operate in an equalizing manner.

The personal income tax by its progressive nature is supposed to reduce income differences directly; in so doing, it would reduce differences in abilities to accumulate capital. But the personal income tax alone is limited in the extent to which it can moderate income differences without seriously impairing incentives for efficient employment of resources and for reallocation of resources from less productive to more productive employments.

The capital gains tax constitutes either a loophole for escaping a part of the personal income tax or a plug for a loophole in the personal income tax, depending on one's definition of income. The capital gains tax is applied to realized appreciation and depreciation in the value of capital assets. Those who can convert a part of their income from capital resources into the form of capital gains have that

---

[9]   An example of such a barrier is provided by professional associations, which control the licensing standards that prospective entrants must meet in order to practice those professions.

part of their remuneration taxed as capital gains at a rate ordinarily below the personal income tax rate. For them, the capital gains tax provides a loophole through which personal income taxes can be escaped. Yet if certain capital gains would escape taxation altogether under the personal income tax, but are covered by the capital gains tax, the latter can be considered as a supplement to the personal income tax. In either case the capital gains tax allows some remuneration from capital resources to be taxed at rates below the personal income tax rates; if differences in opportunities to accumulate capital are to be mitigated, this tax must be revised to prevent individuals from taking advantage of its lower rates.

Estate and gift taxes will play major roles in any tax system designed to reduce differences in capital ownership. The estate taxes in such a system would border on the confiscatory side, above some maximum amount, in order to prevent the transmission of accumulated capital resources from generation to generation. Gift taxes would operate largely to plug estate tax loopholes. They would be designed to prevent transmission of estates by means of gifts from the original owner to heirs prior to the death of the original owner.

Administered Prices

Widespread use is made of administered prices to accomplish the objectives of income redistribution. Examples include wage rates established through collective bargaining, legal minimum wage rates, price supports for farm products, rent controls, and crude oil price controls. Unfortunately many such measures miss their mark. We can seldom be certain that they will accomplish what they are intended to do. Wage rates set above equilibrium levels will generate unemployment. Price controls may deprive some (poor) consumers of goods they would like to have. As we have seen, administered prices in many cases add to rather than decrease income inequalities. In the process they often reduce economic efficiency.

The Negative Income Tax

Measures that redistribute the ownership of labor and capital resources may fall short of accomplishing the desired reduction in income inequalities among households. Supplementary-income transfers from taxpayers to those at the bottom of the income distribution scale may be necessary. Negative income tax proposals provide a means of making supplementary transfers with minimal effects on economic incentives. No widespread use has been made of negative income tax ideas; however, they constitute an interesting possible alternative to such current transfer programs as public assistance, unemployment compensation, food stamps, subsidized housing, and even social security.

The essence of a negative income tax plan is presented in Table 18.3. Two essential elements of it are (1) the income base and (2) the negative tax rate. The income base is the minimum level of income

TABLE 18.3 A negative income tax plan	Income Base	Income Earned	Negative Tax (base − 50% of income earned)	Disposable Income (income earned + negative tax)
	$5,000	$ 0	$5,000	$ 5,000
	5,000	1,000	4,500	5,500
	5,000	2,000	4,000	6,000
	5,000	9,000	500	9,500
	5,000	10,000	0	10,000

below which no household is allowed to fall. The negative tax rate is the percentage of income earned that is subtracted from the income base to determine the size of the subsidy or negative tax that is to be paid the household.

Suppose that the income base and the negative tax rate are set by the appropriate legislative body at $5,000 and 50 percent, respectively. There is nothing sacred about either of these figures—they can be whatever the society, acting through its legislature, wants them to be. If a household earns nothing at all during the year, this fact would be duly reported by an income tax return filed with the appropriate tax collection agency, say the Internal Revenue Service in the United States. The tax collection agency, acting for the government, would then send a $5,000 check to the household, this amount becoming the disposable income of the household. If the household reports an income earned of $1,000, the amount of the check mailed to it is $4,500, leaving it with a disposable income of $5,500. Similarly, an earned income of $2,000 results in a negative tax or subsidy of $4,000 and a disposable income of $6,000. At an earned income level of $10,000 or more per year, the household would receive no negative tax. Under the negative tax scheme a household can always have a larger disposable income if it earns income than it can have if it earns nothing. In addition, the more income it earns, the larger its disposable income will be. Thus, positive incentives to earn are built into the plan. The larger the base and the smaller the negative tax rate, the larger will be the amount of income earned that the household will be allowed to keep, and the higher will be the income level at which the amount of the subsidy to the household becomes zero.

The preservation of incentives to work and earn are important features of the negative income tax plan, but we must be careful not to overstate the case. To put it into proper perspective, suppose we subject a poor individual to three policy options. The first option is to provide the person with no subsidy whatsoever. The second is to provide a direct subsidy in which the welfare payments to the person are reduced dollar for dollar with the individual's earnings. The third is the negative income tax option. How do the three compare with regard to incentives to work and earn?

The first option requires a straightforward use of the income-leisure time indifference map of an individual developed in Chapter 15. Consider Figure 18.3(a) first. The total daily hours of leisure time that could be available for work is $0H$. We draw a dashed vertical axis at H so that daily hours of work are measured to the left from the origin H. If the wage rate is w and the amount of labor performed per day is l ($= h_1H$, h_2H, and so forth), then $l \cdot w$ generates the income line HK. The wage rate w determines and is equal to the slope of HK. Ignoring the other straight-line segments for the present, indifference curve I is the highest the individual can reach. The daily work effort will be h_1H and disposable income in the absence of any taxes is $0D_1$.

To illustrate the second option, suppose in Figure 18.3(a) that the individual can receive a daily welfare payment HE when not working. But if the individual works, the welfare payment is reduced one dollar for every dollar of income earned. The income line becomes EGK. Below work level h_3H the welfare payment exceeds any income the individual could earn so the welfare payment generates the EG portion of the income line. At higher work levels income earned exceeds the welfare payment so the GK portion of the income line becomes relevant. Indifference curve II is the highest that the income line EGK will permit. To reach that level of satisfaction, the individual will elect not to work and will receive the daily welfare payment HE. The welfare payment has destroyed incentives to work. This will be the case for any welfare payment exceeding HJ.

Another possibility exists under the second option. Suppose the individual's indifference map is that of Figure 18.3(b). Again the income line is EGK. If the individual does not work and receives the daily welfare check, the level of satisfaction depicted by indifference curve I' is reached. However, the higher satisfaction level of indifference curve II' is available if the individual works $h_1'H$ hours per day. Work is preferable to welfare in this case, or for any other case in which the welfare payment is less than HJ'.

Under the second option, in which welfare payments are reduced dollar for dollar by income earned, at least some individuals are likely to prefer welfare to work. Since the indifference maps of different individuals will not be the same, the critical welfare pay-

FIGURE 18.3
The effects of welfare
versus the negative
income tax on
incentives to work

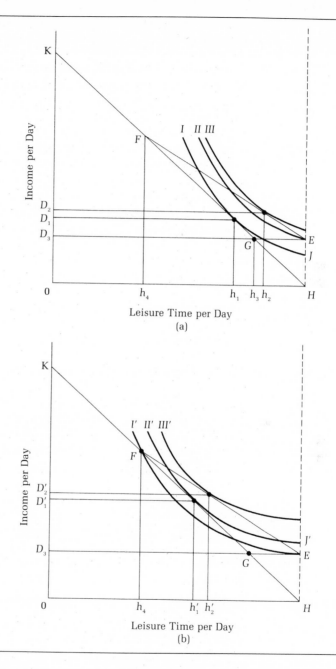

ment level *HJ* varies for different persons. Any given level of daily
welfare payments will be above *HJ* for some persons and below *HJ*
for others. Those in the former group will choose to receive welfare
and not to work.

527   CHAPTER 18   Distribution of Income and Product

For analysis of the third, or negative income tax, option, consider Figure 18.3(a). Suppose the base income for every individual is *HE*—even if the individual does not work. If the individual works, income earned *without the negative tax* would trace out income line *HK* for different numbers of hours worked per day. *With the negative income tax* the income line becomes *EFK*. The *EF* segment of the income line has a smaller slope than *HK*. This is so because the negative tax decreases as income earned increases, reaching zero at some employment level h_4H.[10] With the negative income tax option, the individual chooses to work h_2H hours per day, receiving a disposable income of D_2.

We can now compare the options as they are displayed in Figure 18.3(a). In the absence of any subsidization, the individual wants to work h_1H hours and have a disposable income of $0D_1$. A straight welfare plan in which the subsidy or welfare payment is greater than *HJ* induces the individual not to work. The negative income tax option with a base income of *HE* induces the individual to work h_2H hours, receiving a disposable income of $0D_2$. The negative income tax plan as compared with the welfare payment plan thus preserves some work incentives, but these incentives are not as strong as those provided by the market alone.

In Figure 18.3(b) we compare the three options for an individual for whom either a welfare payment or a negative income tax would be less than *HJ'*. The welfare option drops out because the individual would never choose it, preferring instead to work $h_1'H$ hours per day. With the negative income tax the desired work hours are $h_2'H$ per day. Although the negative income tax preserves some work incentives, those incentives are not as great as the incentives provided by the market.

The negative income tax idea has several appealing features in addition to preserving incentives for resource owners to employ their resources productively. It is simple in concept and could be administered easily by the existing tax-collection mechanism. It does not require a separate bureaucratic agency. It attacks the problem of poverty directly by making subsidy payments only to the poor. If it were

---

[10] Let: Y_e = Income earned
  k = Base income
  t = Fraction of income earned subtracted from base income to determine negative tax
  N = Negative tax
  w = Wage rate
  l = Hours of work per day
  Y_d = Disposable income.

Then: $Y_e = l \cdot w$
  $N = k - Y_e \cdot t = k - l \cdot w \cdot t$
  $Y_d = Y_e + (k - Y_e \cdot t) = l \cdot w + (k - l \cdot w \cdot t)$
  $= k + l \cdot w(1 - t) \qquad l \geqq h_4H$

used, it would eliminate the need for many of the special income-transfer programs now in existence.

Income Redistribution and the Price System

The foregoing discussion suggests that if a society that uses the price mechanism is not satisfied with the income distribution that the price mechanism generates, the most efficient way of redistributing income is to do it outside the operation of the price mechanism itself. Direct government intervention in the pricing of resources, goods, and services is likely to reduce the efficiency with which the economic system operates by distorting price signals and bringing about misallocations of resources. It may also generate unemployment and other surpluses, or, on the other hand, shortages. Redistributions of resource ownership and redistribution of money income by means of taxes and subsidies outside the price mechanism itself are less likely to have adverse effects on efficiency and can get directly at the heart of the problem—alleviation of poverty.

Application: The New Jersey-Pennsylvania Experiment[11]

The U.S. Office of Economic Opportunity, knowing the central importance of incentives in the debate over welfare reform, conducted a large-scale experiment in New Jersey and Pennsylvania between 1968 and 1972 to test the effect of income guarantees on work incentives. At the time most observers expected that the negative income tax proposal would reduce work incentives to some extent. The proposal not only provides grant income, but it lowers the effective market wage rate owing to the tax that is imposed. Both of these factors should cause some reduction in the amount of work supplied. But would the drop in labor supply be large enough to outweigh other advantages of the negative income tax proposal: for example, lower administrative costs than the present welfare system imposes in the form of fewer case workers needed to ensure that recipients comply with its rules and regulations? The key question to be determined was whether or not cash allowances, which decline as hours of work increase, reduce the amount of work done by the recipients *to any significant extent*.

The experiment involved 1,216 families, 725 in the experimen-

---

[11]   This information is drawn from Joseph A. Pechman and P. Michael Timpane, eds., *Work Incentives and Income Guarantees: The New Jersey Negative Income Tax Experiment* (Washington, D.C.: The Brookings Institution, 1975).

tal group and 491 in the control group. They were headed by males aged 18 to 58, had income levels at less than 150 percent of the poverty line, and lived in four urban communities in the two states. No families headed by women or families where the husband and wife were not together were included. The experiment lasted three years and cost $8 million, of which one-third was spent in the form of payments to the families involved. Most of the costs were accounted for by the research effort to determine the consequences of the program. Families in the experiment were placed in different groups according to the various combinations of guaranteed income level and tax rates that yield the average four-week payments shown in Table 18.4. By way of comparison, in Figure 18.3, we assume a single

TABLE 18.4 Average four-week payments to continuous husband-wife families participating in the New Jersey income-maintenance experiment during the second of the three years[a]	Guarantee Level (percent)	Tax Rate (percent)		
		30	50	70
	125	—	$187.28	—
	100	—	123.72	$66.07
	75	$103.54	44.17	34.91
	50	46.23	21.66	—

[a] There is substantial variation within each of the combinations of guarantee level and tax rate owing to differences in family size and earned income.

Source: Albert Rees and Harold W. Watts, "An Overview of the Labor Supply Results," in Joseph A. Pechman and P. Michael Timpane, eds., *Work Incentives and Income Guarantees: The New Jersey Negative Income Tax Experiment* (Washington, D.C.: The Brookings Institution, 1975), p. 76.

combination of cash grant and tax rate. This was done to test two auxiliary hypotheses. First, the experimenters expected that the higher the tax rates the greater the substitution effects and thus the larger the reductions in labor supply at a given level of family satisfaction. Second, for a given tax rate, they anticipated that plans having the more generous payments would show the bigger drops in labor supply.[12]

Some of the results of the experiment are shown in Table 18.5 for families subjected to the 50 percent rate of tax. Overall there was a decline in hours worked of between 5 and 6 percent; the effect was negative, as predicted, but not large. This finding very generally is consistent with the concept of a backward-bending supply-of-labor curve. But Table 18.5 gave the researchers a big surprise in the degree to which the supply response differed among ethnic groups. There

[12] Albert Rees and Harold W. Watts, "An Overview of the Labor Supply Results," *Work Incentives and Income Guarantees*, pp. 60–77. See also Harold W. Watts and Albert Rees, eds., *The New Jersey Income-Maintenance Experiment: Volume II, Labor-Supply Responses* (New York: Academic Press, 1977).

TABLE 18.5
Labor supply response of the family as a whole based on alternative computer models, according to ethnic group, from data generated by the New Jersey negative income tax experiment over different periods of time[a]

	Percent		
	Ethnic group[b]		
Model and variable	Whites	Blacks	Spanish-speaking
Regressions pooled from eighth quarter			
Hours	−8	−3	−6
Earnings	−12	+9	−2
Regressions calculated from averages for twelve quarters			
Hours	−16	+1	−2
Earnings	−8	+13	−28

[a] Includes male heads, wives, and all other household members 16 years of age and over in continuous husband-wife families. The estimates cover the full three years of the work-incentives experiment. The tax rate is 50 percent.

[b] Estimated coefficients are jointly significant at the 1 percent level for whites and blacks, at the 5 percent level for the Spanish-speaking.

Source: Albert Rees and Harold W. Watts, "An Overview of the Labor Supply Results," in Joseph A. Pechman and P. Michael Timpane, eds., *Work Incentives and Income Guarantees: The New Jersey Negative Income Tax Experiment* (Washington, D.C.: The Brookings Institution, 1975), p. 85.

was a moderate and negative effect on the labor supply of white families, a strong and positive effect on the labor supply of black families, and a small but negative effect on the labor supply of Spanish-speaking families. To date the researchers do not have a satisfactory explanation for these striking differences. Their expectation that greater tax rates would cause a greater reduction in labor supply was reflected by the data. The results might have been different if the experiment had been permanent. Three years may be too short a time for some families to adjust to work situations that they could have fitted into if the duration of the experiment had been longer.

Summary

Individual claims to net national product depend on individual incomes; thus, the theory of product distribution is really the theory of income distribution. Marginal productivity theory provides the generally accepted principles of income determination and income distribution. Resource owners tend to be remunerated according to the marginal revenue products of the resources they own, except in cases where resources are purchased monopsonistically.

Incomes are unequally distributed among spending units in the United States. Income differences stem from three basic sources: (1) differences in labor resources owned, (2) differences in capital resources owned, and (3) restrictions placed on the operation of the price mechanism. With regard to the same general skill level, we call these horizontal differences in labor resources. Different individuals also own different kinds of labor, graded vertically from undifferentiated manual labor to top-level professions. Differences in capital resources owned result from disparities in material inheritance, fortuitous circumstances, and propensities to accumulate.

Administered prices for a given resource often lead to unemployment or misallocation of some units of the resource and, hence, to differences in incomes among owners of the resource. The case of monopsony provides an exception. Under monopsony, administered resource prices can offset monopsonistic exploitation of the resources involved.

Attacks on income differences, if society desires to mitigate those differences, should be made by way of redistribution of resources among resource owners. Attacks made by way of administered prices are not likely to accomplish this task. Redistribution of labor resources can be accomplished through measures designed to increase both horizontal and vertical mobility. These will, in turn, increase net national product. The tax system offers a means of effecting redistribution of capital resources. Estate and gift taxes will bear the major burden of effective redistribution and may be supplemented by personal income and capital gains taxes. In addition, a negative income tax plan can be used to accomplish supplemental, direct income transfers to the poor.

These measures can be accomplished within the framework of the price system and the private enterprise economy.

Suggested Readings

Alkinson, A. B. *The Economics of Inequality.* Oxford, Eng.: Oxford University Press, 1975.

Friedman, Milton. *Capitalism and Freedom.* Chicago: University of Chicago Press, 1960, Chaps. 10–12.

Okun, Arthur M. *Equality and Efficiency, the Big Tradeoff.* Washington, D.C.: The Brookings Institution, 1975.

Questions and Exercises

1 In terms of economics only—discounting completely political feasibility—do you think it would be possible to eliminate poverty

a in the United States? Explain why and how.
b in Pakistan? Explain why and how.

2 To what extent would you expect each of the following to contribute to the poverty problem in the United States?
a monopolistic exploitation of resources
b monopsonistic exploitation of resources
c inequalities in labor resources owned
d inequalities in capital resources owned.

3 What impact would you expect licensing laws for particular occupations to have on
a income distribution?
b economic welfare?

4 Price controls and rationing by the government are often suggested as a means of protecting the interests of the poor. Discuss the probable effects of this type of approach to redistribution of the economy's output on
a the efficiency of consumption (*Hint:* Consider a two-good, two-person case in which one person is initially rich and the other is initially poor.)
b the efficiency of production
c the efficiency of the product mix in the economy.

5 Outline a comprehensive income redistribution program that would have minimum adverse effects on economic efficiency.

How the Pieces Fit Together

We try to bring the many facets of microeconomics together in Part Six. It contains little that is new, but it provides a focus and a consistent logical framework that will help us understand what microeconomics is all about. It is especially important that the concepts of *welfare* and *general equilibrium* be kept separate. Maximum welfare is the most desirable state of affairs that we can define objectively, and the conditions that will yield such a state are independent of the type of economic system that may exist. General equilibrium is the state of affairs that a price system will yield, and it may or may not be a maximum welfare situation. A major part of our task is to examine the price system in order to determine how well it performs in a welfare sense.

Equilibrium and Welfare

In this chapter we first review what is involved in the concepts of welfare and equilibrium. Then, we examine the conditions that must be met in order to maximize welfare in the sense of Pareto optimality. Finally, we consider the conditions required for general equilibrium to exist in a private enterprise economic system, and the implications of these conditions for economic welfare.

The Concepts of Equilibrium and Welfare

Welfare and equilibrium are different concepts, although they are frequently confused with one another. We have defined *welfare* as the state of well-being of the persons comprising an economic system. We have defined *equilibrium* as a state of rest, a position from which there is either no incentive or no opportunity to move. We shall look at some of the principal aspects of each of these concepts.

Welfare

Most economic analysis is concerned with the welfare aspects of economic activity—how to achieve maximum or optimum welfare for the population in the economic system. An objective definition of optimum welfare constitutes a major problem. As we noted in the introductory chapter, where only one person is being considered, the concept is straightforward and is synonymous with the well-being of that person. But when more than one individual is at issue, an objective definition of a unique optimum welfare position for the group as a whole becomes impossible since such a definition would require interpersonal comparisons of satisfaction. The Pareto optimum situation, in which no one can be made better off without making someone else worse off, is the best solution that we can attain.

Equilibrium

Equilibrium concepts are important, not because equilibrium positions are ever in fact attained but because these concepts show us the direction in which economic processes move. When equilibrium positions are *stable*—as they have been assumed to be throughout this book—economic units in disequilibrium move toward equilibrium positions. Even as they are doing so, however, changes in consumers' preference patterns, resource supplies, and technology alter the equilibrium positions themselves, thus redirecting the movements that are occurring. If equilibrium positions are *unstable,* disturbances will cause economic units to move farther away from rather than toward such positions.

Partial Equilibrium   A large part of the analytical structure that we have built up is called *partial equilibrium analysis.* It has been concerned with the movements of individual economic units toward equilibrium positions in response to the given economic conditions confronting them. Thus, the consumer, with given tastes and preferences, is confronted with a given income and with given prices of goods and services. Each consumer adjusts his or her purchases accordingly to move toward equilibrium. The business firm—faced with given product demand situations, a given state of technology, and given resource supply situations—moves toward an equilibrium adjustment. The resource owner possesses given quantities of resources to place in employment. There are given alternative employment possibilities and resource price offers. The equilibrium adjustment is made on the basis of the given data. The conditions of demand and of cost in a particular industry engender profits or losses, and these motivate the entry of new firms (if entry is possible) or the exit of existing firms, thus leading toward equilibrium for the industry. Changes in the given data facing economic units and industries alter the positions of equilibrium that each is attempting to reach and motivate movements toward the new positions.

Partial equilibrium is especially suitable for the analysis of two types of problems, both of which we met time and again throughout the book. Problems of the first type are those arising from economic disturbances that are not of sufficient magnitude to reach far beyond the confines of a given industry or sector of the economy. Problems of the second type are concerned with the first-order effects of an economic disturbance of any kind.

As an illustration of the first kind of problem, suppose that the production workers of a small manufacturer of plastic products go on strike. Suppose further the plant is located in a large city and that the workers are fairly well dispersed among the residential areas of the city. The effects of the strike will be limited largely to the company and the employees concerned. Partial equilibrium analysis will provide the relevant answers to most of the economic problems arising from the strike.

As an example of the second type of problem, suppose that a rearmament program increases the demand for steel suddenly and substantially. Partial equilibrium analysis will provide answers to the first-order effects on the steel industry—what happens to its prices, output, profits, demand for resources, the resource prices, and its resource employment levels. However, the first-order effects by no means end the repercussions from the initial disturbance.

General Equilibrium As individual economic units and industries seek equilibrium adjustments to what appear to be given facts, their total group actions change the facts that they face. If some units were in equilibrium and others were not, those in disequilibrium would move toward equilibrium. Their activities would change the facts faced by units in equilibrium and would throw the latter into disequilibrium. General equilibrium for the entire economy could exist only if all economic units were to achieve simultaneous partial, or particular, equilibrium adjustments. The concept of general equilibrium stresses the interdependence of all economic units and of all segments of the economy with each other.

A hard-and-fast line between partial equilibrium analysis and general equilibrium analysis is difficult to draw. Instead of establishing a dichotomy, it will be preferable to think of moving along a continuum from partial to general equilibrium, or from first-order effects of a disturbance into second-, third-, and higher-order effects. For example, in discussing pricing and output under market conditions of pure competition, we were concerned, first, with partial equilibrium, or equilibrium of the individual firm. Next, we extended the analysis to an entire industry and observed the impact of individual firm actions on each other. Finally, we observed how productive capacity is organized in a purely competitive private enterprise economy according to consumers' tastes and preferences. This series of topics represents progressive movement from the application of partial equilibrium analysis to the application of general equilibrium analysis.

General equilibrium theory provides the analytical tools for accomplishing two objectives: (1) from the standpoint of pure theory it provides the means of viewing the economic system in its entirety—the means of seeing what holds it together, what makes it work, and how it operates; (2) and—this objective is really an application of the first one—it permits the determination of the second-, third-, and higher-order effects of an economic disturbance. When the impact of an economic disturbance is of sufficient magnitude to have repercussions throughout most of the economy, general equilibrium analysis provides the more relevant answers regarding its ultimate effects. First comes the big splash from the disturbance. Partial equilibrium analysis handles this. But waves and then ripples are set up from it, affecting one another and affecting the area of the splash. The ripples run farther and farther out, becoming smaller and smaller until eventually they dwindle away. The tools of general equilibrium are required for analysis of the entire series of readjustments.

Suppose that the higher-order repercussions from the increase in demand for steel are to be examined. The first-order, or partial, equilibrium effects are higher prices, greater outputs with given facilities, larger profits, and higher payments to the owners of resources used in making steel. These effects generate additional disturbances. Higher incomes for the resource owners increase demand for other products, setting off disturbances and adjustments in other industries. Demands also increase for steel substitutes, generating another series of disturbances and adjustments. Productive capacity will be diverted from other activities toward the making of steel. Eventually, effects will be felt over the entire economy. If the full impact of such a disturbance is to be determined, general equilibrium analysis must provide the tools to do so.

Since general equilibrium analysis covers the interrelationships of all parts of the economy, it necessarily becomes exceedingly complex. There are two principal variants of it. In the first one, following Walras, most economists find it convenient to discuss general equilibrium in mathematical terms. The interdependence of economic units is shown through a system of simultaneous equations relating the many economic variables to each other. It can be demonstrated that there are as many variables to be determined as there are equations relating them. Solving the system of equations establishes those values of the variables that are consistent with general equilibrium for the economic system. The Walrasian version of general equilibrium provides essentially the theoretical apparatus for understanding the interrelationships of the various sectors of the economy.

The second variant of general equilibrium analysis is Wassily W. Leontief's input-output analysis.[1] The input-output approach is an empirical descendant of the abstract Walrasian approach. It divides the economy into a number of sectors or industries, including households and the government as "industries" of final demand. Each industry is viewed as selling its output to other industries; these outputs become inputs for the purchasing industries. Likewise, each industry is viewed as a purchaser of the outputs of other industries. Thus, the interdependence of each industry on the others is established. Statistical data gathered around the basic framework of the system provide an informative and useful picture of the interin-

---

[1]   For an excellent survey and analysis of this approach, see Robert Dorfman, "The Nature and Significance of Input-Output." Review of Economics and Statistics, 36 (May 1954), pp. 121–33.

dustry flows of goods, services, and resources. The input-output approach has been used extensively by municipalities, states, and regions for economic development purposes.

The attainment of general equilibrium in an economic system does not imply that Pareto optimality is also attained. A price system tends to move the economy toward general equilibrium. Unless pure competition exists in both product and resource markets, however, Pareto optimality will not follow.

The Conditions of Optimum Welfare

Optimum welfare conditions in an economy are usually grouped into three sets. The first consists of the conditions leading to maximum consumer welfare when supplies of goods and services are fixed. The second consists of the conditions of maximum efficiency in production, assuming that resource supplies are fixed. In the third consumer welfare and maximum productive efficiency are brought together to determine conditions under which the outputs of different goods and services are optimal.

Maximum Consumer Welfare: Fixed Supplies

The conditions of maximum consumer welfare with fixed supplies of goods and services per time unit are illustrated in the two-good, two-person model of Figure 19.1. If the distribution of goods X and Y between the two consumers H and J is initially off the contract curve at some such point as D, exchanges can be made that will increase

FIGURE 19.1
Optimum consumer
welfare: fixed supplies

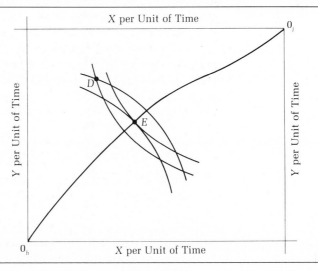

the welfare of either without decreasing the welfare of the other. A movement from distribution D to distribution E increases the welfare of both. Once a contract curve distribution is achieved, any further exchanges can benefit only one consumer at the expense of the other. Any point on the contract curve represents a Pareto optimal distribution of X and Y between the two consumers. Each such point is defined by the condition that:

$$\text{MRS}_{xy}{}^{h} = \text{MRS}_{xy}{}^{j}. \tag{19.1}$$

The condition can be extended to as many goods and services and as many consumers as there are in the economy.

Sometimes there are *externalities* involved in the consumption of a good or service. An externality occurs if the consumption of a good by someone else affects the level of satisfaction attained by any given consumer. Suppose, for example, that H and J are neighbors, that H increases her stereo capacity, and that J, whose musical tastes parallel those of H, can now hear and enjoy the music she plays. J receives an external benefit from H's consumption—his set of indifference curves between music and other goods and services is shifted inward toward the origin of his indifference map. On the other hand, the externality could have operated in the opposite direction. The music played by H could have annoyed J, shifting his set of indifference curves between music and other goods and services outward from the origin of his indifference map.[2]

When an externality in consumption occurs, we can no longer be sure that a point on the contract curve such as E in Figure 19.2 is Pareto optimal. Suppose that J's satisfaction is enhanced by H's increased purchase of music via an expansion of stereo capacity. An exchange of other goods and services for music that moves the consumers from distribution E to distribution F would not change H's level of satisfaction. Suppose that the external benefits that J receives from H's increased consumption of music shift J's indifference curves toward origin 0_j so that the satisfaction level formerly represented by I_j is now represented by I_j'. At point F, J will be at a higher level of satisfaction, represented by I_{j2}', than before; since H's satisfaction has not been lessened, the welfare of the two consumers combined is greater than it was at point E.

Maximum Efficiency in Production: Given Resource Supplies

We turn now to the production side of the picture, holding resource supplies constant.

---

[2]   The preference function of J takes the form of

$$U_J = f(x_J, y_J, x_h),$$

in which x_J and y_J represent J's consumption of two goods, X and Y, and x_h represents H's consumption of X.

FIGURE 19.2
Externalities in
consumption

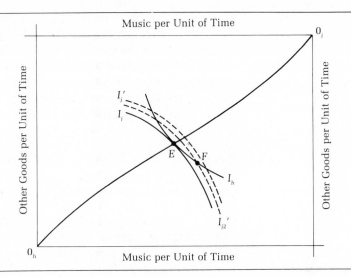

The Conditions of Efficiency: No Externalities   Maximum efficiency
in production refers to Pareto optimality in production processes.
Given the supplies of resources available, these must be allocated
among the production of goods and services in such a way that the
production of any one good cannot be increased unless the production of another is decreased.

    The conditions of efficiency are illustrated in the two-resource,
two-product model of Figure 19.3. Fixed supplies of resources A and

FIGURE 19.3
Optimum productive
efficiency

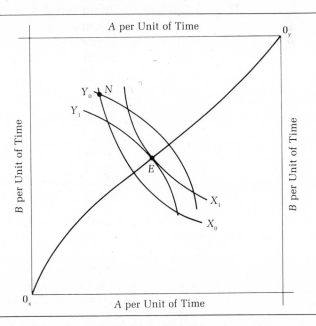

B are used in the production of products X and Y. Any distribution of resources between the two products that lies on the contract curve, such as that at E, is more efficient than is any distribution not on the contract curve, such as that at N. Given any initial distribution such as N, the output of either product can be increased with no sacrifice of the other. It is also possible to increase the outputs of both products by allocating more A and less B to the output of X, and less A and more B to the output of Y, thus moving from N to E. With any distribution such as E, neither product's output can be increased unless some of the other is sacrificed. Any point on the contract curve represents a maximum efficiency allocation of resources. The condition that determines any such point is that

$$MRTS_{ab}{}^x = MRTS_{ab}{}^y. \tag{19.2}$$

These conditions can be expanded to include as many resources and as many goods and services as exist in the economy.

The infinite number of efficiently produced combinations of X and Y shown by the contract curve of Figure 19.3 are also shown by the transformation curve of Figure 19.4. For every combination of X and Y on the transformation curve, resources are allocated to each product in the optimal combinations. The transformation curve is often appropriately called the production possibilities curve. Its slope at any point measures the rate at which one product must be given up to obtain an additional unit of the other, that is, the MRT_{xy}.

The Effects of Externalities   If externalities occur in the production of a good, the contract curve may no longer show the conditions of maximum efficiency. Congested facilities represent a very common type of externality. Suppose, for example, that highways, along with other resources, are used by the producers of wheat and also by the

FIGURE 19.4
A transformation curve

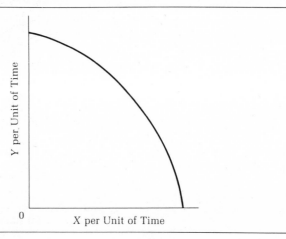

producers of automobiles for getting their commodities to consumers. Initially, these two groups of users cause the highways to be congested to the extent that transportation delays result. In Figure 19.5 the marginal rate of technical substitution between highway facilities and other resources is the same for producers of wheat and producers of automobiles at point E. But this allocation of resources is not necessarily optimal. If highway congestion exists at E, a reduction in the use of the highways by firms in one industry will increase the productivity of highway facilities for those in the other.

Suppose that wheat producers reduce their use of the highways but maintain their output level at w_1 by increasing their use of alternative forms of noncongested transport, thus moving from point E to point F. This move shifts the set of isoquants of automobile producers toward the 0_a origin, and a_1 units of automobiles is now shown by the dashed line a_1'. At point F automobile production will be at a_2', a higher level than before. At the same time there will have been no change in total wheat production. The efficiency of production has been increased by the resource exchange.

Optimal Outputs of Goods and Services

We have not yet determined which of the combinations of products represented by a transformation curve yield optimal welfare to consumers. If we assume that there are no externalities of production,

FIGURE 19.5
Externalities in
production

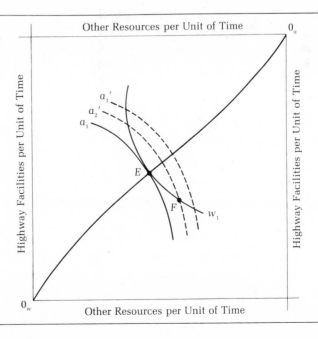

the transformation curve of Figure 19.6 shows the combinations of X and Y that resources A and B can produce when those resources are used efficiently—that is, when $MRTS_{ab}{}^x = MRTS_{ab}{}^y$ for each combination. The slope of the transformation curve at any point, the MRT_{xy}, shows the rate at which it is possible technically to transform Y into X at that combination of goods.

For any combination of X and Y on the transformation curve, an Edgeworth box for consumers can be constructed to show the optimal distributions of supplies making up the combination. For the combination at 0_{j1} in Figure 19.6, the Edgeworth box $0_h y_1 0_{j1} x_1$ is the appropriate one for a two-consumer, two-good model. For the combination at 0_{j2}, the appropriate box is $0_h y_2 0_{j2} x_2$. Note that since the origin 0_h for consumer H remains in a fixed position, H's indifference curves, drawn with respect to the X and Y axes of the transformation diagram, are the same for all possible boxes. The origin of the indifference map for consumer J, however, is different for each different combination of X and Y shown on the transformation curve and for each different box. Consequently, J's set of indifference curves must be redrawn for each different box.

If the combination of X and Y being produced were 0_{j1}, would

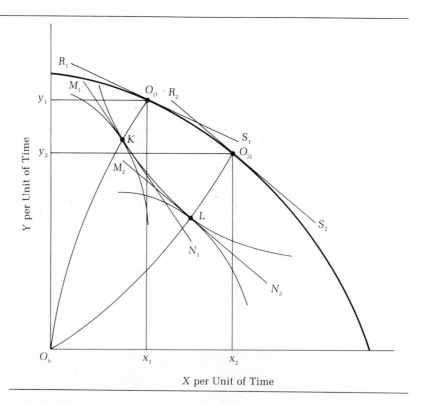

FIGURE 19.6
The full conditions of maximum welfare

this be the optimal output of each product? Since it lies on the transformation curve, the outputs are being produced with maximum efficiency. Moreover, any distribution (such as K) of the output combination between consumers H and J that lies on the contract curve 0_h0_{j1} is a welfare-maximizing distribution of the specific combination. Still, combination 0_{j1} of product outputs, together with distribution K of the products between consumers, does not result in maximum welfare. The slope of line M_1N_1 through point K and tangent to the indifference curves of H and J, measures the MRS_{xy} for both consumers at point K. It indicates the rate at which *both* consumers would be willing to give up Y for X. The slope of R_1S_1 through point 0_{j_1}, tangent to the transformation curve, measures the MRT_{xy} (the rate at which it is technically necessary to give up Y to produce more X). Since $MRS_{xy} > MRT_{xy}$ (that is, consumers are willing to give up more Y to obtain an additional unit of X than is necessary in the production processes), the welfare of both consumers can be increased by increasing the output of X and decreasing the output of Y.

The conditions for optimum welfare in terms of the output levels of X and Y and the distribution of that output between consumers H and J are that

$$MRS_{xy} = MRT_{xy}. \tag{19.3}$$

Consider combination 0_{j2} and distribution L. The lines M_2N_2 and R_2S_2 are parallel, indicating that $MRS_{xy} = MRT_{xy}$; therefore, this is an optimum welfare output combination and distribution. A small movement away from L or away from 0_{j2} will decrease the welfare of at least one of the consumers.

The optimum welfare combination of outputs and distribution of product among consumers is not a unique one, however. There may be an infinite number of output combination-product distribution possibilities at which the $MRS_{xy} = MRT_{xy}$. For output combination 0_{j1}, even though at distribution K the $MRS_{xy} \neq MRT_{xy}$, there may be other distributions on contract curve 0_h0_{j1} at which the $MRS_{xy} = MRT_{xy}$, although it is not certain that there are. The same thing can be said for other output combinations represented by the transformation curve.

Summary of Optimum Welfare Conditions

In summary, then, for Pareto optimality to exist in an economic system three conditions must be met:

1 The distribution of product outputs must be such that the marginal rate of substitution of any one product for any other is the same for all consumers.

2   The allocation of resources must be such that the marginal rate of technical substitution of any one resource for any other is the same in the production of all commodities for which those resources can be used.

3   The outputs of product and their distribution among consumers must be such that the marginal rate of substitution of any one product for any other is equal to the marginal rate of transformation of the products.

The conditions of Pareto optimality leave us uninformed about which of the optimal distributions of product among consumers is the "optimum" optimum and about which of the optimal combinations of product output is the "optimum" optimum. We can eliminate those distributions of any output combination at which marginal rates of substitution are not equal to the corresponding marginal rates of transformation. After these deletions, however, we may still have a great many alternative possibilities.

Private Enterprise and General Equilibrium

Will a private enterprise economic system guided and directed by the price mechanism move toward optimum welfare positions as it moves toward general equilibrium positions? The optimum welfare conditions of the preceding subsection apply to any kind of economic system—socialist, private enterprise, or other. To evaluate the performance of a private enterprise system, then, it is necessary to examine the conditions of the equilibrium toward which it moves in order to determine whether these coincide with the conditions of optimum welfare, or at least approach those conditions. Toward this end we draw on, summarize, and extend the principles developed throughout the book.

Consumer Equilibrium: Fixed Supplies

Consider first the problem of consumers' choice. Assume that the supplies of goods and services are fixed—they automatically come into being on the first of each month. The distribution among consumers may be any distribution, but it will not vary from one month to another. Consumers' preference patterns are fixed. A monetary system exists. The price pattern is initially random. Each good or service is in the hands of many individuals, with the result that pure competition will exist in the event that exchange occurs. What happens at this point if individuals are free to buy and sell, that is, to exchange? Each consumer will seek to maximize satisfaction.

If for two goods—X and Y, priced initially at p_x and p_y—a consumer finds that $MRS_{xy} \neq p_x/p_y$, that individual will want to engage in exchange. Any consumer for whom $MRS_{xy} > p_x/p_y$ will want to sell Y and buy X in order to move to higher indifference curves. Any consumer for whom $MRS_{xy} < p_x/p_y$ will want to sell X and purchase Y in order to move to higher indifference curves.

At the initial price pattern the supplies of some items are likely to be exhausted before all consumers get as much as they desire. The prices of these items will rise, reducing the quantities that consumers want relative to the quantities of other goods. Prices will move to those levels at which consumers are just willing to ration themselves to the entire quantities available per month.

The supplies of other goods may be overabundant at their initial price levels. To reduce the quantities that they have on hand, those who hold surpluses will lower the asking prices. Prices will fall to the levels at which consumers are just willing to take the entire quantities available per month.

General equilibrium exists when goods and services are so priced that each consumer gets the quantity of each of them that he or she desires, relative to the quantities of others, and when there is neither a shortage nor a surplus of any item. Any one consumer H takes a combination of X and Y such that

$$MRS_{xy}{}^h = p_x/p_y.$$

Any other consumer J also takes a combination at which

$$MRS_{xy}{}^j = p_x/p_y.$$

It follows, since p_x/p_y is the same for all consumers, that

$$MRS_{xy}{}^h = MRS_{xy}{}^j. \tag{19.4}$$

All consumers are on the contract curve. Thus, under conditions of pure competition and in the absence of externalities, the conditions of general equilibrium with fixed supplies coincide with the conditions of optimum welfare with fixed supplies.

Producer Equilibrium: Given Resource Supplies

We turn now to the operation of the price mechanism in organizing production. To facilitate the discussion, several assumptions are useful. We shall assume that resource supplies are fixed quantities per month and that their initial prices are random. The range of production techniques is given. We shall start by considering the organization of production in terms of the purely competitive model. Then we shall modify the analysis to take monopoly and monopsony into account.

Pure Competition   Suppose that the fixed supplies that consumers receive are being produced by firms operating in purely competitive industries and that these firms seek to maximize their profits. Confronted with the initial resource prices, each firm attempts to acquire those quantities of different resources at which the marginal revenue product of each resource is equal to its marginal resource cost.

At the initial set of resource prices, firms will find that they are not able to obtain enough of some resources to bring their marginal revenue products into line with their respective marginal resource costs; that is, shortages occur. The prices of these resources will rise, inducing firms to attempt to substitute other resources for them. Prices will reach equilibrium levels when each firm is just able to obtain the quantities that it desires.

Some other resources will not be fully employed when, at the initial prices, every firm takes the quanties at which their marginal revenue products equal their marginal resource costs. Surpluses of these resources will cause those who own them to cut the prices at which they are offered in order to induce firms to substitute them for now relatively more expensive resources. The prices will be in equilibrium when firms are just willing to absorb the entire quantities placed on the market.

General equilibrium exists when each resource is priced so that neither a surplus nor a shortage exists and when each firm is taking that quantity of each resource at which its marginal revenue product is equal to its marginal resource cost. These conditions, together with pure competition in both resource and product markets, lead to important additional consequences, as described below.

Since pure competition exists, the value of marginal product of each resource will be equal to the resource price. For any given resource, A, $MRP_a = MRC_a$ means also that $VMP_a = p_a$ because for any product, X, that A assists in producing, $MR_x = p_x$; and for any firm purchasing A, $MRC_a = p_a$.

When firms using several common resources to produce several products employ resources in profit-maximizing quantities, they will also be employing them efficiently from a Pareto optimal point of view. Suppose that two resources, A and B, are employed by firms producing X and Y. Any firm in industry X employs those quantities of the resources at which

$$MPP_{ax} \times p_x = p_a$$

and

$$MPP_{bx} \times p_x = p_b.$$

Thus,

$$\frac{MPP_{ax}}{p_a} = \frac{1}{p_x} \quad \text{and} \quad \frac{MPP_{bx}}{p_b} = \frac{1}{p_x}.$$

Therefore,

$$\frac{MPP_{ax}}{p_a} = \frac{MPP_{bx}}{p_b} \quad \text{and} \quad \frac{MPP_{ax}}{MPP_{bx}} = \frac{p_a}{p_b},$$

or

$$MRTS_{ab}{}^x = \frac{p_a}{p_b}.$$

Similarly, we can show that

$$MRTS_{ab}{}^y = \frac{p_a}{p_b}.$$

Therefore,

$$MRTS_{ab}{}^x = MRTS_{ab}{}^y, \qquad (19.5)$$

which is the condition for an efficient allocation of any two resources between any two products.

Monopoly and Monopsony   Monopoly in the sale of products will not deter the price system from allocating resources among different products so that they are used efficiently in the production of each, but some degree of monopsony will act as a deterrent. If monopoly exists in the sale of products X and Y, but the firms in both industries purchase resources A and B competitively, we can show that when A and B are purchased in each industry in a manner such that the marginal revenue products of the resources equal their respective resource prices, then

$$MRTS_{ab}{}^x = MRTS_{ab}{}^y.$$

However, if some degree of monopsony exists in the purchase of A and B, then

$$MPP_{ax} \times MR_x = MRC_{ax}$$

and

$$MPP_{bx} \times MR_x = MRC_{bx}.$$

Therefore,

$$\frac{MPP_{ax}}{MRC_{ax}} = \frac{MPP_{bx}}{MRC_{bx}} \quad \text{and} \quad \frac{MPP_{ax}}{MPP_{bx}} = \frac{MRC_{ax}}{MRC_{bx}},$$

or

$$MRTS_{ab}{}^x = \frac{MRC_{ax}}{MRC_{bx}}.$$

We can show similarly that

$$MRTS_{ab}{}^y = \frac{MRC_{ay}}{MRC_{by}}.$$

The firm producing X must pay the same price for resource A as the firm producing Y.[3] But if the elasticity of the supply of A to the firm making X differs from the elasticity of supply of A to the firm making Y, at whatever the supply price of A to both firms may be, then

$$MRC_{ax} \neq MRC_{ay}.$$

Similarly, under the same set of circumstances

$$MRC_{bx} \neq MRC_{by}.$$

Consequently, it is not necessary that

$$MRTS_{ab}{}^x = MRTS_{ab}{}^y, \tag{19.6}$$

and the price system will not necessarily bring about optimum efficiency in the use of the resources in the two industries.

Product Output Levels: Given Resource Supplies

In this subsection we shall continue to trace the implications of the general equilibrium results brought about by the price mechanism. Equilibrium exists when (1) price levels of goods and services are such that there are no shortages and no surpluses, (2) price levels of resources are such that there are no shortages and no surpluses, and (3) firms purchase those quantities of different resources at which their marginal revenue products equal their respective marginal resource costs. Again we shall consider purely competitive markets first and then turn to the effects of monopoly and monopsony.

Pure Competition   Under conditions of pure competition in both product and resource markets, and in the absence of externalities, the allocation of resources and the output levels of product determined by the price system will maximize welfare.

Consider first the allocation of resources between any two products, X and Y. When firms of industry X are using two resources, A and B, and are maximizing profits, then for each firm

$$\frac{MPP_{ax}}{p_a} = \frac{MPP_{bx}}{p_b} = \frac{1}{MC_x} = \frac{1}{p_x},$$

or

$$MC_x = p_x.$$

---

[3]   Rather than assume pure monopsony, in which resource A would be specialized to one firm only, we assume a degree of monopsony in which units of the resource are mobile among a few firms, any one of which buys a sufficient proportion of the total available supply to have an effect on the resource price.

Similarly, for firms in industry Y,

$$\frac{MPP_{ay}}{p_a} = \frac{MPP_{by}}{p_b} = \frac{1}{MC_y} = \frac{1}{p_y},$$

or

$$MC_y = p_y.$$

The MRT_{xy}, at whatever combination of X and Y is being produced, is the measure of the amount of Y that must be given up by the economic system to produce an additional unit of X; MRT_{xy} can be expressed as $\Delta y/\Delta x$.

Since resources are used efficiently in the production of both X and Y, the cost of giving up Δy of Y must equal the cost of adding Δx of X to the economy's output;[4] that is,

$$\Delta y \times MC_y = \Delta x \times MC_x$$

and

$$\frac{\Delta y}{\Delta x} = \frac{MC_x}{MC_y}.$$

Since the price system leads to a product output combination at which

$$MC_x = p_x \quad \text{and} \quad MC_y = p_y,$$

then

$$MRT_{xy} = \frac{\Delta y}{\Delta x} = \frac{MC_x}{MC_y} = \frac{p_x}{p_y}.$$

We can now put the pieces together. The price system induces consumers to establish a price ratio for the supplies of any two goods, X and Y, such that for each consumer

$$MRS_{xy} = \frac{p_x}{p_y}.$$

These prices in turn bring about an allocation of resources between the two goods such that

$$MC_x = p_x \quad \text{and} \quad MC_y = p_y,$$

or

$$\frac{MC_x}{MC_y} = \frac{p_x}{p_y}.$$

---

[4] This relationship must obtain since the identical quantities of resources released in giving up Δy of Y are used to produce Δx of X.

The ratio MC_x/MC_y in turn is the measure of the MRT_{xy}; thus, the price system leads to general equilibrium outputs of X and Y such that

$$MRS_{xy} = MRT_{xy}. \tag{19.7}$$

This condition for general equilibrium is also the condition for a set of optimum outputs of X and Y.

An output combination on the transformation curve, such that $MRS_{xy} \neq MRT_{xy}$, simply means that $MC_x \neq p_x$ and/or $MC_y \neq p_y$. For example, if $MRS_{xy} > MRT_{xy}$, as is the case at point K in Figure 19.6, it follows that $MC_x < p_x$ and $MC_y > p_y$. The price system will bring about an expansion in the output of X and a reduction in the output of Y. These changes will decrease MRS_{xy}, causing p_x to drop and p_y to rise. At the same time they cause MRT_{xy} to rise, increasing MC_x and decreasing MC_y until $MC_x = p_x$, $MC_y = p_y$, and $MRS_{xy} = p_x/p_y$ $= MC_x/MC_y = MRT_{xy}$.

Monopoly   The sale of a product under conditions of monopoly will prevent the attainment of optimal outputs by way of the price mechanism. Suppose that product X is sold monopolistically and product Y is sold competitively. The price system will lead to a set of outputs such that for each consumer

$$MRS_{xy} = \frac{p_x}{p_y}.$$

But profit maximization will induce the monopolist to produce the output at which $MC_x = MR_x < p_x$. Purely competitive producers of Y produce outputs at which $MC_y = p_y$. Thus,

$$MRT_{xy} = \frac{MC_x}{MC_y} = \frac{MR_x}{p_y} < \frac{p_x}{p_y} = MRS_{xy}. \tag{19.8}$$

The output level of X is too small and the output level of Y is too large for optimum welfare.

Summary

In this chapter we summarized the conditions that must be met in an economic system in order to achieve maximum welfare in the sense of a Pareto optimum. Then we summarized the operation of the price mechanism in a private enterprise type of economic system, examining it to see if its results are Pareto optimal. The price system will lead to Pareto optimality if all markets are purely competitive and if no externalities occur in consumption or production. Where selling markets are monopolized, outputs will be short of the optimal quantities. Monopsony in resource purchases has a further adverse effect, in that it leads to inefficiency in the use of resources by the purchasers.

Suggested Readings

Bator, Francis M. "The Simple Analytics of Welfare Maximization." *American Economic Review*, 47 (March 1957), pp. 22–59. Reprinted in William Breit and Harold M. Hochman, eds., *Readings in Microeconomics*, 2d ed. New York: Holt, Rinehart and Winston, 1971, Chap. 32.

Baumol, William J. *Economic Theory and Operations Analysis*, 4th ed. Englewood Cliffs, N.J.: Prentice-Hall, 1977, Chap. 21.

Questions and Exercises

1 It is frequently asserted that the market system underproduces medical services in relation to other goods and services. Two sets of causal factors are cited: (1) blocked entry into medical service professions and (2) externalities in the consumption of medical services. With "Medical Services" on one axis and "Other Goods and Services" on the other axis, show diagrammatically and explain each of these sets of causes. What evidence can you cite with regard to the validity or invalidity of each?

2 You are asked to render a reasoned opinion with regard to whether or not the government should subsidize housing. What will you use as analytical foundations for your opinions? List these and explain each.

3 Suppose that $MRS_{xy} > MRT_{xy}$ in a market economy. Is it possible that general equilibrium exists? Explain.

4 If a market economy in which $MRS_{xy} > MRT_{xy}$ is one of pure competition with no externalities, what can we expect to occur? Explain in detail and illustrate with a diagram.

5 Can you provide a justification solely on economic grounds for
   a a progressive income tax?
   b laws against gambling?
   c state subsidization of education?

**KEY
CONCEPTS**

Process
Process ray
Linearly homogeneous
production function
Isoquants
Isocosts
Optimal solution
Feasible solution
Objective function
Primal problem
Dual problem
Shadow prices

Introduction to Linear Programming

Linear programming is the simplest and most widely used of the mathematical programming techniques that have come into vogue since World War II. It is a technique for solving maximization and minimization problems confronting decision-making agencies subject to certain side conditions or constraints that limit what the agencies are able to do.

Linear programming techniques provide little information regarding the operation of the economy beyond that furnished by the conventional theory of the firm. Their prime virtue is that they provide computational possibilities that are not present in conventional theory, owing to the smooth, continuous, and frequently nonlinear nature of conventional theory's production, cost, and revenue functions. The observable data confronting decision-making agencies are ordinarily not continuous and may not be amenable to marginal analysis or calculus techniques. From an assumption that relations among observable data are linear, straightforward solutions to complex maximization and minimization problems can be obtained through linear programming. Sometimes the distortions resulting from the exclusive use of linear relationships may render worthless the solutions arrived at by means of the technique, but in many cases distortions of this kind may be more or less negligible. Like any other technique, if its results are to be useful, it must be applied with good judgment and common sense.

This chapter presents the nature and method of linear programming. After we establish the assumptions on which linear programming problems rest, we shall formulate and solve graphically a general maximization problem involving one output and two inputs. Then we shall formulate and solve a maximization problem involving multiple outputs and inputs. We shall conclude by considering the dual solution to a maximization problem.

The Assumptions

The linear programming technique rests on several basic assumptions: In the decision making to which it is applied, there are constraints on the decision-making agency; input and output prices are assumed to be constant; and the firm's input-output, output-output, and input-input relations are presumed to be linear. These will be discussed in turn.

The Constraints

In linear programming problems the firm faces various limitations on its activities.[1] There may be quantity limitations on particular kinds of inputs or facilities used by the firm. An automobile final assembly line, for example, can turn out some maximum number of automobiles per twenty-four-hour period. A firm's warehouse space contains a fixed number of square feet. A candy factory can wrap only so many bars per day. The firm's access to credit may be restricted. And so on.

The firm also faces a limited number of alternative production processes. Any one process is defined in terms of a constant ratio of inputs. Suppose process A involves the use of one worker of a given skill and one machine of a given kind and size. Production carried on with process A can be increased or decreased until input quantity limitations are reached, but it always will require one worker per machine regardless of the total number of machines used.

Constant Prices

Linear programming techniques make use of the purely competitive approach to prices. Output prices and input prices are assumed to be unaffected by the actions of any one individual firm. Output prices are the same whether the firm's output is large or small; input prices are the same regardless of how much or how little of the inputs the firm uses. As sellers and buyers, firms are thought of as being price takers rather than price makers.

Linear Relations

Linear programming techniques take advantage of the simplicity of linear relations. In many instances linear relations are found in fact. A firm purchasing an input at a constant price per unit faces a linear total resource cost curve for that input. The total revenue curve from the sale of a product will be linear when the product sells at a constant price per unit. An isocost curve for two inputs will be linear, given the prices of the inputs. An isorevenue curve for two outputs will be linear, given the prices of those outputs.

---

[1] As a matter of convenience, the decision-making agency will be designated as a firm throughout the chapter. Linear programming techniques can be and are used by agencies other than firms, for example, military procurement units.

In other cases, relations among variables that may not actually be linear can be represented usefully by a series of (different) discrete linear relationships or by a single linear relationship. An isoquant, for example, is ordinarily a nonlinear constant product curve for two resources. The linear programming counterpart is a series of connected linear relations. Similarly, actual production functions may very well show nonlinear relations between inputs and outputs. In linear programming problems, they are taken as being homogeneous of degree one.

Maximization Problems

In this section, two maximization problems will be considered. In the first, we shall be concerned with the optimum use of inputs in the production of a single output. In the second, we shall examine the optimum output mix to be produced with particular inputs.

One Output, Two Inputs

In the final maximization problem, we consider two alternative kinds of constraints: (1) cost-outlay limitations and (2) limits to the quantities of inputs available.

Cost Outlay Constraints   Suppose that a firm producing one output X, and using inputs A and B, seeks to maximize output subject to a given cost outlay. This problem is familiar from our previous study of the theory of production and serves as a good introduction to linear programming. However, suppose that the possibilities of continuous substitution between A and B, that characterize the usual theoretical presentation of the problem, are absent. Instead, suppose that there are only four processes—possible ratios of B to A—by which the firm can make the product. The firm faces constant input prices and a constant output price.[2]

The nature of a process is illustrated in Figure A.1. Units of input A per unit of time are measured along the horizontal axis; units of input B per unit of time are shown on the vertical axis. If process C—one of the four processes available to the firm—requires 3 units of input B to every 1 unit of input A, the process can be represented by the linear ray $0C$. Ignore for the moment the scale numbers along $0C$. The various points making up the ray $0C$ show the fixed ratio of B to A, but at different levels of utilization. Similarly, process rays $0D$,

---

[2]   The problem would not be changed if total revenue were stated as the quantity maximized. Since price per unit of output is given, maximization of output also maximizes total revenue.

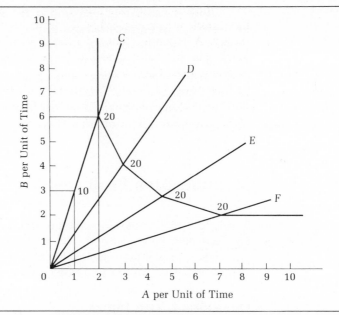

0E, and 0F can be drawn for the other three processes available to the firm. Each process ray shows a given ratio of B to A throughout its length. The ratio of B to A is different for each of the process rays.

The assumption that the production function is homogeneous of degree one enables us to measure product output along each of the process rays. A production function is of this type if, when *all* inputs are increased in a given proportion, output is increased in the same proportion. Focusing for the moment on process ray 0C, suppose that 3 units of B used with 1 unit of A will produce 10 units of output X. The point on 0C representing this combination of A and B can be marked off as 10 units of X. Now if the inputs are doubled to 6 units of B and 2 units of A, output is doubled to 20 units of X. The point on 0C representing the new combination of A and B can be scaled as 20 units of X and will lie twice as far from the origin as the point representing 10 units of X does. The output scale along 0C is thus easily established.

Output scales can be established in a similar way along each of the other three process rays. However, the distance measuring 20 units of output (or any other given quantity of output) will not ordinarily be the same along one process ray as it will be along another. The technological efficiency of the other three processes is assumed to be such that the 20-unit output marks on their respective process rays are those indicated in Figure A.1.

The points on the various process rays representing any given quantity of output can be joined by a series of straight lines, as they are at the 20-unit level in Figure A.1. The resulting kinked curve can be called an isoquant, just as was its counterpart in traditional theory. A different isoquant can be drawn for each possible output level. The higher the output level, the farther from the origin the isoquant lies. The linear segment of an isoquant between any two process rays will always be parallel to the corresponding linear segment of any other isoquant. For example, in Figure A.2 the G_1H_1

FIGURE A.2
Simultaneous use of
two processes

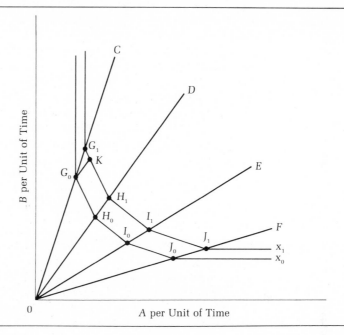

segment of isoquant x_1 is parallel to the G_0H_0 segment of isoquant x_0.[3]

Any point (such as K) on isoquant x_1 represents the simultaneous use by the firm of two processes to produce a given amount of output. In this case the firm would be using processes C and D. The processes are assumed to be technologically independent of one another. The productivity of process C is unaffected by the level at which process D is used and vice versa. Quantity $0G_0$ of X is produced by means of process C. Quantity G_0K $(= H_0H_1)$ of X is produced using process D. The output scale measuring G_0K (or H_0H_1) of X is different from that measuring $0G_0$ of X. The scale of process ray $0D$ is used for the former, while the scale of process ray $0C$ is used for the latter.

---

[3]   This must be so because the sides $0G_1$ and $0H_1$ of triangle G_1H_10 are cut into proportional segments by line G_0H_0; that is, $0G_0/G_0G_1 = 0H_0/H_0H_1$.

In general, we would expect isoquants to exhibit the shapes illustrated in Figures A.1 and A.2. In Figure A.2 suppose that B is capital and A is labor. Continuous substitution of one for the other is assumed to be impossible. Nevertheless, the same general type of reasoning as that used in discussing conventional isoquant shapes still applies. If the firm were using process F to produce a given amount of product, the ratio of labor to capital would be relatively high. Therefore, if the firm were to consider a process using smaller ratios of labor to capital, say, process E, it is likely that it could give up a rather large amount of labor to obtain the additional capital—the amount of output remaining constant. But as the firm moves to processes using relatively smaller ratios of labor to capital, say, processes D and C, the amounts of labor that could be given up to obtain additional units of capital, output remaining constant, would be expected to become smaller and smaller.

The cost constraint on the firm is represented by a conventional isocost curve. Its position and shape are determined by the fixed cost outlay and the fixed prices per unit of the firm's inputs. In Figure A.3

FIGURE A.3
Output maximization,
total cost constraint

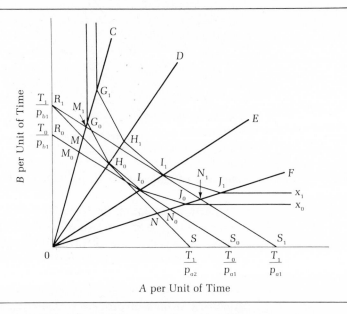

suppose that the cost outlay is T_1 while the prices of A and B are p_{a1} and p_{b1}, respectively. The cost outlay divided by the price of A, or T_1/p_{a1}, establishes point S_1, which is the number of units of A that can be obtained if no B is purchased. Similarly, T_1/p_{b1} is the number of units of B that can be purchased if no A is taken; it is represented by point R_1. A straight line joining R_1 and S_1 is the isocost curve showing the combinations of A and B available with the cost outlay T_1.

The isocost curve has a negative slope equal to

$$0R_1/0S_1 = T_1/p_{b1} \div T_1/p_{a1} = T_1/p_{b1} \times p_{a1}/T_1 = p_{a1}/p_{b1}.[4]$$

The isocost curve and process rays $0C$ and $0F$ place limits on what the firm is able to do. Any point on or within the triangle $0M_1N_1$ is a possible combination of inputs A and B, and will lie on some isoquant of the firm; that is, it will produce some specific level of output. The area bounded by $0M_1N_1$ is called the area of *feasible solutions* to the firm's problem. No production possibilities outside this area are open to the firm.

From the feasible solutions to the firm's problem, the *optimal solution* must be found. This has already been postulated as the one that maximizes the firm's output subject to the cost outlay constraint. The optimal solution will occur at point I_1, at which the isocost curve touches the highest possible isoquant. Output x_1 is the highest output possible with the given cost outlay. The firm will use process E. Cost level T_1 expended on any of the other processes will not produce outputs as high as x_1.

A change in the cost constraint, with the prices of A and B remaining constant, will not affect the process used but will affect only the level at which it is used. Changes in T will shift the position of the isocost curve but will not affect its slope. A reduction in the cost outlay to T_0 shifts the isocost curve to the left parallel to itself to R_0S_0. The area of feasible solutions is now bounded by $0M_0N_0$. The firm maximizes output by using process E at level I_0. The maximum output is x_0. Isocosts parallel to R_1S_1 will always touch those isoquant corners falling along process ray $0E$. This will be so because, due to the assumption that the production function is homogeneous of degree one, the corresponding segments of the various isoquants are parallel to each other.

If the price of A relative to the price of B were to increase enough, the firm would shift to a different process. Suppose that the total cost outlay were to remain the same and that the price of A were to rise to p_{a2}. The restricting isocost curve now becomes R_1S and the area $0MN$ encloses the feasible solutions. To maximize output subject to the constraint, the firm would use process D at level H_0. It is possible, too, that the price of A relative to that of B could change just enough to make the isocost curve coincide with a linear segment

---

[4] The equation of the isocost curve will be

$$ap_{a1} + bp_{b1} = T_1,$$

or

$$b = \frac{T_1}{p_{b1}} - a\,\frac{p_{a1}}{p_{b1}},$$

for which T_1/p_{b1} is the B axis intercept and p_{a1}/p_{b1} is the slope.

of an isoquant, say, a segment corresponding to G_1H_1. If this were the case, processes C and D would be equally efficient. It would make no difference which the firm uses; any combination of the two processes shown by the linear isoquant segment G_1H_1 could be used.

Where the firm is faced by a single constraint, not more than one process is required to maximize whatever the firm is maximizing. In the case at hand, the process to be used will be determined by the ratio of input prices. Once the output-maximizing process has been identified, it becomes apparent that a considerable change in input price ratios may occur without inducing the firm to switch from one process to another. The extent to which input price ratios must change to induce a change in the process used will depend on the number of processes available and the measures of the angles formed by linear segments of the isoquants.

Input Quantity Constraints The optimal solution to the problem of output maximization is different if, instead of being faced with a total cost outlay constraint, the firm is faced with quantity limitations per time period on one or more of its inputs. Common examples of this are warehouse space, number of machines available, size of a drying kiln, and so on. We shall look first at a situation in which only one of two inputs is limited in quantity. Then we shall extend the constraint to include both of the inputs that the firm uses.

In Figure A.4 we assume first that not more than b_0 of B is available to the firm and that A is available in unlimited quantities.

FIGURE A.4
Output maximization, input quantity constraints

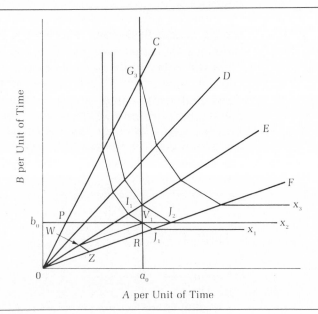

The area of feasible solutions would be on or within triangle $0PJ_2$—the area on or between process rays $0C$ and $0F$ and on or below the horizontal line extending to the right from b_0. There will be some isoquant, the horizontal segment of which coincides with the horizontal line. This isoquant is designated x_2 in the diagram, and represents the highest output level available with quantity b_0 of B. Process F used at level $0J_2$ will maximize the firm's output.

If A were limited to a_0 while B were unlimited in quantity, the area of feasible solutions would lie between process rays $0C$ and $0F$ and on or to the left of a vertical line extending upward from a_0. Output would be maximized by using process C at level $0G_3$ and would be x_3. In each of the two cases, output maximization requires but a single process. In neither case is the ratio of input prices a determinant of the process to be used. Turning now to the case in which both inputs are limited in quantity, assume in Figure A.4 that the availability of input A is limited to a_0, while that of B is limited to b_0. Subject to these limitations, the area of feasible solutions is on or within the polygon $0PV_1R$. The solution lies at point V_1, and the maximum output of the firm is x_1. In the case illustrated, process E and process F will both be used. Quantity $0W$ will be produced using process E, and quantity $WV_1(= ZJ_1)$ will be produced using process F. Conceivably, if the available quantity of A were smaller and that of B were larger, the solution to the problem would fall at an isoquant corner such as I_1. If this were the case, process E only would be required. Again the ratio of the price of A to the price of B plays no part in determining the process or processes to be used.

The problems discussed illustrate a fundamental principle in linear programming techniques. No larger number of processes than the number of constraints placed on the firm will be required in whatever the firm is maximizing or minimizing. In the example in which total cost outlay was the only constraint, one process was required. In the example in which the constraint was the quantity of one input, no more than one process was required. When two inputs were limited in quantity, no more than two processes were required. Where there are more inputs limited in quantity, more processes may be required, but these will not exceed the number of inputs for which there are effective limitations.

Multiple Outputs, Multiple Inputs

Moving now to a more complex problem, suppose that the objective of a firm is to maximize the excess of its total receipts over its total variable costs—that is, its total economic rent as defined in Chapter

15,[5] subject to limitations in the capacities of certain fixed facilities. Suppose the firm produces two kinds of output, X and Y. It has four kinds of facilities, each of which is fixed in capacity. We shall designate these as facilities M, N, R, and S. These could be such things as paint shop capacity, final assembly capacity, packaging capability, and the like.

Rent yielded per unit of X and per unit of Y will depend on the prices received for each of the products and the average variable costs of each. We shall assume that given quantities of variable inputs are required per unit of X regardless of the amount of that commodity produced; therefore, the average variable cost of X will be constant. The same assumption will be made for product Y. Rent yielded per unit of X produced is equal to its price minus its average variable cost and thus will be a constant amount. Rent yielded per unit of product Y is computed in the same way. These can be designated as r_x and r_y, respectively.

If r_x and r_y were \$8 and \$6, respectively, the following *objective equation* could be established showing what it is that the firm wants to maximize:

$$8x + 6y = W. \tag{A.1}$$

Rent yielded per unit of X multiplied by the total amount of X produced will be total rent received from the production of X. Rent yielded per unit of Y multiplied by the quantity of Y produced will show total rent obtained from the production of Y. The sum of the two will be W, or total rent received by the firm.

The objective equation is the equation for a family of *isorent curves*—one for every possible value of W. In Figure A.5 the line FG is the isorent curve for $W = \$120$. It shows all combinations of X and Y that will yield that amount of rent. Its slope is r_x/r_y or, in this case, 8/6. Isorent curves for higher values of W lie farther to the right but have the same slope. Those for lower values of W also have the same slope but lie farther to the left.

The constraints on the firm's activities are the fixed facilities M, N, R, and S. Suppose that we designate the entire amount of each as unity. In Table A.1 that part of each facility required in the production of one unit of X and that part of each required in the production of one unit of Y are shown.

Essentially, Table A.1 defines the processes involved in the problem. There will be two processes used if both outputs are produced. The production of X requires one process—fixed proportions of facilities M, N, S, and R. Similarly, the production of Y requires

---

[5] Maximization of rent also means that profit will be maximized, since profit is equal to rent minus total fixed costs. In the problem being formulated, the firm's fixed costs will not be known. Thus, rent can be computed but profit cannot.

FIGURE A.5
Multiple outputs,
facility constraints

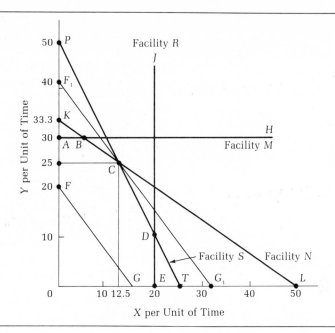

TABLE A.1
Multiple outputs,
facility constraints

Facility	Facility Input per Unit of Output	
	X	**Y**
M	0.0	0.033
N	0.02	0.03
S	0.04	0.02
R	0.05	0.0

one process—fixed proportions of the four facilities, but proportions that are different from those required to produce X.

From Table A.1 we can construct a set of algebraic representations of the constraints placed on the production of X and Y by the fixed facilities. These are

$$0.033y \leq 1 \qquad (A.2)$$

$$0.05x \leq 1 \qquad (A.3)$$

$$0.02x + 0.03y \leq 1 \qquad (A.4)$$

and

$$0.04x + 0.02y \leq 1, \qquad (A.5)$$

in which

$$x \geq 0 \text{ and } y \geq 0.$$

Inequality (A.2) sums up the constraint exercised by facility M. This facility is useful in the production of Y only. It is not useful in the production of X. The amount required in the production of one unit of Y is 0.033 of the entire facility. If we consider (A.2) as an equation, solving for y, we find that the entire facility will permit the production of 30 units of Y per unit of time. It will also permit the production of smaller quantities. Graphically, the horizontal straight line AH in Figure A.5 at 30 units of Y represents the limitations on production inherent in facility M.

Similarly, inequality (A.3) sums up the constraint exercised by facility R, which is used only in the production of X. An amount 0.05 of the entire facility is required for each unit. The maximum quantity of X that facility R will permit is 20 units per time period. This is shown graphically by the vertical line EJ at that output level in Figure A.5.

The production possibilities of facility N are shown by inequality (A.4) and include both outputs. Because 0.03 of facility N are required for a unit of Y and 0.02 of it are required for a unit of X, (A.4) treated as an equation marks off possible combinations of outputs that the facility will allow from those it will not. If x were zero, 33.3 units of Y could be processed by the facility. If y were zero, 50 units of X could be handled by it per time period. Locating these two points at K and L, respectively, the straight line joining them in Figure A.5 is the graphic representation of the equation.

Similarly, (A.5) treated as an equation separates the combinations of X and Y that facility S will permit from those it will not. If no X were produced, y could be 50 units per time period. If no Y were produced, x could be 25 units. The graphic representation of the equation is the line PT in Figure A.5.

The area of feasible solutions, showing all combinations of X and Y that can be turned out per unit of time by the firm, is $0ABCDE$. Facility M limits the firm to combinations equal to or smaller than those represented by AH; facilities M and N limit it to combinations equal to or smaller than those represented by ABL; facilities M, N, and S further limit it to combinations equal to or smaller than those represented by $ABCT$; facilities N, S, and R limit it to combinations equal to or smaller than those represented by BCD; facilities S and R limit it to combinations equal to or smaller than those represented by DE; and facility R limits it to combinations equal to or smaller than those represented by EJ.

The optimal solution to the firm's problem can be found graphically by moving to higher and higher isorent curves until the one just touched by the area of feasible solutions is reached. This will be isorent curve F_1G_1, which is just touched by point C in Figure A.5. No other point either within or on the boundary of the area of feasible solutions touches an isorent curve as high as F_1G_1. Every point other than C on the isorent curve F_1G_1 lies outside the area of feasible solutions. The firm would produce and sell 25 units of Y, receiving rent of $6 per unit. It would produce and sell 12.5 units of X receiving rent of $8 per unit. Thus, the maximum total rent obtainable would be $250 per time period.

The facilities' limitations are not all effective as constraints on the firm. At point C facility M is not used to capacity and, therefore, does not restrict the firm's output. Similarly, facility R is not used to capacity. To produce combination C, only facilities N and S are used to their full capacities. If more of these two facilities were available, the firm could move to a higher isorent curve.

Algebraically, the solution to the problem can be found by examining the "corners" of the area of feasible solutions. We need only to examine the corners since the number of processes involved in the problem will not exceed the number of effective constraints on the firm. Thus, the points at which both X and Y are positive (that is, where two processes are used) and that would be possible optimal solutions must lie at corners formed by two constraints (that is, where two constraints would be effective). A possible optimal solution in which only X is produced would require but one effective constraint and would be the corner at the intersection of the X axis and the constraint that exercises the greatest restriction when used exclusively in the production of X. Similarly, the corner on the Y axis represents the only possible optimal solution if Y alone were produced. If the optimal solution were a zero output for both X and Y, the necessity of a corner solution at the origin is obvious.

Suppose now that we start with the corner at the origin and proceed clockwise around the area of feasible solutions, attempting to find the one at which total rent to the fixed facilities is maximum; that is, at which the objective equation (A.1) yields the maximum W. At 0 we find that W equals zero. To find the coordinates of corner A, we solve the facility M equation (A.2). At this corner x equals zero and y equals 30. Plugging these values for X and Y into equation (A.1), we find that W equals $180. The simultaneous solutions of equations (A.2) and (A.4) for facilities M and N give us corner B, at which y equals 30 and x equals 5. Thus, from equation (A.1), total rent is found to be $220. The simultaneous solution to equations (A.4) and (A.5) for facilities N and S is represented by corner C, where y equals 25 and x equals 12.5. Substituting these values in equation (A.1), total rent is $250. When equations (A.5) and (A.3) for facilities S and R are solved simultaneously for the coordinates of corner D, x equals 20 and y equals 10. Substituting these values in equation (A.1), total rent is $220. The solution to (A.3) provides the coordinates of corner E with x equal to 20 and y equal to zero. Substituting in (A.1) we find that total rent would be $160.

Comparing the results obtained at the various corners shows that corner C provides maximum total rent. In problems where the number of outputs and constraints are too great for graphic analysis, this sort of algebraic examination of the "corners" of the area of feasible solutions can be used to find the one that provides the optimal solution.[6]

Different ratios of r_x to r_y may result in different optimal solutions to rent maximization. The slope of an isorent curve $(-r_x/r_y)$ could conceivably be small enough so that the area of feasible solutions touches the highest isorent curve at point B. Or it could be great enough for the highest possible isorent curve to be touched at point D. If $-r_x/r_y$ were equal to the slope of the line segment CD in Figure A.5 [that is, if the highest attainable isorent curve were to coincide with the graphic representation of equation (A.5)], any combination of X and Y on line segment CD would be an optimal solution to maximization of total rent. In this case the limitations imposed by facility S would be the only effective constraint on the firm.

The Dual Problem

Every linear programming problem has a counterpart problem called its *dual*. The original problem is referred to as the *primal* problem. If the primal problem requires maximization, the dual problem is one of minimization; or if the primal is a minimization problem, the dual is a maximization problem. An illustration of the relationship between a primal problem and its dual is provided in the theory of production and costs. Suppose that the primal problem were that of maximizing output with a given cost outlay. The dual would be that of minimizing costs for the given product output. Whether or not a particular problem to be programmed should be set up for solution in its primal or its dual form depends on (1) which formulation yields the desired information more directly and (2) which can be more easily solved.

In this section the dual of the primal problem of the preceding section will be formulated and solved. In the primal problem we sought the outputs of X and Y that would maximize total rent re-

---

[6]   The method used here is called the complete description method. An alternative is provided by the simplex method. *See* Robert Dorfman, Paul A. Samuelson, and Robert M. Solow, *Linear Programming and Economic Analysis* (New York: McGraw-Hill, 1958), Chap. 4.

ceived by the firm, subject to capacity limitations of its fixed facilities M, N, R, and S. In the dual problem we seek to impute minimum values—sometimes called *shadow prices*—to the firm's fixed facilities, just sufficient to absorb the firm's total rent.

The data available are those of the primal problem. Table A.1 shows the amount of each fixed facility available (one unit of each) and the portion of each fixed facility required in the production of a unit of X and a unit of Y. The contribution per unit of product X to total rent is given as $8; that of a unit of product Y is given as $6. The objective equation of the dual problem can be stated as

$$v_m + v_n + v_r + v_s = V. \tag{A.6}$$

The term v_m denotes the value to be imputed to facility M, while v_n, v_r, and v_s denote, respectively, the values to be imputed to facilities N, R, and S.[7] On the right side of the equation, V denotes the total valuation of the fixed facilities.

The constraints placed on the assigning of minimum values to the fixed facilities are summed up in the following inequalities:

$$0.0v_m + 0.02v_n + 0.04v_s + 0.05v_r \geq 8 \tag{A.7}$$

and

$$0.033v_m + 0.03v_n + 0.02v_s + 0.0v_r \geq 6, \tag{A.8}$$

in which

$$v_m \geq 0, v_n \geq 0, v_s \geq 0, \text{ and } v_r \geq 0.$$

Inequality (A.7) states that the values assigned to the various fixed facilities must be such that the values of productive capacity necessary for the production of one unit of X (*see* Table A.1), when added together, must not be less than the value of a unit of X. Inequality (A.8) states the same thing with respect to the production of Y. Together, and treated as equations, they state that the values assigned to each kind of productive capacity must be such that a dollar's worth of that productive capacity used in producing either X or Y must yield a dollar in rent.

We face the dilemma of having more unknowns than there are equations [treating (A.7) and (A.8) as equations] to solve for the unknowns. However, the linear programming principle cited earlier, together with conventional economic analysis, can rescue us. The linear programming principle tells us that the number of fixed facilities operating as effective constraints on the firm's output

---

[7] In the present problem the coefficient of each of the variables on the left side of the equation will be one since the entire capacity of each fixed facility is taken as being unity. If each fixed facility were to consist of some certain number of units, then the value per unit of each facility would have as its coefficient the number of units of the facility that are available.

should not exceed the number of processes used. There are two processes used—one for producing X and one for producing Y. Consequently, only two of the fixed facilities can be effective constraints on the firm's output, and the other two must be underutilized.

Consider now an underutilized facility from the point of view of conventional economic analysis. A small increase—say, 1 percent—in such a facility would add nothing to the firm's output or total receipts. The marginal revenue product of such an increment would thus be zero and so would its imputed value. Every other 1 percent of the facility would also have an imputed value of zero and so would the whole underutilized facility. Since we must have two underutilized facilities, two of the variables of (A.7) and (A.8) should have values of zero and the other two will take on positive values.

The problem is to find which two of the variables—v_m, v_n, v_s, and v_r—have imputed values of zero and which two have positive values when the firm is minimizing total valuation of the fixed facilities. We can proceed by first assigning values of zero to any two of these, solving for the other two. Then we assign values of zero to another pair (one of the pair may be from the previous pair) and solve for the remaining pair. We proceed in this manner until every possible pair of the variables has been assigned zero values and the corresponding solutions in terms of the remaining variables have been obtained. Six solutions of this sort are possible. We shall examine them in turn.

Suppose, first of all, that v_m and v_n take on values of zero. Equations (A.7) and (A.8) become

$$0.04v_s + 0.05v_r = 8 \qquad \text{(A.7a)}$$

and

$$0.02v_s + 0.0v_r = 6. \qquad \text{(A.8a)}$$

Solving equation (A.8a) for v_s, we find that v_s equals $300. Substituting this value of v_s in equation (A.7a), we find that v_r equals $-\$80$. This is recorded as solution (1) in Table A.2.

TABLE A.2 Imputation of input values	Solution	Imputed Value in Dollars				Total Valuation in Dollars
		v_m	v_n	v_s	v_r	
	(1)	$ 0	$ 0	$300	$-80	—
	(2)	0	200	0	80	$280
	(3)	0	100	150	0	250
	(4)	181.82	0	0	160	341.82
	(5)	66.66	0	200	0	266.66
	(6)	-181.82	400	0	0	—

Second, suppose that v_m and v_s take on values of zero. Equations (A.7) and (A.8) become

$$0.02v_n + 0.05v_r = 8 \qquad \text{(A.7b)}$$

and

$$0.03v_n + 0.0v_r = 6. \qquad \text{(A.8b)}$$

Solving equation (A.8b) for v_n, we find that v_n is \$200. Substituting in equation (A.7b), v_r is found to be \$80. These values are recorded as solution (2) in Table A.2.

Third, let v_m and v_r assume zero values. Equations (A.7) and (A.8) become

$$0.02v_n + 0.04v_s = 8 \qquad \text{(A.7c)}$$

and

$$0.03v_n + 0.02v_s = 6. \qquad \text{(A.8c)}$$

Solving these simultaneously, we obtain v_n equal to \$100 and v_s equal to \$150. These are recorded as solution (3) in Table A.2.

Fourth, let v_n and v_s be zero. Equations (A.7) and (A.8) become

$$0.05v_r = 8 \qquad \text{(A.7d)}$$

and

$$0.033v_m = 6. \qquad \text{(A.8d)}$$

The solutions will be v_r equals \$160 and v_m equals \$181.82. These are shown as solution (4) in Table A.2.

Fifth, if v_n and v_r were zero, equations (A.7) and (A.8) would become

$$0.0v_m + 0.04v_s = 8 \qquad \text{(A.7e)}$$

and

$$0.033v_m + 0.02v_s = 6. \qquad \text{(A.8e)}$$

Solving equation (A.7e) for v_s yields a value of \$200. When we insert this value for v_s into equation (A.8e), v_m becomes \$66.66. These are listed as solution (5) in Table A.2.

Finally, when v_s and v_r take on values of zero, we will have exhausted the possibilities. In this case equations (A.7) and (A.8) become

$$0.0v_m + 0.02v_n = 8 \qquad \text{(A.7f)}$$

and

$$0.033v_m + 0.03v_n = 6. \qquad \text{(A.8f)}$$

In equation (A.7f), v_n is equal to \$400. Substituting this value for v_n

in equation (A.8f), we find that v_m is $-\$181.82$. These are shown as solution (6) in Table A.2.

All six possible combinations of minimum values that may be assigned to the four facilities are shown in Table A.2. Of the six possible solutions, two can be ruled out immediately. Solutions (1) and (6) yield negative values for one variable, thus violating the requirement that imputed values must be zero or larger. To find which of the remaining four solutions will minimize V of the objective equation (A.6), we can evaluate (A.6) using each of the four in turn. The results are listed in Table A.2 in the last column. Thus, of the four solutions, it appears that solution (3) is the one that we seek. Facilities M and R are assigned imputed values of zero. They are the ones that are not fully utilized. Facility N is assigned an imputed value of $\$100$. Facility S is assigned an imputed value of $\$150$. Thus the minimum possible valuation of the fully utilized fixed facilities is $\$250$ when the productive capacity of each of these is equally valuable in the production of either X or Y.

Alternatively, suppose that we look at the problem geometrically. Since facilities M and R have imputed values of zero, the objective equation (A.6) becomes

$$v_n + v_s = V. \qquad (A.6a)$$

This equation yields a family of isovalue curves, each having a slope of -1. If V were $\$300$, then F_1D in Figure A.6 would be the graphic representation of the objective equation. If V were $\$250$, then FG would be its graphic representation. For every different value assigned to V, a different isovalue curve is established. All such curves are parallel to each other.

Equations (A.7c) and (A.8c) are plotted in Figure A.6 as AB and

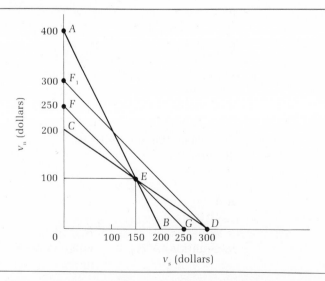

FIGURE A.6
Imputation of input values

CD, respectively. Curve AB shows the minimum possible combinations of values that could be assigned to facilities N and S, such that a dollar's worth of productive capacity would yield a dollar in rent in the production of X. Curve CD shows the minimum possible combinations of values that could be assigned to facilities N and S, such that a dollar's worth of productive capacity would yield a dollar in rent in the production of Y. Pairs of values represented by CE would undervalue the facilities in the production of X. Those represented by EB would undervalue the facilities in the production of Y. Thus, the lines joining A, E, and D represent the minimum possible combinations of values of facilities N and S at which a dollar's worth of productive capacity would produce a dollar's worth of either X or Y. The area above and to the right of AED is the area of feasible solutions to the imputation problem.

The optimal solution is approached geometrically by locating first the lowest isovalue curve touched by the area of feasible solutions. This is curve FG. The pair of values of facilities N and S represented by point E is the optimal solution, with v_n equal to $100 and v_s equal to $250. At no other point on, above, or to the right of AED will the total imputed value, as shown by an isovalue line through that point, be as low. At point E a dollar's worth of productive capacity will produce a dollar's worth of either X or Y or both. It is worth noting that the optimal solution to the dual problem, like that of the primal problem, is a "corner" solution—the "corner" representing the simultaneous solution of two of the linear constraints on the firm.

A comparison of the dual solution with that of the primal problem shows that they provide the same information. In both we found that facilities M and R were underutilized and that only facilities N and S were utilized to capacity. We found that the minimum values that could be imputed to these two facilities total to an amount equal to the maximum rent that they can produce. Further, in the primal problem we found that maximum rent is obtained when 25 units of Y and 12.5 units of X are produced. Twenty-five units of Y, yielding $6 in rent per unit, yield a total rent of $150. Twelve and one-half units of X, yielding $8 in rent per unit, provide a total rent of $100. From Table A.1 we can determine that the production of 25 units of Y requires 75 percent of the capacity of facility N and 50 percent of the capacity of facility S. The production of 12.5 units of X requires 25 percent of the capacity of facility N and 50 percent of the capacity of facility S. From the dual problem, in which v_n and v_s were found to be $100 and $150, respectively, we find that the 75 percent of the facility N used in producing Y is valued at $75, while the 50 percent of facility S used in producing Y is valued at $75. Thus, the total value imputed to that part of facilities N and S used in the production of Y is $150—equal to the total rent that Y yields. Similarly, the

25 percent of facility N used in producing X is valued at \$25, while the 50 percent of facility S used in its production is valued at \$75. The total value of that part of the facilities used in the production of X is \$100—equal to the total rent yielded by product X.

Summary

Linear programming is a technique for solving maximization and minimization problems subject to certain side conditions or constraints. The technique is based on certain assumptions. Decision making is accomplished subject to certain constraints on the decision-making agency; input and output prices are assumed to be constant; and the firm's input-output, output-output, and input-input relationships are assumed to be linear.

The first problem considered was that of maximization of a firm's output (total revenue) subject to the constraint of a given cost outlay to be made by the firm. The production function of the firm was assumed to be linearly homogeneous, and the firm was limited to a choice among four different processes in producing its output. Isoquants and isocosts were established for the firm. The area of feasible solutions to the problem was determined, and then the optimal solution was found at the point where the isocost curve touched a corner of one of the firm's isoquants. Changes in cost outlay, given the prices of inputs, will not alter which of the processes available is the optimal one but will affect only its level of use. Changes in the relative prices of inputs may result in changes in which of the processes available is the optimal one. If the constraints under which the firm maximizes output are quantity limitations on inputs, these rather than input prices determine the process or processes chosen. In general, the number of processes required to carry on its activities will be equal to the number of constraints under which the firm operates.

The second problem was that of maximizing the firm's total rents where multiple outputs are produced and several limited facilities are used to produce them. The processes for producing each output are specified. These, together with constraints, determine the area of feasible output solutions to the problem. If the amount of rent yielded by each output is known, isorent lines for the outputs can be established, and the optimal solution of the problem is that at which the area of feasible solutions just touches the highest possible isorent line. This will ordinarily be at a corner of the area of feasible solutions. Not all input or facility quantity limitations need be effective constraints on the firm. The number of effective constraints will generally be equal to the number of processes used. Changes in relative rents yielded by each output may change the optimal solution and, consequently, the input limitations that act as effective constraints.

Attention was then turned to the dual solution to a linear programming primal problem. For the primal linear programming problem summarized in the preceding paragraph, the dual problem consists of imputing values to the inputs that serve as effective constraints on the firm. The imputed values of the total amounts available of such inputs must be such that their sum will not exceed the firm's total rent. This involves finding the combination of minimum valuations at which a dollar's worth of any one input yields a dollar in rent in any one of the products it is used to produce.

Suggested Readings

Baumol, William J. "Activity Analysis in One Lesson." *American Economic Review*, 48 (December 1958), pp. 837–73.

Dorfman, Robert. "Mathematical or 'Linear' Programming: A Nonmathematical Exposition." *American Economic Review*, 43 (December 1953), pp. 797–825.

Liebhafsky, H. H. *The Nature of Price Theory*, rev. ed. Homewood, Ill.: The Dorsey Press, 1968, Chap. 17.

Wu, Yuan-Li, and Kwang, Ching-Wen. "An Analytical Comparison of Marginal Analysis and Mathematical Programming in the Theory of the Firm." Reprinted in Kenneth E. Boulding and W. Allen Spivey, eds., *Linear Programming and the Theory of the Firm*. New York: McGraw-Hill, 1960, pp. 94–157.

Questions and Exercises

1   In the production of concrete blocks a firm has three possible technological processes available to it. One of these requires 1 unit of labor for every unit of capital used. The second requires 2 units of labor per unit of capital. The third requires 5 units of labor per unit of capital. To produce 100 blocks per day, it takes 5 units of capital and 5 units of labor with Process One, 3 units of capital and 6 units of labor with Process Two, and 2 units of capital and 10 units of labor with Process Three.

   a   Draw the 100-, 200-, and 300-block isoquants.

   b   If the price of capital is $40 per unit and the price of labor is $20 per unit, which process will the firm use? Why?

   c   At the above prices of labor and capital, and with a cost constraint of $480 per day, how many blocks will be produced? Explain.

   d   If the price of labor rises to $32 and the price of capital falls to \$16, how many blocks can be produced with a cost outlay of \$480? Which process will the firm use?

e Suppose that no cost constraint is imposed on the firm but that it is limited to the use of 11 units of capital and 17 units of labor per day. How many blocks per day can it produce and what process should it use?

2 A candy factory can use its facilities to produce 3-ounce candy bars, C, and 1-pound boxes of chocolates, B. The facilities available to it are a kitchen, K, for cooking candy ingredients; a packaging room, P; and a 10-person labor force, L.

The kitchen will cook ingredients for a daily maximum of 600 candy bars, or 240 boxes of candy, or any combination between these limits with a trade-off of 5 candy bars for 2 boxes of candy.

In the packaging room the daily capacity is 800 bars or 106⅔ boxes or any combination between these limits with a trade-off of 15 bars for 2 boxes of candy.

The labor force can cook and package a daily maximum of 1,000 bars or 100 boxes, or any intermediate combination with a trade-off of 20 bars for 2 boxes of candy.

a If the firm's objective is to maximize its total revenue, R, set up and solve the objective function and the constraint inequalities. How many boxes of candy will be produced daily? How many candy bars? (*Hint*: You may find it helpful to plot the problem on graph paper.)

b What values can be imputed to K, P, and L?

GLOSSARY

A   **Alternative cost principle**   The underlying basis of cost—the cost of producing a unit of any good or service—is the value of the resources needed to produce that good or service in their best alternative use.

B   **Budget line or constraint**   All combinations of goods and services available to the consumer when all of the consumer's income (purchasing power) is being utilized, given that income and the prices of the goods and services.

C   **Capital**   The nonhuman ingredients that contribute to the production of goods and services, including land, raw and semifinished materials, tools, buildings, machinery, and inventories.

Cartel   An organization of firms in an industry in which certain management decisions and functions that would otherwise be performed by individual firms are transferred to a group representing them.

Cartel, centralized   A cartel in which the central association or group makes decisions regarding pricing, outputs, sales, and distribution of profits.

Cartel, market-sharing   A cartel in which the market shares of the member firms are determined mutually.

Competition, monopolistic   *See* Monopolistic competition.

Competition, nonprice   *See* Nonprice competition.

Competition, perfect   Pure competition plus an additional condition of perfect knowledge on the part of buyers and sellers which enables them to make instantaneous adjustments to disturbances.

Competition, pure   A market situation in which (1) individual buyers or sellers of an item are too small relative to the market as a whole to be able to influence its price, (2) units of the item are homogeneous, (3) the price of the item is free to move up or down, and (4) units of the item can be sold by any potential seller to any potential buyer.

Competitive goods *See* Substitute goods.

Complementary goods Goods related in such a way that an increase in the consumption of one, holding the consumer's satisfaction level and the quantity consumed of the other constant, increases the marginal rate of substitution of the other for money.

Constant cost industry An industry in which the entry of new firms causes no changes in resource prices or the cost curves of individual firms in the industry.

Constant returns to scale *See* Linearly Homogeneous Production Function.

Contract curve A curve generated in an Edgeworth box showing Pareto optimal distributions of goods (resources) between two consumers (producers).

Cross elasticity of demand The responsiveness of the quantity taken of one item to a small change in the price of another. The elasticity coefficient or measure is computed as the percentage change in the quantity of one divided by the percentage change in the price of the other.

D

Decreasing cost industry An industry in which the entry of new firms causes resource prices to fall, which, in turn, causes the cost curves of each individual firm to shift downward.

Demand The various quantities per unit of time of an item that a buyer(s) is (are) willing to buy at all alternative prices, other things being equal. Demand for an item can be conveniently represented as either a demand schedule or a demand curve.

Diminishing returns, law of The principle stating that if the input of one resource is increased by equal increments per unit of time while the quantities of other inputs are held constant, there will be some point beyond which the marginal physical product of the variable resource will decrease.

Diseconomies, external Forces outside the activities of any single firm causing resource prices to rise and cost curves of the firm to shift upward as new firms enter an industry.

Diseconomies of size The forces causing a firm's long-run average costs to increase as the output level and the size of plant are expanded. These are usually thought to be the increasing difficulties of coordinating and controlling the firm's activities for larger sizes and outputs.

Distribution, output How the output, or net national product, of an economy (usually defined in one-year periods) is shared among individuals and/or families.

Distribution, personal income How the income generated in an economy per time period (for example, one year) is shared among individuals and/or families.

Dual problem The inverse counterpart statement of the primary or primal maximization or minimization problem in linear programming; if the primal problem is to maximize output for a given cost outlay, the dual problem is to minimize the costs of producing whatever that maximum (given) output is.

E

Economic activity The interaction among economic units involved in the production, exchange, and consumption of goods and services.

Economic system The institutional framework within which a society carries on its economic activities.

Economies, external Forces outside the activities of any single firm causing resource prices to fall and cost curves of the firm to shift downward as new producers enter an industry.

Economies of size The forces causing a firm's long-run average costs to decrease as the output level and size of the plant are increased. These are usually thought to be (1) increasing possibilities of division and specialization of labor and (2) greater possibilities of using more efficient technology.

Edgeworth box An analytical device in which the indifference maps (isoquant maps) of the two consumers (producers) are placed over each other, but with one turned 180 degrees from the other. The axes form a box the sides of which measure the total quantities of two products (resources) available to the two consumers (producers).

Efficiency, economic The ratio of the value of outputs obtained from an economic process to the value of inputs necessary to produce them. The higher the value of output per dollar's worth of resource input, the greater is the efficiency of the process.

Efficient distribution of goods A distribution of goods among consumers such that the marginal rate of substitution between any two goods is the same for all consumers.

Efficient distribution of resources   A distribution of resources among products or uses such that the marginal rate of technical substitution between any two resources is the same for each of those products or uses.

Elastic demand   A situation in which the absolute value of the elasticity coefficient is greater than one.

Elasticity of demand, arc   The coefficient of price elasticity measured between two distinct points on a demand curve.

Elasticity of demand, cross   *See* Cross elasticity of demand.

Elasticity of demand, income   The responsiveness of quantity taken of a good to small changes in income, other things being equal. The elasticity coefficient or measure is computed as the percentage change in quantity divided by the percentage change in income.

Elasticity of demand, point   The coefficient of price elasticity measured at a point on a demand curve.

Elasticity of demand, price   The responsiveness of the quantity taken of an item to a small change in its price, given the demand curve. The elasticity coefficient or measure is computed as the percentage change in quantity divided by the percentage change in price.

Engel curve   A curve showing the various quantities of a good or service that a consumer (consumers) will take at all possible income levels, other things being equal.

Equilibrium   A state of rest from which there is either no incentive or no opportunity to move.

Equilibrium, general   Simultaneous equilibrium of all individual economic units and subsections of the economy.

Equilibrium, partial   Equilibrium of individual economic units and/or subsections of the economy with respect to given data or conditions external to the unit or subsection. Changes in those data or conditions will change the equilibrium position of the unit or subsection.

Equilibrium price   See Price, equilibrium.

Expansion path   A curve showing the least-cost (maximum output) combinations of resources for all possible output levels of a firm.

Explicit costs of production   The costs of resources hired or purchased by a firm to use in the process of production.

Exploitation, monopolistic   The difference between what a resource is worth to a firm and what it is worth to consumers; that is, for resource A it is measured by $VMP_a - MRP_a$.

Exploitation, monopsonistic   The difference between what a unit of resource is worth to a firm and what it is paid; that is, for resource A it is measured by $MRP_a - p_a$.

Externalities in consumption   The effects that consumption of an item by one consumer may have on the welfare of others. Externalities may be positive as, for example, when flowers purchased by one person are enjoyed by others as well. They may also be negative as, for example, when one student in a class eats garlic, making the classroom unpleasant for others.

Externalities in production   The effects that production of one product may have on the production possibilities of others. They may be positive, as would be the case if an orchard of fruit trees is grown near a bee farm where honey is produced. They may be negative, as would be the case if one producer pollutes water that another producer must then clean before using.

F

Feasible solutions   The set of possible solutions to a linear programming problem lying within the constraints under which the decision-making unit must operate.

Firms   Single proprietorships, partnerships, and corporations engaged in the buying and hiring of resources and in the production and sale of consumer goods and services or of higher-order capital resources.

Fixed costs   The costs of the fixed resources used by a firm in the short run.

Fixed resources   Those resources used by a firm whose quantity it cannot change in the short run.

G

Gentlemen's agreement   An informal or unwritten agreement among firms with regard to pricing, outputs, market sharing, and other activities of the firms.

H

Households   All unattached individuals and all family units of the economy.

Hypotheses   Tentative statements of causal relations among variables.

I

Implicit costs of production The costs of self-owned, self-employed resources used by a firm in the process of production.

Income consumption curve A curve showing the various combinations of goods that a consumer will take at all possible income levels, given the prices of the goods.

Income distribution, functional The distribution of income by kinds or classes of resources.

Income distribution, personal The distribution of income among households of the economy.

Income effect of a price change That part of a change in quantity taken of a good in response to a price change that results solely from the change in the real income of the consumer occasioned by the price change.

Increasing cost industry An industry in which the entry of new firms causes resource prices to rise, which, in turn, causes the cost curves of each firm to shift upward.

Indifference curve A curve showing the different combinations of two items among which a consumer is indifferent.

Indifference map A family of indifference curves showing the complete set of a consumer's tastes and preferences—the individual's preference rankings of different combinations and sets of combinations—for two items.

Inelastic demand A situation in which the absolute value of the price-elasticity coefficient is less than one.

Inferior goods Goods, the consumption of which decreases as a consumer's (consumers') income(s) increase(s).

Isocost curve A curve showing all combinations of two resources that a firm can purchase for a given cost outlay, given the prices of the resources.

Isoquant curve A curve showing the combinations of resources required by a firm to produce a given level of product output.

Isoquant map The family of isoquant curves of a firm describing the resource combinations required to produce all possible levels of output.

K

Kinked demand curve The demand curve that a firm faces if other firms in the industry would follow price decreases but not price increases. It would have a "kink" or corner in it at the initial price.

L

Labor The capacity for human effort (both of mind and muscle) available for use in producing goods and services, ranging all the way from unskilled, undifferentiated to highly skilled, specialized labor power.

Least-cost combination of resources A combination of resources for a firm at which the marginal rate of technical substitution between the resources is equal to the ratio of the resource prices ($MRTS_{ab} = p_a/p_b$). It is also a combination at which the marginal physical product per dollar's worth of one resource is equal to the marginal physical product per dollar's worth of every other resource

$$\frac{MPP_a}{p_a} = \frac{MPP_b}{p_b}.$$

Limit pricing Price policies followed by the firms in an industry that are designed to discourage entry into the industry by new firms.

Linear programming A technique for solving maximization and minimization problems where the function operated upon is linear and is subjected to linear constraints.

Linearly homogeneous production function A production function with characteristics such that an increase of a given proportion in all resource inputs will increase output in the same proportion; that is, if $x = f(a,b)$, then $\lambda x = f(\lambda a, \lambda b)$.

Living standard The level of well-being or welfare that an economic system provides for the members of a society, usually measured by per capita income.

Long run A planning period long enough for the firm to be able to vary the quantities of all the resources it uses.

Losses The difference between a firm's total costs and its total receipts when total receipts are less than total costs, including as costs the alternative costs of all resources used.

M

Macroeconomics The economics of the economy as a whole—the forces causing recession, depression, and inflation together with the forces resulting in economic growth.

Marginal costs The change in a firm's total costs per unit change in its output level.

Marginal physical product of a resource The change in total output of a firm resulting from a one-unit change in the employment level of the resource, holding the quantities of other resources constant.

Marginal productivity theory The theory that in a private enterprise economy, resource units are paid prices equal to either their values of marginal products or their marginal revenue products. Thus, income is distributed among households according to the relative contributions that the resources they own make to the productive processes.

Marginal rate of substitution The amount of one good or service that a consumer is just willing to give up to obtain an additional unit of another, measured for any combination of goods and services by the slope of the indifference curve through the point representing that combination.

Marginal rate of technical substitution The amount of one resource that a firm is just able to give up in return for an additional unit of another resource with no loss in output. For any given resource combination it is measured by the slope of the isoquant through the point representing that combination.

Marginal rate of transformation The quantity of one product that must be given up in order to produce an additional unit of another. For any given combination of products on a transformation curve, it is measured by the slope of the curve.

Marginal resource cost The change in a firm's total costs resulting from a one-unit change per unit of time in the purchase of a resource.

Marginal revenue The change in a firm's total revenue per unit change in its sales level.

Marginal revenue product The value to a firm of the change in output when the firm changes the level of employment of a resource by one unit. For resource A used in producing product X, it is computed as follows:

$$MRP_a = MPP_a \times MR_x.$$

Marginal utility The change in the total utility to a consumer that results from a one-unit change in the consumption level of an item.

Microeconomics The economics of interacting subunits of the economic system, such as individual consumers and groups of consumers, resource owners, firms, industries, individual government agencies, and the like.

Mobility The capability of a seller to sell to any of various alternative buyers or of buyers to buy from any of various alternative sellers.

Monopolistic competition A market situation in which there are many sellers with no one of them important enough to be able to influence any other seller and with each seller's product differentiated from that of the others.

Monopoly, pure   A market situation in which a single seller sells a product for which there are no good substitutes.

Monopsony   A market situation in which there is a single buyer of an item for which there are no good substitutes.

Most efficient rate of output   The output level at which a firm's short-run average costs are minimum—the most efficient of all possible short-run output levels, given the firm's size of plant.

Most efficient size of plant   That size of plant for which the short-run average cost curve forms the minimum point of the long-run average cost curve—the most efficient of all possible plant sizes for a firm.

N

Nonprice competition   Activities by a firm intended to enlarge its market share without cutting the price of the product. The major forms are (1) advertising and (2) variation in the design and quality of the product.

Normal goods   Goods, the consumption of which increases as consumers' incomes increase, individually or in the aggregate.

Normative economics   Study of the way that economic relationships ought to be. Value judgments play an integral part in the ranking of possible objectives and the choices to be made among them.

O

Objective function   In a linear programming problem the function defining what it is that the decision-making unit wants to maximize or minimize, subject to the constraints that it encounters.

Oligopoly   A market situation in which the number of sellers is small enough for the activities of one to affect the others, and for the activities of any or all of the others to affect the first.

Oligopoly, differentiated   An oligopolistic market situation in which the sellers sell differentiated products.

Oligopoly, pure   An oligopolistic market situation in which the sellers sell homogeneous or identical products.

Opportunity cost principle   *See* Alternative cost principle.

Optimal mix of goods and services   An output mix at which the marginal rate of substitution between any two goods is the same for all consumers and is equal to its marginal rate of transformation, given that all resources are fully employed and that there are no externalities in consumption or production.

Optimal solution   The best (for the decision-making unit) of the feasible solutions to a linear programming problem.

Pareto optimum   A situation in which no event can increase the well-being of one person without decreasing the well-being of someone else.

Plant, size of   *See* Most efficient size of plant

Positive economics   Study of the causal relationships that exist in economics; no value judgments are involved.

Postulates   *See* Premises.

Premises   The bedrock starting point for the construction of a theory, consisting of propositions or conditions that are taken as given or as being so without further investigation.

Price, administered   A price fixed by law, by groups of sellers, by groups of buyers, or by collective actions of buyers and sellers. It is not completely free to move in response to changes in demand and supply.

Price ceiling   An administered level above which the price of an item is not allowed to rise.

Price consumption curve   A curve showing the various combinations of goods that a consumer will take at all possible prices of one, given the price of the others and the consumer's income.

Price discrimination   The act of charging (paying) two or more buyers (sellers) different prices for the same product. It is possible and profitable if (1) buyers (sellers) can be separated into different markets that can be kept apart and (2) the elasticities of demand (supply) at each price level differ among the markets.

Price, equilibrium   That price at which the quantity per unit of time that buyers want to buy is just equal to the quantity that sellers want to sell. It generates neither a surplus nor a shortage. There is no incentive for buyers or sellers to change it. If attained, it will be maintained.

Price floor   An administered level below which the price of an item is not allowed to fall.

Price leadership   A loose form of collusive arrangement in which one firm is identified as the price setter or leader and other firms follow the prices of the leader firm.

Price war   A situation in which rival firms drive prices down through attempts to undercut each other's prices.

Primal problem   In linear programming the original problem stated by the objective function and the constraints placed on the decision-making unit.

Principles   Statements of causal relations that have undergone and survived thorough testing.

Private enterprise system   An economic system characterized by private property rights, voluntary private production, and exchange of goods and services and of resources.

Process   One of several resource proportion possibilities used in producing a good or service. The term is used in linear programming problems.

Process ray   A linear line extending upward to the right from the origin of an isoquant diagram showing a given process at different levels of utilization of that process.

Product differentiation   A situation in which sellers sell essentially the same product but that of each seller has, at least in the minds of the consumers, certain characteristics that distinguish it from the product of other sellers.

Production function   The physical relation between a firm's resource inputs and its output of goods and services per unit of time.

Profits   The difference between a firm's total receipts and its total costs when total receipts exceed total costs, including as costs the alternative costs of all resources used.

R

Rent, economic   The residual left for the fixed resources of a firm after the variable resources have been paid amounts equal to their alternative costs.

Resources   The ingredients available for the production of goods and services that are used to satisfy human wants. They consist of labor resources and capital resources.

S

Shadow prices   Prices imputed to a good, service, or resource that is not priced by the marketplace or that is incorrectly priced by the market.

Shortage   A situation caused by a price below the equilibrium level in which buyers want to buy larger quantities than sellers are willing to sell.

Short run   A planning period so short that a firm is unable to vary the quantities of some of the resources that it uses—usually thought of as the time horizon during which the firm cannot change its size of plant.

Short-run supply curve, firm   A curve showing the different quantities per unit of time of a good that the firm will place on the market at all possible prices. It is that part of the firm's short-run marginal cost curve that lies above the average variable cost curve.

Short-run supply curve, market   A curve showing the different quantities per unit of time of a good that all firms together will place on the market in the short run at various possible prices.

Shutdown price   The price below which the firm would cease to produce in the short run.

Socialistic system   An economic system characterized by governmental ownership or control of resources and of goods and services. Production is carried on by the government, which also specifies the terms or conditions under which exchange may take place.

Substitute goods   Goods related in such a way that an increase in the consumption of one, holding the consumer's satisfaction level and quantity consumed of the other constant, decreases the marginal rate of substitution of the other for money.

Substitution effect of a price change   That part of a change in quantity taken of a good, in response to a price change, that results solely from the change in its price. The effects of the price change on the real income of the consumer, and the subsequent effect of the real income change on the quantity taken, have been eliminated.

Superior goods   *See* Normal goods.

Supply   The various quantities per unit of time of an item that a seller or sellers are willing to sell at all alternative prices, other things being equal. Supply of an item can be conveniently represented as a supply schedule or a supply curve.

Surplus   A situation caused by a price above the equilibrium level in which sellers want to sell larger quantities than buyers want to buy.

T

Tax, excise   A per unit tax on an item. It may be a specific tax based on the physical unit of the item or an *ad valorem* tax based on its price.

Tax incidence   The distribution of a tax among economic units.

Techniques of production   The know-how and the means available for combining and transforming resources into goods and services.

Theory   A set of related principles providing insight into the operation of some phenomenon.

Transformation curve   A curve showing the maximum production possibilities for two products, given the resources available to produce them.

U

Unitary elasticity of demand   A situation in which the absolute value of the elasticity coefficient is equal to one.

Utility   The satisfaction obtained from the goods and services that a consumer consumes.

V

Value of marginal product   The market value of the change in output when a firm changes the employment level of a resource by one unit. For resource A used in producing product X, it is computed as follows:

$$VMP_a = MPP_a \times p_x.$$

Variable costs   The costs of the variable resources used by a firm in either the short run or the long run.

Variable resources   Those resources used by a firm that it can change in quantity in either the short run or the long run.

Very short run   A time period with respect to a given good or service so short that the quantity of it placed on the market cannot be changed.

W

Wants   The varied and insatiable desires of human beings that provide the driving force of economic activity.

Welfare   The level of economic well-being or satisfaction attained by individuals and groups of individuals in the society.

Name Index

Subject Index